THE
ANNUAL REGISTER
Vol. 233

ANNUAL REGISTER ADVISORY BOARD

CHAIRMAN

H. V. HODSON

EDITOR

ALAN J. DAY

ASSISTANT EDITOR

VERENA HOFFMAN

JAMES BISHOP
Editor-in-Chief, The Illustrated London News

FRANK E. CLOSE, PhD
Distinguished Professor of Physics, The University of Tennessee
NOMINATED BY
THE BRITISH ASSOCIATION FOR THE ADVANCEMENT OF SCIENCE

M. R. D. FOOT
Formerly Professor of Modern History, University of Manchester
NOMINATED BY
THE ROYAL HISTORICAL SOCIETY

MICHAEL KASER
Fellow of St Antony's College, Oxford
NOMINATED BY
THE ROYAL INSTITUTE OF INTERNATIONAL AFFAIRS

DEREK MORRIS
Fellow of Oriel College, Oxford
NOMINATED BY
THE ROYAL ECONOMIC SOCIETY

ALASTAIR NIVEN
Literature Director of the Arts Council of Great Britain
NOMINATED BY
THE ARTS COUNCIL OF GREAT BRITAIN

Popperfoto (top), Gamma (bottom)

End of an Empire

Vilnius/Moscow, August-September 1991: As symbols of the Soviet regime come down in the Lithuanian capital (*top*), in the Russian parliament Boris Yeltsin explains to President Gorbachev that things must change (*bottom*).

S. Compoint/Sygma

Aftermath of the Gulf War

Kuwait, April 1991: A salvage team fights to cap one of the hundreds of Kuwaiti oil wells set on fire by retreating Iraqi forces.

THE
ANNUAL REGISTER

A Record of World Events
1991

Edited by
ALAN J. DAY

assisted by
VERENA HOFFMAN

FIRST EDITED IN 1758
BY EDMUND BURKE

Longman

THE ANNUAL REGISTER 1991
Published by Longman Group UK Limited, Longman House.
Burnt Mill, Harlow, Essex, CM20 2JE, United Kingdom

Distributed exclusively in the United States and Canada by Gale Research Company, Book Tower, Detroit, Michigan 48226, USA

ISBN 0-582-09585-9 (Longman)

Library of Congress Catalog Card Number: 4-17979

© Longman Group UK Limited 1992
All rights reserved; no part of this publication may be reproduced,
stored in a retrieval system, or transmitted in any form or by any
means, electronic, mechanical, photocopying, recording or otherwise
without either the prior written permission of the Publishers or a licence permitting restricted
copying issued by the Copyright Licensing Agency Ltd.
33–34 Alfred Place, London, WC1E 7DP

British Library Cataloguing in Publication Data
The Annual Register—1991
 1. History—Periodicals
  909.82'8'05   D410

ISBN 0-582-09585-9

Set in Times Roman by
THE MIDLANDS BOOK TYPESETTING COMPANY LIMITED, LOUGHBOROUGH
Printed and bound in Great Britain by
WILLIAM CLOWES LIMITED, BECCLES AND LONDON

CONTENTS

	PREFACE TO 233rd VOLUME	xv
	EXTRACTS FROM 1791, 1841, 1891 and 1941 VOLUMES	xvi
	EDITORIAL	1

I UNITED KINGDOM

1	The Gulf War, Defence and Europe	5
2	A Depressing Economic Outlook	9
3	The Poll Tax and Local Elections	12
4	Summer Squalls	17
5	This Year, Next Year . . . ?	25
6	The Bumpy Road to Maastricht	29
7	Domestic Affairs in the Final Quarter	33
8	Scotland	36
9	Wales	38
10	Northern Ireland	40

II AMERICAS AND CARIBBEAN

1	United States of America	44
2	Canada	61
3	Latin America: Argentina 66 Bolivia 68 Brazil 69 Chile 70 Colombia 72 Ecuador 73 Paraguay 74 Peru 75 Uruguay 76 Venezuela 77 Cuba 77 Dominican Republic and Haiti 78 Central America and Panama 80 Mexico 83	66
4	Caribbean: Jamaica 85 Guyana 86 Trinidad & Tobago 87 Barbados 88 Belize 89 Grenada 90 The Bahamas 91 Windward & Leeward Islands 91 Suriname 94	85

III WESTERN, CENTRAL AND SOUTHERN EUROPE

1	France 96 Germany 102 Italy 107 Belgium 111 The Netherlands 113 Luxembourg 114 Ireland 115	96
2	Denmark 118 Iceland 120 Norway 122 Sweden 123 Finland 125 Austria 127 Switzerland 129 European Mini-States 132	118
3	Spain 134 Portugal 137 Gibraltar 139 Malta 141 Greece 143 Cyprus 146 Turkey 148	134

IV EASTERN EUROPE

1	Poland 152 Czechoslovakia 155 Hungary 158 Romania 161 Bulgaria 164 Yugoslavia 167 Albania 174	152
2	USSR/Commonwealth of Independent States 177 Baltic States 188	177

V MIDDLE EAST AND NORTH AFRICA

1	Chronology of the Gulf Crisis	191
2	The Gulf War	194
3	Israel	200
4	Arab World 204 Egypt 207 Jordan 210 Syria 212 Lebanon 214 Iraq 217	204
5	Saudi Arabia 220 Yemen 223 Arab States of the Gulf 224	220

6	Sudan 230 Libya 232 Tunisia 235 Algeria 239 Morocco 242 Western Sahara 245	230
VI	EQUATORIAL AFRICA	
1	Ethiopia 248 Somalia 250 Djibouti 251 Kenya 252 Tanzania 254 Uganda 256	248
2	Ghana 257 Nigeria 259 Sierra Leone 262 The Gambia 263 Liberia 264	257
3	Senegal 266 Guinea 267 Mali 268 Mauritania 269 Côte d'Ivoire 269 Burkina Faso 270 Niger 271 Togo 272 Benin 273 Cameroon 274 Chad 275 Gabon and Central African Republic 276 Congo 277 Equatorial Guinea 278	266
VII	CENTRAL AND SOUTHERN AFRICA	
1	Zaïre 279 Burundi and Rwanda 281 Guinea-Bissau and Cape Verde 283 São Tomé & Príncipe 284 Mozambique 284 Angola 287	279
2	Zambia 289 Malawi 291 Zimbabwe 292 Namibia 294 Botswana 296 Lesotho 297 Swaziland 298	289
3	South Africa	299
VIII	SOUTH ASIA AND INDIAN OCEAN	
1	Iran 305 Afghanistan 308	305
2	India 309 Pakistan 313 Bangladesh 316 Nepal 318 Bhutan 320 Sri Lanka 321	309
3	Mauritius 323 Seychelles, Comoros and Maldives 325 Madagascar 327	323
IX	SOUTH-EAST AND EAST ASIA	
1	Myanmar (Burma) 329 Thailand 331 Malaysia 333 Brunei 334 Singapore 335 Indonesia 337 Philippines 339 Vietnam 341 Cambodia 342 Laos 345	329
2	China 346 Taiwan 353 Hong Kong 355 Japan 357 South Korea 361 North Korea 363 Mongolia 364	346
X	AUSTRALIA AND SOUTH PACIFIC	
1	Australia 368 Papua New Guinea 373	368
2	New Zealand 374 South Pacific 378	374
XI	INTERNATIONAL ORGANIZATIONS	
1	United Nations	382
2	The Commonwealth	392
3	European Community	395
4	OECD 404 Comecon 405 Non-Aligned Movement 407	404
5	Conference on Security and Cooperation in Europe European Bank for Reconstruction and Development Council of Europe 414 European Free Trade Association 416 Nordic Council 418	410 412 410
6	African Conferences and Organizations 419 South Asian Association for Regional Cooperation 421 South-East Asian Organizations 423 Pacific Organizations 424 Latin American Organizations 425 Caribbean Organizations 427	419

CONTENTS

XII	DEFENCE AND ARMS CONTROL	
1	New Problems and War in the Gulf	429
2	NATO and the European Dimension	431
3	The START Treaty and Subsequent Initiatives	436
XIII	RELIGION	439
XIV	THE SCIENCES	
1	Medical, Scientific and Industrial Research	445
2	Information Technology	451
3	Environment	455
XV	THE LAW	
1	International Law 461 European Community Law 464	461
2	Law in the United Kingdom	468
3	Law in the United States	473
XVI	THE ARTS	
1	Opera 477 Music 479 Ballet/Dance 483 Theatre 486 Cinema 491 Television and Radio 494	477
2	Art 499 Architecture 502 Fashion 505	499
3	Literature	507
XVII	SPORT	514
XVIII	ECONOMIC AND SOCIAL AFFAIRS	
1	The Economy of the USSR/CIS	525
2	The International Economy	527
3	The Economy of the United States	529
4	The Economy of the United Kingdom	531
5	Economic and Social Data	535
XIX	DOCUMENTS AND REFERENCE	
1	UN Security Council: Gulf Ceasefire Resolution	550
2	Strategic Arms Limitation (START) Treaty	555
3	Commonwealth of Independent States	557
4	Maastricht Treaty on European Union	561
XX	OBITUARY	568
XXI	CHRONICLE OF PRINCIPAL EVENTS IN 1991	582
	INDEX	595

CONTRIBUTORS

EXTRACTS FROM PAST VOLUMES   M. R. D. Foot, Former Professor of Modern History, University of Manchester

PART I
UNITED KINGDOM, SCOTLAND   C. J. Bartlett FRHistS, FRSE, Professor of International History, University of Dundee

WALES   Gwyn Jenkins, MA, Assistant Keeper, Department of Manuscripts and Records, National Library of Wales, Aberystwyth

NORTHERN IRELAND   Sydney Elliott, BA, PhD, Senior Lecturer in Politics, The Queen's University, Belfast

PART II
USA   Neil A. Wynn, MA PhD, Principal Lecturer and Head of History, Polytechnic of Wales

CANADA   David M. L. Farr, Professor Emeritus of History, Carleton University, Ottawa

LATIN AMERICA   Peter Calvert, AM, MA, PhD, Professor of Comparative and International Politics, University of Southampton

THE CARIBBEAN   Julian C. J. Saurin, PhD, Lecturer in International Relations, School of African and Asian Studies, University of Sussex

PART III
FRANCE   Martin Harrison, Professor of Politics, University of Keele

GERMANY   Gordon Smith, BSc(Econ), PhD, Professor of Government, London School of Economics and Political Science

ITALY   Muriel Grindrod, Writer on Italian affairs; formerly Assistant Editor, *The Annual Register*

BELGIUM, NETHERLANDS, LUXEMBOURG   J. D. McLachlan, Managing Director, Marketing, Financial Times Business Information

REPUBLIC OF IRELAND   Louis McRedmond, MA, BL, Formerly Head of Information in Radio Telefís Éireann, the Irish broadcasting service

NORDIC COUNTRIES   Hilary Allen, BSc(Econ), DPhil, Writer on Nordic affairs

AUSTRIA   Angela Gillon, Researcher in West European affairs

SWITZERLAND   Hans Hirter, PhD, Editor, *Année Politique Suisse*. University of Berne

SPAIN, GIBRALTAR   G. A. M. Hills, BA, DLit, Writer and broadcaster on Iberian current affairs and history

PORTUGAL   Manuel Santana, Portuguese Section, BBC World Service

MALTA   D. G. Austin, Emeritus Professor of Government, University of Manchester

CONTRIBUTORS

GREECE	**Richard Clogg,** MA, St Antony's College, Oxford
CYPRUS	**Robert McDonald,** Freelance writer and broadcaster; author on Greece, Cyprus and Turkey
TURKEY	**A. J. A. Mango,** BA, PhD, Orientalist and writer on current affairs in Turkey and the Near East

PART IV

POLAND	**A. Kemp-Welch,** BSc(Econ), PhD, Lecturer in Politics and International Relations, University of Nottingham
CZECHOSLOVAKIA	**Jan Obrman,** Research analyst, Radio Free Europe/Radio Liberty Research Institute, Munich
HUNGARY	**George Schöpflin,** Joint Lecturer in East European Political Institutions, London School of Economics and School of Slavonic and East European Studies, University of London
ROMANIA	**Gabriel Partos,** Senior Talks Writer, BBC World Service
BULGARIA	**Stephen Ashley,** MA, DPhil, Senior Talks Writer, BBC World Service
YUGOSLAVIA	**J. B. Allcock,** MA, PhD, Head of Research Unit in Yugoslav Studies, University of Bradford
ALBANIA	**Richard Crampton,** PhD, Fellow of St Edmund Hall, Oxford; formerly Professor of East European History, University of Kent
USSR/CIS, BALTIC STATES	**Stephen White,** PhD, Professor of Politics, University of Glasgow

PART V

THE GULF WAR	**M. R. D. Foot** (see Extracts from Past Volumes)
ISRAEL	**Noah Lucas,** PhD, Fellow in Israeli Studies, The Oxford Centre for Postgraduate Hebrew Studies
ARAB WORLD, EGYPT, JORDAN, SYRIA, LEBANON, IRAQ	**Christopher Gandy,** Formerly UK Diplomatic Service; writer on Middle Eastern affairs
SAUDI ARABIA, YEMEN	**R. M. Burrell,** Lecturer in the Contemporary History of the Near and Middle East, School of Oriental and African Studies, University of London
ARAB STATES OF THE GULF	**George Joffe,** Consultant Editor, Economist Intelligence Unit; Director of Research, Geopolitics and International Boundaries Research Centre, School of Oriental and African Studies, University of London
SUDAN	**Ahmed al-Shahi,** DPhil, Lecturer in Social Anthropology, Department of Social Policy, University of Newcastle-upon-Tyne
LIBYA, TUNISIA, ALGERIA MOROCCO, WESTERN SAHARA	**R. I. Lawless,** PhD, Reader in Modern Middle Eastern Studies, Centre for Middle Eastern and Islamic Studies, University of Durham

PART VI

ETHIOPIA, SOMALIA, DJIBOUTI	**Christopher Clapham,** MA, DPhil, Professor of Politics and International Relations, University of Lancaster

CONTRIBUTORS

KENYA, TANZANIA, UGANDA	**William Tordoff,** MA, PhD, Emeritus Professor of Government, University of Manchester
GHANA	**D. G. Austin** (see Pt. III, Malta)
NIGERIA	**Robin Theobald,** PhD, Principal Lecturer in Sociology, Polytechnic of Central London
SIERRA LEONE, THE GAMBIA LIBERIA	**Arnold Hughes,** BA, Lecturer in Political Science, Centre of West African Studies, University of Birmingham
CHAPTER 3 (SENEGAL to EQUATORIAL GUINEA)	**Kaye Whiteman,** Editor-in-Chief, *West Africa*

PART VII

CHAPTER 1 (ZAIRE to ANGOLA)	**Robin Hallett,** MA, Writer and lecturer on African affairs
ZAMBIA, MALAWI	**Robin Hallett** (see above)
ZIMBABWE	**R. W. Baldock,** BA, PhD, Senior Editor, Yale University Press; writer on African affairs
NAMIBIA, BOTSWANA, LESOTHO, SWAZILAND, SOUTH AFRICA	**Gerald Shaw,** MA, Associate Editor, *The Cape Times*, Cape Town

PART VIII

IRAN	**Keith McLachlan,** BA, PhD, Professor of Geography with reference to the Near and Middle East, School of Oriental and African Studies, University of London
AFGHANISTAN, INDIA, BANGLADESH, NEPAL, BHUTAN	**Peter Lyon,** BSc(Econ), PhD, Reader in International Relations and Academic Secretary, Institute of Commonwealth Studies, University of London; Editor, *The Round Table*
PAKISTAN	**David Taylor,** Senior Lecturer in Politics with reference to South Asia, School of Oriental and African Studies, University of London
SRI LANKA	**James Jupp,** MSc(Econ), PhD, FASSA, Director, Centre for Immigration and Multicultural Studies, Australian National University, Canberra
SEYCHELLES, MAURITIUS, MALDIVES	**George Bennett,** Former Head, BBC African Service; freelance writer and broadcaster
MADAGASCAR AND COMOROS	**Kaye Whiteman** (see Pt. VI, Ch. 3)

PART IX

MYANMAR (BURMA), INDONESIA, PHILIPPINES	**Robert H. Taylor,** PhD, Professor of Politics, School of Oriental and African Studies, University of London
THAILAND, VIETNAM, CAMBODIA, LAOS	**Jonathan Rigg,** PhD, Lecturer in South East Asian Geography, School of Oriental and African Studies, University of London
MALAYSIA, BRUNEI, SINGAPORE	**Michael Leifer,** BA, PhD, Professor of International Relations, London School of Economics and Political Science
CHINA, TAIWAN, HONG KONG	**Robert F. Ash,** MSc(Econ), PhD, Chairman, Contemporary China Institute and Senior Lecturer in Economics, School of Oriental and African Studies, University of London

CONTRIBUTORS xi

JAPAN	**I. H. Nish,** Emeritus Professor of International History, London School of Economics and Political Science
SOUTH AND NORTH KOREA	**James H. Grayson,** PhD, Director, Centre for Korean Studies, University of Sheffield
MONGOLIA	**Alan Sanders,** FIL, Lecturer in Mongolian Studies, School of Oriental and African Studies, University of London

PART X

AUSTRALIA	**James Jupp** (see Pt. VIII, Sri Lanka)
PAPUA NEW GUINEA	**Norman MacQueen,** Senior Lecturer in Politics, Sunderland Polytechnic
NEW ZEALAND, SOUTH PACIFIC	**Roderic Alley,** PhD, School of Political Science and Public Administration, Victoria University of Wellington

PART XI

UNITED NATIONS	**Granville Fletcher,** Former Chef de Cabinet, UN European Headquarters, Geneva
COMMONWEALTH	**Derek Ingram,** Editor of *Gemini News Service* and author and writer on the Commonwealth
EUROPEAN COMMUNITY	**Michael Berendt,** Expert on affairs of the European Communities
OECD, EFTA	**Roger East,** Editor of *Keesing's Record of World Events*; founder and director of CIRCA Research and Reference Information
COMECON, EUROPEAN BANK FOR RECONSTRUCTION AND DEVELOPMENT	**Michael Kaser,** MA, Reader in Economics, Oxford University and Professorial Fellow of St Antony's College, Oxford
NON-ALIGNED MOVEMENT	**Peter Willetts,** PhD, Senior Lecturer in International Relations, The City University, London
CONFERENCE ON SECURITY AND COOPERATION IN EUROPE	**Adrian G. V. Hyde-Price,** BSc(Econ), PhD, Lecturer, Department of Politics, University of Southampton
COUNCIL OF EUROPE	**Richard Lambert,** Secretary to the UK delegation to the Parliamentary Assembly of the Council of Europe
NORDIC COUNCIL	**Hilary Allen** (see Pt. III, Nordic Countries)
AFRICAN CONFERENCES AND ORGANIZATIONS	**Kaye Whiteman** (see Pt. VI, Ch. 3)
S. ASIAN ASSOCIATION FOR REGIONAL COOPERATION	**Peter Lyon** (see Pt. VIII, Afghanistan, etc.)
S.E. ASIAN ORGANIZATIONS	**D. J. Sagar,** Regional Editor, *Keesing's Record of World Events;* director, CIRCA Research and Reference Information
S. PACIFIC REGIONAL COOPERATION	**Roderic Alley** (see Pt. X, New Zealand, etc.)
LATIN AMERICAN ORGANIZATIONS	**Peter Calvert** (see Pt. II, Latin America)
CARIBBEAN ORGANIZATIONS	**Ciarán Ó Maoláin,** BA, Research Fellow, University of Warwick; writer on Caribbean, Latin American and Pacific affairs

CONTRIBUTORS

PART XII
DEFENCE AND ARMS CONTROL — **Phil Williams,** PhD, Professor of Security Studies, Graduate School of Public and International Affairs, University of Pittsburgh

PART XIII
RELIGION — **Geoffrey Parrinder,** MA, PhD, DD, Emeritus Professor of the Comparative Study of Religions, University of London

PART XIV
MEDICAL, SCIENTIFIC AND INDUSTRIAL RESEARCH — **John Newell,** Editor, Science, Industry, Medicine and Agriculture, BBC World Services
INFORMATION TECHNOLOGY — **David Powell,** A director of Electronic Publishing Services Ltd; editor, *EP Journal*
ENVIRONMENT — **Lloyd Timberlake,** Director for External Affairs, International Institute for Environment and Development (IIED)

PART XV
INTERNATIONAL LAW — **Christine Gray,** MA, PhD, Fellow in Law, St Hilda's College, Oxford
EUROPEAN COMMUNITY LAW — **N. March Hunnings,** LLM, PhD, Editor, *Common Market Law Reports*
LAW IN THE UK — **David Ibbetson,** MA, PhD, Fellow and Tutor in Law, Magdalen College, Oxford
LAW IN THE USA — **Robert J. Spjut,** JD, LLM, Member of the State Bars of California and Florida

PART XVI
OPERA, THEATRE — **Charles Osborne,** Author; opera critic, *The Jewish Chronicle*
DANCE/BALLET — **Jane Pritchard,** Archivist, Rambert Dance Company and English National Ballet
MUSIC — **Francis Routh,** Composer and author; founder director of the Redcliffe Concerts
CINEMA — **Derek Malcolm,** Film critic, *The Guardian*
TV & RADIO — **Raymond Snoddy,** Media correspondent, *The Financial Times*
ART — **Marina Vaizey,** MA, Editor, National Art Collections Fund publications; art columnist, *The Sunday Times*
ARCHITECTURE — **Paul Finch,** Editor, *Building Design*
FASHION — **Bonny Spencer,** Fashion editor, *Bella* magazine
LITERATURE — **Alastair Niven,** Literature director of the Arts Council

PART XVII
SPORT — **Tony Pawson,** OBE, Sports writer, *The Observer;* cricket, football and fly-fishing international

PART XVIII
CHAPTERS 1 to 4
STATISTICS

Victor Keegan, Assistant Editor, *The Guardian*
Sue Cockerill, Former member of the Statistical Department, *Financial Times*

PART XX
OBITUARY

H. V. Hodson, Former editor of *The Annual Register*; Editor, *The Sunday Times*, 1950–61

MAPS

MJL **Graphics**, N. Yorks, YO14 9BE

ACKNOWLEDGEMENTS

THE Advisory Board again gratefully acknowledges its debt to a number of institutions for their help with sources, references and documents, notably the Royal Institute of International Affairs, the US Information Service, the UN Information Centre and the European Commission Office in London. Acknowledgement is also due to the principal sources for the national data sections (showing the situation as at end-1991 unless otherwise stated), namely *Keesing's Record of World Events* (Longman), *People in Power* (Longman) and *World Development Report* (OUP for the World Bank). The Board and the bodies which nominate its members disclaim responsibility for any opinions expressed or the accuracy of facts recorded in this volume.

ABBREVIATIONS

ACC	Arab Cooperation Council
ACP	African, Caribbean and Pacific states associated with EEC
AfDB	African Development Bank
AID	Agency for International Development
AIDS	Acquired Immune Deficiency Syndrome
AMU	Arab Maghreb Union
ANC	African National Congress
ANZUS	Australia-New Zealand-USA Security Treaty
AR	Annual Register
ASEAN	Association of South-East Asian Nations
CAP	Common Agricultural Policy
CARICOM	Caribbean Common Market
CEEAC	Economic Community of Central African States
CFE	Conventional Force Reductions in Europe
COMECON	Council for Mutual Economic Assistance (CMEA)
CSCE	Conference on Security and Cooperation in Europe
Cwth.	Commonwealth
EBRD	European Bank for Reconstruction and Development
EC	European Community
ECO	Economic Cooperation Organization
ECOSOC	Economic and Social Council (UN)
ECOWAS	Economic Community of West African States
EEC	European Economic Community (Common Market)
EFTA	European Free Trade Association
EMS	European Monetary System
ESCAP	Economic and Social Commission for Asia and the Pacific (UN)
FAO	Food and Agriculture Organization
GATT	General Agreement on Tariffs and Trade
GCC	Gulf Cooperation Council
GDP/GNP	Gross Domestic/National Product
IAEA	International Atomic Energy Agency
IBRD	International Bank for Reconstruction and Development
ICBM	Inter-Continental Ballistic Missile
ICO	Islamic Conference Organization
IDA	International Development Association
ILO	International Labour Organization
IMF	International Monetary Fund
INF	Intermediate-range Nuclear Forces
IRA	Irish Republican Army
MBFR	Mutual and Balanced Force Reductions
NAM	Non-Aligned Movement
NATO	North Atlantic Treaty Organization
OAS	Organization of American States
OAU	Organization of African Unity
OECD	Organization for Economic Cooperation and Development
OPEC (OAPEC)	Organization of (Arab) Petroleum Exporting Countries
PLO	Palestine Liberation Organization
SAARC	South Asian Association for Regional Cooperation
SADCC	Southern African Development Coordination Conference
SDI	Strategic Defence Initiative
START	Strategic Arms Reduction Treaty
SWAPO	South-West Africa People's Organization
UN	United Nations
UNCTAD	United National Conference on Trade and Development
UNDP	United Nations Development Programme
UNESCO	United Nations Educational, Scientific and Cultural Organization
UNHCR	United Nations High Commission for Refugees
UNRWA	United National Relief and Works Agency
WHO	World Health Organization

PREFACE

THE recent sequence of years of truly historic international change continued in 1991 with the disintegration of the 70-year-old Soviet empire, the virtual disappearance of communism from the political map of Europe and the birth/rebirth of 15 sovereign republics in the ruin of the ex-USSR. In Yugoslavia, moreover, several more new sovereign states were by year's end about to emerge from another failed communist federation. Unlikely though it seemed at the beginning of the year, these momentous events in Eastern Europe tended to eclipse, as the year progressed, the military drama of the early months, namely the ejection of Iraqi forces from Kuwait by a US-led multinational coalition. Nevertheless, the present 233rd volume of the *Annual Register* includes extensive coverage not only of the demise of the USSR but also of the Gulf War. A special report on the Gulf military campaign appears in Part V, together with a further special chronology of the Gulf crisis.

In recognition that the political structure of Europe is undergoing drastic change, this AR volume departs to some extent from the book's long-established arrangement. In particular, coverage of Western Europe now precedes the old USSR/Eastern Europe section, and there is a new country chapter on the three Baltic republics which achieved independence in 1991. Although, by year's end, there were 12 other sovereign ex-Soviet republics, this volume covers them all in one chapter dealing with the USSR and the successor Commonwealth of Independent States established in December. In view of these developments, and those in Yugoslavia, further changes to the AR structure will have to be made for the 1992 volume.

An innovation in the present volume is that numerical identification has been applied not only to parts and chapters but also to sections within chapters. Designed to enhance the AR as a work of reference, this new system facilitates easy cross-reference within the book, in that the sequential numbering is shown at the head of each page. For detailed investigation of the volume's contents, however, readers are again referred to the comprehensive subject and names index.

The editor and Advisory Board members welcome several new contributors to the AR circle. They also pay tribute to Muriel Grindrod, former assistant editor of the AR, whose contribution on Italy in this volume is the last of a 40-year sequence which will stand as a monument to her deep understanding of Italian affairs.

THE ANNUAL REGISTER

200 years ago

1791. *Abortive Flight of Louis XVI to Varennes.* In the meantime the King [Louis XVI] used the utmost expedition, and arrived the next day [21 June], at noon, at St Menehoud, a place in Champagne, distant from Paris near one hundred and sixty miles: but here, while changing horses, he was recognized by the post-master, who, not being provided with the means of stopping him on the spot, dissembled his knowledge of the King, and sent his son, with the utmost speed, to the next town; where, on disclosing the motive of his coming, he was immediately joined by a number of the national guards, who overpowered some troops that were come to the King's assistance; upon which he was obliged to surrender. The place where he was seized in this manner was Varennes, a town within six leagues of the border of France toward Luxemburgh.

150 years ago

1841. *Irritated Jealousy of France.* Upon the whole, therefore, there was good reason for believing that the irritated jealousy of France would not lead her into any greater folly than that of keeping up, at an enormous cost, *une paix armée*, and indulging in grandiloquent language about the national honour and dignity, while she stood aloof from the attempts that were made to conciliate her wounded pride by the other European Powers.

100 years ago

1891. *Mr Tate's Art Gallery.* The effort to establish an 'English Luxembourg' on the basis furnished by Mr Henry Tate, of Park Hill, Streatham Common, resulted in nothing beyond a display of rivalry among certain cliques of art connoisseurs and of the indifference of the Treasury towards any scheme which might involve the expenditure of public money upon English art. In the first instance, the Trustees of the National Gallery seemed disposed to co-operate with Mr Tate in his efforts to give prominence to pictures of the modern British School. . . It, however, soon became evident that the views of the Treasury had undergone a change, and an alternative site at South Kensington was offered—the East and West Picture Galleries, which had been erected for the Exhibition of 1862.

50 years ago

1941. *Hitler's Invasion of the Soviet Union.* Thus the German invasion of Russia on June 22—launched, as Mr Churchill sarcastically remarked, with scrupulous observance of all Hitler's formalities of perfidy—however much it may have surprised the public, did not catch the Government unawares, and found it not unready to take advantage of the new situation thus created. In a broadcast delivered on the same evening the Prime Minister proclaimed that they were standing now in the fourth great climacteric of the war, the other three being the collapse of France, the repulse of the Nazi air invasion of England, and the passing of the Lease and Lend enactment in the United States. Without retracting any of his previous denunciations of Russian Bolshevism, he said that the fact of outstanding importance at the present juncture was that the Russian leaders had called on their people to resist the invader to the utmost. Since their own one aim was to destroy Hitler, and every vestige of the Nazi regime, it followed that they would give whatever help they could to Russia and the Russian people, and appeal to all their friends and Allies to take the same course.

ANNUAL REGISTER

FOR THE YEAR 1991

EDITORIAL
DEATH-THROES OF AN EMPIRE

THE editorial article in the *Annual Register* for 1990 hailed 'the supreme importance of the ending of the Cold War in radically changing the whole panorama of world affairs in the 1990s'. Events in 1991 fully vindicated that judgment. Even the self-execution of the USSR at the end of the year was logically linked to the same cause by the proposition: 'No end to the Cold War, no end to the Soviet Union'. It was under Mikhail Gorbachev, to whom the world's grateful respect is accordingly due, that the Cold War had been ended: he had striven to the last to preserve the Soviet Union, but in vain; for, once *glasnost* had breached the dyke of communist monopoly rule, no longer could fear of a superpower clash restrain the ever-widening flow of dissent and division. Mr Gorbachev became the symbol of a discarded past, and his resignation at the close of the year justly coincided with the formal demise of the Union itself.

Before its death had been formally certified, republics of the still boneless Commonwealth that was its ghost had appeared at a council meeting of NATO, begging admittance to an organization that had been created primarily to counter the military menace of the Soviet Union. That was the ultimate irony of the revolutionary earthquake that had accompanied the end of the Cold War. There were many other dramatic effects upon the international landscape in 1991.

Unanimity in the UN Security Council—long paralysed by the Cold War partisans' veto—which had been so crucial in the reaction to Iraq's rape of Kuwait in August 1990, was prolonged through the hundred days of fighting and the enforcement of terms of peace. The prestige and authority of the United Nations were enhanced in every theatre of world affairs. Nor did the effect in the Middle East stop at the frontiers of Iraq. No longer classed as clients of one or other of the superpower alliances, its countries and factions re-assorted themselves: Syria, for instance, was no longer seen as a pariah by the West, while the PLO, which had backed Iraq, lost much influence. It is beyond imagining that a Middle East peace conference, with the Arab states, Israel and the Palestinians all present, could have been organized by American leadership when the several participants were patronized either by the USA or by the USSR, and these were mutually hostile in their aims there as elsewhere. Nor could the UN, with the warm support of both Moscow and Washington as well as Western Europe, have brokered a release of hostages in Lebanon, consummated in December, which was one of the happiest events of 1991.

The motives of democracy and nationalism are closely linked. Appeal to the one cause is often disguised appeal to the other. 'Let the people speak', cried Mrs Thatcher in her passionate nationalist onslaught on the transfer of any more power to the European Community. 'Government of the people, by the people, for the people' was, first and foremost, government—the government of a new American nation. Small wonder was it that the tidal wave of democratic aspiration that swept over the Soviet Union and its satellites broke into separatist eddies, swirling among the cultural and linguistic 'nations' which had composed that imperium—not only the submerged previous sovereign states along the Baltic coast but also the other republics and peoples and, beyond the Union, Serbs and Croats, Czechs and Slovaks, and many others. Likewise, when centralized, command economies were abandoned, no practised systems of market-led production and distribution were present to replace them. The result was economic disorder and impoverishment, causing many of the victims to long for a return to the old stagnant certainties.

From these experiences one might sadly conclude that the peoples, nations and tribes of the world are doomed to swing from order to disorder and back again, from authoritarianism and oppression to liberal excess and malign division. However, the family of stable and strong democracies is evidence against such pessimism. They, too, have had a turbulent and bloody past, and they, too, still suffer divisive forces within—in the United Kingdom, for instance, the murderous communal violence in Northern Ireland. But these can be absorbed by the overall regime of democratic government, the rule of law, civic order, mutual tolerance, shared experience and national sentiment. Their example, however, points up the contrast with the condition of many countries, both European neighbours and others in the Third World, which lack those conditions of stability and internal security.

For such countries to acquire the essential bases of order and peace under democratic government will take time, and will suffer setbacks. It will also need the aid, counsel and self-control of their more fortunate fellow nations. Intervention internally—except action by the international community requested by the parties to conflict—would only heighten animosity and risk spreading the infection of war. The welcome of new or revived nations into institutions like the European Community will need to be open but cautious. The decisions of the EC summit at Maastricht in December 1991 were consistent with that theme. British refusal to mount the escalator to federal union, whatever else may be said of it, saved the Community from erecting too stiff a barrier between itself and other European countries which lack the proven experience needed for acceptance as members of such a union. 'Convergence' has to be much more than economic, and is a tough condition even for the Community's present members.

Mutual reduction of armaments began hopefully. If its progress seemed slow, after the swift disappearance of the cause of their excess, this was less for want of will than for clearer recognition of its difficulties: resettlement of demobilized personnel; the verification and disposal of surpluses, especially of nuclear weapons; anxiety over nuclear control in the former Soviet republics; the need to keep in some form the strategic deterrence which had barred world war for 40 years; the heightened dangers of proliferation; and the threat of armed conflict, not between the former superpowers, but among lesser nations and regions, conflict which might embroil the major powers or tempt intervention. The revelation that Iraq had been on the brink of building a nuclear arsenal, as well as an armoury of other weapons of mass destruction, shattered public complacency and disclosed that a world rid of East-West confrontation was still an extremely dangerous place.

So the mood of the Western world, at the end of the year, was sober and apprehensive. Its satisfaction at the collapse and discredit of communism—of which the failed coup by Soviet hard-liners in August appeared to be the last spasm—was much diluted by the spectacle of deadly strife in countries relieved of marxist tyranny only to switch their hate to neighbours of different culture, language, religion or political ambition.

Much of this could have been foreseen. Ideological, authoritarian regimes brook no rivals: dissidence is a crime, non-conformist parties are a conspiracy against the state. So, when such a regime breaks under its own failures and corruption, there is no ready-made alternative offering different policies and attracting popular loyalty. The new banners to which the people rally tend to be those not of substitute governments but of ancient social tribes. History takes over. It was no accident that the ex-communist country of Europe which suffered the worst internal strife in 1991 was Yugoslavia, a compound of peoples roped together in a national state by the greater powers, attempting to construct a unity where none had sprung from earlier history.

Westerners accustomed to thinking of the Soviet Union as a monolithic, deep-founded national entity were swiftly reminded that it was the creature of Russian imperialism, czarist and bolshevik, setting its bounds wider still and wider. The death of empires had been a major theme of world history in the mid-1900s: the Russo-Soviet empire was an anachronism as the century drew to an end. Its fragmentation conformed to all past experience, and in salvaging some form of unity from the debris in the guise of a Commonwealth its leaders were again following an historical example.

The British reservations on monetary union and the social chapter did not prevent the Community from framing a new treaty which advanced it a long way beyond the Treaty of Rome and the Single European Act. Europe, including Britain, signalled that it meant to go on consolidating its authority as a unit in the company of world powers. Renouncing war as an instrument of policy save in self-defence, it would pose no threat to any other nations or group of nations. The danger that it would present to others was that of its taking the path of exclusivity and protectionism. For the economic health, prosperity and good humour of the world much therefore would turn upon the future of GATT. Successful conclusion of the Uruguay Round ought to have been another blessing achieved in 1991. At the end of the year it seemed that five years of negotiation might end in failure, thanks mainly to the grim refusal of EC countries to trim sufficiently its ultra-protectionist system of farm support and agricultural export subsidies. Failure would be an ugly blot on the Community's record and a disaster for the world economy, not least for some of its very poor members.

Besides the Uruguay Round and the resettlement of Eastern and Central Europe and the former Soviet Union, other vital tasks for the statesmen of the world loomed at the end of the year. Among them was relieving the notorious contrast between the poor half of humanity, which had lately grown still poorer, and the other half, which even through economic recession grew even richer, exacerbating a problem of equity which concerned regions and nations as well as the global scene. Other tasks included pacifying the awful internal wars, repressions and revolts which in too many already poor countries had condemned millions to death or destitution; the assertion and defence of human rights, which in some places continued to count for little or nothing; mastering the massive migrations propelled by poverty, suffering and political turmoil, and the consequent racial tensions in reluctant host countries; rescue of the natural environment from progressive degradation; and mastering the effects of the revolution in communications which would surely be one of the most penetrative phenomena of public and private affairs in decades still to be annually registered in these historical volumes.

(London, February 1992)

I UNITED KINGDOM

CAPITAL: London   AREA: 244,100 sq km   POPULATION: 57,200,000 ('89)
OFFICIAL LANGUAGE: English, also Welsh (in Wales)
POLITICAL SYSTEM: parliamentary democracy
HEAD OF STATE: Queen Elizabeth II (since Feb '52)
RULING PARTY: Conservative Party (since May '79)
HEAD OF GOVERNMENT: John Major, Prime Minister (since Nov '90)
PRINCIPAL MINISTERS: Douglas Hurd (foreign and Commonwealth affairs), Norman Lamont (Exchequer), Kenneth Baker (home affairs), Lord Mackay of Clashfern (Lord Chancellor), Tom King (defence), Michael Heseltine (environment), Peter Lilley (trade & industry) (*for full list see* DOCUMENTS)
INTERNATIONAL ALIGNMENT: NATO, OECD, EC, Cwth.
CURRENCY: pound sterling (end-'91 £1=US$1.87)   GNP PER CAPITA: US$14,610 ('89)
MAIN EXPORT EARNERS: machinery and transport equipment, mineral fuels and lubricants, manufactured goods, chemicals, financial services, tourism

1. THE GULF WAR, DEFENCE AND EUROPE

THE news at the start of the year was largely dominated by the Gulf crisis caused by the Iraqi invasion of Kuwait in August 1990. The outcome of various peace moves was anxiously awaited as the deadline of 15 January for an Iraqi withdrawal approached. Coverage of the crisis in the media was more intense than during the Falklands War of 1982. Successive opinion polls reported consistently strong public support for firm action to secure the liberation of Kuwait. Support rose from some 60 per cent in January to over 75 per cent by the middle of February. There was a reluctant but grim readiness to use force if necessary. The main reservation was that the government should act through or with the approval of the United Nations.

The new Prime Minister, John Major, articulated the mood of the majority of the people—notably in his speech of 17 January at the commencement of the fighting. There was no triumphalist or jingoistic rhetoric—this was confined to a minority of the press. National unity was enhanced by the strong support given to government policy by the Liberal Democrats and by about three-quarters of the Labour Party. Neil Kinnock, the Labour leader, tried to maximize party unity with his emphasis on the role of the United Nations, and the need to give sanctions time to prove their efficacy one way or the other.

Even so, four Labour frontbench spokesmen resigned between 15 January and 14 February. Labour backbencher Tony Benn was the most notable of the extreme critics of the government and the war. Less sweeping but thought-provoking criticisms were made by Edward Heath (a Conservative ex-prime minister) and Denis Healey (a former Labour chancellor of the exchequer and spokesman on foreign affairs). Between them they argued that force might worsen rather than ease the problems of the region, and argued that diplomacy and sanctions should be given more time in which to work.

Anti-war groups held rallies and demonstrations both before and after the start of the fighting. Around 30,000 protested against the war in London's Trafalgar Square on 2 February. Sections of the Muslim communities were prominent in these activities, but the crisis also underlined Muslim disunity in Britain.

Some 45,000 British service personnel were ultimately involved in the coalition which drove Iraq from Kuwait between 16–17 January and 28 February. British forces were heavily engaged in some of the most difficult and dangerous operations (see V. 2). Royal Air Force Tornados were used in particularly hazardous low-level strikes against Iraqi airfields; the Royal Navy provided some of the most sophisticated minehunters; and British armoured units were prominent in the fast-moving land offensive. British casualties included 24 killed. Six aircraft were lost to enemy action.

The operation severely stretched many arms of the services, and effectively paralysed for the time being the operational capabilities of British forces in Germany. Allies, notably the United States, played an important part in the movement of personnel and equipment. The Commons defence select committee later expressed concern over the virtual absence of British shipping in the sealift (a consequence of the decline of the nation's merchant marine).

The IRA carried out a mortar attack on Number 10 Downing Street on 7 February while the war cabinet was in session discussing developments in the Gulf. Three bombs were fired from a van parked close to the Ministry of Defence. Four people, including two policemen, were slightly injured. Further explosions at Victoria and Paddington stations on 18 February resulted in the death of one person and injury to 40 others. The IRA was also believed to be responsible for the bomb outside St Albans station which disrupted rail services on 25 February, while on 5 April seven stores in Manchester were damaged by fire bombs.

The Gulf soon demanded further attention. Revolts by Kurdish and Shia rebels against the rule of Saddam Husain were brutally suppressed. By the beginning of April the mass flight of Kurds to the border with Turkey was causing particular concern. Initially the British government seemed anxious not to become involved in the internal politics of Iraq. But the scale of the human catastrophe could not be ignored. Mrs Thatcher in particular caught the attention of the media when she argued on 3 April that 'legal niceties' concerning intervention in the affairs of another state should not be allowed to stand in the way of aid to the Kurds.

Government spokesmen later claimed that plans for an international initiative had begun two days earlier. The sense of urgency was perhaps increased by the number of charges (including some from Tory ranks) of weakness and hesitancy being levelled at the government on other issues. Certainly Mr Major was determined to be seen to be firmly in the lead on the Kurdish question. On 8 April, at a summit of the European Community in Luxembourg, he set out his proposals for the creation of UN-controlled 'safe havens' in northern Iraq, in which Kurdish refugees could receive international aid.

The initiative was taken without reference to Washington, where it was not at first well received. Within two days, however, the Americans were not only lending support but were also prepared to take the initiative in providing military protection for the 'havens' should that prove necessary. British military support was promised a few days later, and the first units began to arrive on 20–21 April. In due course some 5,000 service personnel were deployed in this role. From July a smaller force served in Turkey to provide rapid relief if necessary. But intermittent Iraqi pressure on the Kurds continued.

On 24 April Mr Major followed up his Kurdish initiative by pressing for the creation of a UN register of arms sales in the hope that this might lessen the danger of arms falling into 'unsafe hands' such as the Iraq of Saddam Husain. He won support for this proposal at the summit of the Group of Seven (G7) leading industrial countries which he hosted in London in mid-July. Later reports that Britain had supplied quantities of uranium to Iraq between 1988 and 1990 were answered on 4 August by Peter Lilley, the Trade and Industry Secretary. He reported that the material in question (8.6 tonnes of depleted uranium) was used for medical and industrial purposes.

On a happier note, changes in Middle Eastern politics as a result of the Gulf crisis helped to bring about the release on 8 August of John McCarthy, who had been held for more than five years as a hostage in Lebanon. Jack Mann was freed on 24 September after 28 months of captivity. Finally on 18 November, after almost five years of captivity, came the release of Terry Waite, the special envoy of the Archbishop of Canterbury seized while engaged in negotiating the release of Western hostages in Beirut in January 1987 (see AR 1987, pp. 38, 205, 419). Later in the week Iraq freed Ian Richter, who had been held in captivity since July 1986.

On 14 November Britain joined with the United States in threatening international sanctions against Libya unless it surrendered two intelligence agents accused of the Lockerbie bombing (see AR 1988, p. 38). Colonel Qadafi responded with assurances early in December that Libya had broken off its links with terrorists—including the IRA—and that it was investigating the activities of its own intelligence service.

The speedy ending to the Gulf War also enabled arms cuts and the restructuring of the services to proceed as contemplated. NATO defence ministers on 28 May agreed to streamline allied forces in Europe by the mid-1990s. Tom King, the Defence Secretary, stated that NATO's seven corps would include a rapid reaction force under British command, with Britain supplying two of its four or five divisions. This commitment would absorb nearly half the strength of the much-reduced army of the mid-1990s. An armoured division would be based in Germany, while the second—a mobile division—would be stationed at home and would be free to operate outside the NATO area.

On 4 June Tom King announced that the army would be reduced by some 40,000 soldiers to 116,000 over the next three years. A white paper on 9 July set out in more detail the government's reaction to the implications of the Gulf War and the reduced threat from the USSR (but whose political unpredictability and military strength had still to be 'counter-balanced' in the interest of stability in Europe). The defence budget was expected to fall in real terms by 6 per cent in the next three years, mostly by savings in manpower. The number of combat aircraft was to be slightly increased, whereas there would be falls in the numbers of ships and tanks. The white paper firmly rejected any idea of a distinct European defence organization outside NATO.

Mr King added on 23 July that 22 tank and infantry units would be amalgamated. This meant a fall in the number of infantry battalions from 55 to 38 by 1997. Such changes were bound to excite protests on behalf of many of the historic regiments affected, and criticism was particularly strong in Scotland. There was controversy, too, in Northern Ireland, where the Ulster Defence Regiment was to be merged with the Royal Irish Rangers to form the Royal Irish Regiment.

The Commons defence committee, in the middle of August, fiercely attacked some aspects of government policy, arguing that it lacked a 'coherent strategic overview', and that it was guided by financial rather than military considerations. Service commitments remained much the same despite a cut of one-fifth in personnel. Defenders of the government argued that critics were ignoring its assumption that British forces would rarely be called upon to act on their own in any future 'high intensity conflict'. There were calls during the brief mid-August coup in the USSR (see IV. 2.ii) for delays to the proposed arms cuts. But Mr King replied on 20 August that British arms plans had taken account of the uncertainty surrounding the future of the USSR and were not based on the survival of Mr Gorbachev. The recent changes in Eastern Europe ruled out a surprise attack against NATO. The minister was equally firm in defence of the new policy when the failure of the coup and the break-up of the USSR brought contrary calls for much more radical defence cuts.

The European Community continued to demand much ministerial time and attention. Mr Major was anxious to escape from Britain's relative isolation in the EC under his predecessor without exacerbating tensions on the subject within his own party. Great emphasis was therefore placed on the need for an evolutionary and pragmatic approach.

The Prime Minister made his position clear at the conference of Young Conservatives in Scarborough on 9 February. 'It is simply not enough,' he argued, 'for some people to say, "I don't really like Europe but I will tolerate it", for if we take that view about Europe we will never be at the centre of it and not lead it in the direction in which we wish it to go.' At the same time, he made clear that he had no time for 'impractical dreams'.

He opened the year with two successful visits to Bonn to meet the German Chancellor, Helmut Kohl. During their first meeting, on 11 February, the two leaders agreed that their two parties should cultivate the 'closest possible relationship', and both were anxious to highlight areas of agreement. The second, on 10 March, was in no way upset by a public warning from Mrs Thatcher against the growing power of Germany.

Britain agreed that the nine-nation Western European Union should come under the general direction of the EC. This had implications for European defence. Indeed in the longer term, so Foreign Secretary Douglas Hurd noted, the European role in NATO was likely to outstrip that of the United States. Nevertheless he added a warning that the test of a 'good European' should not be to 'find out what the Americans are doing in order to do something different'.

The headquarters of the European Bank for Reconstruction and Development opened in London on 15 April (see AR 1990, pp. 411, 539). Mr Major stated at the opening ceremony that London was the natural home for Europe's first bank, and was the 'repository' of the skills which Eastern Europe needed for its new economic future.

The Queen's address to Congress on 16 May during her American tour was used as an opportunity by the British government to try to calm fears of the development of a highly protectionist 'fortress Europe' after 1992. The Queen stated that Europe must not be 'enticed into a form of continental insularity' as a consequence of its greater integration. History showed that most progress was achieved when Europeans and Americans acted 'in concert'. The troubled Uruguay Round of the GATT provided the most immediate threat to relations between the United States and Europe. This was also an area where the British were most anxious to act as bridge-builders between the EC and the United States, and where they might hope to preserve the special relationship.

2. A DEPRESSING ECONOMIC OUTLOOK

SOME progress in the control of inflation could at last be recorded. It had been slowly falling from its peak of 10.9 per cent in October 1990. By March 1991 it stood at 8.2 per cent. Cautious cuts in interest and mortgage rates became possible, but falling production figures and soaring unemployment made increasingly gloomy reading. In contrast to the recession in the early 1980s, professionals and the south-east of England were among those seriously affected. Thus unemployment in London in the winter of 1990–91 was growing faster than the national average, although the overall percentage of unemployed was still lower than in the north. Financial institutions were among those to reduce staff. The slump in the housing market was adversely affecting builders, estate agents, architects and related occupations. Even law firms were shedding personnel.

The Labour leader, Mr Kinnock, accused the government on 29 January of following a ruinous economic policy, but the Prime Minister insisted that the battle against inflation had to remain the first priority. Average wage settlements were still disturbingly high. Labour followed up its attack on 10 February by highlighting the number of job losses in high-tech industries. The CBI chairman stated that companies were reporting the lowest demand for their products since October 1980. Figures released on 11 February confirmed that overall there had been a record number of firms going out of business in 1990, and it was soon evident that the trend was still upwards.

On 25 February Labour launched a pre-election campaign entitled *Building a World Class Economy*. In a document, *Modern Manufacturing Strength*, it stressed the primacy of manufacturing in the economy, and outlined tax incentives and other measures to increase investment. It emphasized the need for partnership, not confrontation, between government and industry. Labour envisaged an 'enabling' not a 'command' approach to industry. Economic policy needed to take a long-term view in order to break the 'cycle of boom and bust'. The preparations behind Labour's proposals had included detailed consultation with many industrialists. Government figures released in March acknowledged that employment in manufacturing had fallen below 5 million for the first time on record. Manufacturing as a share of national output had fallen from 28 to 22 per cent since 1979.

Many Conservative MPs were noting with dismay just how much their own constituencies were suffering from rising unemployment. A survey published on 11 February estimated that unemployment had risen five times faster in Tory than Labour seats. Six leading economists headed by Sir Alan Walters (Mrs Thatcher's former personal adviser) warned two days later that the economy could fall into a deep depression unless interest rates were cut. They wanted Britain to leave the European exchange rate mechanism (ERM) and devalue sterling. Many exporters complained that the level of the pound was damaging British competitiveness abroad.

To the delight of Labour, a House of Lords cross-party report of 6 March agreed that more had to be done to strengthen manufacturing, finding that there had been virtually no net investment in the 1980s. The

Thatcherite ideology of leaving industry to market forces had produced a damaging shrinkage of the country's industrial base. The government could do much with tax reliefs and selective aid, and merely by helping to restore faith in manufacturing as a vital and worthy occupation. *The Times* struck a Keynesian note on 1 March when it complained that the 'prolonged idleness of capital and labour', not inflation, was the greatest evil. It was among those calling for a moderately expansionist economic policy.

Norman Lamont, the Chancellor of the Exchequer, presented his first budget on 19 March as a 'budget for business'. His increase in value-added tax (VAT) to 17.5 per cent in order to reduce the poll tax attracted much attention (see next chapter) but Mr Lamont insisted that the control of inflation was his 'central economic aim'. He also intended to create a 'broadly-based tax system' that would allow 'markets to do their job with the minimum of distortion and government interference'. The recession and to a lesser extent the Gulf conflict meant that public sector borrowing might reach £8,000 million in the coming year. There was no scope for an overall reduction in taxes in 1991–92.

The Chancellor planned to help business through the recession in the short term and to encourage investment with an eye to the future. In particular, he announced a stepped cut in corporation tax as an incentive to businesses, with a retrospective reduction of 1 per cent in the tax on profits for 1990–91. There were other miscellaneous measures to assist small companies. But increases in the tax on company cars—with other fiscal changes—threatened to withdraw with one hand some of what had been given with the other. Meanwhile, Mr Lamont made no promises on cuts to interest rates, but said he expected to see an upturn in the economy later in the year. There were small rises in child benefit, and he promised that future increases would be in line with inflation.

John Smith, for Labour, on the second day of the budget debate reminded members of the past errors in government forecasting. Among many criticisms, he described the increase in VAT as 'an inflationary own goal'. Alan Beith for the Liberal Democrats said that the budget was an attempt by the government to get out of a mess of its own making, but it was not providing a strategy that would bring the country safely out of the recession.

Analysts concluded that the budget benefited middle income groups. These would be unaffected by the ending of mortgage interest relief for higher-rate income tax payers. Other critics expressed surprise that the Chancellor had said so little on the recession and done so little (in their view) to try to reverse the downturn. The *Financial Times* was more sympathetic. It thought that the Chancellor had 'played a difficult hand bravely and skilfully . . . He has drawn a line under the Thatcher era'. In contrast, the economics editor of *The Times* complained: 'This should have been the budget for recovery, not a budget for the relief of the poll tax.' Several of the tabloids, however, called it an electioneering move (because of the poll tax relief), and linked the Chancellor with Norman Schwarzkopf, the victorious American commander in the Gulf. Lamont, they said, was another 'Stormin' Norman'.

More bad news on the economy was not long in coming. It is true that opinion polls continued to reassure the Conservatives for the time being, thus encouraging talk of an early election. But Tory opinion was shaken on 18 April when the number of unemployed topped the 2 million mark (the seasonally adjusted figure was 2,092,700) for the first time since December 1988, with the monthly increase itself being the largest registered by the current (20-year-old) system of records. It was also reported that productivity had fallen by 1.8 per cent since March 1990, whereas unit costs had risen by 11.6 per cent. Economic growth since 1979 now averaged only 1.75 per cent per year. But the rate of pay settlements was at last beginning to fall, while the number of days lost through industrial action was at its lowest since 1953. In June the government announced measures to increase the number receiving state assistance to find work (through various training courses and work experience) from 650,000 to 900,000.

The government's privatization programme continued to make progress. One of the most significant steps was the introduction of the Ports Bill in the House of Commons on 16 January. This dealt with the privatization of trust ports with a turnover in excess of £5 million a year and also with the Port of London Authority. The British Technology Group Bill was introduced the following day.

The House of Commons select committee on trade and industry published its conclusions on 21 February concerning the terms of the government's sale of the Rover Group to British Aerospace in 1988 (see AR 1989, p. 34). The report accepted that this might have been the right decision in the context of the government's privatization programme, but it did not believe that the Department of Trade and Industry had 'informed the House of all the terms of the sale'. Lord Young, the then minister responsible for the sale, was unrepentant. Gordon Brown, for Labour, said that the report raised questions about standards of integrity in public life.

3. THE POLL TAX AND THE LOCAL ELECTIONS

SUCH was the attention commanded by events in the Gulf in the first two months of 1991 that Labour had difficulty in mounting an effective attack on the new Prime Minister. Mr Major added to their frustration by blurring the edges of the unpopular policies of his predecessor. Both parties were now competing for the centre ground, to the horror of some of those on the right wing of the Conservative Party. The change was underlined by Mr Heath's commendation of the 'refreshing breeze' that was blowing through the party, though it was evident that too much praise from that quarter could injure as well as help the government by further inflaming those who were still not reconciled to the departure of Mrs Thatcher.

Meanwhile, Labour soon concluded that there were no points to be scored by depicting Mr Major as 'son of Thatcher'. He was more vulnerable to attack over his promise to create a classless society, not least because of the magnitude of the nation's social and economic problems. But Mr Major sought to maintain momentum by underlining his concern to secure higher standards in the public services. In his speech of 9 February to Young Conservatives at Scarborough, for instance, he scarcely mentioned privatization, whereas he stressed the need for quality in the public services. The nation had tolerated standards for 'far too long . . . that are just not good enough'. He singled out education for special attention, with better pay and training for teachers. The Prime Minister continued his bid for the centre ground in a speech at Southport on 23 March with his promise of a 'citizen's charter' to enforce high standards and to afford more protection and right of redress to consumers of such services as British Rail. The first version of the charter appeared in print on 22 July.

But Mr Major and his colleagues knew that the most immediate challenge which they faced at home—apart from the economy—was the future of the community charge, or poll tax. It was costly to administer and difficult to collect. Opinion polls recorded huge majorities against the tax, which was generally seen as Mrs Thatcher's most damaging legacy to her successor. By January the average levels of payment ranged from 82 per cent in shire districts to only 66 per cent in inner London. Defaulters were three times as numerous as under the old rating system. As early as 18 February the government announced a £1,700 million scheme which was expected to cut the payments of half the population of England and Wales in 1991–92.

Yet the albatross around Mr Major's neck seemed as immovable as before. Labour was promising that in office it would speedily replace the poll tax with a modified version of the old rating system to reflect ability to pay. The Ribble Valley by-election on 7 March underlined the vulnerability of the Conservatives. This had been caused by the elevation of the former home secretary, David Waddington, to the House of Lords. A Conservative majority of 19,528 at the general election of 1987 was overturned with a swing of almost 25 per cent to the Liberal Democrats. Their candidate, Michael Carr, secured 22,377 votes and a majority of 4,601. His Tory opponent attributed his defeat to 'the poll tax first, second and last: it didn't matter what we did'. While it was generally agreed that the result was a protest vote, the cause of the protest clearly had to be addressed.

Nevertheless, there was disarray at all levels of the Conservative Party. Mrs Thatcher complained during a visit to the United States that there was a tendency to undermine what she had achieved, and 'to go back to more powers for government'. Some of her strongest supporters wished to preserve the poll tax, while ministers were showered with advice from all sides concerning alternatives to the charge. It was perhaps unreasonable to expect a speedy decision on so complicated a matter, and one which had already done so much damage to the government. But Gordon Brown exercised his right as a spokesman for the opposition to claim on 10 March that the 'iron lady' had been replaced by 'the man of straw'. The honeymoon period which John Major had enjoyed since becoming premier came to an abrupt end.

There was much Conservative relief when the Chancellor, in his budget speech of 19 March, announced that VAT would be increased by 2.5 per cent (to 17.5 per cent) to finance a £140-a-head cut in the poll tax for 1991–92, with the prospect of an average charge of around £252. In the case of the London borough of Wandsworth, the residents would pay nothing, the council having planned to impose a charge of only £136 a head. This sudden action did, however, present problems for local councils, especially those which had already sent out bills. The criticism was also made that this latest increase in the Treasury's contribution to local government revenue represented a further shift of power and discretion to the centre. Locally-raised finance would fall in 1991–92 to 22 per cent of local government expenditure compared with 34 per cent in 1990–91.

Mr Smith for Labour accused the government of making a humiliating U-turn, while Mr Kinnock charged the Tories with wasting £10,000 million on the 'misery and injustice and inefficiency of the poll tax'. The £140 reduction was widely described as a panic attempt to rescue the Conservatives from defeat at the next general election.

On 25 March Nigel Lawson (the former chancellor) intervened in the debate on the future of local taxation with the comment that the government's emphasis on consultation had gone on long enough. 'To govern is to choose', he said. 'To appear to be unable to choose is to appear to be unable to govern.' Over the next four weeks Mr Major and his cabinet were subjected to much criticism on these lines—notably from the opposition, but also from many in their own party. This reached its climax on 10 April when two members of the Bruges Group (noted for its support for Mrs Thatcher's anti-federal approach to the European Community) accused the Prime Minister of 'gesture politics'. More specifically, he was charged with mishandling the crisis over the Kurdish refugees and with apparently acquiescing earlier in the American decision not to continue the Gulf War until Saddam Husain was overthrown.

Mrs Thatcher, as honorary president of the Bruges Group, totally dissociated herself from the statement, while the group itself (with a membership of about 100 Tory MPs) was in 'considerable disarray', according to its chairman. He dismissed the statement as 'poppycock'. Labour provided some distraction with its promise to cut the average household's local tax bill by £140. Chris Patten, the Conservative Party chairman, promptly retorted that the figures were entirely bogus.

The government finally announced the demise of the community charge on 23 April. Its proposals were set out in detail in a consultation document. Michael Heseltine, the Environment Secretary, stated that it would be replaced (though not until 1993) by a new council tax based on property values, with a 25 per cent discount for people living alone. The new tax would be 'substantially lower' than the last average rates bill or current community charge. All homes would be placed in one of seven bands (later increased to eight) according to their market value, and the head of the household alone would be responsible for paying the bill. There would be rebates for those on low incomes. But even some who welcomed the demise of the poll tax were dismayed by the prospects for local democracy when locally-determined revenue was expected to fall to no more than 15 per cent of the total.

Mr Heseltine claimed that the new tax would overcome the most criticized aspects of the rates and the community charge. The opposition retorted that it still retained an element of the poll tax (in fact, two householders would pay more than one) while the narrow banding did not reflect the real gap between the incomes of rich and poor in contrast to its own 'fair rates' proposals.

A consultation paper on the future of local government in England was published on the same day. Great flexibility was promised, with extensive consideration being given to local views and local circumstances. The aim was to arrive 'at the right solution for each community'. Thus there might not be a wholesale abolition of either county or district councils, or even of unitary authorities, though a movement to 'a larger number' of the last-named was 'likely'. A local government commission would oversee the implementation of what was acknowledged to be a tremendously complicated task.

The need for a general election not later than June 1992 began to have an increasing impact on the political debate. Opinion polls tended to favour the government in the early part of the year, and the media required little encouragement to speculate that Mr Major might choose to go to the country as early as June 1991. Politicians of all parties were also manoeuvring for advantage with an eye to the election, and were not averse to flying kites to test the solidity of support both for the parties themselves and for particular policies.

The local elections in England and Wales (but excluding London) at the beginning of May were naturally seen as an all-important test of the feelings of the electorate. Yet the campaigns themselves were relatively unexciting, not least because of the difficulty each party had in explaining its substitute for the poll tax. The outcome was definitely a setback for the Conservatives, though as usual with local elections the results were not easy to interpret.

Some 12,000 seats were contested. The Tories suffered a net loss of 890 seats—worse than Mr Patten, the party chairman, had anticipated. They lost control of 42 councils but added three to the list under their control. Even so, the Tory position overall was reckoned to be worse than in 1983 or 1987. The defeats in the south of England were particularly worrying, and included such places as Guildford, Lewes, Newbury and North Wiltshire, all supposedly Conservative strongholds.

Labour made a net gain of 490 seats, but the Liberal Democrats did even better (despite a fall in their share of the vote since 1987) with no less than 520 new seats. Labour added 12 councils to the number under their control, five fewer than the Liberal Democrats. Labour headed the poll overall, but the Liberal Democrats, with 18 per cent, had done well enough for a 'hung' parliament to seem a possible outcome to a general election.

Paddy Ashdown, the Liberal Democrat leader, immediately announced that if such were the case he would back either a Labour or a Tory government only in return for an undertaking to introduce proportional representation as part of a programme of legislation for a full parliament. Labour retorted that there would be no pacts, no deals. The Prime Minister asserted that proportional representation produced 'not democracy' but 'horse-trading'. Neil Kinnock argued that the local election results justified an immediate general election. A 'dithering' prime minister should not keep the nation in suspense until 1992. Mr Major's verdict was that the result was 'disappointing but bearable'.

Other events in the first half of the year included the decision of the Court of Appeal on 14 March to allow the appeal of the 'Birmingham Six', who had been convicted of murdering 21 people killed by IRA bombs in Birmingham in 1974. The Home Secretary immediately announced that a royal commission would be set up to undertake a wholesale review of the criminal justice system. On 26 June the Court of Appeal quashed the conviction of the 'Maguire Seven' (in 1976 for running an IRA bomb factory in West London), although the judgment itself provoked further controversy. According to Lord Fitt, the former leader of the Northern Ireland SDLP, a new verdict had been invented, namely 'not very guilty'. In October a former home secretary, Douglas Hurd, agreed that a new independent tribunal was needed to take over the task of handling appeals against miscarriages of justice and referring them to the Court of Appeal.

In February two adults died as a result of attacks by dogs, but it was the horrendous injuries sustained by three children in May which focused attention on the American pit bull terrier, a dog bred especially for fighting. New government legislation for the control of some dangerous dogs received the royal assent on 25 July.

On 1 May the government chose to proceed with the enactment of the War Crimes Bill, enabling suspected ex-Nazis in Britain to be brought to trial, despite the opposition of the House of Lords. The Leader of the House of Commons stated that the government would invoke its special powers under the Parliament Acts to secure the royal assent later in the week.

The new Press Complaints Commission took over the duties of the Press Council on 1 January under the chairmanship of Lord McGregor of Durris. As recommended by the Calcutt committee report of June 1990, the new body would be concerned with complaints against newspapers, not with the freedom of the press.

Newspapers were adversely affected by the recession, especially through a slump in advertising. News International's operating profits from newspapers and magazines fell by a quarter. The proprietor of Mirror Group Newspapers, Robert Maxwell (see also I.7), announced on 3 February that he had acquired the title of the short-lived *Sunday Correspondent*, which had gone into liquidation in November 1990. It was incorporated in Mr Maxwell's own weekly newspaper, *The European*, which had been launched in May 1990. At the end of May a merger of the staffs of *The Independent* and its Sunday counterpart was announced. The owners, Newspaper Publishing, suffered a pre-tax loss of £6.4 million in the first six months of 1991. The *Sunday Scot* closed in the middle of July after a four-month existence.

4. SUMMER SQUALLS

THE Labour and Conservative parties became engaged in such fierce battles over the National Health Service (NHS), education and taxation, as well as the state of the economy, that one might have been forgiven for thinking that a general election had been announced for June. There were, for instance, bitter Labour-Conservative exchanges on 12–13 May over tax policies. Labour claimed the existence of a hidden government agenda of VAT increases to meet future increases in public spending and cuts to income tax. This would mean a continuation of the massive redistribution of the burden of taxation from the rich to the poor since 1979. Ministers replied by insisting that tax cuts would not be made at the expense of the public services.

The government had been thrown on to the defensive over the NHS towards the end of April when it became known that two self-governing hospital groups (in London and Bradford) were planning 900 job losses. This was exploited by Labour, though at the same time Mr Kinnock was careful to anticipate Conservative charges of financial irresponsibility by stressing that under a Labour government improvements to public services would be dependent on economic growth. Meanwhile, it was not easy for ministers to persuade patients and the British Medical Association (BMA) that health provision was expanding to keep pace with national needs, even with 4.5 per cent increases in funding in real terms in 1990 and 1991. This encountered the argument that NHS costs tended to rise much faster than inflation.

Both general and local health issues dominated the Monmouth by-election on 16 May, when the Conservatives were defending a majority of 9,350 (their second safest seat in Wales). Indeed, this developed into one of the hardest-fought by-election campaigns of the current parliament as Tories charged Labour with spreading misinformation concerning government health policies. A high turnout of voters (76 per cent) produced a swing of 12.6 per cent against the government, giving the Labour candidate, Huw Edwards, a majority of 2,406 votes and 39.2 per cent of the vote. This was the fifth successive by-election defeat for the Conservatives. If the swing was less pronounced than at Ribble Valley or Eastbourne (in 1990), it was still a disappointing result, given Tory hopes of something better after the departure of Mrs Thatcher and the plan to replace the poll tax.

Controversy persisted after the by-election. Senior Tories, including the Prime Minister, continued for several days to accuse Labour of trying to spread a 'big lie' over government health policies. The general secretary of the Royal College of Nursing intervened on 19 May to insist that, while the trust hospitals were obviously part of the NHS, the real issues were those of under-funding and an internal market that was not working. For the time being Labour clearly held the advantage and was able to play on and increase the public's fears of 'privatization', a 'two-tier health service' and job cuts among staff. Claims by Conservatives that they were trying to make the best use of finite resources prompted the Labour retort that Tory reforms had become a new device for 'rationing health care'. Nor was the image of better management assisted by Health Secretary William Waldegrave's admission to the Commons health service committee on 22 May that many of the 57 hospital trusts had been established before submitting complete business plans to his department.

The week of the Monmouth by-election had been a bad one in general for the government. The latest unemployment figures at 2.2 million were the highest for nearly three years, and the Chancellor did not win any friends with his comment that rising unemployment and the recession were 'a price well worth paying' to get inflation down. Even the stock market was unimpressed when the latter fell to 6.4 per cent, while earlier in the week the governor of the Bank of England had warned against any hasty cuts in interest rates, as it was by no means certain that inflation had been brought under control. Others, however, feared that the high rates might be inflicting long-term damage to the economy.

The week ended with the cabinet under fire from many sides. The *Financial Times* leader of 8 May bore the headline 'A government of amateurs'. The Tories, it said, appeared 'to be adrift, without an overall strategy'. Labour, in contrast, gave the impression of knowing where it was going. *The Times* shared some of the unease, while *The Independent on Sunday* asserted on 19 May that this government 'has the look of death about it'. Some Tory papers called for an end to 'Mr Nice Guy' tactics, and urged ministers to 'get stuck into Labour's front bench'. Ministers, meanwhile, were engaged in the difficult task of trying simultaneously to retain the confidence of the party's right wing, to restore Tory morale as a whole and to adjust their policies in response to the widespread movement of public opinion against Thatcherism.

The government published a green paper, *The Health of the Nation*, on 4 June. The British, despite much advice on healthier life styles, still smoked and drank too much, took too little exercise and ate unwisely. British figures for infant mortality, life expectancy, heart disease and obesity all compared unfavourably with countries such as Japan and many European countries. The green paper outlined an ambitious programme of preventive health care with the aim of reducing premature deaths by some 30 per cent by the year 2000.

Education continued to excite controversy, with further claims of falling standards and criticism of the emphasis on narrow specialization between the ages of 16 and 18. School inspectors reported that the standard of work in 30 per cent of primary schools was 'poor', although a good start was being made to the introduction of the national curriculum. On 23 April the Prince of Wales joined in the attack on the professional educationalists. 'It is almost incredible,' he said, 'that in Shakespeare's land one child in seven leaves primary school functionally illiterate.' He was also dismayed to find that some GCSE literature courses prescribed no Shakespeare.

Both Labour and Liberal Democrats joined in the call for educational reform, the latter going as far as to promise an increase in income tax to pay for change and expansion. Meanwhile, the Department of Education was still struggling with the new national curriculum. Simplified tests for seven-year-olds were announced in September to relieve the burden on teachers; other revisions followed or were in preparation. A parents' charter was announced on 27 September whereby the parents of schoolchildren would be guaranteed extensive information to assist them in the choice of schools. Education Secretary Kenneth Clarke said he intended 'to take the mystery out of education'.

On 20 May the Prime Minister himself helped to launch the government's two white papers for the shake-up of education for all students aged over 16. The changes, he said, would form a main strand of his party's general election campaign. Above all, the reforms were designed to 'break down the artificial barrier' which had for too long divided an 'academic education from a vocational one'. Higher education reforms were spelt out in *A New Framework*, including the creation of a single funding structure for universities, polytechnics and colleges of higher education. Polytechnics would be able to call themselves universities and award their own degrees. The Education Minister added that he expected pure research to remain the province of universities, while the polytechnics concentrated on applied research. The aim was to increase participation in higher education from one in five to one in three by the year 2000. On finance nothing more specific was offered than the comment that the 'real key to . . . cost-effective expansion' lay 'in greater competition for funds and students'.

A second white paper on education and training for the twenty-first century stated that schools would be encouraged to offer a mixture of vocational and academic courses for teenagers over 16. It argued that both sets of qualifications deserved 'equal recognition'. A-levels would remain the 'benchmark of excellence'. But there would also be two new diploma certificates (ordinary and advanced) to provide entry qualifications for further training and higher education respectively. Schools would be allowed to recruit adults and part-time students into their sixth forms. All sixth-form and further education colleges would be removed from local authority control in April 1993, and would be supervised by separate councils for England and Wales. Credits of around £1,000 would be offered to 16- and 17-year-old school leavers to enter training schemes.

The new proposals were the most resolute attempt yet to grapple with Britain's shortage of engineering and other vocational skills. The *National Institute Economic Review* in May 1991 reported that only 30 per cent of the British workforce possessed the important range of qualifications below that of higher national certificates and diplomas, compared with 60 per cent for their counterparts in Germany. This shortage was a serious obstacle to efforts to raise industrial productivity in Britain. The *Review* was highly critical of the recent Youth Training Schemes, and claimed that the number of young people gaining craft-level qualifications in engineering was lower than a decade earlier.

In what was described by Labour's transport spokesman, John Prescott, as a 'massive conversion greater than that of St Paul on the road to Damascus', the Transport Secretary Malcolm Rifkind, on 28 May, announced government plans to stimulate use of the railways. Road congestion, with dire projections of worse to come, and environmental considerations had persuaded ministers to agree to a radical reappraisal of transport policy. Even increases in investment over the last four years to compensate for years of neglect were doing little more than consolidate the rail system as it was. Labour remained unimpressed and dismissed Mr Rifkind's statement as 'vague and empty'.

The privatization of British Rail still remained the government's ultimate objective. In the short-term, the Transport Secretary promised a threefold increase in government grants to enable companies to build their own rail freight sidings. Anyone who wished, he added, would be able to provide rail services for passengers as well as freight with their own staff and rolling stock. 'Monopolies are no more acceptable on the railways than elsewhere', he said, adding that new technology would provide vehicles which could make use of both road and railway.

The government remained committed to its £17,000 million road programme, but, Mr Rifkind warned on 28 May, 'taxpayers cannot by themselves be expected to bear the full costs if our requirements are to be met in the foreseeable future'. Private sector investment was imperative. A three-year research programme into road pricing would be undertaken into the controversial question of charging motorists for the use of scarce road space. But Mr Rifkind emphasized that more roads were not the answer to inner-city transport, asserting that 'more imaginative initiatives' were required. Meanwhile, in June, some relief was given to the recession-hit finances of British Rail and London Regional Transport to the tune of £453 million in grants and additional borrowing.

The management of British Rail was dismayed by the government's decision, announced at the Conservative party conference on 9 October, to opt for a more northerly route (put forward by the Ove Arup group) for the high-speed rail link from the Channel Tunnel to London. This would by-pass Waterloo and reach King's Cross through northern Kent and southern Essex. Such a line was unlikely to open before 2001, and it was intimated that public money might be necessary to help meet the costs—yet another retreat from the Thatcher era. It was argued that this route would facilitate communications with the Midlands, North and Scotland, create fewer environmental problems and assist in the development of east London as envisaged by the Department of the Environment. It was also expected to help to protect a number of Tory seats in the south-east of England. This latest decision, however, did not put an end to the debate over the best, or least damaging, route. It also seemed certain to prolong the contrast between rail travel on the British and French sides of the tunnel.

While England's test cricketers scored a rare victory over the West Indies at the beginning of June, there was little else to cheer the cricket-loving Prime Minister for much of the summer. Almost the only good news on the economic front was that inflation had fallen to 5.8 per cent (according to the headline retail price index). Unease and controversy in Tory ranks also grew as their poll ratings fell sharply behind those of Labour. Rumours added to the tension. Mrs Thatcher found it necessary to repudiate a *Sunday Telegraph* headline of 2 June that she was disappointed in Mr Major, together with claims that she had described the cabinet as the 'B-team' and Mr Major himself as 'grey' and without ideas. She declared she had no regrets over the controversial community charge, and she criticized the rise in VAT to reduce poll tax bills in 1991–92. Sources close to Mrs Thatcher stated that she would continue to support Mr Major, while putting forward her own ideas.

The Prime Minister himself tried to regain the initiative with claims on 3 June that his government had plenty of 'eye-catching ideas'. He dismissed suggestions that he was failing to give firm leadership or was losing his nerve. A leaked Bruges Group document provoked a storm with its claim that Mr Major was frightened to use the veto against a single European currency. Such a failure, it asserted, would 'accelerate a serious split' in the party. On 12 June Nicholas Ridley (a former minister) went so far as to say that some issues were so important that they came before party. But claims, criticisms and controversy of this extreme kind were regarded by most backbenchers as too expensive a luxury for a party which faced a general election within a year. Most rallied behind the government. In September the Bruges Group suffered the resignation of their chairman, Lord Harris of High Cross.

Mr Major told the Welsh Conservative party conference in Swansea on 14 June that he wanted Britain to be at 'the heart of Europe . . . To secure our future we need not abandon our past.' But on a single currency— which he accepted in principle—he insisted that there must be a prior convergence by the European economies and that the final decision must be taken by the British government and parliament. On economic and monetary union, he stated: 'We could say no. If we cannot find common ground, we may have to say no. And if necessary we will.' Earlier, on 31 May, the Chancellor had described a single currency as a 'long way down the road', with any final step being 'a leap in the dark with high risks'. He again pressed the case for the hard ecu.

But government hopes that enough had been said to paper over party cracks and to buy time in Europe were quickly shaken. A meeting of foreign ministers in Luxembourg on 17 June produced almost universal EC support for a future single currency, majority voting even on key political issues, common foreign and defence policies, and a 'federal' destiny. The programme was far too specific and comprehensive for the government to stomach. Above all, Douglas Hurd refused to commit Britain to eventual federal European government. M. Delors, the Commission's president, retorted that 'this is all far too important to take into consideration a momentary political problem in one member state' (a reference to the British government's desire to postpone key decisions until after the general election).

Mrs Thatcher seized the opportunity of a visit to the United States to assume a high profile. In a speech on 17 June, she spoke out against what she described as the 'narrow internationalism of the little Europeans'. The EC's current policies would be damaging to the fledgling democracies of Eastern Europe. 'A new wall, a wealth wall, has arisen . . . to replace the Berlin Wall.' Most Tories, having expected something much more provocative, found this reasonably satisfactory. But a political storm broke a day later. In New York Mrs Thatcher took a much more aggressive line, criticizing many aspects of the EC, and in particular underlining her opposition to a single currency. Parliament, she claimed, had controlled the nation's finances for 700 years. In Britain the executive responded directly to the people whereas control in the EC might pass to a group of people who were not democratically accountable in any way. She added that, with a 'very great effort', she had been 'very quiet at home'. The time had come for more open discussion of momentous issues. It seemed her reservations on the EC included British membership of the ERM.

Her remarks provoked an immediate and ferocious response from Mr Heath. He accused her of leaving a 'ghastly legacy' to her successor. She did not realize that 'we have a European culture as well as individual national aspects'. The European Commission was not 'autocratic in its decision-making'. Mr Patten intervened to urge Tories to unite behind the government. The best safeguard of the achievements of Mrs Thatcher's administrations, he advised, would be a fourth Conservative victory. Many MPs stressed that this was a personal rather than a party quarrel. *The Times* on 20 June added a Shakespearian rebuke:

> Maggie! Ted! Forbear! For shame! Forsooth!
> Yon Eurocaravan rolls on apace,
> With ye twain yapping in its swelling dust
> Your common cry of curs and former years.

Various opinion polls suggested that Mrs Thatcher in particular was out of tune with public feeling, though her support among Tory party workers remained strong.

A Commons debate on 26 June allowed the two ex-prime ministers to continue their battle. While Mrs Thatcher acclaimed Mr Major as a 'leader of vision', she listed five points on which Britain must stand firm in defence of national sovereignty. In effect she called for the European clock to be stopped, and warned against the advance of a federal Europe 'by stealth'. Mr Heath, however, urged the creation of monetary union and a single currency as soon as possible. Labour complained that the government had failed to work out 'a clear negotiating line', although the thinking of its own front bench might not have fared better under close scrutiny. Mrs Thatcher announced on 28 June that she would not stand at the next election, but promised to intensify her struggle against a federal Europe and single currency.

Labour, too, had its problems. The death of the notable left-wing Labour MP, Eric Heffer, necessitated a by-election in Walton, Liverpool, on 4 July in which a Militant-backed 'Real Labour' candidate, Mrs Lesley Mahmood, stood against the official Labour choice. Mrs Mahmood echoed the late Mr Heffer's complaint that Labour had become the 'SDP Mark 2', and defended her earlier campaign against the poll tax (for which she had been expelled from the Labour Party)—'Better to break the law than to break the poor.' Liverpool was described in one report as the poverty capital of Britain (it being estimated that 40 per cent of the inhabitants were living below 'the accepted minimum standard').

Labour had already been embarrassed by left-wing activists during the local elections in Liverpool at the beginning of May. Not only had six official Labour candidates been opposed by members of the 'Broad Left', but five of the latter had been elected to the council. On 22 May the national Labour leadership expelled 25 Liverpool councillors from the party, and set out to discover the identities of those who had worked for the six. This was a follow-up to action already taken against the Militant Tendency in Birkenhead, Bermondsey and Tower Hamlets.

In the July by-election Peter Kilfoyle (Labour) won 21,317 votes against 2,613 for Mrs Mahmood. The Liberal Democrat candidate was a good second, Labour's 1987 majority having been reduced by nearly three-quarters. Later in the month the national Labour leadership sought to consolidate its success against Militant by suspending 147 party members for backing Mrs Mahmood. It also suspended the constituency party in Birkenhead after an 18-month deselection battle had been finally resolved in favour of the sitting MP, Frank Field, a Labour moderate.

Just when the thoughts of MPs might normally have been turning to the summer recess, a financial scandal injected new life into parliamentary debates. On 5 July, as a result of a global operation led by the Bank of England, the Bank of Credit and Commerce International (BCCI) was closed down following the discovery of widespread fraud. This was the world's largest banking disaster. British investors included a number of local authorities (see also I. 8). Investigation by the Serious Fraud Office, however, failed to quieten critics when more evidence appeared of the extent to which BCCI operations had been arousing suspicion from 1987—and even earlier. Further questions were asked regarding the handling of the affair by the Bank of England (which had received firm evidence of huge losses at least as early as the spring of 1990).

On 18 July Mr Kinnock claimed that the scandal went to the heart of the regulation of the financial system. Suggestions that BCCI accounts were being used to fund Palestinian terrorists, and possibly nuclear programmes in Iraq, intensified Labour's pressure for information on ministerial knowledge of what was happening. The Prime Minister on

22 July announced that an official inquiry would be conducted by Lord Justice Bingham. The bitterness of some of the exchanges could be gauged from Mr Major's retort to Neil Kinnock on 23 July: 'If you are saying I am a liar, you had better say so bluntly.' The uproar in the Commons equalled the noisiest of the Thatcher era. Efforts to rescue BCCI came to nothing in the autumn.

5. THIS YEAR, NEXT YEAR . . . ?

DURING the summer the government continued to look anxiously for signs of an economic recovery. In August came news that inflation had fallen to 5.5 per cent, a three-year low, but the unemployment figures showed the biggest July increase since 1945, with 2.37 million out of work. The Bank of England concluded that at best the economy was merely 'bumping along the bottom'. The numbers in arrears with their mortgages had tripled since 1989 while home repossessions had more than doubled compared with the first half of 1990. The biggest increases had occurred in the south-east of England.

Even so, from the end of August several opinion polls broke the sequence of Labour leads, while some economic statistics made more hopeful or at least less gloomy reading. A surprise half-point cut in interest rates on 4 September (a fall from 15 to 10.5 per cent since the autumn of 1990) immediately triggered off talk of a November election. Mr Major was also scoring points for himself and his party as an international leader, whereas Mr Kinnock was seen by many as a vote-loser despite his success in remodelling his party. The Tories tried to turn that achievement against him by suggesting that he lacked political convictions. Mr Lamont labelled him a 'perpetual calendar'.

The first half of September witnessed Britain's worst spate of street violence since 1981. The disorders began in Cardiff, Oxford and Birmingham. Five hours of riot, looting and arson took place on the Meadow Well estate in North Shields on the night of 9–10 September, and further outbreaks occurred in Newcastle on 12–13 September. But the Home Secretary firmly rejected calls for increased local authority spending. Extra funds for the police would have to be at the expense of other services. Labour claimed that government spending curbs were fuelling inner-city discontent as well as weakening the police. The Home Office on 13 September announced an 18 per cent increase in recorded crime in England and Wales in 1990, notably in car crimes.

Meanwhile, the conference season began early in September with the assembly of the Trades Union Congress (TUC) in Glasgow. To the relief of the Labour leadership, a motion for the repeal of all Conservative union legislation since 1979 was heavily defeated. Public sector unions were also warned of the political damage that could be inflicted on

Labour by strikes in the period before the election. But unions did agree to boycott the government's new temporary work scheme for the long-term unemployed. Conservatives, meanwhile, warned of a new era of industrial strife if Labour were returned to office.

The TUC also agreed to come to terms with EC legislation which was largely at odds with Britain's historic adversarial industrial relations. John Edmonds of the General, Municipal, Boilermakers' and Allied Trades Union (GMB) emphasized that unions must change with the times and embrace European practices and institutions, or be left out in the cold. A motion attacking the single union, no-strike deals favoured by Japanese firms received qualified approval. Its accusation that Japanese companies followed an 'alien approach' was strongly opposed by both the AEU engineering union and the GMB. Despite reservations from some skilled workers' unions, the conference supported the call for a statutory minimum wage.

The Liberal Democratic Party conference in Bournemouth (8–12 September) was a confident, disciplined affair. Their leader, Paddy Ashdown, had gained a considerable national reputation (far ahead of his party's modest place in the opinion polls). He took full advantage of this to guide the conference towards a series of tough decisions. Much was made of the argument that Labour could not win. It had, said Mr Ashdown, left a 'huge vacuum and this party intends to occupy it'. The Liberal Democrats had to project a new vision and provide a distinctive and radical programme. It had no future merely 'positioned somewhere between the other two'. Under its new slogan 'Changing Britain for Good', the party was committed to the five Es—education, the enterprise economy, Europe, the environment and electoral reform. Support for economic enterprise would include tough measures against monopolies.

In the run-up to the two main party conferences, the government received the cheering news that inflation had fallen to 4.7 per cent in August. The governor of the Bank of England backed up claims that the recession was ending. The polls, however, began to move back in favour of Labour or at least to suggest a hung parliament. Evidence on the state of the economy remained ambiguous, while the number of business failures reached 900 a week. The Treasury was advising the Prime Minister to wait until 1992 for an election. A decision to this effect was taken during the last weekend in September.

Labour's eight-year-old battle against Militant reached a climax at the opening of its conference in Brighton on 29 September. There was overwhelming support for the leadership's earlier decision to suspend two MPs (Terry Fields, Liverpool Broadgreen, and Dave Nellist, Coventry South East) for their alleged links with the Trotskyist sect (their expulsions followed at the beginning of December). Elections to the national executive committee strengthened Mr Kinnock's influence over the party machine, notably with the election of Gerald Kaufman (shadow spokesman on foreign affairs), while the representation of the far left was confined to Tony Benn and Denis Skinner. Mr Kinnock also refused to be tied by a conference vote in favour of cuts in British defence spending. Indeed, critics of the leadership had little opportunity to make an impact, with Labour now following Tory practice by turning the conference into a well-orchestrated rally.

The main object of Mr Kinnock's conference speech on 1 October was to demonstrate his own eligibility, and that of his party, for office. He had also to overcome the criticism that Labour, in its policy review, had been more successful in jettisoning old thinking than in persuading people that it had strong principles and a clear programme. He argued, for instance, that taxation of the better-off to help the poor was not 'the politics of envy but the ethics of community'. The speech was rapturously received by most delegates and was widely described as his best ever at a conference.

Mr Kinnock affirmed that a Labour government would restore Britain to the first division of European states in terms of economic growth, public services and welfare. The Tories, he insisted, had nothing new to offer in a fourth term—only 'more of the same'. At home he put special emphasis on his party's determination to protect and develop the NHS, whereas a vote for the Tories would be a vote to break up the service. He promised a crusade against child poverty, a national minimum wage, a freedom of information act, a bill of rights, reform of the House of Lords, and devolution 'first to Scotland and then, with consent, to Wales and the regions of England'. In addition, he responded to the recent 'on-off' election speculation and gamesmanship with what was in effect a Labour commitment to fixed-term parliaments.

The shadow chancellor, John Smith, made specific pledges to increase child benefit and state pensions. He promised no cuts in the basic rate of income tax. A Labour government would introduce higher national insurance contributions from the better paid, and there would be a new income tax rate of 50 per cent to be paid by those earning some unstated figure in excess of £30,000 a year. The first call on additional revenue as it became available would be investment in neglected public services.

The debate on the NHS proved to be one of the highlights of the Labour conference. This was an area where delegates were convinced that the public was strongly behind them. Robin Cook promised quick action against the government's policy on trust hospitals, and stated that over the lifetime of the next parliament a Labour ministry would try to correct the underfunding of the service (put at £6,000 million by the BMA). On the same day more details appeared of financial and other problems in one-third of the new trust hospitals. The Prime Minister quickly responded on 4 November with a promise of more money for the NHS. Yet neither party could feel confident that it had complete answers when confronted, for instance, by the fact that London had some of the country's longest hospital waiting lists despite above-average medical provision.

If perhaps the main task of Labour at its conference had been to try to bring its leader's popular rating into line with the party's standing in the opinion polls, that of the Tories as they assembled in Blackpool on 8 October was exactly the opposite. The party chairman, Chris Patten, made an early impression with his attack on Labour as a 'clapped-out relic' of the nineteenth century 'hobbling on its zimmer frame into the sunset'. Labour had no bedrock of principle and was campaigning with 'sleazy' smears against Tory policies. Douglas Hurd balanced a positive attitude towards the EC with the warning that it must not become a 'strait-jacket' of federalism. Mr Lamont tried to cheer delegates with an optimistic prognosis concerning the economy, while Mr Waldegrave offered a spirited defence of Tory policy on the NHS. The patient's charter, he promised, would enshrine free health care for all.

The Tories, despite some early fears to the contrary, managed to avoid serious disputes in the main conference proceedings. The tumultuous ovations accorded to Mrs Thatcher (who did not speak) and to Mr Heseltine (who did) suggested a determination to forgive if not forget the traumatic leadership contest a year earlier (see AR 1990, pp. 34–41). Mr Major's speech—in style as well as much of its substance—discreetly signalled the changes from the Thatcher era, beginning with the replacement of the almost regal 'we' much used by his predecessor by the more modest and at times self-deprecatory 'I'. In general, he set out to capitalize on those of his personal characteristics which were responsible for his current popularity, and which distinguished him from Mrs Thatcher and Mr Kinnock. He reiterated his commitment to the creation of a classless Britain where people would have 'the power to choose and the right to own'. He emphasized that there would be no privatization of the NHS—'Not ever while I'm Prime Minister'. He assured the 'Eurosceptics' that he would put the national interest first at Maastricht and would have no truck with a European super-state.

If some critics looked for more vision and substance from the conference, the majority of delegates went away seemingly happy and reassured. But the cheering news of the day, that inflation had fallen to 4.1 per cent, was balanced by yet more reports of job losses. Labour also showed that it was determined to keep the NHS at the top of the political debate in the run-up to the election. Mr Kinnock insisted that the government was engaged in 'creeping, corrosive' privatization.

6. THE BUMPY ROAD TO MAASTRICHT

DOMESTIC and foreign politics continued to interact, especially given the controversies surrounding British membership of the EC. The likelihood that far-reaching decisions would be taken at the EC summit in Maastricht at the end of the year presented the government with a formidable test of its political skills, both in dealings with its European partners and given the divisions in its own party at home. Meanwhile, the summer gave the Prime Minister several opportunities to star on the international stage.

As chairman of the G7 states, Mr Major hosted the mid-July summit in London and became responsible for the co-ordination of Western moves to assist the USSR. During the attempted Moscow coup in August (see IV.2.ii), the British gave strong political backing to Boris Yeltsin. Nevertheless Mr Major continued to insist—in contrast to Labour's calls for massive assistance on the lines of a new 'Marshall Plan'—that expert help in the development of a market economy and of the USSR's vast natural resources must take precedence. Some Soviets agreed that the USSR was in no state as yet to make full use of large-scale aid.

During a working holiday in the United States, the Prime Minister and President Bush produced a six-point aid plan which Mr Major then outlined to Messrs Gorbachev and Yeltsin in Moscow on 1 September. Mr Major warned that the scale of Western aid would be dependent upon the credibility of Russian reform plans, and upon significant arms cuts. While in Moscow he also discussed the control and siting of Soviet nuclear weapons, and was assured by Mr Gorbachev that all the existing international agreements would be honoured. Britain, after some earlier hesitation, joined its EC partners on 27 August in recognizing the independence of the three Baltic states (see IV.2.i).

From the USSR the Prime Minister flew on to China. This was a more controversial mission, it being the first visit by a Western leader since the Tiananmen Square massacre in 1989 (see AR 1989, 338–40). He defended his trip on the grounds that it was better to talk with the Chinese than engage in armchair denunciations. In particular, he urged the leaders in Beijing to improve their record on human rights. He replied to complaints of past acts of Western aggression against China by declaring that the global movement towards democracy was unstoppable. World opinion would not forget Tiananmen Square. During his stay in China he signed the agreement on the building of the new Hong Kong airport (see IX.2.iii). But complaints persisted that not enough was being done to protect the colony's interests in anticipation of its return to Chinese control in 1997.

At the Commonwealth conference in Zimbabwe (16–21 October) Mr Major argued that the bedrock of the future Commonwealth must be the general application of democracy and good government (see XI.2).

The Harare Declaration cautiously linked economic aid to the human rights record of recipient countries. The Prime Minister also promised to cancel the debts of the poorest countries in accordance with the 'Trinidad terms', whether other creditor nations agreed or not. But Britain remained a lone Commonwealth voice in calling for an early end to sanctions against South Africa.

Nearer home, as preparations intensified for the Maastricht summit, so controversy intensified between opposing factions in the Conservative Party. Tension also increased between the British government and those in Europe who wished to force the pace towards greater unity. There were times when more than the customary forms of bargaining and manoeuvring appeared to be at work. Some of the exchanges became increasingly bad-tempered and dogmatic. Nevertheless, the Prime Minister persevered with his visits to key European capitals and painstakingly tried to lessen differences by personal diplomacy. But he also engaged in some plain speaking. In Paris on 12 September he gave firm backing to the 'wideners'—those who wished to see the EC expand to include Eastern Europe and perhaps ultimately the USSR—as opposed to the 'deepeners' who looked for maximum progress towards greater unity at Maastricht. It was important, he said, not to slam doors in the face of other Europeans. M. Delors retorted that some countries had never wanted more than a 'vague sort of free trade zone'.

The British firmly opposed EC proposals for common immigration, foreign and defence policies. The French were seen as uncomfortably interested in a stronger European defence identity even if they agreed for the time being to the continued primacy of NATO. Mr Major argued on 8 November that any European defence pillar should not duplicate or undermine NATO's present functions. Pressure was also growing in Brussels in favour of a stronger European Parliament, another area where the British entertained reservations.

On 30 October Labour spelt out its terms for acceptance of a single currency. Support for European integration was underlined, but a 'real convergence' of national economies was essential if a union was to succeed. It wanted a central bank to be politically accountable. At the same time, Labour spokesmen attacked ministers for risking national interests while they concentrated on preserving Tory unity. The Liberal Democrats interjected the complaint that both parties were too selective in their commitment to Europe.

The director-general of the CBI on 4 November joined those who were urging the Prime Minister not to sign any deal in Maastricht unless the terms were right. On the same day Mr Hurd accused the EC Commission of trying to penetrate the 'nooks and crannies' of British life. Immigration policy, for instance, had to be based on national backgrounds. 'We cannot harmonize history', opined Mr Hurd. But Tory Euro-sceptics were not reassured. Norman Tebbit, the former party chairman, reinforced his earlier arguments against greater unity and a single currency with the warning that nothing less than 'the loss of the ability to control our lives in this island' was at stake. Mr Ridley on 9 November advised electors to inquire closely into the European opinions of parliamentary candidates. If necessary they should vote against a Tory Europhile.

Mr Major, in his Guildhall banquet speech on 11 November, warned of the 'potential impact' on British influence and prosperity if Britain failed to keep in step with its partners. Although it would be wrong to join a single currency 'now', it would be equally wrong to decide that Britain would never do so. Meanwhile, tensions in Tory ranks gave rise to the election on 13 November for a new chairman of the backbench European affairs committee. This was treated as a test of loyalty to the government. Sir Norman Fowler, a former cabinet minister and a supporter of Mr Major on Europe, was successful. But ministers proceeded more cautiously in the preparations for the Commons debate on Europe of 20–21 November. The motion for debate was phrased in such a way as to maximize party unity—and perhaps also to serve as a warning to their partners on the continent. The motion called for Britain to be at the heart of a Europe which avoided a federal character.

Mr Major used the debate to warn that a deal at Maastricht might be 'genuinely unobtainable'. Mr Kinnock, however, contended that it was not enough for Britain to play for a draw at the summit. No semi-detached arrangement would adequately protect the national interest. Sir Geoffrey Howe, whose differences with Mrs Thatcher over Europe a year earlier had had such momentous consequences (see AR 1990, pp. 38–41), contended that a British veto would not stop the rest of the EC leaving Britain behind.

As expected, Mrs Thatcher made an aggressive speech, issuing warnings against federalism and proposals which involved an unacceptable transfer of responsibility for economic policy from the Commons (which was clearly accountable to the British people) to Community institutions (which were not). While she promised to vote for the government motion, she argued that the issue of a single currency was so fundamental that in certain circumstances it would warrant a national referendum. Paddy Ashdown also called for a referendum, as did some left-wing Labour MPs led by Tony Benn. Fourteen Tories headed by Norman Tebbit took the same line.

Momentarily it seemed as if the government might waver on this issue, but Mrs Thatcher's friends insisted that what she had in mind was an early referendum on a deal at Maastricht, not one at some stage in the later 1990s. Labour was beginning to claim that 'the back-seat driver had seized the wheel'. Mr Major therefore repeated that he saw no need for a referendum. Mr Hurd not only argued that parliament could not shirk its responsibilities, but also reminded Mrs Thatcher of her opposition to the one held in 1975. The government secured a majority of 101 at the end of the two-day debate. Only a handful of Tories dissented or abstained.

Foreign-exchange markets, however, already nervous for other reasons, became even more so as they reflected on the implications of an unsatisfactory outcome at Maastricht. The Bank of England had to intervene on 22 November to protect the pound. On the same day Mrs Thatcher criticized the British and other Western governments for failing to recognize the breakaway republics of Croatia and Slovenia in Yugoslavia. Over the weekend Tory in-fighting escalated until MPs began to remember they had an election to fight in 1992. In the end it seemed that Mrs Thatcher had been weakened by the controversy. Meanwhile, in a House of Lords debate on 25 November, the former prime minister, Lord Callaghan, argued that there was no longer such a thing as 'pure sovereignty'. Concern for it symbolized nostalgia for the past. Mr Kinnock later ruled out a referendum on monetary union, arguing that it was simply a refuge for politicians who were trying to escape from a dilemma.

Expectations of tension and tough bargaining at Maastricht to devise a new European union treaty were amply fulfilled. Only in the early hours of 11 December, after two days of strenuous negotiation, were the final terms of the treaty agreed (see XI.3 and XIX.4), and the Prime Minister was persuaded that he had achieved sufficient concessions to satisfy the bulk of the Tory Party. At one point in the talks, with his mind apparently on the Duke of Wellington at Waterloo, Mr Major spoke of 'hard pounding', adding grimly: 'Let's see who pounds the longest.' Other participants used the analogies of 'street fighting' or 'arm wrestling'.

The British finally secured the right to opt out from the single European currency which their partners hoped to see in being by 1999 at the latest. They also thwarted moves to give the EC new powers over British social and labour law, arguing that these provisions of the European Social Charter threatened to reduce the competitiveness of industry and therefore to put workers' jobs at risk. The other eleven member states were left to proceed independently on this issue. The notorious 'F-word'—federal—was also omitted from the treaty.

The British were reassured on the question of the primacy of NATO despite new plans to strengthen the Western European Union. Greater co-operation in foreign affairs was qualified by the need for a unanimous vote to agree the framework for a joint foreign policy. The British welcomed a declaration reaffirming the EC's readiness to consider applications for membership from democratic European states. They supported the increase in the accountability of the Brussels bureaucracy to the European Parliament.

Much was made by the British negotiators of their diplomatic skill, pragmatism and command of detail, particularly those displayed by the Prime Minister, who claimed that he had won 'game, set and match' at Maastricht. Personal relations with European leaders had not been damaged by controversy to the same degree as in the past. Some of the latter appeared to concede that there existed very real cultural and historical differences between Britain and its continental neighbours. But the German newspaper *Die Zeit* described Britain as an obstructive 'troublemaker' and Mr Major as 'Margaret Thatcher in friendly packaging'. The Belgian Foreign Minister claimed that an attempt was being made to turn Britain into 'the Hong Kong of Europe, with very low social costs'.

Meanwhile, at home, the detailed deliberations within the cabinet and ministerial sensitivity to backbench opinion had greatly reduced Tory divisions. Strong support for the Maastricht deal was forthcoming from major business interests which clearly wanted no trouble from the Euro-sceptics. Mr Kinnock accused the government of 'abdication, not negotiation' at Maastricht, while Roy Hattersley insisted that a Labour government would reverse the opt-out over the social charter. The Employment Secretary conceded that the charter did not require the repeal of government legislation curbing trade union power.

There were fierce parliamentary exchanges on 18–19 December over the outcome at Maastricht and especially over the question of the social charter. Labour accused the government of settling for a down-market economy on the fringe of Europe. Despite Mr Tebbit's bitter attack on the Maastricht terms, only six Tories followed him into the division lobby. The government prevailed by 339 votes to 253.

Later in the month British ministers were dismayed when EC officials dismissed as unacceptable the latest proposals for a compromise within GATT on farm subsidies. They found some support for their position at a meeting of ministers in Brussels on 23 December, but Britain feared a major world economic crisis unless progress was made on this controversial issue.

7. DOMESTIC AFFAIRS IN THE FINAL QUARTER

THE government continued to talk of, and to hope for, an economic upturn before the end of the year. But evidence of a persisting recession continued to outweigh the occasional statistic which promised something better. Early in November the CBI called for a reappraisal by the government of its industrial priorities. Above all, it should follow the example of Germany and Japan in promoting national economic competitiveness, perhaps through the creation of a department of enterprise. Ministers were lacking in 'strategic purpose'.

Inflation averaged only 4 per cent over the two months of October and November, but the pessimism of the CBI seemed to be confirmed by the December survey of industrial trends which reported a decline in factory output for the third month in succession. Unemployment edged above the politically sensitive level of 2.5 million in December, while the underlying trade gap was at its widest since January. An all-party Treasury select committee expressed doubts concerning an early recovery.

Meanwhile, the government continued to press ahead with its trust hospital programme, announcing its approval of 99 more applications for implementation in 1992. At the same time, it continued to try to reassure the public in the face of Labour's charges of 'commercialization' of the NHS (this now being accepted by the opposition as a more accurate description of government policy than 'privatization'). The patient's charter—with its 'ten commandments' relating to the rights of patients—was launched on 30 October and was to be implemented from April 1992. Critics questioned whether the government would provide the resources to fulfil such guarantees as a maximum wait of two years for hospital treatment. On 21 October the government announced additional welfare benefits for the very elderly and most vulnerable with effect from April 1992.

The Children Act 1989, the most sweeping legal reform affecting children in the twentieth century, came into force on 14 October. For the first time parents in a divorce case were compelled to consider the interests of their offspring. Provision was also made to try to improve the handling of child care and suspected child abuse cases by all the parties involved. The act created what were virtually specialized family courts.

The end of October saw the launch of 'Opportunity 2000', a business-led initiative to increase the participation and influence of women in the workforce. Mr Major used the occasion to announce a drive to add to the number of women holding high public appointments. 'Why should half of our population go through life like a hobbled horse in a steeplechase?' he asked. Various efforts to the same end in the past, however, had had only limited success. Britain, for instance, lagged behind many leading European countries in the ratio of women to men in politics.

The impending general election in 1992 compelled the government to content itself with a selective programme in the Queen's Speech on 31 October. The highest priority was to be given to pushing through the council tax. But ministers were also determined to make an impact on education. The Prime Minister offered further assurances on the NHS. But that same evening the Chancellor in his Mansion House speech seemed troubled by the extent to which public spending was soaring above government targets. He reiterated his calls for economic prudence.

In his autumn statement the Chancellor announced an increase of

£11,000 million in government expenditure for 1992–93, and conceded that public spending as a proportion of national income would temporarily rise. The budget of the Transport Department was increased by a quarter, with more funds being given to British Rail and London Underground. Critics, however, complained that the sums in question fell far short of what was needed to bring significant improvements to the rail systems. Additions to the funding for the NHS brought the increase in real terms since 1979 to 50 per cent. Education, inner cities and social security were other major beneficiaries. *The Times* commented that this was 'a pre-election giveaway on a scale not seen for many years' and an 'undeniable' Tory U-turn.

Three by-elections held on 7 November brought no comfort to the government. The Liberal Democrats overturned a Tory majority of some 2,000 in Kincardine and Deeside. Labour won the Tory marginal seat of Langbaurgh, the sort of seat it had to win if it was to secure victory at the general election. On the other hand, the swing (3.5 per cent) was below the critical figure of 8 per cent needed across the nation to put Labour in power in 1992. Labour easily retained the safe Hemsworth seat.

Robert Maxwell, the newspaper proprietor, died on 5 November while cruising in the Canary Islands (see OBITUARY). A month later his great business empire of some 400 interlocking units collapsed, racked by financial scandal and huge debts. All of the Maxwell family's main assets—including Mirror Group Newspapers (MGN) and Maxwell Communication Corporation (MCC)—were put up for sale. Ministers, in response to disclosures concerning the transfer or loan without proper authority of very large sums from MGN pension funds into family private businesses, promised that measures to stop companies acting in this way would be introduced as soon as possible. The Serious Fraud Office began investigations into the Maxwell empire. Meanwhile *The Times* and the *Washington Post* were among those to express concern over the readiness of powerful financial institutions to work with Mr Maxwell, especially after an official inquiry had concluded 20 years earlier that he was unfit to hold the stewardship of a public company.

Early in the morning of 1 December IRA incendiary devices caused fires in several London West End stores. This was the start of a series of incidents. On 15 December, for the first time, prized art treasures were targeted when an incendiary device was set off in the National Gallery. There was little damage. BR's London services were disrupted the following day, and a week later the Underground network was closed during the morning rush-hour.

The rising tide of mortgage repossessions—estimated at 80,000 or more for 1991 and threatening to escalate further in 1992—prompted government action in the third week of December. It was recognized that a recovery in the housing market would be delayed, with all its political and economic implications, as long as large numbers of repossessed homes were being sold at knock-down prices. The Tories, with a general election fast approaching and in view of the massive encouragement which they had given to home ownership since 1979, could not afford to remain inactive on this sensitive subject. On 19 December the Chancellor produced a package which it was hoped would help to kick start the property market and halve repossessions in 1992. Stamp duty on house purchases (up to £250,000) was waived until 1 August 1992. Banks and building societies added further relief by financing schemes to enable defaulting mortgage-holders to become tenants in their own homes. The government agreed that the mortgage interest element in income support for the unemployed should be paid directly to the lenders.

A mass Sunday opening by major retailers in England and Wales in the run-up to Christmas followed the decision of the Attorney-General not to enforce Sunday trading rules under the 1950 Shops Act. Church leaders sent a joint letter of protest accusing the government of conniving at illegal activities and of undermining the traditional Sunday. Many consumers welcomed the move, but sales did not benefit proportionately. A ruling by the European Court of Justice was awaited.

Although 1991 had seen a considerable reduction in the current-account deficit compared with 1990, the underlying trends were worrying. Nor had any other recession since 1945 left the nation with a foreign deficit, an imbalance which existed despite the huge relief given to the balance of payments by North Sea oil, a fact which underlined the disappointing performance of the manufacturing sector since 1979.

8. SCOTLAND

SCOTTISH local authorities continued to suffer from the effects of the poll tax, despite the government announcement on 23 April that it was to be abolished. In November it was reported that almost £1,000 million had not been paid since the introduction of the tax in 1989, a sum equal to the cost of half the annual education budget. The numbers in arrears or refusing to pay continued to rise. The government's proposed substitute for the poll tax, the council tax with its eight bands, was criticized by the opposition parties as cumbersome, unfair and no real solution to the problem of local government funding. The Secretary of State, Ian Lang, retorted that the new tax avoided the pitfalls of the old rating system. He was also planning to strengthen the capping powers against spendthrift councils. Donald Dewar for Labour retorted that fierce capping would injure local democracy.

A consultation document on the future of local government in

Scotland was published on 17 June. In addition, the Secretary of State said that he was impressed by the case for unitary authorities instead of the two-tier structure which had been in operation in mainland Scotland since 1973. The new councils should reflect local allegiances and natural physical boundaries. Several Scottish local authorities were affected by the collapse of the Bank of Credit and Commerce International (see I.4), most notably the Western Isles council which had invested some £24 million with BCCI.

At the Tory party conference in Perth early in May the leadership made other departures from the conservativism of the Thatcher era. Ian Lang stated on 9 May that perhaps Conservative policies had been too often expressed 'in abstract and ideological terms, when we should have been relating them more clearly to everyday issues'. He believed in a 'common-sense', broad and tolerant party. In the NHS he wanted to see more patient's rights, more preventive medicine and better health care. Tenants were entitled to a better service from their landlords.

Despite some resurgence of interest in devolution in the party, the leadership would have none of it. Devolution, it was claimed, would damage business confidence and frighten away foreign investors with the threat of additional Scottish taxes. Proposals for some sort of advisory senate could be justified only if a network of regional assemblies were set up throughout the United Kingdom. In contrast, a few days later the general assembly of the Church of Scotland overwhelmingly backed a call from the former Liberal leader, Sir David Steel, to support the constitutional convention and its bid for a Scottish parliament.

Tory representation in Scotland slumped to nine seats on 7 November, when the Liberal Democrats won the Kincardine and Deeside by-election and thereby jumped to second place behind Labour in the number of Scottish parliamentary seats held. A week later Mr Major responded to questions in the Commons on devolution by insisting that none of the proposed alternatives to the union had 'credibility'.

Meanwhile, the Scottish Nationalists (SNP) were busily presenting themselves as more than a party of protest. On 18 September they set January 1993 as a target date for independence, and proceeded to spell out plans for economic development, full employment and a war on poverty. Scotland, they argued, had the potential to become one of the most prosperous states in Europe. Much was made of opinion polls which indicated up to 37 cent support for independence. In October SNP leader Alex Salmond announced his team for the first government of an independent Scotland.

In general, the first half of the year saw a weakening of the economy and a sharp decline in business confidence, with unemployment reaching 9.2 per cent in mid-summer. Lanarkshire continued to suffer from the decline of the steel industry, while further job losses were in prospect at Ravenscraig and Dalzell. Yarrow Shipbuilders were among several firms to be adversely affected by defence economies. The naval dockyard at Rosyth stood to lose one-fifth of its workforce, while the US nuclear submarine base in the Holy Loch was expected to close in 1992. On the other hand, Japanese investment continued to grow. Scotland was already producing more than a third of Europe's total personal computer output. On 11 November British Rail chose Mossend in Lanarkshire as the Channel Tunnel's Scottish freight terminal. Kvaerner Govan won a record-breaking shipbuilding contract in December.

The new tests in primary schools under the national curriculum were opposed by many Labour councils, teachers and parents. The Convention of Scottish Local Authorities on 1 June called for radical changes to the system. The latest government plans for higher education included the establishment of a single funding council for Scotland's eight universities and 17 central institutions. Four of the latter were deemed eligible for university status.

9. WALES

EVIDENCE of the diverse effects of the recession were to be seen in many areas of Welsh life during the year. Unemployment continued to increase (9.4 per cent by the end of the year) and nearly 2,000 businesses collapsed, a 74 per cent increase on the 1990 total. The manufacturing sector, traditionally crucial to the Welsh economy, continued to suffer from lack of investment and high interest rates. It was reported that since 1975 the number of manufacturing jobs had fallen from 317,000 to 249,000; further decline was expected. Although during the same period the numbers employed in the service sector rose from 527,000 to 670,000, few of these jobs went to those made redundant following the decline of heavy industries. The closure of the Penallta colliery in Ystrad Mynach in November meant that British Coal now had only three working pits and 1,000 miners in south Wales.

In agriculture farm incomes fell to a record post-war low, and there were calls for government support to facilitate adjustment to lower production levels as well as to encourage the recognition of the farmer's role as steward of the countryside. It was also argued that the interests of Welsh farming were not being adequately represented in the European Community. However, rural communities were given a boost by a new 'Rural Initiative' announced by the Secretary of State for Wales, David Hunt, in December.

Welsh Office proposals on local government reorganization in Wales published in June generated much discussion. It was generally agreed that the present two-tier system should be replaced by a single tier but there was no consensus on the size or number of the proposed new authorities. There was wider agreement among local authorities than ever before over the need for some form of Welsh Assembly but the

Secretary of State, in line with Conservative policy on devolution, was unenthusiastic.

Labour won the two by-elections held in Wales during the year. In April Peter Hain, as expected, won at Neath, but the by-election held the following month at Monmouth proved more unpredictable and acrimonious. By concentrating largely on National Health Service (NHS) issues, Huw Edwards, typical of the new breed of Labour candidates, overturned a 9,000 Conservative majority, to win the seat by over 4,000 votes. Labour made further gains in the local government elections in May, but surprisingly lost control of the Taff-Ely council to Plaid Cymru.

The NHS was constantly in the news and the Pembrokeshire health authority became the first in Wales to choose to opt out and become an NHS trust. It was in that part of west Wales, too, that the 'peace dividend' had its greatest effect. Following local and international pressure, the British and US governments decided to scrap their ill-conceived plans to build a military radar installation near St David's. However, the announcement that RNAD Trecwn was to close meant 500 redundancies in an area of already high unemployment.

The Cardiff Bay Barrage Bill, previously a private bill blocked by wrecking tactics in the House of Commons in April, was revived by the government in the Queen's Speech in November. Supporters of the £150 million scheme claimed that the lake created by the one-kilometre-long barrage would regenerate the Cardiff docklands, but there was considerable opposition on environmental grounds. In sponsoring the bill, the Secretary of State argued that the scheme would create 25,000 new jobs.

Cardiff experienced four nights of rioting on the Ely housing estate in September. The riots, sparked off by a dispute between shopkeepers, saw youths attacking police riot squads with petrol bombs and stones.

In October HTV, with a bid of £20.5 million, succeeded in retaining the franchise for broadcasting on the third television channel in Wales and the West of England (see also XVI.1.vi). Redundancies inevitably followed and there was also rationalization in BBC Wales. In December the government appointed the chairman of the Welsh Development Agency, Dr Gwyn Jones, as the new chairman of the Broadcasting Council for Wales and Wales's representative on the BBC's board of governors. This provoked much criticism from opposition MPs, who argued that it was a political appointment, while members of the Broadcasting Council itself feared a conflict of interest.

In sport the Welsh rugby union XV experienced a disappointing World Cup but their soccer counterparts, though failing narrowly to qualify for the finals of the European Championships, defeated the world champions Germany in a memorable match at the National Stadium in June.

10. NORTHERN IRELAND

THE first half of the year was one of progress on the political front as well as on the economic front, as local industry proved resilient in the recession and the events of 'Belfast 1991', especially the Tall Ships event in July, gave a lift to morale. The second half, particularly the regular 'tit for tat' killings and car bombs back in Belfast, led one local Sunday paper to ask whether the province was out of control. It was the year of some eight royal visits, of the retirement of Sir Kenneth Bloomfield as head of the NI civil service and of Lisburn borough's loss of £3 million in the BCCI failure. It was also the year when the 'Peace Train' reached London, and when new community relations schemes took root in local councils.

Agreement by Dublin to permit the Secretary of State to determine the timing of the Republic's entry into political talks paved the way for a new formula presented to the parties on 14 March. By 25 March all participants had endorsed the formula and this was reported to parliament the next day. The aim was, first, a more broadly-based structure than the Anglo-Irish Agreement; second, discussions would focus on relations within Northern Ireland, relations between the people of the island of Ireland and relations between the governments of the United Kingdom and the Republic of Ireland. The talks would have three strands to correspond with the three relationships. The procedure would involve bilateral talks with the parties first, then substantive talks on devolution, then, when Secretary of State Peter Brooke judged it appropriate, the other strands would begin. All strands were to have begun within weeks, but the principle was that nothing was agreed until everything had been agreed.

The prospect of talks was widely welcomed, and after Anglo-Irish conferences on 9 and 26 April a ten-week period was created for talks to begin on 30 April. However, the planned opening of the first phase of talks on 7 May had to be postponed when procedural issues on the venues, procedures and the new principle of an independent chairman for the later stages were permitted to intervene at the expense of trust between the parties. When a chairman was agreed on 14 June the way was clear for talks to begin on 17 June, but there remained only three weeks for discussion before preparations for the next Anglo-Irish conference on 16 July. The Secretary of State ended talks on 3 July to pre-empt a breakdown because Unionists would not talk beyond 9 July, when conference preparations would have begun, and the SDLP would not present specific proposals. Some MPs seemed surprised when he spoke of 'fresh discussions' rather than 'resumed' talks. Questioning produced the frank admission that 'we spent much time on procedural matters relating to strands beyond the first one and that left us inadequate time to address the matter of substance'.

In September Mr Brooke noted the enthusiasm in the community for talks and met local party leaders between 16 and 20 September. However, a new factor had entered government thinking, namely, the possibility of a November general election and its effect on any timetable for talks. When Alliance members met Mr Brooke on 22 October they came away with the impression that there would be no serious proposal for talks before the election. The prospect of a November election passed and a pre-Maastricht meeting between John Major and Charles Haughey in Dublin on 4 December resulted in a commitment to meet twice a year and gave an impetus to talks. As a result, Mr Brooke again met the parties by 12 December and put a new proposal to them in London on 20 December for a response early in January. In his New Year's message, Mr Brooke said that the possibility of talks had improved, and he was pleased that the principles of his March 26 statement still held.

It was a difficult year for politicians. In April the Alliance deputy leader, Gordon Mawhinney, resigned for health and business reasons and was replaced by Seamus Close. In July financial pressure forced the SDLP to dismiss its press officer, and by November the party's overdraft of £150,000 had caused the dismissal of its general secretary. Politicians were not immune from the violence. In September a Sinn Féin councillor, Bernard O'Hagan, was shot dead at Magherafelt technical college. At the end of November there was an abortive attempt on the life of Laurence Kennedy, leader of the Northern Ireland Conservatives. In May Danny Morrison, former publicity director of Sinn Féin, was convicted for false imprisonment and sentenced to eight years' imprisonment. In December the upsurge in violence claimed a victim when Lord Belstead lost his law and order responsibilities to Brian Mawhinney. The last vestiges of the boycott of government ministers by Unionist politicians in protest at the Anglo-Irish conference ended when Belfast lifted its ban and Richard Needham was a visitor on 25 March. However, opposition rallies were still held on the sixth anniversary of the agreement and Unionists refused to take any part in the British-Irish inter-parliamentary body which met in London in June and in Dublin in December.

The year witnessed more deaths from violence (94) than in any year since 1982, but only one more than in 1987 and 1988. Nineteen members of the security forces died, including eight UDR, six RUC and five army personnel; 75 civilians, including paramilitaries, died. In addition, 120 RUC members were wounded as well as 215 soldiers and 410 civilians. November was the bloodiest month, with 17 deaths. The IRA had a wide range of targets, including shopping centres, security bases and the Cabinet in the mortar attack on 7 February on No 10 Downing Street. The year was also remarkable for the increased activity of loyalist paramilitaries. Their body count approached that of the IRA and some actions were of the copy-cat type. For the second year in succession, the IRA called a three-day Christmas ceasefire.

The number of security personnel was increased to meet the level of violence; an extra 500 British troops arrived in March and June to bring the total to 11,000. While there were additions again in September and November, the total was still stated to be 11,000. In fact, the bloodiest month, November, saw some troops drafted back into Belfast and the call-up to temporary full-time duty of 1,200 part-time UDR soldiers. In November the Secretary of State announced an increase of 441 in the RUC establishment requested by the chief constable a year earlier. A new Northern Ireland (Emergency Provisions) Act became law. The official policy remained one of grinding down the terrorists, but the word 'internment' was more frequently heard and debated. Policy was under pressure but change was unlikely due to the proximity of an election and to the talks process.

The defence cuts of the summer contained two proposals affecting Northern Ireland. First, it was proposed that the UDR, which had received the royal colours on its 21st birthday in April, should merge with the Royal Irish Rangers and lose its name. Second, cuts in the size of the Territorial Army, which played no role in local security, saw 36 per cent cuts imposed in Northern Ireland and only 18 per cent elsewhere.

The government viewpoint on the economy was that Northern Ireland was surviving the recession better than the rest of the UK. By December the adjusted unemployment figures showed rises over 20 successive months in Britain but only 12 consecutive months in Northern Ireland. While the mainland figure was 2.5 million (7.8 per cent) in November, it was 102,900 or 14.2 per cent in Northern Ireland. End of year figures for business failures revealed the worst-ever figures, with 563 failures, an increase of 35.3 per cent over 1990. (In Great Britain the comparable figure was 65 per cent.) Finally, the agricultural sector expected a fall of 10 per cent in farm income from an already low level and still had the McSharry EC reforms to face.

The newly-privatized Harland and Woolf declared a profit of £11.7 million over a 16-month period and won an order for six bulk carriers worth £223 million. Shorts (Bombardier) declared a profit of £26.5 million and won a new sub-contract for work on Boeing's new 777 airliner. In November it was announced that Belfast International Airport would be sold. Northern Ireland Electricity, whose generating capacity was currently on offer, declared a profit of £87 million.

The public expenditure figures, published in November, showed an increase of 8.9 per cent, to £7,025 million for 1992/93. Ominously, the figure for criminal damage and personal injury was increased from £42 million to £59 million. The Family Expenditure Survey continued to show the gap in income and expenditure standards from the rest of the

UK. The average weekly household income in the UK in 1989–90 was £336, but in NI it was £232 (Scotland £277).

The Fair Employment Commission issued its first report on those in employment, showing that they divided into 65 per cent Protestant and 35 per cent Catholic, in a population where the overall figures were 62 and 38 per cent respectively. An amendment to the legislation became law in July and the first prosecutions were made.

II THE AMERICAS AND THE CARIBBEAN

1. UNITED STATES OF AMERICA

CAPITAL: Washington, DC   AREA: 9,372,614 sq km   POPULATION: 249,632,692 ('90)
OFFICIAL LANGUAGE: English
POLITICAL SYSTEM: democratic federal republic
HEAD OF STATE: President George Bush (since Jan '89)
RULING PARTIES: Republicans hold presidency, Democrats control Congress
PRINCIPAL CABINET MEMBERS: J. Danforth Quayle (vice-president), James Baker (secretary of state), Nicholas Brady (treasury), Richard Cheney (defence), Manuel Lujan (interior), William P. Barr (attorney-general) (*for full list see* DOCUMENTS)
INTERNATIONAL ALIGNMENT: NATO, OECD, OAS, ANZUS
CURRENCY: dollar (end-'91 £1=US$1.87)   GNP PER CAPITA: US$20,910 ('89)
MAIN EXPORT EARNERS: machinery and transport equipment, agricultural products, chemicals, miscellaneous manufactures

THE year began amid some anxiety and division in the lead-up to outbreak of military conflict in Gulf on 16 January, followed quickly by a wave of nationalism and patriotic celebration with the successful end of 'Operation Desert Storm' on 27 February (see also V.2). The mood of euphoria, which continued through the summer with victory parades across the country, began to evaporate as the limited nature of the allied victory became apparent. The year ended with a sense of gloom and uncertainty due to the deepening economic recession at home.

The popularity of President Bush mirrored these developments. Public opinion polls early in the year showed an approval rating of over 85 per cent as 'Bush mania' followed the allied victory in the Gulf, but in the latter half of the year his popularity plummeted as concern about domestic issues grew. By November his approval rating was back where it was at the end of 1990—below 55 per cent—and one poll in December gave the President an approval rating of only 46 per cent. Political opponents suggested that Mr Bush had a policy for every country but his own. As thoughts began to turn towards the presidential elections in 1992, a growing list of Democratic contenders threw their hats into the ring. With challengers also appearing on the right of the Republican party, the President who had once looked invincible began to appear less and less so.

The greatest challenge to the President's authority in 1991 was over his nomination of a black conservative, Judge Clarence Thomas, to the Supreme Court. The televised confirmation hearings attracted huge viewing audiences and raised several controversial issues, including gender relations at work, sexual harassment and, not least, the confirmation process itself (see below). Sexual relations between men and women were also the subject of another case which attracted enormous television audiences. On 30 March a woman accused the nephew of Senator Edward Kennedy, William Kennedy Smith, of raping her at the Kennedy home in Palm Beach, Florida. The media's fascination with the Kennedy family ensured the widest publicity. Amid general confusion surrounding the affair and in the absence of hard evidence, the Kennedys' past and previous cases of moral failure were dragged up once more. Some newspapers and television stations also took the unusual step of naming the woman involved.

After five weeks of investigation, Mr Smith was charged with sexual battery on 9 May but released on bail. On 11 December, following a ten-day trial in which Senator Kennedy gave evidence on behalf of his nephew, and both Mr Smith and his alleged victim were subjected to a public interrogation, the jury found the defendant not guilty. Although many women suggested that a woman had again been denied justice in the face of entrenched male prejudice and the power of the Kennedy family, the case did raise awareness of the issue of 'date rape'.

Sexual matters of a different nature became subject of public concern when basketball star Earvin 'Magic' Johnson announced early in November that he had been tested HIV positive and was retiring from the sport. The revelation helped to publicize the AIDS risks which even heterosexuals ran, and Mr Johnson said that he would devote himself to educating the public about the virus and the need to practise safe sex. President Bush invited him to join the National AIDS Commission.

While 'Magic' Johnson attracted nothing but sympathy, the American people were at a loss to understand the behaviour of Jeffrey Dahmer, who was charged with 15 murders in Milwaukee on 10 September. Mr Dahmer was arrested in August after police had found several dismembered bodies in his apartment. He confessed to having killed 17 people since 1978. Serial killing and cannibalism were also coincidentally the subject of a number of films, the best-known of which was *The Silence of the Lambs* (see also XVI.1.v).

In America art often appeared to imitate real life, but nature was unpredictable. Not even the presidency could be protected from Hurricane 'Grace' when it struck the east coast in August. The President's holiday home in Kennebunkport, Maine, which had survived Hurricane 'Bob' unscathed, suffered severe damage in the new storm's wake. In the west the long dry summer created problems for farmers as well as fire risks. On 19 October the worst fire in California's history started just outside of San Francisco. By the time the fire was under control 24 people were dead, hundreds had been evacuated from Berkeley, and billions of dollars worth of property had been damaged or destroyed. Southern California experienced an earthquake measuring 6.0 on the Richter scale on 28 June, but this was mild in comparison with that in

San Francisco in 1989 (see AR 1989, p. 46), and only one person was reported killed.

HOME AFFAIRS. The year began as it was to end at home—with concern over the economy (see also XVIII.3). On 4 January President Bush conceded that the country was 'in a slow-down economically, if not a recession'. Such concerns were overlooked for a while pending events overseas. The President's State of the Union address to Congress on 29 January, coming only 13 days after troops were sent into combat in the Gulf, was the first wartime address since Vietnam. Mr Bush said that America was 'standing at a defining hour', and he appealed to Americans to support the war effort in defence of 'a new world order—where diverse nations are drawn together in common cause, to achieve the universal aspirations of mankind: peace and security, freedom, and the rule of law'. Describing America as leading the world 'in facing down a threat to decency and humanity', the President declared: 'Our cause is just. Our cause is moral. Our cause is right.'

Referring to domestic matters, Mr Bush acknowledged that in some regions of the country 'people are in genuine economic distress', but he added that 'there are reasons to be optimistic about our economy'. Pointing to relatively low inflation rates, the absence of high business inventories and record exports, the President promised: 'We will get this recession behind us and return to growth—soon.' Calling for 'long-term investments for the next American century', Mr Bush outlined proposals which included a continued commitment to control federal spending but promised investment 'in America's future—in children, education, infrastructure, space and high technology'. Specific programmes included plans for a new national highway system, investment in research and development, a national energy strategy, banking reform, crime control legislation, control of spiralling health costs and the elimination of political action committees in order to reduce the 'big-money influence in politics'. Proposals to 'put more power and opportunity in the hands of the individual' included incentives to create jobs in inner cities through investment in enterprise zones. On civil rights, Mr Bush urged Congress to 'strengthen laws against employment discrimination without resorting to the use of unfair preferences', a reference to positive discrimination and the use of quotas, which the President opposed.

On 4 February President Bush presented his budget request for fiscal year 1992 (beginning 1 October) to Congress. The figure set was $1,445,900 million, which represented a rise of 2.9 per cent. Adjusted for inflation, this meant a cut in real terms of 1.5 per cent. The detailed proposals included overall cuts in defence spending with the cancellation of various programmes in aircraft, submarine and tank manufacture. The cuts were part of a five-year plan to reduce US armed forces by 25 per cent, and reflected the change in relations with the

Soviet Union. Increased spending was requested for strategic weapons systems, including the anti-missile Strategic Defence Initiative (SDI) and four more B-2 'Stealth' bombers.

The major element of proposals for social spending was the cutting of 'mandatory' spending. Subsidies on Medicare health premiums for individuals and couples earning incomes in excess of $125,000 or $150,000 respectively were to be cut. Subsidies to farmers with high non-farm incomes would end. In education the central element was a request for $6,200 million to be spent on remedial programmes, funding for school districts operating or intending to operate 'voucher' systems enabling parental choice, and an additional $100 million for 'magnet' schools specializing in particular subjects. A record $76,000 million was requested for research and development, an increase of $8,400 million; $43,000 million of this was for military research and the rest for civil programmes in medicine and space. The budget of the National Aeronautics and Space Administration (NASA) was increased from $13,500 million to $14,700 million. Budget Director Richard Darman described the proposals overall as 'reformist' in intention.

The partisan conflict of the previous year over the budget (see AR 1990, pp. 54–8) was not repeated because total spending levels had already been fixed and it was only left to determine priorities. On 17 April, having earlier rejected the President's proposals by 335 votes to 89, the House of Representatives passed a $1,460,000 million budget which cut spending on space and scientific programmes and increased spending on education and medical care for veterans. The Senate passed a roughly similar measure on 25 April. However, on 21 May Mr Bush's defence budget was rejected by the House, which the following day approved its own measure, including cuts in both the SDI and 'Stealth' bomber projects.

In his address to the joint houses of Congress on 6 March on the subject of the Gulf War, Mr Bush placed a crime bill near the top of his domestic agenda. In the legislative proposals he sent to Congress on 11 March, which included heavier sentences for crimes involving the use of firearms and an extension of the death penalty, the President urged congressmen to honour the war veterans by giving them 'an America where it is safe to walk on the streets'. Similar proposals had failed to pass in 1989 because Mr Bush had refused to accede to the demands of Democratic politicians to increase federal funding for local law enforcement.

The Senate approved an omnibus crime bill on 11 July. The legislation included tighter gun controls, an increase in prison sentences, and the imposition of the death sentence for 51 crimes including the use of firearms, hostage-taking and the sale of drugs to minors. The House of Representatives began consideration of an anti-crime bill in September. In May the House had approved the 'Brady Bill' (named after James

Brady, the White House press secretary shot during the assassination attempt on Ronald Reagan in 1981), imposing a seven-day waiting period on the purchase of handguns to allow police checks to be made on would-be purchasers. However, on 17 October the House voted by 247 to 177 votes to remove the clauses outlawing various types of semi-automatic weapons from the anti-crime bill. This came the day after George Hennard had killed 22 people when he ran amuck with two semi-automatic weapons in a cafeteria in Killeen, Texas, before shooting himself. It was the worst mass murder in American history. The Bush administration called for sterner punishment and the expansion of the death penalty as the best deterrent to gun-related crimes.

The issue of law enforcement reached the headlines in another way in March when an onlooker with a video camera happened to film the beating of a black man by members of the Los Angeles police department (LAPD). The film of the incident, which occurred on 3 March, was shown on national television and caused widespread outrage. President Bush said on 21 March: 'What I saw made me sick.' The victim, Rodney King, suffered fractures to the skull, a broken ankle, internal injuries and possible brain damage. The Los Angeles police chief, Daryl Gates, described the events as an 'aberration', but tapes of the radio conversations of the police involved included racially derogatory comments and references to previous acts of violence. On 15 March a grand jury indicted four officers involved in the beating, and Mayor Tom Bradley called upon Mr Gates to resign. When he refused to comply, the Los Angeles Police Commission suspended him from duty, but on 8 April a court ruled that Mr Gates could remain in office pending an official hearing. The commission of inquiry reported on 9 July that they had found that a 'significant number of LAPD officers repetitively misuse force', and called upon Mr Gates to retire. After some delay, he stated that he would give up his post in April 1992.

Race and policing were connected in another incident which had negative consequences in May. Following the shooting of a Hispanic man by a black policewoman in Washington, DC, two days of rioting occurred in the Mount Pleasant–Adams Morgan district of the city. What began as a reaction to the supposed insensitivity of a largely black police force to Hispanic people quickly became an outbreak of looting. Peace was only restored after a curfew had been imposed.

Several nights of rioting also occurred in New York city following an accident in which a car driven by a member of an orthodox Jewish sect ran over and killed a black boy in Crown Heights, Brooklyn, on 19 August. The incident, and the violence which followed, showed the tensions between African Americans and Jews. The conflict was possibly inflamed by the public controversy surrounding a speech on 20 July by a black professor, Leonard Jeffries of City University, who claimed that Jews were involved in a conspiracy against African Americans.

Education was another major issue targeted by the President in his State of the Union addresss, and on 18 April he launched his 'America 2000 Strategy' of educational reform. The proposals, which reflected a widespread concern over educational standards, were described by the President as 'bold, complex and long-ranging reforms' designed to bring about a 'true renaissance in American education'. The measures were largely drawn up by Education Secretary Lamar Alexander, who took up the post in March following the earlier resignation of Lauro Cavazos. They included plans to develop a new nationwide examination system of 'American achievement tests' in core subjects, increased parental choice in schooling for children, a business-financed, non-profit-making organization to develop non-traditional types of school, and ways of encouraging vocational training. Federal funding for education remained limited, and it was still left to states and local authorities to provide over 90 per cent of the educational budget.

There was some concern about Mr Bush's health—and renewed questioning of the suitability of Dan Quayle as Vice-President—when the 66-year-old President was detained in hospital for observation after developing heart problems while jogging on 4 May. Initial tests indicated that the problem was an irregular heartbeat rather than a heart attack, and it was treated with medication. After two nights in hospital Mr Bush returned to work, declaring support for Mr Quayle who, he said, was 'doing a first-class job' and would be his vice-presidential nominee in 1992. Speculation that Mr Quayle might be dropped from the election ticket in favour of General Colin Powell ended when Mr Bush nominated the latter for a second two-year term as Chairman of the Joint Chiefs of Staff. On 9 May it was announced that the President's health problem was due to an over-active thyroid gland (Graves disease), an illness also suffered by his wife since 1989. This coincidence—coupled with the fact that the Bush family dog, Millie, had a similar ailment—led to tests on drinking water in their previous homes, including the Vice–President's residence.

In April questions of ethical conduct were raised in the White House after the *Washington Post* had revealed that Mr Bush's chief of staff, the acerbic and widely-disliked John Sununu, had used military aircraft for personal flights at a cost of over $500,000 to the taxpayer. The flights included skiing trips and visits to see his parents in Florida, and one to his dentist. Further questions were asked in June when Mr Sununu used a White House limousine to travel to a stamp auction, despite a tightening of travel rules among the President's staff. On 19 June Mr Bush acknowledged that there was an 'appearance problem', and on 22 June Mr Sununu made a public statement of regret in which he admitted having made 'mistakes'. Although clearly embarrassed, Mr Bush refused to dismiss Mr Sununu at that stage.

Mr Sununu appeared to have ridden out the storm. However, after he had suggested that the President had 'ad-libbed' a damaging economic proposal concerning credit card interest rates, and postponed a visit to Asia scheduled for late-November because he could not leave Congress without 'adult supervision', the chief of staff resigned on 3 December. Two days later Mr Bush named Transport Secretary Samuel Skinner as Mr Sununu's replacement. The President also named the Commerce Secretary, Robert Mosbacher, as general manager of the Bush–Quayle election campaign for 1992. He subsequently nominated Barbara H. Franklin, whom he described as a 'leader and role model for many women in business', to become the next Secretary of Commerce.

Congressional ethics were again a matter of public interest through the year. On 27 February the Senate ethics committee ruled that no further action should be taken against four of the senators (the 'Keating Five') accused of improper links with Charles Keating, the owner of a failed Arizona savings and loan company. The four were Republican John McCain and Democrats John Glenn, Dennis DeConcini and Donald Riegle. The case of the fifth, Alan Cranston, was to be brought before the full Senate. On 20 June the leading black politician, William H. Gray, resigned as House majority whip to accept the presidency of the United Negro College Fund. Mr Gray refused to comment on the suggestion that he had resigned to avoid a Justice Department investigation into alleged financial improprieties. He said that he wished to spend more time with his family and to influence the next generation of black leaders. In an attempt to prevent a recurrence of some of the past problems, on 17 July the Senate voted to increase senators' annual salaries from $102,000 to $125,000, in exchange for prohibiting honoraria from speeches to political interest groups. The House of Representatives had taken similar action in 1989.

Questions in connection with past relations between the USA and Iran, and the Iran-Contra affair (see AR 1990, pp. 62–3; 1989, pp. 48–9; 1988, pp. 58–9; 1987, pp. 47–51), continued to dog the Bush administration. In May President Bush was forced to respond to charges that he had participated in secret meetings with Iranian officials in Paris in 1980 in which arms were offered in return for delaying the release of US hostages in order to secure an electoral advantage for Ronald Reagan—the so-called 'October surprise' affair. Mr Bush denied the charges, which he described as 'sickening', but allegations continued to be made as new evidence surfaced. Abdulhassan Bani-Sadr, former President of Iran, repeated the charge, first made in his book *My Turn to Speak*, that there had been a deal between Iranians and candidates Mr Reagan and Mr Bush, when he appeared before the House foreign affairs committee on 8 May. Mr Bush described such suggestions as 'grossly untrue, factually incorrect, bald-faced lies'.

On 24 June Senator Albert Gore felt that there was still sufficient evidence to justify a formal investigation of the charges by a bipartisan committee from both houses of Congress. In a television interview on 7 July, Edwin Meese, one of the leading members of the Reagan campaign team, issued a comprehensive denial of the charges, and Mr Bush continued to dismiss them as rumour in a press conference on 12 June. Nonetheless, on 5 August the Speaker of the House, Thomas S. Foley, announced that there would be an official inquiry into the affair involving the Senate foreign relations subcommittee and a House of Representatives task force.

On 8 May President Bush announced the unexpected resignation of William Webster as director of the Central Intelligence Agency (CIA). Mr Webster, aged 67, had held the post for four years. No reason was given for his departure other than that he wished to return to private legal practice. However, a fire in the US embassy in Moscow (which resulted in the loss of computer discs when Russian firemen walked unescorted through the building), following on poor intelligence prior to the Iraqi invasion of Kuwait, was thought to have triggered Mr Webster's resignation. On 14 May Mr Bush nominated Robert M. Gates, the Deputy National Security Adviser and a specialist on Soviet affairs and former deputy director of the CIA, as Mr Webster's successor.

This nomination was bound to face opposition, as Mr Gates had been President Reagan's first choice for the post in 1987 but had withdrawn rather than face questioning on the Iran-Contra affair. On 11 June the Senate intelligence committee decided to delay the Gates hearings when Alan Fiers, head of the CIA's Central American task force from 1984 to 1986, pleaded guilty to two counts of lying to Congress about the affair. In evidence given in return for the acceptance of guilty pleas on lesser charges, Mr Fiers raised new questions about Iran-Contra, the extent of the cover-up and the involvement of top officials such as Mr Gates. In September Mr Fiers's testimony led to the indictment of Clair George, former head of covert operations, on perjury charges.

It was against this background that the hearings began on Mr Gates's nomination. Mr Gates denied charges that he had distorted CIA intelligence reports in the 1980s or that he had any detailed knowledge of the Iran-Contra dealings. He acknowledged that he had made mistakes in the past, but maintained that they were 'well-intentioned and honest'. He claimed that he had 'learned the lessons of Iran-Contra', and promised that, if he were appointed, the CIA would cooperate fully with Congress in future. On 18 October the committee voted 11–4 in favour of his nomination, this decision being confirmed by the full Senate on 5 November.

One possible influential development in this process was the announcement on 16 September by independent prosecutor Lawrence E. Walsh that all charges were being dropped against a former White House aide, Colonel Oliver E. North, who had been a central figure in the Iran-Contra scandal. Colonel North had been found guilty in May

1989 of obstructing Congress and destroying government records, but witnesses in the federal appeals court claimed that they had been influenced by Colonel North's testimony before a congressional investigation, and the charges were dismissed. Colonel North claimed that he had been 'totally, fully and completely exonerated'. His benefits and pension rights as a retired marines officer were restored in the light of the decision. In his book published on 22 October, entitled *Under Fire: An American Story*, Colonel North claimed that President Reagan had known about and supported the arms deal. In a press statement he said that while, as Vice-President, Mr Bush might have known the broad details of his (North's) activities, he had had no specific knowledge of the affair.

On 15 November Admiral John Poindexter, Ronald Reagan's National Security Adviser at the time of the Iran-Contra affair, also had his convictions and six-month prison sentence quashed by an appeal court. The grounds for dismissal were the same as those in the case of Colonel North, that previous testimony to Congress tainted the case against him.

Perhaps also influential in the Senate confirmation of Mr Gates was the knowledge that the process itself had been called into question by another, more protracted and bitter, hearing in the case of Judge Clarence Thomas. On 1 July Mr Bush nominated Judge Thomas to succeed Justice Thurgood Marshall to the Supreme Court. Marshall, aged 82, the only black justice and the only remaining liberal on the Court, had announced his resignation on 27 June.

Judge Thomas's nomination provoked what turned out to be one of the most controversial Senate confirmation hearings in US history. Although a federal appeals court judge, Mr Thomas, a conservative black who had risen from a poor rural background and been educated in Roman Catholic schools, had little judicial experience and was not known as a scholar or author of significant legal decisions. His nomination appeared to be based on his colour and record as chairman of the Equal Opportunities Commission in 1982–90, when his cautious interpretation and application of civil rights legislation angered civil rights organizations. Various groups, including the National Association for the Advancement of Colored People and the National Organization of Women, announced that they would oppose Judge Thomas's confirmation.

The Senate judiciary committee's hearings began on 10 September, and throughout Judge Thomas tried to avoid answering difficult questions or committing himself on controversial issues such as abortion (see XV.3). He was strongly opposed by the Democrats on the committee, led by Senator Edward Kennedy. When the committee voted on 27 September, it was deadlocked along party lines 7–7 (with the exception of one Democrat, who supported confirmation), and the issue was to be left to a full Senate vote scheduled for 8 October. However, new evidence from Professor Anita Hill, a black law teacher at the University of Oklahoma, delayed the vote while her statement to the judiciary committee was heard and considered from 11 to 13 October.

Millions of people watched the televised hearings as Professor Hill claimed that, while she had worked with Judge Thomas in the Education Department and the Equal Opportunities Commission in the early 1980s, he had subjected her to verbal sexual harassment. Judge Thomas vehemently denied the charges and claimed that he was a victim of a 'high-tech lynching' that had destroyed his good name. Despite charge and counter-charge, neither case was proven or disproven, although Judge Thomas appeared to gain public sympathy. When the Senate voted on 15 October, it approved the nomination by the narrowest margin this century—52 votes for and 48 against.

The controversial subject of civil rights again involved the Supreme Court. The Court's decisions in 1989–90 had reversed rulings in the area of employment discrimination, so that Democrats in Congress hoped to regain lost ground through legislation (see AR 1990, p. 63). Having failed to overcome a presidential veto of a bill which put the burden of proof on employers rather than employees in 1990, a similar bill was approved in the House on 4 June. The new measure increased penalties for intentional discrimination and required employers to show that unintentional discrimination was due to business necessity. The bill specifically prohibited racial quotas in terms of fixed proportions of minority workers, but opponents argued that quotas were still implicit in the bill. President Bush said of it: 'You can't put a sign on a pig and say it's a horse.' However, the President eventually approved a compromise bill little different from the one he had vetoed the previous year on 28 December, but he urged that interpretation of it should be limited.

Throughout the summer a number of cities and states experienced financial difficulties as a result of problems in agreeing budgets. At the end of June New York city faced major cuts in services and its workforce as Mayor David Dinkins struggled to close a budget deficit. In the event, the most draconian measures, such as the proposed closure of the zoo in Central Park, were averted by a commitment to raise taxes and shed up to 10,000 city jobs. A last-minute agreement on the budget for the state of New York alleviated the situation by guaranteeing the city $633 million in state funds. On 6 June Bridgeport, the largest city in Connecticut, declared itself bankrupt in an attempt to break out of budget problems. If the city had been able to file for bankruptcy, it could have escaped requirements to balance its budget. The mayor, Mary C. Moran, also hoped to use the crisis to renegotiate contracts with the city's workforce, and city services were drastically cut during the summer. In August, however, the city was denied the right to file for bankruptcy as it had not actually run out of money. Mrs Moran was defeated in the elections in November.

Bridgeport's plight highlighted the crisis throughout the country. At the beginning of July at least ten states, including Connecticut, California and Pennsylvania, had not agreed budgets, and in a number of cases cuts in services other than essentials were introduced. Starting on 11 August from Bridgeport, the Rev Jesse Jackson led a week-long march through Connecticut to the state capital of Hartford in order to publicize the national crisis in a call to 'Rebuild America', but the demonstration remained a low-key affair with little obvious impact.

The roots of the financial crisis were the political conflicts between governors and legislatures over proposed tax increases and cuts in services, the requirements to balance budgets and reductions in federal aid introduced in the Reagan years, as well as the increased welfare expenditures resulting from the deepening economic recession. Despite President Bush's claims at the start of the year that the recession would be brief, there was no sign of a let-up. In January, and in the budget message in February, the White House argued that the economy was basically in a healthy condition and that the fall in consumer confidence was due to uncertainty because of the Gulf War. However, by July nearly 9 million people, almost 7 per cent of the labour force, were officially classed as unemployed, a figure which excluded those who had given up looking. In October General Motors, Ford and Chrysler declared huge losses, and General Motors later announced 21 plant closures and the staggered cut of over 60,000 jobs. On 18 December Alan Greenspan, the chairman of the US Federal Reserve, said: 'It is apparent that the economy is struggling and that there have been some strong forces against moderate cyclical revival.' The White House also acknowledged the problem. Spokesman Marlin Fitzwater said: 'The people of this country know the economy is in trouble and it doesn't make any sense to play games.'

The collapse of banks and major airlines was indicative of the country's economic woes. In January Pan American World Airways (Pan Am), once America's largest airline, and Eastern Airlines, the sixth largest airline, both announced that they had filed for protection from their creditors, i.e. were bankrupt. TWA also faced financial problems in February and was unable to make debt repayments. Attempts to save Pan Am failed, and on 4 December the company ceased all operations.

In January the Bank of New England was closed by the Federal Deposit Insurance Corporation and its assets were seized because of heavy losses. A bank emergency was also declared in the state of Rhode Island, where local banks were closed due to debt repayment defaulting. In May the government declared the Madison National Banks of Washington DC and Virginia insolvent and closed them. On

5 February Treasury Secretary Nicholas Brady proposed measures to reform banking by replacing the four existing regulatory bodies with two, altering certain financial requirements and lifting restrictions on national banking. Moves to rationalize banking and make it easier to operate across state lines were evident in the series of mergers which occurred in July and August, including the $4,500 million merger of BankAmerica Corp of San Francisco and Security Pacific Corp of Los Angeles, to become the second largest bank in the country.

Concern over banking practices and regulation were raised by the unfolding scandal involving the Bank of Credit and Commerce International (BCCI), a huge multinational operation centred in London (but with large holdings in US banks) which appeared to be implicated in arms deals, drug-trafficking and other illegal activities. In August the then director of the CIA, William Webster, ordered a full investigation of any possible links between the agency and BCCI. The bank's activities became the subject of an investigation by the Senate subcommittee on terrorism, narcotics and international operations later in the year (see also I.4).

More financial scandal became apparent on 9 August when Salomon Brothers Inc., the most powerful broker in the US Treasury securities market, admitted to a series of illegal activities in manipulating the auction of securities. The company announced the resignation of three of its most senior executives on 16 August and the dismissal of two directors two days later. As a result, the company was only restricted in future dealings rather than excluded entirely.

The state of the economy led to a fall in popularity and increased criticism of President Bush, who had been thought likely to be invincible in the 1992 elections. In August Albert Gore, widely tipped as a strong contender, joined a list of other senior Democrats, including Senators Sam Nunn and Lloyd Bentsen and Congressman Richard Gephardt, who declared that they would not seek the party's nomination in 1992. The Rev Jesse Jackson also indicated that he would not run in 1992.

By mid-1991 only two people—a former Massachusetts senator, Paul E. Tsongas, and a former mayor of Irvine (California), Larry Agran—had said that they would seek the Democratic nomination. However, in September and October they were joined by Jerry Brown, a former governor of California, Arkansas's Governor Bill Clinton, Senator Tom Harkin of Iowa, Senator Bob Kerrey of Nebraska and Governor Douglas L. Wilder of Virginia. After a period of consideration, Governor Mario Cuomo of New York, sometimes dubbed the 'Hamlet' of American politics because of his indecision, finally announced on 20 December that he would not after all seek the nomination. The governor, whom many commentators thought the best potential challenger to Mr Bush, gave as his reason the unresolved problems in New York state. It was clear, however, that in the event of a deadlock between other candidates, Mr Cuomo might still be drafted in.

Some of the challenges likely to be faced by the President were evident in the November elections. Particularly alarming for Mr Bush was the defeat of his former Attorney-General, Richard Thornburgh, whom the President had supported in his campaign for the Pennsylvania Senate seat. Mr Thornburgh lost to Harris Wofford, a liberal Democrat and former aide to John F. Kennedy, who had been appointed to the seat in April following the death of Senator John Heinz. Mr Wofford had campaigned for national health insurance and action on the economy. Equally embarrassing were the victories of conservatives such as Republican Kirk Fordice, who was elected governor of Mississippi on an anti-welfare, anti-quota ticket with strong racial overtones.

Race was even more of an issue in Louisiana, where David Duke, a former grand wizard in the Ku Klux Klan and founder of the National Association for the Advancement of White People, defeated the incumbent, Buddy Roemer, to become Republican candidate for the governorship. Mr Duke, who was elected to the state legislature in 1989 and claimed to have severed his links with the Klan, was disowned by the Republican party and the White House. His opponent, Democrat Edwin Edwards, was a former governor with a reputation for gambling, womanizing and racketeering. Nonetheless, he won the election by a considerable margin, 61 to 39 per cent, having gained 96 per cent of the black vote. However, the support for Mr Duke in Louisiana and elsewhere was such that the possibility of his entry into the Republican primaries in order to gain influence in the party was one which posed a serious threat to Mr Bush.

Another challenge to Mr Bush came from the conservative Republican, Patrick Buchanan, who announced on 10 December that he would enter the contest for the Republican nomination. Mr Buchanan was a former speech-writer for Presidents Nixon and Ford, and had been President Reagan's director of communications. Calling for a 'new patriotism that puts America first', Mr Buchanan accused Mr Bush of a breach of faith with conservatives and promised to cut both taxes and welfare spending and return to isolationism. Although it was thought that Mr Buchanan really intended to establish a national base for a future presidential bid, many observers believed he could have a damaging effect on Mr Bush's campaign.

FOREIGN AFFAIRS. The early part of the year was dominated by events in the Gulf following the Iraqi invasion of Kuwait. While President Bush tried to be seen to be making every effort to avoid a Gulf war and yet remain uncompromising, there was considerable debate and uncertainty in America as the deadline for armed intervention in the Gulf approached. Some congressmen expressed support for the continuation of reliance on sanctions and appeared to doubt the President's power to commit troops to the Gulf prior to congressional approval.

After three days of often impassioned debate, there were majorities in both houses in favour of the use of force in the vote of 12 January. In the House of Representatives 250 voted for and 183 against the administration's position, while in the Senate the vote was a narrow 52 for and 47 against. Only ten Democrats voted with the majority in the Senate. Most congressional opposition to the war, however, ceased following the launching of 'Operation Desert Storm' on the night of 16 January, as public opinion polls showed that 75 per cent of those asked approved of the war. However, anti-war protests continued and over 100,000 people took part in a demonstration organized by the Campaign for Peace in the Middle East in Washington, DC, on 26 January. Subsequent demonstrations were much smaller, although one person, Gregory Levey, burnt himself to death in protest on 18 February.

The massive allied air offensive against Iraq was followed closely by the American public on television, although the media were generally carefully controlled. While Cable News Network (CNN) reporters gave on-the-spot reports from Baghdad, military personnel used videos to demonstrate the success of 'smart' bombs in hitting military installations and bridges. Overnight the supreme commander of the allied forces, General Norman Schwarzkopf (nicknamed 'Stormin' Norman'), and Chairman of the US Joint Chiefs of Staff, General Colin Powell, became media personalities and popular heroes. The Bush administration was clearly determined to prosecute the war to a successful conclusion, and appeared to have widespread support when, on 22 February, the President rejected the Soviet-backed peace proposal offering a gradual Iraqi withdrawal from Kuwait. Instead, Mr Bush offered no concessions and insisted on the full implementation of UN resolutions, demanding the start of an Iraqi withdrawal by noon the next day. When no such action was forthcoming, the allied ground offensive was launched on 24 February. On 27 February Mr Bush appeared on television to announce: 'Kuwait is liberated; Iraq's army is defeated; our military objectives are met.' A sense of elation swept America.

The widespread mood of national unity and support for action in the Gulf was seen as laying to rest the legacies of involvement in Vietnam 20 years earlier, the so-called 'Vietnam syndrome'. This was especially so because the war in the Gulf was brought to a speedy and apparently victorious conclusion, and did not result in the huge losses anticipated by many Americans. US casualties reflected the one-sided nature of the war, with only 145 killed in action, 121 killed in accidents and under 500 wounded. When Mr Bush went to address a joint session of Congress on 6 March he was greeted with a three-minute ovation.

Victory parades were held across the USA on 8–10 June, ending with a huge celebration in New York city on 10 June, when an estimated 1 million people watched Generals Schwarzkopf and Powell lead 25,000 service personnel in a ticker-tape march down Broadway.

The victory celebrations were hardly dimmed by the allied failure to topple Saddam Husain and the plight of the Kurdish people. There was some criticism of President Bush following General Schwarzkopf's revelation in a television interview on 27 March that the President had terminated hostilities sooner than he (Schwarzkopf) would have preferred, thus possibly preventing the total destruction of Saddam's armed forces. The subsequent refusal of the US government to provide military assistance for Kurdish rebels, seen as a sign of weakness or indecision by some commentators, reflected the concern of the Bush administration not to encourage the disintegration of Iraq and the complete destabilization of the Middle East. This position was reaffirmed in a State Department announcement of 3 April, and on 5 April President Bush himself said that 'it was not an objective of the coalition or the US to overthrow Saddam Husain'. A *New York Times* editorial on 3 April described this hands-off approach as 'shocking', and the President found himself under attack from both left and right. As protest grew, the President was forced to reverse the policy of non-intervention. On 10 April the United States ordered Iraq to cease all military activity north of the 36th parallel, and on 16 April he committed US troops to assist in establishing 'safe havens' for Kurdish refugees in northern Iraq. Sizeable amounts of financial aid were also provided to the refugees by the US government.

In March the White House froze all new arms sales to Middle Eastern countries. Moreover, perhaps as a consequence of the Gulf War and the fears it had unleashed concerning the possible use of chemical and biological weapons, on 13 May, just prior to the resumption of the Geneva Disarmament Conference, Mr Bush announced that the USA would forswear 'the use of chemical weapons for any reason, including retaliation'. He also committed the USA to the destruction of all stocks of such weapons within ten years of an international convention coming into force. On 29 May Mr Bush called specifically for an end to the proliferation of chemical, biological and nuclear weapons in the Middle East, and he proposed an international conference be convened to curb arms sales to the region.

The Gulf War also raised wider issues relating to the Middle East. In a statement made jointly with the then Soviet Foreign Minister, Aleksandr Bessmertnykh, in Washington on 29 January, Secretary of State Baker suggested that, after the conflict was over, removing causes of instability in the region, 'including the Arab-Israeli conflict, will be especially important'. The White House, however, appeared embarrassed by the statement, and the following day Spokesman

Fitzwater stressed that there would be no linkage between the Gulf conflict and the Arab-Israeli confrontation. Nonetheless, in his 6 March address to Congress Mr Bush indicated that a settlement to the conflict would be one of his administration's top priorities in the post-Gulf War period.

Following the President's speech, Mr Baker began a round of diplomatic visits to the Middle East on 7–14 March. This included a two-day visit to Israel, his first since taking office, and also a meeting with a Palestinian delegation approved by the PLO. Mr Baker made three further visits to the region between 8 and 26 April, holding talks in Israel, Syria, Egypt and Jordan in an attempt to initiate a Middle East peace conference. On 1 June President Bush wrote to number of Middle Eastern leaders suggesting that a conference be convened under the joint chairmanship of the USA and Soviet Union, and a date was set in October for meetings to begin. This letter was followed by a further series of visits from Mr Baker, and the conference began in Madrid on 30 October (see also V.3 and V.4.i).

In an attempt not to jeopardize the conference, Mr Bush called upon Congress to delay approval of a $10,000 million loan to Israel. He used all his influence to ensure that the relevant vote was successful, threatening to use his veto if necessary. On 9 October Senate leaders indicated that they would support the President. The US government also urged the Israeli government to stop all further building in occupied territories, and protested when Israeli fighter planes flew over the airspace of Arab countries in a reconnaissance mission to northern Iraq.

The successful convening of the Middle East conference was due in no small measure to the continued improvement in US-Soviet relations. At the end of July Mr Bush met President Gorbachev in Moscow for their third summit conference. The meeting, which had originally been scheduled for February but had been delayed due to the Gulf War, resulted in agreement to sponsor the Middle East peace conference, concessions on trading relations and the signing of the Strategic Arms Reduction Treaty (START) on 31 July (see XII.3 and XIX.2). Both leaders agreed that there had been substantial progress towards developing closer US-Soviet relations. Nonetheless, the US government was concerned about the internal stability of the Soviet Union, and in a speech to the Ukrainian parliament on 1 August Mr Bush said that the USA would not support 'suicidal nationalism'.

Following the attempted coup in Moscow in August, the USA put a temporary hold on all economic aid to the Soviet Union. The new US ambassador to the Soviet Union, Robert Strauss, was instructed not to present his credentials to acting President Yanaev, but as the situation had changed by the time he arrived in Moscow he was able to meet Mr Gorbachev officially on 24 August. The first direct high-level contact with the Soviet and Russian administrations following the coup attempt came during Secretary of State Baker's visit on 10–15 September. One consequence was an agreement on 13 September to stop weapons deliveries to all sides in Afghanistan (see VIII.1.ii).

In a nationally-televised broadcast on 27 September, Mr Bush announced a major disarmament initiative which he said was a response to the developments in the Soviet Union. The President said it was now possible for the USA to take unilateral action 'to make the world a less dangerous place', and he announced the lifting of alert status on all strategic bombers and Minuteman II missiles. He said the USA had abandoned various missile development programmes, and he invited the Soviet Union to begin negotiation on the elimination of all intercontinental ballistic missiles with multiple warheads. Mr Bush described Mr Gorbachev's reciprocal offer of 5 October as 'good news', and said that the USA was 'prepared to discuss all issues'.

On 26 October Mr Bush welcomed the dissolution of the Soviet Union and said: 'I think the whole change toward commonwealth will facilitate further progress in arms reduction.' In a speech from the Oval Office, Mr Bush announced the diplomatic recognition of Russia and five other independent republics. Mr Bush described Boris Yeltsin as Russia's 'courageous President', and acknowledged the achievements of President Gorbachev, who, he said, had enabled the Soviet people to 'cast aside decades of oppression and establish the foundation of freedom'. In a written statement, the President listed Mr Gorbachev's accomplishments as arms control, the reshaping of Europe and an end to Third World conflicts.

At the end of December President Bush set off on his long-delayed ten-day tour of Asia. Declaring that his mission was 'about jobs', Mr Bush included in his party a number of chief executives from US companies. It was hoped that the tour would lead to improved exports for the USA to help the ailing economy—and the President's chances of re-election in 1992.

2. CANADA

CAPITAL: Ottawa   AREA: 9,970,610 sq km   POPULATION: 26,200,000 ('89)
OFFICIAL LANGUAGES: English, French
POLITICAL SYSTEM: federal parliamentary democracy
HEAD OF STATE: Queen Elizabeth II (since Feb '52)
GOVERNOR-GENERAL: Ramon John Hnatyshyn (since Jan '90)
RULING PARTY: Progressive Conservative Party (since Sept '84)
HEAD OF GOVERNMENT: Brian Mulroney, Prime Minister (since Sept '84)
PRINCIPAL MINISTERS: Donald Mazankowski (deputy premier, finance), Joe Clark (constitutional affairs, privy council), Barbara McDougall (external affairs), Marcel Masse (defence), Michael Wilson (international trade, industry & science), Jake Epp (energy, mines & resources), Kim Campbell (justice)
INTERNATIONAL ALIGNMENT: NATO, OECD, OAS, Francophonie, Cwth.
CURRENCY: Canadian dollar (end-'91 £1=Can$2.16, US$1=Can$1.16)
GNP PER CAPITA: US$19,030 ('89)
MAIN EXPORT EARNERS: manufactured goods, fabricated and crude materials, agricultural products, tourism

CONSTITUTIONAL change dominated public affairs in 1991. The Progressive Conservative (PC) administration led by Prime Minister Brian Mulroney brought forth a new set of proposals to reform the country's federal system. This action resulted from the defeat in June 1990 of the Meech Lake Accord (see AR 1990, pp. 70–71), a package of changes designed to satisfy French-speaking Quebec's demand for status in the federation as a 'distinct society'. A widespread disenchantment with the 'closed-door' process through which the Accord was negotiated led to demands for public participation in the second round of constitutional deliberations. The Mulroney government sought to meet this concern by appointing a 12-member commission to gather the views of ordinary Canadians on the objectives for constitutional change. The Citizen's Forum on Canada's Future reported on 27 June that it found a greater attachment to a united Canada than to its regions in all provinces but Quebec. In the latter province opinion was divided between those who favoured Quebec remaining in a revised federal structure and those who advocated a sovereign Quebec, perhaps combined with the rest of Canada in a loose economic association. That Quebec should enjoy a special status ran counter to the belief of a majority of Canadians that in a federation all units should participate on an equal basis. The federal government's 20-year policy of French–English bilingualism in the provision of official services received a mixed reception, the commission found. Outside Quebec it was frequently seen as divisive; inside the province it appeared to be little appreciated. The commission recommended that the bilingualism policy be studied by an independent inquiry.

Eighteen influential members of the Mulroney cabinet spent the summer in drafting a comprehensive set of 28 constitutional proposals. These terms differed from the Meech Lake Accord by attempting to meet the perceived interests of all the regions of Canada, not just the concerns of Quebec. They were put forward, the government emphasized, as a starting-point for discussion and later negotiation among the provinces. The proposals, which were made public on 24 September, were divided into three groups.

1. *Citizenship, shared and diverse elements.* The proposals, meeting a shortcoming brought out in the discussion of the Meech Lake Accord, were introduced by a 'Canada clause' to be entrenched in the constitution. This was a statement defining the core values—gender equality, equal citizenship irrespective of race, colour, creed or disability, Canada's linguistic duality, the protection of the environment, etc.—held by all Canadians. Quebec was to have a 'special responsibility . . . to preserve and promote its distinct society'. The concept was spelled out for the first time: the realities of a French-speaking majority, a unique culture and civil law tradition. Canada's native peoples were to participate in future constitutional deliberations. Their right to self-government was to be recognized in a new constitution and they were to be given distinct representation in a reformed upper house or Senate. The content of aboriginal self-government was to be negotiated with the federal government and the provinces over the next ten years. It would be likely to include control over a native judicial system, education, land and resource management and social welfare structures.

2. *Responsive federal institutions.* The proposals, responding to a demand by the western provinces, recommended a directly-elected Senate with more equitable representation among the provinces. The current 104-member Senate, all of its number appointed by the prime minister, afforded prominence to Ontario, Quebec and the Maritime provinces, the original members of the federation. Quebec, for example, with 6.7 million people, had 24 senators, while British Columbia, with 3.1 million, had only six. New Brunswick, with 720,000 people, had 10 senators; Alberta, with 2.4 million, had six. A parliamentary committee established to study the proposals was given the delicate task of recommending the number of senators which should be assigned to each province. The Senate's powers, in law parallel to those of the House of Commons except for a restriction on initiating money bills, were rarely fully exercised. Under the new proposals they were to be modified. The Senate, for example, would be restricted to a six-month suspensive veto over topics of national importance such as international relations or defence. It would be given a new authority, however, to approve the appointments of the governor of the Bank of Canada as well as the heads of national regulatory and cultural agencies. The House of Commons would continue as a 'confidence chamber', i.e., the prime minister and his cabinet would remain responsible to it and not to the Senate.

3. *Economic proposals looking to a prosperous future.* The current

'common market clause' in the constitution, which forbade barriers to commodity trade among the provinces, would be expanded to encompass the free flow of persons, capital and services. The provinces would be given more authority (in some instances exclusive) in fields of jurisdiction such as job training, immigration, tourism and recreation, mining, forestry, broadcasting and culture. The federal government would be given a new power to make laws 'for the efficient functioning of the economic union' subject to the consent of seven provinces containing 50 per cent of the population of Canada. A new coordinating body, the Council of the Federation, would be created to assist in the management of federal–provincial cooperative arrangements such as shared-cost programmes. The mandate of the Bank of Canada would be changed to enable the bank to concentrate on one task, the preservation of 'price stability', working more closely with the provinces in this endeavour.

The 1991 proposals were received cautiously across the country, being regarded by most Canadians outside Quebec as a useful basis for discussion. Separatist groups in Quebec denounced them as irrelevant to Quebec's real interests, while the governing provincial Liberal Party under Robert Bourassa was divided in its response. In March the party had endorsed a study which recommended a far more sweeping transfer of powers from Ottawa to Quebec than that contained in the proposals. M. Bourassa distanced himself from both the proposals and his party's report, insisting on a free hand to deal with a future federal government constitutional offer. The premier, who had previously held out the European Community as a possible model for Canada, showed nervousness regarding the expanded economic powers to be assigned to Ottawa, claiming the change might weaken Quebec's financial autonomy. In June his government sponsored legislation enabling it to hold a referendum on the future of Quebec, if it believed one to be desirable, no later than October 1992. Canada's Indian leadership criticized the proposals as demeaning to the First Nations by their requirement of a ten-year period to define the content of aboriginal self-government. This delay contrasted, the Indians stated, with the federal government's readiness to deal urgently with Quebec's concerns.

The 28 proposals were given to a joint House of Commons–Senate committee to study and take across the country for public consultation. The committee got off to a shaky start, partisan bickering leading to organizational paralysis. On 13 November the government changed the committee's mandate, dropping the planned 'town hall' hearings in favour of a series of arranged conferences dealing with different aspects of the unity proposals. The committee was also directed to meet with constitutional experts, interest groups and provincial politicians. It was instructed to report to parliament by the end of February 1992, after which the Mulroney government would prepare a revised outline for constitutional change. This would be discussed with all the provinces outside Quebec, approved by parliament, possibly submitted to a nationwide referendum and then used as the basis of negotiations with Quebec. At year's end a definite procedure and timetable for constitutional revision were still unclear. It was apparent, however, that crucial issues regarding the future of Canada would come to a head before the Quebec referendum scheduled for October 1992.

Its standing undermined by recent unpopular policies—notably the Canada-US free trade agreement of 1988 and the goods and services tax (GST) of 1990—the Mulroney government was not in a strong position to initiate major constitutional change. In September a public opinion poll showed that the PC party enjoyed the support of only 17 per cent of decided voters, while 77 per cent of Canadians disapproved of Mulroney's leadership. Nevertheless, the government's majority in the House of Commons remained unshaken. At the end of 1991 the PCs held 159 seats in the 295-seat Commons, the Liberals 81, the New Democratic Party (NDP) 44, the separatist Bloc Québécois 9 and the Reform Party 1. There was also one independent Conservative in the chamber.

There were three provincial general elections in 1991. In New Brunswick the Liberals under Frank McKenna, who won all 58 seats in the legislature in 1987, were confirmed in office with 46 seats in an election on 23 September. A new party committed to cancelling New Brunswick's status as an officially bilingual province carried eight seats, a worrying development in the politics of the Atlantic province. In western Canada two conservative administrations were overthrown by the socialist NDP. British Columbia saw the Social Credit Party, in power for 36 of the last 39 years, swept out of office on 17 October. The NDP, under the moderate leadership of Michael Harcourt, took 51 seats in the legislature, a revived Liberal Party 17 and the Social Credit Party 7. In the prairie province of Saskatchewan, in an election on 21 October, the NDP under another pragmatic politician, Roy Romanow, replaced a PC administration which had been in office since 1982. The NDP won 55 seats, the PCs 10 and the Liberals 1.

The economy showed modest signs of recovery following the recession in 1990. The gross domestic product, on a seasonally-adjusted annual basis, stood at Can$683,600 million at the end of June. Interest rates came down and inflation was checked. In November the consumer price index registered a 4.2 per cent increase over the previous year, some of the rise being attributed to the impact of the GST and other taxes earlier in the year. Unemployment, however, remained disturbingly high, reaching a seasonally-adjusted rate of 10.3 per cent of the labour force in November. Many jobs in manufacturing, especially in Ontario, were lost and the government embarked upon a programme to improve the country's industrial competitiveness.

Under the budget presented on 26 February, additional taxation was imposed to meet the costs of unemployment, depressed wheat prices and the Gulf War. The then Finance Minister, Michael Wilson, promised to hold the federal deficit to the 1990/91 level of Can$30,500 million. Total federal spending was predicted to rise 5.1 per cent to Can$159,000 million in the 1991/92 fiscal year. Restrictions on transfer payments to the provinces for social programmes were continued and the government announced a steep rise in unemployment insurance premiums paid by employees and employers. A public service strike in September and early October saw more than 70,000 federal civil servants leave their jobs for 15 days in protest against a freeze on salary increases. The strikers were ordered back to work by legislation on 2 October.

Canada backed UN military action against Iraq (see V.2) following a House of Commons debate in January. As a consequence, about 4,000 Canadians—sailors, pilots, medical personnel and communications specialists—served in the Gulf theatre. Three ships assisted in the enforcement of UN trade sanctions against Iraq while CF-18 jet fighers flew 2,700 sorties over the Gulf and enemy territory, protecting naval vessels and escorting coalition bombers. Canadian aircraft carried out the first offensive action by Canadian forces since the Korean War in unleashing air-to-ground attacks on Iraqi positions. Prime Minister Mulroney, at the G7 economic summit in July, strongly endorsed a plan for a register of arms sales to be established by the UN.

Canada joined with the United States and Mexico in beginning negotiations in June to establish a North American free trade zone. Although Canadian trade with Mexico represented only 1 per cent of its total trade, Canada joined the talks in order to protect and build upon its own free trade agreement with the United States. The negotiations were expected to run well into 1992.

Prime Minister Mulroney and US President Bush signed a treaty in Ottawa on 13 March to reduce the sulphur dioxide emissions from coal-burning electrical generating plants. The emissions produced acid rain, damaging to forests and lakes on both sides of the border. Canada had sought such an agreement since 1979 and had already begun a programme to curtail emissions. The cutbacks by the two countries would halve trans-boundary flows of sulphur dioxide from 1980 levels by the year 2000.

3. LATIN AMERICA

ARGENTINA—BOLIVIA—BRAZIL—CHILE—COLOMBIA—ECUADOR—
PARAGUAY—PERU—URUGUAY—VENEZUELA—CUBA—
DOMINICAN REPUBLIC AND HAITI—CENTRAL AMERICA
AND PANAMA—MEXICO

i. ARGENTINA

CAPITAL: Buenos Aires   AREA: 2,766,890 sq km   POPULATION: 31,900,000 ('89)
OFFICIAL LANGUAGE: Spanish   POLITICAL SYSTEM: federal presidential democracy
HEAD OF STATE AND GOVERNMENT: President Carlos Saúl Menem (since July '89)
RULING PARTY: Justicialist (Peronist) Party (since Dec '89)
PRINCIPAL MINISTERS: Eduardo Duhalde (vice-president), Guido di Tella (foreign relations), Antonio Ermán González (defence), Domingo Cavallo (economy), José Luis Manzano (interior), Leon Carlos Arslanian (justice)
INTERNATIONAL ALIGNMENT: OAS
CURRENCY: austral (end-'91 £1=A18,521.23, US$1=A9,920.32)
GNP PER CAPITA: US$2,160 ('89)
MAIN EXPORT EARNERS: wheat, other agricultural produce, manufactures

A dramatic transformation in the prospects for the country began on 15 January when President Carlos Menem recalled Dr Guido di Tella from Washington to serve as Defence Minister. Following a further economic crisis at the end of the month, on 29 January Sr di Tella was given the portfolio of external relations, whose former holder, Domingo Cavallo, took over the Ministry of the Economy from Antonio Ermán González, who was moved to defence. Sr Cavallo proceeded to implement a far-reaching programme of economic stabilization, revenue raising and measures to eliminate tax evasion, including a 'fiscal pact' with the Rural Society (SRA). On 27 March the Chamber of Deputies approved a bill for the so-called 'dollarization' of the economy on a parity of 10,000 australes to US$1, backed by foreign exchange or gold reserves at the central bank. By August inflation had fallen to 1.5 per cent, the lowest monthly figure for 17 years. However, the rigours of the austerity programme led to several days of demonstrations by pensioners and *jubilados* in Plaza Lavalle, forcing the government on 5 June to agree to a token 25 per cent increase in minimum benefits.

After a slow start to the privatization programme, the sale was agreed in July of the national airline, Aerolíneas Argentinas, to a consortium headed by Iberia of Spain. On 31 October, after troops had been used to evict strikers from the partially-closed state-owned SOMISA iron works, President Menem issued a decree reversing 40 years of Peronist policy by a sweeping liberalization of economic practices which included abolition of national wage bargaining and of regulations on business contracts and hours of work. During a six-day state visit to the United States in November, President Menem was fêted as the continent's leading free market reformer and US ally. He obtained a promise of debt reduction under the Brady Plan. At the year's end, the sale of 30 per cent of the Buenos Aires telephone company raised nearly twice the amount expected.

Earlier, in March, the President had come under criticism for retaining as his appointments secretary his estranged wife's sister, Amira Yoma, who had been arrested in Spain on suspicion of laundering drug money. Arrested with her was her estranged husband, Ibrahim al Ibrahim, whom Menem had appointed chief of customs at Ezeiza international airport, even though (or perhaps because) he did not speak Spanish. She was eventually dismissed in July only a few days before she was indicted in an Argentine court on the same charges. In the latter part of the year 'Yomagate' became a major topic of gossip, though at the same time support for the ruling Justicialist (Peronist) Party (PJ) strengthened.

On 17 April the President appointed an interventor for the province of Catamarca, whose Peronist governor, Ramón Saadi, had hitherto been a key supporter. Yet in the first round of mid-term provincial and congressional elections on 8 August the Peronists held San Luis and recaptured San Juan from the local Bloquistas. In the second round on 8 September the Peronists won ten of 13 governorships, including that of the province of Buenos Aires, where Vice-President Eduardo Duhalde took 47 per cent of the votes cast. The dissident former military rebel, Aldo Rico, came third, but with only 10 per cent of the vote failed to become a major political force. The Peronists also gained seven seats in the Chamber of Deputies, though this still left them short of an overall majority. Both the Peronist hardliner, Saúl Ubaldini, and Alvaro Alsogaray, former leader of the Union of the Democratic Centre, failed to win election, and four days later former President Raúl Alfonsín announced his intention to resign as leader of the Radical Party (UCR). In the third round on 27 October, the Peronists retained three of the six governorships at stake, though they lost to local candidates in Corrientes, Chaco and Salta.

On 8 January the Supreme Council of the Armed Forces sentenced Mohammed Ali Seneildín and six other officers charged with leading the military rebellion of December 1990 (see AR 1990, p. 75) to indefinite imprisonment and discharge from the service. On 23 February a former member of the customs and border guard, Ismael Abdala, tried to assassinate former President Alfonsín at an election rally, soon after his public criticism of the government's pardon of eight former senior military officers convicted of human rights offences (ibid.). On 21 June Sr Ermán González announced that the armed forces would be cut from 75,000 to 55,000 and the period of conscription reduced from one year to six months. He also confirmed the final cancellation of the Condor missile project, which was to be channelled into peaceful uses. On 31 October the Army Chief of Staff, General Martín Bonnet, resigned in protest at the cuts and was replaced by his deputy, General Martín Balza.

Abroad, concern about Chilean intentions was eased after an agreement on 2 August settling some 22 points of difference on their common frontier, but leaving open the future of the 520-sq-km Laguna del Desierto for settlement by international arbitration. In the latter part of the year, millions of sheep were killed in southern Patagonia when on 8 August Mount Hudson in the Chilean Andes erupted, scattering ash over an enormous area on both sides of the range.

ii. BOLIVIA

CAPITALS: La Paz and Sucre   AREA: 1,099,000 sq km   POPULATION: 7,100,000 ('89)
OFFICIAL LANGUAGES: Spanish, Quechua, Aymará
POLITICAL SYSTEM: presidential democracy
HEAD OF STATE AND GOVERNMENT: President Jaime Paz Zamora (since Aug '89)
RULING PARTIES: Revolutionary Left Movement (MIR) holds presidency, supported by Nationalist Democratic Action (ADN)
PRINCIPAL MINISTERS: Luis Ossio Sanjinés (MIR/vice-president), Carlos Iturralde Ballivián (ADN/foreign affairs), Carlos Saavedra Bruno (MIR/interior & justice), Rear-Adml. Alberto Saínz Klinsky (ADN/defence), David Blanco Zabala (ADN/finance)
INTERNATIONAL ALIGNMENT: NAM, OAS
CURRENCY: boliviano (end-'91 £1=Bs6.97, US$1=Bs3.73)
GNP PER CAPITA: US$620 ('89)
MAIN EXPORT EARNERS: natural gas, tin

THE continued drive for economic stabilization was reflected in a further reduction in budgeted government expenditure and reduction in the national debt. An annual inflation rate of some 12–15 per cent was projected for 1991/92. The basis of this was, however, threatened when the United States forced the resignation on 4 March of Colonel Faustino Rico Toro as head of the Special Force for the Fight Against Drug Trafficking (FELCN), to which he had been appointed on 27 February. On 4 April a reluctant Congress approved the use of US military personnel to train anti-narcotics workers, President Jaime Paz Zamora having given assurances that chemical defoliants would not be used and that peasant producers would not be arrested.

The militarization of the anti-drug campaign brought predictable nationalist resistance among rural workers. The US ambassador, Robert Gelbard, publicly criticized US naval personnel after 'Operation Safe Haven', launched by the Drugs Enforcement Agency (DEA) on 28 June at Santa Ana de Yacuma, failed to capture Erwin Guzmán Gutiérrez, said to be the link with the Cali cartel of Colombia. He later surrendered to the government on 11 July. On 17 July the Minister of the Interior, Carlos Saavedra Bruno, proclaimed a 120-day amnesty period for traffickers to surrender without facing extradition to the USA. In August a major cabinet reshuffle took place with the agreement of the members of the Patriotic Accord (AP). The Foreign Minister, Carlos Iturralde Ballivián, who had been widely criticized, retained his position.

iii. BRAZIL

CAPITAL: Brasília   AREA: 8,512,000 sq km   POPULATION: 147,300,000 ('89)
OFFICIAL LANGUAGE: Portuguese   POLITICAL SYSTEM: federal presidential democracy
HEAD OF STATE AND GOVERNMENT: President Fernando Collor de Mello (since '90)
RULING PARTY: National Reconstruction Party (PRN)
PRINCIPAL MINISTERS: Itamar Franco (vice-president), Francisco Rezek (external relations), Marcílio Marques Moreira (economy), Jarbas Passarinho (justice), João Santana (infrastructure)
INTERNATIONAL ALIGNMENT: OAS
CURRENCY: cruzeiro (end-'91 £1=Cz$1,952.48, US$1=Cz$1,045.78)
GNP PER CAPITA: US$2,540 ('89)
MAIN EXPORT EARNERS: coffee, iron ore, soyabeans, tourism

ON 31 January, after inflation for the month had exceeded 20 per cent, President Collor de Mello announced a new stabilization plan (for March 1990 plan, see AR 1990, p. 77). In addition to imposing an immediate freeze on prices and wages, he abolished the indexation of savings and certificates of deposit, and pooled short-term deposits in a new social development fund to finance the debts of state and local government. The new measures, which led to an immediate crisis in food supplies as supermarket proprietors refused to restock, were unpopular with businessmen, financiers and union leaders alike. On 14 March President Collor announced a National Reconstruction Plan to mark the end of his first year in power. It involved the abolition of state monopolies of telecommunications and fuel, heavy cuts in tariffs, the ending of subsidies, further cutbacks in the public sector and acceleration of the privatization programme.

On 8 April a preliminary agreement was signed with the Paris Club covering arrears of interest due to December 1990, following which the US government withdrew its objection to a new Inter-American Development Bank (IDB) loan to Brazil, for sanitation projects. However, on 8 May the Economy Minister, Zélia Cardoso de Mello, whose high-profile negotiating style, enthusiasm for interventionist measures and much publicized affair with the former minister of justice, Bernardo Cabral, had all made her enemies, resigned. Her successor, Marcílio Marques Moreira (59), a former banker and latterly ambassador to Washington, appointed a more conservative ministry team.

There continued to be widespread criticism of the President, and the state governors refused their support when, after granting large increases to the armed forces, he proposed on 22 August a series of constitutional changes to cut public spending and increase federal revenues. Soon afterwards the President's wife, Rosane Malta, was forced to resign her post as head of the government drought relief agency LBA after allegations in *Jornal do Brasil* that she had authorized large payments to members of her family in the state of Alagoas. In October the President, who meanwhile had dismissed some of his advisers, backed down on the constitutional changes. Lacking support in Congress for his radical plans, he presented instead a much smaller package focusing on fiscal adjustment measures. However, this did not head off proposals to hold a national referendum to curtail his powers.

Armed attacks on rural union leaders continued in the early part of the year. Measures to demarcate a reserve for the Yanomami Indians in Roraima were delayed, and thousands of illegal gold prospectors (*garimpeiros*) again invaded their tribal lands. After a state visit to the United States on 17–20 June, however, President Collor appointed a new head of the National Indian Foudation (FUNAI), Sidney Possuelo, in place of Cantidio Guerreiro Guimarães. He also reactivated some environmental measures, including 'debt for nature' swaps, which he had cancelled on assuming office.

In early June an official report prepared by the federal police in Brasília confirmed concern by human rights organizations about the plight of 'street children'. A total of 4,611 children and adolescents had, it was estimated, been killed over the last three years and thousands more raped, abused and sold into prostitution. Military personnel were reliably reported to have been implicated in the killings. During his pastoral visit between 12 and 24 October, which attracted much less interest than expected, Pope John Paul II appealed for social justice for the street children, but also denounced birth control. (For the arrival of the South American cholera epidemic in Brazil, see XI.6.v.)

iv. CHILE

CAPITAL: Santiago   AREA: 756,000 sq km   POPULATION: 13,000,000 ('89)
OFFICIAL LANGUAGE: Spanish   POLITICAL SYSTEM: presidential democracy
HEAD OF STATE AND GOVERNMENT: Patricio Aylwin Azócar (since March '90)
RULING PARTY: Christian Democratic Party heads 17-party Coalition for Democracy
PRINCIPAL MINISTERS: Enrique Silva Cimma (foreign affairs), Enrique Krauss Rusque (interior), Carlos Ominami Pascual (economy), Alejandro Foxley Rioseco (finance), Francisco Cumplido Cereceda (justice), Patricio Rojas Saavedra (defence)
INTERNATIONAL ALIGNMENT: OAS, NAM
CURRENCY: peso (end-'91 £1=Ch$699.75, US$1=Ch$374.79)
GNP PER CAPITA: US$1,770 ('89)
MAIN EXPORT EARNERS: copper, agricultural products

IN January a congressional committee reported on allegations that payments totalling $3 million had been made by the army to Augusto Pinochet Hiriart, son of former President Augusto Pinochet Ugarte, commander of the army. Though the payments had, it was claimed, been made legitimately to reimburse Sr Pinochet for loans he had secured on behalf of a now-defunct engineering company, the 'Pinocheques' affair cast further doubt on the army's incorruptibility. On 22 January the Chamber of Deputies approved an amendment to the constitution allowing President Patricio Aylwin to release provisionally some 250 political prisoners.

On 4 March the report of the Truth and Reconciliation Commission (CVR), set up in April 1990 under the chairmanship of Raúl Rettig to inquire into human rights violations under General Pinochet's regime, was published.

It documented 2,279 people as having died, including 1,068 by shooting or under torture, and 957 'disappeared' whose ultimate fate remained unknown. In a nationwide television address President Aylwin, who as leader of the Christian Democrats had been among those calling for military intervention in 1973, acknowledged his share of responsibility for the Pinochet regime.

Although the report also noted that 90 members of the security forces had died at the hands of the armed opposition, in an address to 1,500 officers at the Military Academy on 29 March General Pinochet described the report as having no 'historical or legal validity'. Senator Jaime Guzmán Errázuriz, founder and leader of the pro-Pinochet Independent Democratic Union (UDI), also rejected the report. Two days later, on 1 April, he was fatally shot by two gunmen outside the Catholic University. Two members of the Manuel Rodríguez Patriotic Front (FMPR), which had claimed responsibility, were killed eight days later in a shoot-out in Rancagua. Subsequently, from 1 June, the FMPR formally abandoned the armed struggle. Despite the increase in tension, President Aylwin visited European states on 7–25 April without incident. In August he declined a cross-party initiative to extend his mandate from four years to six.

On 2–14 September, 125 unmarked bodies were exhumed from plot 29 of Santiago's general cemetery and were believed to be victims of Pinochet's repression after 1973. The general's comment, that the burial of more than one body in the same grave showed 'great economy', caused widespread revulsion. The government initiated proceedings, not against Pinochet but against a newspaper editor who had described him as 'shameless' and 'sadistic'. However, on 23 September a judge ordered the detention of General (rtd) Manuel Contreras, former head of Pinochet's secret police (DINA), for the murder in Washington of Orlando Letelier (see AR 1976, p. 83). Moreover, when visiting Chancellor Kohl of Germany called the Pinochet regime a 'dictatorship' and likened the general himself to Erich Honecker, the Chilean President expressed his 'solidarity' with his guest.

v. COLOMBIA

CAPITAL: Bogotá   AREA: 1,141,750 sq km   POPULATION: 32,300,000 ('89)
OFFICIAL LANGUAGE: Spanish   POLITICAL SYSTEM: presidential democracy
HEAD OF STATE AND GOVERNMENT: President César Gaviria Trujillo (since Aug '90)
RULING PARTIES: Liberal Party (PL) heads coalition with Social Conservative Party (PSC), National Salvation Movement (MSN), New Democratic Force (NFD) and April 19 Movement Democratic Alliance (ADM-19)
PRINCIPAL MINISTERS: Nohemi Sanín Posada (PSC/foreign affairs), Humberto de la Calle Lombana (PL/interior), Rudolf Hommes Rodríguez (PL/finance), Fernando Carillo Flores (PL/justice), Rafael Pardo Ruedas (PL/defence), Jorge Ospina Sardi (NFD/economic development)
INTERNATIONAL ALIGNMENT: NAM, OAS
CURRENCY: peso (end-'91 £1=Col$1,163,30, US$1=Col$623,09)
GNP PER CAPITA: US$1,200 ('89)
MAIN EXPORT EARNERS: coffee, oil and oil derivatives

IN an important further step towards the restoration of peace, on 15 January Jorge Luis Ochoa, joint leader of the Medellín drugs cartel, surrendered to the authorities and was placed under house arrest. Ten days later, however, in a police operation to free the remaining five of eight journalists seized as hostages by the so-called '*Extraditables*' in mid-1990 (see AR 1990, p. 80), Diana Turbay Quintero, journalist and daughter of former President Julio César Turbay Ayala, was killed, apparently by her captors. President Gaviria Trujillo on 29 January offered to extend his earlier amnesty decree, but not before another of the hostages, Marina Montoya, had already been killed. The remaining three were freed on 5 February and 20 May.

Following the surrender of Sr Ochoa, on 16 February a massive bomb outside La Macarena bullring in the centre of Medellín killed 22 people and injured 135. Nevertheless, the President went ahead with a state visit to the United States on 26-27 February, when he signed a further agreement on collaboration against drug-traffickers. On 19 June, coincident with a vote by the Colombian Congress to repeal legislation permitting extradition of drug-traffickers, the leader of the Medellín cartel himself, 42-year-old Pablo Escobar Gaviria, surrendered. Accused of the murder of hundreds of people, he was taken to a private prison (built to his own design!) to await trial. In August the Minister of Justice, Jaime Giraldo Angel, author of the policy of leniency to drug-traffickers, was forced to resign. In September General Miguel Maza Marquez, who had failed to prevent the assassination of three presidential candidates, was dismissed from his post as director of the Administrative Department of Security (DAS). He was replaced by a lawyer and personal friend of the President, Fernando Britto Ruiz.

Meanwhile, the long dialogue between the government and the

revolutionary left continued. Under a decree of 22 January, the Revolutionary Workers' Party (PRT) laid down its arms, and on 1 March the maoist Popular Liberation Army (EPL) was reborn as the Hope, Peace and Liberty (EPL) party. In return it received two nominated seats in the Constituent Assembly, which met for the first time on 5 February with 73 members, of whom 70 were directly elected. To coincide with the opening of the Assembly, a countrywide offensive was launched by the Revolutionary Armed Forces of Colombia (FARC) and the National Liberation Army (ELN). This led to heavy fighting in several areas, including a clash on the Amazonian frontier near Tabatinga, in which three Brazilian soldiers were killed. Direct talks with their joint directorate, the Simón Bolívar Guerrilla Coordinating Board (CNGSB), eventually began in Caracas on 3 June. One day earlier, the Constituent Assembly had resolved to dissolve the existing National Assembly on 2 July and to empower the President to rule by decree until the new Congress, from which existing deputies and delegates of the Constituent Assembly would be barred, took office on 1 December.

The new constitution, which came into effect at midnight on 5 July, replacing that of 1886, introduced national elections for the Senate, reduced the size of the Legislative Assembly, provided for direct election of departmental governors, created special seats for representation of the indigenous population, banned extradition, established civil marriage and legalized divorce for all citizens. 'Individual' offers of amnesty were made by the government to people who had committed terrorist crimes before 5 July, though a new anti-terrorist law, passed on 26 September, threatened for a time to disrupt the peace talks which had resumed earlier in the month.

In the first elections under the new constitution, held on 27 October, the ruling Liberals (PL) won 58 seats out of 102 in the Senate and 86 out of 161 in the Assembly. The opposition Social Conservative Party (PSC) obtained only 10 Senate and 15 Assembly seats, while the left-wing ADM-19 obtained 9 seats in the Senate and 15 in the House, its support, at 10 per cent, being well down on its 1990 figure.

vi. ECUADOR

CAPITAL: Quito   AREA: 270,500 sq km   POPULATION: 10,300,000 ('89)
OFFICIAL LANGUAGE: Spanish   POLITICAL SYSTEM: presidential democracy
HEAD OF STATE AND GOVERNMENT: President Rodrigo Borja Cevallos (since Aug '88)
RULING PARTIES: Democratic Left allied with Christian Democrats
PRINCIPAL MINISTERS: Luis Parodi (vice-president), Diego Cordovez (foreign affairs), César Verduga (interior), Gen. (rtd) Jorge Félix (defence), Juan Falconi (finance), Pablo Better (industry & trade), Oscar Garzon (energy & mines)
INTERNATIONAL ALIGNMENT: NAM, OAS
CURRENCY: sucre (end-'91 £1=S/.2,424.31, US$1=S/.1,298.51)
GNP PER CAPITA: US$1,020 ('89)
MAIN EXPORT EARNERS: oil and oil derivatives, coffee, bananas

DISAGREEMENT on economic strategy, although it was denied by the government, led to the replacement in January of Jorge Gallardo as Minister of Finance and Public Credit by Juan Falconi, while charges of corruption accounted for the dismissal on 12 March of Diego Tamariz as Minister of Energy and Mines. On 4 September eight dissidents, former members of the guerrilla movement Alfaro Vive, Carajo! (AVC), occupied the British embassy to publicize their demands for the release of their leader, Patricio Baquerizo, but left peacefully after some 30 hours. Three days later, after a demonstration by policemen angered by the judicial system and the media, a dynamite attack severely damaged the Supreme Court building in Quito. In October AVC finally disbanded, its members joining the ruling Democratic Left (ID). Abroad, a fresh conflict with Peruvian forces in the undemarcated frontier region of the Condor mountains was averted by a mutual agreement to withdraw.

vii. PARAGUAY

CAPITAL: Asunción   AREA: 406,752 sq km   POPULATION: 4,200,000 ('89)
OFFICIAL LANGUAGE: Spanish   POLITICAL SYSTEM: republic, emerging democracy
HEAD OF STATE AND GOVERNMENT: President (Gen.) Andres Rodríguez (since '89)
RULING PARTY: Colorado Party
PRINCIPAL MINISTERS: Alexis Frutos Vaesken (foreign affairs), Gen. Orlando Machuca Vargas (interior), Juan José Díaz Perez (finance), Gen. Angel Juan Souto Hernandez (defence), Hugo Estigarribia Elizache (justice & labour), Ualdo Scavone (industry & trade)
INTERNATIONAL ALIGNMENT: OAS
CURRENCY: guaraní (end-'91 £1=G2,447.39, US$1=G1,310.87)
GNP PER CAPITA: US$1,030 ('89)
MAIN EXPORT EARNERS: cotton, soyabeans, meat

IN Paraguay's first-ever municipal elections, which took place on 26 May, the ruling Colorado Party (ANR-PC) gained only 43 per cent of the votes in 154 of the 206 municipalities, against 29 per cent for the opposition Authentic Radical Liberal Party (PLRA). Dr Carlos Alberto Filizzola, a 31-year-old physician and political independent, won the mayorality of Asunción with 34 per cent of the votes cast, defeating the candidates of both major political parties. This led to demands from the Colorado youth wing for the dismissal of the party president, Luis María Argana, and other senior officials described as 'corrupt'.

In Constituent Assembly elections on 1 December, the ANR-PC won a comfortable majority of 57 per cent of the votes, against 28 per cent for the PLRA. The Colorados secured 123 of the 198 seats in the Assembly, which was charged with drafting, within six months, a new constitution to replace that of 1967.

viii. PERU

CAPITAL: Lima AREA: 1,285,000 sq km POPULATION: 21,200,000 ('89)
OFFICIAL LANGUAGES: Spanish, Quechua, Aymará
POLITICAL SYSTEM: presidential democracy
HEAD OF STATE AND GOVERNMENT: President Alberto Keinya Fujimori (since '90)
RULING PARTY: Change 90 heads national unity coalition
PRINCIPAL MINISTERS: Maximo San Roman Caceres (1st vice-president), Carlos Garcia Garcia (2nd vice-president), Alfonso de los Heros Perez Albela (prime minister), Augusto Blacker Miller (foreign affairs), Carlos Boloña Bohr (economy & finance), Gen. E. P. Victor Malca (defence), Augusto Antoniolli Vásquez (justice), Gen. Juan Briones (interior), Victor Joy Way (industry & commerce)
INTERNATIONAL ALIGNMENT: NAM, OAS
CURRENCY: new sol (end-'91 £1=NS1.78, US$1=NS0.95)
GNP PER CAPITA: US$1,010('89)
MAIN EXPORT EARNERS: copper, petroleum products

FOLLOWING major cabinet reshuffles in January and February, the government of President Alberto Keinya Fujimori introduced a package of major changes reversing the land reform legislation of 1969. The measures lifted restrictions on private ownership, allowed endowed land to be used as collateral for loans, and enabled peasant cooperatives to become limited companies. On 1 March the US government suspended $94 million in aid, alleging that Peru had made insufficient progress in combating drug-trafficking. Following further discussions, however, an outline agreement was signed in Lima on 14 May and embodied in a full agreement on 24 July. Aiming to break the alliance of drug-trafficking and insurgency, President Fujimori's government had thus reversed its initial refusal to accept US money for crop substitution. A fresh onslaught by the guerrilla movement Sendero Luminoso had already blacked out Lima, Trujillo and Ica on 6 April, and under cover of darkness bomb and grenade attacks caused extensive property damage. Twelve days later the government extended the state of emergency to a further eight provinces, suspending constitutional guarantees over some two-thirds of the country.

Despite this, incidents continued, including a car bomb attack on the Liberty and Democracy Institute in Lima on 26 April, while further evidence emerged of the involvement of military personnel in death squad activity. Amnesty International claimed that under the Fujimori government 120 people had already 'disappeared', making a total of some 3,700 since 1980. Congress eventually granted the President emergency legislative powers for 150 days from 18 June to deal both with the military emergency and with the economic crisis. Meanwhile, attacks on Japanese aid workers had led to their withdrawal, but not to the cancellation of a $403 million loan. However, it was not until September, when a new currency, the new sol, was introduced to replace the inti, that the country's isolation from the international financial community was formally ended by the endorsement of the IMF of the country's stabilization programme. This enabled the government to reach agreement with the Paris Club on the rescheduling of some $6,600 million of public sector debts.

In October the Senate voted to withdraw congressional immunity from ex-President Alan García Pérez, now a senator, so that he could stand trial on charges of embezzlement centring on the transfer of a third of the central bank reserves to the defunct Bank of Credit and Commerce International. Three former ministers were also accused. President Fujimori's tour to Europe in the same month was generally seen as an attempt to improve Peru's image abroad, which was marred by instability and its poor record on human rights. In further government changes in November, Alfonso de los Heros Pérez Albela was appointed Prime Minister, replacing Carlos Torres y Torres Lara, who had held the post only since February. (For the impact in Peru of the South American cholera epidemic, see XI.6.v.)

ix. URUGUAY

CAPITAL: Montevideo   AREA: 176,200 sq km   POPULATION: 3,100,000 ('89)
OFFICIAL LANGUAGE: Spanish   POLITICAL SYSTEM: presidential democracy
HEAD OF STATE AND GOVERNMENT: President Luis Alberto Lacalle Herrera (since '90)
RULING PARTY: National (Blanco) Party heading coalition with Colorados
PRINCIPAL MINISTERS: Gonzala Aguirre Ramirez (vice-president), Hector Gros Espiell
    (foreign relations), Juan Andres Ramirez (interior), Enrique Braga (economy &
    finance), Mariano Brito (defence), Augusto Montesdeoca (industry & energy)
INTERNATIONAL ALIGNMENT: OAS
CURRENCY: new peso (end-'91 £1=NUr$4,629.83, US$1=NUr2,479.82)
GNP PER CAPITA: US$2,620 ('89)
MAIN EXPORT EARNERS: wool, meat

LACKING as he did a majority in Congress, President Luis Alberto Lacalle Herrera failed in his bid to persuade senators to authorize the privatization of the state-owned telephone service (Antel), airline (Pluna) and port authority. One of the four Colorado members of the government, José Alfredo Solari Damonte, was forced to resign as Minister of Health when his faction, led by former President Sanguinetti, withdrew its support from the National Agreement (CN) government. He was replaced by Carlos Delpiazzo. On 1 October the President signed the State Reform Law, permitting the privatization of public corporations.

x. VENEZUELA

CAPITAL: Caracas AREA: 912,000 sq km POPULATION: 19,200,000 ('89)
OFFICIAL LANGUAGE: Spanish POLITICAL SYSTEM: presidential democracy
HEAD OF STATE AND GOVERNMENT: President Carlos Andrés Pérez (since Feb '89)
RULING PARTY: Democratic Action (since Jan '84)
PRINCIPAL MINISTERS: Armando Durán (foreign affairs), Alejandro Izaguirre Angeli (interior), Roberto Pocaterra (finance), Gen. Fernando Ochoa Antich (defence), Celestino Armas (energy & mines), Alfredo Ducharme (justice)
INTERNATIONAL ALIGNMENT: OAS, NAM
CURRENCY: bolivar (end-'91 £1=Bs113.11, US$1=Bs60.58)
GNP PER CAPITA: US$2,450 ('89)
MAIN EXPORT EARNERS: oil, aluminium

ON 30 April the Foreign Minister, Reinaldo Figueredo Planchart, resigned to seek the leadership of the ruling Democratic Action (AD) party and was replaced by Armando Durán. As a result of the Gulf War, oil revenues increased by some $2,000 million in 1990, generating a substantial trade surplus. Initial optimism about the future, which led the government to budget for substantial debt repayments, brought demands from the Federation of Venezuelan Workers (CTV) for wage increases of 45 per cent. However, realism returned when oil prices quickly dropped back to pre-war levels.

Meanwhile, evidence that the country was increasingly being used as a conduit for drugs and drug-related activities led the government of President Carlos Andrés Pérez to declare 'all-out war' on the problem. The dismissal of the director of military intelligence, General Herminio Fuenmayor, was followed in July by a cabinet reshuffle in which General Fernando Ochoa Antich became Minister of Defence. At the same time, the government followed the general trend by lifting price controls on private goods and services while Congress cut corporation tax and placed a ceiling on taxes in the mining sector. In August the state airline, Viasa, was privatized by sale to a consortium of the Spanish state airline Iberia and the Banco Provincial.

xi. CUBA

CAPITAL: Havana AREA: 115,000 sq km POPULATION: 11,000,000 ('89)
OFFICIAL LANGUAGE: Spanish POLITICAL SYSTEM: republic, one-party communist state
HEAD OF STATE AND GOVERNMENT: President Fidel Castro Ruz (since Jan '59)
RULING PARTY: Cuban Communist Party (PCC)
PRINCIPAL MINISTERS: Gen. Raúl Castro Ruz (1st vice-president, defence), Isidoro Octavio Malmierca Peoli (foreign relations), Gen. Abelardo Colomé Ibarra (interior), Rodrigo García Leon (finance), José López Moreno (planning)
INTERNATIONAL ALIGNMENT: NAM
CURRENCY: peso (end-'91 £1=Cub$1.42, US$1=Cub$0.76)
GNP PER CAPITA: n.a.
MAIN EXPORT EARNERS: sugar and sugar products

AT a speech to commemorate the 30th anniversary of the abortive 'Bay of Pigs' expedition (see AR 1961, pp. 182–3, 192), President Castro reaffirmed his determination to defend 'socialism', if necessary alone, in the face of 'threats of world imperialism and reaction'. Some 85 per cent of Cuba's trade, he confirmed, 'had crumbled in a matter of months' following the collapse of communism in the Soviet Union and Eastern Europe. On the 38th anniversary of his attack on the Moncada barracks, the President on 26 July described the situation in Eastern Europe as a 'disaster' and called on all Cubans to redouble their efforts to resist the economic pressure of the United States. The easing of travel restrictions in August gave rise to fears in the United States of a new 'Mariel exodus' (see AR 1980, p. 85). The unilateral announcement on 11 September by President Gorbachev that 11,000 Soviet troops were to be withdrawn from Cuba was welcomed by the US government, which did not choose to act on his suggestion that US forces should withdraw from their naval base at Guantánamo Bay. Facing a poor sugar harvest and the prospect of the immediate end of Soviet subsidies, the government proceeded to decree a rigorous austerity programme, while harassment of opposition forces increased.

Meanwhile, elections to the National Assembly had been postponed for a year (5 July) to enable it to study 'improvements' to the one-party state. The fourth congress of the Cuban Communist Party (PCC), which would otherwise have clashed with the 11th Pan-American Games in Havana in August, was held behind closed doors in Santiago on 10–14 October. It too rejected both the mixed economy and Western-style multi-party systems, which President Castro was reported to have described as 'garbage'. It also reaffirmed its support for austerity, while seeking as far as possible to shield the gains of the revolution in health and public services. But, by giving official sanction to small-scale traders, it in effect legitimized the active black market. The PCC central committee was enlarged from 146 to 225 members and given extraordinary powers; the politburo, on the other hand, retained only three of its former members, the Castro brothers, as first and second secretaries, and Carlos Rafael Rodríguez, as vice-president.

xii. HAITI AND THE DOMINICAN REPUBLIC

Haiti
CAPITAL: Port-au-Prince   AREA: 27,750 sq km   POPULATION: 6,400,000 ('89)
OFFICIAL LANGUAGE: French, Creole   POLITICAL SYSTEM: military/presidential
HEAD OF STATE AND GOVERNMENT: Joseph Nerette (since Oct '91)
CURRENCY: gourde (end-'91 £1=G9.37, US$1=G5.00)
GNP PER CAPITA: US$360 ('89)
MAIN EXPORT EARNERS: light manufactures, coffee, tourism

II.3.xii HAITI AND THE DOMINICAN REPUBLIC

Dominican Republic
CAPITAL: Santo Domingo   AREA: 48,400 sq km   POPULATION: 7,000,000 ('89)
OFFICIAL LANGUAGE: Spanish   POLITICAL SYSTEM: presidential democracy
HEAD OF STATE AND GOVERNMENT: President Joaquín Balaguer (since Aug '86)
CURRENCY: peso (end-'91 £1=RD$23.66, US$1=RD$12.67)
GNP PER CAPITA: US$790 ('89)
MAIN EXPORT EARNERS: sugar, metals, tourism

FOLLOWING the election of the former Salesian priest Fr Jean-Bertrand Aristide as President of HAITI on 16 December 1990 (see AR 1990, pp. 86–7), an attempt on 6 January to overthrow the interim government of President Ertha Pascal-Trouillot was foiled by the army, led by General Hérard Abraham. Its leader, the hard-line Duvalierist Roger Lafontant, was subsequently, in July, sentenced to life imprisonment with hard labour. Fr Aristide was sworn in on 7 February in Port-au-Prince. In keeping with his role as priest of the poor he forewent his statutory salary ($10,000 per month) and delivered his inaugural address mainly in Creole, which on 29 July he proclaimed joint official language. René Préval, a 48-year-old agronomist of no political affiliation, was appointed Prime Minister and Minister of Defence and Interior, while Marie-Michèle Rey, a senior bank executive, became Minister of Finance. Both the European Community and the United States promised additional aid to facilitate the transition to democracy, and France cancelled debts totalling $55 million.

On 2 July the President dismissed General Abraham as Commander of the Army and appointed in his place General Raoul Cédras, who had supervised the December 1990 presidential elections. But on 29 September a mutiny among junior ranks of the motorized *Engin Lourd* at Frères military camp led to a violent coup in which 26 died (including the Christian Democrat leader, Sylvio Claude). At least 600 people were killed over the next two days and the President himself was saved from the soldiers only by the intercession of the ambassadors of Canada, France, the United States and Venezuela. Meanwhile, General Cédras, whose role in the affair remained ambiguous, called for calm and promised new elections.

On 7 October rebel troops stormed the National Assembly, forced the few deputies present to elect another Supreme Court judge, Joseph Nerette, as interim President, and then drove to the airport to oust the OAS negotiators seeking Fr Aristide's return (see also XI.6.v). The US administration, which had distrusted Fr Aristide's radicalism and sometimes violent rhetoric, resisted pressure to intervene but moved marines to Guantánamo Bay in Cuba in readiness and, on 29 October, imposed strict economic sanctions. At the year's end the army was still in charge, through their nominee as Prime Minister, Jean-Jacques Honorat.

In the DOMINICAN REPUBLIC both President Joaquín Balaguer, aged 84 and virtually blind, and his long-time rival, Juan Bosch Gaviño, aged

82, announced their forthcoming retirements from active politics. In July the government deported some 2,000 Haitian immigrant workers, and claimed that a further 11,000 had left 'voluntarily'. A series of strikes for more pay disrupted the already inadequate electricity service, while rises were conceded to doctors and teachers. On 8 August 62-year-old Salvador Jorge Blanco, President from 1982 to 1986, was sentenced to 20 years' imprisonment for misappropriation of public funds. Later the IMF approved further loans subject to a stringent government austerity programme, the prospect of which caused some unrest.

xiii. CENTRAL AMERICA AND PANAMA

Guatemala
CAPITAL: Guatemala City   AREA: 109,000 sq km   POPULATION: 8,900,000 ('89)
OFFICIAL LANGUAGE: Spanish   POLITICAL SYSTEM: presidential democracy
HEAD OF STATE AND GOVERNMENT: President Jorge Serrano Elías (since Jan '91)
RULING PARTY: Solidarity Action Movement
CURRENCY: quetzal (end-'91 £1=Q9.45, US$1=Q5.06)
GNP PER CAPITA: US$910 ('89)
MAIN EXPORT EARNERS: coffee, sugar, cotton, petroleum, cardamom, bananas

Nicaragua
CAPITAL: Managua   AREA: 120,000 sq km   POPULATION: 3,700,000 ('89)
OFFICIAL LANGUAGE: Spanish   POLITICAL SYSTEM: presidential democracy
HEAD OF STATE AND GOVERNMENT: President Violeta Chamorro (since April '90)
RULING PARTY: National Opposition Union (UNO)
CURRENCY: córdoba (end-'91 £1=C$9.37, US$1=C$5.02)
GNP PER CAPITA: US$830 ('87)
MAIN EXPORT EARNERS: coffee, cotton, sugar, bananas

El Salvador
CAPITAL: San Salvador   AREA: 21,400 sq km   POPULATION: 5,100,000 ('89)
OFFICIAL LANGUAGE: Spanish   POLITICAL SYSTEM: presidential democracy
HEAD OF STATE AND GOVERNMENT: President Alfredo Cristiani (since June '89)
RULING PARTY: National Republican Alliance (Arena)
CURRENCY: colón (end-'91 £1=C14.96, US$1=C8.01)
GNP PER CAPITA: US$1,070 ('89)
MAIN EXPORT EARNERS: coffee, cotton, sugar

Honduras
CAPITAL: Tegucigalpa   AREA: 112,000 sq km   POPULATION: 5,000,000 ('89)
OFFICIAL LANGUAGE: Spanish   POLITICAL SYSTEM: presidential democracy
HEAD OF STATE AND GOVERNMENT: President Rafael Leonard Callejas (since Jan '90)
RULING PARTY: National Party (PN)
CURRENCY: lempira (end-'91 £1=L9.95, US$1=L5.33)
GNP PER CAPITA: US$900 ('89)
MAIN EXPORT EARNERS: bananas, coffee, tourism

Costa Rica
CAPITAL: San José   AREA: 51,000 sq km   POPULATION: 2,700,000 ('89)
OFFICIAL LANGUAGE: Spanish   POLITICAL SYSTEM: presidential democracy
HEAD OF STATE AND GOVERNMENT: President Rafael Angel Calderón Fournier (since May '90)
RULING PARTY: Social Christian Unity Party (PUSC)
CURRENCY: colón (end-'91 £1=C260.66, US$1=C139.61)
GNP PER CAPITA: US$1,780 ('89)
MAIN EXPORT EARNERS: coffee, bananas, tourism

Panama
CAPITAL: Panama City AREA: 77,000 sq km POPULATION: 2,400,000 ('89)
OFFICIAL LANGUAGE: Spanish POLITICAL SYSTEM: presidential
HEAD OF STATE AND GOVERNMENT: President Guillermo Endara (since Dec '89)
RULING PARTY: Authentic Liberal Party (within Civic Opposition Democratic Alliance)
CURRENCY: balboa (end-'91 £1=B1.87, US$1=B1.00)
GNP PER CAPITA: US$1,760 ('89)
MAIN EXPORT EARNERS: bananas, prawns, sugar, canal dues

IN the second round of presidential elections in GUATEMALA on 6 January, Jorge Serrano Elías of the Solidarity Action Movement defeated Jorge Carpio Nicolle of the National Centrist Union (UCN) by 936,338 votes to 438,990 in a very low turnout. Sr Serrano, a conservative businessman and Protestant fundamentalist, succeeded Vinicio Cerezo Arévalo as President on 14 January and immediately announced an emergency economic plan. On 24 and 25 April in Mexico City, government representatives, including for the first time five senior military officers, met with representatives of Guatemalan National Revolutionary Unity (URNG), the umbrella guerrilla organization. After the meeting, President Serrano confirmed that to reach peace it would be necessary not only to disarm the guerrillas but also to strengthen democracy, fight poverty and promote 'the valorization of Maya cultures'. The following day the Interior Minister, Colonel Ricardo Méndez Ruiz, resigned for reasons of health and was replaced by Fernando Hurtado. On 1 May Dianora Pérez of the Democratic Socialist Party was shot by unknown gunmen on the streets of the capital.

However, on 23 July a four-point framework agreement was finally signed in Querétaro, Mexico, and in August for the first time members of the armed services were charged with violations of human rights. Then, on 5 September, the President, who in his inaugural address had described his country's longrunning territorial dispute with Belize (see XI.6.v) as 'belonging to the past', unexpectedly extended full diplomatic recognition to Belize (see II.4.v). The Foreign Minister, Alvaro Arzú Irigoyen, who had already stated that Belize would not be recognized, tendered his resignation, but at the year's end the new government remained firmly in charge.

President Violeta Barrios de Chamorro of NICARAGUA remained in office throughout the year, supported by the Sandinista forces who formally swore allegiance to her and to the constitution on 10 January. On 2 January she had refused to dismiss their commander, General Humberto Ortega Saavedra, despite an official admission that in October 1990 four officers had smuggled 28 Soviet-made anti-aircraft missiles to insurgents in El Salvador. On 2 February 17 of the missiles were formally returned. On 16 February Enrique Bermúdez Varela, a former colonel in the Somozas' National Guard and later a Contra leader (who had been ousted in February 1990 from his position in the so-called National Resistance on account of human rights abuses), was shot and killed in Managua. The Sandinista national (FSLN) directorate denied responsibility.

Meanwhile, proposals by Vice-President Virgilio Godoy and the National Opposition Union (UNO) to repeal the 1990 laws giving retrospective validity to land reform measures of the Sandinista years (known as *la piñata*—the sweet dispenser), led to a boycott of the National Assembly by FSLN deputies from 18 June. The new land law, though passed by Congress in August, was partially vetoed by the President on 11 September, though it still allowed for the return of some $11,000 million worth of property to its former owners. This dispute coincided with the mobilization in June of several hundred former Contras (known as Recontras) in northern Jinotega and followed the repeal on 5 June of a Sandinista law demanding $17,000 million in compensation from the United States for economic damage sustained during the Contra war, in light of the 1986 ruling of the International Court of Justice (AR 1986, pp. 412–3). On 3 September the Minister of the Interior met the Recontra leader, José Angel Morán Flores, but, mindful of the reported remobilization of armed Sandinista groups, he made no concessions and the terrorists were invited to surrender their weapons to a newly-formed National Security Commission.

Meanwhile, the economic situation remained critical. Inflation having reached 13,000 per cent in 1990, on 2 March the gold córdoba was devalued and prices of basic foodstuffs raised by anything up to 400 per cent. With dissatisfaction widespread, a congress of the FSLN on 19–21 July re-elected seven of the nine members of the former national directorate, at the same time endorsing a social democratic platform. Former President Ortega was elected to the new post of secretary-general; his brother, the commander of the army, refused renomination as being incompatible with his national duties.

In January talks between the government and insurgent groups in EL SALVADOR, suspended in September 1990, were resumed in Mexico City, after it had become clear that neither side could gain a significant military advantage. In congressional elections held on 10 March the ruling Nationalist Republican Alliance (Arena) lost its absolute majority in the enlarged 84-member National Assembly, polling 44.3 per cent of the votes cast but winning only 39 seats. The remainder were divided between the Christian Democratic Party (PDC), with 26 seats (28 per cent), the National Conciliation Party (PCN) with 9 (9 per cent), the Democratic Convergence (CD) with 8 (12.2 per cent), and the Nationalist Democratic Union (UDN) and Authentic Democratic Christian Movement (MADC) with one seat each.

While fighting continued over much of the country, at further talks in Mexico City in April agreement was reached on constitutional changes stipulated by the Farabundo Martí National Liberation Front (FMLN) as the precondition for a ceasefire. On 20 May the UN Security Council finally approved the creation of an observer team to monitor human rights violations, and this was deployed on 26 July under pressure from national and international human rights groups. On 16 November the FMLN declared a unilateral ceasefire, and on the last day of the year, in New York, the outgoing Secretary-General of the UN, Javier Pérez de Cuellar, successfully obtained agreement on a staged programme leading to a definitive peace on 1 October 1992 (see also XI.1).

On 26 September the US government cancelled official debts of HONDURAS worth $430 million. An earthquake rated at 7.5 on the Richter scale killed at least 80 people on the Caribbean border region of COSTA RICA and Panama on 22 April.

In elections in PANAMA on 27 January for nine seats in the Legislative Assembly vacant since the 1989 elections, five went to the pro-Noriega National Liberation Coalition (Colina) and four to the ruling Civic Opposition Democratic Alliance (ADOC), which already held 51 of the 58 existing seats. Following disputes within the ruling alliance, on 8 April President Endara dismissed the five Christian Democratic members from his cabinet, accusing them of 'disloyalty and arrogance'. Their leader, Ricardo Arias Calderón, remained one of the two vice-presidents, but his portfolios of interior and justice were given to Juan Chevalier Bravo, a crony of the President, and the ADOC lost its overall majority in the Assembly. On 11 April Panama signed a convention with the United States allowing for the exchange of information concerning money laundering, and this was ratified by the Assembly on 16 July. However, the government's cuts in health, education and social services were so severe that reports of a frustrated military plot on 7 October were widely construed as a distraction.

xiv. MEXICO

CAPITAL: Mexico City   AREA: 1,958,000 sq km   POPULATION: 84,600,000 ('89)
OFFICIAL LANGUAGE: Spanish   POLITICAL SYSTEM: federal presidential democracy
HEAD OF STATE AND GOVERNMENT: President Carlos Salinas de Gortari (since Dec '88)
RULING PARTY: Party of the Institutionalized Revolution (since 1929)
PRINCIPAL MINISTERS: Fernando Solana Morales (foreign relations), Fernando Gutiérrez Barrios (government), Gen. Antonio Riviello Bazán (defence), Pedro Aspe Armella (finance), Ernesto Cedillo Ponce de León (planning & budget), Fernando Hiriart Balderrama (energy, mines & public industries), Enrique Alvárez del Castillo (attorney-general)
INTERNATIONAL ALIGNMENT: OAS
CURRENCY: peso (end-'91 £1=Mex$5,680.57, US$1=Mex$3,042.62)
GNP PER CAPITA: US$2,010 ('89)
MAIN EXPORT EARNERS: oil, motor machinery, coffee, tourism

In 1991 the Mexican Revolution finally ended. On the 53rd anniversary of the nationalization of the country's petroleum industry, on 18 March, the government closed down the capital's largest oil refinery in an effort to combat chronic air pollution. Between 7 and 12 April President Carlos Salinas de Gortari visited the United States and Canada to urge the creation of a North American trading zone on the so-called 'fast track' procedure. At the same time, relations with the European Community were strengthened by the signature in Luxembourg on 26 April of a commercial agreement bringing Mexico within the Community's generalized system of preferences (GSP). During a visit to European states in July President Salinas signed a major agreement on economic cooperation with Italy, particularly on hydrocarbons.

Following strong economic growth, in the mid-term elections on 18 August the ruling Party of Institutionalized Revolution (PRI) regained almost all of its losses in the 1988 elections (see AR 1988, pp. 90–1). With 61.4 per cent of the votes cast, the PRI took 61 of the 64 seats in the Senate and 326 seats in the Chamber of Deputies, including 290 of the 300 directly-elected seats. The new opposition Party of the Democratic Revolution (PRD) obtained only 8.3 per cent of the vote, losing two of its four Senate seats and retaining only 41 seats in the Chamber. Of the remainder, 89 went to the conservative Party of National Action (PAN) and 40 to smaller parties. There were many complaints of irregularities, which a presidential aide admitted to be well-founded. On 29 August the President forced the resignation of the PRI governor-elect of Guanajuato, appointing Carlos Medina Plascencia of the PAN as interim governor pending fresh elections. On 9 October the governor-elect of San Luis Potosí, Fausto Zapata, resigned in similar circumstances, and the President appointed another PRI member, Gonzalo Martínez Corbala, as interim governor.

Following a 13-day siege in late May of the federal prison at Matamoros, Tamaulipas, where a convicted drug dealer, Olivero Chávez Araújo, had continued to run his business from a suite of air-conditioned cells, the Attorney-General, Enrique Alvárez, was forced to resign. In a report published on 18 September, Amnesty International called on the world community to stop ignoring 'the flagrant human rights abuses committed by the Mexican government'.

Though a free trade agreement with Chile was successfully concluded on 22 September, the failure of President Bush to set a clear timetable for the conclusion of the free trade pact with the United States demonstrated that no more progress could be expected until after the US presidential elections. This delay constituted a major setback for President Salinas.

4. THE CARIBBEAN

JAMAICA—GUYANA—TRINIDAD & TOBAGO—BARBADOS—BELIZE—
GRENADA—THE BAHAMAS—WINDWARD AND LEEWARD ISLANDS—
SURINAME

i. JAMAICA

CAPITAL: Kingston   AREA: 11,000 sq km   POPULATION: 2,400,000 ('89)
OFFICIAL LANGUAGE: English   POLITICAL SYSTEM: parliamentary democracy
HEAD OF STATE: Queen Elizabeth II
GOVERNOR-GENERAL: Howard Cooke
RULING PARTY: People's National Party (PNP)
HEAD OF GOVERNMENT: Michael Manley, Prime Minister (since Feb '89)
PRINCIPAL MINISTERS: David Coore (foreign affairs), Hugh Small (finance & planning), K. D. Knight (national security & justice)
INTERNATIONAL ALIGNMENT: NAM, ACP, OAS, Caricom, Cwth.
CURRENCY: Jamaica dollar (end-'91 £1=J$34.94, US$1=J$18.72)
GNP PER CAPITA: US$1,260 ('89)
MAIN EXPORT EARNERS: bauxite/alumina, bananas, sugar, tourism

THE economic development of Jamaica continued to falter and worsen considerably over the year. By the beginning of the last quarter, the People's National Party (PNP) government of Michael Manley was obliged to introduce a 10 per cent general consumption tax; moreover, value-added tax was reintroduced on fuel, thus forcing up public transport costs by as much as 30 per cent. These measures gave further provocation for growing anti-PNP demonstrations. Over the year the general inflation rate rose to 20 per cent; although the economy grew by 3.8 per cent in 1991, the rate of growth was predicted to fall to 2 per cent in 1992. Wage claims by public sector unions, whose employees were particularly hit by inflation, ranged from 35 per cent for teachers, to 50 per cent for postal workers and as much as 70 per cent for some civil servants.

Despite the 22nd consecutive reconfirmation of Mr Manley as president of the PNP, the government was looking distinctly tired and unable to deal with the catalogue of demands placed on it by year's end. It therefore came as no great surprise that, in an attempt to revamp and revitalize his administration, Mr Manley announced a major cabinet reshuffle on 31 December. Commentators noted, however, that the opposition Jamaican Labour Party (JLP) confirmed that, were it in office, it would pursue more or less the same macro-economic policy as the government.

The crisis of confidence in the PNP government was sharply exacerbated by the effects of the removal of all foreign exchange controls, as part of market deregulation. Although the market had been partly loosened in September 1990, the finalization of this process entailed the rate for the Jamaican dollar against the US dollar depreciating from J$8 in January to J$19 by the end of the year.

The controversial return in March to the issue of execution warrants for the carrying out of the death penalty provoked an international outcry against the Jamaican government, in whose prisons 250 people were currently on death row.

ii. GUYANA

CAPITAL: Georgetown   AREA: 215,000 sq km   POPULATION: 796,000 ('89)
OFFICIAL LANGUAGE: English   POLITICAL SYSTEM: cooperative presidential democracy
HEAD OF STATE AND GOVERNMENT: President Desmond Hoyte (since Aug '85)
RULING PARTY: People's National Congress (PNC)
PRINCIPAL MINISTERS: Hamilton Green (1st vice-president & prime minister), Winston Murray (deputy premier, trade, tourism & industry), Keith Stanislaus Massiah (justice), Carl Greenidge (finance), Stella Odie-Ali (home affairs)
INTERNATIONAL ALIGNMENT: NAM, ACP, Caricom, Cwth., OAS
CURRENCY: Guyana dollar (end-'91 £1=G$227.18, US$1=G$121.68)
GNP PER CAPITA: US$340 ('89)
MAIN EXPORT EARNERS: bauxite, sugar, rice

THOUGH general elections were constitutionally due by 28 December (three months after the dissolution of the National Assembly) and were announced by President Desmond Hoyte for 16 December, they were further postponed due to the failure of the government to ensure a clean and fair election, especially since the electoral register was incomplete and replete with errors. Bitter protests by opposition politicians, and by international observers, forced President Hoyte, of the ruling People's National Congress (PNC), to agree to the appointment of Rudolph Collins as chairman of the electoral commission, charged with overseeing the preparation for and conduct of the election. This appointment was intended to compensate for the alleged subservience of the former chairman, Sir Harold Bollers, to the wishes of the PNC government. Faced with particular pressure from the US State Department and the UK Foreign and Commonwealth Office, the government could not risk conducting an inadequately prepared election.

In the event, the elections were postponed yet again. Following a declaration of emergency and the reconvening of the National Assembly, they were now timetabled to take place in mid-1992, upon the proper completion of the electoral list. As a result, the government was subjected to a barrage of criticism from domestic opposition parties, especially from the People's Progressive Party (PPP) under Cheddi Jagan, the Working People's Alliance (WPA) under Clive Thomas and the Guyanese Action for Reform and Democracy (GUARD), for failing to organize the electoral roll and for delaying the election.

On 6 July President Hoyte orchestrated both a cabinet reshuffle and a cut in the number of cabinet posts, from 18 to 11. British accountants KPMG Peat Marwick McLintock recommended the cuts to reduce the duplication of ministerial responsibilities.

Guyana's reintegration into the international economy was confirmed and furthered through a World Bank loan of US$250 million for 'free-market' restructuring. Efforts in this direction, such as reductions in company tax to 35 per cent and simplifications to the consumption taxes, were further recognized when on 30 September the US government confirmed the writing-off of Guyanese government debts of US$112 million. Such restructuring was designed under the government's Economic Recovery Programme (ERP), which was to receive some US$300 million from the Inter-American Development Bank over the next three years. Whichever party won the forthcoming elections, its room for manoeuvre was likely to be severely limited.

iii. TRINIDAD & TOBAGO

CAPITAL: Port of Spain   AREA: 5,128 sq km   POPULATION: 1,300,000 ('89)
OFFICIAL LANGUAGE: English   POLITICAL SYSTEM: parliamentary republic
HEAD OF STATE: President Noor Mohammed Hassanali (since March '87)
RULING PARTY: People's National Movement (PNM)
HEAD OF GOVERNMENT: Patrick Manning, Prime Minister (since Dec '91)
PRINCIPAL MINISTERS: Ralph Maraj (foreign affairs), Wendell Mottley (finance), Keith Sobion (attorney-general), Brian Quei Tung (trade, industry & tourism), Barry Barnes (energy)
INTERNATIONAL ALIGNMENT: NAM, ACP, OAS, Caricom, Cwth.
CURRENCY: Trinidad & Tobago dollar (end-'91 £1=TT$7.96, US$1=TT$4.26)
GNP PER CAPITA: US$3,230 ('89)
MAIN EXPORT EARNERS: oil, chemicals, tourism

CONTINUING decline in the economy and a more effective organization of the opposition, combined with internal dissent in the ruling National Alliance for Reconstruction (NAR), resulted in a huge defeat for the NAR and Prime Minister Robinson in general elections held on 16 December. The NAR retained only 2 of its 33 seats in the House of Representatives. Because the United National Congress, composed of former NAR dissidents led by Basdeo Panday, won 13 seats, the consolation of the NAR becoming the official opposition was also denied. The new government was formed by the victorious People's National Movement (PNM) led by Patrick Manning. The PNM had formed the government between 1956 and 1986, before being ousted by Mr Robinson's NAR.

An issue raised by all parties in the election campaign was the country's ethnic composition and the ethnic distribution of wealth. Whilst all parties claimed to act in the interests of all groups, the PNM tended to attract more support from the urban Afro-Trinidadian electorate, whereas the UNC gained particular support from Indo-Trinidadians.

However, such questions did not distract attention from the increasing economic problems afflicting the country, in a year when both oil production and oil revenues declined and sugar output was also lower. Since taxes from oil accounted for nearly half of total government revenue, declining revenues affected the government's ability to finance public sector programmes. The government was also faced with huge and mounting debts of two state-owned companies, namely the Caroni state sugar company (with debts of TT$3,000 million), and the BWIA regional airline (with debts of TT$4,000 million).

The creation of a new National Trade Union Centre (NATUC) in July, after protracted negotiations among union leaders, further served to unite a fragmented opposition to the then NAR government. Government security services warned of the continuing organization of Muslim fundamentalists of the Jamaat al-Muslimeen, which had been associated with the failed coup attempt of August 1990 (see AR 1990, p. 95). However, there were few overt signs of fundamentalist activity during the election campaign.

iv. BARBARDOS

CAPITAL: Bridgetown   AREA: 430 sq km   POPULATION: 256,000 ('89)
OFFICIAL LANGUAGE: English   POLITICAL SYSTEM: parliamentary democracy
HEAD OF STATE: Queen Elizabeth II
GOVERNOR-GENERAL: Dame Nita Barrow
RULING PARTY: Democratic Labour Party (DLP)
HEAD OF GOVERNMENT: Erskine Sandiford, Prime Minister (since June '87)
PRINCIPAL MINISTERS: Philip Greaves (deputy premier, communications & public works), Maurice King (foreign affairs, attorney-general), Keith Simmons (justice & public safety), Carl Clarke (trade & industry)
INTERNATIONAL ALIGNMENT: NAM, ACP, OAS, Cwth.
CURRENCY: Barbados dollar (end-'91 £1=BDS$3.77, US$1=BDS$2.02)
GNP PER CAPITA: US$6,350 ('89)
MAIN EXPORT EARNERS: sugar, tourism, light manufactures, chemicals

A general election on 22 January resulted in the return of the Democratic Labour Party (DLP) under Prime Minister Erskine Sandiford for a further five-year term. Winning some 49 per cent of the vote, the DLP secured 18 of the 28 seats in the House of Assembly, a loss of 2 seats on its previous holding. The only party to gain was the Barbados Labour Party (BLP), which took 10 seats, partly because of a collapse in support for the National Democratic Party of Richie Haynes, whose split from the DLP in 1989 had weakened the government. Despite the fall in the electorate's confidence in Mr Sandiford, his newly-constituted cabinet of 26 January showed only one new appointment and committed itself to a continuation of the policies of the previous government.

The continuation of austerity measures under the new DLP government stimulated increasing protest from opposition groups through the year, eventually attracting the criticism of DLP members themselves. Gross mismanagement charges had already been levelled at the government in January over plans to increase its central bank overdraft (from 10 per cent of current revenue to 17 per cent) and over the terms of a new loan. In view of the B$313 million budget deficit, however, there were few alternatives open to the government. The major sectors of the Barbados economy—tourism, agriculture and construction—had all suffered declines over the past year and were likely to continue to do so. In spite of this, neither devaluation nor resort to IMF help was at that stage considered necessary, although by mid-year the process of cutting back public expenditure by a planned 7 per cent was taking effect, especially in public works, education and health.

In November the effects of Mr Sandiford's austerity measures provoked an opposition no-confidence motion, although it was withdrawn at the last minute. Opinion polls indicated a clear preference for the BLP, and opposition was further expressed through a series of strikes. Discontent increased following Mr Sandiford's decision to turn, finally, to the IMF for US$58.1 million in loans. Nevertheless, by year's end, the Prime Minister had not acceded to the numerous opposition calls for his resignation.

v. BELIZE

CAPITAL: Belmopan   AREA: 23,000 sq km   POPULATION: 184,000 ('89)
OFFICIAL LANGUAGE: English   POLITICAL SYSTEM: parliamentary democracy
HEAD OF STATE: Queen Elizabeth II
GOVERNOR-GENERAL: Dame Minita Elvira Gordon
RULING PARTY: People's United Party (PUP)
HEAD OF GOVERNMENT: George Price, Prime Minister (since Sept '89)
PRINCIPAL MINISTERS: Florencio Marin (deputy premier, industry & natural resources), Said Musa (foreign affairs & development), Glenn Godfrey (attorney-general)
INTERNATIONAL ALIGNMENT: NAM, ACP, Caricom, Cwth., OAS
CURRENCY: Belize dollar (end-'91 £1=BZ$3.75, US$1=BZ$2.01)
GNP PER CAPITA: US$1,720 ('89)
MAIN EXPORT EARNERS: sugar, citrus products, fish, tourism

IN an announcement on 5 September, which surprised not only the government of Belize but also that of Guatemala, the Guatemalan President, Jorge Serrano Elías, gave a formal public recognition of Belize and agreed to the establishment of official diplomatic relations between the two countries (see also II.2.xii). Since Belize was granted independence in 1981, Guatemala had refused to recognize Belizean rights to self-determination because of its historical territorial claims on Belize. To cement the new relationship, Prime Minister George Price set out to provide access and formal transit zones across Belizean territory for Guatemalan trade, particularly in respect of port facilities at Big Creek. The government also proposed to confirm formally the maritime consequences of the agreement through a Maritime Areas Bill which would limit Belizean territorial waters to three miles but extend the exclusive economic zone (EEZ) in the Bay of Amatique to meet the Honduran EEZ.

vi. GRENADA

CAPITAL: St. George's   AREA: 344 sq km   POPULATION: 94,000,000 ('89)
OFFICIAL LANGUAGE: English   POLITICAL SYSTEM: parliamentary democracy
HEAD OF STATE: Queen Elizabeth II
GOVERNOR-GENERAL: Sir Paul Scoon
RULING PARTY: National Democratic Congress (NDC)
HEAD OF GOVERNMENT: Nicholas Braithwaite, Prime Minister (since March '90)
PRINCIPAL MINISTERS: George Brizan (finance, trade & industry), Francis Alexis (attorney-general)
INTERNATIONAL ALIGNMENT: NAM, ACP, OAS, Caricom, Cwth.
CURRENCY: East Caribbean dollar (end-'91 £1=EC$5.05, US$1=EC$2.71)
GNP PER CAPITA: US$1,900 ('89)
MAIN EXPORT EARNERS: agricultural products, tourism

THE tortuous saga of the 14 people charged with conspiring to murder Maurice Bishop in 1983 (see AR 1990, p. 98) came to a temporary halt when Prime Minister Nicholas Braithwaite commuted the death penalty, originally and controversially imposed in 1986, to life imprisonment on 14 August. Despite repeated calls for a retrial, for further appeal proceedings, including to the UK Privy Council (under the terms of the Eastern Caribbean Supreme Court), the final stay of execution and commuting of the sentences came not through due process of law but from the arbitrary political decision of the Prime Minister.

In attempts to cut public expenditure, a five-year plan announced in October proposed the overhaul of the tax system, the removal of subsidies to publicly-owned business and a reduction in the number of civil servants by over 15 per cent. The principal proposed change in the tax system was to return to a pay-as-you-earn system and away from the inequalities and inefficiencies of value-added tax. Despite such changes, the economic year proved positive for Grenada. Tourism was up by 15 per cent, construction by 12 per cent and transport and communications up by 10 per cent, so that 5 per cent overall growth in GDP was predicted.

The opposition to the ruling National Democratic Congress virtually collapsed with the defection of a third MP of the Grenada United Labour Party (GULP) out of four elected in 1990. The official opposition thereafter consisted of the sole GULP member, Winifred Strachan.

vii. THE BAHAMAS

CAPITAL: Nassau AREA: 14,000 sq km POPULATION: 249,000 ('89)
OFFICIAL LANGUAGE: English POLITICAL SYSTEM: parliamentary democracy
HEAD OF STATE: Queen Elizabeth II
GOVERNOR-GENERAL: Sir Henry Taylor
RULING PARTY: Progressive Liberal Party (PLP)
HEAD OF GOVERNMENT: Sir Lynden O. Pindling, Prime Minister (since Jan '67)
PRINCIPAL MINISTERS: Sir Clement T. Maynard (deputy premier, foreign affairs), Paul L. Adderley (finance), Darrell Rolle (national security), Sean McWeeney (attorney-general)
INTERNATIONAL ALIGNMENT: NAM, ACP, OAS, Cwth.
CURRENCY: Bahamas dollar (end-'91 £1=B$1.87, US$1=B$1.00)
GNP PER CAPITA: US$11,320 ('89)
MAIN EXPORT EARNERS: tourism, petroleum products

IN a supplementary budget on 8 October, prompted by a drop in tourist earnings of at least US$100 million over 1990, the government of Sir Lynden Pindling's Progressive Liberal Party (PLP) was obliged to increase taxes and institute further borrowing to finance the budget deficit. Furthermore, large staff cuts were later proposed in the loss-making airline Bahamasair, from 1,000 to 650. As part of a general and concerted attempt to market the islands' tourist attractions, a National Tourism Board was established in May. The fall in tourism resulted in several demonstrations organized by the Trade Union Congress and the Hotel and Catering and Allied Workers' Union denouncing the increasing number of redundancies in the industry. A survey found that 25 of the Bahamas' 49 MPs were millionaires.

viii. WINDWARD AND LEEWARD ISLANDS

St Kitts & Nevis
CAPITAL: Basseterre AREA: 260 sq km POPULATION: 41,000 ('89)
OFFICIAL LANGUAGE: English POLITICAL SYSTEM: parliamentary democracy
HEAD OF STATE: Queen Elizabeth II
GOVERNOR-GENERAL: Clement Athelston Arrindell
RULING PARTY: People's Action Movement (PAM)
HEAD OF GOVERNMENT: Kennedy A. Simmonds, Prime Minister (since Feb '80)
CURRENCY: East Caribbean dollar (end-'91 £1=EC$5.06, US$1=EC$2.71)
GNP PER CAPITA: US$2,630 ('89)
MAIN EXPORT EARNERS: sugar, agricultural produce, tourism

Antigua & Barbuda
CAPITAL: St. John's AREA: 440 sq km POPULATION: 78,000 ('89)
OFFICIAL LANGUAGE: English POLITICAL SYSTEM: parliamentary democracy
HEAD OF STATE: Queen Elizabeth II
GOVERNOR-GENERAL: Sir Wilfred Ebenezer Jacobs
RULING PARTY: Antigua Labour Party (ALP)
HEAD OF GOVERNMENT: C. Vere Bird Sr, Prime Minister (since Feb '76)
CURRENCY: East Caribbean dollar (end-'91 £1=EC$5.06, US$1=EC$2.71)
GNP PER CAPITA: US$3,690 ('88)
MAIN EXPORT EARNERS: tourism, miscellaneous manufactures

Dominica
CAPITAL: Roseau   AREA: 750 sq km   POPULATION: 82,000 ('89)
OFFICIAL LANGUAGE: English   POLITICAL SYSTEM: parliamentary republic
HEAD OF STATE: President Sir Clarence Augustus Seignoret
RULING PARTY: Dominica Freedom Party (DFP)
HEAD OF GOVERNMENT: Mary Eugenia Charles, Prime Minister (since July '80)
CURRENCY: East Caribbean dollar (end-'91 £1=EC$5.06, US$1=EC$2.71)
GNP PER CAPITA: US$1,680 ('88)
MAIN EXPORT EARNERS: bananas, tourism

St Lucia
CAPITAL: Castries   AREA: 616 sq km   POPULATION: 148,000 ('89)
OFFICIAL LANGUAGE: English   POLITICAL SYSTEM: parliamentary democracy
HEAD OF STATE: Queen Elizabeth II
GOVERNOR-GENERAL: Stanislaus A. James (acting)
RULING PARTY: United Workers' Party (UWP)
HEAD OF GOVERNMENT: John Compton, Prime Minister (since '64)
CURRENCY: East Caribbean dollar (end-'91 £1=EC$5.06, US$1=EC$2.71)
GNP PER CAPITA: US$1,810 ('89)
MAIN EXPORT EARNERS: agricultural products, tourism

St Vincent & the Grenadines
CAPITAL: Kingstown   AREA: 390 sq km   POPULATION: 113,000 ('89)
OFFICIAL LANGUAGE: English   POLITICAL SYSTEM: parliamentary democracy
HEAD OF STATE: Queen Elizabeth II
GOVERNOR-GENERAL: David Jack
RULING PARTY: New Democratic Party (NDP)
HEAD OF GOVERNMENT: James F. Mitchell, Prime Minister (since '72)
CURRENCY: East Caribbean dollar (end-'91 £1=EC$5.06, US$1=EC$2.71)
GNP PER CAPITA: US$1,200 ('88)
MAIN EXPORT EARNERS: bananas, tourism, agricultural produce

Montserrat
CAPITAL: Plymouth   AREA: 102 sq km   POPULATION: 11,900 ('87)
OFFICIAL LANGUAGE: English
POLITICAL SYSTEM: representative democracy under UK rule
GOVERNOR-GENERAL: David G. P. Taylor
RULING PARTY: National Progressive Party (NPP)
HEAD OF GOVERNMENT: Reuben Meade, Chief Minister (since Oct '91)
CURRENCY: East Caribbean dollar (end-'91 £1=EC$5.06, US$1=EC$2.71)
MAIN EXPORT EARNERS: banking, tourism

THE process of regional integration took some small steps forward as a consequence of the meeting of the Windward Islands Regional Constituency Assembly on 7–8 September in Dominica. Although no definite commitments were entered into by the participants (St Lucia, St Vincent & the Grenadines, Grenada and Dominica), broadly federalist proposals for political unity were considered. This more local level of integration was felt to be more feasible and beneficial to these small island states as compared with the looser and more US-leaning Organization of Eastern Caribbean States. The next stage would be a referendum in member states to approve the integration process, followed by parliamentary discussions of the constitutional form and then final popular approval.

The running of the state-owned Sugar Manufacturing Corporation of ST KITTS & NEVIS was contracted out to Booker Tate for two years.

The corporation was expected to lose a further EC$4 million in 1991, despite the gradual recovery of sugar production following the damage caused by Hurricane 'Hugo' in September 1988.

In ANTIGUA & BARBUDA internal strife continued in the ruling Antigua Labour Party (ALP) under the leadership of Vere Bird Sr, centring on an arms-dealing scandal (see AR 1990, p. 101). It prompted a bizarre cabinet reshuffle on 15 March, after five senior ministers had called for Vere Bird to resign and three ministers, including the deputy prime minister, had refused to accept the distribution of new ministerial posts. Whilst the immediate crisis was resolved through the resignation of the disaffected ministers, they rejoined the cabinet on 3 September. After British Airways had annulled its commitment to three weekly Antigua–London flights in July, the new operation of the route was under negotiation.

The Prime Minister of DOMINICA, Eugenia Charles, ran into stiff opposition over her attempts to limit wage negotiation processes and union membership of civil servants. By September the proposed legislation before parliament had to be dropped. Earlier, the budget announced on 24 June proposed a much reduced capital expenditure programme, whilst maintaining existing levels of recurrent expenditure. Since the bulk of the latter was the public salaries bill, further public sector opposition to government plans was defused.

The government of ST LUCIA announced a population control programme in February designed to lower the island's birth rate, which at current rates would lead to a doubling of the population (to 291,000) by 2015. The primacy of the tourist economy over the banana economy was confirmed by the fact that EC$418 million was earned from tourism as against EC$188 million from bananas. According to initial figures, tourist numbers were substantially up over 1990.

Minor cabinet changes were announced in April in ST VINCENT & THE GRENADINES by Prime Minister James Mitchell. The only potential disturbance to the dominance of the ruling New Democratic Party (NDP) was a by-election in October. However, the NDP maintained its monopoly of all 15 seats in the House of Assembly. Shipping registers were boosted when over 100 former Yugoslav ships transferred registration to St Vincent, which could accordingly boast the largest register in the Caribbean.

In a dramatic turn of political fortunes on the UK dependency of MONSERRAT, general elections held on 8 October brought to power the National Progressive Party (NPP), formed just one month before the election under the leadership of Reuben Meade. The NPP won 4 of the 7 Legislative Council seats and in so doing ensured the defeat of Chief Minister John Osborne and his People's Liberation Movement (PLM). The PLM retained only one seat, alongside one each for the National Development Party and an independent.

ix. SURINAME

CAPITAL: Paramaribo   AREA: 163,000 sq km   POPULATION: 437,000 ('89)
OFFICIAL LANGUAGE: Dutch   POLITICAL SYSTEM: republic, under military tutelage
HEAD OF STATE: President Ronald Venetiaan (since Sept '91)
MILITARY LEADER: Lt.-Col. Désiré (Desi) Bouterse
RULING PARTIES: New Front for Democracy and Development, consisting of the Suriname National (NPS), Progressive Reform (VHP) and Unity and Harmony (KTPI) parties, plus the Suriname Labour Party (SPA)
PRINCIPAL MINISTERS: Jules Ajodhia (vice-president, head of government), Subhaas Mungra (VHP/foreign affairs), Siegfried Gilds (SPA/defence), Eddy Sedoc (NPS/finance), Soecil Girvasing (justice & police)
INTERNATIONAL ALIGNMENT: NAM, ACP, OAS
CURRENCY: Suriname guilder (end-'91 £1=SF3.34, US$1=SF1.79)
GNP PER CAPITA: US$3,010 ('89)
MAIN EXPORT EARNERS: bauxite/alumina, aluminium, rice

THE military coup of 24 December 1990 (see AR 1990, p. 102), inspired by the former chief of staff, Lt.-Colonel Desi Bouterse, was followed by promises to hold new elections prepared by an interim government under the premiership of Jules Wijdenbosch of the pro-military National Democratic Party (NDP).

The reassertion of army dominance was apparent in a peace agreement of 26 March with the leader of the rebel Surinamese Liberation Army (or Jungle Commando), which was signed by Lt.-Colonel Bouterse and not by a government minister. Nevertheless, Mr Wijdenbosch's interim government was able to guarantee and oversee a general election on 25 May. The election was monitored by several international organizations, and was judged to be free and fair. It resulted in the overwhelming victory of a newly-formed alliance, the New Front for Democracy and Development, which took 30 of the 51 seats in the National Assembly. A smaller coalition called Democratic Alternative '91, which won 9 seats, shared with the New Front a wish to bar the army from involvement in party politics. However, since Mr Wijdenbosch's NDP won 12 seats, the anti-army coalitions failed to reach the two-thirds Assembly majority required for constitutional changes and selection of the President. Their restraining powers over Lt.-Colonel Bouterse and the army were thus limited.

The consequence of the effective NDP veto was to prolong inter-party negotiations, over both the appointment of a President and the formation of a government, until September. Finally, on 7 September, 645 of the 817 votes cast in the United People's Assembly (convened by the National Assembly) went to the New Front presidential candidate, Ronald Venetiaan, who was able to swear in a new cabinet on 17 September.

On the strength of the apparent success of the democratic restoration President Venetiaan then sought to normalize relations with the Netherlands, the former colonial power and the single largest source of bilateral aid to Suriname. The new President's declaration on 17

October that the New Front government was intent on cutting the defence budget by half and the size of the army by two-thirds was seen as likely to stimulate the transfer of aid from the Netherlands, whilst at the same time testing the strength of the army's commitment to democracy.

# III WESTERN, CENTRAL AND SOUTHERN EUROPE

1. FRANCE—GERMANY—ITALY—BELGIUM—THE NETHERLANDS—
LUXEMBOURG—IRELAND

i. FRANCE

CAPITAL: Paris   AREA: 544,000 sq km   POPULATION: 56,200,000 ('89)
OFFICIAL LANGUAGE: French
POLITICAL SYSTEM: presidential parliamentary democracy
HEAD OF STATE AND GOVERNMENT: President François Mitterrand (since May '81)
RULING PARTIES: Socialist Party (PS) holds presidency; government is centre-left coalition of the PS, Left Radicals (MRG), elements of the Union for French Democracy (UDF) and independents
PRINCIPAL MINISTERS: Edith Cresson (PS/prime minister), Roland Dumas (PS/foreign affairs), Pierre Bérégovoy (PS/economy, trade, finance, industry, posts & telecommunications), Pierre Joxe (PS/defence), Philippe Marchand (PS/interior), Henri Nallet (PS/justice)
INTERNATIONAL ALIGNMENT: NATO (outside command structure), OECD, EC, Francophonie
CURRENCY: franc (end-'91 £1=F9.69, US$1=F5.19)
GNP PER CAPITA: US$17,820 ('89)
MAIN EXPORT EARNERS: machinery and transport equipment, manufactures, chemicals, food and beverages, tourism

FEW years have better illustrated the vagaries of political fortunes. The early weeks were dominated by the Gulf crisis, about which France had special ground for apprehension. Apart from its special relationship with Muslim North Africa, there were fears about the reaction of the country's 3 million Muslims, while a poll in January reported 53 per cent opposition to military intervention. In the event, there was almost no inter-communal friction—then—and opinion swung solidly behind President Mitterrand's leadership. After the allies' lightning victory (see V.2), he reported 'with pride' that France had 'assumed her due rank and role'. A poll registered 83 per cent approval of his actions. The mainstream opposition parties were reduced to peripheral supporting roles; Communist, Ecologist and National Front critics were disavowed by their voters. Indeed, the President had more troubles with his friends than with his enemies. The Defence Minister, Jean-Pierre Chevènement, resigned over the bombing of Iraq and was succeeded by the Minister of the Interior, Pierre Joxe, whose place was taken by Philippe Marchand. Unhappiness on pacifist or anti-American grounds in the Socialist Party (PS) exacerbated its fratricidal divisions. That apart, it was a golden moment for the President.

That moment was short-lived. Domestic problems rapidly returned to the fore: rising unemployment, unhappiness over expenditure cuts of the equivalent of £1,600 million imposed because tax receipts were flagging due to the recession, and renewed unrest in suburbs with a high concentration of immigrants (see AR 1990, p. 142). The refuelling of the previous year's political scandals (see AR 1990, p. 141), while harmful to the entire political class, proved particularly embarrassing for the Socialists. Their opponents regrouped on domestic issues. Michel Rocard met fierce opposition to his legislative programme, which included a reform of public hospitals, measures to transfer funds from rich local authorities to poor ones and provide more social housing, especially for ghetto-dwellers, and an attempt to resolve the Corsican problem by allocating greater powers to the 'impossible' island's elected assembly and a new executive council. Dismissed as inadequate by the Corsican nationalists, the measures were denounced by the right as 'concessions to murderers'. A bill to revise the system of election to regional councils had to be shelved.

In May President Mitterrand dismissed M. Rocard, ostensibly to provide fresh leadership for the challenges of the single European market and legislative elections in 1993. The new Prime Minister, Edith Cresson, who made few ministerial changes at senior level, had previously served as minister for Europe and for trade and industry. She had resigned in frustration some months earlier. She was the first woman to hold the premiership. It was a bold move—and, at least in the short run, a disastrous one. Mme Cresson's popularity fell faster than that of any prime minister for many years; by August it was the lowest of any Fifth Republic prime minister. Misogyny played a part, but her penchant for plain speaking won no friends; she was impulsive and her relations with colleagues were often strained; and she won little praise for grasping a number of nettles left by the Rocard government. Her government brought forward proposals to tackle unemployment, help small business, decentralize government agencies and reorganize higher education. It also took a more interventionist line on industrial organization as a means of confronting the Japanese challenge. A state-sponsored merger of the industrial activities of the Atomic Energy Commissariat and Thomson's civil electronics division, announced in December, was the biggest operation of its kind for many years.

This activity did nothing to dispel the prevailing political malaise. As in 1990, this found expression in boredom and distaste for politics and politicians and in a readiness among a number of groups to take direct action, including hospital staff, magistrates' clerks, policemen and farmers. A series of particularly boorish protests by farmers, angered by falling prices and imports, stirred President Mitterrand to warn that their behaviour was 'endangering the Republic'. But although he summoned the government to stand firm, within days concessions were made to most of the discontented groups.

A major factor in the public's 'moroseness' was the behaviour of the politicians—a slump in parliamentary by-election turnout to a record low of 38 per cent being one of many signs. All the main parties were in disarray, not least the PS, riven by manoeuvring among contenders to succeed M. Mitterrand and fearful of electoral disasters to come. The orthodox right also suffered from personal jockeying for position and its inability to decide how best to meet the populist, xenophobic appeal of Jean-Marie Le Pen's National Front (FN.) The Communist Party leadership beat back all attempts to reform it and continued its march towards marginality. The only parties with the wind in their sails were the Ecologists and the FN, both critics of 'orthodox' politics. The latter's hostility to immigrants struck a responsive note among a third of the electorate. This was not lost on the other parties; after further violent incidents in suburbs with high concentrations of immigrants during the summer, former President Valéry Giscard d'Estaing spoke of an 'invasion' and former prime minister Jacques Chirac of an 'overdose' of foreigners: the 'threshold of tolerance' had been crossed, in their view. Mme Cresson denounced 'demagogy' on immigration but introduced tighter controls on illegal immigration and appeared to endorse accelerating expulsions by chartered aircraft, so earning an approving nod from the FN. However, the government did introduce a series of measures designed to ease the plight of one of the most disfavoured groups—the children of Algerians forced into exile in France for having fought with the French during the Algerian war of independence.

The President himself suffered from the public mood. He had served longer than any of his Fifth Republic predecessors and, at 75, was widely held to have lost his touch and run out of ideas. By the end of the year his standing in the polls had sunk to the lowest level ever. He announced a package of constitutional reforms for 1992. It would take more than this to restore his political fortunes in time for the election challenges of 1992 and 1993—but neither could so experienced and wily a politician safely be buried prematurely.

Economic policy changed little with the new government. Pierre Bérégovoy now headed a 'super-ministry' with responsibility for the economy, trade and finance, industry, posts and telecommunications. Mme Cresson stressed the need for a strong franc, control of inflation and strict restraint in public expenditure. Health insurance contributions were raised to eliminate the social security deficit and, in June, there were increases in some indirect taxes and further expenditure cuts. M. Bérégovoy introduced a 'reasonable and serious' budget in September. While he hailed the fact that France was 'cited as an example abroad', this continuation of austere rectitude deepened his party's gloom. Income would rise 2.6 per cent to some £125,000 million and expenditure by 3.1 per cent to £132,000 million in 1992. With profits taxes cut from 42 per cent to 33.3 per cent and new tax breaks for business, the budget was tailored to help small and medium firms. The greatest increase in expenditure was on debt servicing; beyond that the priorities were justice, higher education, research and the environment. The most encouraging feature of economic performance during the year was that, at 3.1 per cent, inflation was well below German levels—a cardinal policy aim since the early 1980s. However, the economy was slow to pull out of recession. GDP rose only 1.3 per cent in 1991, retail sales were up only 0.8 per cent and industrial investment was stagnant. Unemployment rose steadily to reach 2,860,000 (9.8 per cent) in December. However, the deficit on external trade fell from the equivalent of £5,000 million in 1990 to about £3,000 million. President Mitterrand claimed, with some justification, that 'in the general disorder France has come off better than the rest'. But convincing his countrymen of this was a very different matter.

FOREIGN AFFAIRS AND DEFENCE. In the weeks preceding the allied offensive in the Gulf, French diplomatic activity was intense, with swarms of emissaries vainly attempting directly and through intermediaries to sway the Iraqi leader, Saddam Husain, to the point of stirring a measure of suspicion and derision among France's partners. But while underlining a characteristic French determination not to appear to be tagging along behind the Americans, they did not spare France from the wounded reproaches of her Arab neighbours in North Africa. Considerable effort had to be put into mending fences—which in the case of Tunisia, at least, appeared to have been successful when President Mitterrand visited Tunis in July. He used the occasion to launch a proposed 'Mediterranean summit' for 1992. A meeting between him and President Bush in Martinique in March marked the highest point in Franco-American relations in many years. Hopes of improving relations with Iran had less success. A visit to Tehran by the Foreign Minister, Roland Dumas, in May cleared the way for a resolution of the two countries' differences. However, the assassination in August, allegedly by Iranian agents, of the Shah's last prime minister, Shapour Bakhtiar (see XX: OBITUARY), who had been living in exile near Paris, delayed a full reconciliation, though in December after two years of negotiations agreement was reached on financial issues outstanding since 1979. The total cost to France was reckoned at over £1,000 million.

One notable outcome of the Gulf War was a revived French involvement in the United Nations, long scorned in the Gaullist tradition. In March France took the initiative in promoting a Security Council resolution condemning Iraqi repression of the Kurds, and was also active in the cause of humanitarian aid to Kurdish refugees. In June France put forward proposals for global disarmament and announced that it would sign the 1968 Non-Proliferation Treaty, which it had previously 'shadowed' but declined to sign as an infringement of sovereignty. A visit to New Zealand in April by M. Rocard finally turned the page on the ignominious affair of the *Rainbow Warrior* (see also X.2.i). The year was also notable for France's unwillingness to send troops to Togo, to assist its government against an attempted takeover by the military, and President Mitterrand's encouragement of multi-party democracy at the francophone summit.

Once the Gulf War was over, the chief preoccupation in external policy was Europe. President Mitterrand seemed determined to demonstrate that France had a leading role to play in Eastern Europe despite being overshadowed by the economic strength of Germany. However, he had some difficulty in attuning himself to the 'new Europe'. His apparent acceptance of the August coup in the Soviet Union was widely criticized as weak and fumbling. His proposals for a 'confederation' as an alternative to full Community membership for the former Eastern bloc met a chilly reception, notably from President Havel of Czechoslovakia when he visited Paris in March, especially since M. Mitterrand refused to support speedy Czechoslovak membership of the Community. Later, France tried to block association agreements between the Community and Poland, Hungary and Czechoslovakia because of fears of the impact on its restive farmers, but was then obliged to back down. Subsequently, France agreed to support Czechoslovakia's bid for closer relations with the Community's institutions. Similar agreements were reached with Hungary and Poland. Nevertheless, the deepening of the existing Community remained a first priority; as in the past, it was feared that enlargement might turn the Community into a mere free trade area. Closer union was also seen as a way of binding Germany more surely into the Community. Thus, despite some Gaullist criticism of the loss of national independence implicit in the agreements at the Maastricht EC summit in December (see XI.3 and XIX.3), President Mitterrand was well pleased that Germany was now committed to a single currency and that agreement had been reached on a common foreign and security policy.

For the military the year brought triumph and gloom. The triumph was in the Gulf where, despite British and American criticism of its prickly independence and equipment, once the land war began the French Daguet force was strikingly successful, gaining its objectives ahead of schedule with the loss of only two men in combat (see also V.2). However, given that military planning had not envisaged fighting a fullscale conventional campaign, and the government's decision that conscripts and reservists should not be sent to the Gulf, the war strained France's military capabilities to the limit. And now the government announced that compulsory military service would be cut from 12 months to ten and that, over six years, the army would be reduced by 50,000–70,000 men to 230,000, half of them professionals. The forces in Germany would fall from 50,000 to 30,000 by the end of 1992.

Some units would effectively be 'mothballed' for two months each year. The ensuing reorganization of the army would be comparable in scale to what followed the Algerian war in the 1960s. The proposed S45 mobile nuclear missile programme, once intended to replace a 20-year-old system based on fixed silos, was abandoned—though the new M5 submarine-launched missiles might be adapted to replace existing land-based S3 missiles. The number of Hadès 'pre-strategic' nuclear missiles would also be cut; their role, President Mitterrand made clear, was chiefly as a bargaining counter in nuclear disarmament talks. The first of the new generation of nuclear missile submarines and the nuclear-propelled aircraft carrier *Charles de Gaulle* would enter service late, mainly for budgetary reasons.

OVERSEAS DEPARTMENTS AND TERRITORIES. Réunion experienced its gravest unrest for many years when, in February and March, riots caused eight deaths, many injuries and extensive damage. The spark igniting these events was the closure of a pirate television station that had been on the air for five years, but it was generally recognized that the underlying causes lay in the island's longstanding economic and social problems. The government was already committed to ending inequalities between the overseas departments and metropolitan France, and had just proposed equalization of family allowances and the minimum wage, to be achieved by 1995. However, in April, Louis Le Pensec, Minister for Overseas Departments and Territories, acknowledged that the situation in Réunion called for 'exceptional measures', and the government agreed a 'solidarity pact' of 60 measures which concentrated on improvements in education, training, employment and facilities for young people.

French Polynesia's longrunning political struggles took further twists. In the March elections Gaston Flosse's Tahoeraa Huiraatira party won 18 of the 41 seats and he recovered the presidency of the territorial government after a deal with Émile Vernaudon, who became president of the territory's assembly. However, the introduction of new taxes brought a wave of demonstrations and road blockages which were supported by advocates of independence, followed by clashes between strikers and police at Papeete. M. Flosse denounced the strikes as a politically-motivated attempt to destabilize him, but the new taxes were dropped. In September his alliance with M. Vernaudon broke down and M. Flosse formed a new government with the support of the Here Aia (Love of Country) movement.

ii. GERMANY

CAPITAL: Berlin   AREA: 357,000 sq km   POPULATION: 79,000,000 ('89)
OFFICIAL LANGUAGE: German   POLITICAL SYSTEM: federal parliamentary democracy
HEAD OF STATE: President Richard von Weizsäcker (since July '84)
RULING PARTIES: Christian Democratic Union (CDU), Christian Social Union (CSU) and Free Democratic Party (FDP)
HEAD OF GOVERNMENT: Helmut Kohl (CDU), Federal Chancellor (since Oct '82)
PRINCIPAL MINISTERS: Friedrich Böhl (CDU/head of chancery), Hans-Dietrich Genscher (FDP/foreign affairs), Rudolf Seiters (CDU/interior), Klaus Kinkel (ind./justice), Theo Waigel (CSU/finance), Jürgen Möllemann (FDP/economy), Gerhard Stoltenberg (CDU/defence)
INTERNATIONAL ALIGNMENT: NATO, OECD, EC
CURRENCY: Deutschmark (end-'91 £1=DM2.84, US$1=DM1.52)
GNP PER CAPITA: US$20,440 ('89, West German figure)
MAIN EXPORT EARNERS: machinery and transport equipment, manufactures, chemicals

AFTER its resounding victory in the first all-German elections in December 1990 (see AR 1990, pp. 153–4), the governing coalition of Christian Democrats (CDU/CSU) and Free Democrats (FDP) led by Chancellor Helmut Kohl had dealt with the many problems resulting from unification. The new Germany also had to adjust to the major role it was expected to play in European affairs.

Once the euphoria of German unification had receded, the government lost popularity. In two *Land* elections (Hesse in January and the Rhineland–Palatinate in April) the CDU was ousted from office by the Social Democrats (SPD), while in Hamburg (June) the SPD was returned with an overall majority. This decline in fortunes was in large part due to disenchantment over the rising cost of unification. In February Herr Kohl conceded that he had been over-optimistic in the 1990 election campaign in promising that no-one would be worse off as a result of bringing the two parts of Germany together. From 1 July increases in a range of taxes came into effect.

East Germans certainly regarded themselves as much worse off: on 18 March (the anniversary of the first free election in the former German Democratic Republic—see AR 1990, pp. 147–8) thousands took to the streets in protest at the economic catastrophe and the apparent inability of the federal government to deal with the deteriorating situation. The major cause for concern was the rise in unemployment. The nominal rate was put at 11 per cent, but the real level was far higher, with some estimates at 30 per cent. The true extent of the economic malaise was obscured by such measures as enforced early retirement, retraining schemes, and extensive short-time working. In addition, the flow of people from East to West Germany continued at around 7,000 a month, and there were also about 500,000 daily commuters.

Much of the criticism for the run-down of the eastern economy was directed at the public trustee office (Treuhandanstalt), which had the responsibility for privatizing some 10,000 state-owned enterprises. For many businesses it proved difficult to attract buyers, since they were uneconomic to run, with out-dated equipment and often grossly overmanned. There were also problems relating to rights (former owners could claim back property which had been taken over during the time of the communist regime). Investors would also have to meet the costly environmental standards of West Germany. The head of the Treuhandanstalt, Detlev Rohwedder, came to symbolize the harshness of the policies. He was assassinated in April by a left-wing terrorist organization, the Red Army Faction (RAF). Subsequently, his successor, Birgit Breuel, was given greater scope to save firms from closure if they could be brought up to standard.

Although the most serious effects of the rapid switch to a market system were softened by huge federal subsidies, the social dislocation of eastern Germany's society was apparent. The all-powerful state security police (the 'Stasi') and its vast army of informers had been disbanded, but a legacy of mistrust remained. The dossiers kept on individual citizens (120 miles of files!) were to be opened from January 1992 and would reveal the extent of surveillance and informing, often involving friends and neighbours.

Efforts were made to bring wrong-doers to justice. In September charges were laid against soldiers who had shot people attempting to escape from East to West Germany. Prominent politicians in the former communist regime were also arrested, including Markus Wolf, the spy-chief, who gave himself up in September. But the former leader of the GDR, Erich Honecker, was removed to the Soviet Union in March by the Soviet military. The German government sought his extradition, but an impasse was reached at the end of the year when Herr Honecker took refuge in the Chilean embassy in Moscow.

It had already been decided the previous year that Berlin would be the official capital city of Germany, but it was not until June that a Bundestag vote was taken on whether the seat of the government and parliament would move from Bonn to Berlin. The issue split the parties, and on a free vote Berlin won narrowly by 338 votes to 320. In December it was announced that for an interim period ten ministries would move to Berlin and eight stay in Bonn. However, the Bundesrat, the upper house representing the *Länder* governments, voted in July to remain in Bonn. In Berlin, Eberhard Diepgen (CDU) was elected (January) to be the governing mayor, and the CDU formed a grand coalition with the SPD.

One of the most contentious and worrying political issues was the extent of migration into Germany, especially the rise in the number of those seeking political asylum. In 1990 the number had reached 190,000, and it rose again in 1991 to 250,000. Proposals by the CDU/CSU to amend the constitution (currently giving an unqualified right to claim political asylum) to make it easier to refuse entry to 'economic migrants' were rejected by the SPD and FDP. Eventually, in October, a compromise was reached on a procedure to speed up decisions, so that claims would be settled within six weeks. Hitherto, some cases, going through the courts on appeal, had taken years to reach a final decision. That the issue had strong political implications was shown by the *Land* election in Bremen (September) where the vote for the SPD (seen to be unwilling to take a tough line) fell very sharply, whilst an extreme right-wing party, the German People's Union (DVU), made significant gains. Anti-foreigner outbreaks increased in the second half of the year, particularly in eastern Germany; attacks on hostels where asylum-seekers were lodged became commonplace. However, there were fewer ethnic Germans from Eastern Europe and the Soviet Union resettling in Germany (around 340,000 as against 400,000 in 1990).

Several changes took place in the leading ranks of the major parties. For the CDU, Wolfgang Schäuble (who had survived an assassination attempt in 1990 which left him permanently paralysed) switched from the Interior Ministry in November to become leader of the parliamentary party, replacing Alfred Dregger, who retired. Herr Schäuble, despite his disability, was thought to be a possible successor to Herr Kohl, as was Volker Rühe, the secretary-general of the CDU. At one time, Lothar Späth, until January the minister-president of Baden-Württemberg, had been regarded as a contender, but he was forced to resign because of allegations of impropriety in his dealings with certain business concerns. The CDU also faced problems with the party's personnel in the former GDR, since the CDU there had inherited many who in one way or another had been associated with the communist system. The same applied to the FDP: the deputy minister-president of Saxony-Anhalt, Gerd Brunner, was forced to resign in August because of his involvement with the Stasi.

For the SPD, the most important change was the resignation of Hans-Jochen Vogel as leader of the parliamentary party; he was succeeded by Hans-Ulrich Klose, formerly party treasurer. Previously, Herr Vogel had also been chairman of the national SPD, but after the 1990 election he resigned, to be succeeded by Björn Engholm, minister-president of Schleswig-Holstein, the party's likely choice to be the new chancellor-candidate.

The Greens, after their serious setback in 1990, when the West German Greens failed to retain any seats in the Bundestag, made a recovery in *Land* elections, especially in Hesse and Bremen. In both states the party joined an SPD-led coalition, an indication that the Greens were becoming acceptable as partners in government. At the same time, many in the radical, fundamentalist wing of the party, including its most prominent figure, Jutta Ditfurth, left in protest at the more moderate course that was being taken. The remnant of the once-significant popular movements in eastern Germany (known as 'Bündnis '90') announced in September that it would become a federal-wide party. The Greens argued, however, that the two parties should merge, since they both appealed to the same kind of electorate.

That green/environmental measures had become leading concerns for all parties was shown by the government's decision in March to shut down the Kalkar fast-breeder reactor, entailing the write-off of a huge capital investment programme. In September the Environment Minister, Klaus Töpfer, stated that the nuclear reactor at Greifswald (eastern Germany) would be decommissioned. Herr Töpfer was also prominent in announcing measures to combat the wasteful habits of a throw-away society.

The year saw the Federal Republic much concerned with foreign affairs, and in consequence also a target for criticism. Most problematic was the position taken by Germany in the course of the Gulf conflict, since for political and constitutional reasons the government was unwilling to intervene actively on the side of the allies, and this provoked hostile comment in both the USA and Britain. In January the government dispatched airforce units to Turkey (a NATO member) but they were only to be employed if Turkey was attacked; even this modest assistance met with opposition in Germany. Germany, however, did agree in January to make a substantial contribution in support of the USA of DM 14,000 million. In January, too, Herr Kohl declared that in future the united Germany would have to assume a greater measure of international responsibility.

Of most concern to German public opinion were the events in the Soviet Union, especially the fear that there could be further destabilization in Eastern Europe. In April the Bundestag ratified the new treaty relationships with the Soviet Union. President Yeltsin of Russia visited Bonn in November; his promise that the Volga republic for German-speaking Russians would be re-established was welcomed, not least because it was hoped that the pressure of ethnic Germans migrating to Germany would be thereby eased. Relations with Poland were also put on a firmer footing. In June a 'good neighbour' treaty was signed by the two countries and ratified by the Bundestag in October. A special concern of the Federal Republic was to secure equitable treatment for ethnic Germans in Poland, and on the Polish side there was a desire to work for closer association with the European Community (EC). In April the requirement for Poles to have visas to travel to Germany was dropped, although this liberalization sparked off hostile demonstrations against Polish visitors in eastern Germany.

The outbreak of civil war in Yugoslavia (see IV.1.vi) quickly led German public opinion to side with Slovenia and Croatia and to vocal demands for recognizing their independence. Eventually, the government expressed its intention to establish diplomatic relations with the two states early in 1992. Chancellor Kohl and the Foreign Minister, Hans-Dietrich Genscher, then put pressure on the governments of other

European Community (EC) countries to follow the German lead, and in December they agreed to do so. But there was some resentment felt at being pushed to take what some regarded as a decision with possibly dangerous consequences for the whole region.

In numerous ways the German government sought to hasten the process of European integration. One initiative, taken along with France, was aimed at creating a specific European defence identity: in October the two governments agreed to set up a joint, 50,000-man army corps. Although this new formation was not intended to weaken Germany's NATO commitments, it was unclear what its relationship with NATO would be. The government also reduced its own Bundeswehr structures, announcing a scaling-down of the number of bases in April from 688 to 473. The American and British governments also decided to prune back their armed forces serving in Germany.

The German government was prominent in supporting moves towards the closer integration of the EC at the Maastricht summit in December. Germany favoured the creation of a federal system, increased powers for the European Parliament, a general rule of majority voting in the Council of Ministers, and the adoption of a common foreign policy. Of greatest importance was the agreement to establish a currency union, since it was evident that, because Germany had the strongest economy, the monetary disciplines enforced by the Bundesbank would have to be followed by the other countries. Nevertheless, fears were voiced in Germany that the effects of the union would be to weaken German currency stability. The president of the Bundesbank, Karl Otto Pöhl, resigned at the end of October and was succeeded by the vice-president, Helmut Schlesinger, who had a reputation for adhering to strict monetary discipline.

There was international concern at the end of the year when the Bundesbank raised its bank rate to the level of 9.5 per cent. Most other members of the EC's exchange-rate mechanism (ERM) felt obliged to follow suit, despite the fact that many were suffering from recession. The rise in German interest rates was primarily in response to domestic factors, since inflation was forecast to rise to near 5 per cent in 1992 compared with 3.5 per cent in 1991. A major concern was the high level of wage demands of 10 per cent or more. At the same time, unemployment looked set to rise substantially above the 1991 overall rate of 6 per cent; with a large number of short-time working agreements expiring at the end of the year, eastern Germany would be badly affected. Nonetheless, there was optimism that economic growth would continue: up to 10 per cent in eastern Germany, although only 1.5 per cent in the west.

As had become usual, German tennis players were dominant at Wimbledon where Steffi Graf and Michael Stich won the two singles finals (see XVII.3). But perhaps the most evocative event in the year, and of great symbolic import, occurred in August. The remains of Frederick the Great of Prussia, which had been moved to western Germany towards the end of World War II, were reinterred in the grounds of Sanssouci at Potsdam. It was feared that the ceremony, attended by Chancellor Kohl, would be the occasion for nationalist flag-waving. In the event, it turned out to be a remarkably low-key affair, to the relief of most Germans.

iii. ITALY

CAPITAL: Rome   AREA: 301,000 sq km   POPULATION: 57,500,000 ('89)
OFFICIAL LANGUAGE: Italian   POLITICAL SYSTEM: parliamentary democracy
HEAD OF STATE: President Francesco Cossiga (since July '85)
RULING PARTIES: Christian Democratic (DC), Socialist Unity (PSU), Social Democratic (PSDI) and Liberal (PLI) parties
HEAD OF GOVERNMENT: Giulio Andreotti (DC), Prime Minister (since July '89)
PRINCIPAL MINISTERS: Claudio Martelli (PSU/deputy premier, justice), Gianni De Michelis (PSU/foreign affairs), Vincenzo Scotti (DC/interior), Guido Carli (DC/treasury), Paolo Cirino Pomicino (DC/budget), Salvatore Formica (PSU/finance), Virginio Rognoni (DC/defence)
INTERNATIONAL ALIGNMENT: NATO, OECD, EC
CURRENCY: lira (end-'91 £1=Lit2,149.75, US$1=Lit1,151.45)
GNP PER CAPITA: US$15,120 ('89)
MAIN EXPORT EARNERS: machinery and transport equipment, manufactures, chemicals, agricultural products, tourism

THE year opened with the Christian Democratic Prime Minister, Giulio Andreotti, aged 72, still presiding over the five-party coalition government he had formed in 1989. This government, Signor Andreotti's sixth, and unusually long-lived by Italian standards, consisted of his own Christian Democrats (DC), still easily the largest party, the Socialists, accounting for some 14 per cent of the electorate and now officially called the Socialist Unity Party (PSU), and three smaller centrist parties, the Social Democrats, Republicans and Liberals. Some such coalition had characterized virtually all Italian governments since 1948. It also demonstrated continued unwillingness to admit into the government the Communists, the country's second largest party, which in the past had at times accounted for a third of the electorate.

The Communist Party had recently changed its character, and under its leader, Achille Occhetto, decided to alter its name to Democratic Party of the Left (PDS) and replace the hammer-and-sickle emblem with an oaktree (see AR 1990, pp. 155–6). Its congress in Rimini in early February endorsed these proposals, despite objections from marxist hardliners. The confused state of the party seemed likely to lose it support, and the ambitious Socialist leader, Bettino Craxi, seized this opportunity to press for radical changes in the political system, hoping himself to secure more left-wing support. In mid-March he called for a presidential republic, possibly on French lines, in which the president would be given greater executive power and would be directly elected by the voters instead of by parliament as at present. He also suggested a change in the existing proportional representation system of voting: a cut-off point, possibly of 5 per cent, below which parties would not be admitted to parliament. Such a proposal would obviously be strongly contested by three of the five coalition parties, the Republicans, Social Democrats and Liberals, each of whom had less than five per cent of the total vote.

Signor Craxi was not alone in calling for radical reforms of the post-war political system. President Francesco Cossiga himself, now in the sixth year of his seven-year term of office, had recently repeatedly called for drastic changes in the 1948 constitution. This caused a clash with the government headed by his own former DC party, whose membership card Signor Cossiga had destroyed on being elected President in 1985 to show that he intended to be above the party fray. Neither President Cossiga nor Signor Craxi wanted to precipitate a time-consuming general election in the parliament's last year. But as a result of their pressure for change, Signor Andreotti on 29 March tendered his resignation. On 5 April President Cossiga asked him to form a new cabinet, which he did on 12 April, the key posts remaining unchanged. But the three Republican Party ministers refused to take up the posts they had been offered, saying that these were not what they had been promised, and on 15 April their party decided not to back the new government. It was therefore only a four-party coalition which presented itself to parliament, securing a vote of confidence in the Chamber on 19 April and in the Senate the next day.

The support in the country as a whole for constitutional change was demonstrated in a referendum held on 9 June. The change being voted on was relatively minor: it abolished a system of preferential votes that had allowed local political leaders to receive blocks of such votes from a given area in exchange for favours, thus enabling Mafia chiefs to acquire political influence. But although most of the political parties had advised voters to boycott the referendum, there was an exceptionally high turnout of 62.5 per cent, well above the required 50 per cent minimum. Moreover, over 95 per cent of the voters supported the proposed change, which was seen in part as an anti-Mafia measure.

The Mafia itself continued to present a serious problem not only in Sicily and Calabria but also in hitherto orderly northern towns such as Bologna. A parliamentary commission reporting on criminal gangs in Calabria in late May said that nearly 130 persons had been killed there since January; the gangs now depended less on drug-trafficking and relied more on extortion and misuse of government expenditure. At the end of October the government launched a new élite corps of fighters to combat the Mafia.

Dissatisfaction with the central government in Rome was also shown in the development of *leghe*, or leagues. These started out as grass-roots political movements in northern Italy, where the Lombard League, aiming at more regional autonomy, did well in regional elections in 1990 (see AR 1990, p. 156), and had since spread to many central and southern regions. In local elections in the northern industrial town of Brescia on 25 November, for example, the Lombard League got over 24 per cent of the total vote, marginally ahead of the hitherto predominant Christian Democrats. Some commentators accused the *leghe* of racism and of tapping fears of foreign immigrants who, coming especially from Senegal and North Africa, presented particular problems in tourist cities such as Florence. The hitherto lax immigration laws were tightened up and the immigrants' status was more clearly defined. In the autumn and winter new fears arose of a possible influx of refugees from Yugoslavia.

By then Italy had already experienced an influx of unwanted refugees from Albania, fleeing from impossible living conditions there. Early in March some 20,000 refugees came in Albanian ships to the southern Italian ports of Bari, Brindisi and Otranto. The government tried to persuade the Albanian government to check the flow, and the Foreign Minister, Gianni De Michelis, visited Tirana offering emergency aid. Meanwhile, the refugees were housed in camps in Bari and Brindisi, and attempts were made to disperse them to other parts of Italy. The government fixed the date of 15 July for the repatriation of those who had been unable to find work or did not qualify as political refugees, but a fresh wave attempted to land in August, about half of whom were sent back under police escort. On 24 August the Interior Minister, Vincenzo Scotti, went to Tirana to sign an agreement with Albania which would allow Italian ships to patrol the Albanian coast to prevent further waves of illegal immigrants.

During the Gulf War Italy cooperated with the United Nations, offering transport facilities and sending a contingent of Tornados and some ships (see V.2), and subsequently sending army and air force humanitarian missions to the Kurds. In the Yugoslav crisis, Signor De Michelis, a Socialist from Venice, formed part of the 'troika' of EC foreign ministers (from past, present and future countries holding the rotating six-month EC presidency) seeking to monitor the situation there (see IV.1.vi). Italy also formed part of the 'Hexagonale' conference of central and southern European countries, founded in 1989 by Signor De Michelis. Originally consisting of Italy, Yugoslavia, Austria and Hungary, it was subsequently joined by Czechoslovakia (when it became the 'Pentagonale') and then by Poland.

In the EC itself, Italy had always been strongly federalist in theory but had recently become more pragmatic, seeking to combine strong adherence to NATO with an EC defence policy. To this end Italy and Britain, early in October, submitted to the EC foreign ministers a joint paper proposing that the EC should make use of the Western European Union as its defence component. This move was in part an expression of Italy's wish to strengthen Britain's position in the EC as a counterpoise to Germany and France. Mr Major visited Rome on 27 November for talks with Signor Andreotti, who in a pre-Maastricht interview said that his two priorities there would be social policy and the powers of the European Parliament. He added that economic and monetary union (EMU) would be 'revolutionary' for Italy because it would lead to the imposition of budgetary discipline. This view was echoed by the Italian Treasury Minister, Guido Carli. Incidentally, for all its federalist enthusiasm for the EC, Italy had easily the worst record in complying with EC directives.

On 19–20 December Boris Yeltsin, the Russian President, spent two days in Rome. Though Russia was not yet fully recognized as legal heir to the Soviet Union, the Italian authorities treated this as a state visit, and he stayed in the Quirinale palace as guest of President Cossiga. Apart from meeting political leaders and visiting the Pope, the main object of the visit on the Russian side was financial. Italy had for long been the Soviet Union's second largest trading partner after Germany, and Italian export credits of 1,500,000 million lire (£750 million), which had been suspended after the attempted Moscow coup in August, were now unblocked. Mr Yeltsin was also hoping that his meetings with Italian businessmen, including Gianni Agnelli of Fiat and Carlo De Benedetti of Olivetti, would result in further promises of economic aid and investment. Fiat already had strong post-war links with Russia, where Fiat cars had been produced in Togliattigrad, named after the early Italian Communist leader, Palmiro Togliatti. Italy also had trade links with other East European countries, notably Poland, where Fiat was embarking on a joint venture to produce Fiat 500s, and in Czechoslovakia and Hungary, where Olivetti had set up its first East European subsidiary company.

In some ways, this flourishing outlook on the East European trade front seemed to be reflected in the economy in general. Car sales, for example, dropped by less than 1 per cent in 1991, and there was widespread evidence of consumer spending. But inflation remained above 6 per cent, labour costs were rising and industrial production was running at 2.4 per cent below that of 1990. An overall growth rate of no more than 1 per cent was expected in 1991, abnormally sluggish for Italy. On top of this, there was the enormous and uncontainable annual budget deficit, about which President Cossiga, in one of his attacks on Italian bureaucracy, said: 'If an individual managed his financial affairs in the way the government is running those of the nation, he would end up in prison.' The budget for 1992, announced on 30 September, aimed at reducing the deficit through tax increases, but the governor of the Bank of Italy on 28 October attacked it as inadequate, as also did the IMF (on 18 November) in saying that it relied too much on temporary measures. The government had in May introduced a package of taxes on luxury goods, and in July the Prime Minister published the names of 240,000 ascertained tax evaders for 1983–85, but this step seemed unlikely to strike terror into the heart of the hardened tax evader. And, of course, no statistics could keep track of the daily acts of production and transmission that made up the black market, estimated at accounting for something between 10 and 20 per cent of official GDP.

iv. BELGIUM

CAPITAL: Brussels   AREA: 30,500 sq km   POPULATION: 10,000,000 ('89)
OFFICIAL LANGUAGES: French & Flemish
POLITICAL SYSTEM: parliamentary democracy, devolved federal structure based on language communities
HEAD OF STATE: King Baudouin (since July '51)
RULING PARTIES: Christian People's Party (CVP/Flemish), Christian Social Party (PSC/Walloon), Socialist Party (SP/Flemish) and Socialist Party (PS/Walloon) continued in caretaker coalition after November elections
HEAD OF GOVERNMENT: Wilfried Martens (CVP), Prime Minister (since Dec '81)
PRINCIPAL MINISTERS: Philippe Moureaux (PS/deputy premier, Brussels, institutional reform, education), Willy Claes (SP/deputy premier, economic affairs & planning, education), Jean-Luc Dehaene (CVP/deputy premier, communications, institutional reform), Melchior Wathelet (PSC/deputy premier, justice, middle classes), Wivina De Meester-Demeyer (CVP/budget, scientific policy), Mark Eyskens (CVP/foreign affairs), Philippe Maystadt (PSC/finance), Guy Coëme (PS/defence)
INTERNATIONAL ALIGNMENT: NATO, OECD, EC, Benelux, Francophonie
CURRENCY: Belgian franc (end-'91 £1=BF58.55, US$1=BF31.36)
GNP PER CAPITA: US$16,220 ('89)
MAIN EXPORT EARNERS: machinery and transport equipment, manufactures, chemicals, agricultural products

FROM very early in the year it was apparent that the spirit of cooperation among the coalition government's five partners was wearing thin. Whether on major international issues such as the Gulf War (which the Socialists opposed, whereas the Christian Socials supported the allies), or important domestic issues like the next stage of government devolution to the linguistic regions (on which the Walloon parties went in for delaying tactics), the coalition parties were clearly engaged in preparing their positions for the forthcoming general elections.

It was the issue of arms sales to the Middle East that provided the trigger for the collapse of the coalition. The French-speaking parties (Wallonia had the main weapons factories) were in favour of the sales, while the Volksunie, a moderate Flemish nationalist party, and the Flemish wing of the Socialist Party objected on moral grounds. A possible compromise solution was unacceptable to the Volksunie, which left the government on 29 September. A cobbled-together coalition of the other four parties lasted little more than a week before squabbling on relatively petty regional issues caused it to collapse.

A general election followed on 24 November. None of the main political parties appeared to the electorate to have any new policies, and it was clear that popular dissatisfaction with them was increasing. In particular, hostility towards Belgium's large immigrant population was growing and some extreme solutions were aired by extremist parties. Questions of 'law and order' and the environment were also prominent in the election campaign.

Insofar as the election results constituted both a protest against the ineffectiveness of the main parties and also a major voicing of concern about the perceived dangers of high immigration, they shifted the balance of political power and made formation of a new government extremely problematic. The previous main coalition partners, the Flemish and Walloon wings of the Christian Social and Socialist parties, lost 13 of their 134 seats in the 212-member lower house. While they still had sufficient seats to form a majority government, they by no means possessed the two-thirds majority necessary to pass further devolution legislation. The Volksunie lost 6 of its 16 seats and diminished in status as a worthwhile coalition partner. The opposition Liberals gained an extra seat in Flanders but lost ground in Wallonia, which left the party two seats down overall, rendering it hardly credible as leader of a new coalition. The gainers were the Flemish extremist Vlaams Blok (from 2 seats to 12), the Ecolo (green) Party (from 3 seats to 10) and a new Flemish extremist party called the Van Rossem List, which took 3 seats.

In view of the outcome, Prime Minister Wilfried Martens tendered his resignation on 25 November but was asked to continue in a caretaker capacity pending the formation of a new government. Initial efforts to that end made no progress, however. As the year closed, the general expectation was that a new government would not be formed easily or quickly.

Economic growth slowed markedly during the year. Industrial output, though improving from the very weak performance of the early months, was only slightly above the 1990 level, as a result of the feeble inflow of new orders. Building was especially hard hit. Business investment increased by a very modest 1.5 per cent, reflecting low utilization of existing production capacity and uncertainty about sales prospects. Unemployment rose sharply as economic activity declined. However, the slackness in demand brought a benefit in the shape of a very slow rate of price increases.

In September Belgium sent troops to Zaïre, its former colony, to oversee the evacuation of Belgian citizens following widespread rioting (see also VII.1.i). This move was widely considered to mark the end of the close relationship with Zaïre, in which Belgium still had extensive commercial interests.

v. THE NETHERLANDS

CAPITAL: Amsterdam   AREA: 37,000 sq km   POPULATION: 14,800,000 ('89)
OFFICIAL LANGUAGE: Dutch   POLITICAL SYSTEM: parliamentary democracy
HEAD OF STATE: Queen Beatrix (since April '80)
RULING PARTIES: Christian Democratic Appeal (CDA) & Labour Party (PvdA)
HEAD OF GOVERNMENT: Ruud Lubbers (CDA), Prime Minister (since Nov '82)
PRINCIPAL MINISTERS: Wim Kok (PvdA/deputy premier, finance), Hans van den Broek (CDA/foreign affairs), Ien Dales (PvdA/home affairs), Relus ter Beek (PvdA/defence), Koos Andriessen (CDA/economic affairs), Ernst Hirsch Ballin (CDA/justice)
INTERNATIONAL ALIGNMENT: NATO, OECD, EC, Benelux
CURRENCY: guilder (end-'91 £1=f3.20, US$1=f1.71)
GNP PER CAPITA: US$15,920 ('89)
MAIN EXPORT EARNERS: oil and gas, machinery and transport equipment, chemicals, agricultural products

AN austerity programme, severe by Dutch standards, introduced by the Christian Democrat/Labour coalition government in February led to a shift of political support away from the coalition parties in the provincial elections held on 6 March. The Labour Party's share of the vote fell from 32 per cent at the 1989 general elections to only 20 per cent, as many of its supporters switched to the more radical Democrats '66, whose share surged from 8 per cent to 16 per cent. The Christian Democrats held on to one-third of the vote. The main opposition party, the right-wing People's Party for Freedom and Democracy, increased its representation from 15 to 16 per cent.

This political realignment became more accentuated as the year progressed, with opinion polls by late July suggesting that the Labour Party could lose half of its seats in parliament in the event of a general election. The most acute problems for Labour related to the coalition's proposals to tighten the eligibility requirements, and reduce the benefits of, the widely-abused industrial disability system, and in particular the linkage of benefits to private-sector wages. As tensions mounted between the coalition partners, the government came close to falling; only a last-minute compromise enabled it to survive a no-confidence vote on 29 August. Nevertheless, several important members of the Labour Party resigned, including the chairman, Marjanne Sint.

A further politically destabilizing factor was the growing public hostility towards the influx of refugees, asylum seekers and economic migrants. A number of efforts were made by the government both to reduce the flow and to limit domestic movement of asylum seekers and prospective immigrants, including a proposal, eventually rejected, to set up special centres for deportees. Legislation was proposed, amid heated debate, to monitor the ethnic composition of the population by adding data on ethnic origins to existing statistical returns.

Unsurprisingly, an official visit by the Japanese Prime Minister in July generated strong emotions, especially among World War II prisoners in the former Dutch East Indies. It was widely considered that the argument of Prime Minister Lubbers, to the effect that Japan was too important a nation for the Netherlands not to maintain close ties with it, cost him significant political support.

The legalization of euthanasia was provided for in a parliamentary bill submitted in November. This step would remove the uncertainty under previous legislation as to the position of doctors involved in euthanasia, who technically had been liable to imprisonment.

The logic of the austerity programme was developed further in the 1992 budget presented on 17 September, providing for more government spending cuts. Large-scale protest strikes took place, halting many public services as well as private-sector companies. Nevertheless, the government stood firm on its proposal to reduce the budget deficit further. Efforts to discourage energy consumption, as part of a campaign to shift from fossil to renewable fuels, intensified in mid-July when the government announced the introduction of an 'eco-tax' on petroleum and its products, natural gas and electricity.

Economic growth slowed sharply in 1991, mainly as a result of a major decline in both public and private investment. This was partially offset by strong expansion in personal consumption, as unemployment fell and wage increases were relatively large. Taken together, these developments contributed to a faster rise in prices.

vi. LUXEMBOURG

CAPITAL: Luxembourg AREA: 3,000 sq km POPULATION: 377,000 ('89)
OFFICIAL LANGUAGE: Letzeburgish
POLITICAL SYSTEM: parliamentary democracy
HEAD OF STATE: Grand Duke Jean (since Nov '64)
RULING PARTIES: Christian Social People's Party (PCS) and Luxembourg Socialist Workers' Party (LSAP)
HEAD OF GOVERNMENT: Jacques Santer (PCS), Prime Minister (since July '84)
PRINCIPAL MINISTERS: Jacques Poos (LSAP/deputy premier, foreign affairs), Jean Spautz (PCS/interior), Jean-Claude Juncker (PCS/finance, labour, budget), Robert Goebbels (LSAP/economy)
INTERNATIONAL ALIGNMENT: NATO, OECD, EC, Benelux, Francophonie
CURRENCY: Luxembourg franc (end-'91 £1=LF58.55, US$1=LF31.36)
GNP PER CAPITA: US$24,980 ('89)
MAIN EXPORT EARNERS: basic manufactures, machinery and transport equipment, tourism, financial services

THOUGH the steel industry, still a dominant element of the economy, was suffering from lower demand, leading to a sharp decline in output, other sectors performed well in 1991. Consequently, overall economic growth quickened and the Grand Duchy appeared largely immune (apart from the steel industry) to the international business recession. There was a consumer spending boom, fuelled by tax cuts and by an average 7.5 per cent wage increase, and yet inflation remained well under control at around 3.8 per cent. Normally tranquil labour relations were upset in July by a one-day strike by the country's four banking unions, called against new contract conditions.

The 1992 budget, announced in September, showed the usual healthy surplus even after provision for further improvements to the economic infrastructure, designed to encourage foreign investment in manufacturing. The government also announced its intention to increase investment aid to companies in order to foster diversification. The aim was to help restore the role of manufacturing, which with the expansion of the financial and services sector had declined to only a quarter of domestic product.

The banking authorities inevitably became involved in the scandal and shut-down of the Bank of Credit and Commerce International (BCCI), which was registered in Luxembourg. The effectiveness of the regulatory mechanisms governing Luxembourg's important banking sector came under heavy local and international criticism, causing considerable governmental concern about its liberal approach to banking controls.

Luxembourg's turn in the presidency of the European Community (EC) in the first half of 1991 placed Foreign Minister Poos in the international limelight, as the EC sought to mediate in the Yugoslav crisis (see IV.1.vi) and grappled with its own plans for closer economic and political union (see XI.3). In February the government authorized the United States to use Luxembourg's airport for military transit in connection with the Gulf War.

vii. REPUBLIC OF IRELAND

CAPITAL: Dublin   AREA: 70,280 sq km   POPULATION: 3,500,000 ('89)
OFFICIAL LANGUAGES: Irish, English
POLITICAL SYSTEM: parliamentary democracy
HEAD OF STATE: President Mary Robinson (since Dec '90)
RULING PARTIES: Fianna Fáil (FF), Progressive Democrats (PD)
HEAD OF GOVERNMENT: Charles Haughey (FF), Prime Minister/Taoiseach (since March '87)
PRINCIPAL MINISTERS: John P. Wilson (FF/deputy premier/Tánaiste, marine), Gerard Collins (FF/foreign affairs), Bertie Ahern (FF finance), Ray Burke (FF/justice & communications), Desmond J. O'Malley (PD/industry & commerce)
INTERNATIONAL ALIGNMENT: neutral, OECD, EC
CURRENCY: punt (end-'91 £1=IR£1.07, US$1=IR£0.57)
GNP PER CAPITA: US$8,710 ('89)
MAIN EXPORT EARNERS: tourism, machinery and transport equipment, chemicals, agriculture

THE conclusion in January of an agreement between government, unions and employers, called the Programme for Economic and Social Progress (PESP), augured well with its provision for improvements in health, education and employment over the coming three years. The promise of cumulative pay rises of 14.5 per cent in the same period looked like a credible guarantee of industrial peace since inflation in the Republic was a mere 2.6 per cent, the lowest in any country of the European Community (EC). Opinion polls showed public satisfaction with the coalition government of Fianna Fáil and the Progressive Democrats, led by Charles Haughey as Taoiseach (Prime Minister), to be exceptionally high.

The difficulty of meeting the PESP objectives soon became apparent, however, as cost-cutting exercises in state companies like the Post Office, the Aer Lingus airline and the electricity service threatened redundancies and in several cases caused work stoppages. Farmers became increasingly anxious about the impact of proposed changes in the EC's common agricultural policy, which would reduce or eliminate the subsidies on which they had become dependent. A substantial drop in emigration came about, not from a growth in job opportunities at home but from the contraction of employment in recession-hit Britain. In particular, Irish graduates with technical and professional qualifications, who had been much in demand in the later 1980s, could no longer find openings in the United Kingdom. The increase in redundancies and unemployment put a strain on the social services, casting a doubt over the possibility of implementing the PESP in full.

Other factors compounded the mounting discontent. The poor condition of the road network in rural areas, and urban dissatisfaction with politically-contrived revisions of planning regulations, evoked much debate. So did allegations of malpractice in the Irish beef industry, made on a Granada TV's *World in Action* programme in May, which resulted in the establishment of a sworn public inquiry. The government's competence both in policy-making and in protecting the public interest was by now seriously in question. In local authority elections at the end of June, Fianna Fáil suffered heavy defeats and lost control of many municipalities and county councils, including the cities of Dublin, Cork, Limerick and Galway. Labour and independent candidates, including the Greens, gained most from this debacle.

A succession of financial scandals came to light in September and October. Some senior executives of a food-processing firm, until recently state-owned, were found to have made substantial personal profit from selling another company to their employers during the course of privatization. It was alleged that Irish Telecom bought new premises at an inflated price, to the benefit of a private vendor, and that the government had made a grant from public funds to encourage the purchase of property for university development at what seemed excessive cost. In several cases tax liabilities had been minimized by the use of 'off-shore' companies set up in Jersey, the Isle of Man or Cyprus.

Apart from the university incident, none of these, or lesser transactions revealed at the time, touched the government directly. But some of the beneficiaries were thought to typify a slick entrepreneurialism associated with an element in Fianna Fáil. The government was held to have been negligent in supervising the use of state money. With income tax levels high and wage-earners' tax being deducted at source, anger was voiced over the revelation that the wealthy people could keep down their liabilities by resorting to sophisticated schemes for tax avoidance. The government set up a plethora of inquiries, but most had still to report by the year's end.

Fianna Fáil now slumped in the opinion polls to record low levels, as also did approval for Mr Haughey himself. The Taoiseach made matters worse by inept comments on radio. The fear grew within Fianna Fáil that the party would lose massively if a general election were called while Mr Haughey still led it. The Minister for Finance, Albert Reynolds, and the Minister for the Environment, Padraig Flynn, as well as three junior ministers, joined in a revolt against Mr Haughey but a motion of no-confidence in his leadership was defeated decisively at a parliamentary party meeting on 10 November, on a vote by open roll-call. It was widely believed that many members of parliament who backed the Taoiseach did so on the unspoken understanding that he would resign in the early months of 1992. The dissident ministers were dismissed and the Minister for Labour, Bertie Ahern, was moved to finance, the most important departmental ministry in the Irish system.

Another consequence of the scandals became evident in December when the trade unions proved exceptionally obdurate in the face of government decisions to delay the payment of certain public sector pay awards under the PESP agreement because of the worsening pressure on state finances. Union leaders made it clear that their members would insist on the letter of the agreement since, as it seemed to them, the government had not prevented well-off businessmen from making personal fortunes with the aid of taxpayers' money while avoiding payment of their own fair share to the exchequer.

Anglo-Irish relations were relatively happy throughout the year, although Dublin and London continued to differ over extradition. The major grievance in Ireland concerned the decision of an English magistrate (later overturned) to send an accused person forward for trial on charges other than those on which he had been extradited from the Republic. General satisfaction greeted the release of the 'Birmingham Six' in March (see also I.3). The Foreign Minister, Gerard Collins, and the British Northern Ireland Secretary, Peter Brooke, worked in close harmony to bring the talks on the future of the North to fruition (see also I.10). Mr Brooke won admiration in the Republic for his efforts to keep the Northern parties in meaningful discussion, but also for his determination, shared by Mr Collins, to proceed with a scheduled meeting of the Anglo-Irish Conference in July despite the likelihood that the Unionists would abandon the talks if it went ahead—as, in fact, they did.

The Maastricht meeting of EC heads of government in December presented few problems for the Republic, since progress towards political union and, in particular, a single currency had long been accepted as EC objectives by the coalition and the major opposition party, Fine Gael. Some anxiety over the assistance to be provided for poorer EC countries in the evolution towards a 'new Europe' was expressed, as well as doubts concerning the ultimate arrangements for defence (which would require a modification of Irish neutrality). However, the need for a constitutional referendum on the Maastricht agreement in 1992 meant that serious controversy was deferred for the time being.

Mrs Mary Robinson received much praise for the discharge of her duties as President of Ireland in her first year of office, especially for the concern she showed towards the disadvantaged in Irish society—the itinerants, the inner-city unemployed, the people of the depopulated western seaboard—as well as her encouragement of visits to the presidential residence by groups representing every political persuasion in the North. Very limited funding reduced the impact which might have been made by the EC designation of Dublin as European 'City of Culture' in 1991. Nevertheless, the capital recorded two notable cultural achievements in the outstanding success of the Abbey Theatre's production on Broadway of Brian Friel's play *Dancing at Lughnasa* and the enthusiastic reception of Alan Parker's film *The Commitments*, based on a story by Dublin schoolteacher Roddy Doyle and performed by a cast of young Dubliners, many of them amateurs (see also XVI.1.v).

2. DENMARK—ICELAND—NORWAY—SWEDEN—FINLAND AUSTRIA—SWITZERLAND—EUROPEAN MINI STATES

i. DENMARK

CAPITAL: Copenhagen   AREA: 43,000 sq km   POPULATION: 5,100,000 ('89)
OFFICIAL LANGUAGE: Danish
POLITICAL SYSTEM: parliamentary democracy
HEAD OF STATE: Queen Margrethe II (since Jan '72)
RULING PARTIES: Conservative People's Party (KF) and Venstre Liberals (V)
HEAD OF GOVERNMENT: Poul Schlüter (KF), Prime Minister (since Sept '82)
PRINCIPAL MINISTERS: Uffe Ellemann-Jensen (V/foreign affairs), Henning Dyremose (KF/finance), Anders Fogh Rasmussen (V/economic affairs) Hans Engell (KF/justice), Knud Enggaard (V/defence), Thor Pedersen (V/interior, Nordic affairs)
INTERNATIONAL ALIGNMENT: NATO, OECD, EC, Nordic Council
CURRENCY: krone (end-'91 £1=DKr11.05, US$1=DKr5.92)
GNP PER CAPITA: US$20,450 ('89)
MAIN EXPORT EARNERS: agricultural produce, machinery and transport equipment, manufactures

POUL Schlüter's minority coalition of Conservatives and Liberals survived the year despite holding less than one-third of the Folketing's seats. This was possible because of the basic consensus between the centre-right parties and Social Democrats on the broad aims of economic policy (low inflation, sound external finances, export-led growth) and its main means (tight fiscal policy, a fixed exchange rate within the EC's exchange rate mechanism and greater savings incentives).

In late January the 1991 budget was passed with the centre parties voting in favour and the Social Democrats abstaining. On 6 February the public sector unions accepted a two-year wage agreement in line with Denmark's low inflation rate of 2.5 per cent. Subsequent private sector agreements were equally low. The current account was in surplus for a second year, and the trade surplus was 6 per cent of GDP.

Major structural problems remained. Unemployment was 10.8 per cent. In May the non-socialist parties and Social Democrats agreed a reform of unemployment benefits making them less generous. The budget deficit was still a large 4.5 per cent of GDP. The projected 1992 deficit, agreed in a six-party budget compromise on 5 December, was no lower, despite spending cuts.

The consensus was even more evident in foreign policy, where old divisions over NATO and the EC had ended in the light of German unification. Non-socialists and Social Democrats supported a continued American presence in Europe as a counter-balance to an enlarged Germany, together with further EC integration to bind Germany into Western Europe. During the Gulf War Denmark sent a corvette to the war zone. In April the government and moderate opposition parties agreed on a 1991/92 defence budget with only moderate spending cuts. In the EC negotiations on economic and political union, Denmark supported the goal of EMU, subject to holding a referendum. However, it opposed giving the EC a genuinely federal character, or a defence role likely to weaken NATO.

The main threat to the government came from the long-running 'Tamilgate' scandal, on which a public judicial inquiry heard starkly conflicting evidence from ministers, civil servants and the Prime Minister himself. It was seeking to establish whether a former Conservative justice minister, Mr Ninn-Hansen, should be impeached for acting illegally in halting (in 1987) the administrative process by which families of Tamil refugees were brought to Denmark. The inquiry's conclusion was expected in 1992.

On 23 March Denmark and Sweden signed an agreement to build a rail and motorway bridge across the Öresund between Copenhagen and Malmö. This was another stage in the ambitious project to connect Jutland with Zeeland and Sweden. However, problems plagued the construction work already underway in the Great Belt. In July Denmark won an interim judgment against Finland's attempt to stop construction of the suspension bridge between Zeeland and Sprogø (see XV.1.i). But in October, already behind schedule, the two tunnels being bored in the same area were flooded. The contractors then refused to continue boring, pending further geological surveys.

Following a general election in Greenland on 5 March, Lars Emil Johansen, who had replaced Jonathan Motzfeldt as leader of Siumut, became Prime Minister at the head of a left-wing coalition of Siumut and Inuit Ataqatigiit. The election loser was the conservative Atassut party, which lost three of its 11 seats in the 27-seat parliament.

ii. ICELAND

CAPITAL: Reykjavik   AREA: 103,000 sq km   POPULATION: 254,000 ('89)
OFFICIAL LANGUAGE: Icelandic
POLITICAL SYSTEM: parliamentary democracy
HEAD OF STATE: President Vigdís Finnbogadóttir (since Aug '80)
RULING PARTIES: Independence Party (IP), Social Democratic Party (SDP)
HEAD OF GOVERNMENT: Davíd Oddsson (IP), Prime Minister (since April '91)
PRINCIPAL MINISTERS: Jón Baldvin Hannibalsson (SDP/foreign affairs), Fridrik Sophusson (IP/finance), Thorsteinn Pálsson (IP/ fisheries, justice, ecclesiastical affairs), Jón Sigurdsson (SDP/industry & commerce)
INTERNATIONAL ALIGNMENT: NATO, OECD, EFTA, Nordic Council
CURRENCY: króna (end-'91 £1=ISK104.25, US$1=ISK55.84)
GNP PER CAPITA: US$21,070 ('89)
MAIN EXPORT EARNERS: fish and fish products, tourism

ICELAND demonstrated early support for the Baltic states' struggle for independence (see IV.2.ii). Foreign Minister Jón Baldvin Hannibalsson visited Lithuania on 18–22 January, followed a week later by a parliamentary delegation. On 11 February the Allting voted to establish diplomatic relations with Lithuania as soon as possible. On 26 August Iceland became the first state formally to establish diplomatic relations with all three Baltic states.

In March the outgoing Allting voted in favour of abolishing its division into two chambers and sitting in future as one. This constitutional change was confirmed by the new Allting in May, following a general election on 20 April. This resulted in a victory for the Independence Party (IP) under its new leader, Davíd Oddsson, a former mayor of Reykjavik. Of 11 parties standing, five won seats in a turnout of 89.6 per cent. The results were as follows (1987 figures in brackets):

	% of votes	seats
Independence Party	38.6 (27.2)	26 (16)
Progress Party	18.9 (18.9)	13 (13)
Social Democrats	15.5 (15.2)	10 (10)
People's Alliance	14.4 (13.3)	9 (8)
Women's Alliance	8.3 (10.1)	5 (6)
Citizens' Party/Liberals	1.2 (10.9)	0 (7)
Other parties	3.1 (4.4)	0 (1)

The election campaign revealed sharp differences over Europe and economic policy between the Social Democrats and their coalition partners, the Progress Party and People's Alliance. The Social Democrats therefore chose after the election to form a government with the IP rather than continue the previous coalition. The new government, with Mr Oddsson as Prime Minister, took office on 30 April. It was supported by 36 of the Allting's 63 members. Each party had five ministers.

The new government's programme included completion of the EC-EFTA negotiations on a European Economic Area; exploitation of Iceland's energy resources and industrial development, including construction of a controversial aluminium smelter by the Atlantal consortium; privatization and greater scope for market forces; and continuation of the no-devaluation policy established in December 1989. Preparations were begun to link the króna to the European Community's ecu in 1993.

Inflation had fallen rapidly as a result of the hard króna and the national wage agreement of February 1990 (see AR 1990, p. 169), which was due to expire on 15 September. Negotiations to renew this important agreement were complicated by the severe economic problems which emerged after the election. Acting on the advice of Iceland's marine scientists, the government in the summer announced large cuts in the permitted 1991–92 capelin catch, exacerbating the fishing industry's problems and causing a downward revision of forecast economic growth and government tax revenues. The forecast budget deficit had already been revised sharply upwards. Refusing to increase taxes, the government in its September budget proposed public expenditure cuts and the introduction of user charges for public services. In November the Atlantal consortium announced an indefinite delay in construction of the aluminium smelter due to world over-capacity and falling prices.

Under the EC-EFTA agreement, which was concluded on 21 October, Iceland achieved its main objective. Tariffs would be removed from nearly all Iceland's fish exports to the EC without Iceland in return having to open its fishing grounds to Community fishermen or permit foreign investment in the fishing industry.

On 27 December the government decided that Iceland would leave the International Whaling Commission on 30 June 1992, on the grounds that it had become an anachronistic and ineffective organization.

iii. NORWAY

CAPITAL: Oslo   AREA: 324,000 sq km   POPULATION: 4,200,000 ('89)
OFFICIAL LANGUAGE: Norwegian
POLITICAL SYSTEM: parliamentary democracy
HEAD OF STATE: King Harald V (since Jan '91)
RULING PARTY: Labour Party (minority government)
HEAD OF GOVERNMENT: Gro Harlem Brundtland, Prime Minister (since Nov '90)
PRINCIPAL MINISTERS: Thorvald Stoltenberg (foreign affairs), Sigbjoern Johnsen (finance), Finn Kristensen (petroleum), Johan J. Holst (defence), Kari Gjesteby (justice), Odrunn Pettersen (fisheries)
INTERNATIONAL ALIGNMENT: NATO, OECD, EFTA, Nordic Council
CURRENCY: krone (end-'91 £1=NKr11.17, US$1=NKr5.98)
GNP PER CAPITA: US$22,290 ('89)
MAIN EXPORT EARNERS: oil and gas, machinery and transport equipment, manufactures, chemicals, fish

KING Olav V died on 17 January, aged 87 (see XX: OBITUARY). The second king of independent Norway, he had reigned since 1957. He was succeeded by his son, who became King Harald V.

Economic trends in the spring gave grounds for some optimism. Inflation was under 4 per cent, the current account again in surplus, GNP growth forecast at 3.5 per cent, the spring wage agreements moderate, interest rates lower and the krone strong. On the other hand, unemployment was about 5 per cent, the banks were revealing increasingly serious losses, and the budget deficit was rising. In February the government established a NKr 5,000 million bank insurance fund to underpin guarantee funds already operating. In May it proposed a NKr 10,000 million infrastructure investment programme to promote growth and employment. In June a broad Storting majority approved a new tax system, intended to promote enterprise and saving. This followed Sweden's example by lowering tax rates while broadening and simplifying the tax base.

Gro Harlem Brundtland's minority Labour government faced an opposition deeply divided over Europe and economic policy. The government looked for support for its economic measures from the centre parties and the Socialist Left. The controversial EC-EFTA negotiations for a European Economic Area (EEA) were supported by the Conservatives and the Progress Party (both also favouring EC membership) and by the Christian People's Party. Polls showed public opinion equally divided over Norway's relations with the EC. Labour's strategy was to conclude an EEA treaty in 1991 but to postpone a decision on EC membership until the party's national congress in 1992. It maintained this position despite Sweden's membership application in July and indications that Finland might also apply.

In local elections on 8–9 September the two parties opposing both EC membership and the EEA negotiations—the Centre Party and the Socialist Left—increased their vote. Labour's share was its lowest since the 1920s, while the Progress Party lost half its support. The

Conservatives and Christian People's Party maintained the support they had received in the 1989 general election. Over one-third of the electorate failed to vote.

The EEA agreement concluded on 21 October found broad support in parliament and public opinion despite opposition from the Centre Party, the Socialist Left and fishermen's organizations. It seemed likely to receive the necessary three-quarters Storting majority for ratification in 1992. EC fishermen would take a larger catch in Norwegian waters in return for expanded duty-free access for Norwegian fish in EC markets.

By autumn the economic outlook had deteriorated. Labour's expansionary 1992 budget, passed in November, projected an increased budget deficit of NKr 24,000 million, even allowing for state petroleum revenue. The budget aimed to reduce unemployment by stimulating the depressed on-shore economy. The Central Bank warned that such a large deficit could push up interest rates and weaken confidence in the krone.

The seriousness of Norway's banking crisis became apparent in mid-October when Christiana, the second-largest bank, was declared technically insolvent. The government was forced to act to save the entire banking system from collapse. It made clear its determination to allocate whatever resources were required to keep the system intact, while forcing through reforms to put it back on a sound basis. On 17 October the government announced a new NKr 11,500 million support arrangement for the banks, and a further NKr 6,000 million for the bank insurance fund. The requirement for state aid was expected to last into 1992.

iv. SWEDEN

CAPITAL: Stockholm   AREA: 450,000 sq km   POPULATION: 8,500,000 ('89)
OFFICIAL LANGUAGE: Swedish
POLITICAL SYSTEM: parliamentary democracy
HEAD OF STATE: King Carl XVI Gustav (since Sept '73)
RULING PARTIES: Moderate Unity Party (MSP), Liberal Party (FP), Centre Party (CP), Christian Democratic Community Party (KDS)
HEAD OF GOVERNMENT: Carl Bildt (MSP), Prime Minister (since Oct '91)
PRINCIPAL MINISTERS: Bengt Westerberg (FP/deputy premier, health & social affairs), Gun Hellsvik (MSP/justice), Margaretha af Ugglas (MSP/foreign affairs), Anders Björck (MSP/defence), Anne Wibble (FP/finance)
INTERNATIONAL ALIGNMENT: neutral, OECD, EFTA, Nordic Council
CURRENCY: krona (end-'91 £1=SKr10.37, US$1=SKr5.55)
GNP PER CAPITA: US$21,570 ('89)
MAIN EXPORT EARNERS: machinery and transport equipment, timber and wood products, iron and steel, tourism

FACED by deep recession and an election in September, the minority Social Democratic government of Ingvar Carlsson nevertheless continued its anti-inflationary strategy and programme of transforming

Sweden into a social market economy. Its major tax reform, shifting the burden from incomes onto goods and services (see AR 1990, p. 173), came into effect on 1 January. The budget on 10 January contained a tight fiscal policy and public expenditure cuts, despite rising unemployment. On 14 February the government published a programme for growth, including higher spending on transport and communications, lower import tariffs on food, and measures to increase competition in the agricultural and retail sectors.

On 17 May the krona was pegged to the European Community's ecu, within narrow bands, so that devaluation was ruled out as a policy option. On 14 June the Riksdag approved a government proposal to apply for EC membership. A fortnight later, on 1 July, Mr Carlsson personally delivered Sweden's application to the European Commission in Brussels.

Public opinion polls pointed to an election defeat for the Social Democrats but no stable non-socialist alternative. A new anti-tax, pro-alcohol populist party called New Democracy, founded in February, attracted much attention. The Moderates and Liberals presented a joint economic programme promising lower taxes and reduced public expenditure, privatization and an end to 'corporatist' collective bargaining. But it was clear that they would require the support of the Centre and Christian Democratic parties in order to form a government.

The election on 15 September produced the Social Democrats' worst result since 1928. Two hitherto-unrepresented parties entered parliament—New Democracy and the Christian Democrats—but the Greens this time failed to cross the 4 per cent threshold. On a turnout of 85 per cent (low for Sweden), the results were as follows (1988 figures in brackets):

	% of votes	seats
Social Democrats	37.6 (43.2)	138 (156)
Moderates	21.9 (18.3)	80 (66)
Liberals	9.1 (12.2)	33 (44)
Centre Party	8.5 (11.3)	31 (42)
Christian Democrats	7.1 (2.9)	26 (0)
New Democracy	6.7 (–)	25 (–)
Left Party	4.5 (5.6)	16 (21)
Greens	3.4 (5.5)	0 (20)
Others	1.2 (2.0)	0 (0)

Mr Carlsson's government resigned on 16 September. The following day the Moderate leader, Carl Bildt, was asked to form a coalition. On 3 October he was elected Prime Minister of a four-party minority centre-right coalition of Moderates, Liberals, Centre Party and Christian Democrats commanding 170 of the Riksdag's 349 seats.

The new government's programme included the negotiation of EC membership; greater choice in health and social service provision; encouragement of foreign investment; and measures to improve economic efficiency including privatization, deregulation, lower taxes and public spending, and higher spending on infrastructure, education and research.

On 5 November the government announced a SKr 9,000 million cut in public expenditure, the first step in a planned annual reduction to lower the tax burden from 55 per cent to 40 per cent of GDP. On 6 November it announced cuts in VAT on food and transport, with the ultimate aim of reaching EC levels. Economic and monetary policy would be determined by the aim of achieving the criteria laid down for entry into the third stage of EC economic and monetary union in the later 1990s. By mid-November the government had also announced measures to privatize 35 state-owned companies, lift restrictions on foreign ownership of companies and shares, and to cut business taxes.

Following the Finnish devaluation on 15 November (see III.2.v), the Swedish krona came under intense pressure. In three weeks the Central Bank used a quarter of its reserves to defend the currency within its 1.5 per cent band against the ecu. On 5 December it raised short-term interest rates by 6 per cent, to 17.5 per cent. Pressure on the krona then eased, with the result that interest rates fell slightly. But Mr Bildt's aim of reviving the Swedish economy had been made more difficult.

v. FINLAND

CAPITAL: Helsinki AREA: 338,000 sq km POPULATION: 5,000,000 ('89)
OFFICIAL LANGUAGES: Finnish & Swedish
POLITICAL SYSTEM: presidential democracy
HEAD OF STATE: President Mauno Koivisto (since Sept '81)
RULING PARTIES: Centre Party (KESK), National Coalition Party (KOK), Swedish People's Party (SFP), Finnish Christian Union (SKL)
HEAD OF GOVERNMENT: Esko Aho (KESK), Prime Minister (since April '91)
PRINCIPAL MINISTERS: Paavo Väyrynen (KESK/foreign affairs), Mauri Pekkarinen (KESK/interior), Hannele Pokka (KESK/justice), Elisabeth Rehn (SFP/defence), Iiro Viinanen (KOK/finance)
INTERNATIONAL ALIGNMENT: neutral, OECD, EFTA, Nordic Council
CURRENCY: markka (end-'91 £1=Fmk7.73, US$1=Fmk4.14)
GNP PER CAPITA: US$22,120 ('89)
MAIN EXPORT EARNERS: timber and wood products, manufactures, machinery and transport equipment, tourism

ON 1 January Finland's trade with the Soviet Union moved onto a hard-currency basis. On 13 January demonstrators in Helsinki protested outside the Soviet embassy against the use of force in Lithuania (see IV.2.ii). These events both symbolized and were part of major changes in Finland's relations with the Soviet Union during 1991. Trade with that country fell to 5 per cent of Finland's exports, increasing its dependence on Western markets. Following the attempted August coup in Moscow (see IV.2.i), Finland proposed a renegotiation of the 1948 Treaty of Friendship, Cooperation and Mutual Assistance. On 22 September the two countries agreed to replace it by a treaty modelled on those concluded by the Soviet Union with Germany and France.

Mr Holkeri's coalition of Conservatives, Social Democrats and the Swedish People's Party fought a general election on 17 March with Finland in severe recession. Unemployment and the current-account deficit were rising, GNP and investment contracting. Interest rates were high to defend the government's hard markka policy, which the forest industry and exporters blamed for falling market shares.

The Conservatives and Social Democrats lost heavily in the election. The Centre Party gained 15 seats and again became the largest party in the 200-seat parliament. On a turnout of 72 per cent, the results were as follows (1987 figures in brackets):

	% of votes	seats
Centre Party	24.9 (17.6)	55 (40)
Social Democrats	22.1 (24.1)	48 (56)
Conservatives	19.3 (23.1)	40 (53)
Left Alliance	10.1 (13.4)	19 (20)
Swedish People's Party	5.4 (5.3)	12 (13)
Greens	6.8 (4.0)	10 (4)
Christian League	3.1 (2.6)	8 (5)
Rural Party	4.9 (6.3)	7 (9)
Liberals	1.2 (1.0)	1 (0)
Others	2.2 (2.6)	0 (0)

The Social Democrats chose to go into opposition. In November they elected Ulf Sundqvist as chairman in place of Pertti Paassio. On 26 April a four-party coalition of the Centre Party, Conservatives, Swedish People's Party and Christian League took office, with Centre leader Esko Aho as Prime Minister.

The new government pledged to maintain its predecessor's hard markka policy. But in May, in order to help industry, it announced plans to provide Fmk 7,000 million in aid by shifting the burden of social security contributions from employers to employees. It also proposed a two-year wage freeze and promised public expenditure cuts in the 1992 budget. On 7 June it pegged the markka to the ecu at the existing level, provoking intense controversy between the supporters and opponents of devaluation. On 21 October the central employers' and employees' organizations concluded a 22-month wage agreement which would cut real incomes by 4 per cent and industry's wage costs by nearly 7 per cent.

However, by mid-November the pressure for devaluation had become irresistible. The metal workers had rejected the October wage agreement and interest rates had reached 30 per cent, as the Bank of Finland sought to defend the markka. On 14 November, in a severe setback for the government's economic strategy, the markka was floated. The next day it was devalued by 12.3 per cent against the ecu. The government said it would defend the new rate. On 28 November the unions accepted a 22-month wage freeze.

By the autumn the Conservatives and Social Democrats had declared in favour of EC membership. Polls showed public opinion in favour. The government was due to reach a decision by early 1992, so that it could, if an application was made, participate in the 'first wave' of post-Maastricht EC entry negotiations with Sweden and Austria.

vi. AUSTRIA

CAPITAL: Vienna   AREA: 84,000 sq km   POPULATION: 7,600,000 ('89)
OFFICIAL LANGUAGE: German   POLITICAL SYSTEM: federal parliamentary democracy
HEAD OF STATE: Federal President Kurt Waldheim (since July '86)
RULING PARTIES: Social Democratic (SPÖ) and People's (ÖVP) parties
HEAD OF GOVERNMENT: Franz Vranitzky (SPÖ), Federal Chancellor (since June '86)
PRINCIPAL MINISTERS: Erhard Busek (ÖVP/vice-chancellor), Aloïs Mock (ÖVP/foreign affairs), Ferdinand Lacina (SPÖ/finance), Franz Löschnack (SPÖ/interior), Werner Fasslabend (ÖVP/defence), Nikolaus Michalek (non-party/justice)
INTERNATIONAL ALIGNMENT: neutral, OECD, EFTA
CURRENCY: schilling (end-'91 £1=Sch19.96, US$1=Sch10.69)
GNP PER CAPITA: US$17,300 ('89)
MAIN EXPORT EARNERS: basic manufactures, machinery and transport equipment, chemicals, tourism

THE year saw the lavish bicentenary celebrations of Mozart's death (see XVI.1.i and ii), as well as the first Austrian space flight, as part of a Soviet mission to the *Mir* space station in October. It also saw the remarkable discovery on 19 September of the 'first Tyrolean', whose mummified body emerged from the ice of the Niederjoch glacier on the Austro-Italian border complete with remains of clothes and weapons preserved by the ice for some 4,000 years.

It was also a year marked by real progress towards Austria's goal of joining the European Community (EC). The Commission's positive opinion on Austria's application was issued on 31 July, and on 22 October political agreement was reached in the negotiations between the EC and EFTA countries (including Austria) on the creation of the so-called European Economic Area (see XI.3 and XI.5.iii). On 3 December Austria signed a transit traffic agreement with the Community, and on 4 December the Federal Chancellor, Dr Franz Vranitzky, announced that the mandate for membership negotiations would be issued in mid-1992, with actual negotiations expected to begin in early 1993. It was in this context that Dr Vranitzky's Socialist Party decided at its congress in June to confirm its alignment with the moderate European left by reverting to its original name of Social Democratic Party of Austria (while retaining the familiar abbreviation SPÖ).

When hostilities in the Gulf began on 15 January, the Austrian government took steps immediately to offer humanitarian and medical assistance to those caught up in the fighting. Subsequently, the law governing the import, export and transit of military equipment was amended to facilitate Austrian compliance with decisions of the UN Security Council (in which Austria had just begun a two-year term as a non-permanent member). But public opinion was uneasy, and the government's decision on 5 February to permit the transit of 103 US armoured tank recovery vehicles was criticized as inconsistent with Austria's neutral status.

The flow of economic refugees from Eastern Europe continued to agitate public opinion. In fact, the rate of migration slowed during the year, and the visa requirement temporarily imposed on Polish citizens from September 1990 (see AR 1990, p. 176) was allowed to lapse on 31 August. On 4 December new asylum legislation was enacted, introducing abbreviated procedures for dealing with 'unfounded' applications for political asylum from those whose identity or citizenship could not be established, or who came from countries where it was generally agreed that no danger of persecution existed.

There was no question, however, about the genuine need of the 20,000 or more displaced Yugoslavs who had taken refuge in Austria by the end of the year. Austrian public opinion strongly supported Slovenian and Croatian aspirations to independence, as it had those of the Baltic states (formally recognized on 28 August). However, within the grand coalition between the SPÖ and its junior partner, the People's Party (ÖVP), opinions were divided on when and in what company to recognize the breakaway republics. Dr Vranitzky's determination to keep in step with EC policy finally carried the day. On 19 November the federal government announced that Austria would, in parallel with the EC, withdraw some trade privileges enjoyed by Yugoslavia. On 30 November the foreign ministers of the six-nation regional cooperation group known as the Hexagonale, meeting without Yugoslavia, decided that in view of the crisis the Yugoslav presidency of the grouping should be curtailed by six months and transferred to Austria.

Economically, Austria continued to avoid the worst effects of recession. In the 1991 draft federal budget presented to parliament on 27 February, the budget deficit was further reduced, to a projected 3.3 per cent of GDP. Although the economic growth rate for 1991 dropped slightly by comparison with the previous year, to 3 per cent, unemployment rose only marginally to 5.8 per cent, and inflation held steady at 3.3 per cent. Nonetheless, it was a difficult year for the government. Apart from predictable SPÖ/ÖVP disagreements over foreign policy, the continued weakness of the ÖVP raised a question mark over the stability of the coalition. In spite of another change of leader on 28 June (when Erhard Busek succeeded Josef Riegler), the ÖVP steadily lost ground against the growing electoral challenge on its right wing from Jörg Haider's Freedom Party (FPÖ). The SPÖ itself was embarrassed by reminders of old scandals when prison sentences were handed down on 1 February in the Noricum illegal arms sale trial and, on 12 March, in the Lucona trial (see AR 1989, p. 174).

Meanwhile, the FPÖ continued to fan the flames of anti-immigrant prejudice and to benefit from the general mood of disenchantment with the cosy arrangements of the grand coalition among many ordinary Austrians. Dr Haider himself suffered an unexpected setback on 21 June when he was voted out as state governor of Carinthia for having said in the provincial assembly that the Third Reich had pursued a 'sound employment policy'. But when Austrian voters had the opportunity to register their views, in four provincial elections during the latter part of the year, the FPÖ made some spectacular advances. In Burgenland on 23 June the FPÖ took only one seat from the ÖVP, and the balance of forces in the assembly remained much as before. In Styria on 22 September, however, the ÖVP vote plummeted and the FPÖ more than tripled its vote. In Upper Austria on 6 October the FPÖ again did well, increasing its vote from 5 to nearly 18 per cent, while the ÖVP lost its absolute majority, and the SPÖ also suffered losses. In Vienna on 10 November the SPÖ retained its overall majority but the FPÖ overtook the ÖVP as second-largest party, winning nearly 23 per cent of the votes.

By the end of the year each of the three main parties was fielding a candidate for the presidential election due in April 1992 (the controversial incumbent, Dr Kurt Waldheim, having announced in June that he would not after all seek a second term). Political attention was focused on whether the ÖVP could be tempted into a 'small' coalition with Dr Haider, in return for the transfer of FPÖ votes to the ÖVP candidate in the second round of voting.

vii. SWITZERLAND

CAPITAL: Berne   AREA: 41,300 sq km   POPULATION: 6,850,000 ('90)
OFFICIAL LANGUAGES: German, French, Italian, Rhaeto-Romanic
POLITICAL SYSTEM: federal canton-based democracy
RULING PARTIES: Christian Democratic People's (CVP), Radical Democratic (FDP), Social Democratic (SPS) and Swiss People's (SVP) parties
HEAD OF STATE AND GOVERNMENT: Flavio Cotti (CVP), 1991 President of Federal Council, Minister of Interior
OTHER MINISTERS: René Felber (SPS/vice-president, foreign affairs), Otto Stich (SPS/finance), Jean-Pascal Delamuraz (FDP/economy), Adolf Ogi (SVP/communications & energy), Arnold Koller (CVP/justice), Kaspar Villiger (FDP/defence)
INTERNATIONAL ALIGNMENT: neutral, OECD, EFTA
CURRENCY: Swiss franc (end-'91 £1=SwF2.53, US$1=SwF1.35)
GNP PER CAPITA: US$37,800 ('90)
MAIN EXPORT EARNERS: financial services, machinery, chemicals, tourism

SWITZERLAND celebrated its 700th anniversary with festivities and all kinds of other manifestations throughout the year. This event was not only a review of the past but also served as a good reason for a wide debate on the future of the nation. Many politicians, intellectuals and citizens expressed their conviction that one of the main principles of Swiss politics, armed neutrality, could soon lose its meaning and usefulness. The political integration of Western Europe fostered this sentiment, as did the end of the Cold War.

The most important political event of the year was nevertheless the elections for the National Council (parliament) held on 20 October. Two of the three main political parties, the Radical Democrats (FDP) and the Christian Democrats (CVP), tried to keep the campaign on a low profile. They refrained, in view of diverging opinions among their own members, from taking a clear position on the issues of European integration and the growing number of persons seeking asylum in Switzerland. This reticence did not pay off. The FDP lost 7 of its 51 parliamentary seats and the CVP 6 of its 42; in contrast, the other two government parties, the Social Democrats (SPS) and the People's Party (SVP), maintained their position. The winners were mainly to be found on the right of the political spectrum. The populist Automobile Party (with the slogan 'free highways for free citizens') and the Swiss Democrats (formerly National Action Against Foreign Infiltration of People and Homeland), both resolutely opposed to European Community (EC) membership and immigration from Third World countries, augmented their representation by 6 and 2 seats respectively. Also on the winning side was the Green Party, which benefited from the disintegration of some smaller and more radical green and leftist formations. The results were as follows (comparable 1987 figures in brackets):

	% of vote	seats
Radical Democrats (FDP)	21.0 (22.9)	44 (51)
Social Democrats (SPS)	18.5 (18.4)	42 (41)
Christian Democrats (CVP)	18.2 (20.0)	36 (42)
Swiss People's Party (SVP)	11.9 (11.0)	25 (25)
Green Party	6.1 (4.8)	14 (9)
Swiss Liberal Party (LPS)	3.0 (2.7)	10 (9)
Automobile Party	5.1 (2.6)	8 (2)
Swiss Democrats	3.3 (2.8)	5 (3)
Other parties (6)	12.9 (14.8)	16 (18)

In spite of their overall losses in the elections and a call from right-wingers that the Social Democrats should be evicted from government, the four ruling parties saw no necessity for a change in the composition of the Federal Council. In December all seven members were re-elected by the new parliament for another term. Party leaders and analysts pointed out that under the Swiss political system, where any parliamentary decision could be challenged by a popular vote, it was not wise to exclude any important party from participation in government. The French-speaking SPS Vice-President, René Felber, was elected to the annually-rotating post of President of the Federal Council for 1992.

Some new tendencies emerged in discussions on whether Switzerland should apply for full membership of the EC. In October the government, together with the other EFTA member countries, signed a treaty with the EC for the creation of the European Economic Area (EEA) (see also XI.3 and XI.4.iii). The Treaty required to be ratified both by parliament and by a popular vote. Until this moment, the Federal Council had defended the treaty with the argument that it could be a convenient means of taking part in the European integration without being full member of the Community. Now the government expressed for the first time the idea that the EEA might be only an intermediate arrangement and that Switzerland should become prepared to join the EC. This change of mind was welcomed by the SPS and the trade unions, which had both already formally decided to support such a policy. The FDP and the CVP were less enthusiastic and proposed that Switzerland should first make up its mind about the EEA treaty and only then decide any further steps.

Whereas Switzerland had to make some substantial concessions during the negotiations for the EEA, separately-conducted talks with the EC for a treaty on transport matters ended in a most satisfactory way. The Community accepted that the Swiss weight limit for trucks using its roads could remain at 28 tonnes, with a limited number of exceptions being permissible only if the transport capacity of the Swiss railroad system should prove insufficient. With the object of preventing such a situation, the Swiss parliament approved a project for the construction of two new railway tunnels through the Alps.

After many years of surpluses, the state of the federal finances changed for the worse. Following an anticipated balance in 1991, a deficit of more than SwF 1,000 million was budgeted for 1992. The tax reform adopted by parliament in 1990 (see AR 1990, p. 179) did not secure the approval of the people and was rejected by a majority of 54 per cent in a referendum. The project had proposed, among other measures, the replacement of sales tax by a value-added tax (VAT). Polls taken after the vote showed that opposition was not especially directed against VAT, but in a more general way against taxes and the danger of their being increased by government.

The first results of the national census conducted on 1 December 1990 showed that Switzerland had experienced, over the past decade, the largest proportionate increase in population of any Western European country apart from Iceland. The increase from 6,370,000 to 6,850,000 (plus 7.5 per cent), was mainly due to immigration. Persons seeking asylum represented a growing percentage of this immigration, and the number of new applications reached another all-time high in 1991.

On 14 June about 500,000 women went on a nationwide strike to protest against all kinds of unequal treatment in society. This action did not bring any immediate improvements, but it was considered by the organizing committee as an important step in the struggle for a society in which the sexes enjoyed not only the same formal rights but also the same opportunities.

Having persisted throughout the 1980s, economic growth came to an abrupt halt in the second half of the year. The number of unemployed reached 60,000 (1.9 per cent of the workforce), the highest level since 1939. In spite of the recession, prices continued to boom, with the inflation rate rising to a ten-year high of 5.9 per cent.

viii. EUROPEAN MINI-STATES

Andorra
CAPITAL: Andorra la Vella   AREA: 460 sq km   POPULATION: 51,500 ('90)
OFFICIAL LANGUAGE: Catalan
POLITICAL SYSTEM: qualified democracy
HEADS OF STATE: President Mitterrand of France & Bishop Joan Martí Alanis of Urgel (co-princes)
HEAD OF GOVERNMENT: Oscar Ribas Reig, President of Executive Council (since '90)
CURRENCY: French franc & Spanish peseta
MAIN EXPORT EARNERS: tourism, banking, smuggling

Holy See (Vatican)
CAPITAL: Vatican City   AREA: 0.44 sq km   POPULATION: 760 ('90)
OFFICIAL LANGUAGES: Italian & Latin
POLITICAL SYSTEM: theocracy
HEADS OF STATE: Pope Paul II (since '78)
HEAD OF GOVERNMENT: Most Rev Angelo Sodano, Secretary of State (since Dec '90)
CURRENCY: Vatican lira (pegged to Italian lira)

Liechtenstein
CAPITAL: Vaduz   AREA: 160 sq km   POPULATION: 29,000 ('90)
OFFICIAL LANGUAGE: German
POLITICAL SYSTEM: parliamentary democracy
HEAD OF STATE: Prince Hans Adam II (since Nov '89)
RULING PARTIES: Patriotic Union (VU) & Progressive Citizens' Party (FBP)
HEAD OF GOVERNMENT: Hans Brunhart (VU), Prime Minister (since '78)
CURRENCY: Swiss franc   GNP PER CAPITA: US$15,000 ('89)
MAIN EXPORT EARNERS: manufactured goods, tourism

Monaco
CAPITAL: Monaco-Ville   AREA: 1.95 sq km   POPULATION: 28,000 ('90)
OFFICIAL LANGUAGE: French
POLITICAL SYSTEM: constitutional monarchy
HEAD OF STATE: Prince Rainier III (since '49)
HEAD OF GOVERNMENT: Jacques Dupont, Minister of State (since April '91)
CURRENCY: French franc
MAIN EXPORT EARNERS: tourism, financial services

San Marino
CAPITAL: San Marino   AREA: 60.5 sq km   POPULATION: 23,000 ('90)
OFFICIAL LANGUAGE: Italian
POLITICAL SYSTEM: parliamentary democracy
HEADS OF STATE AND GOVERNMENT: Captains-Regent Edda Ceccoli I & Marino Riccardi I
RULING PARTIES: Christian Democratic and Democratic Progressive parties
CURRENCY: Italian lira
MAIN EXPORT EARNERS: tourism, agricultural products

III.2.viii EUROPEAN MINI-STATES

THE Holy See, Liechtenstein, Monaco and San Marino continued, as sovereign states under international law, to play their due part in the structures of the Conference on Security and Cooperation in Europe (CSCE), following their signature of the Charter of Paris for a New Europe in November 1990 (see AR 1990, p. 569). Liechtenstein now had the additional responsibility of full membership of the United Nations, which it had joined in 1990 (see AR 1990, p. 387). It also, on 22 May, became the seventh member of the European Free Trade Association (EFTA), having previously had associate status through its customs union with Switzerland (see XI.5.iv). The co-principality of Andorra (under Spanish episcopal and French joint suzerainty) became a full member of the European Community (EC) customs union on 1 July.

Internally, politicians in Andorra pursued their quest for consensus on a written constitution that would bring the co-principality more into line with West European democratic practice. In Liechtenstein, the 53-year-old ruling coalition of the Patriotic Union (VU) and Progressive Citizens' Party (FBP) took steps to correct some early-year economic shakiness. It also kept a close eye on the political debate in Switzerland on whether to follow Austria and Sweden in applying for EC membership (see III.2.vii). Although Prince Hans Adam averred in August that EC membership was impracticable for his 'small principality', few doubted but that Liechtenstein would follow a Swiss move to join, if and when it came.

Monaco's voters went to the polls in March and elected a new town mayor in the person of Anne-Marie Campora, from the progressive Évolution Communale list. In San Marino, the local Communists continued as the junior coalition partner to the Christian Democrats but now called themselves the Democratic Progressive Party. By the year's end they were just about the only Communists (or ex-Communists) left in government anywhere in Europe.

3. SPAIN—PORTUGAL—GIBRALTAR—MALTA—GREECE—CYPRUS—TURKEY

i. SPAIN

CAPITAL: Madrid   AREA: 505,000 sq km   POPULATION: 39,000,000 ('89)
OFFICIAL LANGUAGE: Spanish   POLITICAL SYSTEM: parliamentary democracy
HEAD OF STATE: King Juan Carlos (since Nov '75)
RULING PARTY: Spanish Socialist Workers' Party (PSOE)
HEAD OF GOVERNMENT: Felipe González, Prime Minister (since Nov '82)
PRINCIPAL MINISTERS: Narcís Serra Serra (deputy premier), Julian García Vargas (defence), José Luis Corcuero (interior), Francisco Fernández Ordóñez (foreign affairs), Carlos Solchaga (economy & finance), Tomas de la Quadra Salcedo (justice)
INTERNATIONAL ALIGNMENT: NATO, OECD, EC
CURRENCY: peseta (end-'91 £1=Ptas180.65, US$1=Ptas96.80)
GNP PER CAPITA: US$9,330 ('89)
MAIN EXPORT EARNERS: tourism, transport equipment, agricultural products, minerals and base metals

ON 13 January Alfonso Guerra announced his resignation as Deputy Premier. He did so at an unimportant meeting of the ruling Socialist Workers' Party (PSOE) in the provincial city of Caceres, western Spain. He kept his other post, that of deputy secretary-general of the PSOE, so as to continue, from that position of authority, to urge the party to pursue a policy of what he called 'democratic socialism' towards 'the transformation of capitalism', and to oppose the 'social democratic' ideas prevalent in the cabinet. At the PSOE conference the previous November he had steered through a policy document for the following decade which contained marxist overtones little to the liking of the social democrats, especially the Minister of Economy and Finance, Carlos Solchaga, who described himself as a pragmatic liberal social democrat.

Sr Guerra's resignation, which Prime Minister Felipe González accepted the following day, came at an awkward moment. The Cortes was due to discuss what Spain's role in the Gulf War should be. Ever since the dispatch the previous August of three frigates to the Gulf, there had been demonstrations against Spanish participation in the operation. That Spain was providing substantial logistical support to the allied forces—indeed, that aircraft carrying 45 per cent of all US forces en route to the Gulf had refuelled in Spain—was not likely to remain a secret. Opinion polls revealed that only 30 per cent of the population wanted Spain to participate. Nevertheless, on 18 January the government requested and received from the Cortes, by a large majority of both PSOE and opposition deputies, authority to provide whatever 'logistical, humanitarian and political support' it could to the allied forces.

Sr González delayed appointing a successor to Sr Guerra until 11 March. He then elevated to the post his Minister of Defence, Narcís

Serra, who was succeeded by Julian García Vargas. A man of like mind to his predecessor, Sr García Vargas in April sent 600 members of the Spanish parachute brigade, all professional soldiers, to take part in the protection of the Kurds on the Iraq-Turkey border. In other, less important, cabinet changes made following Sr Guerra's resignation, Sr González strengthened the moderate, social democratic, faction of the government.

As details emerged of the conduct of the Gulf War, a bill was introduced in the Cortes to reduce compulsory military service from 12 to nine months. This intensified a longstanding debate among senior officers, political leaders and the general public on whether Spain should opt for wholly professional, in lieu of mixed professional/conscript, armed services. Self-evidently, conscripts could not be trained to master such sophisticated weapons as had been used in the Gulf. An opinion poll in April revealed that the option had the full support of 57 per cent of all adult Spaniards and 80 per cent of those aged 18 to 24. Nevertheless, the existing professional element in the services was over 30 per cent under strength. The civilian labour market offered far better pay and career prospects, and a higher quality of life and status in society, than the services. Ex-regulars did not easily find employment.

On 22 April Sr García Vargas declared in the Cortes that Spain had neither the financial resources nor the manpower to opt for exclusively professional armed services. Spain's birth rate was now next to the lowest in the European Community (EC). On the same occasion, the new Defence Minister reiterated the Spanish view that Western Europe should hasten to assume greater responsibility for its own defence (see AR 1990, p. 183), and that this responsibility should be assumed either by the EC or the Western European Union (WEU). In October, bearing in mind the differences of opinion on political union and a common defence and security policy within the EC, Spain joined Germany and France in advocating that the WEU should undertake that responsibility. The compromises arrived at by the Maastricht EC summit in December (see XI.3 and XIX.3) pleased Spain well enough. It would have preferred greater powers to have been given the EC on foreign and defence policies, but it was proud to have been the leader on 'economic and social cohesion', and to have got its way.

Two more of the projected six agreements on the coordination of the Spanish with other NATO forces (see AR 1990, p. 182) were signed during the year—in January the one covering operations in the western Mediterranean, and in April the one relating to the defence of Spanish territory. As expected, there was no progress towards agreement on Spain's role in the defence of the Strait of Gibraltar. Spain made known its view that, irrespective of who held sovereignty over the Rock, Spain should be the country primarily responsible in that area.

King Juan Carlos, addressing the UN General Assembly in October, referred to Gibraltar as 'a colonial problem . . . to which Spaniards are particularly sensitive', and which remained unresolved in accordance with the UN resolutions on decolonization. The subject figured on the agenda of several meetings during the year between the foreign ministers and the prime ministers of the United Kingdom and Spain (see also III.3.iii), but there was no progress towards a settlement of the issue. Spain persisted in its lack of understanding of why Britain could not give orders to a colonial government. In June Spain warned that it would not sign the EC External Frontiers Convention, because in its opinion the convention, as worded, would give the Gibraltarians the power to control entry into Spain. Spain was prepared to cede this power to the sovereign states of the Community but not to a colony of any of them. It accordingly demanded a separate Hispano-British agreement with reference to the Gibraltar frontier. Britain, in reply, offered to allow a footnote to be added to the convention, stating that its coming into effect would be without prejudice to negotiations on Gibraltar, but Spain was not satisfied. Sr González stated categorically that Spain would not sign the convention if the problem of Gibraltar were not resolved.

The struggle between the two factions in the PSOE revived in April. Sr Guerra and his supporters insisted that the party's manifesto for the May regional and municipal elections should contain a firm commitment to finance the building over the next four years of 400,000 houses and to help their purchasers with mortgages at interest rates well below the market levels. Sr Solchaga angered the Guerra faction by pointing out that the enormous cost to the Treasury of such a plan could be met only if government expenditure on other social necessities were substantially reduced. Sr González dampened the consequent altercation by agreeing to the inclusion of the commitment to build and the exclusion of the promise of low-interest mortgages.

In the elections the PSOE retained control of 13 of the 17 autonomous regional governments but lost power in the cities of Seville and Valencia. Unable to dislodge the social democratic faction from the central government, Sr Guerra and his followers began in November to argue that the best-qualified bodies to allocate public funds for social services were the regional governments and local mayors. They therefore advocated the transfer to such bodies of 50 per cent of the moneys destined for those services in the national budget, or currently controlled by Sr Solchaga's ministry.

The Basque separatist ETA kept up its acts of terrorism throughout the year, but there were two developments offering some hope for a more peaceful future. In 1990 ETA had brought a halt to the construction of a motorway across the province of Gipuzkoa, to link San Sebastian with Pamplona, after inflicting damage estimated at $10 million. It alleged that it was motivated by environmental considerations. However, this defence of its actions was destroyed by an ecological survey carried out by the EC, which then granted $60 million towards the construction of the motorway. In August the Basque Nationalist Party negotiated an end to the terrorist campaign over the motorway, through Herri Batasuna, ETA's political arm. In November Herri Batasuna announced that over the following five months it would carry out a debate within the party, at all levels and with 'other individuals', on whether 'a new way' other than violence might lead to a more rapid realization of its aim, namely the creation of an independent and socialist Basque nation-state.

ii. PORTUGAL

CAPITAL: Lisbon   AREA: 92,000 sq km   POPULATION: 10,300,000 ('89)
OFFICIAL LANGUAGE: Portuguese
POLITICAL SYSTEM: presidential/parliamentary democracy
HEAD OF STATE: President Mário Soares (since March '86)
RULING PARTY: Social Democratic Party (PSD)
HEAD OF GOVERNMENT: Anibal Cavaco Silva, Prime Minister (since Nov '85)
PRINCIPAL MINISTERS: Joaquim Fernando Nogueira (presidency & defence), Jorge Braga de Macedo (finance), Manuel Dias Loureiro (home affairs), João de Deus Pinheiro (foreign affairs), Alvaro Laborinho Lucío (justice)
INTERNATIONAL ALIGNMENT: NATO, OECD, EC
CURRENCY: escudo (end-'91 £1=Esc251.60, US$1=Esc134.76)
GNP PER CAPITA: US$5,682 ('90)
MAIN EXPORT EARNERS: tourism, basic manufactures, textiles, agricultural products

THE political year began with presidential elections on 15 January, resulting in the re-election of President Mário Soares with a landslide majority over the right-wing candidate, Basilio Horta. Despite the reservations of some Social Democrats (PSD), Prime Minister Cavaco Silva persuaded his party that cohabitation with the Socialist (PS) President had worked, and would continue to work, and that an artificial conflict should be avoided by not running a PSD candidate. From then on the PSD, as the ruling party, concentrated on preparing the ground for the forthcoming parliamentary elections.

It was on the foreign affairs front that the government achieved its first major success. On 31 May the government was able to announce the terms of a peace agreement and ceasefire in the 16-year-old Angolan civil war (see VII.1.vi). This marked the culmination of nearly two years of negotiations between the warring parties, chaired by Secretary of State for Foreign Affairs, Durão Barroso.

During much of the summer the 52-year-old Prime Minister travelled the country, inaugurating public works and seeking to impress voters as the symbol of stability and prosperity. In the parliamentary elections, held on 6 October, the voters gave the PSD a second consecutive absolute majority after an electoral campaign dominated much more by the Prime Minister's strong and self-confident personality than by issues. The results of the elections, for an Assembly reduced from 250 to 230 seats, were as follows (1987 figures in brackets):

	% of votes	seats
Social Democrats (PSD)	50.4 (50.2)	135 (148)
Socialists (PS)	29.3 (22.2)	72 (60)
Communists (CDU)	8.8 (12.1)	17 (31)
Democratic Social Centre (CDS)	4.4 (4.4)	5 (4)
National Solidarity (PSN)	1.7 (–)	1 (–)
Democratic Renewal (PRD)	0.7 (4.9)	0 (7)

The PS opposition, led by the soft-spoken intellectual mayor of Lisbon, Jorge Sampaio, did little more than criticize a growing gap between rich and poor and warn of austerity ahead. The Socialists increased their share of the vote, but were still left in opposition. Soon afterwards, Sr Sampaio's leadership came under challenge from Antonio Guterrez, who decided not to apply for re-selection as PS parliamentary leader in order to run for the post of party secretary-general.

The Communists, embarrassed by their leadership's failure to condemn the unsuccessful coup in Moscow in unequivocal terms, continued to lose ground. The electoral result contributed to a further wave of major defections, including that of Barros Moura, a prominent Euro-MP, who resigned his seat and started moves towards the creation of a new left-wing party.

Sr Cavaco Silva's PSD managed to retain most of the right-wing vote plus the centre and part of the centre-left electorate. The scale of the boom transforming Portugal, which achieved a growth rate of 3 per cent in 1991, could be seen in the extent of new buildings and motorways, built with a considerable flow of European Community (EC) aid. Remarkable progress was made, with inflation falling to 8.5 per cent, although further progress was deemed necessary before the escudo could enter the EC's exchange rate mechanism (ERM). Foreign investment continued to pour in ($6,000 million in 1991), but the government's priority was to reduce bank borrowing rates while reducing the budget deficit by an accelerated programme of privatization. Exports grew, but not as fast as imports, which were sucked in by rising private demand and the strength of the escudo. As a result of the international recession, exports contracted, particularly in Portugal's main European markets. The budget deficit remained high at 5.6 per cent of GNP, of which, by the end of 1991, the current-account deficit was expected to be a manageable 1 per cent.

In early November, in anticipation of Portugal's assumption of the rotating EC presidency for the first half of 1992, the Prime Minister announced a small government reshuffle. In the principal change, Finance Minister Miguel Beleza, who had apparently disagreed with the Prime Minister over how to fight inflation, was replaced by Jorge Braga de Macedo, a 43-year-old academic. Sr Cavaco Silva had insisted that reducing inflation and the budget deficit were priorities that could be achieved without resorting to austerity. He was quoted as saying: 'Maintaining a high growth rate is the only way to have a fiscal dividend without having to raise taxes.'

The privatization programme progressed too slowly for many critics. The government pointed to difficulties in removing constitutional barriers to denationalization and to the effects of the Gulf War on the capital market. After a delay for the elections, privatizations were resumed in November with the second stage of the sale of the country's two biggest commercial banks and of the first tranche of the oil company Petrogal. Up to 80 per cent of the proceeds from privatizations were used to repay public debt and to improve the balance sheets of some public companies. However, the process became a focus of criticism from such disparate forces as conservative industrialists, stockbrokers, trade unionists and opposition Socialists. The process was said to be clouded in illegalities and secrecy, such as buy-back agreements with employees and purchases on credit, which perverted the philosophy of 'people's capitalism'. The government denied any illegalities and no charges were upheld. However, the confidence of small investors was shaken after it was learnt that profits for some companies privatized in 1990 were far lower than had been forecast in privatization prospectuses.

In an election year the government made little effort to restructure Portugal's outdated and under-capitalized textile sector or the chronically inefficient agriculture sector. Unemployment was kept at a very low 4.2 per cent of the workforce, but was bound to rise as a result of the backward state of these two low-wage sectors and the social costs of their restructuring. In late July discontent among farmers from the centre and north of Portugal blocked traffic on summer roads in a series of protests outside the control of the established farming unions. However, in general, public-sector strikes were short-lived and ineffective, while the private sector remained almost strike-free.

Proud of the highest growth rate in Europe and buoyed by political stability as confirmed in the parliamentary elections, Sr Cavaco Silva's PSD government ended 1991 in a mood of quiet self-confidence, and was looking forward to its presidency of the EC.

iii. GIBRALTAR

CAPITAL: Gibraltar   AREA: 6.5 sq km   POPULATION: 31,000 ('89)
OFFICIAL LANGUAGE: English   POLITICAL SYSTEM: UK dependency, democracy
HEAD OF STATE: Queen Elizabeth II   GOVERNOR: Adml. Sir Derek Reffell
RULING PARTY: Socialist Labour Party (SLP)
HEAD OF GOVERNMENT: Joe Bossano, Chief Minister (since March '88)

IN February Chief Minister Joe Bossano refused, as in previous years, to attend the annual meeting of the British and Spanish foreign ministers to review the state of the Brussels process. Similarly, he refused to put before the Assembly for ratification the UK-Spanish agreement on the joint use of Gibraltar's airport, as this was linked to that process (see AR 1990, p. 186). In May Spanish Prime Minister Felipe González, on an official visit to London, called on Britain 'to adopt a more imaginative approach' towards overcoming the differences between the two countries over Gibraltar. Mr Bossano's reaction was to equate Sr González's attitude to the Gibraltarians with that of General Franco.

In the UK House of Commons on 16 July, Tristan Garel-Jones, the Foreign Office minister responsible for Gibraltar, expressed the opinion that the effort of imagination called for by Sr González had to be made by Gibraltar and Spain as well as by Britain. He believed that the future of the Rock, as of the United Kingdom and Spain, lay within the European Community (EC), and that 'there was just a chance' that the problem of Gibraltar might be 'resolved within the EC'. The leaders of the three political parties in Gibraltar took this to mean that, were the Community to develop into a federal state, Gibraltar could become a colony of the EC rather than of the United Kingdom. They rejected the idea unanimously. Mr Garel-Jones was given an unfriendly reception by Mr Bossano's supporters when he paid a private visit to Gibraltar at the end of that month.

All this while, much publicity was given in Gibraltar to the opinion of one British specialist in international law that the article in the 1713 Treaty of Utrecht on the surrender of Gibraltar to Britain did not rule out independence for it. Addressing a Commonwealth parliamentary conference in India on 27 September, Mr Bossano appealed to the audience to press Britain and Spain 'to recognize the right to self-determination and right to independence . . . of the people of Gibraltar'. He explained that his government was boycotting the Brussels process negotiations because it was expected to participate in them 'as part of the UK delegation'. On his return to Gibraltar, Mr Bossano declared that 'if the people desired it' he was prepared to challenge the UK-Spanish view that the Treaty of Utrecht ruled out the conversion of Gibraltar into an independent state.

The leaders of the opposition Labour and Social Democratic parties acquiesced in what Mr Bossano had said in India. These parties were in disarray. Mr Montegriffo resigned the leadership of the Social Democrats and his seat in the Assembly, after the legal firm in which he worked had called on him to choose between continued employment and his political role. His place in the party was taken by another young lawyer, Peter Caruana, who in a by-election for the seat had a comfortable majority over his sole Labour opponent. Adolfo Canepa, the Labour leader, came under heavy pressure from his colleagues to resign after another Labour member in the Assembly had crossed over to the Social Democrats.

To challenge both opposition parties, and possibly the ruling Socialist Labour Party, a new party was formed during the autumn, namely the Gibraltar National Party led by Joe Garcia, the editor of a local weekly journal, hitherto a staunch supporter of Mr Bossano. In December it issued its manifesto, more a draft for a new constitution than a political programme. The new party proposed the conversion of the colony into 'a constitutional monarchy within the parameters of the EC, a royal city-state with the Queen as queen of Gibraltar'. On 10 December Mr Bossano surprised Gibraltarians by announcing that there would be a general election in January 1992.

Throughout the year work continued apace on the construction of substantial buildings, mostly to facilitate the expansion of Gibraltar as an off-shore financial centre. However, the impasse over the airport tended to leave Gibraltar at a disadvantage with similar centres elsewhere in Europe.

iv. MALTA

CAPITAL: Valletta   AREA: 316 sq km   POPULATION: 350,000 ('89)
OFFICIAL LANGUAGE: Maltese & English
POLITICAL SYSTEM: parliamentary democracy
HEAD OF STATE: President Vincent Tabone (since April '89)
RULING PARTIES: Nationalist Party (NP)
HEAD OF GOVERNMENT: Edward Fenech Adami, Prime Minister (since May '87)
PRINCIPAL MINISTERS: Guido De Marco (deputy premier, foreign affairs, justice), George Bonello Du Puis (finance), Ugo Mifsud Bonnici (education, interior)
INTERNATIONAL ALIGNMENT: NAM, Cwth
CURRENCY: lira (end-'91 £1=Lm0.57, US$1=Lm0.30)
GNP PER CAPITA: US$5,830 ('89)
MAIN EXPORT EARNERS: tourism, manufactured goods, machinery

THE year was dominated by economic interests. The tone was set by Dr Fenech Adami in an address to the local chamber of commerce on 5 June. With his key economic ministers by his side, the Prime Minister noted: 'This is the third consecutive year of solid growth. Malta today has the lowest unemployment rate for many years, with rising incomes, booming investments, brisk savings, low inflation and profits running high.' The onset of the Gulf War (see V.2) had earlier aroused apprehension about Malta's principal revenue source, tourism, since it still constituted 27 per cent of GNP. In fact, having suffered an estimated drop of 22,000 in the first half of the year, tourist arrivals picked up by mid-summer, while the shortfall in revenue was partly met by an increase in exports of manufactured goods to the European Community (EC).

The latter trend gave extra point to Malta's bid for full membership of the EC, which now took 75 per cent of the islands' total exports despite competition from Spain, Portugal and Greece. The protocol covering the existing trade agreement was confirmed in April when both the European Parliament and the EC Council of Ministers agreed to extend the first stage of Malta's association to the end of 1991. Meanwhile, the government continued to prepare the economy in the hope of full membership, establishing a stock exchange in Valletta, pressing forward with construction of a new airport terminal, extending the local dry dock and free port facilities, and forcing inflation down under an agreement between government, employers and the trade unions. The government noted with interest Dublin's plea for extra financial help from Brussels, once the Channel Tunnel was open, when the Irish Republic would be the only EC member not to be connected with the European mainland. It was perhaps a hopeful precedent for future island members.

The ideological gap between the ruling Nationalist and opposition Labour parties was narrower now, but the latter continued to voice its suspicions about EC entry, fearing the loss not only of capital but also of labour once the internal market was completed. Labour leaders were also less sympathetic than the government towards Western, particularly US, policy in the Gulf.

Malta continued to be represented at a variety of international conferences, among them the Commonwealth heads of government meeting in Harare (see XI.2), the conference in May of 'non-aligned European states' in Liechtenstein and, a new venture, preliminary meetings for a Mediterranean oil and gas exhibition and conference to be held in Malta in January 1992. Relations with Libya continued to improve during the year: the foreign ministers of the two countries met regularly and a new trade agreement in August gave promise of increasing Maltese imports into Libya.

On a more sombre note, many Maltese were filled with anxiety over the unravelling of investigations into the Lockerbie airliner crash of December 1988 (see AR 1988, p. 38). It became known that the Scottish police had visited Valletta as early as August 1989 to inquire into the activities of a suspected Arab terrorist who had visited Malta the previous year and was now serving a life sentence in Sweden. The strong probability was that the bomb had begun its journey in Malta to Frankfurt before being transferred to the Pan Am flight to New York (see also I.1 and V.6.ii).

v. GREECE

CAPITAL: Athens   AREA: 132,000 sq km   POPULATION: 10,000,000 ('89)
OFFICIAL LANGUAGE: Greek   POLITICAL SYSTEM: parliamentary democracy
HEAD OF STATE: President Konstantinos Karamanlis (since May '90)
RULING PARTY: New Democracy (ND)
HEAD OF GOVERNMENT: Konstantinos Mitsotakis, Prime Minister (since April '90)
PRINCIPAL MINISTERS: Tzannis Tzannetakis (deputy premier), Athanasios Kanellopoulos (deputy premier), Antonis Samaras (foreign affairs), Yannis Varvitsiotis (defence), Nikolaos Kleitos (interior), Yannis Paliokrassas (finance), Michalis Papaconstantinou (justice)
INTERNATIONAL ALIGNMENT: NATO, OECD, EC
CURRENCY: drachma (end-'91 £1=Dr327.7, US$1=Dr175.52)
GNP PER CAPITA: US$5,350 ('89)
MAIN EXPORT EARNERS: tourism, merchant marine, textiles, agricultural products

THE year was a gloomy one for Greece. There was little sign of the economic turn-around promised by Konstantinos Mitsotakis's New Democracy government. Terrorism continued without effective countermeasures. Atmospheric pollution reached record levels in the capital. Hopes that Cyprus would be included in attempts to bring about a Middle East peace settlement were frustrated. Moreover, the break-up of the Yugoslav federation and the prospect of an independent Macedonia, coupled with continuing tensions in relations with Turkey, created a high degree of public unease.

In January the European Community (EC) granted a loan of 2,200 million ecu but with stringent conditions. Only half the loan was to be released initially, with the remainder to be paid in two instalments by 1993, provided that the rate of inflation was reduced from over 20 to less than 10 per cent, and was accompanied by a large reduction in the public-sector deficit. A measure of the government's financial desperation was the ill-conceived plan to sell off to the highest bidder 35 islets in the Bay of Argolis and the Saronic Gulf. This was abandoned in the light of vociferous protests, not only on the part of the opposition but from within the ranks of New Democracy itself, and amid rumours of an expression of interest by a Turkish multi-millionaire.

The row over the proposed sale of the islands was one of the factors leading to the dismissal on 26 October of Miltiades Evert, the Minister to the Prime Minister and a leading contender for the eventual succession to the leadership of New Democracy. A number of other senior ministers resigned or were dismissed in the course of the year. On 9 January Vasilis Kondoyiannopoulos resigned as Minister of Education and Religious Affairs, following the death of a school-teacher in a riot in one of the 1,000 secondary schools that had been under occupation since mid-December 1990 in protest against measures to tighten discipline and over inadequate funding. The teachers' union as a consequence went on strike. Following a violent demonstration on 10 January by teachers, pupils and parents, the new minister, Georgios Souflias (hitherto responsible for the economy and tourism), withdrew the offending measures and promised additional funding. On 25 October anarchists exploited another demonstration by high-school students, who were protesting against the reintroduction of end-of-year examinations, to cause extensive damage to the historic buildings of the Athens Polytechnic.

Mr Mitsotakis took over responsibility for the economy, reflecting the high priority afforded to the economic situation. The new Minister of Tourism, Yannis Kefaloyiannis, resigned on 2 September in protest against the relaxation of controls on hotel building on the shoreline. Stavros Dimas resigned as Minister of Industry, Energy and Technology while accompanying Mr Mitsotakis on a visit to the Soviet Union in July. He had fallen foul of the Prime Minister's daughter, Mrs Dora Bakoyianni, who was herself dismissed as under-secretary in the Ministry to the Prime Minister in a cabinet reshuffle on 7 August. Stephanos Manos was removed at the same time as Minister for the Environment, to be replaced by Achilleas Karamanlis, the brother of President Konstantinos Karamanlis. The cabinet was reduced in size from 43 to 36.

There were also important changes on the left of the political spectrum. On 27 February Aleka Papariga, a conservative, was elected secretary-general of the Communist Party of Greece (KKE). Moreover, on 18 March Maria Damanaki (39) succeeded Kharilaos Florakis as leader of the Alliance of the Left and Progress, a coalition of the orthodox and reform communist parties. Greece now had a party leader who was not a septuagenarian. In July the KKE withdrew from the Alliance and Ms Damanaki and other reformists were suspended from the KKE central committee. The following month the KKE leadership came out in support of the anti-Gorbachev plotters in the Soviet Union and made clear its disquiet at subsequent developments.

On 11 March the corruption trial arising out of the Bank of Crete scandal (see AR 1988, pp. 192–3; 1989, pp. 186–8) got under way before a special tribunal appointed by parliament. Five former Panhellenic Socialist Movement (PASOK) ministers, including former Prime Minister Andreas Papandreou (who refused to attend the court), were indicted. The trial was adjourned for 11 days in April following the heart attack and subsequent death of the principal defendant, Agamemnon Koutsogiorgas, who had been accused of receiving a $1,300,000 bribe in return for legislation intended to protect the former owner of the Bank of Crete, George Koskotas, from investigation. Mr Koskotas, after dropping his fight against extradition from the United States, alleged in court testimony in July that he had been blackmailed into channelling funds to PASOK under the threat of the nationalization of his bank. By the year's end, no verdict had been reached.

The year was punctuated by terrorist attacks, responsibility for many of which was claimed by the shadowy '17 November' group which had carried out assassinations over many years with apparent impunity. On 12 March a sergeant in the US army stationed in Greece was killed. On 19 April a Palestinian blew up himself and six bystanders with a bomb intended for the British consulate in Patras. On 17 July the Turkish consul and two members of the consular staff were injured in a bomb attack. In September seven daily newspaper editors were briefly imprisoned for defying a government ban on publishing the communiques of terrorist groups, including '17 December'. The latter claimed responsibility for the shooting on 7 October of the Turkish press attaché, Cetin Gogu, the day before the Prime Minister was due to leave for Istanbul to attend the funeral of the Ecumenical Patriarch Dimitrios I (see XX: OBITUARY). There were also a number of rocket attacks during the year, including one on a luxury hotel in the suburbs of Athens on 31 March.

Relations with Greece's neighbours were tense throughout the year. Polemics between Greece and Turkey continued, with passions being inflamed by the death of 34 Greek tourists in an (apparently not politically-motivated) arson attack on a bus in Istanbul during the Orthodox Easter holiday. The call in May for a Greek-Turkish federation and joint exploration for oil in the disputed waters of the Aegean by the New Democracy minister without portfolio and maverick musician-cum-politician, Mikis Theodorakis, was not well received. Rumours that the border might be sealed prompted some 3,500 Albanians, mainly members of the Greek minority, to flood across the frontier between 31 December 1990 and 1 January 1991. In mid-January the Prime Minister visited Albania to urge members of the Greek minority to remain in situ in the hope of better times. On 20 January the government declared that no-one would be allowed to cross the frontier without a visa. At the end of the year large numbers of illegal Albanian immigrants were rounded up and returned to Albania, on the grounds that they were responsible for a crime wave. This move prompted vigorous protests from the Albanian government.

In February a US State Department report alleging 'economic and social discrimination against the Muslim minority in Western Thrace', and recognizing the existence of a small Slav Macedonian minority in Greece, caused a storm of protest. The growing antagonism between Serbia and Croatia caused considerable alarm, with the government making no secret of its sympathy for the Serbian cause and its wish to see the maintenance of federal Yugoslavia. The prospect of the emergence of an independent Macedonia prompted the Foreign Minister, Antonis Samaras, repeatedly to declare that Greece would never recognize a state calling itself Macedonia. In December, at the Maastricht EC summit, Greece achieved a major foreign policy objective, namely admission to the Western European Union. In mid-July President Bush, to the accompaniment of violent protests and unprecedented security precautions, visited Greece on his way to Turkey. In the course of his visit he thanked Greece for its contribution, in the shape of a frigate, to the allied effort in the Gulf War (see V.2).

The 77-year-old Ecumenical Patriarch Dimitrios I died in Istanbul on 3 October and was succeeded by the 51-year-old Bartholomaios, Metropolitan of Chalcedon, who was elected by the 15-member Holy Synod.

vi. CYPRUS

CAPITAL: Nicosia   AREA: 9,250 sq km   POPULATION: 706,900 ('91)
POLITICAL SYSTEM: separate presidential democracies in Greek area and in Turkish Republic of Northern Cyprus (recognized only by Turkey)
HEAD OF STATE AND GOVERNMENT: President Georgios Vassiliou (since Feb '88); Rauf Denktash has been President of Turkish area since Feb '75
PRINCIPAL MINISTERS: (Greek Cyprus) Georgios Iacovou (foreign affairs), Georgios Syrimis (finance), Christodoulos Veniamin (interior), Andreas Aloneftis (defence), Nikolaos Papaioannou (justice)
INTERNATIONAL ALIGNMENT: (Greek Cyprus) NAM, Cwth.
CURRENCY: Cyprus pound (end-'91 £1=C£00.81, US$1=C£00.44)
GNP PER CAPITA: Greek Cyprus US$9,010 ('91), Turkish Cyprus $3,600 ('91)
MAIN EXPORT EARNERS: tourism, textiles, agricultural products

THE year began with seemingly good prospects for a peace settlement. Elections on 20 May to the 56-seat Greek Cypriot parliament gave a clear victory to parties supporting President Vassiliou's efforts at a constitutional settlement. The conservative Democratic Rally again took 19 seats (and helped an allied Liberal candidate to win a seat); the communist AKEL gained three to take 18; and the Democratic Party of former President Spyros Kyprianou, which had spearheaded the 'rejectionist' front, lost five to stand at just 11. The socialist EDEK party took the remaining seven seats.

The US government, which during the Gulf crisis had insisted on the need for international implementation of UN resolutions, felt morally obliged to involve itself actively in the search for a Cyprus solution. President Bush proposed a UN-sponsored high-level meeting which would directly involve the Greek and Turkish governments in the negotiating process for the first time since the 1970s. He offered himself as a 'catalyst' in the process, and during meetings with Prime Minister Mitsotakis of Greece and President Özal of Turkey in July secured their agreement to 'a well-prepared meeting' chaired by the UN Secretary-General. After considerable wrangling, Greece reluctantly agreed to quadripartite talks involving the Greek and Turkish governments and the two Cypriot communal leaders.

During July and August the special representatives of the UN Secretary-General, Oscar Camilion and Gustave Feissel, conducted intensive negotiations with officials in Athens and Ankara, moving on to Cyprus during the first fortnight of September. There, assisted by a third

UN representative, they held daily talks with the leadership of both communities. The first sign that the process was going off the rails came at a meeting between the Greek and Turkish Prime Ministers in Paris on 12 September on the fringes of the conference of the European Democrat Union, when the two leaders acknowledged 'some differences of view'. The UN Secretary-General, Javier Pérez de Cuellar, subsequently implied that Prime Minister Yilmaz of Turkey, then locked into a fierce general election battle (which he lost—see III.3.vii), had indicated that he would not attend the proposed conference personally.

Moreover, in a report on his mission of good offices submitted on 8 October, Sr Pérez de Cuellar referred to a more fundamental problem. Mr Denktash, he said, was insisting that each Cypriot community had sovereignty—including the right of secession—which it would retain after the establishment of a federation. The UN Secretary-General concluded that this was contrary to his agreed mandate, which was to 'preserve the sovereignty, independence and territorial integrity of the state of Cyprus'.

This position was reaffirmed by the UN Security Council in resolution 716 of 11 October. Having persistently argued that the UN had been wrong in 1964 to acknowledge the solely Greek Cypriot administration as the legitimate government of the island, Mr Denktash angrily dismissed the resolution. He said that it was the equivalent of starting a game as a loser because the 'referees have already determined the scores', adding that his administration would stay away from the playing field until 'balance is established'.

On 13 October there were by-elections for 12 of the 50 seats in the Turkish Cypriot Assembly. The seats had been held by pro-settlement opposition MPs who had boycotted the Assembly since the May 1990 elections because of the alleged bias of the electoral law in favour of the ruling National Unity Party (NUP), which supported a separatist line. In a 67 per cent turnout, the NUP took 11 of the 12 seats, giving it a total of 45 in the Assembly.

On the Turkish mainland, the 20 October general elections produced a hung parliament and, after prolonged negotiations, a conservative-socialist coalition under veteran politician Süleyman Demirel. Because of the precarious nature of the coalition, neither party could be seen to be making concessions regarding Cyprus. Mr Demirel accordingly adopted the line that a Cyprus settlement should be pursued between the island's communities under UN auspices. On his retirement as UN Secretary-General at year's end, Sr Pérez de Cuellar expressed disappointment that after 16 years' close association with the Cyprus issue he had in the end failed to secure a solution.

In the course of 1991, the Republic of Cyprus was removed from the World Bank list of developing countries after average annual income had risen above $9,000, making it the 24th richest country in the world on a per capita basis. In the 'Turkish Republic of Northern Cyprus', per capita income remained at around $3,600. Ending such economic disparity was one of the principal factors motivating Turkish Cypriots who favoured a federal settlement.

vii. TURKEY

CAPITAL: Ankara AREA: 781,000 sq km POPULATION: 57,000,000 ('90)
OFFICIAL LANGUAGE: Turkish
POLITICAL SYSTEM: parliamentary democracy
HEAD OF STATE: President Turgut Özal (since Nov '89)
RULING PARTIES: True Path Party (DYP) and Social Democratic Populists (SHP)
HEAD OF GOVERNMENT: Süleyman Demirel (DYP), Prime Minister (since Nov '91)
PRINCIPAL MINISTERS: Erdal İnönü (SHP/deputy premier), Hikmet Çetin (foreign affairs), Seyfi Oktay (justice), Nevzat Ayaz (defence), Ismat Sezgin (interior), Sümer Oral (finance)
INTERNATIONAL ALIGNMENT: NATO, OECD, ICO, ECO
CURRENCY: lira (end-'91 £1=LT9,518.63, US$1=LT5,092.90)
GNP PER CAPITA: US$1,456 ('89)
MAIN EXPORT EARNERS: textiles, iron and steel, agricultural products, tourism

THE prestige won by President Turgut Özal in the ranks of the allies during the Gulf War did not avert the defeat of the Motherland Party, which he had founded, in the general elections in October.

Under President Özal's leadership, Turkey made three major contributions to the defeat of the Iraqi dictator Saddam Husain: it closed down the twin pipeline from Kirkuk to the Turkish Mediterranean terminal at Yumurtalik; it tied down a considerable part of the Iraqi army on its frontier; and, most important, it allowed the use of bases on its territory by allied warplanes in offensive operations against Iraq (see also V.2). In so doing, Turkey disregarded Saddam Husain's threat to retaliate, which was not implemented. But the war caused losses to the Turkish economy, through the cessation of trade and commercial relations with Iraq and Kuwait, the need to procure crude oil from more distant sources, the decline in revenue from tourism and the effects of the general world recession. While most of these losses would have been inevitable, whatever the policy pursued by Turkey, the willing promptness of President Özal's support for the allied cause was rewarded with grants and credits amounting to some US$4,000 million.

However, the political consequences of the Gulf War were mixed. Its effect in strengthening Turkey's relations with the United States was illustrated by President Özal's visit to Camp David on 22–24 March, and President George Bush's return visit to Turkey on 20–21 July. But any hope that President Özal may have entertained that US influence would hasten Turkey's admission as a full member of the European

Community was disappointed. In an attempt to remove one obstacle to admission, President Bush secured the agreement of both President Özal and of the Greek Prime Minister, Konstantinos Mitsotakis, to a conference where the two were to have been joined by the leaders of the Greek and Turkish communities in Cyprus. However, the quadripartite conference, which had first been proposed by President Özal in 1990, could not convene in the absence of sufficient common ground for the solution of the Cyprus problem (see III.3.vi).

The Gulf War also exacerbated the Kurdish problem as both an external and an internal threat to Turkey. On his return from the United States at the beginning of April, President Özal learned that hundreds of thousands of Iraqi Kurds had fled to the Turkish frontier from the advance of Saddam Husain's troops, who had crushed their rebellion. Turkey's refusal to admit the refugees, coupled with its insistence that conditions should be established for their return home, led to the creation for them of a safe haven in northern Iraq by the force of allied arms. However, the safe haven was also used by terrorists of the PKK (Kurdish Workers' Party), who could thus increase their attacks on Turkish security forces in their campaign to carve out an independent (or, at least, autonomous) Kurdish area in south-eastern Turkey. Syria, which President Özal visited at the end of the Gulf War as a member of the anti-Iraqi coalition, did not close the camps of the PKK (or of ethnic Turkish left-wing terrorists) in the Bekaa valley of eastern Lebanon or expel the PKK leader, Abdullah Öcalan, from his refuge in Damascus. Moreover, any loss of direct Syrian support to the PKK was made good by Saddam Husain when the terrorists transferred their forward bases to northern Iraq.

Efforts by the Turkish government, under President Özal's direct guidance, to parry the threat by a policy of liberalization at home, coupled with incursions against terrorist bases in northern Iraq, did not improve the security situation. The lifting of the ban on the use of the Kurdish language and of the proscription of marxist and religious political parties was welcomed by liberal opinion abroad, which was, however, critical of Turkish cross-border operations.

At home, criticism of Mr Özal's use of the presidential office—which had been conceived as one of an impartial, and largely ceremonial, arbiter—for the direct formulation of policy intensified as the Gulf War put a stop to economic growth. Moreover, a split developed inside the ruling Motherland Party, when the First Lady, Semra Özal, was elected on 3 March, on a second attempt, to the leadership of the Istanbul provincial organization, against the votes of religious conservatives. The latter included the President's cousin, Hüsnü Dogan, whose dismissal as Minister of Defence weakened Özal's original nominee, Prime Minister Yildirim Akbulut. At its convention on 15 June, the Motherland Party removed Mr Akbulut from the leadership, replacing him with the former

Foreign Minister, Mesut Yilmaz, who formed a new administration on 23 June.

As public opinion surveys showed a disastrous loss of support for the Motherland Party, Mr Yilmaz gambled on calling general elections a year before the term of parliament was due to expire, while seeking to allay dissatisfaction by implementing large increases in wages, salaries and farm support prices. The decision to hold early elections made it impossible to amend the consitution, as President Özal had suggested earlier. But the Motherland Party did succeed in making minor modifications to the electoral law.

These modifications did not save its fortunes. In the elections, held on 20 October, the Party of the Right Path (or True Path Party), led by Mr Özal's rival for the votes of the centre-right, ex-prime minister Süleyman Demirel, came first with 178 seats in the 450-member parliament and 27 per cent of the total poll. The Motherland Party was second with 115 seats and 24 per cent of the popular vote. The Social Democratic Populist Party (SHP), led by Professor Erdal Inönü, was third with 88 seats and a 20 per cent share of the poll. It was a disappointing result for the left, notwithstanding an electoral alliance between the Social Democrats and the (largely Kurdish) Toiling People's Party, some 20 of whose members were elected on the SHP ticket. The fundamentalist Welfare Party, led by Professor Necmettin Erbakan, having also formed an alliance—with the racist Nationalist Labour Party of Colonel (rtd) Alpaslan Türkeş—increased its share of the poll to 17 per cent and won 62 seats. However, soon after the election, Mr Türkeş and 17 of his supporters broke from the fundamentalists and returned to their old party. Finally, the Party of the Democratic Left, led by Bülent Ecevit (also a former prime minister), received 11 per cent of the total vote and secured 7 seats in parliament, having for the first time exceeded the minimum 10 per cent needed for parliamentary representation.

On 20 November Mr Demirel formed a coalition government with the SHP, whose leader became deputy prime minister. The government, in which Mr Demirel's party held most of the economic portfolios and in which the SHP secretary-general, Hikmet Çetin, became Foreign Minister, was confirmed in office by parliament on 30 November by 280 votes to 164.

On 6 December both Mr Demirel and Mr Inönü went to the Kurdish-speaking south-eastern region, where the Prime Minister proclaimed his recognition of Kurdish identity and promised that if Saddam Husain attempted any fresh outrage against the Kurds he would find Turkey facing him. However, any hopes that terrorism would be ended by these declarations of principle, or by simultaneous promises by the government to make good all deficiencies in the practice of democracy, were quickly disappointed. On 25 December the reality of the guerrilla war in the south-east was brought home to the inhabitants of Istanbul when a department store belonging to the brothers of the emergency governor of the south-eastern region, Necati Çetinkaya, was set on fire by PKK terrorists, with the loss of 11 lives. At the same time, difficulties were made for the coalition by radical statements in parliament by Kurdish nationalists elected as members of the SHP. Left-wing terrorism, which had earlier claimed the lives of five serving or retired generals, continued with the murder of the deputy commissioner of the Istanbul police on 4 December.

Turkey's regional influence grew as a result of the dissolution of the Soviet Union. Turkey was the first foreign country to recognize the independence of Azerbaijan in November. In December it extended recognition to all the other ex-Soviet republics. The presidents of Kazakhstan, Turkmenia, Uzbekistan and Kirghiza visited Ankara, where they declared that their Turkic republics would give priority to Turkey in establishing their foreign relations.

After a slight drop in overall economic activity in the first half of the year, growth resumed slowly in the third quarter. The slowdown did not affect the inexorable rise in prices, and the urban consumer price index (usually taken as a measure of inflation) rose by 71 per cent over the year. However, Gulf aid, the fall in oil prices and rising exports all but wiped out the deficit in the external current account, thus giving the Demirel government the chance to attract fresh funds. Moreover, Turkey's integration in the world market was advanced by the signature of a free trade agreement with the European Free Trade Association.

Economic difficulties did not prevent progress in major public works. The twin tunnels designed to draw water from the newly-built Atatürk dam on the Euphrates to irrigate the northern Mesopotamian plain were completed, and work continued on the conversion of Ankara and Istanbul to natural gas, and on the construction of a motorway from the Bulgarian frontier to Ankara and beyond.

IV EASTERN EUROPE

1. POLAND—CZECHOSLOVAKIA—HUNGARY—
ROMANIA—BULGARIA—YUGOSLAVIA—ALBANIA

i. POLAND

CAPITAL: Warsaw AREA: 313,000 sq km POPULATION: 37,900,000 ('89)
OFFICIAL LANGUAGE: Polish POLITICAL SYSTEM: presidential democracy
HEAD OF STATE: President Lech Walesa (since Dec '90)
RULING PARTIES: Citizens' Centre Alliance heads coalition
PRINCIPAL MINISTERS: Jan Olszewski (prime minister), Leszek Balcerowicz (finance),
 Krzystof Skubiszewski (foreign affairs), Vice-Adml. Piotr Kolodziejczyk (defence)
INTERNATIONAL ALIGNMENT: towards Western Europe
CURRENCY: zloty (end '91 £1=Zl.19,526.00, US$1=Zl.10,458.00)
GNP PER CAPITA: US$1,790 ('89)
MAIN EXPORT EARNERS: engineering equipment, coal, metals, agricultural produce

THIS was the second year of economic 'shock therapy' and the first of competitive elections. The latter resulted in a hung parliament (Sejm) unable to form the strong government necessary to keep economic reform going. Moreover, the powers of President Walesa grew steadily throughout the year, leading to increased tension within the Polish constitution.

On 4 January the President's nominee as Prime Minister, Jan Bielecki, was approved by the Sejm by 276 votes to 58, with 52 abstentions. In his acceptance speech on 5 January, Mr Bielecki pledged to develop the free-market policies introduced by his precedessor (see AR 1990, p. 115). To emphasize continuity and to reassure Western creditors, the architect of the former policy, Leszek Balcerowicz, remained Finance Minister. Also retained were the Foreign and Defence Ministers.

This was widely regarded as an interim administration, intended to last only until a general election in the spring; but it remained in office until October, whilst a new constitution was being hammered out. It thus held power at a time of major upheavals in East-West relations as a new international order was created following the collapse of the Soviet Union (see IV.2.i).

On 21 January the governments of Poland, Hungary and Czechoslovakia announced their withdrawal from the Warsaw Pact, to take effect on 1 July. All three countries expressed their readiness for closer relations with NATO, possibly resulting in eventual membership. Poland also protested to the Soviet Union over the 50,000 Red Army troops still stationed on its territory. Until a timetable for their removal was agreed, transit rights would be denied across Polish territory for Soviet military forces and equipment due to return home from eastern Germany.

Poland's reintegration into the world economy continued to be overshadowed by a hard currency debt. Borrowings and outstanding interest, built up in the 1970s and 1980s to the Paris Club of 17 creditor nations and to commercial banks, had reached $48,500 million. In March Poland suspended interest payments to its commercial creditors, demanding debt reductions. On 15 March the Paris Club took the unprecedented step of writing off one half of Poland's inter-governmental borrowings. This was, however, conditional upon Poland's adherence to an IMF programme for monetary stabilization, as a necessary prelude to radical restructuring of the whole economy. On 20 March the United States promised to cut bilateral debts of $2,900 million by 70 per cent, as a token of its commitment to Poland's democratic transition. Germany and France had already made similar reductions.

As part of its IMF agreement, Poland undertook to reduce government spending by a third. In order to achieve fiscal equilibrium, harsh cuts were made successively to social projects and welfare benefits. These continued throughout the year, as the budget deficit still overshot previously-agreed targets. The shortfall was exacerbated by a drop in revenues, as state sector output fell and the rate of privatization proved much slower than reformers had planned, partly because of domestic political opposition. There was a substantial reduction of the original number of enterprises whose ownership was to be transferred to the people through share distribution (see AR 1990, p. 115).

Recession deepened during the year, further jeopardizing the country's political future. Output fell by 3 per cent (following a fall of 13 per cent in 1990). Partly by means of harsh government penalties for inflationary settlements, wages in the state sector were contained and the previous year's record inflation of up to 550 per cent was reduced to 60–80 per cent. But unemployment doubled to 12 per cent. There was anxiety amongst policy-makers and the public alike that the government-sponsored recession could not be overcome without a major injection of Western capital. But that in turn would add to unemployment by improving productivity.

Salvation was sought in an association agreement with the European Community (EC), signed in December. This relaxed EC constraints on previously-sensitive imports of Polish agricultural products, as well as textiles, steel and chemicals. The prospect of full membership was also reiterated, though both sides recognized that this was still a distant goal, contingent upon much greater progress in economic restructuring.

The rapid introduction of competitive elections, to replace the partly-free parliament elected under the 'round table' agreement of April 1989, was proposed by President Walesa on 7 March. His impatience with the pace of democratic change was understandable: Poland, the pioneer in 1989, was now alone in having a communist-dominated parliament. But parliament rejected his proposed constitutional amendments and postponed its own dissolution until October. The members of the old communist *nomenklatura* and the new democratic forces both hoped to regroup during the interval.

The following months saw hectic political manoeuvring, largely regarded with indifference by a majority of the population. The one potentially explosive issue—anti-abortion legislation sponsored by the Roman Catholic Church—was defused in May, when the Sejm rejected highly restrictive legislation. An amendment was passed (by 208 votes to 145, with 14 abstentions) to transfer the question to a wider review of social legislation, leaving constitutional implications to a commission of the Ministry of Justice.

In June the prolonged constitutional wrangle between President Walesa and the outgoing parliament over a new electoral system was resolved. The new law combined proportional representation on a constituency basis with a small number of seats reserved for 'national lists' of candidates from the most successful political groupings. So great was the propensity towards pluralism, highly reminiscent of the 1920s, that voters eventually faced a ballot paper with 67 parties. Of these, 29 won at least one seat, but perhaps the most significant statistic was that 56.8 per cent of the electorate did not vote.

The new Sejm covered a wide political spectrum. The ex-communist Democratic Left Alliance came a close second to the post-Solidarity party headed by former Prime Minister Mazowiecki, namely the Democratic Union. Prime Minister Bielecki (whose Liberal-Democratic Congress had come sixth in the poll) was asked to continue in office until a successor could be appointed. But on 29 October, two days after the vote, President Walesa proposed himself as Prime Minister, citing the pre-war precedent of Marshal Pilsudski. This suggestion galvanized the new deputies into action.

Following the failure of the Democratic Union to form a coalition, attempts were made to align the centre-right deputies of the Catholic Electoral Action Party (headed by Justice Minister Chrzanowski), the Polish Peasant Party and the nationalist Confederation of Independent Poland. However, despite tacit support from the Catholic Church, such a potential grouping could not agree an economic programme. In particular, the peasantry sought relief from the former government's austerity programme.

A key role in the negotiations was played by Jan Olszewski, a member of the Citizens' Centre Alliance and an independent lawyer with a long record of defending human rights cases. After a series of difficult meetings with Mr Olszewski, President Walesa nominated him as Prime Minister on 6 December on condition that he could obtain a majority within the Sejm. After initially giving up this task, Mr Olszewski obtained the necessary majority. The President confirmed him in office and the year ended as it had begun with a new Prime Minister about to form a government.

ii. CZECHOSLOVAKIA

CAPITAL: Prague   AREA: 128,000 sq km   POPULATION: 15,600,000 ('89)
OFFICIAL LANGUAGES: Czech, Slovak
POLITICAL SYSTEM: federal parliamentary democracy
HEAD OF STATE: President Václav Havel (since Dec '89)
RULING PARTIES: coalition of Civic Democratic Party (CDP), Civic Movement (CM), Civic Democratic Union–Public against Violence (CDU–PAV) and Christian and Democratic Union/Christian Democratic Movement (CDU/CDM)
PRINCIPAL MINISTERS: Marian Čalfa (CDU-PAV/prime minister), Václav Klaus (CDP/deputy premier, finance), Pavel Hoffman (ind./deputy premier), Pavel Rychetsky (CM/deputy premier, legislative affairs), Jozef Miklosko (CDM/deputy premier, human rights), Jiri Dienstbier (CM/deputy premier, foreign affairs), Lubos Dubrovsky (CM/defence), Jan Langos (CDU-PAV/interior), Vladimir Dlouhy (CM/economy)
INTERNATIONAL ALIGNMENT: towards Western Europe
CURRENCY: koruna (end-'91 £1=K50.32, US$1=K26.95)
GNP PER CAPITA: US$3,450 ('89)
MAIN EXPORT EARNERS: machinery, chemicals and fuels, manufactured goods

CZECHOSLOVAKIA'S second year of democracy was marked by significant changes in the political spectrum, the beginning of privatization, removing the vestiges of the country's communist past and almost complete emancipation from Soviet dominance. The single most important development, however, was a virtual deadlock over the question of power-sharing between the two constituent republics and the federation. Despite calls by President Václav Havel for new constitutions before the end of 1991, it proved impossible to agree on the fundamental issue of Czechoslovakia's future constitutional status. The first stages of the discussion on the new republican and federal constitutions involved only the leaders of the two republican parliaments and governments. The two sides quickly became deadlocked over when to adopt these constitutions. Although the leaderships of the Czech and Slovak parliaments finally agreed that the constitutions should be preceded by an inter-republic treaty clearly defining the distribution of power between federal and republican institutions, they disagreed on the significance of the treaty. The Czech representatives considered it a legislative initiative of the two national parliaments, which would not affect the position of the Federal Assembly. Slovak officials insisted that the treaty should be considered a binding document, on at least an equal footing with the federal constitution.

After long parliamentary disputes, the Federal Assembly eventually adopted a law in July permitting a referendum on the country's constitutional set-up. Hopes that a referendum could solve the conflict remained unfulfilled, as Federal Assembly deputies were unable to agree on the wording of the question to be put to the vote. Three attempts by nationalist deputies in the Slovak National Council to declare sovereignty by adopting a so-called 'full' constitution (meaning one not deriving from the federal constitution) narrowly failed. Confronted with the virtual deadlock in the talks between the two republics as well as growing nationalism in Slovakia, President Havel proposed a series of constitutional changes which, among other things, would have given him the power to dissolve the Federal Assembly if necessary and to call a referendum without parliamentary approval. The President's suggestions were, however, immediately criticized by leading politicians in both republics. Thus the constitutional stalemate persisted and there was no solution in sight, as the country seemed to slide toward disintegration.

Major changes occurred in the Czechoslovak political spectrum during 1991. While President Havel remained the most popular actor on the political stage and an important integrating element, his once-dominant role was diminished to some degree by the gradual emergence of strong political parties. The country's previously leading political forces—the Civic Forum (CF) in the Czech Republic, and its Slovak counterpart, Public against Violence, which had scored an impressive victory in the June 1990 elections (see AR 1990, p. 120)—split into a number of separate parties. On the Czech side, Finance Minister Václav Klaus established the conservative Civic Democratic Party and Foreign Minister Jiri Dienstbier the left-of-centre Civic Movement. Other deputies in the Federal Assembly and the Czech National Council (parliament) left the CF and joined the ranks of the Social Democratic Party, which had previously not been represented in any of the three parliaments. Public against Violence disintegrated in March, when Vladimír Mečiar, the then Slovak Prime Minister, founded the nationalist Movement for a Democratic Slovakia. After Mr Mečiar had lost a vote of confidence in the Slovak National Council and had been replaced by Ján Čarnogurský, the movement quickly became a strong opposition force with which the ruling Slovak coalition of Christian Democrats, the tiny Democratic Party and the remnants of Public against Violence had to reckon. Faced with a dramatic drop in public support, Public against Violence eventually transformed itself into the Civic Democratic Union, which was ideologically close to Václav Klaus's Civic Democratic Party.

In view of the parliamentary elections scheduled for June 1992, several parties decided to form pre-election coalitions. The Communist Party, which had gained a respectable 10 per cent in the June 1990 elections, maintained a low profile and seemed to benefit only from the tactical mistakes of the other political parties. In late 1991 the party split into three formations, each of which had a different ideological orientation. Polls throughout the year indicated that while conservative and right-of-centre parties enjoyed relatively strong support in the Czech republic, there was a significant shift toward nationalist and leftist movements in Slovakia.

Efforts to deal with Czechoslovakia's communist past continued throughout the year. In October the Federal Assembly approved a law providing for the dismissal of officials who had been high-ranking Communist Party officials before November 1989 or had collaborated with the notorious state security police. The law was to remain in effect for five years and could affect hundreds of thousands of people, including such personalities as Alexander Dubček. Although the measures taken were popular among most Czechs and Slovaks, some critics condemned the law as 'institutionalized revenge'.

With the adoption of several laws in the Federal Assembly, Czechoslovakia entered the crucial phase of privatization. In January price controls were removed and internal convertibility of the koruna introduced. Owing to a relatively strict fiscal policy, the exchange rate of the koruna against major Western currencies remained fairly stable throughout the year. Also in January the process began of auctioning off some 70,000 small state-owned businesses (referred to as 'small privatization'), as did the restitution of property confiscated after February 1948. Industrial production decreased by about 10 per cent and construction by almost 34 per cent. Inflation rose sharply in the first months of 1991 (by about 40 per cent), but remained fairly stable for the rest of the year. Despite several wage increases secured by the maturing trade unions, wages failed to keep pace with price increases. The unemployment rate reached some 6 per cent, which was considerably lower than had been predicted by the government. However, Slovakia, with its less developed infrastructure and heavy industries (including armaments), was harder hit by unemployment than the Czech republic. Moreover, Slovakia's proximity to the Soviet Union, and its considerable reliance on the Soviet market and Soviet supplies, did further damage to its economic performance. Despite the hardships that accompanied economic reform, there were no major strikes and no significant social tensions. It was widely expected that unemployment would increase dramatically once the so-called 'large privatization' of state-owned companies had got under way, probably in 1992.

Czechoslovakia's reorientation of its foreign-trade policy was best illustrated by the fact that exports to members of the former Council for Mutual Economic Assistance (CMEA) dropped by 55 per cent in 1991 and trade with the West started to increase. An important indicator of Czechoslovakia's current international standing was the extent of inward foreign investment. About 3,000 joint ventures were operating by year's end, among them such powerful partnerships as the car manufacturers Škoda and Volkswagen. However, economists predicted that foreign capital would start flowing into the country only after the conflict over the constitutional structure of Czechoslovakia had been resolved.

In the foreign political sphere, Czechoslovakia continued to strengthen its ties with the West, while abandoning some of its idealistic rhetoric of the early post-communist period. In 1991 its foreign policy was marked by an almost complete emancipation from Soviet dominance. The last Soviet troops stationed in Czechoslovakia since the military intervention of August 1968 left the country; the Warsaw Pact and the CMEA were dissolved; and the two states initialed a friendship treaty, which, unlike all previous treaties between Czechoslovakia and the USSR, omitted any provision that effectively limited Czechoslovak sovereignty. After the coup attempt in Moscow in August and the subsequent onset of the disintegration of the USSR, Czechoslovakia quickly adapted its foreign policy, recognizing the independence of the three Baltic republics and, after that republic's overwhelming vote for independence, the Ukraine.

Czechoslovakia also continued to improve relations with its other neighbours, signing or initialing friendship treaties with a number of West European states. The most significant of these was a treaty with Germany, which stated that neither party had any territorial claims on the other, that all conflicts would have to be solved in a peaceful manner and that ethnic minorities in both countries would be granted full rights. Other successes of Czechoslovakia's foreign policy included the country's admission as a full member of the Council of Europe (see XI.5.2); its association accord with the European Community (see XI.3); and the establishment of diplomatic relations with previously-shunned states, such as Saudi Arabia and South Africa.

The fact that Czechoslovakia was not able to gain any kind of security guarantee from the North Atlantic Treaty Organization (NATO) was considered a failure for foreign policy. Moreover, the poor performance of the Conference on Security and Cooperation in Europe in crisis management during the continuing Yugoslav conflict was also a disappointing reflection on Czechoslovak diplomacy, since Foreign Minister Dienstbier was among its main protagonists (see XI.5.i).

iii. HUNGARY

CAPITAL: Budapest   AREA: 93,000 sq km   POPULATION: 10,600,000 ('89)
OFFICIAL LANGUAGE: Hungarian   POLITICAL SYSTEM: multi-party democracy
HEAD OF STATE: President Árpád Göncz (since Aug '90)
RULING PARTY: coalition led by Hungarian Democratic Forum (HDF)
HEAD OF GOVERNMENT: József Antall, Prime Minister (since May '90)
PRINCIPAL MINISTERS: Géza Jeszenszky (foreign affairs), Lajos Für (defence), Péter Boross (interior), Mihaly Kupa (finance), István Balsai (justice)
INTERNATIONAL ALIGNMENT: towards Western Europe
CURRENCY: forint (end-'91 £1=Ft142.34, US$1=Ft76.24)
GNP PER CAPITA: US$2,590 ('89)
MAIN EXPORT EARNERS: machinery and transport equipment, agricultural products, basic manufactures

THE year in Hungary passed off without any major upsets, but there were numerous indications that the political process was marked by a growing sense of dissatisfaction with the newly-instituted democratic process. The chief problem was the slow pace of change, especially in the economic sphere. To an extent, this was inherent in the nature of the situation. The transformation of a communist economy into a marketized one was always going to be hard. In particular, the dismantling of the state-supported industrial complex posed, it seemed, near-insuperable difficulties.

The new parliamentary system coalesced into a very clearly divided ruling coalition and opposition, with the Prime Minister, József Antall, dominating the scene to a great extent. This had its drawbacks, as Mr Antall was neither an experienced politician nor a practised administrator, with the result that the government's strategy seemed hesitant and dilatory. A major programme of economic transformation, known as the Kupa Plan after its author, the Finance Minister, was announced in February, but was never fully adopted by the coalition itself. The pace of privatization, which unlike the Polish and Czechoslovak projects was to be achieved entirely through private investment from within Hungary and from the West, was slow. The recession in the West was no help in this respect. Nevertheless, Hungary received well over half of all the Western investment going to the post-communist countries. If nothing else, this was a sign of Western confidence in the country and of the higher level of adaptation to Western requirements in terms of simplifying the bureaucracy and legal procedures.

Overall, in terms of foreign trade, Hungary performed reasonably well. In respect of the domestic economy, the rate of inflation reached around 35 per cent at the end of year, but analysts suggested that it was on the decline and would fall to around 20–25 per cent in 1992. This was achieved largely through tighter budgetary controls. The new law governing the National Bank, which came into effect in November, provided for a considerable degree of independence for its chairman, this being regarded as an essential precondition for economic success. The negative side was a rising tide of poverty. Unemployment reached 7.3 per cent towards the end of the year and was increasing. Those on or below the minimum acceptable level were dangerously close to two-fifths of the population and would constitute fertile ground for any demagogic populism.

Indeed, there was no shortage of potential demagogues and populists. Within the Hungarian Democratic Forum (HDF), the largest component in the ruling coalition, the populist current continued to insist on Hungarian nationalism as the only salvation. And the pre-eminent figure in the Smallholders Party (one of the smaller coalition partners), József Torgyán, emerged as an effective spokesman for elements impatient with the democratic process. He was highly unpopular with the opposition, which regarded him as a dangerous authoritarian.

Currents of authoritarianism could also be found in the HDF. The chairman of its parliamentary group, Imre Kónya, was responsible for a document that in effect called for the abolition of media freedom, at any rate in the electronic media. In this, Mr Kónya was giving expression to a widespread view in the government that it was not receiving fair treatment in the media and that it should do something to remedy this. In consequence, relations between government and media deteriorated, as the latter concluded that it was the target of a government campaign.

Nor were relations harmonious between the government and President Árpád Göncz. The presidency had been conceived of as a fairly weak institution, but President Göncz sought to invest it with a degree of authority and influence, something to which the government objected. The conflict between the two was eventually referred to the constitutional court, which ruled more in favour of the government than of the president.

The court was called on again, over the legality of the so-called Zétényi-Takács law on political justice. Named after the two deputies who launched it, this measure would make it possible to institute proceedings against senior figures of the communist era on charges of murder or treason. The court had still to report by the end of the year. The law was strongly opposed by the opposition and much of the legal establishment, which felt that it set aside the presumption of innocence.

The opposition itself was experiencing difficulties in adjusting to its role. Just as the government found it hard to come to terms with the demands of exercising power, so the opposition had some trouble in constructing a consistent line on what it should be doing. Should it maintain an all-out critique of everything initiated by the coalition or should it seek to emerge as a responsible alternative with an eye on the next elections? In the event, the chairman of the Alliance of Free Democrats, János Kis, decided to resign and Péter Tölgyessy was elected as his successor. Mr Tölgyessy was expected to adopt a more combative stance, one more geared to the demands of day-to-day politics than his predecessor's approach as head of the largest opposition party.

The most positive development for the opposition was that it consistently out-performed the coalition in the opinion polls. However, it was Fidesz (the Alliance of Young Democrats) which benefited particularly, regularly receiving the backing of 25–30 per cent of those polled; the Free Democrats and the Hungarian Socialist Party (the successor to the communists) did less well.

In foreign affairs, Hungary had two overriding concerns: relations with the West and the Yugoslav crisis (see IV.1.vi). Its strategy towards the West was essentially aimed at gaining acceptance as a serious, normal European country and, ultimately, admission to the European Community (EC) and NATO. These were long-term objectives, obviously. In the shorter term, integration was being pursued with the other two Central European states, Poland and Czechoslovakia, notably at two summits held in Visegrád and Cracow. With respect to Yugoslavia, Hungary instinctively supported Crotia and Slovenia and recognized them in December, following the German and EC decisions to that effect. The problem of the 400,000-strong Hungarian minority in Serbia exercised the Budapest government greatly, especially as it was powerless to do anything to prevent anti-Hungarian measures from being implemented by the Serbs.

iv. ROMANIA

CAPITAL: Bucharest   AREA: 237,500 sq km   POPULATION: 23,200,000 ('89)
OFFICIAL LANGUAGE: Romanian
POLITICAL SYSTEM: emerging democracy
HEAD OF STATE: President Ion Iliescu (since Dec '89)
RULING PARTIES: National Salvation Front (NSF), National Liberal Party (NLP), Romanian Ecological Movement (REM) Agrarian Democratic Party (ADP)
HEAD OF GOVERNMENT: Theodor Stolojan, Prime Minister (since Oct '91)
PRINCIPAL MINISTERS: Adrian Năstase (foreign affairs), Gen. Nicolae Constantin Spiroiu (defence), Mircea Ionescu-Quintus (justice), Victor Babiuc (interior), George Danielescu (economy & finance)
INTERNATIONAL ALIGNMENT: towards Western Europe
CURRENCY: leu (end-'91 £1=354.18 lei, US$1=189.70 lei)
GNP PER CAPITA: US$2,540 ('81)
MAIN EXPORT EARNERS: oil, raw materials and metals, machinery and transport equipment, chemicals, tourism

THE second year under the post-Ceaușescu regime was marked by persistent political instability, worsening economic problems and deep-rooted social discontent. Together, these circumstances led to riots by miners in September which brought down Prime Minister Petre Roman after 21 months in office.

The year opened with Mr Roman already under attack from two quarters. The opposition parties, in and out of parliament, continued their criticism of him for failing to broaden economic reform, beyond implementing massive price rises, and for harbouring many ex-communist officials in the government bureaucracy. Meanwhile, many of these former communists within Mr Roman's ruling National Salvation Front (NSF) did their utmost to obstruct his market-oriented economic policies. These conservatives enjoyed the sympathy of President Ion Iliescu, whose personal relations with Mr Roman gradually deteriorated as their political views diverged.

Nonetheless, Mr Roman managed to consolidate his position as the NSF leader at the party's first national congress in March, when several of his closest supporters were elected to senior posts. Two small groups of conservatives opposed to his policies broke away from the NSF, and one of his most outspoken critics, Alexandru Bîrlădeanu, the 80-year-old president of the Senate, was expelled from the party.

Following the party congress—and in the wake of demonstrations against wide-ranging price rises in April—Mr Roman reshuffled his government. He had been seeking to form a coalition to broaden his political base, but his attempts to persuade the main opposition parties to join his administration failed in the face of their reluctance to become associated with an increasingly unpopular government. In any case, the posts on offer were relatively insignificant. The sham coalition that Mr Roman eventually formed had only two ministers who were not closely linked to the NSF. However, the Prime Minister persevered with his attempts to attract wider support by concluding a so-called Charter for Reform and Democracy with several less important political parties in July.

Meanwhile, growing economic hardship fuelled greater social discontent. In 1990 demonstrations had been staged mostly by students and opposition activists disillusioned by the continuing influence of ex-communist officials at all levels of authority. In 1991 they were increasingly joined by industrial workers protesting against falling living standards and worried by emerging unemployment. It was, ironically, the coalminers of the Jiu valley—earlier the mainstay of NSF (see AR 1990, pp. 128–9)—who finally toppled Mr Roman's government when thousands of them descended on Bucharest in September to demand higher wages and the Prime Minister's dismissal. In the ensuing riots, several people were killed and hundreds were injured.

In the midst of the riots, Mr Roman announced on 26 September that he was handing back his mandate. President Iliescu quickly accepted this decision, interpreting it as amounting to the Prime Minister's resignation. Mr Roman later claimed that the miners' violent action had been orchestrated by ex-communists opposed to his reforms. In fact, Theodor Stolojan, a 48-year-old economist entrusted with forming the new government, was a more committed advocate of market-oriented policies than his predecessor. An independent technocrat, he had resigned as finance minister from Mr Roman's government in March because he considered that the price liberalization planned at the time was not sufficiently far-reaching.

Mr Stolojan succeeded, where Mr Roman had failed, in forming a coalition government. The new administration announced in October had 16 NSF members or allies, four National Liberals (NLP) and two ministers from smaller parties. The price of enticing the NLP into the coalition was giving its representatives two important portfolios, economy and finance (George Danielescu) and justice (Mircea Ionescu-Quintus). The NLP's decision to join the government was a blow to the anti-NSF alliance of opposition parties, called the National Convention for the Creation of Democracy (NCCD), even though its leadership renewed its pledge to run candidates jointly with other NCCD parties in the elections scheduled for 1992. In any case, throughout the year the NCCD alliance failed to make political capital out of the NSF's rapidly declining popularity. The only parties to increase their approval rating in opinion polls were the nationalists associated with the Vatra Românească movement.

One of Mr Stolojan's first tasks was to steer Romania's new constitution through parliament. It was approved overwhelmingly in November and confirmed in a referendum on 8 December by a majority of 77 per cent of those voting. The new constitution accorded considerable powers to the President. But some of the strongest criticism directed against it came from the ethnic Hungarian community, who claimed that it provided insufficient guarantees for minority rights. Relations between the different ethnic communities had already come under further strain in October following the publication of a parliamentary report which accused ethnic Hungarians in Covasna and Harghita counties of having murdered seven Romanian policemen during the anti-Ceaușescu revolution of December 1989 as part of a campaign to intimidate Romanians in these predominantly Hungarian-populated areas.

Underlying all the political instability, social malaise and ethnic squabbles, there was immense financial hardship for many, as Romania belatedly embarked on the road to a market economy. In April all food prices were liberalized, except for a basket of 12 staple items whose prices could not be increased by more than 125 per cent. In an attempt to prevent a wage/price spiral, pay compensation was set at only 60 per cent of the price rises. Living standards dropped even further with the introduction of personal income tax ranging from 6 to 45 per cent of earnings.

Other measures were also introduced in April to speed up the transition to a market economy. A new foreign investment law offered a range of tax incentives to boost the inflow of capital from the outside world. In August the long-awaited privatization law was enacted, setting aside 30 per cent of the assets of state-owned enterprises for Romanian citizens in the form of free vouchers, with the rest being made available to anyone wishing to invest.

Steps were also taken to make the leu convertible. In April, it was devalued from 35 lei to 60 lei to the US dollar; in November, something akin to a free-float rate was introduced, which settled at approaching 200 lei to the dollar. These measures combined with pledges to curb drastically the budget deficit and to eliminate price distortions, helped to persuade the IMF to extend its facilities to Romania. But IMF assistance, along with loans by foreign governments and commercial lenders worth hundreds of millions of dollars, were suspended or postponed in the wake of the miners' riots and the fall of Mr Roman's government.

In general, though, Romania's relations with the outside world improved considerably during the year. In April President Mitterrand led a large delegation of French officials and business executives to Bucharest to rebuild the traditionally good relations between the two countries. Playing host to the French President was just part of Romania's efforts to forge closer links with the West.

But Romania's main foreign policy preoccupations were nearer home. The disintegration of Yugoslavia (see IV.1.vi) was perceived in Bucharest as a potential threat to Romania's own stability. Romania and Greece were the only two of Yugoslavia's seven neighbours to stay on friendly terms with the Serbian leadership. The break-up of the Soviet Union (see IV.2.i) was seen in a different light—one that could provide Romania with fresh opportunities. But Romania adopted a very cautious approach, to the extent that in April it became the only one of the Kremlin's former allies to sign a friendship treaty with the Soviet Union which was widely regarded as restricting Romania's future options in choosing other allies. Ratification of the treaty by the Romanian parliament was delayed to the point where it lost its validity with the dissolution of the Soviet Union.

The break-up of the Soviet Union brought demands from Romanian nationalists for the unification of Romania and the newly-independent ex-Soviet republic of Moldova (Moldavia), in view of the latter's ethnic Romanian majority. Both Romanian and Moldovan leaders resisted these demands, knowing that Moldova's large Slavic minority was bitterly opposed to this. Nevertheless, Romania registered a territorial claim to an adjoining region of newly-independent Ukraine which, as Northern Bukovina, had belonged to it in 1918–40. Relations with Hungary remained frosty as the dispute over the rights of Romania's Hungarian minority in Transylvania showed no signs of being resolved.

v. BULGARIA

CAPITAL: Sofia AREA: 110,000 sq km POPULATION: 8,600,000 ('91)
OFFICIAL LANGUAGE: Bulgarian POLITICAL SYSTEM: parliamentary democracy
HEAD OF STATE: President Zhelyu Zhelev
RULING PARTY: Union of Democratic Forces (UDF)
HEAD OF GOVERNMENT: Filip Dimitrov, Prime Minister (since Oct '91)
PRINCIPAL MINISTERS: Stoyan Ganev (deputy premier, foreign affairs), Nikolai Vasilev (deputy premier, education & science), Ivan Kostov (finance), Dimitur Ludzhev (defence), Yordan Sokolov (interior), Ivan Pushkarov (trade & industry)
INTERNATIONAL ALIGNMENT: towards Western Europe
CURRENCY: lev (end-'91 £1=L32.24, US$1=L17.27)
MAIN EXPORT EARNERS: machinery and equipment, agricultural produce, tourism

THE chief event of 1991 was the general election on 13 October, the second free multi-party ballot since the collapse of the communist dictatorship. It resulted in a narrow four-seat victory for the Union of Democratic Forces (UDF) over the ex-communists of the Bulgarian Socialist Party (BSP). The UDF took 110 seats in the reduced 240-seat

National Assembly, as opposed to 106 for the BSP; the remaining 24 seats were won by the Movement for Rights and Freedoms (MRF), representing Bulgaria's ethnic Turkish and Pomak Muslim minorities.

The UDF at once formed its own cabinet, relying on the parliamentary support of the MRF and excluding the ex-communists from power for the first time since the pro-Soviet putsch of 1944. The UDF's 36-year-old Prime Minister, Filip Dimitrov, promised to start rapid privatization of the economy and quickly demonstrated his commitment to profound political change by appointing the former deputy prime minister, Dimitur Ludzhev, as the first civilian Defence Minister since 1934. Another early measure was the Restitution Act, passed in November, which sequestered the assets of the BSP and its former satellite organizations, among them Bulgaria's largest trade union confederation.

Until October, Bulgaria had been ruled by a multi-party government, which had included BSP and UDF representatives. Considerable hope was invested in this uneasy coalition when it was created in December 1990 under the non-party Prime Minister, Dimitur Popov, a former magistrate (see AR 1990, p. 133); but it must be said that its record in office was mixed. Its greatest achievement was to preserve calm in the country and win public acceptance of severe price reforms and interest-rate increases, imposed by the UDF Finance Minister, Ivan Kostov, as part of the shift to a market economy. The legislative success of the coalition, however, was hampered by its divisions and the bitter inter-party feuding and obstructiveness of the BSP majority in the Assembly. A land reform measure was passed, intended to return farms confiscated by the communists up to a limit of 30 hectares, but its implementation was slow. A foreign investments law and measures on banking and commercial practice were denounced by the UDF as excessively restrictive.

The main item of legislation was the new, democratic constitution, promulgated on 12 July after a bitter controversy, fuelled by UDF radicals demanding a public referendum. Criticism that the constitution was insufficiently democratic and would shield former communists from legal accountability did not prevent it from securing the votes of 309 of the then 400 MPs, following a split in the UDF. Two centrist groupings broke away, later to contest the October election separately as the UDF-Liberals and UDF-Centre; but both were eliminated, failing to gather the 4 per cent share of the vote needed to enter the new Assembly. The election proved equally disastrous for Bulgaria's two rival Agrarian Unions, even though Viktor Vulkov, a leader of the larger group, had served as deputy prime minister and foreign minister under Mr Popov.

The constitution was also denounced by the MRF, on the grounds that it contained no text on minority rights. The MRF frequently found itself at the centre of controversy during the year, provoking charges from the BSP and Bulgarian nationalists that it was intrinsically separatist and violated the Law on Political Parties. Nevertheless, its popularity grew, partly as a result of its successive school boycotts and demonstrations, which, in November, secured the restitution of Turkish-language teaching in schools, long since banned under communism. Pressure from the USA and the European Community, as well as Turkey, ensured that the MRF was permitted to participate in the October election, even though it had been denied leave to register as a political party by the law courts. Its return of 24 seats gave it the balance of power, but the MRF's leader, Ahmed Dogan, declined to press for a coalition. Nevertheless, the UDF still had to endure charges from nationalists that its government, and President Zhelev, had become political captives of the ethnic Turks.

The BSP's shift to crude nationalism was a reaction to its continuing fall in popularity, illustrated by the 13 per cent drop in its vote in the October poll. Such pressures caused the Socialists to become seriously split between a social democratic wing, grouped around the former prime minister, Andrei Lukanov, and more conservative neo-marxists, led by party chairman Aleksandur Lilov. The predominance of the latter trend was clinched at a post-electoral congress on 16 December, when Mr Lilov stepped down in favour of a 32-year-old unknown, Zhan Videnov, while retaining an important input into party policy as head of a new research centre.

The BSP was damaged by the reluctance of its leaders to make an open denunciation of the failed hardline coup in the USSR in August (see IV.2.i), whereas President Zhelev did condemn it, to his great international credit. The BSP was also hurt by the trial of the ex-dictator, Todor Zhivkov, which opened on 25 February and dragged on inconclusively throughout the year while Mr Zhivkov slandered witnesses and charged up to $10,000 for a press interview. Verdicts were reached, however, in other more minor corruption cases. One saw the communist former deputy premier, Grigor Stoichkov, gaoled for his part in covering up the impact of the 1986 Chernobyl disaster in Bulgaria.

In foreign policy, the year confirmed Bulgaria's increasingly pro-Western orientation. Diplomatic contacts and trade links increased with its Balkan neighbours, especially Greece and Turkey, which were respectively its third and fourth most important trading partners after the former USSR and Germany. Although the government reached no global agreement on the rescheduling of the $11,000 million foreign debt with the international banks, Bulgaria secured fresh loans of $503 million from the IMF and $250 million from the World Bank to fund price reforms and moves towards internal currency convertability. The US granted most-favoured-nation trading status and strongly supported the election victory of the UDF. Bulgaria was also deeply affected by the break-up of Yugoslavia and the ensuing civil war in Croatia (see IV.1.vi). There was a surge of public sympathy for the independence aspirations of the neighbouring republic of Macedonia, whose Slav majority was seen as having a close ethnic, cultural and linguistic affinity with Bulgaria. Macedonia's prime minister, Nikola Kljusev, made a historic visit to Sofia in the summer, which led President Zhelev to pledge Bulgaria to recognize independent Macedonia as soon as it became practically possible.

vi. YUGOSLAVIA

FEDERAL CAPITAL: Belgrade   AREA: 255,804 sq km   POPULATION: 23,914,977 ('91)
OFFICIAL LANGUAGES: Serbo-Croat, Macedonian & Slovene
POLITICAL SYSTEM: nominally socialist federal republic, but undergoing civil war
FEDERAL GOVERNMENT Branko Kostić (vice-president of federal presidency), Ante Marković (federal premier), Budimir Lončar (foreign affairs), Veljko Kadijević (defence) (federal government effectively ceased to exist from Nov '91)
PRESIDENTS OF THE REPUBLICS: Bosnia/Hercegovina—Alija Izetbegović; Croatia—Franjo Tudjman; Macedonia—Kiro Gligorov; Montenegro—Momir Bulatović; Serbia—Slobodan Milošević; Slovenia—Milan Kucan
INTERNATIONAL ALIGNMENT: NAM, OECD (observer)
CURRENCY: dinar (end-'91 £1=Din37.08, US$1=Din20.36)
GNP PER CAPITA: US$2,520 ('91)
MAIN EXPORT EARNERS: machinery (esp. transport equipment), metals and metal manufactures, textiles and related products, agricultural products and food

THE election of Kiro Gligorov as the president of the Macedonian Assembly on 27 January rounded off the business of the old year, following the installation in each of Yugoslavia's six republics of governments which had won freely-contested elections (see AR 1990, pp. 134–5). The nationalistic ambitions of newly-installed republican leaderships soon brought them into conflict with each other, and with a federal government whose own credibility was eroded by its inability to secure cooperation around the Marković economic reform package. By the end of the year, the Yugoslav federation had effectively ceased to exist, as Slovenia and Croatia, the leading secessionist republics, stood poised to achieve full international recognition as independent states.

The constitutional question of the relative priority of republican or federal law was put to the test early in the year when the Slovene Assembly, on 20 February, passed a proposal for the dissolution of the federation. The following day the Croatian parliament (Sabor) adopted legislation which formally declared that republican law could overrule that of the federation. Croatian and Slovene proposals for reform were immediately rejected by the federal government.

IV EASTERN EUROPE

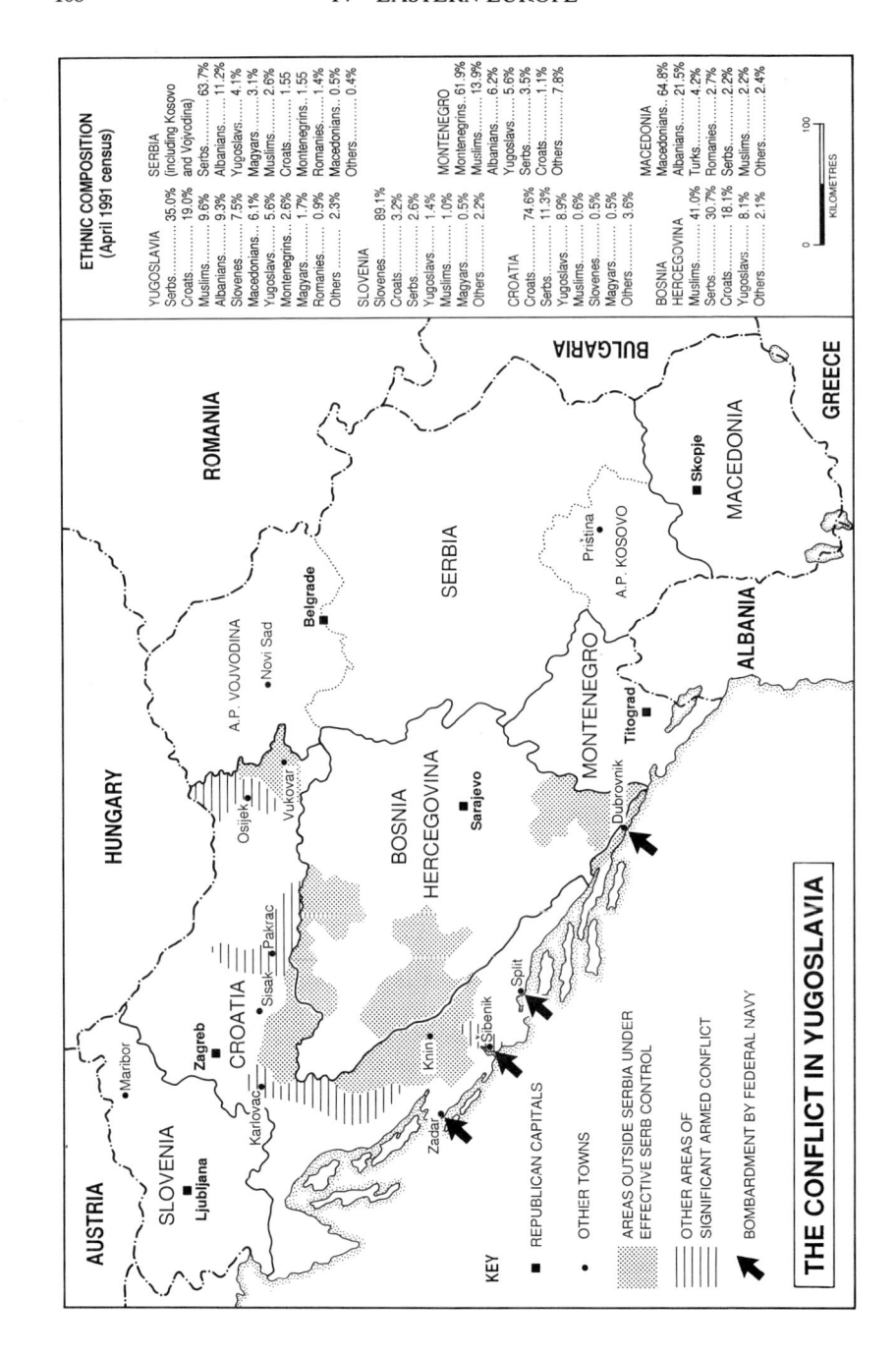

THE CONFLICT IN YUGOSLAVIA

ETHNIC COMPOSITION
(April 1991 census)

YUGOSLAVIA
- Serbs.............35.0%
- Croats............19.0%
- Muslims............9.6%
- Albanians..........9.3%
- Slovenes...........7.5%
- Macedonians........6.1%
- Yugoslavs..........5.6%
- Montenegrins.......2.6%
- Magyars............1.7%
- Romanies...........0.9%
- Others.............2.3%

SLOVENIA
- Slovenes..........89.1%
- Croats.............3.2%
- Serbs..............2.6%
- Yugoslavs..........1.4%
- Muslims............1.0%
- Magyars............0.5%
- Others.............2.2%

CROATIA
- Croats............74.6%
- Serbs.............11.3%
- Yugoslavs..........8.9%
- Muslims............0.6%
- Slovenes...........0.5%
- Magyars............0.5%
- Others.............3.6%

SERBIA
(including Kosovo and Vojvodina)
- Serbs.............63.7%
- Albanians.........11.2%
- Yugoslavs..........4.1%
- Magyars............3.1%
- Muslims............2.6%
- Croats.............1.5%
- Montenegrins.......1.5%
- Romanies...........1.4%
- Macedonians........0.5%
- Others.............0.4%

MONTENEGRO
- Montenegrins.....61.9%
- Muslims...........13.9%
- Albanians..........6.2%
- Yugoslavs..........5.6%
- Croats.............3.5%
- Serbs..............1.1%
- Others.............7.8%

MACEDONIA
- Macedonians......64.8%
- Albanians.........21.5%
- Turks..............4.2%
- Romanies...........2.7%
- Serbs..............2.2%
- Muslims............2.2%
- Others.............2.4%

BOSNIA HERCEGOVINA
- Muslims...........41.0%
- Serbs.............30.7%
- Croats............18.1%
- Yugoslavs..........8.1%
- Others.............2.1%

KEY
- ■ REPUBLICAN CAPITALS
- • OTHER TOWNS
- AREAS OUTSIDE SERBIA UNDER EFFECTIVE SERB CONTROL
- OTHER AREAS OF SIGNIFICANT ARMED CONFLICT
- ➤ BOMBARDMENT BY FEDERAL NAVY

Similar issues were raised on 18 March when the Serbian parliament (Skupština) completed its unilateral abrogation of the autonomy of the provinces of Kosovo and Vojvodina (see AR 1990, pp. 135–6). The anomaly of there continuing to be 'representatives' in the federal collective presidency of provinces which no longer existed was turned to use by Serbia in May, when the Serbian-led bloc successfully obstructed the normal process of rotation which would have permitted the Croatian member of the presidency (Stipe Mesić) to take the chair. Claiming that his support for Croatian autonomy rendered him unfit to hold federal office, Serbia and its allies at first vetoed his accession, thus effectively suspending a constitutional convention. On 21 May, after a week of intense and acrimonious negotiation, Mr Mesić announced that he had assumed the chair. In view of the turn which events rapidly took, it was unclear in what sense he ever exercised his presidential function.

The failure to resolve the constitutional question fuelled, and was exacerbated by, the continuing deterioration of Serb–Croat relations in several localities. Fighting broke out in the vicinity of the western Slavonian town of Pakrac (Croatia) in early March, and continued with increasing severity along several stretches of the Croatian–Bosnian border into May (see accompanying map). Parts of these areas were occupied by units of the federal army (JNA), with the declared aim of keeping the warring factions apart. Croatian sources accused the Serb-dominated army of, in effect, abetting Serb secessionism. Major incidents at this time included the death of a soldier during demonstrations in Split; the blockade of the Croatian police post at Kijevo, near Knin; and the killing of 12 Croatian policemen on 2 May in an ambush at Borovo Selo, near the Serbian border in eastern Slavonia. Croatian public opinion was enraged by rumours that atrocities had been committed on the bodies of the policeman.

On 9 May the federal presidency finally agreed to grant special powers to the JNA, following what amounted to an ultimatum. The agreement gave legal cover to the virtual freeing of the army from effective federal government control, although throughout the second half of the year there were numerous indications of a power struggle within the JNA.

Following the example of Slovenia (see AR 1990, p. 135), the Croatian government in February declared its intention to conduct a referendum on the future of the republic within the federation. Anxiety on the part of the republic's 531,000 Serbs led to a declaration on 28 February by the Serbian National Council (see AR 1990, p. 137) that it would hold its own referendum on the possible separation of Serb enclaves in Croatia and their incorporation into Serbia. This was held on 12 May (a week before the official Croatian referendum) and was declared to have produced a massive majority in favour of secession. The formation of the Serbian autonomous region of 'Krajina' was formally announced, incorporating initially six communes in western Croatia, centred upon the town of Knin. A provisional government headed by a local dentist, Milan Babić, was announced on 29 May.

The spiral of mutual distrust was given a further twist when, in early May, several large Croatian firms and government departments began to dismiss Serb employees who were unwilling to sign loyalty oaths to the Croatian government. The official Croatian referendum on autonomy on 19 May recorded over 93 per cent support for the creation of a 'sovereign and independent state' of Croatia.

The growth of inter-ethnic distrust was not confined to Croatia, however. The Serb minority in Bosnia also declared autonomy (on 25 April), in the region around Drvar, while on 13 May a National Council of the Sandžak was inaugurated with the intention of defending the interests of ethnic Muslims, especially in Serbia. The process of fragmentation was to continue throughout the year. An assembly of local Serbs was held in eastern Hercegovina on 27 May, and on 12 September this region also declared its autonomy. Similar events on 25–26 June led to the controversial declaration of the autonomous Serb region of 'Slavonija, Baranja and Western Srem' in the area of Croatia between Osijek and the Danube. The process was carried to absurdity in Bosnia, where several such Serb units consisted of no more than single villages.

In Slovenia, the resignation of Vice-President Jože Mencinger in mid-April, on the grounds of his disagreement with the economic stance taken by the DEMOS coalition government, was interpreted by many observers as an indication of the weakening commitment of the Slovenes to secession. Nevertheless, the anticipatory measures which he designed subsequently successfully guided the economic aspects of Slovenia's independence process.

Numerous attempts were made within the federal presidency to broker agreement in advance of the coming into effect of the Slovene and Croatian declarations of intent. To this end, a succession of 'summits' took place throughout May, June and July, mostly held in villas which had once belonged to the late President Tito. The last of these, in Ohrid (Macedonia) on 22 and 23 July, managed to secure the extrication of JNA forces from Slovenia, but failed to resolve the disputes over the status of Serb minorities in Croatia and Bosnia/Hercegovina.

Outside the country, the deteriorating political situation was followed with concern, especially within the European Community (EC). A 'troika' of ministers from Italy, Luxembourg and the Netherlands visited Yugoslavia on 3–4 April in order to clarify the situation and voice their collective anxiety. This was followed on 29–30 May by the visit of Jacques Santer, Prime Minister of Luxembourg (which then held the EC presidency), and Jacques Delors, president of the European Commission. They let it be known that the EC was strongly opposed to any modification of either the external or the internal borders of

Yugoslavia—views which were echoed by President George Bush of the USA. On 19 June the Yugoslav situation featured on the agenda of the CSCE council of ministers, meeting in Berlin.

Meanwhile, the Yugoslav economy continued to decline, in the absence of agreement on the implementation of the Marković reforms and of any solution to the constitutional crisis. On 16 April Serbian textile and metal workers went on strike in protest against the slump in their living standards. As if signalling its determination to scuttle the Marković programme, the Serbian republican government accepted the strikers' principal demands the following day.

The anticipated declarations of independence by the republics of Slovenia and Croatia took place on 25 and 26 June respectively, with elaborate public ceremony in the latter case. The following day the JNA moved into Slovenia, with the declared aim of securing Yugoslavia's international borders. The federal forces were met by vigorous and highly effective resistance from Slovene territorial units, with the result that a ceasefire was declared after only two days. Having fielded an estimated 25,000 men, the JNA was both outnumbered and outwitted by the Slovenes. Reports indicated that over 6,000 JNA deserters either joined the Slovene forces or fled abroad, and that about 4,600 men were captured (meaning that the JNA lost more than 40 per cent of its strength). The reported death toll was 36 JNA soldiers, five members of the Slovene armed forces, five civilians and 10 foreign nationals.

The EC 'troika' continued its attempts to broker a reconciliation, making three visits to Yugoslavia between 29 June and 7 July. A CSCE meeting in Prague on 3 July passed on the task of mediation to the EC. The principal success of these efforts was to provide a framework for a reasonably dignified withdrawal by the JNA from Slovenia, under the supervision of the newly-founded mission of EC peace monitors, the first of which arrived in Slovenia on 15 July.

As armed conflict eased in Slovenia, however, it escalated in Croatia. The declarations of autonomy by Serbs in the Knin 'Krajina' and in five additional communes in the 'Banija' area (on the Bosnian border south of Zagreb) had been accompanied over several months by the systematic arming and organization of the Serb population. By contrast with Slovenia, the Tudjman government in Zagreb had apparently made relatively little preparation for the forcible securing of its independence. Official response to JNA troop movements was tentative, unplanned and relatively ineffective. A 'war cabinet' was not formed until 17 July, nor were the economic dimensions of independence properly addressed. In a belated attempt to reassure Serbs living within the republic that their security was not threatened by an independent Croatia, on 1 August President Tudjman appointed two Serbs and a Muslim to ministerial posts. However, this apparently more conciliatory stance was obscured by the simultaneous reversal of the military policy of non-confrontation.

Unlike the Slovenes, the Croats were poorly equipped. Partly as a consequence, the first phase of Croat resistance to JNA occupation took the form of a number of sieges of federal military installations. Especially heavy fighting was reported around the Borongaj barracks in Zagreb.

The declaration of independence by Croatia also signalled the opening of a new front in eastern Slavonia. The sporadic fighting which had taken place in several Danubian villages since the clash in Borovo Selo in early May escalated in June into a systematic attempt by the JNA and Serbian irregulars to appropriate the region. Hungarian villages (principally in the commune of Beli Manastir) as well as Croatian settlements were cleared. Nevertheless, Croatian irregulars mounted sustained and effective resistance in Vukovar, which finally fell on 17 November after a siege of 86 days.

The military successes of the JNA disguised its intrinsic weakness, which became ever more apparent during the late summer. Massive rates of desertion were reported; restrictions were placed upon the cross-border movement of men of military age. The late summer draft was estimated to have raised only about a third of the expected manpower, and the JNA was staffed increasingly by reservists. Attempts to secure footholds for federal forces on the Croatian coast, and especially control over important military installations in Šibenik and Zadar, were prevented during September. On 22 September agreement was negotiated allowing the JNA to withdraw its besieged forces from the barracks in Zagreb and several other Croatian bases.

In retrospect, the turning-point of the war was probably the siege of Dubrovnik, which was mounted at the end of September by a mixture of JNA troops and Montenegrin territorials. As a target, Dubrovnik was strategically important for its port of Gruž and airport at Čilipi. Its capture would have satisfied the long-standing Serbian aim of access to the sea, through the Serb-controlled enclaves of eastern Hercegovina. However, enormous international protest, popular and official, greeted the assault on one of Europe's great historic cities. This accelerated the growing isolation of Serbia and the residue of the federal government, while boosting the Croatians' campaign for international recognition of their independence. On 31 October a flotilla of relief ships was finally permitted to reach the city, accompanied by Mr Mesić, and a ceasefire took effect in Dubrovnik in mid-November.

Continuing international mediation efforts, meanwhile, included a further unsuccessful visit by the EC 'troika' on 2–4 August and meetings of senior CSCE officials in Prague on 8–9 August and 3–4 September. Initially, it appeared that internal endeavours to negotiate peace would be more successful, as the federal presidency declared a further ceasefire on 6 August. However, the collapse of this and subsequent internal agreements helped to persuade the federal government to accept, on 3

September, the EC's proposal for a peace conference. This convened at the Hague on 7 September under the chairmanship of Lord Carrington; two days later the EC peace monitors were deployed in Croatia. But although the Hague conference quickly led to further ceasefire declarations, the complete mutual distrust between the warring parties, and the lack of central control over irregulars on both sides, ensured that these too were short-lived.

Lack of progress at the Hague resulted in the imposition of EC economic sanctions against Yugoslavia on 15 November (these being directed, from 2 December, specifically against Serbia and its ally Montenegro). At the same time, the UN began to explore the prospects of involvement, sending Cyrus Vance and Marrack Goulding to Yugoslavia on a fact-finding mission. On the basis of their preliminary report, the Security Council on 27 November requested a further report on the feasibility of sending a peace-keeping force.

International intervention did little to retard the movement towards the separation of other Yugoslav republics. A referendum in Macedonia on 8 September yielded a 95 per cent majority (in a 75 per cent poll) in favour of independence 'with the right to join an alliance of sovereign states'. On 18 September the Macedonian Sobranie (parliament) adopted a declaration on sovereignty and independence. On 22 September the Kosovo Assembly, which had been set up 'in exile' (see AR 1990, pp. 136–7), also passed a resolution declaring the province to be a sovereign republic.

Further effect was given to the Croatian independence drive by the withdrawal of Croatian representatives from the federal government on 12 September. The economic disintegration of the federation was underlined on 8 October, when the Slovene republic launched its own currency, the tolar (a derivative of the old Austrian thaler).

Assaults by Serb and JNA forces on Croatian cities such as Dubrovnik, Osijek and Vukovar increased the perception of the Serbs as intransigent in negotiation. The result was a growing international movement to precipitate change through the recognition of Croatia and Slovenia, articulated most vocally by Austrian, German and Italian leaders. Despite resistance from British, French and American official opinion, the summit of EC heads of government at Maastricht on 10 December agreed in principle to recognition early in 1992, conditional upon their receiving a satisfactory report from the French jurist Robert Badinter. Confirmed by the EC foreign ministers on 16 December at Germany's insistence, the prospect of recognition raised as many questions as it settled. The EC's invitation to other republics to apply for recognition by 23 December was interpreted within Serbia as provocative and partisan. Bosnia/Hercegovina, Macedonia and the Kosovo government-in-exile all filed applications. Each of these areas, whether or not they asserted independence, contained the ingredients of serious internal, even international, conflict. Nevertheless, by late December, the Vance mission had succeeded in reaching a negotiated ceasefire with all parties (the 15th such agreement) and had prepared the ground for the intervention of a UN peace-keeping force.

Because of the conflict in Slovenia and Croatia, developments in Kosovo tended to be overlooked in the world's press. Following the suspension of the provincial Kosovo constitution by Serbia in March, the use of the Albanian language in official documents and public financial transactions was declared illegal. Thereafter, the replacement of Albanian officials and other professional workers by Serbs gathered pace. In September an attempt began to redress the ethnic 'imbalance' in Kosovo, by implanting Serb settlers from the war zones in Croatia. Several Albanian-language educational institutions were closed. A determined campaign, led by the (Albanian) Democratic League of Kosovo, sought to channel resistance into non-violent modes of expression.

vii. ALBANIA

CAPITAL: Tirana   AREA: 29,000 sq km   POPULATION: 3,000,000 ('89)
OFFICIAL LANGUAGE: Albanian   POLITICAL SYSTEM: emerging democracy
HEAD OF STATE: President Ramiz Alia since Nov '82
HEAD OF GOVERNMENT: Vilson Ahmeti, Prime Minister (since Dec '91), heading caretaker cabinet of non-party technocrats
CURRENCY: lek (end-'91 £1=AL10.03, US$1=AL5.37)
GNP PER CAPITA: US$820 ('81)
MAIN EXPORT EARNERS: crude oil, minerals, agricultural products

IN 1991 Albanians saw an extension of their individual freedoms and the further reintegration of their country into the international community, but they did not find political stability.

The extension of individual freedoms was registered in the steady release of political prisoners, in the restoration of public Muslim worship (symbolized by the reopening of the Etem Bcy mosque in Tirana on 18 January), in the right to own motor cars and in the freedom to run private businesses and to wear beards.

Reintegration into the international community received a major boost with the restoration of relations with the United States on 15 March. On 29 May relations were formally restored with the United Kingdom; in August the Soviet embassy in Tirana was reopened; and in the following month formal contact was established between Albania and the Vatican. In November Albania sent delegates to a meeting of the Group of 24 and in December attended the summit of the Islamic Conference Organization in Dakar as an observer. It was also admitted to the European Bank for Reconstruction and Development.

Internal political evolution was dominated by extra-parliamentary protest action. In January a wave of strikes forced the government to postpone elections, due in February, until the end of March in order to give the opposition more time to prepare for the campaign. The main opposition parties had now crystallized into the Democratic Party (DP), the Republican Party, the Ecology Party and the Agrarian Party, of which the DP was the largest. There were also a number of organizations representing social or ethnic groups. All were vigorously opposed to the communist Party of Labour (PLA).

Of the social groups, the students were amongst the most vocal. Early in February they issued a list of demands which included an improvement in living conditions, the renaming of Tirana's Enver Hoxha University and an end to the compulsory teaching of marxism-leninism. The agitation spread rapidly and on 18 February 700 activists announced they were going on hunger strike. Two days later a massive demonstration in Tirana's central Skanderbeg Square toppled Hoxha's statue before being suppressed by police backed by tanks. Though peace was restored, President Ramiz Alia thought it advisable to sack Prime Minister Adil Carcani, replacing him with Fatos Nano.

A further register of social unrest came at the beginning of March when over 20,000 Albanians fled by sea to Italy (see also III.1.iii). Although military action was taken to prevent further exodus, throughout the remainder of the year there were periodic attempts at mass breakouts, many of which ended in bloodshed.

The opposition parties insisted that the March exodus had been engineered by the PLA in order to influence the elections, which were held in two rounds on 31 March and 7/14 April. The results were a major blow to the opposition, in that the PLA took 60 per cent of the votes and 169 of the 250 seats. The DP had 75 seats, the National Veterans' Committee 1, and Omonia (an organization representing the Greek minority) 5. The PLA's victory had been won in the rural constituencies, though the anti-communist urban intelligentsia inflicted humiliation upon President Alia, who failed to win his seat in Tirana.

Opposition anger over the results could not be contained, most seriously in Shkodër, where serious disturbances on 2 April resulted in the death of at least four people, including the local DP leader. A later parliamentary investigation blamed the violence on the security police, responsibility for which was transferred in May from government to state control. But the so-called 'Shkodër massacre' was to remain a factor in national affairs for the remainder of the year.

Under an interim constitution adopted by parliament on 29 April, the country was renamed the 'Republic of Albania', i.e. without the adjectives 'socialist' or 'people's'. Mr Alia was confirmed as President and on 3 May a new government was constituted, again with Mr Nano as Prime Minister.

These changes did not pacify the Union of Independent Trade Unions, which had put forward a number of sectional and general demands on 29 April. Strikes were again ordered and by the end of May as much as half the workforce was involved. On 29 May there was another huge demonstration in the centre of Tirana. President Alia sacked Mr Nano and on 4 June formed a 'government of national solidarity', which included nominees and representatives of the main opposition groups, with Gramoz Pashko of the DP as Deputy Prime Minister. The new Prime Minister was Ylli Bufi of the PLA, who promised rapid privatization (including that of land), economic liberalization and the depoliticization of state institutions, the police and education. In June the 10th congress of the PLA decided on fundamental changes to that party, which was renamed the Socialist Party of Albania (SPA).

By the end of August, however, demonstrations had begun again. There were increasingly loud calls for the end of SPA domination over the media, for a proper investigation into the Shkodër massacre and for the abolition of the secret police. By September and October popular passions were further inflamed by the decline in food supplies, which in turn led to increasing anarchy in the countryside. By November the hard-pressed government had to admit that parts of the north-east of the country were beyond state control; in desperation it agreed to bring forward the next elections from May–June 1992. But the 'government of national solidarity' was doomed. Defections from the cabinet, together with yet more demonstrations in Tirana, persuaded Mr Bufi to leave office. He was replaced on 14 December by Vilson Ahmeti, a non-party intellectual.

Mr Ahmeti announced that his first priority was to preserve public order but, perhaps to contain popular discontent, he also sounded the patriotic bell, insisting that Albanians in Yugoslavia must be allowed their due rights and protesting to the UN on 28 December at the treatment of ethnic Greek Albanian refugees in Greece (see also III.3.v). Mr Ahmeti also determined that a general election should be held on 1 March 1992.

2. USSR/CIS—BALTIC STATES

i. USSR/COMMONWEALTH OF INDEPENDENT STATES

CAPITAL: Moscow   AREA: 22,402,000 sq km   POPULATION: 290,000,000 ('91)
PRINCIPAL OFFICIAL LANGUAGE: Russian
HEAD OF STATE: President Mikhail Gorbachev (resigned Dec '91)
PRESIDENTS OF THE REPUBLICS: Armenia—Levon Ter-Petrosyan; Azerbaijan—Ayaz Mutalibov; Belorussia—Stanislav Shushkevich; Georgia—Zviad Gamsakhurdia; Kazakhstan—Nursultan Nazarbayev; Kirghizia—Askar Akayev; Moldavia—Mircea Snegur; Russian Federation—Boris Yeltsin; Tadjikistan—Rakhman Nabiyev; Turkmenia—Saparmurad Niyazov; Ukraine—Leonid Kravchuk; Uzbekistan—Islam Karimov
CURRENCY: rouble (end-'91 £1=R3.08, US$1=R1.65)
MAIN EXPORT EARNERS: oil and oil products, machinery and equipment

In that the USSR did not cease to exist de jure until the last days of 1991, the process of disintegration leading to the creation of the successor Commonwealth of Independent States is covered below in a single section. However, because they achieved internationally-recognized independence in mid-1991, the three Baltic republics of Estonia, Latvia and Lithuania are allocated a separate section in this chapter.

IF 1989 was Eastern Europe's *annus mirabilis*, 1991 produced a series of changes in the Soviet Union that were still more remarkable because they took place in a country in which communist rule had not originally been an external imposition. The decisive moment was probably in August, when a short-lived coup attempted to remove Mikhail Gorbachev from power. The plotters, it emerged, had wished to prevent the signature of a new treaty that would have replaced the union established in 1922 with a loose confederation. The result of their action was to accelerate a process of disintegration which, by the end of the year, had led to full independence in the three Baltic republics and to a limited form of association among the others, most of which had declared themselves sovereign states. Still more remarkable, the August coup, launched in the name of maintaining central control, led swiftly to the suspension or suppression of the Communist Party throughout the former USSR and to the abolition of the Soviet parliament and presidency. President Gorbachev, whose position disappeared, finally resigned on 25 December, bringing to an end more than six years of *perestroika*. For all the dramatic character of these changes, however, there was one constant: a deepening economic crisis, which (by the end of 1991) appeared to be resolvable only with the aid of the USSR's former competitors.

Mikhail Gorbachev's customary summer sojourn in the Crimea was abruptly interrupted this year when on the afternoon of 18 August he was visited by four emissaries from Moscow and placed under house arrest because he refused to approve a state of emergency. In the early hours of 19 August a self-styled 'national emergency committee' informed a startled world that the President was 'unwell' and was therefore unable to perform his duties; his responsibilities

IV EASTERN EUROPE

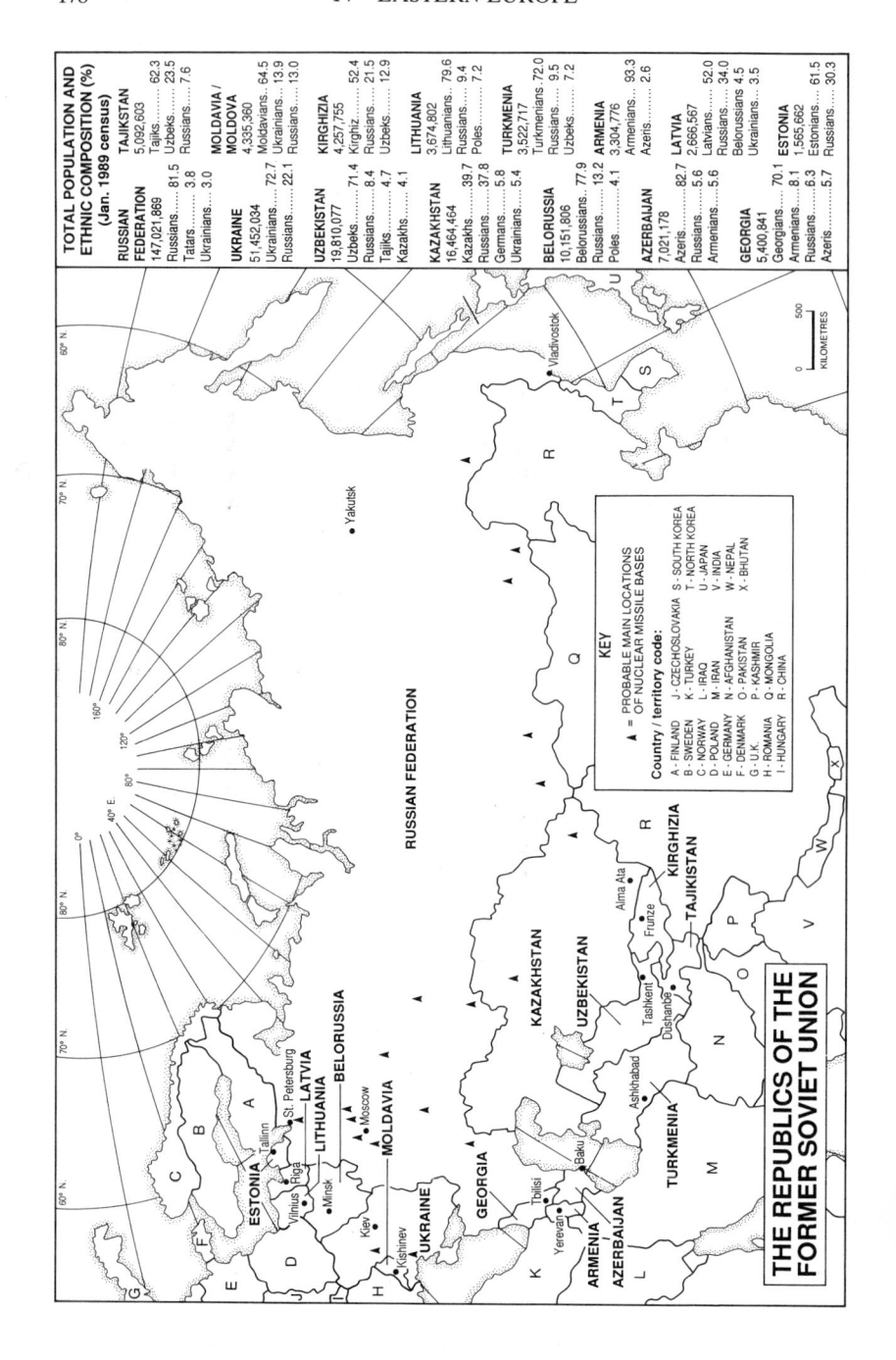

THE REPUBLICS OF THE FORMER SOVIET UNION

TOTAL POPULATION AND ETHNIC COMPOSITION (%)
(Jan. 1989 census)

RUSSIAN FEDERATION	147,021,869	
Russians		81.5
Tatars		3.8
Ukrainians		3.0
UKRAINE	51,452,034	
Ukrainians		72.7
Russians		22.1
UZBEKISTAN	19,810,077	
Uzbeks		71.4
Russians		8.4
Tajiks		4.7
Kazakhs		4.1
KAZAKHSTAN	16,464,464	
Kazakhs		39.7
Russians		37.8
Germans		5.8
Ukrainians		5.4
BELORUSSIA	10,151,806	
Belorussians		77.9
Russians		13.2
Poles		4.1
AZERBAIJAN	7,021,178	
Azeris		82.7
Russians		5.6
Armenians		5.6
GEORGIA	5,400,841	
Georgians		70.1
Armenians		8.1
Russians		6.3
Azeris		5.7
TAJIKISTAN	5,092,603	
Tajiks		62.3
Uzbeks		23.5
Russians		7.6
MOLDAVIA / MOLDOVA	4,335,360	
Moldavians		64.5
Ukrainians		13.9
Russians		13.0
KIRGHIZIA	4,257,755	
Kirghiz		52.4
Russians		21.5
Uzbeks		12.9
LITHUANIA	3,674,802	
Lithuanians		79.6
Russians		9.4
Poles		7.2
TURKMENIA	3,522,717	
Turkmenians		72.0
Russians		9.5
Uzbeks		7.2
ARMENIA	3,304,776	
Armenians		93.3
Azeris		2.6
LATVIA	2,666,567	
Latvians		52.0
Russians		34.0
Belorussians		4.5
Ukrainians		3.5
ESTONIA	1,565,662	
Estonians		61.5
Russians		30.3

KEY

▲ = PROBABLE MAIN LOCATIONS OF NUCLEAR MISSILE BASES

Country / territory code:

A - FINLAND
B - SWEDEN
C - NORWAY
D - POLAND
E - GERMANY
F - DENMARK
G - U.K.
H - ROMANIA
I - HUNGARY
J - CZECHOSLOVAKIA
K - TURKEY
L - IRAQ
M - IRAN
N - AFGHANISTAN
O - PAKISTAN
P - KASHMIR
Q - MONGOLIA
R - CHINA
S - SOUTH KOREA
T - NORTH KOREA
U - JAPAN
V - INDIA
W - NEPAL
X - BHUTAN

were to be assumed by his Vice-President, Gennadii Yanaev. The committee, it later emerged, had eight members. Apart from Mr Yanaev himself, it included the KGB chairman, Vladimir Kryuchkov, Defence Minister Dmitry Yazov, Interior Minister Boris Pugo and Prime Minister Valentin Pavlov. The three other members were of less prominence, namely Oleg Baklanov (deputy chairman of the Defence Council), Vasily Starodubtsev (chairman of the USSR Farmers' Council) and Alexander Tizyakov (president of the Association of State Enterprises).

In a series of decrees, the emergency committee suspended the activities of all parties (other than those that supported the emergency), banned the publication of all but a small number of newspapers (including *Pravda*) and prohibited meetings, strikes and demonstrations. In a 'message to the Soviet people', broadcast on the morning of 19 August, the committee referred to 'extremist forces' which were exploiting national feelings and attempting to 'destroy the Soviet Union'. It promised to restore order and to deal with the food and housing problems, while honouring international obligations and restoring pride in the Soviet motherland.

The coup, it soon became clear, had been poorly planned. Indeed, two of its principal members, Mr Yanaev and Mr Pavlov, appeared to be drunk for most of its duration. It was opposed from the outset by the Russian President, Boris Yeltsin, who made a dramatic call for resistance on 19 August. Standing on one of the tanks stationed outside the Russian parliament building in Moscow, he called for a general strike against a 'rightist, reactionary, anti-constitutional coup'. Later the same day, Mr Yeltsin declared himself to be in charge of the Soviet Union's security forces on Russian territory until constitutional order had been restored. Huge demonstrations in front of the Russian parliament ('White House') on 20 August were addressed by former Foreign Minister Eduard Shevardnadze and other democrats. The critical moment was the evening of 20 August, when large numbers of Muscovites defied the curfew and remained assembled to defend the parliament building against an expected attack by pro-coup forces. That night three men were killed—one shot and two crushed by tanks on the Moscow ring road—but the attack on the building itself did not materialize. It later emerged that substantial sections of the armed forces had declared against the coup, and that the elite KGB 'Alpha' anti-terrorist group had rejected an order to storm the Russian parliament.

On 21 August the coup began to collapse. Media restrictions were lifted, the troops began to be withdrawn and a statement by President Gorbachev, announcing that he was again in control of the country, was broadcast nationally. The USSR Supreme Soviet Presidium declared the actions of the emergency committee illegal, and the Procurator-General's office announced that criminal proceedings for high treason had been instigated against its members. One of the coup leaders, Boris Pugo, committed suicide; several others went to the Crimea to seek Mr Gorbachev's forgiveness; and still others, such as Foreign Minister Aleksandr Bessmertnykh, tried to explain why they had (in his case) suffered a sudden 'cold' during the emergency. Mr Bessmertnykh was dismissed two days later.

The most ambiguous figure of all was the Chairman of the Supreme Soviet, Anatoly Lukyanov, an old college friend of the Soviet President. He had refused to denounce the coup at the time and was accused of being its 'chief ideologist'. He resigned his position on 26 August and by the end of the month was one of the 14 people involved in the coup who had been arrested and charged with high treason.

President Gorbachev was flown back to Moscow in the early hours of 22 August, where he later addressed a crowded press conference. He thanked Mr Yeltsin personally for securing his release, as well as the Russian parliament, and began to describe the difficult conditions under which he had been held. He had refused to accept the conditions which his captors had tried to dictate to him, and had been able to rig up a makeshift radio to listen to Western broadcasts, notably the BBC World Service. There was some surprise that the Soviet leader continued to defend the Communist Party, whose role in the attempted coup was obscure. He was clearly dismayed when Mr Yeltsin signed a decree suspending the party in the Russian Federation in the course of the Soviet President's appearance before the Russian parliament on 23 August.

However, when the complicity of the party leadership became clear, President Gorbachev resigned the general-secretaryship (on 24 August) and called on the central committee to take the 'difficult but honourable decision to dissolve itself'. On 29 August the USSR Supreme Soviet suspended the activities of the party throughout the Soviet Union; its bank accounts and financial operations were frozen, and its buildings placed under the control of local soviets.

The coup had a still greater impact on the structure of the Soviet state, accelerating its disintegration and the achievement of full independence by the Baltic republics of Estonia, Latvia and Lithuania (see IV.2.ii). Earlier in the year, none of the three Baltic states had taken part in the referendum on the future of the Soviet Union held on 17 March. The first exercise of its kind ever to be conducted, it asked voters throughout the Soviet Union whether they considered it 'necessary to preserve the Union of Soviet Socialist Republics as a renewed federation of equal, sovereign republics in which the human rights and freedoms of all nationalities [would] be fully guaranteed'. Voter turnout was officially put at 80 per cent, although six republics (Armenia, Georgia and Moldavia as well as the Baltic republics) took no official part in the proceedings. Of those who voted, 76.4 per cent supported the proposition, while 21.7 per cent voted against; this meant that a 'yes' vote had been cast by just over 61 per cent of registered electors, or about 56 per cent of all Soviet citizens of voting age.

Matters were further complicated by the fact that four of the nine republics in which the exercise took place asked questions which modified or added to the formulation approved by the central authorities. The vote in the Russian Federation approved not simply a 'renewed federation', but also (by a majority of 70 per cent) a directly-elected Russian presidency. This was seen to represent a political victory for Boris Yeltsin and his supporters.

Mr Yeltsin was again successful in the Russian presidential elections on 12 June, which were contested by six candidates. Mr Yeltsin took 57 per cent of the vote on a 75 per cent turnout, well ahead of former Prime Minister Nikolai Ryzhkov (17 per cent), who took second place. Mr Yeltsin's vice-presidential candidate was Alexander Rutskoi, a fighter pilot who had left the Communist Party to become head of a more liberal grouping, the Democratic Communist Party of Russia. Under Mr Yeltsin's leadership, the Russian Federation began to play an increasingly assertive role in broadening the rights of all republics and of the Federation itself. Following Mr Yeltsin's visit to the United States in June, it was announced on 23 June that the republic would have its own counsellor in the Soviet embassy in Washington and its own representative in the Soviet UN mission.

A vote in Leningrad, at the same time as the Russian presidential elections on 12 June, had meanwhile approved a proposal that the city should revert to its original name of St Petersburg—this decision was subsequently confirmed by the Russian parliament. A Russian television service was launched in May, broadcasting six hours a day on the Soviet Union's second channel; agreement was also reached to establish a Russian KGB. In September the second television channel was transferred entirely to the Russian service, and the Novosti news agency—which had been taken under Russian control following the attempted coup—was absorbed within the Russian Information Agency.

Mr Yeltsin had called for the resignation of President Gorbachev in a controversial television interview in February. Moreover, in a speech on 9 March—which he later regretted—he went so far as to call upon Soviet democrats to 'declare war' on Mr Gorbachev. These differences notwithstanding, the Soviet President and his Russian critic were among the parties that concluded an historic agreement on 23 April at Novo-Ogarevo, a government dacha outside Moscow. The agreement, described as the '9 plus 1' accord because it had been concluded by nine republican heads of state as well as the Soviet President, covered a series of actions that were to be taken in every sphere, but particularly in the Soviet economy. Public order was to be restored by banning strikes in key industries, ensuring the fulfilment of the 1991 budget, moderating price rises and increasing compensation for the less affluent. At the same time, a new union treaty would be signed within three months and a new constitution would be adopted which would be followed by elections at all levels of government.

President Gorbachev was accordingly able to announce on 24 July that the nine republics had reached agreement on a new union treaty. As published in the central press, it specified that defence, foreign policy, energy, communications, transport and budgetary matters would be decided 'jointly' by the centre and the republics, but that in all other matters republican laws would have priority over those of the union as a whole. On 12 July the draft treaty was approved by the Supreme Soviet, after it had received the endorsement of eight of the nine republics (the Ukrainian decision was still pending).

It was this version of the union treaty which was to have been signed by Russian and other representatives on 20 August—a weakening of central authority that the attempted coup launched one day beforehand was apparently intended to prevent. In the event, the coup discredited the draft treaty and led to a series of declarations of republican independence which, by the end of the year, had led to the abolition of the USSR itself. Ukraine was the first to declare its independence, on 24 August; Moldavia (Moldova) followed on 27 August, and Azerbaijan on 30 August. The Belorussian president, Nikolai Dementei, who had expressed support for the coup, resigned on 25 August, shortly after which the republican parliament voted to declare the 'political and economic independence of Belorussia'. The Uzbek parliament voted similarly on 31 August. Tajikistan voted for independence on 9 September, Armenia on 23 September, Turkmenia on 27 October and Kazakhstan on 16 December. (The three Baltic republics had meanwhile secured acceptance of their independence from the State Council.) By the end of the year, Russia was the only republic that had not adopted a declaration of this kind.

Republican declarations generally took a common form, including a change of name (dropping 'soviet socialist' from their title) and an assertion of ownership of the enterprises and natural resources located on their territory. Most republican leaders resigned from the Communist Party, whose activities were generally banned (although in some Central Asian republics the party was able to reconstitute itself under a new name). The newly-independent republics also became more assertive on matters of defence and foreign policy, applying (in a few cases) to join the United Nations and (more generally) seeking to establish their own armed forces.

The Ukrainian supreme soviet, for instance, passed laws on 23 October creating a legal basis for the republic to have its own army, air force and navy, although it was also announced that the Ukraine would eventually become nuclear-free. In Georgia, where Zviad Gamsakhurdia had led a nationalist coalition to power in October 1990 (see AR 1990, p. 111), a referendum on 26 March produced a 99 per cent majority for independence, with the result that the republican supreme soviet voted to this effect on 9 April. Mr Gamsakhurdia himself won 87 per cent of the vote on 26 May in a contest with five other candidates to become the republic's first-ever elected President. His increasingly dictatorial tendencies, however, led to domestic tensions. Prime Minister Tengiz Sigua resigned (18 August), opposition leaders were arrested (September) and a mounting wave of popular opposition left the President (by the end of the year) facing a battle for survival.

The draft union treaty, which was to have been signed on 20 August, was clearly superseded by those developments. As the Kazakh President, Nursultan Nazarbaev, told the USSR Supreme Soviet in early September, only a much looser confederation would satisfy the aspirations of the republics which still wished to conclude some kind of association. In the end, ten republics—including some that had declared independence—agreed a joint statement which indicated that a loose 'union of sovereign states' would be established based on Russia and the Central Asian republics. Mr Gorbachev, for the time being, would remain President; but he was to rule through a Council of State on which all the ten participating republics would be represented. Management of the economy was to be entrusted to an inter-republican committee headed by the Russian Prime Minister, Ivan Silaev. The old Soviet parliament was to be replaced by a two-chamber Supreme Soviet, and in due course a new Soviet constitution would be presented for approval leading in 1992 to presidential and, perhaps, multi-party elections.

These were intended to be interim arrangements only. Further negotiations then took place in which President Gorbachev sought to establish the basis of a more substantial political union. Eventually, on 14 November, nine of the original 15 republics (i.e. excluding the Baltic states, Georgia, Armenia and Moldavia) reached agreement on another version of the 'union of sovereign states'. This agreement, like those that had preceded it, envisaged a directly-elected presidency and a bicameral legislature. Central authority would be limited to those spheres of activity which had been specifically delegated to it by the members of the union. A referendum in the Ukraine on 1 December, however, resulted in a majority of over 90 per cent in favour of a fully independent status. This vote appeared to convince President Yeltsin that it would be unprofitable to pursue the goal of political union any further. On 8 December, at a country house outside Minsk, the capital of Belorussia, the three Slav republics (Russia, Belorussia and Ukraine) concluded an agreement establishing an entirely new entity, the 'Commonwealth of Independent States', with its headquarters in Minsk. The new Commonwealth was not a state, but would nonetheless provide for unitary control of nuclear arms, a single currency and a 'single economic space'. The USSR, as a subject of international law and a geopolitical reality, was declared no longer in existence, and the three republics individually denounced the 1922 treaty through which it had originally been established (see XIX.3:DOCUMENTS).

The new Commonwealth declared itself open to other Soviet republics, as well as to states elsewhere that shared its objectives. On 21 December, in Alma-Ata (Kazakhstan), a further agreement was signed by the three original members and by eight of the other nine republics, namely Armenia, Azerbaijan, Kazakhstan, Kirghizia, Moldavia, Tajikistan, Turkmenia and Uzbekistan (but not Georgia). This declaration committed those who signed it to recognition of the independence and sovereignty of other members, respect for human rights including those of national minorities, and observance of existing boundaries. Relations among the members of the Commonwealth were to be conducted on an equal, multilateral basis, but it was agreed to endorse the principle of unitary control of strategic nuclear arms and the concept of a 'single economic space'. Each member of the Commonwealth was entitled, at the same time, to seek to achieve a non-nuclear or neutral status. The USSR as such was held to have 'ended its existence', but the members of the Commonwealth pledged themselves to discharge the obligations that arose from the 15,000 or so international treaties and agreements to which the USSR had been a party. In a separate agreement, the heads of member states agreed that Russia should take the seat at the United Nations formerly occupied by the USSR, and a framework of inter-state and inter-governmental consultation was established.

Following these developments, Mr Gorbachev resigned as USSR President on 25 December. His offices in the Kremlin were occupied by representatives of the Russian government, on 26 December the upper house of the USSR Supreme Soviet voted a formal end to the original treaty of union (which had not, in fact, provided for any procedure of this kind).

Underlying and contributing to the process of disintegration was an economic situation that was critical as the year began and graver still by the time it ended. The official plan results for 1990, released in January, showed that national income had fallen by 2 per cent, produced national income by 4 per cent and labour productivity by 3 per cent. Industrial output was down by 1.2 per cent and agricultural output by 2.3 per cent. Oil and coal, iron and steel, tractors and computer equipment, fertilizer and paper—all contracted. Admittedly, not everything declined. For example, the state debt had risen by more than a quarter; money incomes had gone up by 11 per cent; and inflation (reflecting these various circumstances) had increased to an annual rate of 19 per cent by the end of the year (unofficial sources put it much higher). Moreover, the trade deficit had risen from 3,400 million roubles in 1989 to 10,000 million roubles in 1990, even though overall trade volume had fallen by 7 per cent. Nor was it simply a matter of monetary aggregates, as the plan report also made clear. There was more crime; fewer schools and hospitals were built; and environmental conditions worsened considerably. Mr Gorbachev, his spokesman Gennady Gerasimov explained, had not won the Nobel Prize for economics. Anyone who read these results would have understood why.

The central government made an attempt to deal with some of these difficulties with an 'anti-crisis programme', launched by Prime Minister Pavlov on 22 April. Its central element was a sharp increase in state retail prices (beef, for instance, rose from 2 to 7 roubles a kilo), combined with a move towards free or 'agreed' prices for many others. These increases were combined with a more limited set of measures for the 'social compensation' of poorer sections of the community. As Mr Pavlov told the Supreme Soviet, the general level of retail prices was expected to rise by about 60 per cent in 1991. There would be fixed state prices for some basic commodities: meat, milk, tea, salt, children's goods and so forth. The price of medicines, coffee, energy, vodka and some other commodities would remain at the same level for the time being. About 30 per cent of retail trade, however, would be conducted at market prices, which should balance supply and demand. About 85 per cent of the increase in prices was to be returned in the form of social benefits, with priority being given to students, the handicapped, pensioners, and large and single-parent families. There would, Mr Pavlov warned, be further 'liberalization' of this kind in the future.

Market-oriented reforms were taken forward through other measures. In May the Supreme Soviet approved legislation that provided for the operation of wholly foreign-owned companies anywhere on Soviet territory. A Russian law that came into effect on 1 July gave official recognition to the concept of unemployment, hitherto formally outlawed since the closure of the last labour exchanges in 1930. Legislation on the 'basic principles of de-statification and privatization of enterprises' was adopted by the USSR Supreme Soviet in July. It envisaged the denationalization of 40–50 per cent of state assets by the end of 1992, rising to 60–70 per cent by 1995. Two distinctive approaches to economic reform began to emerge by the summer. One, Grigory Yavlinsky's 'grand bargain', envisaged large-scale technical and financial assistance from the West tied to a five-year programme of transition to a market economy. The other, associated with Prime Minister Pavlov, placed less emphasis on foreign economic assistance and rather more upon the restoration of planning discipline. A joint anti-crisis programme, approved by President Gorbachev and representatives of ten republics in July, leaned towards Mr Pavlov's approach; its stated objective was to build a 'socially-oriented market economy within a single, union-wide economic space'. More specifically, the programme included measures for coordinating the actions of central government and the republics, cutting budgetary expenditure, putting investment on a commercial rather than non-repayable basis, and social protection for the mass of the population. A coordinated approach to economic reform acquired further form when on 18 October the leaders of eight republics signed an agreement establishing an 'economic community'. It provided for the free movement of goods, services and labour, a common monetary and banking system, a coordinated policy on budgets and taxation, and price reform, with controlled prices for key goods and services.

The making of economic reform, as the year advanced, in fact became increasingly the prerogative of individual republican governments, as it became clear that at least the largest of them, the Russian, intended to press boldly forward towards a fully market system. President Yeltsin, speaking to the Russian Congress of People's Deputies in October, put forward a radical plan that involved financial discipline and privatization. At some risk to his own position, he proposed himself to discharge the duties of prime minister in addition to those of president until the reform process had been completed. The Yeltsin programme, which was approved on 1 November, included a tough monetary and financial policy and was widely compared to the 'shock therapy' that had already been implemented in Poland. Mr Yeltsin was given additional powers to implement his programme of reform on the same date, when lower levels of government were subordinated to the Russian presidency and local elections postponed until 1 December 1992. The liberalization of prices, a key element in the Russian reforms, was due to start in mid-December but was postponed until 2 January 1992. Such was Russia's economic influence that the other republics in the new Commonwealth were effectively obliged to follow suit. It was less clear how the reforms would be greeted by the general public, particularly by groups like the coal miners (who had taken extended industrial action in the spring) and by the increasingly militant and often unofficial labour unions.

In the sphere of international relations, the year began with the Soviet Union in broad agreement with its Western counterparts that Iraq's invasion of Kuwait could not be justified and that its forces must be unconditionally withdrawn (see AR 1990, p. 114). There was some evidence, during 1991, that Soviet perceptions of the war differed, at least in emphasis, from those of the allied powers. Speaking in Minsk, President Gorbachev asked why Iraq had been seen as an aggressor but not Israel, which had also violated UN resolutions. And why had the United States, which had invaded Grenada and Panama, been allowed to give lectures about the rights of man? However, his statement on the outbreak of the Gulf War (see V.2) emphasized that everything must be done to bring it to an end in cooperation with other countries and the United Nations. Foreign Ministry spokesmen took the same line, while urging a more broadly-conceived approach to Middle Eastern problems as a whole.

The year was otherwise remarkable for the closer integration of the Soviet Union into the world community. Full diplomatic relations were restored with Israel, after trading relations had been established the year before, and diplomatic relations were established for the first time with South Africa. Mr Gorbachev made the first-ever visit by a Soviet leader to South Korea in April and was also the first Soviet leader to visit Japan in the same month, where his discussions were inconclusive because of continuing differences over the fate of the southern Kurile islands (see also IX.2.iv).

It was also a year of moves towards greater integration of the USSR into the global economy, particularly at the Group of Seven summit in London on 15–17 July. President Gorbachev accepted an unprecedented invitation to be present for this gathering, at which discussions were dominated by the question of Western economic assistance to the Soviet Union. Some states (especially Germany) were willing to consider substantial assistance in the near future, while others (particularly the USA and Japan) opposed any further financial aid in advance of far-reaching economic reform. There were also divisions within the Soviet Union itself as to the policy that should be followed, so that the programme outlined by Mr Gorbachev included no more than modest moves towards privatization and military conversion in exchange for large-scale Western assistance.

The G-7 leaders eventually reached a general agreement to support 'moves towards the political and economic transformation of the Soviet Union' and expressed their readiness 'to assist the integration of the Soviet Union into the world economy'. Moreover, after a meeting with President Gorbachev (who explained that he had not come as a supplicant), they approved a more specific programme of assistance. This included special association with the IMF and World Bank, increased technical assistance, the promotion of Soviet trade and follow-up reports and visits.

July was also the occasion for a third and, as it transpired, final summit meeting between Presidents Gorbachev and Bush. The meeting, originally scheduled for February, was finally held in Moscow on 30–31 July. Despite acknowledged differences between the two sides over the pace of Soviet economic reform and policy towards the Baltic republics, the meeting was hailed by a Soviet government spokesman as an 'outstanding international event'. The most significant single development was the signing of a Strategic Arms Reduction Treaty (START) which committed each side to reduce its stock of strategic weapons by 30 per cent (see XII.3 and XIX.2). The Soviet Union also obtained most-favoured-nation status for its trade with the United States, while five bilateral agreements were signed on the prevention and management of industrial accidents, technical cooperation, civil aviation safety and other matters.

In wide-ranging talks on international and regional issues, the two leaders agreed, in particular, to convene a Middle East peace conference later in the year (see V.4.i). While in Moscow, President Bush held separate talks with President Yeltsin of Russia and the Kazakh President, Nursultan Nazarbaev, and he addressed the Ukrainian parliament on 1 August. Soviet-American relations were further improved by the announcement, in September, that the Soviet Union would be withdrawing 11,000 of its troops from Cuba and 'de-ideologizing' its relationship with the Castro administration (see also II.3.xi). The West was also gratified by the return of Mr Shevardnadze to the renamed and reorganized External Relations Ministry on 19 November, less than a year after his resignation from the post (see AR 1990, p. 114). As it turned out, however, the central USSR government structure was to expire little more than a month later.

ii. ESTONIA—LATVIA—LITHUANIA

Estonia
CAPITAL: Tallinn   AREA: 45,000 sq km   POPULATION: 1,600,000 ('91)
POLITICAL SYSTEM: emerging democracy
HEAD OF STATE: President Arnold Rüütel (since March '90)
PRINCIPAL MINISTERS: Edgar Savisaar (prime minister), Lennart Merri (foreign affairs)

Latvia
CAPITAL: Riga   AREA: 64,000 sq km   POPULATION: 2,700,000 ('91)
POLITICAL SYSTEM: emerging democracy
HEAD OF STATE: President Anatolijs Gorbunovs (since March '90)
PRINCIPAL MINISTERS: Ivars Godmanis (prime minister), Janis Jurkans (foreign affairs)

Lithuania
CAPITAL: Vilnius   AREA: 65,000 sq km   POPULATION: 3,700,000 ('91)
POLITICAL SYSTEM: emerging democracy
HEAD OF STATE: President Vytautas Landsbergis (since March '90)
PRINCIPAL MINISTERS: Gediminas Vagnorius (prime minister), Algirdas Saudargas (foreign affairs)

THE achievement of full independence by Estonia, Latvia and Lithuania in 1991 marked the historic and, in the end, speedy culmination of a process which began several years previously.

Incorporated into the USSR in 1940 under the terms of the Nazi-Soviet Pact of 1939, the three Baltic states had begun openly to press for a change in their status in the late 1980s. There had been demonstrations in 1987 on the anniversary of the pact, with several thousand involved in Estonia and up to 10,000 in Latvia (see AR 1987, p. 107). The text of the pact had become public in 1988, but nationalist pressure had meanwhile broadened into a widely-supported and sustained challenge to the whole structure of the Soviet state. Low birthrates and the attraction of higher living standards had led, particularly in Latvia, to anxiety about the immigration of non-nationals; and there was concern about the environmental damage that had been suffered as a result of decisions about economic development being taken in Moscow rather than in the republics themselves. Popular movements, ostensibly 'in support of *perestroika*' but in fact for the strengthening of local autonomy, had come into existence in all three republics in October 1988. There had also been considerable opposition to the changes proposed in the Soviet constitution later that year on the grounds that they were unduly centralizing in character (see AR 1988, pp. 110–11).

All three republics had been allowed to adopt a form of republican economic self-management from January 1990, but pressure for reform had continued and led to a massive demonstration on 23 August 1989, the 50th anniversary of the Nazi-Soviet Pact, when an estimated 2 million citizens had joined hands across the republics in the biggest demonstration yet seen (see AR 1989, pp. 101–2). Matters had reached a new stage with the election of nationalist majorities to the parliaments of all three republics in the spring of 1990. The Lithuanian parliament, hoping to anticipate Mr Gorbachev's acquisition of extensive presidential powers, had agreed to reaffirm the republic's declaration of independence of 1918 and had declared its incorporation into the USSR in 1940 to be illegal; it had also elected a new President, Vytautas Landsbergis, from the nationalist movement Sajudis. The declaration had not been accepted by the Soviet authorities and an economic blockade had later been imposed. These pressures notwithstanding, Estonia and Latvia had adopted more cautiously-worded resolutions in support of a transition to full independence, on 30 March and 4 May 1990 respectively. The matters at issue had then become the subject of Soviet-Baltic negotiations, but it was not until the following year, in the wake of the abortive Soviet coup of August 1991 (see IV.2.i), that all three republics were able to translate these declarations into reality and to resume their independent place in international affairs.

An outcome of this kind had seemed uncertain at the start of the year, when military action in the three republics had appeared to suggest a harsher policy by the central government towards nationalists and radicals. The use of military force in Latvia and Lithuania was justified by Moscow on the grounds that the Soviet constitution was being violated—in particular, that the civil rights of the non-indigenous population were being infringed and that the call-up of recruits into the armed forces was being impeded. In Lithuania 13 protesters died and 230 were injured on 13 January when troops stormed the television centre in Vilnius. In Latvia four died in a battle for government buildings in Riga on 20 January. President Gorbachev, speaking before the loss of life, claimed that local leaders were using 'slogans of democracy as a cover for a policy aimed at restoring a bourgeois system'; Boris Yeltsin, more forthrightly, described the action of the authorities as an 'offensive against democracy'. At least to some observers, the action in the Baltic republics represented an attempt by hard-line party and military officials, organized in a shadowy 'Committee of National Salvation', to seize power and overthrow the nationalist administrations. Whether they had taken such action with the authorization of President Gorbachev remained unclear, although it was widely agreed that he had failed to respond adequately to the loss of life.

The action of the central authorities, in any event, served to rally local opinion still more closely behind the nationalist leaderships. When the issue of full independence was put to the Baltic populations in the spring it received overwhelming endorsement. The Lithuanian vote, on 9 February, produced a majority of 90 per cent on an 84 per cent turnout. In Latvia and Estonia, on 3 March, there were majorities for independence of 74 and 78 per cent respectively on similar turnouts. The votes had little constitutional significance (although Iceland, for instance, moved at once to establish diplomatic relations with Lithuania). They nonetheless strengthened the authority of the republican leaderships as they gradually extended their effective control over local affairs while simultaneously withdrawing from the work of all-union institutions.

During the attempted coup in Moscow, on 20 and 21 August respectively, Estonia and Latvia formally declared themselves independent. The Lithuanian parliament had voted to this effect on 11 March 1990 (see AR 1990, p. 110). The independence of all three republics was recognized by the Russian Federation led by Mr Yeltsin, and finally, on 6 September, the USSR State Council—established just after the abortive coup—took the same position. The three states—which in their own view were reaffirming rather than gaining their independence at this time—were admitted to the Conference on Security and Cooperation in Europe on 10 September (see XI.5.i) and to the United Nations a week later (see XI.1).

V MIDDLE EAST AND NORTH AFRICA

1. CHRONOLOGY OF THE GULF WAR 1991

National and international aspects of the Gulf crisis feature extensively in the present volume, notably in the following part, which includes maps illustrating the conflict. Readers are also referred to the entry 'Gulf Crisis' in the index for guidance on other relevant coverage.

JANUARY

3   King Husain of Jordan in London for talks on Gulf crisis.
4   EC Foreign Ministers met in Luxembourg to consider Gulf crisis; French Foreign Minister put forward seven-point peace plan.
6   UK Prime Minister John Major began three-day visit to Gulf.
8   US Secretary of State Baker held crisis talks with President Mitterrand in Paris.
9   US Secretary of State and Iraqi Foreign Minister Tariq Aziz held fruitless talks in Geneva; Aziz refused a letter from President Bush to President Saddam Husain.
10 UK ambassador and remaining diplomats left Baghdad.
11 UN Secretary-General met EC Foreign Ministers in Geneva to discuss crisis.
12 Both houses of US Congress voted to authorize military action in Gulf, first time it had given such approval since World War II.
13 UN Secretary-General in Baghdad for talks with Saddam; he later had talks in Paris with President Mitterrand who had been attempting independent French peace initiative; US Secretary of State in London for talks as Britain ordered out more Iraqi embassy staff.
14 PM Major in Paris for crisis talks with President Mitterrand; France announced that Foreign Minister Dumas would go to Baghdad in last-ditch peace effort.
15 UN resolution 678 (of 29 Nov. 1990) approving use of force in Gulf became effective, Iraq having failed to meet deadline for withdrawal from Gulf.
    In UK, government had majority of 477 at end of debate on Gulf confrontation.
16 Gulf deadline officially expired at 5 am GMT, 8 am local time in Saudi Arabia; at night, allied forces launched massive bombing raids against military targets in Kuwait and Iraq at the start of 'Operation Desert Storm' for the liberation of Kuwait; these air raids continued nightly for the duration of the campaign.
18 Iraq launched Scud missiles against Israel, causing minor injury to 15 people in Tel-Aviv and Haifa; in course of the war, Israel was hit by 39 Scuds which killed 13 people, directly or indirectly, and injured 200.
19 In wake of second Scud missile attack, world leaders urged Israel not to retaliate in interest of preserving anti-Iraq coalition.
    All foreign correspondents ordered out of Baghdad.
20 US planes began attacking Iraq on northern front out of Turkey's Incirlik airbase.
    Patriot missiles destroyed first of many Scud missiles fired by Iraq at Dhahran air base and Riyadh, Saudi Arabia.
21 US installed Patriot air defence systems in Israel to counter Scud missile attacks.
    Iraq paraded seven allied POWs on TV and announced that they and others would be used as 'human shields' at potential strategic targets.
    In UK, House of Commons debated Gulf War.
    British navy took offensive action in Gulf for first time.

22 Iraq reported to have blown up installations at Walfra oilfield in Kuwait, causing dense smoke.
23 As Iraq launched its fourth Scud missile attack (which was intercepted by Patriot defence system), Israeli cabinet agreed a policy of restraint and non-retaliation.
  Chairman of US Joint Chiefs of Staff, Gen. Colin Powell, announced that allied air forces had now achieved air superiority over Iraq and would concentrate on severing supply lines between Iraq and its ground forces in Kuwait.
24 Allied forces retook Qaruh Island, first piece of Kuwait to be liberated; a Saudi pilot shot down two Iraqi jets flying in Saddam's first air offensive.
25 Crude oil pumped by Iraq from Mina al-Ahmadi station in Kuwait formed a slick 30-miles long and 8-miles wide; scientists predicted death of 1–2 million birds in world's worst-ever spillage; US fighters bombed complex on 27 Jan. in attempt to stem flow.
28 More than 100 Iraqi planes reported to have flown to Iran to seek shelter from allied bombing.
  Planned Moscow summit between Presidents Bush and Gorbachev, scheduled for Feb. 1991, postponed because of war.
29 French Defence Minister Jean-Pierre Chevènement resigned because of his opposition to French involvement in war; he was succeeded by Pierre Joxe.
29 In his State of the Union address, President Bush appealed for nation's support in seeking to drive Saddam out of Kuwait.
30 Hundreds of Iraqi soldiers and 12 US marines died in first land battle of war; Iraqi raiders had occupied town of Khafji on Saudi-Kuwait border.
31 Britain agreed to US request to station B52 bombers in UK to undertake bombing missions against strategic sites in Iraq.

FEBRUARY

3 US confirmed that seven marines had died under fire from their own side.
4 Iranian President Rafsanjani offered to mediate between Saddam and US; US battleship *Missouri* began shelling Iraqi ground forces in Kuwait.
5 Iraqi government announced ban on sale of all fuel oil.
6 King Husain of Jordan, in TV address, paid tribute to people and armed forces of Iraq.
8 US Defence Secretary Cheney and Gen. Colin Powell on weekend visit to Saudi Arabia to assess effects of allied offensive.
10 Soviet envoy Evgenii Primakov began new mission to Baghdad.
11 Chancellor Kohl and PM Major held talks in Bonn on Gulf and other issues.
13 Several hundred Iraqi civilians died when US planes bombed a bunker in Baghdad; allies claimed it was a military communications centre.
15 Iraq's Revolutionary Command Council issued statement offering to withdraw from Kuwait but conditions attached were immediately rejected by President Bush.
18 Iraqi Foreign Minister Tariq Aziz in Moscow to discuss a Soviet peace plan; further talks were held on 21 Feb.; on 22 Feb. USSR announced that Aziz had accepted its plan, but the terms were not acceptable to coalition partners.
21 British troops began biggest artillery bombardment since Korean war on Iraqi targets near northern border of Saudi Arabia; Saddam ruled out surrender, declaring 'the mother of battles will be our victory'.
22 President Bush gave Iraq ultimatum to pull out of Kuwait by 5 pm GMT on 23 Feb. or face ground war; he said Saddam had launched a scorched-earth policy in Kuwait; more than 150 oil wells were reported on fire.
24 At dawn (1 am GMT), allied forces launched ground offensive to liberate Kuwait; US announced surrender of 5,500 Iraqi troops in first hours; Iraqi troops blew

up public buildings and hotels in Kuwait City; 300 oil-wells reported on fire; in UK, the Queen made unprecedented broadcast to the nation.
15 Twenty-eight US troops died in Iraqi Scud missile attack in Saudi Arabia as ground offensive continued.
26 President Saddam, broadcasting on Iraqi radio, announced withdrawal from Kuwait; US planes bombed retreating Iraqi troops, thousands of whom surrendered to allies; nine British soldiers died in accidental attack by US plane during a tank battle.
27 Allied forces entered Kuwait city and Kuwait was declared liberated; almost all the country's oil wells were now on fire; exiled Emir declared three months of martial law to restore order to devastated country; Iraqi Foreign Minister wrote to UN agreeing to rescind Iraqi annexation of Kuwait and pay reparations; allied forces surrounded Republican Guard troops near Basra, having undertaken a massive flanking manoeuvre across southern Iraq; UK Foreign Secretary Hurd in Washington for talks with President Bush and Secretary of State Baker.
28 President Bush announced suspension of hostilities in Gulf from 5 am GMT; Iraq informed UN that it agreed to comply fully with resolution 660 and all other Security Council resolutions; 175,000 Iraqi POWs were held by allies.

MARCH

2 UN Security Council passed resolution 686 by 11 votes to 1 with three abstentions; it called for release of all POWs before final Gulf ceasefire could be signed.
3 Gulf commander Gen. Norman Schwarzkopf and other allied generals met defeated Iraqi commanders in a desert tent to conclude ceasefire terms; they agreed arrangements for release of POWs and Iraqis gave details of minefields in Iraq and Kuwait.
4 Kuwait's Crown Prince and Prime Minister returned to their homeland; exchange of allied and Iraqi POWs commenced.
6 UK PM Major was first allied leader to visit Kuwait city; his one-day visit to Gulf included talks with King of Saudi Arabia.
President Bush addressed joint session of Congress on ending of Gulf War.
7 US Secretary of State Baker began 10-day tour of Gulf; at meetings with Arab and Israeli leaders he discussed a new world order; first servicemen returned home from Gulf.
14 Emir of Kuwait returned to his homeland after seven-months' exile.
15 In Iraq, US troops reoccupied positions in Euphrates valley to deter Saddam's troops from crushing anti-government rebellion.
20 Kuwait's cabinet resigned; it was blamed for failing to restore public services after liberation.
22 UN sanctions committee agreed to lift restrictions on food and other essentials to Iraq amid mounting fears of famine and epidemics there.
25 Iraqi government forces bombed northern city of Kirkuk, held by Kurdish insurgents; loyalist troops reported to have suppressed three-week rebellion in southern Iraq.

APRIL

3 UN Security Council adopted resolution 687 on terms of full ceasefire in Gulf (see XIX.1).
9 UN Security Council approved resolution 689 on establishment of demilitarized zone between Iraq and Kuwait.
11 Gulf War ceasefire formally came into effect.

2. THE GULF WAR

HOSTILITIES began at 0800, local time in Kuwait, on 16 January 1991 (0500 GMT, midnight New York time), when the UN ultimatum ran out (see AR 1990, pp. 566).

Iraq remained the sole combatant against the UN coalition, in which 29 states took an active part.* The USA provided much the largest contingent of fighting troops, over 400,000 strong; the United Kingdom, which provided the next largest, only fielded a tenth as many. They came from every continent and from diverse religious, political and social cultures, including marxist and Muslim as well as Christian and agnostic, Arab and Slav as well as Latin and Anglo-Saxon. The presence of strangers with entirely foreign customs—such as women wearing visible trousers, or driving motor vehicles—was upsetting to Saudi Arabian society; but the upset was overridden by the urgency of the war's aim, to get the invader out of Kuwait. It had taken prodigious efforts by supply staffs to get the combatants to the theatre of war in time, with adequate supplies of ammunition, fuel and food.

The Americans' predominance in numbers made it clear that the supreme commander should be an American. He was H. Norman Schwarzkopf, a 56-year-old US Army three-star general of forceful personality with plenty of combat experience (in Vietnam), unlike most of those under his command, who were young and green. The British commander on the spot, Lieutenant-General Sir Peter de la Billière, had the advantage of having fought in the Middle East before, in a small, important but unpublicized Special Air Service (SAS) operation in Oman in 1959. He had also commanded the SAS in the Falklands campaign of 1982 (see AR 1982, pp. 7–21).

The presence of an ex-SAS general at once raised the concept of a move to eliminate Saddam Husain himself, and thus bring the war to an abrupt end. As it turned out, this was impossible, for no one could get close to him without marrying into his family—a step no one in the allied special services thought of taking, till too late. The Iraqi leader kept himself very much to himself, behind a bodyguard of his own relatives—a protection against his own officers as well as foreign enemies. He spent most of the war inside a deep bunker.

Saddam Husain commanded the fourth-largest armed forces in the world, battle-hardened by their eight years' war with Iran. His available army on the Kuwaiti front was estimated at 580,000-strong—superior to the coalition's in size. Size in this case was counterbalanced by

---

*They were Argentina, Australia, Bangladesh, Belgium, Canada, Czechoslovakia, Denmark, Egypt, France, Germany, Greece, Italy, Kuwait, Morocco, the Netherlands, New Zealand, Niger, Norway, Oman, Pakistan, Poland, Qatar, Saudi Arabia, Senegal, Spain, Syria, the United Arab Emirates, the United Kingdom and the United States.

V.2 THE GULF WAR 195

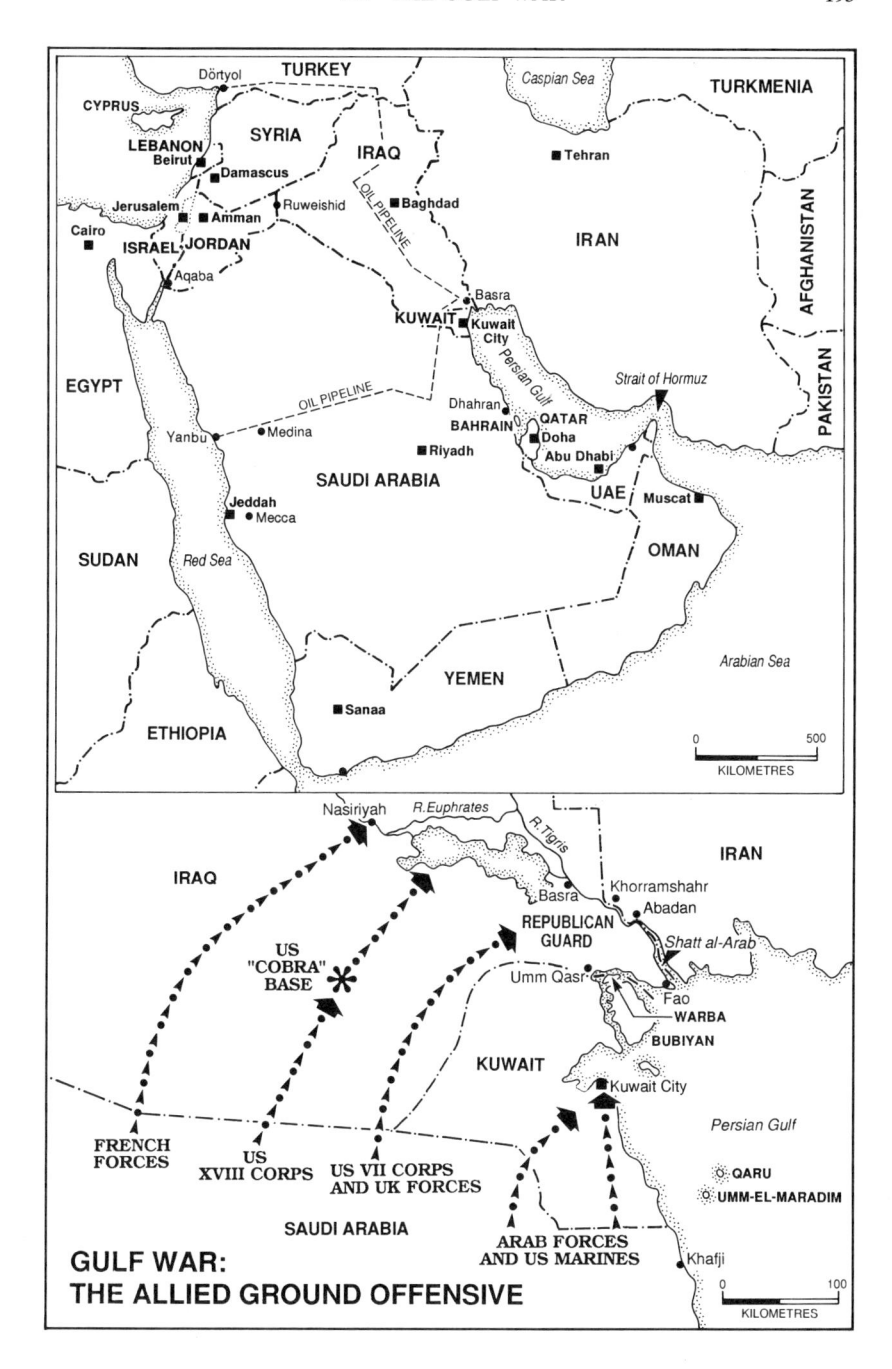

**GULF WAR:
THE ALLIED GROUND OFFENSIVE**

technology: the coalition's forces were much better equipped for their tasks. There was a vast disparity in technical capacity between the two sides. The allies—overwhelmingly, the Americans—had full control of all the latest gadgets; the Iraqis were several stages behind. Most of their equipment had come from the USSR, and had not been latest off the production line even there. Moreover, the Soviet authorities, though officially neutral in the war, had provided vital intelligence before it began about the exact performance of much of the equipment they had handed over. The Americans must have contemplated bringing the war to a sudden stop with a nuclear strike, against which Iraq was as powerless as any other state; but evidently they decided that a use of nuclear weapons would be counter-productive, after the bad press they had accumulated ever since 1945.

The first military task for the coalition was to secure air superiority. From the first night of the campaign (16/17 January), heavy allied air raids shook Baghdad and attacked Iraq's main centres of communication, by rail, road and radio. American bombers used to be notorious for inaccuracy of aim—ask any elderly Pisan. This time they and other allied bombers operated on the whole with surgical precision. The exactness of their target-finding depended partly on greatly improved equipment, and partly on target marking, carried out for them by British and American special troops, who would disguise themselves as locals and carry homing devices which they planted right at the points that needed to be attacked.

These special troops succeeded in avoiding any publicity at the time. All the same, the war was much set about with reporters from the news media, about whose role the commanders on each side made a mistake. The Iraqis reckoned that plenty of combat photography from the battlefield would work to their advantage, because the Vietnam War had shown that the American public could not stand the immediacies of conflict brought into their homes by television. They therefore welcomed Western television reporters in Baghdad during the run-up to the war, and, even after hostilities were well launched, kept—on a tight rein, but kept—a team from the American Cable News Network (CNN), who constantly televised coverage of what was going on round them. By contrast, the American high command, believing that it had lost the war in Vietnam because subversive telecasters had twisted the minds of American viewers by slanted reporting, was decidedly hostile in principle to the presence of reporters at all.

As it turned out, the CNN reports were recognized outside Iraq as having been prepared under duress, and therefore carried no especial weight. At the same time, reporting from the coalition side, thanks to a combination of censorship and goodwill, gave a fair enough account of what was happening without souring too many of the coalition's supporters into demanding that the war should be ended forthwith.

As was usual in wars, each side accused the other of atrocities. Tales of torture came out of occupied Kuwait, and whenever an allied bomb missed its mark—as was bound sometimes to happen—CNN produced pictures of civilian casualties.

Popular news media in the West, anxious to press an analogy between Saddam Husain and Adolf Hitler, postulated a resistance movement in Kuwait. Real evidence was slender. Acts of resistance heroism there undoubtedly were; but, to create the sort of organized, armed resistance movement that the Special Operations Executive and the Office of Strategic Services had supported in 1940–45, there had been neither time nor opportunity.

As well as resistance, there was its obverse, collaboration. Many (not all) of Kuwait's inhabitants of Palestinian origin welcomed and helped the invaders, providing labour and advice about where to loot. The Iraqi army followed sound mediæval precedent in looting Kuwait city thoroughly. Shops and houses from which the owners had fled, or of which the owners were suspect, were stripped of television sets, washing machines, freezers, fine carpets—anything portable and desirable. This activity went on steadily while battles raged elsewhere.

Iraq's anti-aircraft (AA) defences, such as they were, figured prominently among early coalition targets. In the course of the whole campaign the coalition lost 67 aircraft, for over 110,000 sorties flown—an acceptable rate of loss. On the first night, only one aircraft failed to return. The highly centralized Iraqi system never recovered from that initial attack, which knocked out most of the ground control interception centres from which the whole AA effort was to have been directed. Iraqi light AA guns remained alert and operational, and scored occasional successes against low-flying allied aircraft; but after the first night the country lay open to leisurely and accurate high-level attacks, which proceeded to demolish (for example) all the main road bridges over the Euphrates. Saddam Husain had his anti-aircraft commander executed.

On the second night of the war (17/18 January), the Iraqis used a few of their Scud ground-to-ground missiles, descendants of the Nazis' V2s, some against Saudi Arabia, some against neutral Israel. They were rumoured in Israel to be armed with chemical warheads; the rumour turned out untrue, but gas masks were distributed all over the country and dutifully worn during air raid alerts. The six missiles that hit Israeli territory in this initial attack killed nobody. Nor did they provoke what had evidently been the Iraqi aim: an Israeli act of war against Iraq, which would almost certainly have unsettled some of the coalition's Arab members. Israel did declare itself to be in a state of war (on 19 January), but it took no offensive action at all. Further Iraqi Scuds fired at Saudi Arabia on 18/19 January were all successfully intercepted by US Patriot anti-missile missiles. The Israelis had just received some Patriots, but evidently had not yet learned to use them properly. The missile attacks continued, with similar results, except that the Israelis rapidly learned to use their Patriots, suffering a total of two direct and 11 indirect fatalities from Scuds. The Iraqis were known to have 108 mobile Scud launchers; tracking them down and directing bombers onto them became another special forces' task, fairly successfully concluded. The one really successful Scud, right at the end of the war, hit a barracks at Dhahran in Saudi Arabia by chance, killing 28 American soldiers. The weapon, supposed to induce terror, failed to do so.

Air superiority, at once attained, was soon turned into air supremacy. Attacks on Iraqi airfields provoked, not counter-attacks by Iraqi fighters, but the desertion or flight of some 150 Iraqi warplanes (out of a total of some 750) into Iran, where they and their pilots were interned for the duration.

A few coalition air crews were captured by the Iraqis, after ejecting from their damaged aircraft. Some of them appeared on CNN's broadcasts, looking the worse for wear; after the war it was confirmed that they had been tortured. Saddam Husain announced that they were going to be placed round strategic targets in Iraq—a contravention of the Geneva convention on prisoners-of-war (though lawyers doubted whether the convention necessarily applied to the Gulf operations). Several more were rescued by helicopter missions into the Iraqi desert or by air/sea rescue craft in the Persian Gulf.

Coalition naval activity in the Gulf was intense. US navy aircraft played a full part in the air attacks on Iraq; plenty of publicity was given to the arrival of US marines and other commando-style units. No-one outside General Schwarzkopf's innermost circle realized then that this was part of a deception plan. Kuwaiti commandos took part, on 24 January, in the recapture of some offshore islands; the Royal Navy began that day the process of sinking the Iraqi navy, most of which was on the bottom by the end of the war. In any case, the main Iraqi naval effort seemed to be devoted to moving loot out of Kuwait rather than to naval business proper.

As a retaliation against coalition activity at sea, Iraq began releasing oil from Kuwaiti storage tanks at the head of the Gulf, thus creating a vast oil slick, which moved slowly south-eastward, damaging bird life and threatening some Saudi water supplies. Moreover, from 23 January the oil wells in Kuwait began to burn; by the end of the war, over 600 of them had been set ablaze. Some of them burned till November. A few may have been set on fire by allied bombing; igniting the rest can only have been an act of spite by the Iraqis.

On 29 January the Iraqis mounted their only ground attack of the war. It was aimed at Khafji, a Saudi coastal town ten miles south of the Kuwaiti border which had already been abandoned by its inhabitants. The attack was ill coordinated—over half the troops allotted to it never reached the battle. Saudi and Qatari troops, aided by US marines, repelled it within 48 hours. The 400-strong Iraqi battalion that took Khafji lost 65 dead and then surrendered. Eleven US marines were killed, seven of them in a single incident by friendly fire. Of 17 small boats full of Iraqi commandos, intended to make a simultaneous assault by sea, 14 were sunk and three ran ashore.

A feature of the Khafji episode was that the main Iraqi force approaching overland had its tank turrets reversed, as if surrendering; moreover, the infantry with the tanks had their hands up. As they closed the coalition positions, and Saudi troops came out to accept the surrender, the tank turrets turned round and the Iraqi infantry opened fire. This may only have been a *ruse de guerre*; it may also have been meant to show the rest of the Iraqi army that attempts to surrender would not necessarily work. Coalition commanders also noted that, although the complicated Iraqi attack plan was several times dislocated, no attempt was made to revise it on the spot. Moreover, Saddam Husain announced the complete success of the attack, regardless of the facts. This was taken by General Schwarzkopf's staff as a sign that he would be susceptible to well-organized deception, with which they got busy.

Just as, before the war began, amateur strategists and earnest politicians had urged that sanctions should be used instead of war, after it started there was an agitation to maintain pressure by air attack, without an advance on the ground. Others pointed out that history contained hardly any examples of strategic success through air attack alone. General Schwarzkopf himself always intended a ground attack, and was confirmed in his intention after a visit on 9 February from his immediate US superiors, General Powell, the US Chief of Staff, and Richard Cheney, the Defence Secretary. He kept the media, and the world, interested in the threats of combined operations in the Persian Gulf, while he prepared to outflank the Iraqi armies in and north of Kuwait by delivering a 'left hook' so deep that, unless the Iraqis reacted to it, they would be altogether cut off from their base. Meanwhile, air attacks continued to keep Iraqi communications cut and persistently bombarded the Republican Guard, reputedly the fighting core of the Iraqi army, where it was stationed north of the Kuwaiti border. Diplomatic efforts continued to try to remove the Iraqis from Kuwait on terms acceptable to the UN as well as the USA. They failed, although the ground attack was put off for three days to give them further chances of succeeding.

The onslaught began at 0400 local time on Sunday, 24 February. Within 100 hours it had attained complete success. A French light division provided a flank guard on the extreme left; it advanced 100 miles in the first 24 hours. An American armoured corps, including the British first armoured division, delivered the main punch, while Egyptian, Saudi and American troops engaged the enemy's attention closer to Kuwait city. Iraqi conscripts near the frontier surrendered in droves—20,000 were taken prisoner on the first day—and, tank for tank, the Republican Guard proved much inferior to its assailants. Mines had been expected to present a problem, especially if they were gas mines. Gas mines were indeed found, but none exploded. Nautical mines scored two hits on US warships in the Gulf, neither fatal. Land mines were swept away by flail tanks or safely lifted by engineers. Sand berms round Iraqi positions were breached with no trouble by armoured bulldozers. In short, the land battle followed the pattern of the air battle: coalition techniques were far in advance of Iraqi ones and the Iraqi army showed even less fight than the air force.

On 25 February, as Iraqi broadcasts were still claiming successes, Saddam Husain ordered his troops to withdraw from Kuwait. Even at this stage, Iraqi soldiers could not resist the temptation to loot. A four-mile traffic jam of Iraqi vehicles, caught withdrawing along the Mutla ridge north of Kuwait, was shot up on 26 February by American aircraft. The whole convoy caught fire. A few hours later, when allied troops reached the wreckage, it stank about equally of dead flesh and of looted scent. On 27 February President Bush decided that enough was enough, with the result that hostilities ceased the following day.

Casualties on the allied side turned out to have been ludicrously light: fewer than 200 dead all told, of whom about a quarter had been accidentally killed by their own side. The extent of the Iraqi casualties remained unknown. Estimates varied between a minimum of 8,000 dead and a maximum of over 16 times that number. Certainly, scores of thousands of Iraqi soldiers deserted.

3. ISRAEL

CAPITAL: Jerusalem   AREA: 22,000 sq km   POPULATION: 5,010,000 ('91)
OFFICIAL LANGUAGE: Hebrew
POLITICAL SYSTEM: parliamentary democracy
HEAD OF STATE: President Chaim Herzog (since May '83)
RULING PARTIES: coalition led by Likud with small religious and nationalist parties
HEAD OF GOVERNMENT: Yitzhak Shamir, Prime Minister (since Oct '86)
PRINCIPAL MINISTERS: David Levi (deputy premier, foreign affairs), Moshe Nissim (deputy premier, trade & industry), Moshe Arens (defence), Yitzhak Modai (finance), Dan Meridor (justice), Arie Deri (interior), David Magen (economy & planning)
CURRENCY: new shekel (end-'91 £1=NIS4.26, US$1=NIS2.29)
GNP PER CAPITA: US$9,790 ('89)
MAIN EXPORT EARNERS: diamonds, machinery, agricultural produce, tourism

LIKE other states in the region, Israel was seized throughout January and February by the impact upon it of Saddam Husain's aggression and the Arab–Western coalition's military campaign to liberate Kuwait (see V.2). Beginning on the second night of the war (18/19 January), Iraq attacked Israel with a sustained barrage of Scud missiles, totalling 39 in all during the six weeks of the war. Yet Saddam failed to accomplish his apparent aim of drawing Israel into the battle in order to undermine the solidarity of the Arab powers arrayed against Iraq. The USA applied heavy pressure on Israel to refrain from a military response. Fear of chemical warheads, and an apparent lack of intelligence about Iraqi capacity, made Israelis nervous. But, while reserving the right to retaliate at a time and in a manner of its own choosing, the government appreciated the wisdom of passivity while the American-led forces were clearly doing everything they could, if indeed without great success, to destroy Iraq's missile fire-power.

An unexpected result of the engagement was the participation for the first time of US soldiers on Israeli soil, to assist in the speedy deployment of Patriot missiles against the Scuds. The performance of the Patriots was not completely satisfactory to the Israeli military, but they did much to sustain the morale of the public, tired out by weeks of taking nightly shelter in sealed rooms wearing gas masks. The Scuds, aimed mainly at the civilian populations of metropolitan Tel Aviv and Haifa, in the event took a remarkably light toll. There were no more than two directly-attributable fatalities and a further 11 indirect deaths from heart attacks, suffocation due to improper handling of gas masks, and the like. Some 200 were injured, and over 1,600 families lost their homes. There was extensive damage to over 4,000 buildings.

The brunt of the attack fell in the vicinity of Tel Aviv and Ramat Gan. Although there was an exodus to Jerusalem and Eilat from the targeted areas of the coastal plain, an atmosphere of calm stoicism prevailed. Opinion surveys showed support from three-quarters of the population for the government's policy of refraining from immediate military retaliation. While the Israelis sweated in their sealed rooms, the Palestinians of the occupied West Bank were placed under curfew. There was evidence that they celebrated the arrival of every missile from Iraq, by dancing on the roofs of their houses. This support for the Iraqi dictator lost the Palestinians sympathy among the dovish left of Israeli politics and contributed to a hardening of the prevailing right-wing nationalist sentiment in Israel.

Israel's restraint earned it some credit with the US administration, with the result that relations with Washington, having been placed under strain due to Israel's colonizing activity on the West Bank, improved for a while. Defence Minister Arens visited Washington in February in the midst of the war to discuss strategic coordination and increased military and economic aid to Israel. After a year of stalling on the issue owing to suspicion that Israel was investing heavily in construction on the West Bank, US Secretary of State James Baker finally signed a loan-guarantee of $400 million for housing new immigrants, conditional on assurances that the money would not be spent in the occupied territories.

Following the war, relations between Israel and the USA soured again due to an apparent Israeli reluctance to enter peace negotiations. Secretary Baker in March began a tireless round of Middle East capitals aimed at persuading Israel and the Arabs to join in a regional peace conference. The US government exerted exceptional leverage on Israel by witholding from it, at least until the new year, loan guarantees to a total of $10,000 million which Israel needed for the housing of new immigrants. President Bush took a tough stand against congressional sentiment on the issue. As though to counter intemperate accusations made in Israel that he was anti-Israel and anti-semitic, he gave a lead in late September to a successful campaign in the UN General Assembly to rescind its 'Zionism is racism' resolution of 1975 (see XI.1 and XIII).

In September, after the Arabs had all fallen into line, Prime Minister Shamir finally succumbed to US pressure for a peace conference. He later yielded also on Israel's preference for a Middle Eastern venue, by agreeing to participate in preliminary peace talks at Madrid in October (see also V.4.i). At the same time, Mr Shamir made it clear that Israel would not consider giving up any occupied territory in return for peace. In a surprise stroke, as though to give added emphasis to Israel's firmness on the issue of territory, Mr Shamir announced on the eve of the talks that he personally would head the Israeli delegation to Madrid. He thereby snubbed Foreign Minister David Levy, whose reputation was that of a conciliatory negotiator and who, in a fit of pique, refused to attend himself.

The drama of Madrid generated some cautious optimism among the public, but the government's lack of enthusiasm for the talks discouraged expectations of progress. As though to give emphasis to this downbeat verdict on the process, Mr Shamir assured the public that not an inch of land would be negotiable. Nor did he do anything to persuade the right-wing fringe parties to withdraw their threat to leave the government if discussion of autonomy on the West Bank took place on the basis of the formula agreed at Camp David between Egypt and Israel. When the talks moved to Washington in December, the last days of the year were spent by Israelis and Palestinians sitting in the corridors locked in a procedural wrangle about the extent of the Palestinian delegation's separate standing. Mr Shamir seemed able, in effect, to slow down the process of negotiation without incurring a political penalty at home. His posture was successfully portrayed to the peace-hungry Israeli public as strong rather than negative.

In a year that began and ended with the major dramas of war and peace, no event so captured the imagination of the public as the influx of Ethiopian Jews (Falashas) at the end of May. The massive overnight airlift of 14,000 destitute people, dubbed 'Operation Solomon', was organized in secrecy. Meantime, the immigration of Jews from what was still the Soviet Union continued at a reduced rate compared with the peaks of 1990. At the year's end, it was estimated that some 145,000

Russians had arrived, compared with 185,000 in the previous year. In consequence Israel's population rose above the 5 million mark.

Friction, disgruntlement and occasional despair characterized the adjustment of the Russian immigrants, as a shortage of housing and a dearth of employment opportunities took their toll in morale. It was widely assumed that many of the Russians would leave Israel if the gates were opened to them elsewhere. The shortage of employment was not due entirely to the pressure of mass immigration; rather, it reflected the general condition of recession in the economy. Inflation was only slightly higher, at 18 per cent compared with 17.6 per cent in 1990, and devaluation of the currency was controlled at a moderate rate. Nevertheless, deep economic malaise and a steady increase in the chronic budget deficit were unaffected by government efforts to increase taxes and keep public spending down. Pressures from military spending and for public housing were the most intense. At the same time, the religious parties and other special interest groups haggled to exact material benefits in return for their support for the 1992 calendar year budget. This resulted in the Knesset's failure to approve the NIS 108,000 million budget package by the set deadline of 31 December, so that the government entered the new year technically in an unfunded state.

The government's narrow majority in the Knesset was increased by two extra votes in February by the controversial inclusion of the Moledet party in the coalition. Regarded as the furthest to the right of all parties in the Knesset and separated from the outlawed Kach only by a terminological hair's-breadth, Moledet stood for the 'transfer' to neighbouring Arab states of the Palestinian population of the occupied territories. In late December two votes were in turn lost by the coalition. Agriculture Minister Rafael Eitan, leader of Tsomet, announced his resignation when it became clear that Mr Shamir would violate an undertaking to allow a free vote on the issue of electoral reform. Mr Shamir fiercely opposed direct elections for the post of prime minister, a proposal advanced because of the substantial vote for numerous smaller parties in recent Knesset elections. At a convention of the ruling Likud in December, he forced through a rejection of the proposed reform, making it clear that he would penalize any supporters of the measure when it came to a vote in the Knesset.

Indeed, Mr Shamir seemed not uncomfortable with his power in thrall all year to the will of the extremist right-wing and religious fringe. Although the figures were shrouded in mystery, it was known that vast sums were being spent on expensive West Bank settlement, against the better judgement of the military. Housing Minister Ariel Sharon set the pace, using provocative statements and actions at every opportunity. But he was undoubtedly backed by the Prime Minister and, if not unanimously, by the government itself. It came to appear that Mr Shamir and his colleagues were even willing, in the end, to risk all American aid, if that proved to be the cost of creating irrevocable 'facts' in the occupied territories.

In April, after a four-year term, General Dan Shomron relinquished his baton as Chief of Staff and handed over to Ehud Barak, his deputy. In December the retiring air force chief, Avihu Bin-Nun, delivered a withering blast of criticism of the government. Forced by Defence Minister Arens and Chief of Staff Barak to apologize for his insubordination, on pain of dismissal in his last week in the job, General Bin-Nun acknowledged his political indiscretion. However, he could not withdraw the force of his comments, to the effect that the government had allowed policy guidance on matters of security to drift into a state of anarchy.

The Palestinian uprising continued sporadically through the year, while an increase in vigilantism among the West Bank settlers defied and disturbed the military authorities. Leaders of the Jewish settlements were galvanized by the peace negotiations to mobilize their energies with a view to undermining any practical possibility of Palestinian autonomy.

In October the Soviet Union and Israel restored diplomatic relations, which had been broken off following the war of 1967. The new Soviet ambassador presented his credentials to the Israeli President in the last week of December, fully expecting that in the new year he would become plenipotentiary of Russia. At the same time, Israel made plans to send emissaries to the independent republics of the old Soviet Union.

4. ARAB WORLD—EGYPT—JORDAN—SYRIA—LEBANON—IRAQ

i. THE ARAB WORLD

THE defeat of Iraq in the Gulf War (see V.2) made the Arab peoples more anti-Western, not only in Jordan and Yemen, whose leaders had supported Saddam Husain, and in North Africa, hitherto preoccupied with its own affairs, but even in Syria, whose government had joined the allies. The expatriate Palestinian leadership, having also backed Saddam, looked foolish and many innocent Palestinians in the Gulf were penalized for its mistakes. The war gravely damaged Iraq and Kuwait, and other countries suffered interruption of their lucrative Gulf trade and workers' remittances. The crisis showed up Arab folly and reminded the Americans how unpopular Israeli intransigence had made them in this vital region; but by discrediting the PLO in Tunis it encouraged the pragmatism of educated Palestinians in the occupied territories (OT). The collapse of Soviet power also improved the chances of peace.

Fresh moves towards a settlement began on 6 March, when President Bush declared that it was time to end the Arab-Israeli conflict. Five days later Secretary Baker returned, on the first of his many 1991 visits, to a very disturbed Middle East. Many ordinary Palestinians were reported to have cheered as Iraq's Scud missiles reached Israel (see V.3). The Israelis had disregarded a UN Security Council resolution criticizing their conduct in the OT, where they were still meeting disorder by shooting rioters and intensifying illegal expulsions. But on 25 March the PLO leader, Yassir Arafat, mentioned the possibility of a UN-policed buffer zone between Israel and a demilitarized Palestinian state. A month later Israel's Prime Minister, Mr Shamir, while still refusing to surrender any of the OT, suggested that his successor might in five years' time be ready for territorial compromise.

Mr Baker's discussions concerned the modalities rather than the substance of negotiation. On the latter the two sides seemed irreconcilable, with the Israelis tirelessly insisting that they would never trade territory for peace. Even the modalities were controversial. Israel aimed to push the UN aside, reduce the role of the superpowers and deal separately with each Arab state, while refusing to negotiate with the PLO at all. The Arabs, and especially the Palestinians, wanted one grand continuing conference chaired by the UN.

On 1 June Mr Baker formally proposed to the governments concerned that the conference should be chaired jointly by the USA and the USSR; delegations should be Israeli, Egyptian, Syrian, Lebanese and Jordanian–Palestinian; others, including the UN, should attend as observers. Once opened, the conference would divide into separate bilateral negotiations, but the plenum would periodically re-convene. He reportedly promised Jerusalem to support its contention that the PLO and residents of East Jerusalem should not officially participate, but also urged Israel not to expand its settlements on the West Bank.

Mr Shamir at once rejected most of this, refusing any role to the UN and claiming the right to veto Palestinians nominated to the joint Palestinian–Jordanian delegation. After many negotiating shuttles, Mr Baker secured Arab agreement, with even Syria accepting (in mid-July). Jerusalem delayed its acceptance till August and then hedged it with conditions. Mr Bush propitiated Jewish sentiment by proposing the repeal of the 1975 UN General Assembly resolution equating Zionism with racism.

The Palestinians spoke with several voices. The diaspora rejectionists opposed the planned conference, as did Hamas, the Islamic fundamentalist organization in the OT. Increasingly, however, the decisive voices came from the more Westernized people there; Mr Baker regularly met them, despite Israeli disapproval. Mr Arafat and the PLO mainstream followed; the rejectionist PFLP withdrew. On 18 October the PLO's central council voted to participate in the conference and claimed that the Palestinian delegation there would be 'directed' by the PLO. This was an overstatement of the PLO's role.

Hoping, doubtless, to encourage realism in Jerusalem as well as Arab goodwill, Washington in October succeeded in persuading Congress to delay guaranteeing a $10,000 million loan to Israel, to cover the absorption of incoming Soviet Jews.

Events in the OT themselves looked unpropitious for the conference. No-one, apparently, could stop the Israelis extending Jewish settlements. There were regular assassinations of settlers and of Palestinian collaborators. Murdered settlers were outnumbered by Palestinians shot by Israeli occupying troops. Israel continued illegally deporting Arab 'inciters'.

On 18 October a joint letter from Presidents Bush and Gorbachev invited the front-line Arab states, and the Palestinians as part of the Jordanian delegation, to attend a peace conference in Madrid on 30 October; the UN, the European Community and the Gulf Cooperation Council (GCC) were also invited. Four days later there would be bilateral negotiations and, after that, multilateral talks on regional issues.

This letter avoided a crucial issue: which Palestinians should join the Jordanian delegation and what would be their relation to the PLO. A rough and ready solution was reached. There would be no overt PLO representation among the 14 Palestinians nominated; but regular contact with the PLO leadership, through advisers led by Faisal Husaini, appeared to be winked at by the US and Israeli governments. Israel later abandoned its attempt to have the most effective Palestinian, Mrs Hannan Ashrawi, arrested in Israel for meeting PLO leaders; the US dropped its initial refusal of visas to PLO members.

The conference opened in the Spanish capital on 30 October as planned, with much Syrian and Israeli rhetoric for the record, but progressed only slowly to the bilateral stage. Israel, the most reluctant participant, objected to meeting anywhere outside the Middle East, aiming to lure the Arabs to Jerusalem and thus obtain their de facto recognition. Eventually, the USA unilaterally moved the conference to Washington, where the Israelis, claiming they could not be ready by the date suggested, arrived five days late. Meanwhile, US officials had attempted to promote discussions of substance by inquiring from various participants what concessions they might make in exchange for their known main desideratum (e.g. for Syria, the return of the Golan heights). The Washington meetings were dominated by Israel's refusal to negotiate separately with Jordan and the Palestinians, so that their talks stayed, literally, in the corridor. The delegates finally went into recess on 18 December.

In all this the Arab League, hamstrung by Iraq's continued membership, proved marginal. Inter-Arab consultation was not conducted in the League but in Damascus, at an ad hoc meeting on 23 October of those directly affected, with observers representing the Gulf and Maghreb states.

The Gulf War produced a plan for a permanent Arab peacekeeping force, to be manned by Egypt and Syria (both with sizeable forces already in place) and financed by the GCC. But there was considerable fear of the cost and a tendency to regard Western backing and Iranian cooperation as essential. Egypt opposed the latter, while Iran itself was suspicious. Nothing was achieved in repeated consultations, so that the group's final communique made no mention of an Arab force for the Gulf. Meanwhile, the Egyptian and Syrian troops had gone home.

The discovery of Iraq's non-conventional arsenal (see V.4.vi) had shown how dangerous was the proliferation of such weapons. In March President Mubarak of Egypt proposed that the Middle East, including Israel, should be made free of nuclear weapons. In May President Bush advocated an end to the proliferation of non-conventional weapons in the area and that leading arms-supplying countries should curb deliveries. In July the five permanent Security Council powers agreed to establish a weapons-free zone in the Middle East, the final goal being the elimination of surface-to-surface missiles. They called on regional governments to accept international control on their nuclear activities, sign the forthcoming treaty on chemical weapons and stop importing weapons-grade nuclear materials.

ii. EGYPT

CAPITAL: Cairo   AREA: 1,000,000 sq km   POPULATION: 51,000,000 ('89)
OFFICIAL LANGUAGE: Arabic   POLITICAL SYSTEM: presidential democracy
HEAD OF STATE AND GOVERNMENT: President Mohammed Husni Mubarak (since '81)
RULING PARTY: National Democratic Party (NDP)
PRINCIPAL MINISTERS: Atif Sidqi (prime minister), Kamal Ahmed Ganzouri (deputy premier, finance, economy & planning), Boutros Boutros Ghali (deputy premier, foreign liaison), Yusuf Amin Wali (deputy premier, agriculture), Gen. Mohammed Hussein Tantawi Sulayman (defence), Amr Mohammed Moussa (foreign affairs), Mohammed Abdel-Halim Moussa (interior), Mohammed al-Razaz (finance), Farouk Seif al-Nasr (justice)
INTERNATIONAL ALIGNMENT: NAM, Arab League, OAPEC, ACC, OAU, ICO, Francophonie
CURRENCY: Egyptian pound (end-'91 £1=LE6.20, US$1=LE3.32)
GNP PER CAPITA: US$640 ('89)
MAIN EXPORT EARNERS: oil and gas, cotton, tourism, agricultural produce

EGYPT'S role in the Gulf War (see V.2) strengthened its international prestige and status but divided it further from the pro-Iraq feelings of some Arab governments and most Arab peoples. Nor did the whole Egyptian public support President Husni Mubarak on this issue. The war also damaged Egypt's already ailing economy, though bringing help to its finances. But at least America's increased commitment to the Arab-Israeli peace process, by creating distance between Washington and Jerusalem, alleviated the embarrassment of Egypt's friendship with the West and its relations with Israel.

The war brought protests, and demands for the return of Egyptian troops, from fundamentalists of the Muslim Brotherhood and Al Jihad and from left-wing, anti-American opponents of the government; these continued until the ceasefire. On 24 January President Mubarak explained to parliament how persistently he had intervened with Saddam Husain in an attempt to prevent war, and attacked Saddam's bad faith. Government pronouncements stressed that Iraq's territorial integrity must be preserved and that Arab troops must not be asked to invade it; although Saddam's attempt to link his aggression with the Arab-Israeli question was inadmissible in Egypt's view, the latter must be addressed as soon as the former had been settled. The Egyptian leader also opposed any involvement of Israel in the war.

The land war, in which about 35,000 Egyptians participated and nine were killed, brought together Egypt and Syria, the most important non-Gulf Arab countries in the coalition. Later, their Foreign Ministers issued a call for a permanent Arab peacekeeping force (see V.4.i).

President Mubarak was keen to help solve the Middle East's political problems. In March he stressed that the war had been one of legitimacy versus anarchy, not East versus West, and urged that the whole area, including Israel, should be free of nuclear weapons. This theme was resumed in July, when the Egyptian Foreign Minister supported the Security Council's plea for a Middle East free of nuclear weapons. In the autumn Egypt attended, as an observer, the Middle East peace negotiations in Madrid and Washington.

There was less to sour Egyptian-Israeli relations than in previous years, but Israel's behaviour in the occupied territories was a constant irritant. In July President Mubarak supported Secretary Baker's suggestion that the Arabs should stop boycotting Israel in exchange for a freeze on settlement.

Pro-Iraqi sentiment in Algeria, Tunisia and Morocco made for friction in Egyptian relations with those countries. Requirements for visas, not hitherto needed, were imposed, from fear that the three states might issue passports to Palestinian terrorists. Oddly, relations improved with Libya, which President Mubarak himself visited. He condemned Sudan's support of Iraq; a special guard was put on the High Dam; and the Egyptian University's branch in Khartoum was closed. The election in December of Egypt's Deputy Prime Minister, Boutros Boutros Ghali, as Secretary-General of the UN was a feather in Egypt's cap (see XI.1).

President Mubarak was much on tour, often hunting for money. The Gulf War greatly increased Egypt's burdens: thousands more of its migrant workers returned, fewer tourists came (until later in the year), less shipping used the Suez Canal and some oil companies seemed reluctant to renew their concessions. Unemployment was reportedly over 17 per cent, and by July the government estimated that the crisis had cost Egypt US$20,000 million.

The financial effects of the war were not wholly unfavourable, however. Members of the coalition forgave Egypt about $13,000 million of its debts (Britain cancelled $550 million), and this greater generosity must also have affected negotiations with the IMF. In April the latter promised Egypt a stand-by loan and creditors then agreed to reschedule and write-off much of Egypt's debts over the next few years. Nevertheless, Egypt's indebtedness was still some $40,000 million at year's end.

The debt rescheduling agreement was linked to the implementation of economic reforms, which included a 10 per cent sales tax (except on food), 30 per cent increases in energy prices and an income-tax floor of LE2,000, later raised to LE3,000. The government also planned to rationalize part of the state sector by running it on commercial lines with minimum state intervention. The IBRD and IDA approved loans to support the government's structural adjustments and to establish a social fund to help those who lost jobs through the reforms and the Gulf War. In February a free market in foreign exchange had been opened, cutting the value of the Egyptian pound against the dollar by 10 per cent. In October the foreign exchange regime was further liberalized by the unification of the commercial and central bank markets.

There was a major cabinet reshuffle in May, following the appointment of the then Foreign Minister, Esmat Abdul Meguid, as secretary-general of the Arab League. He was replaced by Egypt's representative at the UN, Amr Muhammad Musa. The Defence Minister was replaced by the commander of the Egyptian forces in the Gulf, and new ministers were appointed for oil, education and local affairs (a new post).

Apart from agitation against Egypt's support for the anti-Iraq coalition, there seemed to be less internal effervescence. In January the police mounted a campaign in Upper Egypt against drug-dealers and terrorists, while drug-dealing by parliamentary deputies also came under investigation. In September there was inter-confessional violence, with attacks on Coptic churches. In April Khalid Abdul Nasser (see AR 1990, p. 205) was acquitted on charges of subversion.

The Arab world's leading performer and composer of music, Muhammad Abdul Wahhab, died on 4 May.

iii. JORDAN

CAPITAL: Amman   AREA: 97,000 sq km   POPULATION: 3,900,000 ('89)
OFFICIAL LANGUAGE: Arabic   POLITICAL SYSTEM: monarchy
HEAD OF STATE AND GOVERNMENT: King Husain ibn Talal (since Aug '52)
PRINCIPAL MINISTERS: Field Marshal Sharif Zaid ibn Shaker (prime minister, defence), Dhuqan al-Hindawi (deputy premier, education), Ali al-Suhaymat (deputy premier, transport), Kamil Abu Jabir (foreign affairs), Basil Jardana (finance), Yusuf al-Mubayyidin (justice), Jawdat al-Subul (interior)
INTERNATIONAL ALIGNMENT: NAM, Arab League, ACC, ICO
CURRENCY: dinar (end-'91 £1=JD1.25, US$1=JD0.67)
GNP PER CAPITA: US$1,640 ('89)
MAIN EXPORT EARNERS: phosphates, chemicals, cement

THE Gulf War (see V.2) aggravated Jordan's economic situation, as popular xenophobia and fundamentalist influence made it even harder for King Husain to recover from his mistake in supporting Saddam Husain. But his doggedness (and Western magnanimity) succeeded in restoring relations, even with the less forgiving anti-Saddam Arabs. The King later accepted an invitation for Jordan to attend the Madrid peace conference (see V.4.i). Popular and political opposition forced him to bring back a strong and tried Prime Minister.

On 1 January King Husain reshuffled his government, apparently to conciliate pro-Iraqi feeling and to reflect fundamentalist strength in parliament; Tahir al Masri, the new Foreign Minister, was a Palestinian. Seven Muslim Brothers, with two other fundamentalists, were now in the cabinet, one holding the important portfolio of education. The King also approved the proposed National Charter legalizing political parties. Next day he started for Europe in the hope of preventing war. Its outbreak two weeks later intensified anti-Western feeling, and a parliamentary resolution reviled America, once King Husain's friend, as 'the Great Satan'.

This feeling mounted in February, when Jordanians were killed in allied attacks on the Jordan-Iraq highway; one such attack was condemned by the UN Secretary-General. On 6 February the King made a violently pro-Iraqi broadcast. The Saudis banned trade with Jordan, provoking anti-Saudi riots, and the USA started to review some of its aid; in contrast, Japan and the European Community allocated larger slices of theirs to Jordan. The last-minute Soviet peace initiative was welcomed by Jordan, as it had earlier proposals by Iran, with whom Jordan had just restored relations. The Foreign Minister was leaving on another peace-making tour in Europe when the land war started.

The coalition's lightning victory changed the mood in Jordan. Saddam Husain's pictures began to disappear and on 1 March the King welcomed the liberation of Kuwait and pleaded for a general reconciliation, to include the question of Palestine. Kuwait received this frostily but Jordan's former Western friends were more forgiving. A British minister was in Amman on 11 March, and President Bush fought hard with

Congress before being forced to sign a bill suspending US aid. Jordan certainly needed it; according to the Prime Minister, the war had cost Jordan billions, and UNICEF reported that many more families were now below the poverty line than a year earlier.

The fundamentalist deputies, besides backing Saddam, were unrealistic in their economics and reactionary in their politics. They tried to segregate girls from boys at school and urged that the Sharia (Islamic law) should govern the new National Charter which King Husain had approved on 9 June. Ten days later he accepted the resignation of the Prime Minister, Mudar Badran, who was thought too close to the fundamentalists, and replaced him with Foreign Minister Tahir al Masri. The fundamentalist ministers were dropped at the King's behest. On 7 July a royal decree ended most of the restrictions under martial law; later, however, members of an extremist organisation confessed to having planned bombings and attacks on Western diplomats.

Meanwhile, on 1 June, the USA launched its proposed peace conference, at which Jordan was to share a delegation with the Palestinians. The US invitation was accepted on 21 July, but this was condemned in parliament; two ministers threatened resignation. The Prime Minister tried to reassure opponents that the essential point—Israeli withdrawal from the occupied territories, including East Jerusalem—had already been secured. The King said that the PLO should leave these issues to those resident in the territories. But opposition to Jordan's attendance at the conference continued.

On 25 September the King prolonged the parliamentary recess till December. A week later the Foreign Minister of three months resigned, together with four other ministers opposed to Jordanian participation in the peace conference; he was replaced by Kamil Abu Jabir, a US-trained academic. On 6 October 49 deputies protested against Jordan's proposed attendance at the conference and urged the Prime Minister to resign. Several newspapers were confiscated for criticizing the King and the government; a Muslim Brotherhood demonstration was banned.

King Husain told a large meeting of officials on 13 October that the invitation to the peace conference had been unconditionally accepted; the crisis, he said, had made him consider, but reject, the possibility of abdication. On 26 October the Prime Minister published the names of the Jordanian delegates—diplomats, civil servants and academics—and the delegation duly left for Madrid.

Under parliamentary pressure, Prime Minister Tahir al Masri resigned on 16 November; he was replaced by the King's cousin, Field Marshal Sharif Zaid ibn Shaker, well-known for a safe pair of hands in emergencies (see AR 1989, p. 205). He secured a vote of confidence, but 27 deputies voted against him. Addressing the new parliamentary session, the King concentrated on the economy and the need for austerity.

This could not be denied. Jordan's parlous finances (with foreign debts estimated in November at $8,000 million) were further strained by the cost of providing somehow for the thousands of its subjects fleeing from Iraq and Kuwait, where PLO misjudgements and the crimes of a few collaborators had discredited all Palestinians. This mass arrival altered the character of Amman, turning it, according to one journalist, from an extended village into a metropolis; he estimated that, besides 300,000 Jordanian passport holders, there were 150,000 refugees trying to secure visas for other countries. The situation was aggravated by a drought which lowered the water level in a major dam by more than 50 per cent.

iv. SYRIA

CAPITAL: Damascus   AREA: 185,000 sq km   POPULATION: 12,100,000 ('89)
OFFICIAL LANGUAGE: Arabic   POLITICAL SYSTEM: presidential
HEAD OF STATE AND GOVERNMENT: President Hafiz al-Asad (since March '71)
RULING PARTY: Baath Arab Socialist Party
VICE-PRESIDENTS: Abdul Halim Khaddam, Zuheir Masharqa
PRINCIPAL MINISTERS: Mahmud Zuabi (prime minister), Gen. Mustafa Tlas (deputy premier, defence), Salim Yassin (deputy premier, economic affairs), Faruq al-Shara (foreign affairs), Khalid Ansari (justice), Mohammad Harbah (interior)
INTERNATIONAL ALIGNMENT: NAM, Arab League, OAPEC, ICO
CURRENCY: Syrian pound (end-'91 £1=LS39.34, US$1=LS21.07)
GNP PER CAPITA: US$980 ('89)
MAIN EXPORT EARNERS: oil, cotton, textiles

THE country's participation in the Gulf War (see V.2) gave President Hafiz al-Asad leverage with the victorious coalition but reportedly displeased most Syrians. It was not surprising therefore that, in a conscious demonstration of Arab nationalism, Syria should often seem to obstruct, without irrevocably imperilling, the subsequent peace process. The USSR's collapse left him no alternative policy. Other gains from Syria's new leverage were that it now had a relatively free hand in Lebanon (see V.4.v) and could also collect a fair amount of cash.

Foreseeing Iraq's attempt to disrupt the coalition by involving Israel, Foreign Minister Faruq al-Shara had already warned the Israelis not to retaliate against an Iraqi attack. President Asad sent a last-minute appeal to Saddam Husain to quit Kuwait. Implacable as he was towards Saddam, he feared the break-up of Iraq; in talks with Ankara and Tehran he committed himself to its territorial integrity.

The 'Damascus declaration' of 6 March advanced a plan for a permanent Arab peacekeeping force in the Gulf, manned by Egypt and Syria and financed by the GCC. However, nothing more was achieved on this plan, despite repeated consultations (see V.4.i).

In Lebanon the war benefited Syria by ending Iraq's ability to interfere, discrediting Yassir Arafat and the PLO, once an obstacle to Syria's ambitions, and generally averting Western criticism. Syria's new agreement with the Lebanese government, signed in Damascus on 22 May, enshrined its special position there. Nevertheless, Syria's interests still did not always coincide with Lebanon's. The latter was anxious to coax the Israelis out of southern Lebanon and naturally opposed provocative anti-Israel activity there; Syria tended to see these activities as a useful counter with which to bargain for the Golan.

Syria sought to pursue simultaneously the recovery of the Golan, the satisfaction of moderate Palestinian objectives and the securing of support from the USA, which alone could overcome Israeli resistance. This was not an easy path, and Syria moved only slowly towards acceptance of President Bush's proposals of 1 June. They reportedly included an assurance that the USA would not recognize Israel's claim to have annexed the Golan, which would be treated as subject to UN resolutions 224 and 238 and therefore a proper topic for discussion.

Syrian acceptance of the US invitation became known in mid-July, when Secretary Baker confirmed that Syria would accept the presence of a UN observer at the conference as meeting its requirement for a UN role. At end-July President Asad, in a press interview, praised Mr Bush's intervention, while the Foreign Minister said that the US President had spoken of a comprehensive peace based on UN resolutions 242 and 338. Reportedly, this position was officially notified to Syria by Mr Baker in Damascus on 18 September. The USA by then stood high with the Arabs for its firmness over Israel's request for loan guarantees (see V.3).

Before the Madrid conference, Syria further improved its relations with the West. In Beirut the final release of Western hostages had begun, a process to which Syria certainly contributed. There were storms ahead, however. Although the opening stage of the conference in Madrid began well, the Syrian Foreign Minister soon introduced acrimony by responding to Israeli charges of Syrian state terrorism by making a personal attack on the Israeli Prime Minister Mr Shamir. The last days of the conference in 1991 were dominated by Palestinian, not Syrian, issues.

The start of negotiations inevitably raised the subject of Syria's relations with the PLO. On 3 March General Mustafa Tlas, the Defence Minister, had declared that no-one now respected Yassir Arafat, whose Palestinian opponents were honourably received by the Syrian Foreign Minister. But some softening was observable a week later, when Syria released 300 out of 400 Palestinians, mostly from Mr Arafat's Fatah wing. In late May President Asad received a high-level PLO delegation.

On 2 December President Asad was confirmed as President in elections in which he was the only candidate. This was followed by the release of some 2,800 political prisoners, most of them Muslim Brothers, always his most determined opponents.

The economy benefited from increased foreign aid, particularly payments from the Gulf states in recognition of Syria's role in the war. In early spring the European Community approved loans of $205 million. Oil production was expanding and was expected to reach 550,000 b/d by the end of 1991. Increased foreign exchange receipts allowed Syria to pay off some of its $16,000 million external debt (owed mostly to the USSR). The IBRD and IMF were still owed about $360 million. In July these bodies had discussions in Damascus on possible measures of economic liberalization. Parliament approved legislation to encourage investment and reducing top rates of income tax. Budgeted expenditure in 1991, as approved in November, was up 37 per cent on the 1990 figure.

v. LEBANON

CAPITAL: Beirut   AREA: 10,000 sq km   POPULATION: 2,670,000 ('85)
OFFICIAL LANGUAGE: Arabic   POLITICAL SYSTEM: presidential, based on power-sharing
HEAD OF STATE AND GOVERNMENT: President Elias Hrawi (since Nov '89)
RULING PARTIES: government of national unity
PRINCIPAL MINISTERS: Omar Karami (prime minister), Michel al-Murr (deputy premier, defence), Ali al-Khalil (finance), Faris Buwayz (foreign affairs), Maj.-Gen. Sami al-Khatib (interior), Khatchik Babikian (justice)
INTERNATIONAL ALIGNMENT: NAM, Arab League, ICO, Francophonie
CURRENCY: Lebanese pound (end-'91 £1=LL1,646.9, US$1=LL882.11)
GNP PER CAPITA: n.a.
MAIN EXPORT EARNERS: agricultural products, precious metals and jewels

SYRIA was now supporting the Lebanese government. The Maronite, Shia and Palestinian irregulars had been weakened by General Michel Aoun's overthrow (see AR 1990, pp. 213–4), Iran's declining interference and the PLO's humiliating mistakes. They were partly disarmed, although Israel's retention of its 'security zone' in southern Lebanon incited continued Shia violence. The economic benefits of pacification were balanced by losses from the Gulf War. All but two Western hostages had been released by year's end; but many Lebanese were still held by Israel.

The Lebanese army was deployed throughout greater Beirut. The new government of Omar Karami was less dominated by militia leaders and had the support of a parliamentary majority (albeit not overwhelming). In January the army began disarming the militias. In February, with Syrian encouragement, it deployed southwards and the two Shia militias, Amal and Hizbullah, started withdrawing. The Palestinians were forced to do so after one of their factions supported the army. Meanwhile, the government had resumed control of Beirut port from the Christian militias; it reopened on 15 March. Later that month the government set 30 April for the dissolution of the militias, to be followed by a gradual further extension of government control.

Palestinian non-cooperation gave the (Maronite) Forces Libanaises (FL) a pretext to do likewise. But by mid-May the disarmament of the FL, Amal and the Druze PSP seemed complete, and the government had closed the last illegal ports. The problems posed by other militias—Palestinian and Hizbullah—remained, however. The former demanded recognition of their status as soldiers fighting Israel, and Hizbullah still relied on its Iranian paymasters.

The government now began to normalize parliament, as provided for in the 1989 Taif Agreement, and to regulate its relations with Syria. On 9 May the electoral law was amended to fill, by nomination, 32 of the 99 existing seats which had become vacant since 1972 and to create nine new Muslim seats, so that Muslims and Christians would each have 54 members in the new 108-seat Assembly. A new treaty sanctifying Syria's special position was signed on 22 May in Damascus. Lebanon would not harbour forces hostile to Syria, Syrian forces could legally be deployed in the Beqaa and two standing Syrian–Lebanese councils would coordinate policy.

This formalization of Syria's *fait accompli*, though constituting its first formal recognition of Lebanese independence, angered some Maronite leaders. Moreover, Israel's displeasure was signalled by air attacks in early June, the heaviest since its 1982 invasion. Later, at the Madrid and Washington peace conference sessions, the Lebanese delegation carefully followed the Syrian line.

Israel persisted in occupying, with its surrogates, a significant part of southern Lebanon, from which it mounted attacks on others, with resulting friction and violence. This occupation was itself provoking attacks on Israeli forces. Lebanon appealed against it, citing UN Security Council resolution 425 of 1978. In November three Lebanese soldiers and one Irish soldier serving with the UN were killed in attacks from the security zone. The Lebanese army wished to enter Jezzine, outside the zone, but in August Israel reportedly installed forces there. Later, efforts by the Lebanese delegation in Madrid to secure US intervention were understood to have resulted in a US request to Israel to assist the peace process by stopping military activity in southern Lebanon.

The kidnapping and detention of Western nationals by clandestine groups almost ended. Between August and December successive releases of five American, three British and other hostages included, on 18 November, that of Terry Waite, the Archbishop of Canterbury's special envoy, captive since 1987. Britain and the USA paid no obvious price for them, though Washington's decision to return to Iran monies deposited by the Shah had perhaps helped. The bodies of two American hostages who had been killed by their captors were returned. This left two Germans, whom relatives of two Lebanese terrorists imprisoned in

Germany had kidnapped in order to secure their kinsmen's release. The German government resisted this pressure.

Less straightforward was the question of hundreds of Lebanese, including Sheikh Obeid (see AR 1989, p. 211), held by Israel and that of the latter's six or seven servicemen missing in action. To assist the release of Western hostages, Israel released successive groups of these Lebanese but insisted that the bulk—and Sheikh Obeid in particular—would be detained until it received news of its servicemen, of whom only one was believed still alive. No-one in Lebanon seemed able or willing to give all of this information and little progress was made.

The Lebanese economy should have benefited from the partial pacification. Customs revenues, no longer purloined by the militias, were again accruing to the state, but were being calculated at an absurdly out-of-date exchange rate. The Lebanese pound fell overall by a further 25 per cent. The budget deficit entailed huge borrowings, service on which now accounted for 25 per cent of expenditure. Lebanon's foreign-exchange income suffered severely from the Gulf War, which interrupted its trade and workers' remittances. It was calculated that 800,000 people had become homeless during the civil war.

In other ways, Lebanon seemed to be approaching normality. In August parliament approved an amnesty for crimes during the civil war, except the 1975 massacre of Palestinians which started it and murders of leading politicians. General Aoun was pardoned and left for France; the $30 million he had secreted there was frozen. The militia leaders began to lose their baleful influence. Nabih Berri, head of Amal, resigned from the government. This, and Druze leader Walid Jumblatt's allegations of corruption, seemed intended to discredit a government which had reduced militia power. Whether or not Mr Jumblatt's accusations were justified, people had noticed that, in nominating deputies to parliament, President Elias Hrawi had found room for his own son and son-in-law.

The more hopeful atmosphere generated by the decline in violence was spoilt in November and December by explosions in Beirut. They could not be firmly attributed, but a man who confessed to a bombing at the American University implied that it had been commissioned by a pro-Israeli group.

vi. IRAQ

CAPITAL: Baghdad AREA: 438,000 sq km POPULATION: 18,300,000 ('89)
OFFICIAL LANGUAGE: Arabic POLITICAL SYSTEM: presidential
HEAD OF STATE AND GOVERNMENT: President Saddam Husain (since July '79), also Chairman of Revolutionary Command Council and Prime Minister
RULING PARTY: Baath Arab Socialist Party
PRINCIPAL MINISTERS: Mohammed Hamzah al-Zubaydi (prime minister), Tariq Aziz (deputy premier), Watban Ibrahim al-Hasan (interior), Ahmada Husayn Khudayyir (foreign affairs), Usamah Abd al-Razzaq Hummadi al-Hithi (industry & military industrialization, oil), Ali Hasan al-Majid (defence), Shabib Lazim al-Maliki (justice)
INTERNATIONAL ALIGNMENT: NAM, Arab League, OPEC, OAPEC, ACC, ICO
CURRENCY: dinar (end-'91 £1=ID0.59, US$1=ID0.32)
GNP PER CAPITA: n.a.
MAIN EXPORT EARNERS: oil and gas

THE UN-supported coalition defeated Iraq (see V.2) and maintained economic sanctions against it; but this left President Saddam Husain in power, ruthlessly suppressing revolts in the Kurdish north and Shia south.

The Iraqi leader rejected all the opportunities, offered by the UN Secretary-General, the USA and many other governments, to withdraw without bloodshed or loss of Iraqi territory. On 16 January the American-led coalition began air attacks on military and non-military targets. Despite efforts to make them accurate, there were many civilian casualties. Saddam responded by firing missiles at Israel, hoping to disrupt the coalition by exploiting anti-Israel and anti-US popular sentiment within its Arab members. Israel did not retaliate, so the tactic failed (see V.3).

Allied airmen shot down were used as human shields for Iraqi military targets. Oil was released into the Gulf and wells ignited, putting the whole region's ecology at risk. Iraqi aircraft, powerless against the coalition's air assault, were flown to Iran.

Diplomacy continued, but in vain. On 10 February Evgenii Primakov, a Soviet diplomatist with Iraqi experience (see AR 1990, p. 218), reached Baghdad; Iraqi envoys visited Moscow and Tehran. Iraq steadily refused to leave Kuwait. On 15 February Saddam offered withdrawal in return for an immediate ceasefire, cancellation of all Iraq's debts, payment for damage suffered, Israel's evacuation of the occupied territories and removal from the Gulf of foreign military bases. The Iraqi government, while remaining bellicose, purported to accept a Soviet peace plan which Washington thought inadequate.

Soviet and Iranian efforts were still proceeding when, their ultimatum of 22 February having expired, the allies launched a ground offensive on 24 February, occupied Kuwait city three days later and ended hostilities on 28 February. A formal ceasefire followed on 3 March. In four days, over 150,000 Iraqi soldiers had surrendered or been captured and many thousands had died.

It was assumed that allied action or internal revolt would now rid the world of Saddam Husain. But the allies renounced any advance on Baghdad, while Saddam, having kept his most loyal units in reserve, soon parried or crushed outright the Kurdish and Shia revolts which had begun by 1 March and at first carried everything before them. By 30 March Kirkuk, principal city of Kurdistan, and Kerbela, centre of Shia dissidence, had been retaken and many people killed, particularly in the south.

Saddam had already, on 16 March, promised reform. A week later a new Prime Minister, Saadun Hammadi, was appointed. A Shia and a technocrat, leading a cabinet containing nine other newcomers, Mr Hammadi announced that reconstruction and reform could begin 'now that sectarian sedition was dead'. However, Saddam himself, with his two most permanent henchmen, Tariq Aziz and Taha Yasin Ramadan, remained in charge.

The allies' decision to relinquish southern Iraqi territory held at the ceasefire prevented their protecting those Shias whom the allied victory, and some allied pronouncements, had encouraged to rebel, though they did initially stop Saddam using his air force against them. Allied forces operating from Turkey established a Kurdish 'safe haven' and excluded Iraqi forces. But the last allied troops had left Kurdistan by 15 July. The Kurdish leaders, seeing little hope from the allies, began negotiations with Saddam, based on the abortive autonomy agreement of 1970. But they could not agree among themselves: the Barzani faction was readier to compromise than that of Jallal Talabani, so that the negotiations achieved little.

The Kurdish people suffered intensely, sent trekking to and fro by the erratic movements of allied and Iraqi forces and harassed by summer heat and winter cold. By December an Iraqi blockade of Kurdistan had continued for two months, although the Kurdish leaders had in November, at Baghdad's demand, withdrawn all their forces south of Arbil in exchange for Baghdad's promise—not long observed—to lift the blockade. The only restraints on the government were the continued presence of US troops in south-east Turkey and of UN officials in northern Iraq; on 24 November agreement was reached with Baghdad to prolong their relief operations. In December these officials reported that 200,000 Kurds had fled their homes since October to avoid Iraqi shelling, besides the 600,000 left homeless after the Kurdish uprising.

Iraq's defeat, and the hardships imposed by UN sanctions, did not force Saddam from power in a military coup or popular revolt. His propaganda aimed to convince Iraqis that their sufferings resulted from allied actions, not from his own; years of his ubiquitous police state had left army and people reluctant to confront the regime, from which both had formerly derived material benefit.

Thus Saddam had to surrender few of his powers or ambitions. The Prime Minister appointed in March, Mr Hammadi, was dropped in September, when Saddam declared that no one pursuing Western ideas of democracy would ever be allowed in the leadership. He was replaced by Mohammed Hamzah al-Zubaydi, hitherto deputy premier. The regime was increasingly controlled by relations or cronies of Saddam. His cousin, Ali Hasan al-Majid, notorious for his cruelties to Kurds and Kuwaitis, became successively Minister of Interior and then of Defence (having been replaced in the former post by Saddam's half-brother). Another half-brother ran the security services. Stories of plots against Saddam, of Mr Hammadi's involvement in them and of mass executions of officers, like much in Saddam's Iraq, could not be reliably checked. Meetings of Iraqi exiles in Washington and Damascus posed little threat to the regime.

Saddam clung also to his non-conventional arsenal. The UN continued hunting the mass destruction weapons which Iraq was believed to be holding or preparing and which UN resolution 687 (see XIX.1: DOCUMENTS) required it to notify and destroy. Successive Iraqi denials or partial disclosures were investigated and exposed. By October the UN or its agencies had sent missions to search for nuclear, biological and chemical weapons, often against determined Iraqi opposition, one team being detained for several days. Though Iraq had not, apparently, had a germ warfare programme, it had accumulated lethal chemical weapons and might retain its nuclear weapons development programme. As late as November, further stocks of enriched uranium were discovered. Huge long-range guns (see AR 1990, p. 215) were—but only in late autumn—discovered and destroyed.

Should the allies, despite the sufferings of the Iraqi people, honour their pledge to maintain sanctions until Saddam fell? Or should they follow the pleas of many governments and international philanthropic bodies to lift sanctions and leave him in place? He exploited this dilemma by encouraging such pleas with statistics of deprivation, while steadfastly refusing the palliative of Security Council resolution 706, authorizing Iraq to sell $1,600 million's worth of oil to buy essential food and humanitarian supplies (see XI.1). Iraqi representatives denounced this resolution, and another allotting 30 per cent of Iraq's future oil sales as reparations to its victims, as violations of sovereignty. They demanded instead the release of $4,000 million of Iraqi assets blocked abroad, substantially less than its many unpaid debts.

As 1991 ended, Iraq's economy and people were in a desperate state. True, international organizations reported that it had, despite sanctions, imported around 600,000 tonnes of wheat during 1991; but its monthly import needs were put at 200,000 tons. Power stations and electricity grids had been destroyed, water purification and distribution systems heavily damaged. Iraq, said one observer, had been thrown back into the pre-industrial age, but was still shackled by the technological needs which that age had created.

5. SAUDI ARABIA—YEMEN—ARAB STATES OF THE GULF

i. SAUDI ARABIA

CAPITAL: Riyadh   AREA: 2,150,000 sq km   POPULATION: 13,200,000 ('90 est)
OFFICIAL LANGUAGE: Arabic   POLITICAL SYSTEM: monarchy
HEAD OF STATE AND GOVERNMENT: King Fahd ibn Abdul Aziz (since June '82), also Prime Minister
PRINCIPAL MINISTERS: Crown Prince Abdallah (first deputy premier), Prince Sultan (second deputy premier, defence), Prince Nayef (interior), Prince Saud al-Faisal (foreign affairs), Muhammad Ali Aba al-Khalil (finance & national economy), Hisham Nazer (petroleum), Mohammed ibn Ibrahim ibn Jubair (justice)
INTERNATIONAL ALIGNMENT: NAM, Arab League, OPEC, OAPEC, GCC, ICO
CURRENCY: riyal (end-'91 £1=SRls7.02, US$1=SRls3.76)
GNP PER CAPITA: US$6,020 ('89)
MAIN EXPORT EARNERS: oil and gas

ONCE again Saudi Arabia faced a difficult year, as it sought to come to terms with the results of the Iraqi invasion of Kuwait (see AR 1990, pp. 219–21). The early weeks were occupied by military preparations for, and the implementation of, the coalition's counter-attack. But the process of readjustment after hostilities ceased on 28 February was, perhaps, even more difficult; for some of the effects of the allied military action were unforeseen and uncomfortable. The kingdom also had to try and cope with other changes which occurred within the wider Islamic world—in particular the emergence of fledgling republics in the Muslim areas of the former USSR (see IV.2.i). Again, the process promised to be both complex and, potentially, unsettling.

The air war against Iraq began on 16 January and many Saudi airfields were used throughout that campaign (see V.2). Two days later religious officials justified the war in their Friday sermons by calling Saddam Husain 'an enemy of God'. On 20 January the first Iraqi Scud missiles were fired at Riyadh and Dhahran and war was brought much closer for many Saudi families. Other such attacks followed later and on 25 February an Iraqi Scud missile killed 28 US troops, and injured nearly 100 others, at their base near Dhahran. At a meeting with President Mubarak on 2 February King Fahd announced that Egyptian and Saudi forces would not fight inside Iraq. On 29 January Iraqi troops began to move into the deserted Saudi border town of Khafji, but they were expelled by Saudi and US troops within 36 hours.

The land campaign was launched from Saudi territory on 24 February. Saudi and Kuwait troops took control of Kuwait city on the morning of 27 February and the preliminary ceasefire was implemented the following day. In the kingdom—as elsewhere—there was great relief, and no little public surprise, that the campaign was over so quickly and at such a small cost in human terms to the coalition partners. Neither was the ecological damage to the country's Gulf coastline, caused by the spillage of Kuwaiti crude oil, as great as had initially been feared.

Saudi sensitivity about the presence of so many non-Muslim, and some female, troops on its territory had already become clear (see AR 1990, p. 219). Riyadh was keen to see them depart as quickly as was possible and prudent. Hopes of forming some kind of defensive military cooperation alliance between Saudi Arabia, the other smaller members of the Gulf Cooperation Council (GCC) and the two major Arab partners in the coalition, Egypt and Syria, did not materialize (see V.4.i). At the end of the year Saudi Arabia and the other GCC states were still debating how best to ensure their future security. It was announced that the kingdom's armed forces would be expanded, and a policy from the past was again pursued, that of arms purchases from the USA, Britain and France. Much new high technology weaponry was ordered. A previous large arms deal with Britain (see AR 1989, p. 216) experienced some difficulty over payments, and negotiations were conducted to resolve the issue.

Saudi Arabia received an unusually high number of distinguished overseas visitors, both civilian and military. Prolonged exposure to a large contingent of foreign journalists was an unusual, and not always welcome, experience. In February the government placed restrictions on their activities and movements, and was clearly relieved when they departed. Some Saudis had, however, enjoyed the Western television coverage of the kingdom, and their voices were raised asking the government to implement democratic political reforms. A different and potentially more serious challenge, however, came from another quarter.

During the summer and autumn a number of taped cassettes were made by militant Islamic leaders criticizing the ruling family for religious laxity, corruption and lack of respect for Muslim values. They also deplored the need to seek Western, particularly American, military assistance. The authors of these messages called for sweeping reforms in certain government ministries and the ending of the country's close and extensive ties with the West; they also wanted the religious classes to have a more powerful voice in the country's future governing structure. At first the government did not seem to have been greatly worried by this domestic opposition; but when some of the criticisms became highly personal, and when demands were made to end modern education for women, the government felt compelled to act. Very senior religious figures were called upon to verify the religious credentials of the ruling family, and to support its announced policy of establishing a Consultative Council and of promulgating a code of law. In December King Fahd stated that details of the new political system would be published by the end of February 1992. The announcement of such a timetable was seen, in itself, as both unusual and significant.

The militant Muslim critics also condemned the US-sponsored Middle East peace conference in Madrid. While Saudi Arabia was not, formally, a party to those talks, it had encouraged other Arab governments to attend and the Saudi ambassador to Washington was present when they began. Diplomatic relations with Tehran were restored in March, and Iranian Muslims took part in the annual pilgrimage in June for the first time for four years. The event was marred by the crash of a Nigerian airliner on 11 July shortly after it took off from Jeddah. The 247 returning pilgrims and 14 crew were killed. In another tragedy, over 600 people drowned when a ferry en route from Jeddah to the Egyptian port of Safaga sank on 14 December.

The impending war with Iraq caused the government to delay publishing the budget in January. In May the kingdom contracted a loan of $4,500 million from foreign banks, this becoming another source of criticism for the Islamic militants. The needs of the war, and a lack of exports from Iraq and Kuwait, meant that oil production remained high throughout the year. The kingdom also produced a record wheat harvest of over 4 million tonnes, some of which was sold abroad at highly subsidized prices. The government considered reducing the price it paid to wheat farmers from over $400 per tonne to a level closer to the world market level of around $135 per tonne.

In September the Saudi ambassador at the United Nations was elected as president of the General Assembly. In October the kingdom provided emergency relief aid for the USSR of over $1,000 million. As it became clear that the Soviet Union would disintegrate, the government tried to establish diplomatic and religious links with the southern Muslim republics. In part this was because it feared that Tehran was seeking greater influence in that region. The government also tried to encourage greater unity among the various Afghan guerilla groups in the hope that the withdrawal of Soviet support would cause the regime of President Najibullah in Kabul to collapse (see VIII.1.2).

ii. YEMEN

CAPITAL: Sanaa   AREA: 540,000 sq km   POPULATION: 11,000,000 ('90 est.)
OFFICIAL LANGUAGE: Arabic   POLITICAL SYSTEM: presidential democracy
HEAD OF STATE AND GOVERNMENT: President (Gen.) Ali Abdullah Saleh (since '90)
VICE-PRESIDENT: Ali Salim al-Bid (since May '90)
PRINCIPAL MINISTERS: Haidar Abu Bakr al-Attas (prime minister), Hasan Mohammed Makki (first deputy premier), Gen. Mujahid Yahya Abu Shawarib (deputy premier, internal affairs), Gen. Salih Ubayd Ahmed (deputy premier, defence), Abdul Karim al-Iryani (foreign affairs), Alwi Salih al-Salami (finance), Abdel Wasi Ahmed Sallam (justice)
INTERNATIONAL ALIGNMENT: NAM, Arab League, ACC
CURRENCY: rial & dinar (end-'91 £1=YRls24.26 or YD0.87, US$1=YRls12.99 or YD0.47)
GNP PER CAPITA: US$650 ('89)
MAIN EXPORT EARNERS: oil, agricultural products

As for many states in the Middle East, political events in Yemen were dominated by the war with Iraq over Kuwait (see V.2) and its aftermath. The newly-united state had incurred the wrath of Saudi Arabia for its initial reluctance to condemn Baghdad's invasion, and for its voting record on various UN resolutions (see AR 1990, p. 222–3). Relations with Riyadh did not improve appreciably in 1991 and Yemen's economy suffered a severe blow as a result of the expulsion of over one million Yemeni workers from Saudi Arabia. This placed the government under considerable strain. Not only was there a very steep and damaging decline in remittance income, but also many of the returning Yemenis were, in effect, refugees from the war, so that temporary camps had to be established to house them. There were reports of the ill-treatment of some Yemenis in Saudi Arabia, and much bitterness was generated by the speed and manner of their expulsion. In late January and early February a number of pro-Iraqi demonstrations took place in Sanaa and elsewhere. The American, Egyptian, Japanese and Turkish embassies were attacked, but damage was slight and no one was seriously injured.

Nevertheless, in a somewhat unexpected move on 17 September, President Ali Abdullah Saleh called for the final settlement of the country's borders with Saudi Arabia and Oman, an issue of great sensitivity in the past. At the end of October two French ministers visited Yemen and praised the country for its continuing attempt to maintain democratic rule—an experience which remained unique in the Arabian peninsula. Hopes were expressed that this visit might pave the way for enhanced contacts with, and aid from, Western Europe, since US financial assistance had been reduced very sharply in January following Yemen's votes at the UN.

The one relatively bright aspect of the economy was an expansion in oil production and exploration in both the former states. By the end of the year more than 15 foreign companies were active in the petroleum and gas sector. In late May the government announced that it intended to establish a free trade zone at Aden, but hopes for a rapid recovery in the economic fortunes of that port were not realized. Some older economic habits died hard: new trade and cooperation agreements were signed with Cuba in May and with Vietnam in June. Other economic agreements were negotiated with Japan, China, Iran and Germany. Progress on the unification of the currency was slow, and both the rial (northern) and the dinar (southern) remained in circulation.

The domestic political scene was lively and occasionally violent. In mid-May a referendum was held on the proposed new constitution. The exercise was opposed by several Islamically-inspired groups who wanted religious law (the Sharia) to be the sole guiding principle in the new constitution. According to the government, the referendum boycott called for by the religious groups was unsuccessful: the turn-out figure was reported to be 72 per cent, with over 98 per cent of those voting favouring the proposed changes. In June a draft law on political parties was issued, and by the end of the year more than 35 were said to be in operation, some of them owing more to tribal allegiance than to ideological commitment.

In July the death sentences passed in 1987 on the former president of South Yemen, Ali Nasser Muhammad, and five of his aides were annulled (see AR 1987, pp. 213–4). In September the politically prominent director of the Central Highlands development project, Hassan al Hurraibi, was assassinated. On 19 October a serious clash occurred in Sanaa and nine people were reported dead after an army officer shot and killed a traffic policeman. A number of arrests were made and the President appealed for calm at a time of economic difficulty. That latter fact was emphasized when the government announced reductions in public expenditure in November. At the end of a difficult year the country's new-found political unity had been maintained, but economic prospects were not reassuring.

iii. ARAB STATES OF THE GULF

United Arab Emirates
CONSTITUENTS: Abu Dhabi, Dubai, Sharjah, Ras al-Khaimah, Fujairah, Umm al-Qaiwin, Ajman
FEDERAL CAPITAL: Abu Dhabi   AREA: 77,000 sq km   POPULATION: 1,500,000 ('89)
OFFICIAL LANGUAGE: Arabic
POLITICAL SYSTEM: federation of monarchies
HEAD OF STATE AND GOVERNMENT: Shaikh Zayad bin Sultan al Nahayyan (Ruler of Abu Dhabi), President of UAE (since '71)
CURRENCY: dirham (end-'91 £1=Dh6.87, US$1=3.68)
GNP PER CAPITA: US$18,430 ('89)
MAIN EXPORT EARNERS: oil and gas

Kuwait
CAPITAL: Kuwait AREA: 18,000 sq km POPULATION: 2,000,000 ('89)
OFFICIAL LANGUAGE: Arabic
POLITICAL SYSTEM: monarchy
HEAD OF STATE AND GOVERNMENT: Shaikh Jabir al-Ahmadal Jabir as-Sabah (since '77)
CURRENCY: dinar (end-'91 £1=KD0.53, US$1=KD0.28)
GNP PER CAPITA: US$16,150 ('89)
MAIN EXPORT EARNERS: oil and gas

Oman
CAPITAL: Muscat AREA: 300,000 sq km POPULATION: 1,500,000
OFFICIAL LANGUAGE: Arabic
POLITICAL SYSTEM: monarchy
HEAD OF STATE AND GOVERNMENT: Shaikh Qaboos bin Said (since '70)
CURRENCY: rial (end-'91 £1=OR0.72, US$=OR0.38) GNP PER CAPITA: US$5,220 ('89)
MAIN EXPORT EARNERS: oil and gas

Qatar
CAPITAL: Doha AREA: 11,400 sq km POPULATION: 422,000 ('89)
OFFICIAL LANGUAGE: Arabic
POLITICAL SYSTEM: monarchy
HEAD OF STATE AND GOVERNMENT: Shaikh Khalifah bin Hamad al-Thani (since '72)
CURRENCY: (end-'91 £1=QR6.81, US$1=QR3.65) GNP PER CAPITA: US$15,500 ('89)
MAIN EXPORT EARNERS: oil and gas

Bahrain
CAPITAL: Manama AREA: 685 sq km POPULATION: 489,000 ('89)
OFFICIAL LANGUAGE: Arabic
POLITICAL SYSTEM: monarchy
HEAD OF STATE AND GOVERNMENT: Shaikh Isa bin Sulman al-Khalifah (since '61)
CURRENCY: dinar (end-'91 £1=BD0.70, US$1=BD0.38) GNP PER CAPITA: US$6,340 ('88)
MAIN EXPORT EARNERS: oil and gas, aluminium

THE war between the US-led and UN-authorized multinational coalition and Iraq over the latter's occupation of Kuwait, and its aftermath, dominated Gulf affairs during 1991. All the Arab Gulf states contributed men, financial support or facilities to the coalition (see also V.2). Units from most of them participated in the 100-hour-long ground war to liberate Kuwait which began on 24 February, or in the month-long air war which preceded it. In the aftermath of the war, all of the member-states of the Gulf Cooperation Council (GCC) were closely involved in attempts to create a viable security structure for the region.

In the wake of the GCC heads of state meeting in Doha in late December 1990—which proposed, through Omani prompting, to create a security system involving the GCC states and Iran and set up a US$15,000 million fund to aid countries adversely affected by the crisis—a new security proposal emerged from a meeting of the six GCC states with Egypt and Syria in Damascus on 6 March (see also V.4.i). The Damascus Declaration proposed that Syria and Egypt should provide the forces required for regional security, while the GCC states would finance the operation and supplement Syrian and Arab units with their own armed forces. The proposal rapidly ran into difficulties, however, as Egypt became increasingly incensed at insensitive Kuwaiti treatment of its nationals in the newly-liberated emirate, and as it became obvious that several GCC states did not want a close defence link with Egypt and Syria.

At GCC Foreign Ministers' meetings in June and September little attention was paid to the Damascus proposals. Moreover, although the GCC Foreign Ministers did meet their Syrian and Egyptian counterparts in Kuwait in July, no progress on the proposals occurred there either. Instead, the Foreign Ministers agreed in June that the GCC secretary-general, Abdallah Bishara, should represent the GCC states at the US-sponsored Middle East peace conference. In September they authorized the GCC to reopen negotiations over the proposed EC-GCC economic agreement designed to liberalize trade, particularly in petrochemical exports to Europe. Although outline agreement had been achieved in 1990, negotiations had stalled over the details of actual tariff levels and the transition periods involved.

The fact was that southern GCC states—Oman and the UAE—were anxious for a regional security system involving Iran, while their northern colleagues—particularly Kuwait and Bahrain—preferred defence links with Western powers. Saudi Arabia wavered between the two options. The result was that the GCC heads of state meeting in December emphasized the GCC's conviction of the need to improve relations with Iran, while Kuwait had signed defence agreements with the USA, the UK and France by the end of the year. Egypt, in anger at Kuwait's implicit rejection of the Damascus Declaration proposals, refused a proposed $250 million Kuwaiti loan intended to ease the reintegration of former migrants forced out from Kuwait.

Kuwait's agreement with Washington envisaged the pre-positioning of military equipment, the training of Kuwaiti forces, the upgrading of airforce facilities at a cost of $350 million and the grant of extraterritorial rights to US forces—1,500 of whom were still in the emirate by the end of the year. Bahrain signed a similar agreement with Washington in October during Shaikh Isa's visit to the American capital. At the same time, Kuwait, Bahrain and Qatar improved relations with Iran. Bahrain appointed a new ambassador to Tehran in January and Shaikh Hamad bin Khalifah al-Thani visited Tehran in November to arrange agreements on improved trade relations and a 2,000-km water pipeline to Doha.

The aftermath of the war was most strongly felt in Kuwait. Despite the creation of a 15-km-deep demilitarized zone along the emirate's common border with Iraq, which under Security Council resolution 687 (see XIX.1) was monitored by a UN observer mission, there were constant cross-border incidents. At the end of August Kuwait charged that Iraqi forces had invaded the northern Kuwaiti island of Bubiyan again—claims treated with scepticism in Western circles. In September there were incidents around border posts, and in October further incidents at sea. At the same time, the United Nations proceeded to demarcate the frontier between the two states in accordance with the 1963 border agreement. This ensured that the problem of access to the Iraqi port of Umm Qasr would bedevil relations in the future, although Kuwait proposed to build a 175-km fence along the border.

Kuwait also continued to maintain that Iraq was still holding its nationals as prisoner, claiming that 2,242 were still missing at the end of the year. Iraq countered by refusing to move on the issue until Kuwait released the stateless Kuwaiti nomads (*bidouns*) that it was holding. Indeed, the issue of Kuwait's treatment of non-Kuwaiti elements in its population caused considerable friction with Western states throughout the year. Shortly after the Emir's government was restored to Kuwait, it became clear that the authorities were intending to force many non-Kuwaiti nationals out of the country, however long they might have been living there, in order to ensure that the 750,000–800,000 Kuwaiti nationals should, in future, be a majority inside the emirate.

By the end of the year, the pre-war 400,000-strong Palestinian population of Kuwait had shrunk to 50,000 persons. The same happened to the *bidouns*, originally 200,000-strong, who had formed the backbone of the Kuwaiti army before the crisis and whose expulsion resulted in the reduction of Kuwait's armed forces from 14,000 to 5,000 men. Egyptians (originally 250,000) and other Arabs (originally 150,000) were also reduced, to around 50,000 for each group, while the 400,000-strong Asian community fell to 150,000. It was expected, however, that the Asian and Egyptian communities would be built up again, simply because of the resulting labour shortage. Indeed, the expulsions produced major problems within the administration, where Palestinians had provided a complete stratum of essential middle management. The expulsions were accompanied by serious human rights abuses, involving the disappearance of up to 1,000 Palestinians and angry complaints from Western observers. Particular attention was drawn to a series of political assassinations, to detention conditions for Palestinians and *bidouns* and to a series of trials held under martial law. Eventually, martial law was ended in June and the National Council was recalled. The latter decision followed the resignation of the government amid evidence of a policy split between the al-Jabir and the al-Salim wings of the ruling family.

Despite promises given during the government's exile in Taif, the Emir announced, shortly after returning to Kuwait in April, that democratic elections to a restored National Assembly would be delayed until October 1992. Proposals were made for women to be given the vote, a move which would enlarge the electorate from 67,000 to around 130,000. Despite opposition protests and the welding together of the nine opposition movements into a single front, the government proved obdurate. Eventually support for the opposition melted away as the authorities generously compensated Kuwaitis for the losses incurred during the war. At the end of the year, in a gesture designed to garner further public support, the Kuwaiti government settled all outstanding debts, estimated at $20,000 million, from the 1982 Souk al-Manakh unofficial stock exchange crisis.

Recovery from the war was, however, faster than anticipated. The 600 oil well fires (out of 1,080 original producing wells) were extinguished by 6 November, after an operation costing $2,000 million. The fires destroyed 3 per cent of Kuwait's recoverable reserves, while 60 per cent of Kuwait's surface area was contaminated by oil spills. Crude production rose to 500,000 b/d by the end of 1991, with targets of 1.6 million b/d being set for the end of 1992 and 2 million b/d by January 1994. Kuwait's three major refineries at Mina Ahmadi, Mina Abdullah and Shuaiba were to be rehabilitated to improve refined output from 170,000 b/d by the end of 1991 to 400,000 b/d in 1993. Both developments were expected to increase oil-based revenues from $7,000 million in 1992 to $10,000 million in 1993.

Although a UN mission in March estimated the damage caused to Kuwait by the war at $23,000 million, including $8,500 million in lost opportunity cost of oil exports, local consultants estimated that total costs would be closer to $88,000 million by the end of 1993. Of this, $22,000 million represented payment for allied military costs and $20,000 million reconstruction costs. With its revenues averaging only $11,000 million annually, Kuwait therefore had to dip into its massive foreign assets to cover these costs. It also raised a $5,000 million loan to cover short-term costs.

The other GCC states were far less seriously affected by the conflict although the UAE lost 17 men and paid $5,500 million towards the costs of the war. Political problems abounded, however, particularly between Bahrain and Qatar. The Bahraini authorities were furious when Qatar unilaterally placed their sovereignty dispute over the Hawwar islands and the two reefs of Fasht al-Dibal and Qitat Jaradah before the International Court of Justice in mid-year. Bahrain had wanted, instead, to continue Saudi mediation over the issue. Bahrain and Qatar each improved their relations with the USA and Iran, while the UAE sought closer relations with its traditional arms supplier, France, during a visit to Paris by Shaikh Zayad in September. Oman finally ratified its border agreement with Saudi Arabia during a visit by Sultan Qaboos to Riyadh.

The anticipated democratization of the Gulf regimes in the wake of the war against Iraq failed to materialize. In addition to Kuwait's decision to delay elections, the Bahraini authorities explicitly discounted any such initiatives, while no hint of any change emerged in the UAE. In Qatar, the Advisory Council was revamped to bring in some new faces. In Oman, however, a start was made on a process of guided democratic reform. A new Regional Assembly Council was inaugurated at the start of November, in which a representative from each of the 59 *wilayas* (districts) was to sit. Three candidates were nominated for each *wilaya* and elections were then held to select the actual representative. The Council was to be purely consultative, however, like the State Consultative Council.

All of the states profited from the virtual removal of OPEC crude production quotas in response to the crisis in oil supply caused by the Iraqi invasion of Kuwait. In the UAE, towards the end of the year, production in Abu Dhabi was cut back from 2.5 million b/d at the start of May to 1.9 million b/d at the end of the month, while Dubai continued to produce its habitual 410,000 b/d. In Oman, production remained at 700,000 b/d, the level it had reached in 1990, while Qatar retained a production level of 400,000 b/d. Even in Bahrain, attempts were made to improve the output of Bapco's Sitra refinery, which depended on Saudi crude inputs, from 250,000 b/d to 360,000 b/d. Qatar also brought the first phase of its North Gas Field on stream in September and issued contracts for the second phase. Downstream development was hampered, however, by a lack of adequate finance. Japanese purchases of liquified natural gas from the field were expected to start in 1997.

GCC banking and finance sectors continued to be depressed as a result of the confidence lost during the war. Offshore banking units in Bahrain saw their profits remain static, as their assets declined by 14.8 per cent in the first half of the year. The major problem, however, afflicted the UAE, where the Abu Dhabi authorities were caught by surprise by the collapse of the transnational banking group based there, the Bank of Credit and Commerce International (BCCI). Their anger at incurring losses of around $10,000 million was compounded by what the authorities saw as high-handed behaviour by the Bank of England in handling the crisis (see also I.4). The crisis had a knock-on effect in Oman, too, where BCCI held 40 per cent of the stock of the sultanate's largest private bank, the National Bank of Oman. There, BCCI local assets of $250 million were sold off to cover the losses.

Notwithstanding the sudden rush for Kuwaiti reconstruction contracts, general uncertainty was reflected in continued delays in development projects and in cautious national budgets during 1991. In Dubai, the Jebel Ali and the Port Rashid freeports were amalgamated, in order to shrug off threatened competition from Bahrain. In Bahrain itself, a new development bank was founded in order to stimulate future development in the private sector designed to ease the growing job shortage on the island. The UAE federal budget, published at the start of July, proposed expenditure 17 per cent below the figures published in the draft budget one month earlier. Expenditure in the Qatari budget remained static, although revenues were expected to rise by 8.4 per cent. Oman introduced its fourth five-year plan at the start of 1991, with expenditure set to rise by 10.2 per cent to $24,545 million. All in all, it seemed to be a year of consolidation for the GCC in the wake of the war against Iraq.

6. SUDAN—LIBYA—TUNISIA—ALGERIA—MOROCCO—WESTERN SAHARA

i. SUDAN

CAPITAL: Khartoum   AREA: 2,500,000 sq km   POPULATION: 24,500,000 ('89)
OFFICIAL LANGUAGE: Arabic
POLITICAL SYSTEM: military regime
HEAD OF STATE AND GOVERNMENT: Lt-Gen. Omar Hasan Ahmed al-Bashir, Chairman of Revolutionary Command Council (since June '89)
PRINCIPAL MINISTERS: Brig.-Gen. Zubir Mohammed Saleh (deputy premier, interior) Ahmad Salul (foreign affairs), Brig. Ahmad Mahmud Hasan (justice), Abdul Rahman Mahmoud Hamdi (finance & economic planning)
INTERNATIONAL ALIGNMENT: NAM, Arab League, OAU, ACP, ICO
CURRENCY: Sudanese pound (end-'91 £1=Lsd28.10, US$1=Lsd15.05)
GNP PER CAPITA: US$480 ('88)
MAIN EXPORT EARNERS: cotton, agricultural products

DESPITE the strong control exercised by the military government and the National Islamic Front (NIF) over the army, the police, civil and diplomatic services, security organizations and other institutions, the regime was challenged by two unsuccessful coups. As a result 28 serving army officers were executed and 15 others were arrested, together with a number of retired army officers and civilians. Sudan's international status suffered from the fundamentalist nature of its government, the continuing civil war in the south and its continued support of Iraq even after the liberation of Kuwait. To salvage its tarnished reputation, the government declared an amnesty for political prisoners, including the former prime minister, Sayyid Sadiq al-Mahdi. In response to its isolation, the regime hosted a conference in April at which representatives of Muslim Brotherhoods, communists and nationalists from Arab and Muslim countries set up an international secretariat. Khartoum was chosen as its headquarters and Dr Hasan al-Turabi, the NIF leader, was elected as permanent secretary.

As promised, the regime implemented the federal system by dividing the country into nine states, each with its own governor and a cabinet of ministers, and each responsible for local administration and collection of taxes. In March the Sharia (Islamic) criminal laws were re-activated, entailing punishments like amputation and death for various crimes. These laws and federalism were rejected by the Sudan People's Liberation Army (SPLA), under the leadership of Colonel John Garang. Many attempts to settle the civil war failed, including one sponsored by Nigeria, which was postponed due to a rift between Colonel Garang, who wanted a unified Sudan, and Riak Machar and Lam Akol (SPLA commanders), who favoured secession by the south. The SPLA continued its military successes: it was reported that some of its forces entered southern Darfur and that Juba was shelled.

Despite international pressure, the regime refused to admit the existence of famine in Kordofan and Darfur, though it later appealed for relief supplies. An estimated 7 million people were affected by the drought in eastern and western Sudan. The UN Food and Agriculture Organization (FAO) appealed for one million tonnes of food aid but only half of this amount was pledged. The International Development Association approved an emergency loan of $16 million to provide medicines, water supply and agricultural equipment. The UN High Commission for Refugees completed its biggest-ever refugee airlift, of 50,000 Ethiopian soldiers who had taken refuge in Sudan after the collapse of the Mengistu regime (see VI.1.i). With an estimated one million displaced people in the country, the government intended to move 300,000 displaced southerners from Khartoum to the Upper Nile. 'Operation Lifeline Sudan 3' started during the year, it being expected that about 500,000 tonnes of food would be delivered to people affected by the civil war in the south.

Protest marches against the regime's policies continued. The University of Khartoum, the barometer of the capital, was closed when a student was killed during clashes with the police. The fear of a counter-coup by the army prompted the head of the state, General Omar al-Bashir, to announce without explanation the retirement of the army Chief of Staff, General Ishaq Ibrahim Omer. Two ministerial reshuffles took place in tandem with a policy of replacing government employees by those sympathetic to the regime.

Relations with Egypt deteriorated because of that country's participation in the anti-Iraq coalition in the Gulf War (see V.2 and V.4.ii). Sudan was warned of severe consequences if it allowed Iraqi forces to attack the Aswan High Dam. Support for Iraq continued, but the Gulf conflict caused many Sudanese workers to return home from Iraq and Kuwait, having lost their employment and savings. Chad strengthened its trade relations and cooperation with Sudan after the overthrow of President Hissène Habre in December 1990 (see AR 1990, p. 274). Libya, one of Sudan's few Arab allies, agreed in May to meet Sudan's fuel needs. With the exception of humanitarian aid, relations with many Western, African and Arab countries declined, even though the Sudanese government sent delegations to these countries. On the other hand, Sudan forged a new alliance with Iran during a visit to Khartoum by President Rafsanjani in December. It was reported that an agreement was concluded for the development of military ties, trade and exchange of expertise; also that Iranian revolutionary guards were to be sent to Sudan to train the Sudanese army and security organizations. Western and some Arab governments were consequently alarmed that Sudan could become a base for the spread of Islamic fundamentalism and for attacks on Western targets.

As a result of the Gulf War and the internal civil war, Sudan suffered a considerable loss of financial backing. The government embarked on austerity measures, raising the price of fuel and basic commodities, phasing out subsidies, devaluing the pound and introducing a 10 per cent cut in all chapters of the budget. It also began the privatization of Sudan Airways, Sudan Shipping Line and other state-owned enterprises such as tanneries, banks and hotels. In response to spiralling inflation and the scarcity of essential commodities, the government announced salary increases for its employees ranging from 45 to 100 per cent.

During 1991 Sudan received $35 million from various Western donors to help drought and famine-stricken areas. But it received only $24 million in official loans and aid from Western countries, Japan and OPEC. Trade protocols, amounting to $167 million were concluded with China, Pakistan and Libya, envisaging the import of fuel, machinery, textiles and medicines in exchange for livestock and agricultural products. Due to Sudan's non-servicing of its international debts and lack of projects, the World Bank decided to close its office in Khartoum by the end of the year.

ii. LIBYA

CAPITAL: Tripoli AREA: 1,760,000 sq km POPULATION: 4,400,000 ('89)
OFFICIAL LANGUAGE: Arabic
POLITICAL SYSTEM: socialist 'state of the masses'
HEAD OF STATE: Col. Muammar Qadafi, 'Leader of the Revolution' (since '69)
GOVERNMENT LEADERS: Maj. Abdul Salem Jalloud ('Libyan number two'), Muftah al-Usta Umar (sec.-gen. of Gen. People's Congress), Omar Mustafa al-Muntassir (planning & economy), Ibrahim Bashari (foreign affairs), Abdullah Salem al-Badri (petroleum), Farhat Sharnanah (economy & foreign trade)
INTERNATIONAL ALIGNMENT: NAM, Arab League, OPEC, OAPEC, AMU, OAU, ICO
CURRENCY: dinar (end-'91 £1=LD0.50, US$1=LD0.27) GNP PER CAPITA: US$5,310 ('89)
MAIN EXPORT EARNERS: oil and gas

AT a summit meeting held in Tripoli between Libya, Egypt, Syria and Sudan on 3 January, Colonel Qadafi announced that Libya would be on the same side as Egypt if war broke out in the Gulf. On 19 January, three days after US-led coalition forces attacked Iraq (see V.2), the Libyan leader led a mass demonstration demanding an end to the bombing but without expressing support for Iraq. The following day, the Saudi Arabian ambassador to Libya was given permission to make a statement on Tripoli radio explaining his government's position. In speeches on 26 January and 20 February Colonel Qadafi criticized President Saddam Husain of Iraq for ignoring his peace initiatives and accused Baghdad of supporting anti-Libyan forces in Chad. He condemned Iraqi missile attacks on Israel, declaring that they merely revived international sympathy for the Jewish state. Shortly before the ground war began, the Libyan media denounced America's failure to liberate Kuwait and described Western reporting on the war as deceptive and misleading. The subsequent rapid defeat of Iraqi forces and the supremacy of US military technology were reported to have seriously alarmed Libya's military leadership.

President Mubarak of Egypt was believed to have played an important part in persuading the Libyan leader to show restraint during the Gulf crisis, as relations between the two countries continued to improve. While President Mubarak resisted Colonel Qadafi's unification plans, closer links offered the prospect of much-needed economic opportunities for Egypt, especially the employment of Egyptian manpower. Libya had offered to resettle one million Egyptian farmers on lands to be irrigated by the Great Man-made River scheme, the first phase of which was inaugurated on 28 August. For Libya, Egypt remained a key ally and intermediary in its efforts to improve relations with the West and the conservative Arab states. In March Colonel Qadafi abolished immigration and customs controls for Egyptians entering Libya; reciprocal measures were taken by Egypt in August. But within a week the flood of visitors resulted in the re-establishment of checkpoints on both sides of the border. A security agreement on the movement of citizens across the border was signed on 23 August.

In contrast, progress towards further integration with Libya's Maghreb neighbours and with Sudan was limited. Although Colonel Qadafi assumed the presidency of the Arab Maghreb Union (AMU) on 1 January for a period of six months, he was absent for the summit held in Rabat on 15–16 September. When the headquarters of AMU institutions were allocated, Libya was offered only the Maghreb University and Academy of Sciences, the least important. Although Libya and Sudan signed 'minutes of integration' followed by an agreement on freedom of movement, residence, work and ownership on 19 June, the unification process lacked real substance. Colonel Qadafi's proposals for a tripartite union of Libya, Egypt and Sudan were firmly rejected by President Mubarak. Addressing the General People's Congress (GPC, parliament) on 17 June, the Libyan leader expressed his disappointment at the Sudanese government's failure to implement the *jamahiriya* system.

On 18 February the new Chadian leader, Idriss Deby, who had ousted President Hissène Habré from power in December 1990, visited Tripoli and, in an address to the GPC, thanked Libya for its contribution to his military victory. He carefully avoided responding to Colonel Qadafi's references to a union between the two countries and requested Libya's practical participation in the reconstruction of Chad. The thorny question of the Libyan prisoners-of-war in Chad who had joined the military wing of the opposition National Front for the Salvation of

Libya and received CIA training (see AR 1990, p. 274), continued to cause problems. When some 350 of these Libyan dissidents appeared in Kenya, Libya issued a statement on 14 February accusing the Kenyan government of accepting $5 million from the USA for its part in 'kidnapping' the prisoners of war. At the GPC on 11 June, Secretary Abd al-Raziq condemned the evacuation of the Libyan prisoners-of-war as 'an act of international piracy' by the USA.

On 26 June Amnesty International criticized Libya for continuing human rights violations and stated that hundreds of political prisoners were being detained without trial and were vulnerable to torture and ill-treatment. Earlier that month the US deputy assistant secretary of state for human rights commented on the use of torture during interrogation and the absence of basic legal freedoms and rights in Libya. Islamist groups were believed to be particularly vulnerable to such abuses. In August Colonel Qadafi denounced the Muslim Brotherhood and several other fundamentalist movements, calling on Libyans to liquidate any person found to be a member of these parties.

Colonel Qadafi's restraint during the Gulf crisis did not result in improved relations with either the USA or Britain. On 2 January President Bush renewed US sanctions against Libya for another year because of its support for international terrorism. On 30 April the Office of Foreign Assets Control of the US Treasury listed 48 banks, companies and organizations which it accused of assisting the Libyan regime to get round the US embargo. In particular, US sanctions continued to deny Libya access to much-needed new equipment and technology for the oil industry, which in turn prevented it from increasing production to full capacity during the Gulf crisis.

Overtures by Libyan officials anxious to restore diplomatic links with London were firmly rejected by the British Foreign Office. In early June Conservative MP Teddy Taylor had returned from a private visit to Libya, carrying a proposal for renewed relations and a Libyan donation of £250,000 to a police charity as an apology for the murder of policewoman Yvonne Fletcher in London in 1984 (see AR 1984, pp. 39–40). At the same time, Ali Abdul al-Treiki, Libya's ambassador to the UN, stated that Libya no longer had links with the IRA and that, once diplomatic relations were restored, his government would disclose the names of IRA members who had received Libyan arms. Britain refused to open negotiations, demanding clear evidence that Libya was no longer engaged in terrorism.

On 30 October a French magistrate issued international arrest warrants for four Libyan officials, including Abdallah Sannousi (Colonel Qadafi's brother-in-law and head of the Libyan secret services), in connection with investigations into the bombing of a French airliner over the Sahara in 1989, in which 171 people died. Two weeks later US and UK investigators charged two Libyan Arab Airlines officials, Abdel

Basset al-Megrahi and al-Amin Khalifah Fahima, with the bombing of Pan Am flight 103 over Lockerbie (Scotland) in 1988, causing the deaths of 270 people (see AR 1988, p. 38). Their report placed sole responsibility for the attack on the Libyan security authorities. In a joint statement on 27 November, Britain and the USA repeated their demands for the extradition of the two Libyans and the payment of compensation to the victims of the attack. A declaration by Britain, the USA and France called on Libya to cease all forms of terrorist action and all assistance to terrorist groups. On 28 November Roland Dumas, the French Foreign Minister, previously an advocate of better relations between the European Community and Libya, threatened to break off diplomatic relations with Tripoli unless the Libyan authorities handed over the four Libyans accused of blowing up the French DC-10.

In response, Libya denied any involvement in the two incidents, reaffirmed its condemnation of all forms of terrorism and called for an inquiry into the indictments by a neutral international body. Libyan diplomats began an intensive campaign in the Arab world to counter the British and American accusations. An announcement on 15 November that contracts of non-Arab expatriate workers would not be renewed was interpreted as an attempt to pre-empt further sanctions by the West. As a precaution, Libya began to transfer its liquid holdings from Britain and France to Geneva and the Gulf.

Reports in early December, quoting official Libyan sources, said that six men indicted in connection with the two bombings had been detained in Libya for questioning; there was, however, no question of handing them over, as such an action would violate Libyan law. In an interview broadcast on British television on 27 December, Colonel Qadafi again refused to hand over the two men accused of involvement in the Lockerbie bombing but stated that Britain and the USA could send independent judges to the trial in Tripoli. In a separate interview, Foreign Minister Ibrahim Bashari offered to send Libyan judges to Washington or London to discuss the case. Britain and the US dismissed both offers. On 26 December President Bush announced that the USA would extend sanctions on Libya for a further year.

iii. TUNISIA

CAPITAL: Tunis   AREA: 164,000 sq km   POPULATION: 8,000,000 ('89)
OFFICIAL LANGUAGE: Arabic   POLITICAL SYSTEM: presidential
HEAD OF STATE AND GOVERNMENT: Gen. Zayn al-Abdin Ben Ali (since Nov '87)
RULING PARTY: Constitutional Democratic Rally (RCD)
PRINCIPAL MINISTERS: Hamid Qarwi (prime minister), Habib Ben Yahya (foreign affairs), Abdullah Khalal (interior), Abderrahim Zouari (justice), Abdelaziz Ben Dhia (defence), Mohammed Ghanouchi (finance), Sadok Rabah (economy)
INTERNATIONAL ALIGNMENT: NAM, Arab League, OAPEC, AMU, OAU, ICO
CURRENCY: dinar (end-'90 £1=TD1.62, US$1=TD0.87)   GNP PER CAPITA: US$1,260 ('89)
MAIN EXPORT EARNERS: tourism, oil and gas, phosphates, olive oil

WITH pro-Iraqi feeling running high among Tunisians at all levels of society, the army and security forces were put on alert as the 15 January UN deadline to Iraq approached. As the allies launched their first wave of air attacks against Iraq, opposition groups and the ruling Rassemblement Constitutionnel Démocratique (RCD) organized a demonstration of over 6,000 people in Tunis. Further street protests, most of them peaceful, took place in late January and early February not just in Tunis but throughout the country. In a survey carried out in early February, 93 per cent of Tunisians interviewed expressed their support for Iraq; 57 per cent approved of the annexation of Kuwait; and 53 per cent saw the war as above all a struggle against Western imperialism. President Ben Ali probably voiced the feelings of the majority of Tunisians when he condemned the bombing of Iraq and claimed that the war was being undertaken primarily 'to prevent the rebirth of the Arab nation, leaving it weakened and dependent'.

When the scale of the Iraqi defeat became known, most Tunisians were stunned. Throughout the war the local media had continued to report Iraqi 'successes'. The end of hostilities brought relief for the government, which had found itself torn between the strong pro-Iraqi feelings of ordinary Tunisians and the need, for economic reasons, to maintain good relations with the West and the conservative Gulf monarchies. The government moved swiftly to try to repair relations with members of the anti-Iraq coalition. Satisfaction was expressed at the recovery of Kuwaiti sovereignty and in April Foreign Minister Habib Ben Yahya met US Secretary of State James Baker in Damascus, the first high-level contact since Washington slashed its financial assistance programme to Tunisia in February. In March Tunisia attended the first post-war meeting of the Arab League's ministerial council in Cairo and in May the Foreign Minister met President Mubarak of Egypt.

The authorities continued their crackdown on the Islamic Nahda party, accusing it of involvement in terrorist activities. In January there were violent clashes on the streets between Nahda supporters and the security forces. Under renewed pressure from the government, divisions within the organization intensified. Following a violent attack on RCD headquarters in Tunis on 17 February by a group who, when arrested, confessed that they belonged to Nahda, three members of the party's executive committee resigned. Including one of the party's leaders, Abdelfattah Mourou, the three denounced the attack and pledged their commitment to political change through peaceful means. Exiled leader Rached Ghannouchi stated that the Nahda leadership had not planned the attack, but further resignations followed leaving the party without effective leadership inside Tunisia.

On 25 March police raided premises in Tunis University used by the Union Générale Tunisienne des Étudiants (UGTE), an organization closely associated with the Islamic opposition. They seized materials which, the authorities claimed, implicated the UGTE in recent violence. All the union's activities were then suspended. Further unrest on university campuses resulted in the deaths of two students on 8 May in clashes with riot police.

On 22 May the Interior Minister, Abdullah Kallel, announced that the authorities had uncovered a fundamentalist plot to seize power by force and to set up an Islamic state. Of the 300 people arrested, 100 were members of the armed forces. According to the minister, Nahda planned to create violent unrest and disorder throughout the country in order to provoke army intervention; Nahda militants within the armed forces would then seize power. However, the captured arms put on display would have posed little threat to Tunisia's well-equipped security forces. The Nahda leadership denied any involvement in the alleged plot and Mr Ghannouchi repeated Nadha's commitment to multi-party democracy. Police mounted a major hunt for Nahda members and international warrants were issued for Mr Ghannouchi and other leaders in France.

In September President Ben Ali announced that the authorities had discovered a large arms cache in south Tunis which he described as the final link in the 'diabolical plot of religious extremists'. When the captured weapons were finally put on display, foreign observers expressed serious doubts about the existence of an Islamist plot to overthrow the state. Rather, they saw it as merely an excuse for the government to mount a new wave of arrests of Nahda militants and to maintain a strong police presence in the troublesome universities. The offensive against Nahda brought allegations of human rights abuses from Amnesty International, the US deputy assistant secretary of state for human rights and the Ligue Tunisienne des Droits de l'Homme. In response to claims of torture, the President ordered an official inquiry into the allegations and announced the appointment of a presidential adviser on human rights.

In the aftermath of the Gulf War, the legal opposition parties asked the government to reopen discussions about political reforms, requesting that they be allowed regular access to the media and financial support from the state. In his Independence Day address on 20 March, President Ben Ali responded positively and reaffirmed his commitment to political plurality. The parties were invited to participate in discussions on a new five-year development plan and to take part in regional economic and social councils. They were also given some access to state television and radio, while each party was granted TD50,000 in financial assistance and a further TD30,000 towards the cost of publishing its newspaper.

Nevertheless, all six legal opposition parties boycotted parliamentary by-elections held in nine constituencies on 13 October. Although President Ben Ali proposed that the ruling RCD would not contest them, the opposition parties felt that the proposal would not give them sufficient representation in the Chamber of Deputies. In a speech on 7 November the President reaffirmed his commitment to dialogue with the legal opposition, but Mr Ghannouchi called for a united front against the government. Mr Mourou, who resigned from Nahda in February, appeared to have abandoned his plan to form a rival moderate Islamist party, stating that the government made no distinction between violent and non-violent parties.

On 9 October three Islamists convicted of taking part in the attack on RCD headquarters in February were hanged after the President had rejected appeals for clemency. They were the first executions of political dissidents since Mr Ben Ali took power in 1988. In a cabinet reshuffle on 10 October, Interior Minister Khalal, responsible for the government's campaign against Nahda, was promoted to the rank of minister of state, making him the most senior cabinet member after the Prime Minister. At the same time, Abdelaziz Ben Dhia, a close aide of the President, replaced Habib Boulares as Minister of Defence. Analysts suggested that the reshuffle increased hardline elements in the government and thus strengthened the President's hand in his moves to eradicate Nahda.

On the economic front, the government reported considerable success in limiting the damage resulting from the Gulf crisis. At the beginning of the year growth in GDP was revised down to zero as tourism revenues collapsed. But at the end of November Planning and Regional Development Minister Mustapha Nabli announced that GDP was expected to grow by 3.2 per cent in 1991. This improvement was accounted for by a good cereal harvest, a 10 per cent rise in the value of exports and a smaller fall in earnings from tourism (20 per cent as opposed to 35 per cent) than originally forecast. The current-account deficit for 1991 was expected to be $500 million rather than the original estimate of $650 million. In early December loans of over $100 million were agreed with the Arab Fund for Economic and Social Development and the European Investment Bank. In October Mr Nabli announced that the economic liberalization programme would be accelerated 'to establish an open, competitive and liberal economy'. The government had requested a $400 million loan from the IMF/World Bank to support economic restructuring.

iv. ALGERIA

CAPITAL: Algiers   AREA: 2,382,000 sq km   POPULATION: 24,400,000 ('89)
OFFICIAL LANGUAGE: Arabic   POLITICAL SYSTEM: presidential
HEAD OF STATE AND GOVERNMENT: President Bendjedid Chadli (since Feb '79)
RULING PARTY: National Liberation Front (FLN)
PRINCIPAL MINISTERS: Sid-Ahmed Ghozali (prime minister, economy), Lakhdar Brahimi (foreign affairs), Maj.-Gen. Khaled Nezzar (defence), Gen.-Maj. Larbi Belkheir (interior), Hamadani Benkhelil (justice), Abdennour Keramane (mines, industry)
INTERNATIONAL ALIGNMENT: NAM, Arab League, OPEC, OAPEC, AMU, OAU, ICO
CURRENCY: dinar (end-'91 £1=DA39.51, US$1=DA21.16)
GNP PER CAPITA: US$2,320 ('89)
MAIN EXPORT EARNERS: oil and gas

As the US-led allied forces attacked Iraq on 16 January (see V.2), a wave of protest swept through Algeria as massive anti-war demonstrations were organized in Algiers and other cities by all leading political groups. Tens, sometimes hundreds, of thousands of Algerians from all walks of life took to the streets to voice their support for Iraq and to condemn the West, especially the USA but also France. The largest demonstrations were led by the opposition Front Islamique du Salut (FIS), which demanded the setting-up of training camps for volunteers for Iraq, and took a decidedly anti-government line. Within the FLN government, the strongest condemnation of the allied operation came from the Foreign Minister, Sid-Ahmed Ghozali. Security was tightened and almost all foreign correspondents were banned from entering the country. During the war many Algerians believed reports in the media about Iraqi successes, drawing heavily on official Iraqi communiques. Allied statements were dismissed as merely propaganda. The scale of Iraq's defeat therefore came as a stunning blow to ordinary people. On the streets tensions increased perceptibly.

A revised electoral law passed on 1 April by the National Assembly, which was still dominated by the FLN, provoked strong criticism from the FIS and some other opposition parties. The new legislation brought in single-member constituencies, with the two leading candidates going forward to a second stage of voting if no candidate won an absolute majority in the first round. Proxy voting was strictly limited and the use of mosques for electoral campaigning was banned—factors believed to have contributed to the sweeping victory achieved by the FIS in the local and provincial elections in June 1990 (see AR 1990, pp. 238–9). The FIS also attacked a second law on changes to electoral boundaries resulting from a decision to increase the number of Assembly deputies from 295 to 542. Even after revisions, the new law gave the most densely-populated coastal areas, containing the major cities where the FIS had swept to power in the 1990 elections, a relatively low representation compared with the sparsely-populated south, where the FLN had won most of the seats. On 3 April President Chadli announced that general elections would be held on 27 June, although in the event they did not take place until 26 December.

In the run-up to the original election date, the FIS continued its attack on the new electoral laws and accused the government of carrying out an organized campaign against it. There were reports of widening divisions within FIS ranks between the 'moderate' and 'radical' wings and suspicions that rival Islamist parties, Hamas and the Mouvement de Nahda Islamique, were being encouraged by the presidency. The FIS called for presidential elections and made repeated threats of a general strike. Tensions with the army mounted as the FIS leader, Dr Abassi Madani, warned that any military intervention to stop a general strike would be resisted 'to the point of annihilation'. When the strike was called on 25 May, there was only a limited response, and a march organized by the FIS in Algiers on the 26 May was quickly dispersed by riot police. However, further demonstrations by FIS supporters, who were now calling for the setting up of an Islamic state and the resignation of President Chadli, provoked new clashes with the security forces. An appeal for calm by President Chadli was ignored as riot police struggled to disperse marches by tens of thousands of FIS supporters.

As Algiers was brought to a halt by marches and demonstrations, the Interior Ministry, on 3 June, issued a stern warning against unauthorized demonstrations and threatened to arrest and prosecute their organizers. Clashes nevertheless continued, as armed FIS supporters set up barricades in two of the city's main squares, transforming them into battlefields. On 4 June, in a dramatic midnight announcement, President Chadli declared a state of siege, cancelled the elections set for 27 June and accepted the resignation of Prime Minister Mouloud Hamrouche and his government. By the early hours of the morning the army had occupied key positions in Algiers. Armed with extensive powers amounting almost to martial law, the military then re-established relative peace in the streets of the capital.

President Chadli named the outgoing Foreign Minister, Mr Ghozali, as the new Prime Minister. The FIS called off the strike and the President agreed to hold both parliamentary and presidential elections before the end of the year and to change the disputed new electoral laws. After two weeks of intensive consultations, Mr Ghozali announced a 'non-partisan' government, consisting largely of technocrats. General Khaled Nezzar remained at the Ministry of Defence with responsibility for administering the state of siege. Hocine Benissad, who had close links with the leadership of the Front des Forces Socialistes (FFS), was appointed Economy Minister. Lakhdar Brahimi, one of the most respected diplomats in the Arab world and former deputy secretary-general of the Arab League, became Foreign Minister. The new government included the Arab world's first minister for human rights, namely Ali Haroun, a lawyer. At the end of an FLN central committee meeting in late June, President Chadli announced his resignation as leader of the party.

During the first weeks of the state of siege, the army arrested at least 2,500 Islamists in a major crackdown on FIS activities. After further violent clashes Dr Madani and another FIS leader, Ali Benhaj, were arrested on 1 July accused of having 'formented, organized, unleashed and led an armed conspiracy against the security of the state in an attempt to take power'. There were police raids on mosques, FIS offices and the homes of FIS leaders. Human rights activists announced that some 8,000 people had been arrested and 300 killed since early June. On 2 July Prime Minister Ghozali confirmed that the two FIS leaders would be tried.

In an attempt to end the political crisis, Mr Ghozali called a meeting of all political parties on 30 July–2 August to discuss conditions for general elections. The FIS refused to attend; the FFS walked out as soon as the meeting began; and the FLN delegates left later in protest. A second meeting also failed to reach agreement. When the Ghozali government eventually brought a revised electoral law to parliament, it was passed (on 13 October) only after several key amendments had been inserted. Proxy voting was not abolished—husbands or wives could vote by proxy by producing their marriage certificate; parliament was increased in size from 377 to 430 seats; and the minimum age for candidates was raised from 25 to 28. Almost immediately, President Chadli announced that general elections would be held on 26 December.

The state of siege was lifted on 26 September. On 4 October tens of thousands of FIS supporters held a peaceful mass meeting declaring that the party would only participate in elections if their leaders were released. But the army remained vigilant. In a cabinet reshuffle at the end of October General Larbi Belkhair, a key figure in the military establishment, was appointed to the Interior Ministry, with responsibility for the general elections. Prime Minister Ghozali was given personal charge of the economy, replacing Hocine Benissad. In November an appeal to allow the imprisoned FIS leaders to stand in the elections was rejected. Speaking on the 20 November, the party's interim leader, Abdelkader Hachimi, threatened to boycott the elections and 'to exert every available means, within the framework of the law, so that there will be no elections'. It was not until 14 December, after a vigorous internal debate, that the FIS announced it would participate in the elections.

The government's economic reforms were challenged not only by the opposition parties but also from within the FLN establishment. At the end of August parliament rejected cuts in subsidies, which had been demanded by the IMF as part of a standby loan agreement approved in June. The announcement of a 22 per cent devaluation on 29 September demonstrated the government's commitment to radical restructuring of the economy in line with IMF recommendations. In December parliament approved major revisions to the hydrocarbons law reversing the previously unchallenged monopoly of the state in the oil and gas sectors. The new legislation formed a key element in the government's strategy to increase export revenues by encouraging new exploration and increasing output from existing fields.

The first results of the general elections on 26 December indicated that the FIS had won outright in 188 of the 430 constituencies. The FFS was in second place, with 25 seats, and the ruling FLN relegated to third place with only 15 seats. An estimated 7.8 million people voted out of 13.3 million eligible voters. Actual voting figures indicated that the FIS had won 3.3 million votes, the FLN 1.6 million and the FFS 510,000. Almost a million voting papers were disqualified. Second round elections were scheduled to take place on 16 January 1992 in 199 constituencies where no candidate had won at least 51 per cent of the vote. In most cases it would be a straight fight between the FIS and FLN. Victories in only 28 constituencies would give the FIS the parliamentary majority needed to form a government. President Chadli promised to honour the election results whatever the final outcome, but there was uncertainty whether the army would accept an Islamist government.

v. MOROCCO

CAPITAL: Rabat   AREA: 460,000 sq km   POPULATION: 24,500,000 ('89)
OFFICIAL LANGUAGE: Arabic   POLITICAL SYSTEM: monarchy
HEAD OF STATE AND GOVERNMENT: King Hassan II (since '61)
RULING PARTIES: Constitutional Union heads coalition
PRINCIPAL MINISTERS: Azzedine Laraki (prime minister), Abdel Latif Filali (foreign affairs), Mohammed Berrada (finance), Driss Badri (interior, information), Moulay Mustapha Ben Larbi Alaiou (justice), Moulay Driss Alaoui M'Daghri (energy and mines)
INTERNATIONAL ALIGNMENT: NAM, Arab League, AMU, ICO
CURRENCY: dirham (end-'91 £1=DH15.02, US$1=DH8.04)
GNP PER CAPITA: US$880 ('89)
MAIN EXPORT EARNERS: phosphates, agricultural products, tourism

As the Gulf War broke out on 16 January (see V.2) popular protest mounted throughout the country against the US-led coalition's attack on Iraq. At first the government banned all public demonstrations, closed schools and universities to prevent student unrest and sent the army and security forces out in strength to preserve public order. On 15 January, in a televised address to the nation, King Hassan had warned that he would declare a state of siege if there were any signs of disorder. On 22 January opposition parties demanded that Moroccan troops should be withdrawn from the anti-Iraq coalition because its aim was no longer the liberation of Kuwait but the destruction of Iraq.

In the face of rising tensions, the authorities finally agreed to allow trade unions to hold a one-day general strike on 28 January in support of the Iraqi people. It passed off peacefully. Permission was then given for mass pro-Iraqi demonstrations in the capital, Rabat, on 3 February. On that day, an estimated 300,000 Moroccans marched through the streets chanting slogans against the USA and France and burning Western flags, in probably the biggest demonstration to be held in the country since independence. With the military and security forces on high alert, the marchers dispersed peacefully and there were no reports of any incidents. The Moroccan Red Crescent was given permission by the King to collect donations to be used for humanitarian aid to the Iraqi people. Nevertheless, King Hassan firmly refused opposition demands for the withdrawal of Moroccan forces from the Gulf. He declared that the decision to send troops was a royal prerogative and that any further criticism would invoke severe punishment for lese-majesty or treason. He stressed, however, that the role of the Moroccan forces in Saudi Arabia was purely defensive.

On 19 January King Hassan appealed to Saddam Husain to agree to a peace initiative from the Maghreb states that would have involved the withdrawal of Iraqi forces from Kuwait and their replacement by troops from the Maghreb. On 25 January Morocco joined the other members of the Arab Maghreb Union (AMU), Yemen and Sudan in requesting that the UN Security Council should propose a ceasefire, but the proposal was rejected by the Council until Iraq had complied with its existing resolutions. Morocco also joined other AMU foreign ministers on 20 February in condemning the bombing of Iraq by coalition forces and calling upon Iraq to accept UN Security Council Resolution 660 (see AR 1990, p. 561).

The Iraqi Deputy Prime Minister, Saadun Hammadi, visited Morocco on 12–13 February to request the withdrawal of Moroccan forces from the Gulf. The request was ignored by King Hassan but officials stressed that in no circumstances would Moroccan troops take part in military action against another Arab state. King Hassan failed to attend a meeting of Arab members of the coalition in Cairo in February, and in early March Morocco was the only Arab participant not present at a meeting with foreign ministers of the Gulf Cooperation Council in Damascus. King Hassan was also absent from the third AMU summit held in Ras Lanuf (Libya) on 10 March, after the other members had declined his request for a postponement. Nevertheless, the union survived the tensions provoked by the Gulf crisis, on which its five member states achieved a measure of agreement. At the AMU summit in Casablanca, in September, it was announced that the headquarters of the union would be located in Morocco.

By a delicate balancing-act during the Gulf crisis, King Hassan successfully appeased popular pressure at home without jeopardizing continued financial support from Saudi Arabia and the Gulf states. In November it was announced that Saudi Arabia had written off debts of $2,800 million and that other Gulf states were expected to follow, bringing the total to $3,600 million. After the damaging effects of the war, especially on Morocco's important tourist sector, economic prospects improved significantly, enabling the government to announce that it no longer needed to go ahead with the second phase of its debt restructuring agreements under the Brady Plan.

Relations with Western Europe remained tense during the Gulf War, as the Moroccan immigrant communities were threatened with deportations, increased police harassment and racial violence. After the hostilities France in particular moved quickly to improve relations with the Maghreb states. The French Foreign Minister, Roland Dumas, visited Rabat in April and renewed an invitation to King Hassan from the French President to visit France. In June France expelled a Moroccan dissident, Abd el Moumen Diouri, who was preparing to publish a book called *A qui appartient le Maroc?*, investigating the finances of the royal family and the activities of French banks in Morocco. However, a Paris court ruled that the expulsion (on the grounds of Mr Diouri's earlier contacts with Iraq) was unjustified, so that he returned to Paris on 16 July. Tensions affecting Moroccan immigrant communities continued. In May some 5,000 illegal Moroccan immigrants were expelled from Spain, while in Brussels violent clashes occurred between police and Moroccan workers. In July King Juan Carlos of Spain visited Rabat and signed a treaty of friendship. During the visit, Prime Minister Felipe González signed an accord on the peaceful resolution of disputes and the promotion of Mediterranean development and security.

On 26–27 September King Hassan paid a state visit to Washington, his first US visit since George Bush became President. Before the visit the Pentagon announced the sale of 20 F-16 fighter aircraft to Morocco, to a total value of $250 million. The US Defence Department said that the sale would contribute to national security by helping to improve the security of a friendly country which constituted a force for political stability and economic progress in North Africa.

On 1 May (Labour Day), in Casablanca, the country's two major trade unions held their first-ever joint march. The participants were the Union Générale des Travailleurs du Maroc (UGTM), allied to the opposition Istiqlal party, and the Confédération Démocratique du Travail (CDT), allied to the Union Socialiste des Forces Populaires (USFP). Attended by up to 200,000 people, the event generated calls for more representative democracy. In December two major political parties, the Istiqlal and the USFP, announced that they had formed a common front to campaign for 'authentic democracy'. They demanded an independent judiciary and greater powers for parliament; guarantees for free elections; a reduction in the voting age from 21 to 18 and the preparation of new electoral lists and boundaries; new guarantees for human rights and civil liberties; and a development programme that would increase access to jobs, education, health and housing.

Islamist groups, who had been allowed to take part in demonstrations during the Gulf War, were also active in the Labour Day marches and in clashes between students and police at Hassan II University in Casablanca in April. In November violent clashes, resulting in many arrests, were reported between Islamist and left-wing students in Oujda, Fez, Meknes and Kenitra. *Al Ittihad al-Ishtiraqi*, the USFP newspaper, reported that Islamists had butchered three left-wing students in the border town of Oujda and that during the unrest police had arrested several Islamist militants from neighbouring Algeria.

In February King Hassan approved recommendations by the Royal Consultative Council on Human Rights. However, in a report released in March, Amnesty International again condemned Morocco for human rights violations. There were also calls for an improvement in Morocco's human rights record from the European Parliament and the Organisation Marocaine des Droits de l'Homme. At the beginning of the year King Hassan granted a royal pardon to the family of Mohamed Oufkir, the former minister of the interior who planned an assassination attempt on the King in 1972. However, Amnesty International reported in March that it could not confirm that the family, who had been detained for 18 years without being charged or brought to trial, were at liberty. Another well-known political prisoner, Abraham Serfaty, leader of the illegal Ilal Amam movement, was released from gaol and expelled to France on 13 September. On 23 September an airforce lieutenant, Embarek Touil, became the first military prisoner involved in the 1971 and 1972 coup attempts to be released. Some observers argued that these releases were intended to improve Morocco's human rights record in preparation for the King's state visit to the USA.

vi. WESTERN SAHARA

CAPITAL: Al Aaiún   AREA: 252,000 sq km   POPULATION: 164,000 ('82)
STATUS: regarded as under its sovereignty by Morocco, whereas independent Sahrawi
    Arab Democratic Republic (SDR) was declared by Polisario Front in 1976.

IN April the UN Security Council approved resolution 690 calling for the implementation of the Secretary-General's proposals for a referendum in Western Sahara, originally set out in an interim report published in June 1990 (see AR 1990 , pp. 244–5). During the first phase of the peace plan, personnel of the UN Mission for the Referendum in the Western Sahara (MINURSO), made up of 1,695 troops, 300 police and 800 civilians, would be deployed in the territory before a ceasefire came into effect. In the second phase, a 20-week transitional period leading up to the referendum, Moroccan forces in the territory would be reduced to 65,000 and, together with Polisario forces, would be monitored by MINURSO military observers; and a UN identification commission would identify those eligible to vote. It was later announced that the ceasefire would start on 6 September, the referendum being scheduled for early 1992.

Moroccan government sources made few comments on the resolution but the opposition press was hostile, rejecting the referendum as a threat to Morocco's sovereignty and territorial integrity. A spokesman for Polisario stated that the front would accept the results of the referendum. In May King Hassan visited Western Sahara and at the end of the month held three days of talks in Oran with President Chadli of Algeria which centred on recent developments in the disputed territory. In June King Hassan granted an amnesty to all members of Polisario imprisoned since the conflict began in 1976.

In July Morocco submitted to the UN a list of 120,000 people who, it claimed, were Sahrawi refugees living in Morocco and were therefore eligible to vote in the referendum in addition to the 70,204 voters on the list drawn up by the UN (based on the 1974 census carried out by the Spanish colonial authorities). This issue was discussed at a meeting between the Moroccan Foreign Minister, Abdel Latif Filali, and the UN Secretary-General, Sr Pérez de Cuellar, in Geneva in August. The UN refused to accept block lists and insisted that the case for each voter had to be considered individually. Morocco used this dispute as a pretext to delay the entry of the advance party of MINURSO on 10 August.

Renewed fighting broke out in Western Sahara in early August, less than a month before the UN ceasefire was due to come into effect. On 10 August Polisario claimed that Morocco had launched a large-scale assault against its positions in the north-east of the territory around Bir Lahlou and Tifariti. Moroccan sources described the aerial attacks and troop build-up as only a 'mopping up' operation directed against Polisario infiltrators into the area between the defensive walls and the frontier. Fighting continued, with Polisario claiming that some 100,000 Moroccan troops were involved in fighting on several fronts. In the absence of detailed information, it was difficult to assess the scale of the attacks. However, Polisario appeared to have suffered a serious military setback.

On 21 August King Hassan called for a postponement of the peace plan, arguing that the UN had not honoured its commitment to draw up accurate electoral lists. Opposition parties continued to maintain that a referendum was unnecessary because there was no doubt that the 'Saharan provinces' were Moroccan. There was strong pressure on the King not to allow the referendum unless he could be sure that Moroccan claims would be upheld. In spite of these political differences and the continued fighting, Sr Pérez de Cuellar insisted that he wished to keep to the timetable already set for the referendum, with the result that a formal ceasefire was declared in Western Sahara on 6 September. In the preceding week, after the fighting around Tifariti and Bir Lahlan had apparently died down, UN forces were able to move in to monitor Moroccan and Polisario troop deployments. General Armand Roy of Canada, the UN military mission commander, arrived in El-Ayoun on 5 September.

At the end of September Polisario claimed that Moroccan fighter planes had violated the ceasefire and that 35,000 to 40,000 Moroccans had entered the territory since 6 September. Morocco maintained that the new arrivals were Sahrawis who had taken refuge in Morocco when Western Sahara was under Spanish control and were now returning 'to do their national duty' by taking part in the referendum. Rabat also accused Polisario of using the ceasefire to strengthen its military positions in the disputed territory.

In mid-November *The Independent* (London) carried a story alleging serious misconduct by UN officials sympathetic to Morocco, who were accused of passing sensitive information, supplied to them by Polisario, to the Moroccans. This information was believed to have contained the names of dead Sahrawis whose identity, Polisario argued, could then be claimed by Moroccans entering the territory to take part in the referendum. Polisario called for an immediate investigation, but on 18 November the UN Secretary-General strongly denied the allegations.

On 15 November it was reported that Sr Pérez de Cuellar had agreed to widen the criteria used to identify those eligible to vote in the referendum but that Morocco was pressing for further concessions, a move being resisted by Polisario. By early November only 450 members of MINURSO had arrived in El-Ayoun. Although the Secretary-General's special representative, Johannes Manz, had arrived in the territory by then, serious doubts were being expressed whether the referendum would go ahead as scheduled in January 1992.

VI EQUATORIAL AFRICA

1. ETHIOPIA—SOMALIA—DJIBOUTI—KENYA—TANZANIA—UGANDA

i. ETHIOPIA

CAPITAL: Addis Ababa   AREA: 1,220,000 sq km   POPULATION: 49,500,000 ('89)
OFFICIAL LANGUAGE: Amharic   POLITICAL SYSTEM: in transition
HEAD OF STATE: President Meles Zenawi (since July '91)
PRINCIPAL MINISTERS: Tamirat Laynie (prime minister), Wolde Mariam Germai (finance), Shiferaw Wolde Mikael (justice), Seyoum Mesfin (foreign affairs), Kuma Demeksa (interior)
INTERNATIONAL ALIGNMENT: NAM, OAU, ACP
CURRENCY: birr (end-'91 £1=Br3.85, US$1=Br2.06)   GNP PER CAPITA: US$120 ('89)
MAIN EXPORT EARNERS: coffee, agricultural produce

PRESIDENT Mengistu Haile-Maryam fled in May, when the Ethiopian People's Revolutionary Democratic Front (EPRDF) seized the capital, Addis Ababa, and established a provisional government. The Eritrean People's Liberation Front (EPLF) took control of Eritrea and set the region on the road to full independence.

The Mengistu regime's military position deteriorated rapidly in the early months of the year. The EPRDF, a coalition led by the Tigré People's Liberation Front (TPLF), launched an offensive in north-west Ethiopia late in February. By early April it had advanced rapidly down the western side of the country through Gonder and Gojjam regions and into Welega. Resistance from demoralized government forces was slight. At the same time, the EPLF moved southwards down the Eritrean coast from Massawa, until by early April it was in a position to threaten the vital port of Assab. Deputy Prime Minister Tesfaye Dinka was appointed Prime Minister on 26 April and formed a government of technocrats, but attempts to find a political solution came to nothing.

As the EPRDF advanced towards Addis Ababa, President Mengistu fled to Zimbabwe on 21 May. Vice-President Tesfaye Gebre-Kidan took over as acting President, as the army collapsed and the navy and much of the airforce fled abroad. Some 15,000 Ethiopian Jews (Falashas) were airlifted to Israel just before the regime fell (see also V.3). Peace talks chaired by US Assistant Secretary of State Herman Cohen opened in London on 27 May; but, with the EPRDF already moving on Addis Ababa, these provided no more than a diplomatic setting for the transfer of power. The EPRDF entered the capital with US approval on 28 May, to prevent a threatened breakdown of order. Its forces stormed the presidential palace and set up a new regime with its leader, Meles Zenawi, as interim President.

The EPRDF rapidly assumed control over the rest of the country, apart from Eritrea, though widespread looting occurred in parts of southern Ethiopia in the interval between regimes. In Addis Ababa, demonstrations against the new government were suppressed with some loss of life, and several massive explosions in ammunition dumps were ascribed to saboteurs. Generally, however, the change of regime was peaceful. A national conference, in which a large number of political groups took part, was held in Addis Ababa on 1–5 July. It established an 87-member Council of Representatives which on 10 July appointed Meles Zenawi as President of a transitional government. This was to hold power until elections were held in 1993. EPRDF vice-president Tamirat Laynie became Prime Minister, and a council of ministers, carefully chosen to represent different regional and ethnic groups, was installed on 10 August. This took little more than a caretaker role, and an economic policy announced in August differed little from that followed by the Mengistu regime after March 1990. While welcoming private enterprise, it retained state ownership of agricultural land and major industries.

In Eritrea, the old government's remaining forces surrendered to the EPLF late in May. The EPLF refused to take part in the Addis Ababa government, but agreed to postpone a referendum on Eritrean independence for two years. However, a provisional government of Eritrea under the EPLF leader, Isayas Afewerki, was established on 30 May, from which date Eritrea became independent in all but name. The provisional government rapidly expelled over 125,000 non-Eritreans from the region, including not only Ethiopian government soldiers and officials and their dependents but also many long-term residents. The central government made no attempt to claim jurisdiction over Eritrea, and recognized its right to independence after a referendum. However, the government in Asmara refused to acknowledge that Eritrea was even formally part of Ethiopia with the result that the territory entered a diplomatic limbo which complicated relations with the outside world. The government offered assurances that a multi-party political system with free elections would be established once Eritrea became independent, but in the interim the EPLF retained tight control. On 1 September Isayas Afewerki issued a warning against movements seeking continued union with Ethiopia, and there was no attempt to reconcile Eritrean political movements which had been opposed to the EPLF.

Further complications arose from Eritrean control over all of Ethiopia's coastline, including the port of Assab, which contained the country's only oil refinery and provided the major access point for famine relief. The Addis Ababa and Asmara governments agreed that Assab should be a free port, but the refinery remained out of operation and relief shipments were delayed. Transport inland was periodically interrupted by Afar dissidents, but the Eritreans denied allegations that they were deliberately obstructing or diverting food aid.

Lawlessness increased, especially in southern Ethiopia, as a result of the proliferation of weapons and the relaxation of the central control imposed by the ousted Mengistu regime. At the same time, the new government's policy of regional autonomy encouraged the growth of local political movements. One of these, the Oromo Liberation Front (OLF), while taking part in the provisional government in Addis Ababa, was often at odds with the EPRDF at local level. Outbreaks of violence in Hararghe region badly affected relief supplies to refugees fleeing the fighting in Somalia, while in south-western Ethiopia several hundred thousand refugees fled back into southern Sudan (see V.6.i). In the historically famine-prone areas of the north, however, the end of the war aided relief and rehabilitation, and the main rains were generally good.

ii. SOMALIA

CAPITAL: Mogadishu   AREA: 638,000 sq km   POPULATION: 6,100,000 ('89)
OFFICIAL LANGUAGE: Somali & Arabic   POLITICAL SYSTEM: in transition
HEAD OF STATE: Ali Mahdi Mohammed, interim President (since Jan '91)
PRINCIPAL MINISTERS: Umar Arteh Ghalib (prime minister), Ahmed Shaikh Hassan (interior), Abdullah Shaikh Ismail (foreign affairs)
INTERNATIONAL ALIGNMENT: NAM, OAU, ACP, Arab League, ICO
CURRENCY: shilling (end-'91 £1=SoSh4908.57, US$1=SoSh2629.12)
GNP PER CAPITA: US$170 ('89)
MAIN EXPORT EARNERS: livestock, agricultural produce

THE fall of President Siyad Barre in January brought no respite from civil war. The numerous movements opposed to him proved unable to put together any viable regime, and much of the country collapsed into anarchy. The northern region declared itself independent.

At the start of the year, President Siyad still clung to power, though much of the capital, Mogadishu, was controlled by the opposition United Somali Congress (USC). Attempts to negotiate a ceasefire failed, and foreigners (including all embassies) were evacuated. President Siyad fled the capital on 26 January, but remained at large in the south of the country. On 29 January the USC leader, Ali Mahdi Mohammed, was sworn in as President, despite opposition from other movements and some factions in the USC itself. The recently-appointed Prime Minister, Umar Arteh Ghalib, remained in office under the new government. The Somali National Movement (SNM) took full control of the northern region but refused to participate in the Mogadishu government. A projected conference for national reconciliation was abandoned, as traditional clan divisions were reflected in the various movements. The USC represented the Hawiye clans around Mogadishu, the SNM the northern Isaaq, the United Somali Front (USF) the Issa, and the Somali Patriotic Movement (SPM) and Democratic Front for the Salvation of

Somalia (DFSS) different groups among the Darod. Ex-President Siyad's supporters, also Darod, regrouped as the Somali National Front (SNF). Other factions included the Somali Democratic Movement (SDM) and Democratic Alliance of Somalia (DAS).

The SNM set up its own government in the northern region (former British Somaliland), which it declared to be an independent state on 18 May. The SNM leader, Abdel-Rahman Ahmed Ali, became its president. The secession was not recognized by any government, but the European Community (EC) assisted the SNM in implementing relief projects. In the south, fighting between rival groups alternated with attempts at reconciliation. Leaders of the USC, DFSS, SPM and SDM met in Djibouti in June, and again (with DAS and USF participation) in July. They confirmed Ali Mahdi Mohammed as interim President for two years. At a USC congress on 4–5 July, however, the leader of a rival faction, General Mohammed Farah Aydid, was elected as chairman.

Fighting between the two USC factions broke out in Mogadishu in early September, causing several hundred deaths, while further conflicts occurred in south-western Somalia. Despite a ceasefire, a new cabinet appointed on 1 October, with SPM and SDM participation, was denounced by General Aydid. From November intensified fighting resumed between the USC factions, a UN report estimating that some 20,000 people (including some foreign aid workers) had died by the end of the year. On 14 December President Ali Mahdi Mohammed appealed for UN, EC and OAU intervention.

These conflicts drastically affected relief efforts, especially the distribution of food and medical supplies. While some relief agencies continued to work under appalling conditions, others were withdrawn. Starvation and disease were rife, and by September 80 per cent of the population were estimated to be under-nourished. While in some localities clan elders were able to maintain order, Somalia as a state effectively ceased to exist.

iii. DJIBOUTI

CAPITAL: Djibouti   AREA: 23,000 sq km   POPULATION: 411,000 ('89)
OFFICIAL LANGUAGES: Arabic & French
POLITICAL SYSTEM: presidential, one-party state
HEAD OF STATE: President Hassan Gouled Aptidon (since '77)
RULING PARTY: Popular Rally for Progres (RPP)
PRINCIPAL MINISTERS: Barkat Gourad Hamadou (prime minister, planning & land development), Ismail Ali Youssouf (defence), Moussa Bouraleh Robleh (finance & economy), Moumin Bahdon Farah (foreign affairs), Ahmed Bulaleh Barreh (interior), Ougoute Hassan Ibrahim (justice)
INTERNATIONAL ALIGNMENT: NAM, OAU, ACP, Arab League, ICO, Francophonie
CURRENCY: Djibouti franc (end-'91 £1=DF310.00, US$1=DF166.04)
GNP PER CAPITA: US$480 ('81)
MAIN EXPORT EARNERS: agricultural products

PRESIDENT Hassan Gouled retained power amid conditions of continued political uncertainty. In January a former prime minister, Ali Aref Bourhan, and other members of the Afar community were arrested and charged with an attempted coup d'état. In March a congress of the ruling Rassemblement Populaire pour le Progrès reaffirmed its commitment to a single-party state. Fighting in Ethiopia and Somalia led to a further refugee influx, including members of the former Ethiopian regime's armed forces. Allegations of forced repatriation to Ethiopia were denied. Several armed clashes between ethnic groups within Djibouti were reported, and a substantial incursion of Afars from Ethiopia/Eritrea occurred late in the year; Afar dissidents took over much of the north. Djibouti provided a base for French forces engaged in the Gulf War (see v.2) and received aid from France and the Gulf states.

iv. KENYA

CAPITAL: Nairobi   AREA: 580,000 sq km   POPULATION: 23,500,000 ('89)
OFFICIAL LANGUAGE: Kiswahili   POLITICAL SYSTEM: presidential
HEAD OF STATE AND GOVERNMENT: President Daniel Arap Moi (since '78)
RULING PARTY: Kenya African National Union (KANU)
PRINCIPAL MINISTERS: George Saitoti (vice-president, finance), Wilson Ndolo Ayah (foreign affairs), Davidson Ngibuni Kuguru (home affairs), Zachary Onyonka (planning & national development)
INTERNATIONAL ALIGNMENT: NAM, OAU, ACP, Cwth.
CURRENCY: shilling (end-'91 £1=Ksh52.42, US$1=Ksh28.07)
GNP PER CAPITA: US$360 ('89)
MAIN EXPORT EARNERS: coffee, tea, petroleum products, tourism

UNTIL late in the year President Daniel Arap Moi turned his back on the pro-democracy movement sweeping across much of Africa. He argued that the effect of introducing a multi-party system would be socially disruptive and politically destabilizing, and described pro-democracy leaders as traitors and anarchists. However, opposition to the Kalenjin-dominated government was no longer the preserve of the Mwakenya movement (see AR 1987, p. 239) or of other radical clandestine groups, but attracted support across a broad front. Opposition leaders were lawyers and politicians (including former cabinet ministers), academics, businessmen and churchmen. They established the Forum for the Restoration of Democracy (FORD)—an essentially middle-class, pro-capitalist group which was itself divided on the pace and scale of reform. The government reacted to dissident activity by a spate of arrests—for example, of Gitobu Imanyara, the editor of the highly critical *Nairobi Law Monthly*, at the beginning of March (he was released in May) and of the ex-MP George Anyona in July. It also seized passports, including that of former Vice-President Oginga

Odinga, and banned pro-democracy rallies. In November, those who tried to organize an opposition rally in Nairobi were charged with contravening the Public Order Act, and security forces used tear gas and batons to prevent the rally from taking place.

Internal critics of President Moi's repressive regime received external backing. In July Africa Watch published a 329-page report detailing human rights abuses in Kenya, including the alleged use of torture in the country's prisons. In September Douglas Hurd, the British Foreign Secretary, spoke in favour of multi-party democracy during a visit to Kenya, but Britain failed to follow the lead of the United States and the Scandinavian countries in reducing the level of its aid. In late November donors attending a World Bank consultative group meeting in Paris announced that they were withholding for six months their response to Kenya's request for new aid (of some US$2,000 million over the next two years). The meeting warned that further help would depend on the government's progress in instituting economic and political reforms. Having taken some remedial action before the Paris meeting, President Moi reacted to its decision by announcing that his government was committed to 'a new era of openness and accountability'.

Much international attention focused on a judicial committee of inquiry (in Kisumu) into the murder in February 1990 of Dr Robert Ouko, Kenya's highly-respected Foreign Minister (see AR 1990, pp. 250–1). John Troon, an ex-Scotland Yard detective, gave evidence in November which linked Dr Ouko's death to his determination to expose allegations of high-level corruption involving some of his cabinet colleagues and also to a personal dispute with Nicholas Biwott, then Minister of Energy, during a visit to Washington in January 1990. Mr Troon then named Mr Biwott, President Moi's closest political ally, and Hezekiah Oyugi, head of internal security, as principal suspects. President Moi, who had transferred Mr Biwott from energy to industry in late October (when he had also put Mr Oyugi in charge of the state motor company) reacted by dismissing Mr Biwott from the government. He also halted the judicial inquiry and asked the police to conduct further investigations, as Mr Troon had recommended in his (unpublished) original report. In late November Mr Biwott, Mr Oyugi and three others were held by the police for questioning in connection with the murder, but only Jonah Anguka, a district commissioner from the Rift Valley area, was charged. Mr Biwott and Mr Oyugi were released for lack of evidence.

In December parliament amended the constitution to end the legal monopoly of power of the Kenya African National Union (KANU) and to allow other political parties to be registered. The opposition, worried that a snap election might be called, split into two factions, one called the National Democratic Alliance, associated with Oginga Odinga and backed by prominent opposition figures such as Paul Muite (chairman of the Kenya Law Society), and the other led by Martin Shikuku, a former MP. A general election was not held but other significant political events occurred. On 23 December President Moi dismissed Peter Aloo Aringo as Manpower Minister, for calling for reform within KANU. Over the next week five other members of the government resigned, including Mwai Kibaki, Minister of Health and a former national vice-president. The former ministers gave election rigging, mismanagement of the economy and the alleged cover-up of Dr Ouko's murder as their reasons for resigning. The President claimed that KANU would be strengthened rather than weakened by their departure.

On the economic front, the government made sharp cuts in the budgets of ministries and state enterprises early in the year. In mid-April it announced that the latter were to be the subject of a long-term programme of reform and/or divestiture; a parastatal reform committee was appointed. The budget for 1991/92, presented in June, proposed to rationalize the tax structure and impose stricter control of government expenditure. The deficit was to be reduced from 5.3 per cent of GDP in the 1990/91 financial year to 2 per cent in 1991/92; a 4 per cent growth rate was predicted—again optimistically—for 1991/92.

Nineteen girls died and 71 others were raped or brutalized by boys at St Kizito boarding school, Meru district, in July. This sad incident led women's movements to draw attention to their inferior position in Kenyan society (there were only two women MPs). The African Medical and Research Foundation (AMREF) set up a trachoma control unit to support its mobile health teams in Masailand, where over half the children were found to be suffering from trachoma.

President F. W. de Klerk of South Africa and Queen Elizabeth II made short visits to Kenya in June and October respectively. In the latter month the government was again accused of providing the Renamo rebel movement in Mozambique with financial and material assistance, but Kenyan officials claimed that they were merely working to secure a peace agreement in that strife-torn country (see VII.1.v).

v. TANZANIA

CAPITAL: Dar es Salaam/Dodoma   AREA: 945,000 sq km   POPULATION: 23,800,000 ('89)
OFFICIAL LANGUAGES: Swahili & English
POLITICAL SYSTEM: presidential, one-party state
HEAD OF STATE AND GOVERNMENT: President Ali Hassan Mwinyi (since '85)
RULING PARTY: Chama cha Mapinduzi (CCM)
VICE-PRESIDENTS: John Malecela (prime minister), Salmin Amour (president of Zanzibar)
PRINCIPAL MINISTERS: Stephen Kibona (finance), Ahmed Hassan Diria (foreign affairs), Augustine Lyatonga Mrema (interior)
INTERNATIONAL ALIGNMENT: NAM, OAU, ACP, Cwth.
CURRENCY: shilling (end-'91 £1=Tsh435.03, US$1=Tsh233.01)
GNP PER CAPITA: US$130 ('89)
MAIN EXPORT EARNERS: coffee, cotton, tropical foodstuffs

IN March President Ali Hassan Mwinyi appointed a 20-member presidential commission to test public opinion over a 12-month period as to whether Tanzania should continue with single-party government or adopt a multi-party system. If the latter were favoured, the commission was to make recommendations on a number of other issues such as the future role of the army. The commission was chaired by the Chief Justice and included 10 Zanzibaris. Supporters of multi-partyism, who included lawyers, academics and radical churchmen, rejected the commission on the ground that it was essentially a committee of Chama cha Mapinduzi (CCM), the ruling party. On 21 March the President banned all opposition political groups, pointing out that Tanzania was still constitutionally a one-party state. Despite this ban, the *Family Mirror*, an independent newspaper which was forthright in its support of multi-partyism, carried strong attacks on CCM policies. Public debate increased, but was still restrained. In November the police arrested two leading pro-democracy campaigners and charged them with founding unlawful societies.

Though the political liberalization issue remained unresolved at the year's end, Tanzania had been committed to economic liberalization since reaching agreement with the IMF in 1986. The government continued to pursue a flexible exchange rate and to implement the second phase of the Economic Recovery Programme (ERP), adopted in July 1989. It aimed at strengthening the social services, rehabilitating transport and communications, and increasing agricultural production. Agriculture employed 90 per cent of the labour force and accounted for 66 per cent of GDP and 80 per cent of export earnings (mainly from coffee). Manufacturing contributed some 4 per cent of GDP, but output was constrained by foreign-exchange shortages and rising import costs. International support was still essential to rehabilitate the economy, but reliance on external loans and assistance was to be gradually reduced. Budget proposals for 1991/92 included improving existing development structures; simplifying tax procedures and improving tax collection; increasing the export of non-traditional commodities such as vegetables, flowers, fruit and meat; freeing the banks of government interference; and introducing new austerity measures, such as reducing the size of the government workforce.

A former director of the US Agency for International Development (USAID) in Tanzania alleged in November that foreign aid had benefited urban and rural elites rather than the poorest people. The Swedish International Development Agency (SIDA) temporarily froze its development aid to Tanzania. In December a new trade union federation was registered, called the Organization of Tanzania Trade Unions (OTTU). Unlike the former federation, it was to be independent of the ruling party, have its own constitution, elect its own leaders and introduce economic projects to enable it to stand on its own feet.

Early in the year Zanzibar had to introduce a supplementary budget to make up the substantial deficit in its budget for 1990/91; this resulted mainly from increased oil prices occasioned by the Gulf crisis. Zanzibar, too, adopted an economic liberalization policy, aiming to become a regional trading centre. It took steps to improve the administration of its parastatal companies, to encourage private investment, to reduce dependence on imported foodstuffs, and to fight unemployment, which was made worse by the depressed state of the cloves industry.

vi. UGANDA

CAPITAL: Kampala   AREA: 240,000 sq km   POPULATION: 16,800,000 ('89)
OFFICIAL LANGUAGE: English   POLITICAL SYSTEM: presidential
HEAD OF STATE AND GOVERNMENT: President Yoweri Museveni (since Jan '86)
RULING PARTY: National Resistance Movement (NRM) heads broad-based coalition
PRINCIPAL MINISTERS: George Adyebo (prime minister), Eriya Kategaya (first deputy premier), Paul Semogerere (second deputy premier, foreign affairs), Abubakar Mayanja (third deputy premier), Crispus Kiyonga (finance), George Kanyeihamba (justice), Joshua Mayanja-Nkangi (planning & economic development)
INTERNATIONAL ALIGNMENT: NAM, OAU, ACP, Cwth.
CURRENCY: shilling (end-'91 £1=Ush1721.22, US$1=Ush921.92)
GNP PER CAPITA: US$250 ('89)
MAIN EXPORT EARNERS: coffee, cotton

IN January President Yoweri Museveni appointed George Adyebo, a 43-year old economist, as Prime Minister in place of the elderly Samson Kisekka, who became Deputy President and Minister of the Interior. Mr Adyebo was a Langi and his appointment maintained the government's communal balance. In July the President cut the size of the government from 72 to 42—22 ministers, 10 ministers of state and 10 deputy ministers. Under a World Bank reform package the number of state employees was again drastically reduced. On the other hand, civil service wages were increased very substantially, possibly to discourage corruption. Fringe benefits were also cut. Attempts to stimulate private-sector activity included plans to privatize several of the country's 112 public enterprises. The marketing of coffee, the mainstay of the economy, was liberalized by ending the monopoly of the Coffee Marketing Board; four co-operative unions were licensed to export coffee. A new regulatory body for the coffee industry—the Uganda Coffee Development Authority—was established.

Sporadic rebel guerrilla activity continued in parts of northern and eastern Uganda, causing many deaths. Omara Atubo, Minister of State for Foreign Affairs, and Andrew Adimola, a former high commissioner in London, were charged with treason in May for their alleged support of the rebels. Despite such outbreaks of dissident activity (there was also cattle-rustling in the north-east), the overall security situation improved, enabling the government to pursue its twin objectives of achieving national reconciliation and rehabilitating the economy. Though political party activity was still suspended, the government, with its mandate extended to January 1995, allowed a free and frank debate to take place on Uganda's future constitution. The constitutional commission, appointed in February 1989, continued its work.

It did so in economic conditions which, by the end of the year, were grim for the ordinary man. There were steep rises in the cost of medicine and medical services, clothing, rents, electricity and postal services, while food prices were up by 50 per cent. The main features of the Economic Recovery Programme (1988–92) remained in place, namely continued currency devaluation, increased producer prices for agricultural crops, and structural and public sector reforms. In his July budget speech, Crispus Kiyonga, the Minister of Finance, pointed out that after three years of economic expansion averaging 6.6 per cent per annum growth for 1990/91 had slowed down to an estimated 4.7 per cent, partly because of the collapse of the international coffee price. The budgetary objectives for 1991/92 were to sustain a GDP growth rate of at least 5 per cent; to bring down inflation to 15 per cent; and to strengthen the balance-of-payments position by increasing exports. The economy, however, remained heavily dependent on external foreign assistance.

The Ugandan AIDS Control Programme estimated that 1.2 million peple were infected with the HIV virus; the President urged Ugandans to use condoms. Preliminary steps were taken to revive some aspects of the former East African Community, which had collapsed in 1977 (see AR 1977, p. 353). The governments of Uganda, Tanzania and Zambia sought foreign aid to launch a new airline, to be called Africa Joint Air Services. Relations with Rwanda remained strained following the invasion of that country the previous year by Rwandan refugees living in Uganda (see AR 1990, p. 256).

2. GHANA—NIGERIA—SIERRA LEONE—THE GAMBIA—LIBERIA

i. GHANA

CAPITAL: Accra   AREA: 240,000 sq km   POPULATION: 14,400,000 ('89)
OFFICIAL LANGUAGE: English   POLITICAL SYSTEM: military regime
HEAD OF STATE: Flt-Lt Jerry Rawlings, Chairman of Provisional National Defence Council (since '81)
PRINCIPAL MINISTERS: P. V. Obeng (chairman of committee of secretaries), Kwesi Botchwey (finance & economic planning), Obed Y. Asamoah (foreign affairs), Mahamad Idrisu (defence), G. Tandoh (justice), Nana Akuko Sarpong (interior)
INTERNATIONAL ALIGNMENT: NAM, OAU, ACP, Cwth.
CURRENCY: cedi (end-'91 £1=C730.47, US$1=C391.25)
GNP PER CAPITA: US$390 ('89)
MAIN EXPORT EARNERS: cocoa, gold, minerals

THE tide of democracy which was said to be rising throughout the world left its mark on Ghana too. The year was full of commission reports and government statements foreshadowing the move away from military rule to a restoration of civilian government on the base of a new constitution and free and fair elections.

At the beginning of January, 13 local opposition groups came together to form a Coordinating Committee of Democratic Forces (CCDF). The ruling Provisional National Defence Council (PNDC) tried to respond to its demands and in August Flight-Lieutenant Rawlings inaugurated a Constituent Assembly of 258 members to draft a constitution for what would be the Fourth Republic (after those of 1960–66, 1969–72 and 1979–81). A timetable was drawn up. The Assembly would complete its work by the end of the year, then political parties would be 'unbanned' and a referendum held on the new constitution, followed by local, national and presidential elections in the last quarter of 1992.

Such were the hopes and expectations. The future was to be secured by a return to the past. In May the earlier forum, the National Council for Democracy and the Movement for Freedom and Justice (see AR 1990, p. 258), presented a report to the PNDC urging reform; at the end of July a committee of experts, appointed by Flight-Lieutenant Rawlings, made recommendations about the shape of the government-to-be. In general—to be successful—politics must go with the grain of society; in Ghana that meant a revival of old antagonisms between those who opposed and those who supported the late Kwame Nkrumah. Left and right ideologies? Or factions of rival interests? More the latter; and, since parties were still outlawed, societies were founded. Danquah-Busia clubs were inaugurated in Accra, Koforidua, Nkawkaw and Kumasi. In reply, Kwame Nkrumah welfare societies were formed. And true to past form, various splinter movements began to emerge, as well as various possible presidential candidates.

The year ended with delay. The Constituent Assembly had not finished its task. Ghanaians would have to wait and see what was recommended—a presidential/vice-presidential system on American lines, a president/prime minister on the French model, a simple return to Westminster, or a new amalgam of the past.

Meanwhile, the country went through bad and good times. The dark side was still that of a harsh dictatorial regime. In June all three of the country's universities were closed (and stayed closed) when students complained of their poor living conditions. On 23 September 150 market women paraded naked through the streets of the capital in protest against high prices. Nurses, too, went on a series of strikes, followed by doctors and laboratory technicians. Then, on 21 October, two former politicians were detained, namely Nana Okutwer Bekow and Kwesi Armah; the former was then released without explanation. On 12 November the security forces arrested George Naykene, editor of the

Accra weekly, *Christian Chronicle*, for publishing reports of corruption among members of the former Armed Forces Revolutionary Council. Protests from the Ghana Journalists Association succeeded only in ensuring a future trial on the charge of criminal libel.

On the bright side of the year had to be placed evidence of economic recovery. The last day of 1991 was also the tenth anniversary of Flight-Lieutenant Rawlings' (second) seizure of power. In a new year's broadcast he admitted the economic hardship of the past decade but spoke soberly of better times to come. There was substance to his message. Cocoa production was up from 153,000 tonnes in 1983 to 300,000 tonnes; farmers' incomes had also increased despite falling world prices. Production of maize, yams, cassava, rice, fruit and cotton had all increased substantially in response to the internationally-assisted recovery programme. Gold output, too, was up: new mines were opened after many years of declining production. On 21–27 October, the Confederation of British Industry and the West Africa Committee held a conference in Accra under the title 'Ghana: Africa's Golden Opportunity'. And as if to cap the country's return to fortune, in September, in Italy, Ghana's 'Black Starlets' football team won the under-17 World Cup.

Other notable international events included Ghana's representation at Harare for the Commonwealth heads of government meeting (see XI.2), a World Health Organization forum (4–6 December) and the 10th ministerial meeting of the Non-Aligned Movement (NAM) in Accra (2–7 September), when representatives of 96 governments met in the new pink International Centre built on the former race-course (see XI.4). Ghanaians were bemused by the initials NAM, the local Akan word for 'meat'. Good times were surely coming.

ii. NIGERIA

CAPITAL: Abuja   AREA: 924,000 sq km   POPULATION: 113,800,000 ('89)
OFFICIAL LANGUAGE: English   POLITICAL SYSTEM: military regime
HEAD OF STATE AND GOVERNMENT: President (Gen.) Ibrahim Babangida (since '85)
PRINCIPAL MINISTERS: Vice-Adml (rtd) Augustus Aikhomu (vice-president), Maj.-Gen. Ike Nwachuku (foreign affairs), Lt-Gen. Sanni Abacha (defence), Abubakar Alhaji (finance & economic planning), Jibril Aminu (petroleum), Prince Bola Ajibola (justice), Maj.-Gen. A. B. Mamman (interior), Chu Okongwu (budget & planning)
INTERNATIONAL ALIGNMENT: NAM, OAU, OPEC, ICO, ACP, Cwth.
CURRENCY: naira (end-'91 £1=N18.36 US$1=N9.83)   GNP PER CAPITA: US$250 ('89)
MAIN EXPORT EARNERS: oil and gas

THE most significant developments of 1991 took place during the closing months of the year. At the end of November restrictions were placed upon the movement of citizens in order that the long-awaited census could take place. The exercise was fraught with difficulties, not least because of its sheer scale: 200,000 enumeration zones requiring 500,000 enumerators using every means of transport—from four-wheeled jeeps to canoes—to reach the remotest corners of the country. Added to this was the political sensitivity of the census: with population density forming the basis of revenue allocation, over-reporting and the manipulation of results had discredited all previous attempts since independence. Notwithstanding these difficulties, the exercise proceeded in an orderly fashion, with a claimed 99.7 per cent of the population participating. However, the real test of success would not come until the results were published in March 1992.

On 12 December President Ibrahim Babangida fulfilled a longstanding commitment to relocate the seat of the federal government when, with his family and personal staff, he left Lagos for the new federal capital of Abuja. To mark the occasion, at a ceremony held in Lagos city hall, the President was presented with a scroll which decreed that henceforth 12 December would be celebrated in the state as Ibrahim Babangida Day. The federal capital territory of Abuja had first been designated in a proclamation of 1975, when there had been 19 Nigerian states. Despite intense pressure for more states during the Second Republic (1979–83) none had been created until 1987, when Katsina had been formed out of northern Kaduna and Akwa Ibom from southern Cross River. The 1987 changes had rekindled the clamour for new states, to which the Armed Forces Ruling Council (AFRC) had initially seemed unresponsive. However, on 27 August 1991, on the sixth anniversary of his coming to power, the President announced the formation of nine new states, bringing the total to 30. The decision was justified in terms of the principles of 'social justice', 'development' and a 'balanced federation'.

The unexpected creation of the new states, necessitating various administrative changes, gave rise to some concern about the AFRC's commitment to returning the country to civilian rule in 1992, especially since there seemed to be a growing personality cult surrounding the President and his wife. However, confidence that the transition programme was still on course was renewed with the holding of gubernatorial primary elections in October. Whilst these were generally peaceful, the publication of their results unleashed a torrent of accusations of ballot-rigging and other irregularities within the two state-sponsored parties, the Social Democratic Party (SDP) and the National Republican Convention (NRC). Such was the degree of intra-party dissension that Vice-President Augustus Aikhomu called publicly upon the warring factions to resolve their differences, whilst the chairman of the National Electoral Commission (NEC), Professor Humphrey Nwosu, cancelled results in nine states and ordered a re-run under NEC supervision.

The fact that internal wrangling was much more serious within the

SDP was thought to explain that party's patchy performance in the actual gubernatorial (and state assembly) elections held on 14 December. The outcome was that the NRC secured the governorships of 16 states, while the SDP was victorious in 12 (elections in two states being postponed). One major surprise was that Lagos, traditionally a stronghold of social democracy, went to the rightist NRC. A second was that Kano, formerly the main power base of the radical People's Redemption Party (under the Second Republic), also went to the NRC.

At the beginning of 1991 the Budget and Planning Minister, Chu Okongwu, found himself in the happy situation of presiding over the first budget surplus for ten years. The temporary oil price boom produced by the Gulf War enabled Nigeria to reduce its enormous rolled-over deficit of N 22,000 million as well as to build up its foreign-exchange reserves. Whilst affirming the government's commitment to ongoing large-scale capital projects in steel, agriculture and water supply, Mr Okongwu stressed his determination to hold down expenditure with the aim of achieving an end-of-year surplus. However, as early as mid-year, hopes of attaining this goal were dashed by an announcement by the governor of the central bank, Alhaji Abdelkadir Ahmad, of a record deficit for the first six months of 1991 of N 19,560 million. Three principal factors were thought to underpin this apparently inexorable drift into the red: the falling price of oil, the declining value of the naira and the costs of debt servicing. Mr Okongwu's budget assumed an oil price of at least US\$21 per barrel and an exchange rate of N 8 per US\$1. In fact, the oil price for most of the year was around \$18, while the naira hovered around 10 to the dollar. The latter factor increased the price of imports, not least of military hardware. High levels of military spending were thought to lie behind significant off-budget items of expenditure.

At the beginning of the year Nigeria reached agreement with the Paris Club regarding the further rescheduling of that part of its foreign debt owed to official creditors (approximately \$17,500 million). However, since the accord was based on an oil price of \$23 per barrel, actual net repayments resulted in an unexpected \$500 million shortfall on the original budget. With hefty repayments also due early in 1992 under a London Club agreement with private creditors, the long-sought goal of keeping debt-servicing below 30 per cent of export earnings seemed as elusive as ever.

Meanwhile, ordinary Nigerians continued to endure falling living standards, high levels of unemployment (especially among the young), a chronic shortage of housing and appalling transport difficulties. Not surprisingly, the grim cycle of daily life produced manifold social tensions, which expressed themselves not only in alarming levels of personal violence (such as acid attacks on political opponents) but also in a number of serious mass outbursts. In February Lagos experienced two days of rioting, apparently triggered by the state authority's demolition of shops belonging to illegal traders. In April violent religious clashes in Katsina were followed by a rampage in Bauchi by supporters of the Islamic Movement of Nigeria. But whereas the Katsina disturbances involved an intra-Islamic feud between overly-enthusiastic Shia proselytes and local Muslims, the Bauchi outburst took on a more disquieting anti-Christian tone. There at least 40 people were killed and 30 buildings, including churches, were burned down. Hostility to Christianity also lay behind the most serious outbreak of the year, in October, when thousands of Muslims in Kano stormed the emir's palace to protest against a five-day revivalist campaign to be led by a German preacher. In three days of rioting and looting at least 100 people were killed.

On the international stage Nigeria continued to maintain a high profile on the African continent. In June the 27th session of heads of state of the Organization of African Unity was held in Abuja, as was the 14th summit of the Economic Community of West African States (ECOWAS) the following month (see also XI.6.i). President Babangida's wife, Maryam, was in September awarded the 1991 Africa Prize for Leadership for the Sustainable End of Hunger (jointly with Professor Wangari Maathi of Kenya) for her 'better life for rural women' project. Other Nigerians who achieved international prominence in 1991 were the writer Ben Okri, who was awarded the Booker Prize (see XVI.3), and the Minister of Petroleum, Jibril Aminu, who was chosen as president of OPEC.

iii. SIERRA LEONE

CAPITAL: Freetown   AREA: 72,000 sq km   POPULATION: 4,000,000 ('89)
OFFICIAL LANGUAGE: English   POLITICAL SYSTEM: presidential
HEAD OF STATE AND GOVERNMENT: President Joseph Saidu Momoh (since '85)
RULING PARTY: All-People's Congress (APC)
PRINCIPAL MINISTERS: Abdulai Conteh (first vice-president, rural development, internal affairs), John Bandala Dauda (second vice-president, justice), J. S. A. Funna (finance & economic planning), A. R. Dumbuya (foreign affairs)
INTERNATIONAL ALIGNMENT: NAM, OAU, ICO, Cwth.
CURRENCY: leone (end-'91 £1=Le766.10, US$1=Le410.33)
GNP PER CAPITA: US$220 ('89)
MAIN EXPORT EARNERS: diamonds, coffee, cocoa

PRESIDENT Joseph Momoh faced further difficulties during 1991. In addition to an economic crisis, exacerbated by years of mismanagement, world recession and the effects of the Gulf War and fighting in Liberia (see VI.2.v), the President had to contend with two new challenges: mounting demands for political reform and invasion from neighbouring Liberia. Demands for a review of the 1978 single-party constitution had been conceded in October 1990 with the creation of a constitutional review commission under Peter Tucker (see AR 1990, p. 263). While the commission undertook its work, demands for the abolition of the single-party system grew, particularly among the intelligentsia and professions. Even as the Tucker report was presented to the President on 28 March, opponents of the government, styling themselves the Revolutionary United Front and led by ex-Corporal Foday Sankoh (gaoled in 1971 for participating in an earlier coup attempt), invaded the country along its border with Liberia. Supported by elements of Charles Taylor's National Patriotic Forces of Liberia, aggrieved by Sierra Leone's participation in the ECOWAS intervention in Liberia, the insurgents overran four districts in the Eastern and Southern provinces, causing considerable death and destruction and forcing an estimated 200,000 people to flee. With military assistance from Nigeria and Guinea, the inexperienced and under-manned army gradually halted and then pushed back the invaders, so that by December most of the seized territory had been recovered. However the cost of reconstruction was enormous, with the loss of export earnings from the affected area being estimated at nearly Le 3,000 million.

On the political front, despite extending its life until the constitutional reforms were implemented, the ruling All-People's Congress faced the inevitable loss of its political monopoly. Despite his earlier objections to a multi-party system, President Momoh accepted the Tucker report with only minor modifications. Following parliamentary approval and a national referendum in August, the multi-party constitution came into effect in October. The new constitution, additionally, restricted the presidency to two terms, barred MPs from cabinet office and created a new State Advisory Council, of 12 paramount chiefs and 10 nominated members. Six new parties had received official recognition by December. Anticipating the possible demise of the APC, several prominent members switched their support to the new parties. This forced President Momoh to carry out a major reorganization of his cabinet in September in anticipation of the multi-party elections delayed until early 1992.

iv. THE GAMBIA

CAPITAL: Banjul   AREA: 11,300 sq km   POPULATION: 849,000 ('89)
OFFICIAL LANGUAGE: English   POLITICAL SYSTEM: presidential democracy
HEAD OF STATE AND GOVERNMENT: President Sir Dawda Kairaba Jawara (since '70)
RULING PARTY: People's Progressive Party (PPP)
PRINCIPAL MINISTERS: Bakary Bunja Darbo (vice-president), Omar Sey (external affairs), Saihou S. Sabally (economy), Lamin Kiti Jabang (interior), Hassan Jallow (justice)
INTERNATIONAL ALIGNMENT: NAM, OAU, ACP, ICO, Cwth.
CURRENCY: dalasi (end-'91 £1=D16.99, US$1=D9.10)   GNP PER CAPITA: US$240 ('89)
MAIN EXPORT EARNERS: groundnuts, groundnut products

ON 18 February (Independence Day) all remaining prisoners gaoled for their part in the attempted coup of 1981 were amnestied by the President, Sir Dawda Jawara. Possible new military disaffection was adroitly handled in June, when 60 members of the Gambian contingent sent to Liberia as part of the ECOWAS mediating force demonstrated in front of State House, demanding payment of overdue allowances and the dismissal of the Gambian army commander, Colonel Momodou N'Dow N'Jie. The arrears were quickly paid and Colonel N'Dow N'Jie replaced. With elections due in 1992, a new opposition party appeared in September. Led by a political newcomer, Dr Lamin Bojang, the Gambian People's Democratic Party drew support from defectors from the main opposition group, the National Convention Party. The ruling People's Progressive Party (PPP) also faced a crisis in December when, quite unexpectedly, President Jawara announced his intention not to seek re-nomination for the presidential election in 1992. Following a national demonstration in Banjul by the PPP, the President relented and agreed to stand for a further term.

Hopes of improved relations with Senegal followed the signing in January of a new Treaty of Friendship and Co-operation to replace the lapsed Senegambia confederation. Annual meetings of the two heads of state and the establishment of a joint commission to implement further agreements formed part of the treaty. Both countries also attended a meeting of the River Gambia Development Organization in July and cooperated in trying to resolve the Liberian crisis. The Senegalese leader, President Abdou Diouf, replaced Sir Dawda as chairman of ECOWAS.

v. LIBERIA

CAPITAL: Monrovia AREA: 97,750 sq km POPULATION: 2,500,000 ('89)
OFFICIAL LANGUAGE: English POLITICAL SYSTEM: presidential
HEAD OF STATE AND GOVERNMENT: Amos Sawyer, President of interim government
PRINCIPAL MINISTERS: Peter Naigow (vice-president), Edward Kesselly (defence),
    Gabriel Matthews (foreign affairs), Amelia Ward (economy & planning), Philis
    Banks (justice)
INTERNATIONAL ALIGNMENT: NAM, OAU, ACP
CURRENCY: Liberian dollar (end-'91 £1=L$1.87, US$1=L$1.00)
GNP PER CAPITA: US$450 ('89)
MAIN EXPORT EARNERS: iron ore, rubber, coffee

AFTER a year of intensive and often fruitless negotiations, in Monrovia as well as neighbouring states, the outlines of a final peace settlement were agreed at a fourth meeting of the warring factions and ECOWAS mediators at Yamoussoukro in Côte d'Ivoire in October. A tentative arrangement was reached to allow ECOMOG (ECOWAS Monitoring Group) to supervise the disarmament and encampment of the rival warring factions. These were the National Patriotic Front of Liberia (NPFL) led by Charles Taylor, the Independent Patriotic Front of Liberia (IPFL) led by Prince Yormie Johnson, and the rump national army, Armed Forces of Liberia (AFL) formerly loyal to the deposed and murdered head-of-state, Samuel Doe (see AR 1990, pp. 264–5). A national elections commission would then arrange for countrywide multi-party elections under international supervision (by former US President Carter's INN organization) some time in 1992. Already some six political parties were in existence. A fourth military faction, the United Liberation Movement for Liberian Democracy (ULIMO), though not present at Yamoussoukro, agreed to the ceasefire separately. Led by Raleigh Seekie, ULIMO was drawn from anti-Taylor Muslim-Mandingo and Krahn groups which had been harshly persecuted by the NPFL.

Earlier talks in Monrovia, Togo and Côte d'Ivoire, between the rival factions and the ECOWAS-backed interim national government led by Dr Amos Sawyer, had collapsed principally because of the intransigence of Mr Taylor. As the leader responsible for the overthrow of the much-hated Doe regime, he bitterly resented the Nigerian-dominated ECOMOG military presence, which underpinned Dr Sawyer's interim presidency. The NFPL was in effective control of 12 of Liberia's 13 counties (and virtually all its natural resources) and had conducted its own separate elections the previous year, in which Mr Taylor had been chosen as president. The NFPL leader also feared that discredited former politicians would get back to power following fresh elections. Further difficulties arose from the shifting position of Prince Johnson, whose support during the year veered between Dr Sawyer and the NPFL, and from the need to establish consensus among the ECOWAS mediating countries themselves, given that Côte d'Ivoire and Burkina Faso supported Mr Taylor. Finally, there remained the enormous cost of national rehabilitation and an external debt of over $3,000 million.

3. SENEGAL—GUINEA—MALI—MAURITANIA—CÔTE
D'IVOIRE—BURKINA FASO—NIGER—TOGO—BENIN—CAMEROON—
CHAD—GABON AND CENTRAL AFRICAN REPUBLIC—CONGO—
EQUATORIAL GUINEA

i. SENEGAL

CAPITAL: Dakar   AREA: 196,000 sq km   POPULATION: 7,200,000 ('89)
OFFICIAL LANGUAGE: French   POLITICAL SYSTEM: presidential democracy
HEAD OF STATE AND GOVERNMENT: President Abdou Diouf (since '81)
RULING PARTY: Socialist Party (PS) heads coalition with Senegal Democratic Party (PDS) & Party of Independence and Labour (PIT)
PRINCIPAL MINISTERS: Habib Thiam (PS/prime minister), Abdoulaye Wade (PDS/minister of state), Famara Ibrahima Sagna (PS/economy, finance & planning), Medoune Fall (PS/armed forces), Serigne Lamine Diop (PS/justice), Djibo Ka (PS/foreign affairs), Khary Dieng (PS/interior), Amath Dansokho (PIT/urban planning & housing)
INTERNATIONAL ALIGNMENT: NAM, ACP, ICO, Francophonie
CURRENCY: CFA franc (end-'91 £1=CFAF484.50, US$1=CFAF259.51)
GNP PER CAPITA: US$650 ('89)
MAIN EXPORT EARNERS: agricultural products and fish, chemicals

THE year contained a number of political surprises, which meant that in spite of the continuing fragility of the economy the year ended with a more relaxed political atmosphere than at its start. The major political development was the entry into a government coalition of the main opposition party, the Senegal Democratic Party (PDS). The leader of the opposition, Maître Abdoulaye Wade, became Minister of State (without portfolio) and three other senior party figures were given ministries. The leader of a less significant grouping, Amath Dansokho of the Party of Independence and Labour (PIT), also obtained a ministry. This had the effect of defusing the sourness which had existed between government and opposition since the violent ructions of the 1988 elections. A key element in the new atmosphere were the concessions made by President Abdou Diouf to the opposition's demands for a fairer electoral code. This, it was reckoned, would lead to a more peaceable election next time round in 1993.

Many Senegalese wondered whether Maître Wade had been out-manoeuvred in being absorbed into the government. Even though there was no merger of parties, his PDS would be associated with the economic hardship imposed by the observation of structural adjustment programmes. Here, Senegal's earlier model performance was now being criticized by the World Bank and the International Monetary Fund because it was increasingly straying from economic targets. However, the new stability of the coalition (despite certain frictions arising from 'co-habitation') reassured donors, and further IMF credits were agreed in the second half of the year.

The peace agreement signed in May with secessionists in the southern province of Casamance was also reassuring for donors. The PDS claimed an influential role in brokering the deal, and the new political climate certainly facilitated peace in the region, where the PDS had strong support. Nevertheless, there was further violence in Casamance at the end of the year. The PDS was also active in supporting new government initiatives on regional integration, notably when President Diouf became chairman of the Economic Community of West African States (ECOWAS) in July.

ii. GUINEA

CAPITAL: Conakry   AREA: 246,000 sq km   POPULATION: 5,600,000 ('89)
OFFICIAL LANGUAGE: French   POLITICAL SYSTEM: military regime
HEAD OF STATE AND GOVERNMENT: Brig.-Gen. Lansana Conté, Chairman of Transitional Committee for National Recovery (since '84)
PRINCIPAL MINISTERS: Maj. Jean Traoré (foreign affairs), Maj. Abdourahmane Diallo (defence), Edouard Benjamin (economy & finance), Maj. Facine Touré (justice), Alhassane Conde (interior)
INTERNATIONAL ALIGNMENT: NAM, OAU, ACP, ICO, Francophonie
CURRENCY: Guinean franc (end-'91 £1=GF1,521.83, US$1=GF815.21)
GNP PER CAPITA: US$430 ('89)
MAIN EXPORT EARNERS: bauxite, oilseeds

THE slowness of the transition from military to civilian government, announced originally as a five-year programme in 1988, came under increasing pressure from a growing number of opposition groups, but the government of President Lansana Conté more or less held firm. In January the Military Committee for National Recovery, set up after the 1984 coup, was dissolved, and replaced by a Transitional Committee for National Recovery. This took the emphasis off the military nature of the government. In September the President announced that parliamentary elections would be held before the end of 1992, followed by presidential elections in 1993; moreover, the present restriction of parties to two would be changed when a new law on parties came into force in April 1992. The move followed several months of agitation and discontent, including a general strike in June. There was also trouble in May and June when an opposition leader, Alpha Condé, returned and was so harassed by the authorities that he had to seek refuge in the Senegalese embassy. He was eventually expelled to Senegal.

iii. MALI

CAPITAL: Bamako   AREA: 1,240,000 sq km   POPULATION: 8,200,000 ('89)
OFFICIAL LANGUAGE: French   POLITICAL SYSTEM: transitional military/civilian
HEAD OF STATE: Lt-Col. Amadou Toumani Touré, Chairman of Transition
   Committee for the Salvation of the People (since March '91)
PRINCIPAL MINISTERS: Soumana Sacko (prime minister), Bassary Touré (economy & finance), Mamadou Ouattara (justice), Lt-Col. Kanfougouna Kone (defence), Tiébilé Dramé (foreign affairs)
INTERNATIONAL ALIGNMENT: NAM, OAU, ACP, ICO, Francophonie
CURRENCY: CFA franc (end-'91 £1=CFAF484.50, US$1=CFAF259.51)
GNP PER CAPITA: US$270 ('89)
MAIN EXPORT EARNERS: cotton, agricultural products

THIS was the year of the second coup d'état in Mali's history, the first having been when the military originally took over in 1968. This time, however, it was a coup which, though led by the army colonel commanding the paratroop regiment, Amadou Toumani Touré, was designed to take the army definitively out of the political arena. It followed several weeks of mounting protests against the government of General Moussa Traoré. He had resisted pressures to democratize his regime, either in the direction of allowing multi-partyism or of holding a national conference, which in other African countries had become a passport to such democratization. It was estimated that between 200 and 300 were killed in the demonstrations. The army's refusal to go on killing unarmed civilians was one of the main motives for the takeover.

The coup took place on 26 March and was marked by the arrest of President Traoré, his wife and several ministers. A 17-member National Reconciliation Council was quickly succeeded by a 25-member Transition Committee for the Salvation of the People, on which civilians had 15 seats. A programme was announced for a return to civilian rule early in 1992, with a multi-party constitution, and an all-civilian transitional government was appointed. The new Prime Minister was Soumana Sacko, a former minister of finance who had resigned because of the malpractices of the previous regime. He was known as 'Zorro' because of his reputation as an anti-corruption crusader.

Progress in the transition was hampered somewhat by the recrudescence of the revolt of the nomadic Touareg peoples in the north of the country. This was despite the signature of a peace agreement in January in Tamanrasset (Algeria), under the auspices of Mali, Niger, Algeria and Libya (all with Touareg populations). In fact, Touareg insurgency continued through the year, and there was some suspicion that the (Touareg) Popular Front for the Liberation of Azaouad (FPLA) was being financed and encouraged from Libya.

iv. MAURITANIA

CAPITAL: Nouakchott   AREA: 1,000,000 sq km   POPULATION: 1,900,000 ('89)
OFFICIAL LANGUAGES: French & Arabic   POLITICAL SYSTEM: military regime
HEAD OF STATE AND GOVERNMENT: Col. Moaouia Ould Sidi Mohamed Taya, Chairman of Military Council of National Salvation (since '84)
PRINCIPAL MINISTERS: Hassiny Ould Didi (foreign affairs), Ahmed Ould Minnih (interior), Sow Adema Samba (justice), Sidi Mohamed Ould Boubaker (finance), Mouhamedou Ould Michel (planning)
INTERNATIONAL ALIGNMENT: NAM, Arab League, ICO, OAU, ACP, AMU, Francophonie
CURRENCY: ouguiya (end-'91 £1=UM156.25, US$1=UM83.69)
GNP PER CAPITA: US$500 ('89)
MAIN EXPORT EARNERS: iron ore, fish

ALTHOUGH Colonel Moaouia Ould Sidi Mohamed Taya had promised a return to democratic practices when he seized power in 1984, this had so far only extended to the holding of municipal elections. In April, however, influenced by the democratic pressures increasingly evident in Africa, he announced a full return to civilian rule, with an 'unlimited number of political parties'. The move followed the distribution of anonymous tracts calling for more democracy, which Arab nationalist elements close to the government were thought to have been resisting on the grounds that it was a French-inspired campaign.

A new constitution describing Mauritania as an 'Islamic Arab and African republic' was approved in a referendum on 12 July by what was described as a 'sweeping victory'. Official figures said that 97.94 per cent of votes cast were in favour of the new constitution, and that more than 85 per cent of the electorate took part in the poll. Opposition parties, dominated by black Mauritanians from the south, claimed that these figures were doctored, since they had called for a boycott. In August the creation of political parties was permitted and preparations were made for parliamentary and presidential elections, which after several delays were scheduled for January 1992.

v. CÔTE D'IVOIRE

CAPITAL: Abidjan   AREA: 322,000 sq km   POPULATION: 11,700,000 ('89)
OFFICIAL LANGUAGE: French   POLITICAL SYSTEM: presidential
HEAD OF STATE AND GOVERNMENT: President Félix Houphouët-Boigny (since '60)
RULING PARTY: Democratic Party of Côte d'Ivoire (PDCI)
PRINCIPAL MINISTERS: Alassane Ouattara (prime minister, economy & finance), Amara Essy (foreign affairs), Léon Konan Koffi (defence), Emile Constant Bombet (interior), Jacqueline Lohoues Oble (justice)
INTERNATIONAL ALIGNMENT: NAM, OAU, ACP, Francophonie
CURRENCY: CFA franc (end-'91 £1=CFAF484.50, US$1=CFAF259.51)
GNP PER CAPITA: US$790 ('89)
MAIN EXPORT EARNERS: cocoa, coffee, timber

AFTER the turbulence of 1990, during which President Houphouët-Boigny was re-elected for a five-year term in his first contest with an opponent (see AR 1990, p. 269), emphasis was placed in 1991 on trying to achieve economic recovery. It was generally a quiet year, although there was serious student unrest in May, followed by rumours of a coup attempt at the end of July. The Prime Minister, Alassane Ouattara, had some successes to report, especially in the area of government reform, privatization and improved revenue collection. However, the continuing poor performance of the main exports, coffee and cocoa, on the world markets meant that he appeared to be fighting an uphill battle. Towards the end of the year the government faced unrest from trade unions and students, but the new freedoms of multi-partyism and an independent press meant that society had some safety-valves, even if Abidjan's notorious crime wave continued unabated.

President Houphouët-Boigny himself was increasingly involved in the peace process in Liberia (see VI.2.v), with Yamoussoukro, his home town, hosting four successive reconciliation summits. Ivoirian support for the Liberian rebel leader Charles Taylor became increasingly controversial as he continued to obstruct the peace process.

vi. BURKINA FASO

CAPITAL: Ouagadougou   AREA: 275,000 sq km   POPULATION: 8,800,000 ('89)
OFFICIAL LANGUAGE: French   POLITICAL SYSTEM: transitional
HEAD OF STATE AND GOVERNMENT: Capt. Blaise Compaoré, Chairman of Popular Front (since '87)
PRINCIPAL MINISTERS: Issa Dominique Konate (external relations), Frédéric Assomption Korsaga (finance & planning), Benoit Lompo (justice), Lassane Ouangraoua (defence)
INTERNATIONAL ALIGNMENT: NAM, OAU, ACP, ICO, Francophonie
CURRENCY: CFA franc (end-'91 £1=CFAF484.50, US$1=CFAF259.51)
GNP PER CAPITA: US$320 ('89)
MAIN EXPORT EARNERS: cotton, agricultural produce

CAPTAIN Blaise Compaoré, who appeared to start the year in a relatively strong political position, found himself politically isolated by December, grouped with those African leaders trying to resist political change. Having agreed to allow pluralism both of political parties and the media (which were made legal in April), on 2 June he secured a massive majority in a referendum on a new multi-party constitution. He then established a coalition government with several of the important opposition parties. By August, however, this had fallen apart, and he entered the December presidential election facing a boycott by the 20 parties of the opposition Coalition of Democratic Forces (CFD), who were calling for a national conference to be convened before elections. Since Captain Compaoré polled only 573,186 votes of a possible 2.7 million, the opposition called for the election to be invalidated. Some serious violence occurred, in which Clément Ouedraogo, who had been in the government until forming his own opposition party in April, was killed in a bomb explosion. The government then postponed parliamentary elections indefinitely and proposed the convening of a 'national forum', which would not have the same powers as a national conference. Thus the year ended in total political stalemate.

vii. NIGER

CAPITAL: Niamey   AREA: 1,267,000 sq km   POPULATION: 7,400,000 ('89)
OFFICIAL LANGUAGE: French   POLITICAL SYSTEM: transitional
HEAD OF STATE: President (Brig.) Ali Saibou (since '87)
PRINCIPAL MINISTERS: Amadou Cheiffou (prime minister, defence), Mohammed Mousa (interior), Hassane Hamidou (foreign affairs), Souna Issake (justice), Laoual Chaffani (economy & finance)
INTERNATIONAL ALIGNMENT: NAM, OAU, ACP, ICO, Francophonie
CURRENCY: CFA franc (end-'91 £1=CFAF484.50, US$1=CFAF259.51)
GNP PER CAPITA: US$290 ('89)
MAIN EXPORT EARNERS: uranium, metal ores

IN a year in which 'national conferences' on political change led to serious upsets elsewhere in Africa, Niger staged its own very quietly, and took all the resultant changes in its stride. This was, in part, due to the cooperative attitude of the President, Brigadier Ali Saibou, who seemed less fussed about retention of power than some of his presidential counterparts. The movement to democracy had begun in 1990 (see AR 1990, p. 271); by the beginning of 1991 political party creation was legalized. The trade union federation was de-linked from the former ruling party, the National Movement for a Development Society, which held a congress in March to transform itself into a 'simple political party'. Niger's national conference began on 27 May. Although not without upsets and disagreements, it proceeded relentlessly on its way, assuming sovereignty and suspending the constitution. Eventually, after 4½ months, it gave birth to a transitional programme due to be completed in January 1993. On 26 October Amadou Cheiffou was appointed as Prime Minister, charged with running the programme through to parliamentary and presidential elections. The programme also provided for economic measures designed to clean up public finances, relaunch the modern sector of the economy and reduce the budget deficit. One of the first problems the new Prime Minister had to face, however, was a series of attacks in the north from Touareg rebels, an insurgency parallel to that affecting Mali since 1990 (see VI.3.iii).

viii. TOGO

CAPITAL: Lomé AREA: 57,000 sq km POPULATION: 3,500,000 ('89)
OFFICIAL LANGUAGES: French, Kabiye & Ewe
POLITICAL SYSTEM: transitional
HEAD OF STATE: President Gnassingbe Eyadema (since '67)
PRINCIPAL MINISTERS: Joseph Kokou Koffigoh (prime minister, defence), Abdou Touré Tchiaka (foreign affairs & cooperation), Kwami Kouma Alfred Tordjo (justice), Elias Kwassivi Kpetigo (economy & finance), Kokouvi Masseme (interior)
INTERNATIONAL ALIGNMENT: NAM, OAU, ACP, Francophonie
CURRENCY: CFA franc (end-'91 £1=CFAF484.50, US$1=CFAF259.51)
GNP PER CAPITA: US$390 ('89)
MAIN EXPORT EARNERS: phosphates, cocoa

THE democracy movement, under way since the riots of October 1990 (see AR 1990, p. 272), gained in strength in the first few months of 1991. More concessions were extracted from a reluctant President Gnassingbe Eyadema each time there was a further round of strikes and demonstrations. Having already accepted multi-partyism at the beginning of the year, by April, when there was serious loss of life in Lomé (including some gruesome reprisal killings by the armed forces), the President conceded the idea of a national forum. After a general strike in June, this became a full-dress national conference. Although the President later claimed that he had never conceded that the conference should acquire full sovereignty, when it was convened in July this was what happened.

Like the national conferences held in some other African countries (Benin, Togo, Niger), the meeting in Lomé became a major catharsis session, in which long-term opponents of the Eyadema regime listed its serious offences, ranging from corruption to murder. The army, a majority of whom were from President Eyadema's own ethnic group (the minority Kabye from the central-north region), were distressed at much of the proceedings. Presumably with the President's blessing, the army tried to dismiss the conference before it ended, but was thwarted by the intervention of international 'friends' (notably France, Germany and the USA).

Thus Mr Eyadema, although remaining as honorary President, was stripped of nearly all of his powers, which were given to a transitional government headed by Joseph Kokou Koffigoh, who had been one of the leaders of the democracy movement. Leading soldiers remained discontented, however. In early October they made an unsuccessful attempt to kidnap Mr Koffigoh, but were said to have been dissuaded by the President. In November, after the interim Assembly decided to implement a national conference decision proscribing the former ruling Rally of the Togolese People (RPT), soldiers besieged the Prime Minister in his official residence for about ten days, before blasting their way into the building to capture him. Due to French pressure, he was not killed;

rather, he was taken to President Eyadema (whose pretence to be above the struggle had by now worn extremely thin) and forced to accept compromises. These included the unbanning of the RPT and a coalition government including Eyadema supporters, although Mr Koffigoh resisted the dissolution of the interim Assembly. Even so, now that the army had shown its muscle, prospects for a smooth transition to democracy in 1992 looked bleak.

ix. BENIN

CAPITAL: Porto Novo   AREA: 113,000 sq km   POPULATION: 4,600,000 ('89)
OFFICIAL LANGUAGE: French   POLITICAL SYSTEM: presidential democracy
HEAD OF STATE AND GOVERNMENT: President Nicéphore Soglo (since April '91)
PRINCIPAL MINISTERS: Desiré Vieyra (minister of state), Theodore Holo (foreign affairs), Richard Adjaho (interior), Paul Dossou (finance), Yves Yehouessi (justice), Paul Dossou (finance)
INTERNATIONAL ALIGNMENT: NAM, OAU, ACP, Francophonie
CURRENCY: CFA franc (end-'91 £1=CFAF484.50, US$1=CFAF259.51)
GNP PER CAPITA: US$380 ('89)
MAIN EXPORT EARNERS: cotton, palm products

THIS was an important year, in which Benin's new pioneering role as a champion of democracy was crowned with a free presidential election on 24 March, in which the incumbent, Mathieu Kerekou, was voted out of office, to be replaced by Nicéphore Soglo. Mr Soglo had in fact been ruling the country as Prime Minister with virtually full powers since the national conference of February 1990 (see AR 1990, p. 272) while General Kerekou had become virtually ceremonial President, in spite of having ruled the country for 18 years. To have held the election at all, amid rumblings that sections of the army were unhappy and with President Kerekou retaining control of the presidential guard, was an achievement. When Kerekou, with only 32 per cent of the vote against Mr Soglo's 67 per cent, graciously conceded defeat, and gave up power at the beginning of April, it seemed like a minor miracle. It was the first time on the mainland of Africa that an incumbent President had lost an election and given up power (the only precedents so far, both earlier in 1991, being the island states of Cape Verde and São Tomé and Príncipe—see VII.1.iii and iv).

It was true that General Kerekou had been given immunity from prosecution, even though, as the national conference of 1990 had shown, he had quite a lot to answer for. Moreover, Mr Soglo was so ill at the handover ceremony that he had to be flown to Paris for treatment. There were rumours in Cotonou that the new President was the victim of witchcraft, but officially the problem was said to be typhoid fever and sciatica. Three months passed before he was well enough to take over the reins of government properly, during which time the government was in the hands of Desiré Vieyra, Minister of State and Mr Soglo's brother-in-law.

Democracy continued to function, and even to spring surprises, as when an opposition deputy, Adrien Houngbedji, used the unstable multi-party situation created by the elections of February to secure election as president of the National Assembly over President Soglo's preferred choice. Moreover, aid began to pour into Benin, which became the first of the new African democracies to receive a massive debt cancellation. On the other hand, the trade unions and students were looking fairly restive by the end of the year, as the government's austerity measures began to bite.

x. CAMEROON

CAPITAL: Yaoundé   AREA: 475,000 sq km   POPULATION: 11,600,000 ('89)
OFFICIAL LANGUAGES: French & English   POLITICAL SYSTEM: transitional
HEAD OF STATE AND GOVERNMENT: President Paul Biya (since '82)
RULING PARTY: Cameroon People's Democratic Movement (RDPC)
PRINCIPAL MINISTERS: Sadou Hayatou (prime minister), Edouard Akame Mfoumou (defence), Kis Justin Ndioro (finance), Jacques-Roger Booh-Booh (foreign affairs), Douala Montome (justice)
INTERNATIONAL ALIGNMENT: NAM, OAU, ACP, ICO, Francophonie
CURRENCY: CFA franc (end-'91 £1=CFAF484.50, US$1=CFAF259.51)
GNP PER CAPITA: US$1,000 ('89)
MAIN EXPORT EARNERS: oil, cocoa, coffee, aluminium

As in many other African countries, the democracy movement exercised a powerful influence in Cameroon. President Paul Biya was, however, unwilling to accept that his country came into the same category as those which had been ruled by military men. Although Cameroon was a single-party state, he believed that, since he had been democratically elected, he did not need to rush change. Although he had accepted the idea of multi-partyism in 1990 (see AR 1990, p. 273), he was in no hurry to implement it. Nor did he see why a national conference was necessary. In that position, he frequently managed to wrongfoot himself in the face of mounting opposition, and usually found himself making concessions three months too late.

Thus the story of 1991 was of a long series of protest campaigns organized by a vocal and active opposition (which had begun to be recognized in February). This campaign, which took the form of strikes and demonstrations in the major towns, culminated in a six-month operation known as 'ghost towns', where each town shut down for much of the week. This had a devastating effect on the country, both in terms of economic activity and investment confidence, as well as on the collection of government revenue. The high-handed attitude of the security forces and political police kept public indignation and protest at a high level, in spite of the appointment in April of a Prime Minister,

Sadou Hayatou, with a better sense of public relations. However, by November, when it was agreed that multi-party elections would be brought forward, the government had managed to divide the multitude of opposition parties. An important segment of moderates agreed to the holding of the elections without a prior national conference, which had been a major opposition demand.

Friction between the francophone and anglophone communities (the anglophones were in the forefront of political protest) was partly appeased by the establishment of Cameroon's first English-language university in Buea, balanced by a francophone one at Ngaounderé. Yaoundé University retained the status of a national bilingual university, in line with the bilingualism written into the constitution.

xi. CHAD

CAPITAL: N'djaména   AREA: 1,284,000 sq km   POPULATION: 5,500,000 ('89)
OFFICIAL LANGUAGES: French & Arabic   POLITICAL SYSTEM: presidential
HEAD OF STATE AND GOVERNMENT: President (Col.) Idriss Deby (since Dec '90)
PRINCIPAL MINISTERS: Jean Alingue Bawoyeu (prime minister), Ahmad Soungui (foreign affairs), Col. Abbas Koty (defence), Manasse Nguayalbaye (economy & finance), Youssouf Togoimi (justice)
INTERNATIONAL ALIGNMENT: NAM, OAU, ACP, ICO, Francophonie
CURRENCY: CFA franc (end-'91 £1=CFAF484.50, US$1=CFAF259.51)
GNP PER CAPITA: US$190 ('89)
MAIN EXPORT EARNERS: cotton, agricultural products

THE year began with President Idriss Deby, who had seized power in December 1990 (see AR 1990, p. 274), announcing a 30-month transition to civilian multi-party rule. This was in line with his commitment on taking power, and pressures from the French, but the realities on the ground made it look increasingly improbable. He had come into Chad from Sudan with 50,000 warriors, many from his own Zaghawa people, who expected to be retained in the new army, thus creating a serious problem of demobilization. Although the French helped with both funds and training, the Zaghawa remained a problem through the year because of their own lawlessness, which added to the general insecurity prevalent in the country. This was compounded by the threat from troops loyal to former President Hissène Habré. Mr Habré himself was in Dakar (Senegal), and was blamed for having looted the treasury on leaving (as well as having killed 300 political prisoners). But his loyalists were in Niger, and in September they crossed the border and attacked a barracks after first provoking an army mutiny. Soon after Christmas they launched a serious attack from near Lake Chad and threatened the capital. This necessitated the sending of a further 450 French troops, adding to the 1,200 already stationed in Chad.

Colonel Deby's regime was also weakened by internal conflicts. The arrest of Interior Minister Abbas Bada Maldoum in October lost the President the support of the influential Hadjerai ethnic group. Moreover, the main Zaghawa leader, Abbas Koty, also proved difficult, as Colonel Deby was not considered a proper Zaghawa. Understandably, there were delays in setting up a transitional programme, despite much clamour, especially from the students and trade unionists of southern Chad. At the end of the year President Deby was still talking of a 'form' of national conference in May 1992, if the security situation was under control by then.

xii. GABON AND CENTRAL AFRICAN REPUBLIC

Gabon
CAPITAL: Libreville   AREA: 268,000 sq km   POPULATION: 1,100,000 ('89)
OFFICIAL LANGUAGE: French   POLITICAL SYSTEM: presidential
HEAD OF STATE AND GOVERNMENT: President Omar Bongo (since '67)
RULING PARTY: Gabonese Democratic Party (PDG)
CURRENCY: CFA franc (end-'91 £1=CFAF484.50, US$1=CFAF259.51)
GNP PER CAPITA: US$2,960 ('89)
MAIN EXPORT EARNERS: oil and gas, manganese

Central African Republic
CAPITAL: Bangui   AREA: 623,000 sq km   POPULATION: 3,000,000 ('89)
OFFICIAL LANGUAGE: French   POLITICAL SYSTEM: presidential
HEAD OF STATE AND PARTY LEADER: President (Gen.) André Kolingba (since '81)
RULING PARTY: Central African Democratic Assembly (RDC)
CURRENCY: CFA franc (end '91 £1=CFAF484.50, US$1=CFAF259.51)
GNP PER CAPITA: US$390 ('89)
MAIN EXPORT EARNERS: coffee, diamonds, timber

AFTER the upsets of 1990, in which President Bongo survived a national conference and had to call in French troops (see AR 1990, p. 275), this was a quiet year in GABON. The temporary oil price boom arising from the Gulf crisis brought a small windfall, although economic austerity was maintained. The President travelled little, as managing multi-partyism and staying on top was very time-consuming. In June Prime Minister Casimir Oye Mba was dismissed after opposition protests which culminated in a general strike, only to be reappointed as head of a greatly reshuffled new government.

President André Kolingba of the CENTRAL AFRICAN REPUBLIC was another African leader in the position of having reluctantly to make concessions under pressure from an active democracy movement. Having vaguely accepted multi-partyism late in 1990 (see AR 1990, p. 276) in March he appointed a Prime Minister, Edouard Frank, in an attempt to hold the tide. Mr Frank, however, although well respected, was unable to prevent continuing strikes and protests, which continued through the year, in spite of the legalization of political parties. At the end of the year it was still impossible to tell whether President Kolingba had agreed to a national conference, which would be likely to seal his political fate.

xiii. CONGO

CAPITAL: Brazzaville   AREA: 342,000 sq km   POPULATION: 2,200,000 ('89)
OFFICIAL LANGUAGE: French   POLITICAL SYSTEM: transitional
HEAD OF STATE: President (Col.) Denis Sassou-Nguesso (since '79)
PRINCIPAL MINISTERS: André Milongo (prime minister), Édouard Ebouka-Babackas (economy, finance & planning), Alexis Gabou (interior), Jean-Balise Kokolo (foreign affairs), Jena-Martin M'Bemba (justice)
INTERNATIONAL ALIGNMENT: NAM, OAU, ACP, Francophonie
CURRENCY: CFA franc (end-'91 £1=CFAF484.50, US$1=CFAF259.51)
GNP PER CAPITA: US$940 ('89)
MAIN EXPORT EARNERS: oil and gas, timber

As one of Africa's most highly educated and politically conscious countries, the Congo not surprisingly made up for lost ground in 1991, moving to the forefront of the 'new democracy' movement in Africa. It started the year having already legalized political parties and abolished the official credo of marxism-leninism (see AR 1990, p. 276). On 25 February President Denis Sassou-Nguesso opened a national conference which was to prove one of the political marathons of the year—not as long as that in Niger but certainly more turbulent. Watching the televised proceedings became a national pastime, as the conference moved immediately to assume the country's sovereignty. Part of the process was the pillorying of Colonel Sassou-Nguesso and his colleagues, in spite of the President's appeal for 'the end of all sectarianism and petty political intrigues'.

Eventually, in June, the conference president, Mgr Ernest Kombo, proclaimed the meeting closed, after the election of a 153-member Higher Council of the Republic, composed of representatives of political parties and non-governmental associations. Also elected was a Prime Minister—former World Bank official André Milongo, who narrowly defeated Pascal Lissouba, himself a former Prime Minister. The rest of the year saw Mr Milongo wrestling with an intractable economic situation. In spite of the country's oil base, he encountered a surprising lack of enthusiasm in international circles when he travelled in search of aid. It was said that more evidence was needed of the Congo's willingness to undertake restructuring, especially of its top-heavy civil service. Meanwhile, stripped of his powers, President Sassou-Nguesso sulked in his tent, biding his time.

xiv. EQUATORIAL GUINEA

CAPITAL: Malabo AREA: 28,000 sq km POPULATION: 407,000 ('89)
OFFICIAL LANGUAGE: Spanish POLITICAL SYSTEM: military regime
HEAD OF STATE AND GOVERNMENT: Col. Teodoro Obiang Nguema Mbasogo,
    President of Supreme Military Council
RULING PARTY: Democratic Party of Equatorial Guinea (PDGE)
PRINCIPAL MINISTERS: Capt. Cristiano Seriche Bioko (prime minister), Santiago
    Eneme Owono (foreign affairs), Melanio Ebendeng Nsomo (defence), Antonio
    Fernando Nve Ngu (economy & finance), Silvestre Siale Sale Bileka (justice)
INTERNATIONAL ALIGNMENT: NAM, OAU, ACP, Francophonie
CURRENCY: CFA franc (end-'91 £1=CFAF484.50, US$1=CFAF259.51)
GNP PER CAPITA: US$330 ('89)
MAIN EXPORT EARNERS: cocoa, timber, coffee

IN spite of having been massively re-elected in 1990 (see AR 1990, p. 277), when his party was likewise returned to power, President Teodoro Obiang Nguema Mbasogo was obliged in the course of 1991 to concede a transition to multi-partyism which would mean going through the whole business of elections again. An extraordinary congress of the ruling Democratic Party of Equatorial Guinea (PDGE) in August decided on the change to 'multi-partyism in accord with the country's socio-political realities' and approved the drafting of a new law regulating freedom of expression.

The new constitution was massively approved in a referendum on 16 November. The participation rate was 94.26 per cent, of which 98.36 per cent voted in favour. Following this exercise, the Spanish Prime Minister, Felipe González, visited the country, in the context of his work as a mediator between the government and opposition groups in exile in Spain. His visit was expected to lead to a return of exiled opponents of the government.

VII CENTRAL AND SOUTHERN AFRICA

1. ZAÏRE—BURUNDI AND RWANDA—GUINEA-BISSAU AND
CAPE VERDE—SÃO TOMÉ & PRÍNCIPE—MOZAMBIQUE—ANGOLA

i. ZAÏRE

CAPITAL: Kinshasa   AREA: 2,345,000 sq km   POPULATION: 34,500,000 ('89)
OFFICIAL LANGUAGE: French   POLITICAL SYSTEM: presidential
HEAD OF STATE AND GOVERNMENT: President (Marshal) Mobutu Sese Seko (since '65)
RULING PARTY: Popular Movement of the Revolution (MPR)
PRINCIPAL MINISTERS: Nguza Karl I Bond (prime minister), Mandungu Bula-Nyati (interior), N'gbanda Nzambo Ko Atumba (defence), Babeni Adehito Nzenegya (external relations), Moamba Mulunda (finance), Mokuba (justice)
INTERNATIONAL ALIGNMENT: NAM, OAU, ACP, Francophonie
CURRENCY: zaïre (end-'91 £1=Z117,295.00, US$1=Z62,825.40)
GNP PER CAPITA: US$260 ('89)
MAIN EXPORT EARNERS: copper, other minerals, oil

THE flood waters of political discontent continued to rise, but they were not yet strong enough to sweep away a President who had ruled the country autocratically for 26 years. Indeed, in the most politically confusing year of Zaïre's recent history, there was one clear constant: the determination of President Mobutu Sese Seko to hold on to power at whatever cost. In this the President succeeded, revealing yet again his remarkable political adroitness, his skill in manipulation and propaganda, refined by years of experience. But at the year's end his position looked less assured than it had ever been and it was widely assumed that his days of power must now be numbered.

In 1990 the President had attempted to control the tides of change by announcing an end to one-party rule (see AR 1990, p. 278), although in the new dispensation only three parties, one of them his own Popular Movement of the Revolution (MPR), were to be allowed. This restriction proved impossible to enforce. Registration of parties started in January; by the middle of the year at least 159 parties could be identified. They could be divided into three main groups: the Consensus Group, embracing 110 parties prepared to collaborate with the President; the Cartel Group, of 40 parties whose position varied according to the issues at stake; and the Rejectionists. Though numbering only nine parties, the Rejectionists opposed any form of collaboration with the President and enjoyed by far the widest and most vociferous support. The most important Rejectionist parties were the Union for Democracy and Social Progress (UDPS) under the leadership of Étienne Tshisekedi, the Union of Federalists and Independent Republicans (UFERI) founded by Nguza Karl I Bond, Joseph Ileo's Christian Social and Democrat Party

(PDSC) and the veteran Antoine Gizenga's Unified Lumumbist Party (PALU).

Zaïrean politicians of this new generation were profoundly influenced, as their predecessors had been in the late 1950s, by developments taking place elsewhere in Francophone Africa, where many countries had embarked on 'national conferences' as a means of bringing about effective reform. Particularly inspiring was the national conference held in Brazzaville, the capital of Congo (see VI.3.xii), whose proceedings were transmitted live in Kinshasa on radio and TV. Reluctantly, President Mobutu accepted that a national conference should be held in Zaïre, but set about ensuring that it was packed with his own nominees. Originally scheduled to begin in April, the conference never really got under way, to the exasperation of the opposition, which had planned to make it into a sovereign body with sufficient powers to control the President. Exasperation was not confined to the Rejectionists. In July 130 parties agreed to come together to form what was designated the Sacred Union to put pressure on the President.

This uncertain situation was rendered all the more confusing at the end of September when soldiers in Kinshasa started rioting and looting shops, businesses and private houses in the richer suburbs. Their example was followed over the next few days by soldiers in other towns, the disturbances resulting in a reported death toll of over 100 people. There were no reports of attacks on Europeans, but the French and Belgian governments sent in military detachments to protect and help evacuate their nationals, 20,000 of whom left the country. The riots constituted a major disaster for the country's already shaky economy. The correspondent of *The Times* (1 November) wrote: 'Every key city in the country has been wrecked utterly and commercial activity brought to a standstill.'

The soldiers had taken to the streets, it was said, because the government was no longer able to pay them. Three weeks after the riots the President announced that all civil servants and military personnel were to receive 1,000 per cent pay increases (orders being placed with a firm in Munich to print the notes required). Thus inflation was made still more onerous for ordinary Zaïreans. In Kinshasa it was widely believed that the government itself had set the riots in motion as a device for distracting attention from the political crisis. On 30 September the President succeeded in persuading the most prominent of his opponents, Mr Tshisekedi, to become Prime Minister, a post which he had turned down two months earlier. This time, however, the President's familiar tactic of coopting a dangerous opponent did not work. There was a bitter argument, apparently over the President's determination to reserve the defence portfolio for his own nominee. On 21 October Mr Tshisekedi was dismissed and replaced by Mungul Diaka, a politician who had spent some time in exile (see AR 1980, p. 245).

The opposition reacted by announcing that it was setting up a 'parallel government' under Mr Tshisekedi, for which foreign support was sought. In November all the opposition newspapers were forced to close down after bomb attacks or threats against their premises. Meanwhile, the President publicly stated that elections should be held within the next few months, while the Diaka government reconvened the national conference, although to little effect. At the end of November cracks appeared in the opposition front when Nguza Karl I Bond agreed to act as interim Prime Minister under President Mobutu, who demoted Mr Diaka to the rank of minister of state. The Sacred Union responded by expelling UFERI from its ranks and roundly condemning Mr Nguza, who nevertheless attracted several opposition factions into his new government. The key portfolios continued to be held by Mobutu supporters.

In their despair some Zaïreans looked to the outside world—especially to the United States, France and Belgium—to rescue them from impending disaster. There had been a sharp deterioration in the relations between President Mobutu and his main Western supporters in 1990 (see AR 1990, p. 279), resulting in the cutting off of most aid. Displeasure turned to exasperation as it became clear that the President was resorting to every trick at his disposal to retain power. There were heated arguments in Washington, Paris and Brussels between those who believed that the time had come to cease supporting the Mobutu regime and those who warned that the President's removal would lead to even greater confusion. However, the general view of Western governments was that little could be gained by becoming more deeply involved in a country whose strategic significance had faded with the ending of the Cold War. As for the Organization of African Unity, it lacked the resources to mount any effective form of intervention.

ii. BURUNDI AND RWANDA

Burundi
CAPITAL: Bujumbura   AREA: 28,000 sq km   POPULATION: 5,300,000 ('89)
OFFICIAL LANGUAGES: French & Kirundi   POLITICAL SYSTEM: military regime
HEAD OF STATE AND GOVERNMENT: Maj. Pierre Buyoya, Chairman of Military
    Council for National Salvation (since Sept '87)
CURRENCY: Burundi franc (end-'91 £1=FBu352.25, US$1=FBu188.67)
GNP PER CAPITA: US$220 ('89)
MAIN EXPORT EARNERS: coffee, tea

Rwanda

CAPITAL: Kigali   AREA: 26,300 sq km   POPULATION: 6,900,000 ('89)
OFFICIAL LANGUAGES: French & Kinyarwanda   POLITICAL SYSTEM: presidential
HEAD OF STATE AND GOVERNMENT: President (Maj.-Gen.) Juvénal Habyarimana (since '73)
PRINCIPAL MINISTERS: Sylvestre Nsazimana (prime minister, justice), Casimir Bizimungu (foreign affairs), Benoft Ntiguirwa (finance)
CURRENCY: Rwanda franc (end-'91 £1=RF221.19, US$1=RF118.47)
GNP PER CAPITA: US$320 ('89)
MAIN EXPORT EARNERS: coffee, tea, tin

PRESIDENT Pierre Buyoya of BURUNDI responded to the winds of change by announcing in November that a referendum for a new constitution would be held early in 1992. In the same month there were reports of fighting in the vicinity of the capital, Bujumbura, between security forces and guerrillas of the Tanzanian-based Party for the Liberation of the Hutu People (Palipehutu).

Following the late-1990 invasion of northern RWANDA by a military force made up largely of Tutsi refugees long resident in Uganda and organized as the Rwandan Patriotic Front (FRP), serious fighting was reported in January and February, followed by a ceasefire in March. There were further reports of fighting in June and again in November. The Organization of African Unity attempted to lessen the tension by sending military observers to monitor a ceasefire and by arranging summit meetings to bring together President Habyarimana and the heads of state or senior representatives of Rwanda's neighbours. At a meeting in Dar es Salaam in February, President Habyarimana accepted the right of Rwandan refugees, reckoned to number 500,000 in Uganda and 270,000 in Burundi, to return to their homeland.

The President also showed himself willing to accept constitutional changes that would allow the introduction of a multi-party system. But many Hutu, alarmed by the Tutsi invasion, were less conciliatory. Some 4,000 people, suspected of complicity with the invaders, were detained in the aftermath of the invasion. In February, at a trial in Kigali where defence lawyers were intimidated by threatening crowds, seven suspects were condemned to death. Certain Hutu publications began producing virulently anti-Tutsi propaganda. In such an atmosphere, liberal reforms were clearly going to be very difficult to implement. Moreover, the task of absorbing large numbers of Tutsi refugees, in a country where rapid population growth was putting heavy pressure on natural resources (see AR 1990, p. 281), presented colossal difficulties.

iii. GUINEA-BISSAU AND CAPE VERDE

Guinea-Bissau
CAPITAL: Bissau   AREA: 3,600 sq km   POPULATION: 960,000 ('89)
OFFICIAL LANGUAGE: Portuguese   POLITICAL SYSTEM: presidential
HEAD OF STATE AND GOVERNMENT: President (Brig.-Gen.) João Vieira (since '80)
RULING PARTY: African Party for the Independence of Guinea and Cape Verde (PAIGC)
CURRENCY: peso (end-'91 £1=PG9,367.50, US$1=PG5,017.41)
GNP PER CAPITA: US$180 ('89)
MAIN EXPORT EARNERS: groundnuts, agricultural products

Cape Verde
CAPITAL: Praia   AREA: 4,000 sq km   POPULATION: 361,000 ('89)
OFFICIAL LANGUAGE: Portuguese   POLITICAL SYSTEM: emerging democracy
HEAD OF STATE: President Antonio Mascarenhas Monteiro (since March '91)
RULING PARTY: Movement for Democracy (MPD)
HEAD OF GOVERNMENT: Carlos Veiga, Prime Minister (since Jan '91)
CURRENCY: Cape Verde escudo (end-'91 £1=CVEsc137.32, US$1=CVEsc73.55)
GNP PER CAPITA: US$780 ('89)
MAIN EXPORT EARNERS: cashew nuts, fish

IN May GUINEA-BISSAU took a first step towards multi-party democracy when the National Assembly deleted from the constitution clauses guaranteeing a one-party state. But it was not until November that the Supreme Court legalized the first opposition party, the Democratic Front. This was led by a dissident economist, Aristides Menezes, who called for a free-market economy. Opposition to the government was reported to be strongest among the Balante, the country's largest ethnic group.

CAPE VERDE became the first ex-Portuguese territory in Africa to hold free elections. In polling for the National Assembly held on 13 January, the newly-formed Movement for Democracy (MPD) won a decisive victory over the ruling African Party for the Independence of Cape Verde (PAICV), winning 56 of the 79 seats. A similar result was produced by the presidential election four weeks later. Aristides Pereira, President since 1975 and regarded as the founder of the nation, was beaten by the MPD's candidate, Supreme Court judge Antonio Mascarenhas Monteiro, who won 75 per cent of the votes.

The two results were interpreted as evidence that the 'veterans of the independence struggle' had lost their appeal to an impatient younger generation. The new Prime Minister, Carlos Veiga, a 41-year-old lawyer, was described as 'aggressively pro-capitalist', advocating an economic policy that would attract investment in tourism and the fishing industry. One of the first acts of the new government was to abolish the political police and order a commission of inquiry into the misuse of state funds. In foreign policy there was talk of supporting Unita in Angola and the MNR in Mozambique.

iv. SÃO TOMÉ & PRÍNCIPE

CAPITAL: São Tomé   AREA: 965 sq km   POPULATION: 120,000 ('89)
OFFICIAL LANGUAGE: Portuguese   POLITICAL SYSTEM: emerging democracy
HEAD OF STATE: President Miguel Trovoada (since March '91)
RULING PARTY: Democratic Convergence Party (PCD)
PRINCIPAL MINISTERS: Daniel Lima dos Santos (prime minister), Albertino Braganca (defence), Norberto Costa Alegre (economy & finance), Alda Bandeira (foreign affairs)
INTERNATIONAL ALIGNMENT: NAM, OAU, ACP
CURRENCY: dobra (end-'91 £1=Db449.64, US$1=Db240.84)
GNP PER CAPITA: US$340 ('89)
MAIN EXPORT EARNERS: cocoa, copra

THE process of political change begun in August 1990, when a referendum showed that 72 per cent of the electorate were in favour of multi-party democracy (see AR 1990, p. 283), was carried a stage further in January when elections for the National Assembly gave the newly formed Democratic Convergence Party (PCD) 30 seats out of 55. Most of the remainder went to the Movement for the Liberation of São Tomé and Príncipe (MLSTP), which had ruled the islands as a one-party state since 1975. In the presidential elections held in March, President Manuel Pinto da Costa decided not to stand, thus allowing an easy victory to Miguel Trovoada, who stood as an independent but with the backing of the PCD. Mr Trovoada had been Prime Minister from 1975 to 1979, when he had quarrelled with President Pinto da Costa and had been dismissed and detained (see AR 1980, p. 248). From 1981 to 1990 he had lived in exile in Paris.

v. MOZAMBIQUE

CAPITAL: Maputo   AREA: 800,000 sq km   POPULATION: 15,900,000 ('90)
OFFICIAL LANGUAGE: Portuguese   POLITICAL SYSTEM: presidential
HEAD OF STATE AND GOVERNMENT: President Joaquim Chissano (since '86)
RULING PARTY: Front for the Liberation of Mozambique (Frelimo)
PRINCIPAL MINISTERS: Mario de Graça Machungo (prime minister, planning), Lt-Gen. Alberto Joaquim Chipande (defence), Pascoal Mocumbi (foreign affairs), Edmundo Carlos Alberto (interior), Eneias da Conceiçao (finance), Ossmane Ali Dauto (justice)
INTERNATIONAL ALIGNMENT: NAM, OAU, ACP
CURRENCY: metical (end-'91 £1=Mt3,211.05, US$1=Mt1,719.90)
GNP PER CAPITA: US$80 ('89)
MAIN EXPORT EARNERS: sea food, cashew nuts

THERE was no perceptible abatement of the civil war that had ravaged Mozambique since the late 1970s, despite the fact that in July 1990 representatives of the Frelimo government and of the rebel National Resistance Movement (MNR or Renamo) had met face to face for the first time in Rome to commence negotiations (see AR 1990, p. 284). The same pattern was maintained throughout 1991: negotiations in Rome, fighting in Mozambique. A statement made by rebel leader Afonso

Dhlakama in October attempted to rationalize this situation: 'It is usual in Africa to negotiate while fighting because the government is never a voluntary party to negotiations. We cannot abandon the armed struggle.'

Already in 1990 the Frelimo government had met the MNR's initial demands by renouncing marxism-leninism and introducing constitutional changes that envisaged the eventual holding of elections on a multi-party basis. However, the rebels clearly considered that they had more to gain by continuing the war, in which they were reckoned to have control of one-third of the country and to operate with little restraint in another third. Assured of the support of a wide range of private backers in South Africa, the United States, Portugal, Kenya and other countries, they could shrug aside much of the opprobrium with which their movement, guilty of countless well-authenticated atrocities, was regarded by the international community.

In December 1990 the two sides agreed on a 'mini-ceasefire' along the two lines of rail connecting Zimbabwe with Beira and Maputo. A joint verification commission, made up of representatives of Frelimo and the MNR together with members from eight other countries (including Britain), was set up to monitor the ceasefire but could not prevent some infractions. The negotiations in Rome were subject to repeated interruptions and breakdowns, but in November agreement was reached on two protocols. Under protocol 1 the MNR agreed that once a full ceasefire had been signed it would accept laws made by the government in Maputo, in return for an undertaking by Frelimo not to hinder the MNR's international publicity campaign. Protocol 2 guaranteed to the MNR, after a ceasefire, full recognition as a political party and equal access to the media. In return, the MNR would agree to accept the government's right to register political parties.

Within days of these protocols being agreed, the MNR appeared deliberately to have increased its military pressure on the government, by launching a series of attacks on suburban areas of both Maputo and Beira. In the Maputo area many similar attacks had taken place during the year, and the city's electricity supply had frequently been disrupted. The situation of the country as a whole was summarized by a correspondent of the *Financial Times* (in September) as follows: 'Mozambique is still a patchwork of no-go areas frequented by the MNR and outposts of government control, mostly provincial capitals or district resettlement centres where rural dwellers are herded together to wait for food aid.'

The progress of military operations in Zambezia, the country's most populous province, with the richest agricultural potential, aroused the greatest interest. In the first half of the year the Naparama popular movement led by Manuel Antonio (see AR 1990, p. 285) extended its activities from Nampula province into northern Zambezia, freeing areas from MNR control. The Namaprama militia was armed only with spears, its members' morale strengthened by their conviction that the 'vaccination' carried out on each man by Mr Antonio provided invulnerability against bullets. This belief was painfully challenged when the MNR sent some of its best-equipped guerrillas into the area and won a resounding victory in September by capturing Lalaua, an important town in northern Nampula. But even as the morale of the Naparama was declining, a new more puritanical group known as Mukuepa emerged, attracting supporters by promising that peace would return if the people accepted complicated taboos and magic vaccination. Frelimo's attitude towards these grassroots movements was ambivalent; useful allies in the present, they could become a threat to the government's authority in the future. At the same time, Frelimo's rural policy was clearly changing, with officials trying to win the support of traditional chiefs whom the party had for long denounced for their collaboration with the Portuguese colonialists.

Some 7,000 Zimbabwean troops remained in Mozambique, but under the terms of the December 1990 ceasefire agreement they were restricted to guarding the two rail corridors. The MNR took advantage of the new situation to step up its activities in Tete province, knowing that it would no longer have to face counter-insurgency operations mounted by the Zimbabweans. To maintain the size of their respective armed forces, both sides resorted to drastic methods, with the Frelimo government press-ganging recruits and the MNR kidnapping often very young boys. In some areas it was hard to distinguish the operations of the rival armed forces from pure banditry.

Following the drastic cutback in assistance from the former Eastern bloc countries, Mozambique could be seen as totally dependent on aid from the West. In 1991 donors pledged $1,200 million, it being reckoned that similar sums would be required throughout the 1990s. In its first years in power in the late 1970s, the Frelimo government had laid great stress on self-reliance; by the 1990s it found itself probably the most dependent government in the world on the charity of others. Moreover, such economic statistics as were available provided no evidence of any substantial improvements. Faced with deteriorating conditions and the unabated misery of so many of the people, it was hardly surprising that some aid workers should give way to expressions of despair.

The Frelimo government's manifold difficulties were given a further twist in June with the discovery of a coup attempt, the first in the country's history. The plotters, arrested before a shot was fired, included the Minister of the Interior, two very senior retired army officers and two brothers of the late President Samora Machel. No statement as to their motives was available, but it was assumed that they opposed the government's abandonment of marxism-leninism and its willingness to negotiate with those so long denounced as 'bandits' and 'traitors'.

Little was heard during the year of the new parties which emerged at the end of 1990: the Liberal and Democratic Party of Mozambique (PALMO), whose programme strongly criticized the dominant role of whites, Asians and people of mixed race in the economy, and the National Mozambique Union (Unamo), which was supported by MNR dissidents. There was also talk of the founding of a Christian Democratic Party, which would enjoy the support of the powerful Roman Catholic Church. The significance of these political tendencies could be assessed only when it became possible to hold genuinely free elections—at year's end still a remote prospect.

vi. ANGOLA

CAPITAL: Luanda   AREA: 1,247,000 sq km   POPULATION: 9,700,000 ('89)
OFFICIAL LANGUAGE: Portuguese   POLITICAL SYSTEM: emerging democracy
HEAD OF STATE AND GOVERNMENT: President José Eduardo dos Santos (since '79)
RULING PARTY: Popular Movement for the Liberation of Angola—Workers' Party (MPLA-PT)
PRINCIPAL MINISTERS: Fernando José França Van-Dúnem (prime minister), Col.-Gen. Pedro Maria Tonha 'Pedale' (defence), Lt.-Col. Pedro de Castro Van-Dúnem 'Loy' (external relations), Lazaro Manuel Dias (justice), Aguinaldo Jaime (finance)
INTERNATIONAL ALIGNMENT: NAM, OAU, ACP
CURRENCY: kwanza (end-'91 £1=Kw164.92, US$1=Kw88.33)
GNP PER CAPITA: US$610 ('89)
MAIN EXPORT EARNERS: oil, coffee, diamonds

ON 31 May Angola's 16-year-long civil war was brought formally to an end when the President José Eduardo dos Santos, head of the MPLA government, and Dr Jonas Savimbi, leader of Unita, signed what became known as the Estoril Accord, an elaborate document running to over 60 pages. The solemnity of the occasion was emphasized by the presence at the ceremony of the US Secretary of State, the Soviet Foreign Minister, the UN Secretary-General and the current chairman of the Organization of African Unity, President Museveni of Uganda. That the ceremony and the final negotiations should have taken place in Lisbon was testimony to the important role of the Portuguese government in acting as a mediator between the two sides. Even more important in bringing about the final agreement was the decision of the United States and the Soviet Union to put pressure on Unita and the MPLA respectively in order to ensure an ending of the war. No Cuban or South African representative was present at the final ceremony. The Cubans withdrew their last troops from Angola in the last week of May, a month ahead of schedule. Dr Savimbi expressed his gratitude to South Africa by visiting Pretoria immediately after the ceremony.

The Estoril Accord confirmed the ceasefire that had come into operation on 15 May. A joint political and military commission, made up of representatives of the two sides together with US, Soviet and

Portuguese officers, was established to monitor the ceasefire. It was agreed that the military forces of the two sides, thought to number more than 200,000 men, should be reduced and merged to form a national army of 50,000, a process to be assisted by a military mission with Portuguese, French and British members. Finally, the two sides agreed to the holding of a general election between September and November 1992, although details of the legal framework were left to the members of the political and military commission to work out. In June the UN Security Council approved the maintenance in Angola of a UN Verification Force, 400-strong, to supervise the peace accord.

On 26 March Angola ceased to be a one-party state when the National Assembly passed legislation making provision for a multi-party system. Within weeks, more than 20 political groups had emerged in Luanda. But the regulations laying down conditions that parties had to meet before they could be registered and allowed to compete in an election were very stringent: each party had to produce evidence of 3,000 supporters spread out over at least 14 of the country's 18 provinces. It therefore seemed unlikely that any other party would be in a position to field candidates to oppose the MPLA and Unita.

There was, however, ample evidence of discontent—at least in the capital Luanda, the only part of the country where opinion could be gauged on the style and performance of Unita and the MPLA. As regards Unita, the personality cult surrounding Dr Savimbi was described by one observer who attended the party's seventh congress (held at Jamba in March) as 'among the most grotesque in the entire African continent'. Dr Savimbi was re-elected party leader by 3,069 votes out of a possible 3,080. In Unita-controlled territory, criticism of the leadership was ruthlessly discouraged. In contrast, far greater freedom of expression was possible in areas controlled by the MPLA. But the party that had ruled Angola since 1975 had to its discredit an appalling record of failure in its economic and social policies. In part, such a failure could be ascribed to the war, but blame also had to be put on the government's rigid adherence to an inflexible system of centralized control inspired by marxism-leninism.

The MPLA was clearly divided between hardliners and reformers, with the former still controlling important sections of the country's massive bureaucracy. 'Economic reform is being held back', one diplomat exclaimed frankly, 'by an ungodly alliance of ideologues and crooks hiding behind ideologues who have vested interests in the black market and the controlled economy. Many MPLA people are grabbing as much as they can before tomorrow comes because they know that tomorrow will not belong to them.'

In September President dos Santos visited Washington to learn from President Bush that the US government would establish formal diplomatic relations with Luanda only when Angola had a government given legitimacy by free elections. From Washington President dos Santos went to London to plead for foreign investment and an alleviation of the country's debt burden, currently standing at $7,000 million. Meanwhile, his rival, Dr Savimbi, had paid his first visit to Luanda since the end of the war, it being announced later that Unita would open an office in the capital.

During the year the enclave of Cabinda, which produced 60 per cent of Angola's oil output, was the scene of developments with serious implications for any future Angolan government. For many years the Front for the Liberation of the Enclave of Cabinda (FLEC) had engaged in spasmodic guerrilla operations, its aim being to secure a measure of self-determination for the people of Cabinda and a fairer share of its oil wealth. Its most effective tactic was the kidnapping of foreign oil workers, thus deterring further foreign investment in the enclave's oil industry. Observers reckoned that FLEC, in spite of being weakened by internal divisions, enjoyed the support of 90 per cent of Cabinda's population; but the movement was not represented in the negotiations leading up to the Estoril Accord. A strike by workers at an oil production centre in July was accompanied by political demands supported by FLEC, which made it clear that the new MPLA-Unita alliance had little relevance to the problems of Cabinda.

Nevertheless, no serious breaches of the general ceasefire were reported in the seven months after the signing of the peace agreement. Members of the MPLA and Unita forces moved to specially-designated marshalling areas, from which most of them would be demobilized, and engineers began removing mines from the main roads. Thus the year ended on a reasonably optimistic note.

2. ZAMBIA—MALAWI—ZIMBABWE—NAMIBIA—BOTSWANA—
LESOTHO—SWAZILAND

i. ZAMBIA

CAPITAL: Lusaka   AREA: 750,000 sq km   POPULATION: 7,800,000 ('89)
OFFICIAL LANGUAGE: English   POLITICAL SYSTEM: emerging democracy
HEAD OF STATE AND GOVERNMENT: President Frederick Chiluba (since Nov '91)
RULING PARTY: Movement for Multi-Party Democracy (MMD)
PRINCIPAL MINISTERS: Levy Mwanawasa (vice-president), Benjamin Y. Mwila (defence), Vernon J. Mwaanga (foreign affairs), Emmanuel G. Kasonde (finance), Newstead L. Zimba (home affairs), Roger Chongwe (legal affairs)
INTERNATIONAL ALIGNMENT: NAM, OAU, ACP, Cwth.
CURRENCY: kwacha (end-'91 £1=K162.99, US$1=K87.30)
GNP PER CAPITA: US$390 ('89)
MAIN EXPORT EARNERS: copper, zinc, cobalt

IN one of the very few genuinely free elections to be held in post-colonial Africa, President Kenneth Kaunda and the United National Independence Party (UNIP) were defeated on 31 October by the newly formed Movement for Multi-Party Democracy (MMD). In the presidential election, Frederick Chiluba of the MMD won 75 per cent of the votes. In the election for the National Assembly, the MMD won 125 of the 150 seats. Only in Eastern province did UNIP achieve any success, winning all 19 of the seats. Zambia had been ruled as a one-party state from 1972 to 1990, President Kaunda himself having been in power since the country achieved independence in 1964. The October 1991 elections were thus a real turning-point in the country's history.

The MMD, founded in 1990 (see AR 1990, p. 289), held its first national convention in February. Mr Chiluba, chairman-general of the Zambian Congress of Trades Unionists, was elected as the party's president, decisively defeating his closest rival, the veteran politician Arthur Wina. The election for the 38 posts on the MMD national executive committee was described by observers as the fairest election of its kind so far held in Zambia. The committee, as finally elected, represented a broad cross-section of the community. It contained representatives of all ethnic groups, including three Europeans and an Asian, as well as a wide range of occupations (academics, businessmen, other professionals and farmers) and some politicians who had grown disillusioned with UNIP.

The election was monitored by no less than 2,000 observers. Some came from the Commonwealth, the Organization of African Unity and the Carter Foundation (an organization founded by ex-President Jimmy Carter of the USA), others from the Zambian election monitoring coordinating committee representing local churches, law associations and women's groups. During the election campaign some unfair practices were noted, such as UNIP candidates using public funds to pay for advertising. On polling day, however, no incidents of violence were reported and relatively few of intimidation (in some rural areas headmen threatened to expel villagers who voted for the MMD). President Kaunda made no attempt to dispute the result, conceding defeat after a third of the results had been announced. Mr Chiluba was sworn in as President on 2 November.

'We want change, we want change' had been the cry of the crowds at election meetings. Soaring inflation and high unemployment affected the lives of most families in urban areas. The MMD pledged itself to reduce spending on the security services, to privatize loss-making parastatal organizations and to find ways of diversifying the economy away from its dependence on copper (supplies of which were fast diminishing, even though copper still brought in 90 per cent of foreign-exchange earnings). But with free-marketeers, social democrats and old-style marxists all present in its ranks, the MMD had no precisely-defined ideology to present to the electorate.

In the last weeks of President Kaunda's rule, two major economic problems reappeared in an acute form. The first related to the people's staple food, namely maize. With state marketing boards paying ludicrously low prices, many farmers had either ceased growing maize or smuggled their produce across the frontiers to Zaïre and Malawi, where prices were three times as high. For the urban population the price of maize was kept artificially low by subsidies reckoned to cost the government $500,000 a day. With an election pending and fearing food riots, President Kaunda refused to raise prices, a policy which contributed to the second problem. The government's insistence on maintaining maize subsidies exasperated the country's aid donors. After Zambia had defaulted on a $10 million repayment, the World Bank and the IMF retaliated by suspending negotiations which could have provided Zambia with a desperately-needed $200 million.

ii. MALAWI

CAPITAL: Lilongwe   AREA: 118,500 sq km   POPULATION: 8,200,000 ('89)
OFFICIAL LANGUAGE: English   POLITICAL SYSTEM: presidential, one-party state
HEAD OF STATE AND GOVERNMENT: President Hastings Kamuzu Banda (since '66)
RULING PARTY: Malawi Congress Party (MCP)
PRINCIPAL MINISTERS: Maxwell Pashane (without portfolio), Louis Chimango (finance), Robson W. Chirwa (trade & industry)
INTERNATIONAL ALIGNMENT: NAM, OAU, ACP, Cwth.
CURRENCY: kwacha (end-'91 £1=MK4.90, US$1=MK2.62)
GNP PER CAPITA: US$180 ('89)
MAIN EXPORT EARNERS: tobacco, tea, sugar

APPARENTLY insulated from the winds of change blowing through so many other countries in Africa, Malawi continued to be totally dominated by a President generally thought to be in his nineties and by his closest associates. 'The Malawi system', in the words of Life President Dr Hastings Kamuzu Banda, 'is that Kamuzu says it's that and then it's finished'. However, a foreign correspondent expelled in 1990 described Malawi as 'a land of zombies where no one speaks because no-one dares to speak'. In June the British press provided an example of Malawian methods. *The Observer*, after publishing a critical article on the country by Julie Flint, a highly esteemed foreign correspondent, came out two issues later with a contrite apology to the Life President. It was noted that Lonrho, the company directed by Tiny Rowland, proprietor of *The Observer*, had substantial business interests in Malawi.

Against this gloomy picture had to be set the fact that, in contrast with its neighbours (not only war-torn Mozambique but also Zambia and Tanzania), Malawi remained a country of stability and order. Moreover, the willingness of the government and people to welcome and make available land for one million refugees from Mozambique provided an impressive example to the rest of the world.

A number of political detainees released during the year included the country's leading poet, Jack Mapanje, who had been detained since 1987 (see AR 1987, p. 275). The releases were in all probability the result of pressure from the European Community on the issue of human rights.

iii. ZIMBABWE

CAPITAL: Harare   AREA: 390,000 sq km   POPULATION: 9,500,000 ('89)
OFFICIAL LANGUAGE: English   POLITICAL SYSTEM: presidential
HEAD OF STATE AND GOVERNMENT: President Robert Mugabe (since Dec '87, previously Prime Minister)
RULING PARTY: Zimbabwe African National Union–Patriotic Front (ZANU-PF)
PRINCIPAL MINISTERS: Simon Muzenda (vice-president), Joshua Nkomo (vice-president), Didymus Mutasa (senior minister, political affairs), Bernard Chidzero (senior minister, finance, planning & development), Nathan Shamuyarira (foreign affairs), Emmerson Munangagwa (justice), Richard Hove (defence), Moven Mahachi (home affairs)
INTERNATIONAL ALIGNMENT: NAM, OAU, ACP, Cwth.
CURRENCY: Zimbabwe dollar (end-'91 £1=Z$9.41, US$1=Z$5.04)
GNP PER CAPITA: US$650 ('89)
MAIN EXPORT EARNERS: tobacco, gold, tin

ZIMBABWE was host in October to the 28th Commonwealth heads of government meeting in Harare (see XI.2) and to a state visit by Queen Elizabeth II, her first visit to the country since 1953. President Robert Mugabe was chairman of the Commonwealth meeting, responsible for its agenda and a party to its resolutions. The assembled leaders' forceful recommendations on human rights and freedom of expression appeared to have a salutary impact on the host nation, where tolerance of dissentient views in the press and broadcasting media was more evident than in the previous 11 years of the country's independent existence.

In terms of the economy, the priority of Mr Mugabe's ZANU-PF government was to tackle the problems identified late in 1990 (see AR 1990, p. 294) as standing in the way of Zimbabwe's prosperity. In January the government launched its five-year Economic Structural Adjustment Programme (ESAP), which sought to stimulate the country's increasingly stagnant and uncompetitive economy towards an annual growth rate of 5 per cent. Measures adopted included a major deregulation of the economy, the relaxation of controls on imports and foreign exchange, the institution of export incentives and the encouragement of foreign investment. At a meeting in Paris in March, donor agencies such as the World Bank and the IMF pledged US$700 million (contingent, interestingly, on a positive assessment of the country's human rights record) towards the ESAP initiative, the balance of the projected $16,000 million reform programme coming from cost-cutting and increased efficiency within Zimbabwe itself. The 1991/92 budget, published on 25 July, forecast a reduced deficit of 7.6 per cent of GDP, representing an improvement on the previous year's figure of 10.3 per cent and on course for a target of 5 per cent by 1994/95.

The immediate impact of ESAP was painful. The broadening of the open import licence list led to a surge in imports, while exports remained depressed by the international economic downturn. The removal of retail price controls, along with a 50 per cent increase in the cost of fuel after the Gulf War, pushed inflation close to 30 per cent. To control the money supply and check the trading imbalance, the government raised interest rates and, in the three months to September, engineered a 40 per cent depreciation in the value of the Zimbabwean dollar. Rising commodity prices and shortages of bread, sugar, maize and cooking-oil hit the poorly-paid and the unemployed in particular. The President maintained that the spirit which had brought about Zimbabwe's independence 'must now be demonstrated in attaining the goals of our economic struggle'.

Signs of the government's resulting unpopularity were manifest in low attendance at ZANU-PF rallies, continued unrest at the University of Zimbabwe and increasingly widespread press criticism. Particular targets were the government's slowness in implementing reductions in the size of the civil service and executive (see AR 1990, p. 294), its failure to make progress in the provision of low-cost housing and its plans for the introduction of school fees. The ZANU-PF administration remained in a strong position, however, thanks to a sizeable and loyal army, to division and disorganization within the opposition ZUM party (led by Edgar Tekere) and to the likelihood that, in the four years remaining before new parliamentary and presidential elections, clear benefits of the economic reform strategy would be evident.

The manufacturing sector suffered most from the 'frictional negative consequences' of ESAP, hit by the rising cost of raw materials, transport delays and a flood of competing imports. Agriculture remained the backbone of Zimbabwe's prosperity, employing 70 per cent of the total labour force and contributing 11 per cent of GDP. The 1990/91 rains, disappointing though not disastrous, led to a fall in the yield of the principal food crops and to the need, unprecedented in the country's history, to import maize, hitherto a valuable source of export revenue. Cash crop production on communal farms was worst affected. By contrast, tobacco farmers produced a record crop of 155,000 tonnes, which fetched high prices on the world markets. An outbreak of foot-and-mouth disease led to a repeat of the 1989 ban on beef and dairy exports to the European Community. In his fourth State of the Nation speech, on 13 December, President Mugabe outlined the government's intention, as part of the national development plan, to bolster the agricultural sector against natural disasters. Provision for improved water resources and irrigation projects in the communal and resettlement areas, together with the decentralization of veterinary and animal management activities, marked a step towards self-sufficiency and food security in rural areas.

In pursuance of plans announced earlier for the redistribution and resettlement of rural land (see AR 1990, p. 293), the government acquired approximately 35,000 hectares during 1991, sufficient for 2,000 families, and at a cost of Z$8 million. In response to the shortage of available land, and its spiralling cost, particularly in white-owned agricultural areas, a draft Land Acquisition Bill empowering the expropriation of privately-held land was announced in December. It was accompanied by a proposed Land Tax Bill which sought, as the President somewhat elliptically explained, to 'encourage efficient utilization of land in the large-scale commercial farming sector'.

Apart from the Commonwealth heads of government meeting, the country was the venue for an historic meeting between the African National Congress and Pan Africanist Congress of South Africa to discuss a common strategy in their negotiations with the Pretoria government (see VII.3). In February, at a crucial stage in the Gulf conflict, Zimbabwe assumed the presidency of the UN Security Council. The candidature of the Senior Minister of Finance, Economic Planning and Development, Dr Bernard Chidzero, for the post of UN Secretary-General—which he narrowly lost to Dr Boutros Boutros Ghali of Egypt (see XI.1)—confirmed Zimbabwe's raised profile in international politics.

iv. NAMIBIA

CAPITAL: Windhoek   AREA: 824,000 sq km   POPULATION: 1,700,000 ('89)
OFFICIAL LANGUAGES: Afrikaans & English
POLITICAL SYSTEM: presidential democracy
HEAD OF STATE: President Sam Nujoma (since March '90)
RULING PARTY: South West Africa People's Organization (SWAPO)
PRINCIPAL MINISTERS: Hage Geingob (prime minister), Theo-Ben Gurirab (foreign affairs), Peter Mueshihange (defence), Hifikepunje Pohamba (home affairs), Ngarikutuke Tjiriange (justice), Otto Herrigel (finance), Andimba Toivo ja Toivo (mines & energy)
INTERNATIONAL ALIGNMENT: NAM, OAU, SADCC, ACP, Cwth.
CURRENCY: South African rand (end-'91 £1=R5.14, US$1=R2.75)
GNP PER CAPITA: US$1,030 ('89)
MAIN EXPORT EARNERS: minerals

IN January Namibia and Denmark signed a development assistance agreement which would bring R 18 million in aid to the country. A sum of R 9 million was earmarked for budgetary support and most of the rest for the development of education and agriculture. Among other aid agreements was one with Florida State University, which signed a $15 million contract to help reform primary education in Namibia.

In February Finance Minister Otto Herrigel introduced an Additional Appropriation Bill, noting that Namibia had overspent by R 164.7 million in its first year of independence. Government spokesmen stressed their commitment to a stable political and economic environment and a free enterprise culture which would attract investment from abroad. After visiting Namibia in September, Stephan Denning, director of the southern African department of the World Bank, complimented the Namibian government on its prudent management of the economy. He pledged the World Bank's continued support in the realization of Namibia's undoubted economic potential. According to Mr Denning, Namibia did not need large-scale immediate access to the World Bank's resources because of the availability of generous assistance from many donors.

Talks between Windhoek and Pretoria on the future of Walvis Bay (a South African enclave within Namibian territory and Namibia's only deep-water port) ended in apparent stalemate in March. The Foreign Ministers of South Africa and Namibia, Pik Botha and Theo-Ben Gurirab, said that they would have to report back to their governments. In May, however, both governments reported progress in resolving the dispute after further talks in Windhoek. It appeared that a solution might yet be found in a system of joint administration of the enclave and a number of offshore islands, pending eventual final settlement of the question. South Africa, it was concluded, had agreed in principle to renounce sovereignty over Walvis Bay.

Negotiations between the European Community and the Namibian government on a new fishing agreement were broken off in May after a court in Windhoek sentenced five Spanish trawler captains to heavy fines and the seizure of their vessels. The Spanish government delivered a far-reaching apology to Windhoek for the infringements of Namibia's territorial fishing rights, promising legal restraints against Spanish trawlers fishing without licence. Other countries, including the Japanese, had concluded agreements to fish legally inside the Namibian exclusive economic zone immediately after independence.

When US Vice-President Dan Quayle visited Namibia in September, it was disclosed that the US government would provide $2.7 million for light aircraft and a patrol boat, for the protection of the country's marine resources.

v. BOTSWANA

CAPITAL: Gaborone   AREA: 580,000 sq km   POPULATION: 1,200,000 ('89)
OFFICIAL LANGUAGE: English   POLITICAL SYSTEM: presidential democracy
HEAD OF STATE AND GOVERNMENT: President Quett Masire (since '80)
RULING PARTY: Botswana Democratic Party (BDP)
PRINCIPAL MINISTERS: Peter Mmusi (vice-president, local government & lands), Gaositwe Chiepe (external affairs), Festus Mogae (finance & planning), Patrick Balopi (home & labour)
INTERNATIONAL ALIGNMENT: NAM, OAU, ACP, Cwth.
CURRENCY: pula (end-'91 £1=P3.88, US$1=P2.08)
GNP PER CAPITA: US$1,600 ('89)
MAIN EXPORT EARNERS: diamonds, copper-nickel, beef

PRESENTING his budget to parliament in February, Finance Minister Festus Mogae said that GDP per capita had risen from 70 South African rands 25 years ago to R 6,700 in 1991. However, a drop in diamond revenue had given the country its first budget deficit in nine years. The Botswana Defence Force was allocated R 310 million in the budget, much of it apparently earmarked for a big new base to be built near Gaborone.

In March Botswana stockbrokers reported considerable appreciation in the value of share portfolios in the Gaborone stock market over the previous 12 months. This was attributed to the continued steady rate of growth of the country's economy, which had maintained one of the highest growth rates in the world in recent years. There was also a low level of liquidity, while a shortage of stocks had tended to push prices higher.

In June President Quett Masire opened a R 1,300 million soda ash and salt project, which was a joint venture between the Botswana government (48 per cent) and a South African consortium (52 per cent). Mr Masire said that the plant would eventually produce 10 per cent of Botswana's national export earnings.

Following the collapse of the Bank of Credit and Commerce International (BCCI), First National Bank of South Africa took over the former BCCI affiliate in Botswana, the Bank of Credit and Commerce. The bank would operate as First National Bank of Botswana Ltd.

A government white paper on tourism was published in August, foreshadowing the introduction of legislation to regulate tourism and tourist accommodation. The new policy was to promote low-volume, high-cost tourism, it was stated. Henceforth tours would have to be operated by companies incorporated and registered in Botswana, and audited locally.

In November some 70,000 state and public-sector employees took industrial action in support of a 154 per cent pay rise, claiming that the government had reneged on an agreement with their union to pay such an increase. About 12,000 of the strikers were dismissed by the government management agency on 6 November.

vi. LESOTHO

CAPITAL: Maseru AREA: 30,000 sq km POPULATION: 1,700,000 ('89)
OFFICIAL LANGUAGES: English & Sesotho POLITICAL SYSTEM: monarchy, under military rule
HEAD OF STATE: King Letsie III (since Nov '90)
HEAD OF GOVERNMENT: Col. Elias Ramaema, Chairman of Military Council (since April '91)
PRINCIPAL MINISTERS: A. L. Thoalane (finance, planning & economy), Capt. Pius Molapo (foreign affairs), Kgotsi Matete (interior), A. K. Maopoe (justice)
INTERNATIONAL ALIGNMENT: NAM, OAU, ACP, Cwth.
CURRENCY: maloti (end-'91 £1=M5.14, US$1=M2.75)
GNP PER CAPITA: US$470 ('89)
MAIN EXPORT EARNERS: diamonds, wool

MAJOR-General Justin Lekhanya was ousted as the head of Lesotho's ruling Military Council in a bloodless coup staged by junior officers in April. He was succeeded by Colonel Elias Phisoana Ramaema (57), who said the new government was committed to return to democratic rule by June 1992.

Colonel Ramaema repealed an order by the military which banned party political activity. Yet the future seemed uncertain. The new military ruler followed the example of his predecessor in refusing demands by the junior officers for more pay and insisting that the country could not afford to meet their demands. Lesotho had been cutting public expenditure to comply with stringent conditions imposed by the International Monetary Fund.

Towards the end of May rioting broke out in Maseru, directed against Asian-run businesses. A number of Chinese businessmen and their families took refuge across the border in South Africa. The disturbances appeared to have been sparked off by an incident in which a young woman was killed after allegedly stealing a shirt. Shops were looted and a Chinese businessman was stoned to death.

With the departure from power of Major-General Lekhanya, a movement began for the deposed King Moshoeshoe II to return to Lesotho. He had been stripped of his powers in February 1990 (see AR 1990, p. 297) and exiled to Britain after refusing to approve changes in the administration which had been proposed by the military. His return would mean that his son, King Letsie III, who had succeeded him, would have to step down in his favour.

In September Lesotho signed a $110 million loan agreement with the World Bank in respect of the first phase of the Lesotho Highlands water project.

vii. SWAZILAND

CAPITAL: Mbabane   AREA: 17,350 sq km   POPULATION: 761,000 ('89)
OFFICIAL LANGUAGES: English & Siswati   POLITICAL SYSTEM: monarchy
HEAD OF STATE AND GOVERNMENT: King Mswati III (since '86)
PRINCIPAL MINISTERS: Obed Dlamini (prime minister), Sibusiso Barnabas Dlamini (finance), Sir George Mbikwakhe Mamba (foreign affairs), Prince Sobandla (interior), Zonke Amos Khumalo (justice)
INTERNATIONAL ALIGNMENT: NAM, OAU, ACP, Cwth.
CURRENCY: emalangeni (end-'91 £1=E5.14, US$1=E2.75)
GNP PER CAPITA: US$900 ('89)
MAIN EXPORT EARNERS: sugar, agricultural products

THERE were some signs in 1991 that Swaziland might modernize its political system, although little progress was made in this direction by the end of the year. There was pressure from various sources outside the country for Swaziland to abandon its use of detention without trial. A statement by the US embassy said that the detention law had 'a chilling effect on democratic processes'. Four detainees were treated in hospital in March for the effects of a prolonged hunger strike. In all, six people were in detention at that stage, including a member of the Swazi royal family, Prince Mfanasibili, who had been rearrested in August 1990 after his acquittal on a charge of high treason (see AR 1990, p. 298). The six detainees were released in April and Prince Mfanasibili was granted a pardon by King Mswati III. The Prince blamed his detention on an allegedly corrupt group of influential people and said he had forgiven them.

In June 20 coal miners trapped underground at the Emaswati mine were rescued after a huge drilling rig from Witbank in the Transvaal was employed to drive a borehole 65 metres deep to reach them. The men were brought to safety in a rescue capsule.

In September King Mswati visited the United States and had two days of talks in Washington aimed at encouraging American aid and investment in Swaziland.

Dr Ambrose Zwane, the veteran opposition political leader, denounced the country's system of government in October as undemocratic and unworkable. Dr Zwane, leader of the banned Ngwane National Liberatory Congress (NNLC), called for democratic elections in a multi-party system. He welcomed the review of local political structures currently being undertaken by a special committee appointed by King Mswati. Political parties had been banned in the kingdom since 1973. However, hopes for speedy political change were dashed in November when King Mswati said that the present system should not be abandoned.

3. SOUTH AFRICA

CAPITAL: Pretoria   AREA: 1,220,000 sq km   POPULATION: 35,000,000 ('89)
OFFICIAL LANGUAGES: Afrikaans & English
POLITICAL SYSTEM: presidential, under white minority rule (democracy for whites, partial representation for coloureds and Asians)
HEAD OF STATE AND GOVERNMENT: President F. W. de Klerk (since Sept '89)
RULING PARTY: National Party (NP)
PRINCIPAL MINISTERS: R. F. (Pik) Botha (foreign affairs), Gerrit van N. Viljoen (constitutional development), Roelf Meyer (defence), George S. Bartlett (minerals & energy), Kobie (H. J.) Coetsee (justice), Barend J. du Plessis (finance), Gene Louw (home affairs)
CURRENCY: rand (end-'91 £1=R5.14, US$1=R2.75)
GNP PER CAPITA: US$2,470 ('89)
MAIN EXPORT EARNERS: precious and base metals, minerals

EVENTS in the first half of the year left no doubt that the transition from apartheid to multi-party democracy would be turbulent. There was a resurgence of factional violence between rival black groups, notably the African National Congress (ANC) and the rather more conservative Inkatha Freedom Party, based in the province of Natal. Yet it appeared that much of the violence could be laid at the door of shadowy right-wing forces opposed to a negotiated settlement. In spite of the violence, the movement towards negotiation was maintained and South Africa's isolation in the international community began to ease. As the year was ending, a multi-party conference to plan the transition finally got under way.

There was a growing conviction on the part of the ANC that President de Klerk's National Party (NP) government was failing in its duty to keep the peace and, in particular, was allowing Inkatha supporters, brandishing spears and clubs, to march unhindered through township streets, attacking and killing ANC supporters and other residents. As Rand township violence reached unprecedented levels of intensity in the first half of the year, the ANC concluded that the de Klerk government and Inkatha, as the principal beneficiaries of the violence, politically speaking, were actively condoning killing expeditions by Zulu hostel-dwellers. The repeated attacks on commuters in trains and at bus and taxi queues, carried out by masked gunmen using AK-47 assault rifles, likewise gave rise to acute concern.

Claims were made—at first unsubstantiated—that elements in military intelligence and the Special Forces of the South African Defence Force (SADF) were linked with the attacks on commuters. The ANC in particular suspected that it was becoming the victim of a destabilization campaign conducted on the same lines as the SADF's covert support for the Renamo terrorists in Mozambique (see VII.1.v). While the good faith of President de Klerk himself was not in question, it appeared to the ANC that elements in his security forces might still be carrying on the clandestine divide-and-rule tactics of the Botha era. Then death squads under police and military control had assassinated militant opponents of apartheid rule and had actively promoted hostilities between rival groups in the black community.

The violence, including a series of attacks on ANC activists by unidentified assassins, reached such a pitch by April that Nelson Mandela, president of the ANC, called on the government to sack both the Minister of Defence, General Magnus Malan, and the Law and Order Minister, Adriaan Vlok. If this was not done, he said, the ANC would consider withdrawing from negotiations with the government. Mr Mandela also issued an 'open letter' to President de Klerk, demanding that the government restore law and order in the townships. The ANC's suggestion that it might withdraw from negotiations was at first derisively brushed aside as a propaganda ploy. But it soon became clear that the organization was profoundly concerned about the violence and feared that the climate for negotiation was evaporating.

The ANC's own hands were by no means spotless. The campaign of violent insurrection waged by Umkhonto we Siswe (the ANC's military wing) had been suspended in August 1990 under the Pretoria Minute (see AR 1990, p. 302), and no-one doubted that the suspension had been scrupulously maintained. Yet the ANC's furious propaganda campaign against black local authorities and the continuing feud with Inkatha certainly stirred up tensions and led to violence at the local level. Non-ANC civic leaders, including the pro-Inkatha mayor of Soweto, fell victim to shootings, petrol bombings or hand-grenade attacks. Policemen were also singled out as targets. Factional violence was rife in some of the huge squatter settlements such as those at Inanda, outside Durban, or at Crossroads and Khayelitsha, outside Cape Town, in which local Tammany-style bosses were building rival power bases among the newly-arrived immigrants from the impoverished tribal areas. Commercial rivalries, as in a vicious Capone-style 'taxi war' in the Cape Peninsula, also took a steady toll in lives, and again there were allegations of police siding with one faction or another.

There was no clear pattern in the violence. A fair conclusion was that all three of the principal parties—the ANC, Inkatha and the state authorities—should bear a share of the blame for a culture of violence which was threatening to get out of hand. Criminal violence, notably armed robbery, was also causing anxiety in the cities and was not always distinguishable from the political variety.

By mid-year both the NP government and the ANC seemed to be dragging their heels on the negotiation trail. But appearances were deceptive. In spite of the wrangling over who was to blame for the violence, the movement towards negotiation went ahead steadily. The process had been given a massive boost when President de Klerk announced at the opening of parliament that he would introduce legislation during the session to repeal the bedrock statutes of the apartheid era. These were the Population Registration Act, providing for racial classification of all South Africans; the Group Areas Act, providing for racial zoning of residential areas; and the Land Acts, which set aside most of the land in the country for the white minority and confined black rights of land ownership to 13 per cent of the country, situated in the impoverished, overcrowded rural reserves. The parliamentary session saw the entire legislative underpinning of the apartheid system finally swept away.

In April President de Klerk visited Britain, Ireland and Denmark and obtained a loan of R 850 million via a consortium of German banks, the first important foreign loan since the easing of financial sanctions. In the following month, however, the industrial share index of the Johannesburg stock exchange lost 36 points, which was seen as reflecting a depression in investor confidence as a result of the continuing township violence. The Minister of Law and Order, Mr Vlok, announced in parliament on 6 May that 771 people had been killed in unrest since the start of the year, compared with 754 deaths in the same period in the previous year.

In a bid to get to grips with the violence, President de Klerk convened a summit meeting of all political groups on 24-25 May. The ANC and other extra-parliamentary parties declined to attend, protesting that the state was part of the problem. The meeting went ahead anyway and resolved that a second peace conference should be convened in September under the auspices of the churches and that a representative forum be instituted to negotiate proposals to end the violence. A week before the second peace conference was due to take place there was a renewed flare-up in which 23 Inkatha supporters were mowed down by automatic fire while marching to a rally. In the following week the death toll on all sides rose to 142.

The killing which sparked the renewed violence was seen by the ANC as an attempt by extremist right-wing forces to derail the peace process. It did not do so. The ANC attended the second peace conference, as did Inkatha and the NP as well as representatives of the government and the police. In fact, all other significant groups except the far-right Conservative Party attended. On 14 September a 'national peace accord' was adopted, with codes of conduct, mechanisms and procedures for monitoring unrest, investigating incidents and securing the peace. It was resolved that a standing commission on political violence and intimidation should be set up, as well as representative committees at the local level to monitor and investigate violence. The commission was duly appointed by President de Klerk, under the chairmanship of Mr Justice Goldstone, and it began work immediately.

The ANC's suspicions of collusion between the security forces and Inkatha had been substantiated in dramatic fashion some weeks earlier when documentary evidence came to light showing that R 250,000 had been channelled to Inkatha by the security police to fund a party rally.

It was also disclosed that a further R 1.5 million had been handed over to Inkatha by security police for the use of Inkatha's trade union arm. President de Klerk went on national television to give wide-ranging assurances that clandestine funding by government agencies would be curbed. He assured the country that 'relentless action' would be taken against members of the security forces who were found to be guilty of organizing or promoting violence. All secret funding of political parties or organizations by the state would be cancelled, subject to contractual obligations. An investigation by the pro-NP *Citizen* newspaper showed that 39 secret projects were run by the police and two by the SADF. (On 25 July Pik Botha, Minister of Foreign Affairs, disclosed that well over R 100 million had been spent from secret state funds to aid opponents of SWAPO in the Namibian independence elections in the previous year.)

In his televised statement, the President said that covert funding had been instituted at a time when South Africa was at war with the ANC, resulting in the use of violence and extraordinary strategies on both sides. There had been a change of circumstances since the signing of the Groote Schuur and Pretoria minutes in 1990, and the support of political parties or movements with state funds was now unacceptable. However, President de Klerk's assurances did little to make good the damage to his credibility, particularly in ANC quarters. It was pointed out that he had given similar assurances to parliament 12 months earlier, promising a review of all secret projects, yet the Inkatha funding had continued until exposed in the media.

President de Klerk took no further action in the immediate aftermath of the 'Inkathagate' scandal, as it became known, but on 29 July he unexpectedly reshuffled his cabinet. Both Mr Vlok and General Malan were relegated to minor portfolios and replaced by Hernus Kriel and Roelf Meyer respectively. The new Law and Order Minister, Mr Kriel, had held the planning, provincial affairs and housing portfolios and was generally regarded as a much tougher politician than Mr Vlok, likely to make a better job of controlling the police. The new Defence Minister, Mr Meyer, was seen as a liberal-minded member of parliament, strongly in favour of the de Klerk reforms and highly regarded by the ANC.

In July the government's reform initiative was rewarded internationally in a number of ways. In the USA President Bush formally scrapped the Comprehensive Anti-Apartheid Act sanctions and laid the groundwork for possible legal action to roll back state and local sanctions laws. South Africa's membership of the International Olympic Committee was restored, opening the way for unified non-racial sports bodies to be accepted into world competition. The Israeli government lifted economic and cultural sanctions imposed in 1987. The International Cricket Council welcomed South Africa back into world cricket with immediate effect. The International Confederation of Free Trade Unions announced that it would grant R 30 million in aid to the South

African trade union movement. Restored diplomatic relations with Hungary were upgraded to ambassadorial level, among a number of other such steps broadening South Africa's representation in world capitals. In August the US Transport Department announced that all aviation restrictions against South Africa had been lifted.

During the year trade missions came to South Africa from Britain, North America, the European Community, Eastern Europe and the Far East, creating hopes of a steady increase in South Africa's share of world trade. The Commonwealth heads of government meeting in Harare voted to scrap all people-to-people sanctions against South Africa and to lift other sanctions in stages as the country took further steps to establish a non-racial democratic society (see XI.2). Meanwhile, the Taiwan government announced that it would invest $200 million in a petrochemical plant in South Africa. Nevertheless, violence in the country continued to scare off most investors.

In August three people were killed and scores injured in running battles between white right-wingers and police in the western Transvaal town of Ventersdorp, as members of the militant neo-nazi Afrikaans Resistance Movement (AWB) sought to prevent President de Klerk from addressing an NP rally in the town. There were some indications, including by-election results, that President de Klerk was losing support in the traditional Afrikaner heartlands. In the marginal NP-held seat of Virginia (Orange Free State), for example, the right-wing Conservative Party polled 7,980 votes to the NP's 4,814 at a November by-election.

Meanwhile, the ANC was getting its house in order for serious negotiations, holding a national congress in July which was the biggest such gathering ever held in South Africa, attracting 2,500 delegates. The congress elected Cyril Ramaphosa, the competent and respected general secretary of the National Union of Mineworkers, to the key post of ANC secretary-general. The ailing Oliver Tambo, who had led the ANC from abroad during the 30 years in which it was a banned organization, was succeeded as president by Mr Mandela, who had been a prisoner on Robben Island for most of that time. Walter Sisulu was elected deputy president, Thomas Nkobi was re-elected treasurer general and Jacob Zuma stepped into the new post of deputy secretary-general. In a pre-negotiation show of muscle, the alliance of the ANC, the South African Communist Party and the COSATU trade union federation staged a successful two-day work stayaway in November to protest against the new value-added tax (VAT) system, which, they said, had been introduced without adequate consultation with the unions.

Concern grew throughout the year at the extent of unemployment in the squatter camps outside the big cities and in the black community generally. In August the government announced a R 1,000 million allocation of funds to 667 socio-economic projects which would create 59,000 jobs. With unemployment at 60 per cent in some areas, the problem seemed insurmountable, however, and potentially explosive unless a revived economy could produce growth rates of the order of those achieved in countries of the Pacific Rim. By December, conscious of the stagnating economy, all the major parties seemed determined to bring violence under control and to get down to serious negotiations. A return of calm and stability, it was thought, would restore confidence and create the economic buoyancy to underpin the transition. After remarkably successful preliminary discussions, it was agreed to call a conference to frame a declaration of intent and set up an interim administration to run the country during the negotiations. Designated the Convention for a Democratic South Africa (CODESA), the conference began in Johannesburg on 20 December.

After decades of racial conflict, South Africa was at last on the road to a constitutional settlement and, it was hoped, a non-racial democracy.

VIII SOUTH ASIA AND INDIAN OCEAN

1. IRAN—AFGHANISTAN

i. IRAN

CAPITAL: Tehran   AREA: 1,650,000 sq km   POPULATION: 54,900,000 ('90)
OFFICIAL LANGUAGE: Farsi (Persian)   POLITICAL SYSTEM: Islamic Republic
RELIGIOUS LEADER: Ayatollah Seyed Ali Khamenei (since June '89)
HEAD OF STATE AND GOVERNMENT: President (Hojatolislam) Hashemi Ali Akbar Rafsanjani (since July '89)
OTHER SENIOR LEADERS: Hossain Moussavi (presidential adviser), Hassan Ebrahim Habibi (vice-president), Seyed Mhajerani (vice-president, legal & parliamentary affairs), Massoud Roghani Zanjani (vice-president, planning and budget), Reza Amrollahi (vice-president, atomic energy), Mansour Razavi (vice-president, state employment), Mehdi Manafi (vice-president, environment), Hassan Ghafurifard (vice-president, physical education), Ayatollah Mehdi Karrubi (speaker of Majlis)
PRINCIPAL MINISTERS: Ali Akbar Velayati (foreign affairs), Gholamreza Agazadeh (oil), Abdollah Nouri (interior), Mohsen Nourbakhsh (economic affairs and finance), Hujatolislam Ismail Shostari (justice)
INTERNATIONAL ALIGNMENT: NAM, OPEC, ICO, ECO
CURRENCY: rial (end-'91 £1=Rls119.00, US$1=Rls63.74)
GNP PER CAPITA: US$3,230 ('89)
MAIN EXPORT EARNERS: oil and gas, carpets

THERE were strong reverberations within Iran from the Iraqi invasion of Kuwait and the resultant Gulf War. Promised benefits to Iran by way of Iraqi concessions under UN resolution 598 of 1987, including the settlement of most outstanding disputes on Iranian terms negotiated in the second half of 1990 (see AR 1990, p. 306), appeared to dissipate. The build-up of US and allied forces in the Persian Gulf ran directly contrary to Iranian policy goals, while the military reinforcement of Saudi Arabia also caused unease by the beginning of 1991. The government of Iran attempted to defuse the Kuwait issue by acting as a peace-maker. Shuttle diplomacy between Tehran and Baghdad led to a personal and apparently successful effort by President Rafsanjani in January to persuade Saddam Husain to withdraw from Kuwaiti territory. In the event, this failed and the Iranian stance against Iraq hardened in consequence.

Iran became enmeshed as a bystander in the war over Kuwait. In the last week of January more than 100 Iraqi aircraft, including the majority of the Iraqi Airlines fleet, fled to Iran seeking asylum from allied air raids. In the border areas there was an increasing flow of refugees as Iraqis fled, first from allied bombing and later, after the ceasefire of 28 February, in far greater numbers when Shias fought with the Iraqi army in the south and the Kurdish rebellion was crushed in the north (see V.4.vi). In April Iranian officials reported that 350,000 Shia and 770,000 Kurdish refugees had entered Iran from Iraq. Meanwhile, Iraq failed to ratify its earlier agreements on UN resolution 598 and showed open hostility towards the Islamic republic. The Iranian government demonstrated great self-restraint by not intervening on the side of the Shia faction in southern Iraq, despite considerable domestic pressures to do so.

In the aftermath of the war in Kuwait, Iran was isolated. It was given no role in the new regional defence arrangements envisaged under the Damascus Agreement signed between the Arabian peninsula states Egypt and Syria in March (see V.5.iii). Even though this accord proved to be stillborn, Iranian policy developed rapidly in the changed regional circumstances. Efforts were made to set up a political axis with Saudi Arabia. The Iranian Foreign Minister, Ali Akbar Velayati, undertook the pilgrimage to Mecca, and Prince Saud al-Faisal, his Saudi counterpart, travelled to Tehran in June. Other links with the peninsula were also carefully cultivated through a series of official exchange visits.

Other areas of foreign policy underwent change as recognition grew in ruling circles that, without normalization of relations, Iran would not get access to the finance, technology and markets necessary for its drive to economic development. Closer links were sought during the year with the countries of the European Community, but progress was slow. The British demanded freedom for all hostages in Lebanon, the release of Roger Cooper from gaol in Iran and cancellation of the *fatweh* against the life of Salman Rushdie (see AR 1989, pp. 298, 493-4, 538). Mr Cooper was set free in March and the British hostages were released one by one later in the year (see V.4.v). But the *fatweh* against Mr Rushdie inevitably remained, since it was not capable of formal annulment. Relations with France continued to be strained by the failure of the two sides to agree on the repayment to Iran of monies outstanding from a $1,000 million loan made to France by the late Shah. There was also outrage in France in September when Iranian officials appeared to be implicated in the murder in Paris of Dr Shapour Bakhtiar (see XX: OBITUARY), a former prime minister who had become leader of a small opposition group (see also III.1.i). A proposed visit to Iran by President Mitterrand was postponed indefinitely in the wake of Bakhtiar's death.

The disintegration of the USSR posed serious difficulties for Iran, which it handled extremely well overall. The Iranian authorities carefully avoided comment during the August coup attempt in Moscow and maintained strictly formal relations with the separate republics, despite the obvious temptation to support pro-Islamic movements for autonomy in the southern region. A series of province-to-province agreements on trade and transit facilities were signed between Iranian provincial authorities and their counterparts in the southern republics. The President of Azerbaijan visited Tehran on 16 August for official talks. In September Iran recognized the three Baltic republics. President

Yang Shangkun of China visited Iran in early November, giving rise to speculation that a Sino-Iranian link for the exchange of atomic technology was under consideration.

In mid-year there were sporadic riots in a number of Iranian towns against economic difficulties and the activities of government agents on matters such as enforcement of the dress code for women. In August a series of unexplained arson attacks occurred in the country's principal bazaars, while in October widespread anti-government protests were reported to have broken out in Tehran. The mujahideen Khalq rebel organization increased its international activities from its base in Iraq but it posed little threat within Iran. Despite widespread apathy and occasional violence, President Rafsanjani gradually consolidated his position during the year. He was aided by a modest upturn in the economy, slowly improving living standards and an apparent determination by the population at large not to involve itself in changing the regime by violent means. Ayatollah Khamenei, the country's spiritual guide, remained in political alliance with President Rafsanjani, but he came under attack from hardline elements and from the influential Shia religious establishment, which questioned his standing as an Islamic jurist.

Iranian sources put the rate of growth in the economy at 10.1 per cent for the year ending 20 March 1991, the first time that real growth had been achieved since the mid-1980s. Expansion was largely fed by rising oil revenues, gains in productivity in existing industrial plant and a good performance by agriculture. The government did much to encourage the private sector by easing financial regulations, though the level of confidence in the regime on the part of individual capitalists remained low. The 1991/92 budget provided for a 54 per cent increase in spending. There was continued heavy dependence on oil revenues, which were forecast at $23,000 million. Outgoings were expected to amount to Rls 8,516,300 million, with a deficit of Rls 1,346,000 million. No less than Rls 2,653,100 million was allocated for the economic development plan.

Iran began to draw appreciably on foreign loans during 1991. Iranian credit-worthiness was endorsed by the World Bank, which allotted a loan of $250 million for reconstruction of the earthquake-devastated northern areas of Gilan and Zanjan (see AR 1990, p. 308). It was announced that in all a total of $27,700 million of credits would be sought abroad over the next five years, including a measure of foreign investment in Iran. Difficulties with the exchange rate were manifest throughout the year. On 20 January the central bank lowered the competitive rate, hoping to undermine the free market in the rial. The move failed and for the rest of the year the government gradually transferred the pricing of commodities from the official rate to a new floating rate. At year's end the free market rate for the rial remained low.

A number of long-term economic problems remained as a legacy of a protracted period of revolution and war. The population continued to grow rapidly at an estimated 3.4 per cent annually, adding to problems of unemployment. The flight of people from the land to the cities went on unabated. Inflation was officially put at 9 per cent in 1991, mitigated in part by subsidized food supplies. But higher levels of inflation adversely affected urban peoples in particular, as prices of accommodation, clothing and consumer goods rose by an estimated 20 per cent in the year.

ii. AFGHANISTAN

CAPITAL: Kabul   AREA: 650,000 sq km   POPULATION: 15,000,000 ('88 est.)
OFFICIAL LANGUAGES: Pushtu & Dari (Persian)   POLITICAL SYSTEM: presidential
HEAD OF STATE AND GOVERNMENT: President Mohammed Najibullah (since '87, previously Chairman of Revolutionary Council)
RULING PARTY: Homeland Party
PRINCIPAL MINISTERS: Fazl Haq Khaleqiar (prime minister), Abdol Samad Salim (deputy premier, economy), Abdol Wakil (foreign affairs), Raz Mohammad Patkin (internal affairs), Mohammad Hakim (finance), Maj.-Gen. Mohammad Aslam Watanjar (defence), Gholam Mahaynodin Daraz (justice)
INTERNATIONAL ALIGNMENT: NAM, ICO
CURRENCY: afghani (end-'91 £1=Af99.25, US$1=Af53.16)
GNP PER CAPITA: US$168 ('82)
MAIN EXPORT EARNERS: agricultural products

THE year again demonstrated President Najibullah's remarkable tenacity of purpose in holding on to office, despite the final withdrawal of Soviet troops in February 1989 (see AR 1989, p. 300). Undoubtedly this continuance was aided by the disagreements and divisions amongst the various anti-government mujahideen guerrilla groups opposed to his regime. Such divisions remained a crucial factor throughout the year, despite the capture of the town of Khost by mujahideen at the end of March.

In mid-September the Soviet Union and the USA agreed to stop supplying arms to, respectively, the Afghan government and the rebel groups trying to overthrow it. January 1992 was set as the deadline. This important step towards de-escalating the civil war of more than a decade was agreed by James Baker, the US Secretary of State, and Boris Pankin, the then Soviet Foreign Minister. Subsequently, there were unsubstantiated press reports that President Najibullah was trying to revive earlier plans to arrange a return from exile of Afghanistan's frail 76-year-old King Zahir Shah, deposed in 1973, in an attempt to arrange or anticipate a settlement. On 18 September the President announced that he had restored citizenship to Zahir Shah and to 19 members of the royal family. On 4 November Zahir Shah was stabbed in the face and throat by a man posing as a journalist at his villa in Rome. The former monarch escaped with minor wounds and said that he was ready to assume his 'moral duty' to return to Afghanistan.

Five days of talks were held in Moscow on 11–15 November between a mujahideen delegation and Soviet and Russian officials. A joint statement released afterwards said that the two sides had 'confirmed the necessity of transfer of the entire state power in Afghanistan to an interim Islamic government'. It continued: 'Within two years, from the moment of transfer of power from the Kabul regime to the interim government, general elections will be held in Afghanistan with the assistance of the Islamic Conference Organization and the UN.' The communique signed by Mr Pankin included a denunciation of the Soviet invasion of Afghanistan in 1979 and a Soviet commitment to assist in post-war reconstruction.

All nine of the Iran-based Shia mujahideen groups and four of the seven Pakistan-based Sunni groups appeared to be willing to negotiate with the Kabul government. As for the Kabul government, it welcomed the Moscow talks as part of continuing international efforts to resolve the Afghanistan issue. Dialogue between Afghans, it said, was the only way to achieve peace.

2. INDIA—PAKISTAN—BANGLADESH—NEPAL—BHUTAN—SRI LANKA

i. INDIA

CAPITAL: New Delhi   AREA: 3,287,000 sq km   POPULATION: 844,00,000 ('91)
OFFICIAL LANGUAGES: Hindi & English   POLITICAL SYSTEM: parliamentary democracy
HEAD OF STATE: President Ramaswamy Venkataraman (since '87)
RULING PARTIES: minority government led by Congress (I)
HEAD OF GOVERNMENT: P. V. Narasimha Rao, Prime Minister (since June '91)
PRINCIPAL MINISTERS: Madhavsinh Solanki (external affairs), Manmohan Singh (finance), Sharad Pawar (defence), S. B. Chavan (home affairs), Madhav Rao Scindia (justice)
INTERNATIONAL ALIGNMENT: NAM, SAARC, Cwth.
CURRENCY: rupee (end-'91 £1=Rs48.00, US$1=Rs25.71)
GNP PER CAPITA: US$340 ('89)
MAIN EXPORT EARNERS: precious stones, textiles, tea, tourism

IT was a year of cataclysmic and often puzzling changes on the world scene and within India itself, as old orders yielded to new. Some rites of passage removed features which had dominated India for many years. Rajiv Gandhi's assassination attracted most attention and comment from the world's media, but other matters obtruded, notably an early general election and the return of Congress (I) to power, albeit as a minority government. The year was also marked by the inception of major changes in national economic management; two rupee devaluations; continuing violence in and over Punjab, Kashmir, Assam and elsewhere; and reappraisal of the country's foreign policy in the face of the changing world scene.

The precarious minority government of the Chandra Shekhar (S) faction of the Janata Dal, formed only four months earlier in November 1990 (see AR 1990, pp. 313–4), collapsed on 6 March when the Prime Minister resigned. Mr Shekhar was unwilling or unable to continue accommodating the demands made by Congress (I) as the price of its support or neutrality in parliament. The immediate cause of the rupture was Congress (I) indignation over alleged surveillance of Mr Gandhi's house in New Delhi. More fundamentally, the Congress (I) leader was optimistic about his chances in new general elections. After some procedural complications, President Ramaswamy Venkataraman eventually obliged by dissolving parliament on 13 March and ordering that it be reconvened on 5 June, thus ensuring a long election campaign. Mr Shekhar was asked to continue as head of a caretaker government pending the outcome of the elections, which were originally set for 20, 23 and 26 May, until the assassination of Mr Gandhi on 21 May threw this timetable awry.

The 46-year-old former prime minister (see XX: OBITUARY) died instantly in a bomb explosion at a Congress (I) election rally at Sriperumpudar in the southern state of Tamil Nadu, 45 km from Madras. Fifteen other people were killed in the explosion, including the young Tamil girl who was carrying the bomb. Suspicion concerning responsibility immediately focused on the militant Liberation Tigers of Tamil Eelam (LTTE), against whose separatist struggle in Sri Lanka Indian troops had been deployed in the late 1980s under Mr Gandhi's premiership. Hundreds of exiled LTTE activists were rounded up by the Indian authorities, who by 29 May were convinced that the Tigers had been involved. Two commissions of inquiry were set up by the government to investigate the assassination, but prospects of a speedy conclusion receded when a prime suspect, who was a known LTTE activist, committed suicide on 20 August as police were storming his hideout in Bangalore (see also VIII.2.vi). Meanwhile, Rajiv Gandhi had been cremated in New Delhi on 24 May, near the spots where his mother Indira (assassinated in 1984), his brother Sanjay (killed in a plane crash in 1980) and his grandfather Jawaharlal Nehru had also been cremated. Numerous foreign leaders attended the funeral.

Because of the assassination, the second and third rounds of the election were postponed until 12 and 15 June. In the interim, Congress (I) was faced with the problem that there was no obvious successor to Mr Gandhi. Attempts by some party veterans to persuade his widow Sonia, an Italian-born Christian, to accept the leadership were unsuccessful. After extensive consultations and much manoeuvring, the Congress (I) central working committee on 29 May unanimously elected P. V. Narasimha Rao, a 70-year-old southerner, as party president. Because of Mr Rao's ill-health, this was widely construed at the time as a stop-gap measure.

The two June voting rounds were largely violence-free (except in

Bihar), in contrast to the 20 May round, when over 100 people were killed in election-related clashes in several states. Because of their troubled internal situations, elections were postponed in Punjab and in Jammu and Kashmir. Only about half the eligible electorate went to the polls, compared with over 80 per cent in both the 1989 and the 1984 elections. The results showed appreciable Congress (I) gains in terms of seats (from 197 in 1989 to 225 this time), largely on the strength of what appeared to be a sympathy vote in the southern states. But in the northern 'Hindi belt' Congress (I) was decimated, much of its traditional support in these states transferring to the Hindu-revivalist Bharatiya Janata Party (BJP), which took 119 seats as against 85 in 1989. The BJP also increased its share of the popular vote, from 11.4 to 19.9 per cent, whereas Congress (I) slipped from 39.5 to 37.3 per cent. Of the other main formations, Janata Dal slumped from 143 to 55 seats, while the Communist Party of India (Marxist) (CPI-M) won a creditable (given world trends) 35 seats. At least 17 other parties also gained representation in the new Lok Sabha.

In post-election negotiations between the parties, Congress (I) ruled out any political deal with the BJP but quickly secured pledges of qualified external support or abstention from both Janata Dal and the Left Front (of the CPI-M and allies). Having with some difficulty secured election as Congress (I) parliamentary leader, Mr Rao was the following day sworn in as India's ninth Prime Minister since independence in 1947. Sensibly, he spent most of his first five days persuading his main rival for the leadership, Sharad Pawar (chief minister of Maharashtra), to join the cabinet as defence minister. There were thus 15 cabinet ministers (excluding the Prime Minister), as well as 35 ministers of state and seven deputy ministers. Six of the new appointees were women, including one cabinet minister. On 15 July the new minority government obtained the confidence of the Lok Sabha by 241 votes to 111, with 112 abstentions.

Pursuant to the new Prime Minister's inaugural pledge to give primacy to the economy, his experienced Finance Minister, Manmohan Singh, immediately launched a series of reform measures to tackle India's economic crisis, particularly the massive foreign debt of $70,000 million and chronic shortage of foreign exchange. On 1 and 3 July the rupee was devalued against the US dollar by 8 and 10 per cent respectively, while on the latter date the Reserve Bank of India raised the bank rate by 1 per cent, to a record 11 per cent. With the aim of making the rupee fully convertible for trade purposes within three to five years, the government also gave notice of the withdrawal of export subsidies and the linking of foreign-exchange allocations for imports to the achievement of export sales. Dr Singh followed up on 24 July by announcing a more open and liberal industrial policy and by presenting to parliament a 1991/92 budget which combined austerity with financial orthodoxy to such an extent that the BJP opposition was not alone in claiming that the government had bowed to the diktat of the International Monetary Fund (IMF).

The Finance Minister told the Lok Sabha on 18 December that the government had categorically ruled out a third devaluation of the rupee in the near future. He accused 'interested parties' within the country and outside of spreading devaluation rumours and of thus deterring non-resident Indians and others from investing in India. Referring to a letter of intent to the IMF, which he had placed before parliament on 16 December, Dr Singh asserted that it showed no deviation from the government's stated policies. Economic problems had to be faced, he said, otherwise there was a possibility of the country disintegrating.

According to an official projection made in the last quarter of 1991, India would need to create 10 million jobs each year for the next ten years in order to reach a state of near-full employment by the turn of the century. It was made by India's Planning Commission in a paper formulating an approach to the eighth five-year plan, beginning in April 1992. In a speech on 23 December to the National Development Council (India's highest economic decision-making body, including all state chief ministers as members), Mr Rao called for a nationwide programme to eradicate poverty during the forthcoming plan period. Most experts commented, however, that this target would be virtually impossible to achieve within the prescribed time-frame. Preliminary results of India's 1991 census, made public on 25 March, showed a total population of 843,930,861—over 160 million more than in 1981. Recent demographic trends indicated that India could overtake China as the world's most populous country by the year 2011. In face of the rapidly rising population, as well as an AIDS epidemic, official tolerance of explicit advertisements for contraceptives became increasingly evident.

India's foreign policy attracted some sharp criticism in 1991, from articulate Indians as well as from informed foreigners, for its alleged timidity and lack of adaptability in a rapidly-changing international environment. This was somewhat ironic in view of the fact that Mr Rao's longest and most successful previous ministerial tenure had been as minister of external affairs. Towards the end of the year there were indications that Indo-American relations were improving, amid much press speculation that the Indian government was planning to purchase substantial amounts of defence equipment from the United States. Nevertheless, India's continued opposition to the Nuclear Non-Proliferation Treaty regime remained a major restraint in relations with Washington, however much it was recognized that, with the demise of the USSR, India needed to reevaluate its role in world affairs. At the same time, a desire for continuity was apparent in the declared intention of both Moscow and New Delhi that the 1971 Indo-Soviet treaty of friendship and mutual co-operation would be renewed at least between the Russian Federation and India.

Improving relations with China were signalled in particular by an official six-day visit by Premier Li Peng to India in December, the first by a Chinese Prime Minister to India for 31 years. The visit provided further evidence that India's overall geostrategic situation had changed much more emphatically than had the power relations in its own region of South Asia. Indeed, relations with Pakistan and with Sri Lanka were distinctly uneasy and at times openly acrimonious, with India accusing Pakistan of aiding and abetting terrorism in Punjab and Kashmir (see also VIII.2.ii) and disagreeing with both countries on the future of the South Asian Association for Regional Cooperation (see XI.6.ii). At least in declaratory terms, Indian leaders continued to affirm a belief in the efficacy of non-alignment, despite the patent post-Cold War disarray of the Non-Aligned Movement (see XI.4.iv).

ii. PAKISTAN

CAPITAL: Islamabad   AREA: 804,000 sq km   POPULATION: 109,900,000 ('89)
OFFICIAL LANGUAGE: Urdu   POLITICAL SYSTEM: nominal parliamentary democracy
HEAD OF STATE: President Ghulam Ishaq Khan (since Aug '88)
RULING PARTY: Islamic Democratic Alliance (IJI), dominated by Muslim League
HEAD OF GOVERNMENT: Nawaz Sharif, Prime Minister (since Nov '90)
PRINCIPAL MINISTERS: Sayed Ghaus Ali Shah (defence), Choudhry Shujat Hussain (interior), Sartaj Aziz (finance & economy), Hamid Nasir Chattha (planning & development), Choudhary Abdul Ghafoor (justice)
INTERNATIONAL ALIGNMENT: NAM, ICO, ECO, SAARC, Cwth.
CURRENCY: rupee (end-'91 £1=PRS44.00, US$1=PRS23.57)
GNP PER CAPITA: US$370 ('89)
MAIN EXPORT EARNERS: cotton, textiles, rice

PRIME Minister Nawaz Sharif, in office since November 1990 (see AR 1990, p. 317), faced no serious challenge in 1991, but he failed to consolidate his position and had to deal with dissent within his ruling Islami Jamhoori Ittehad (IJI) coalition as well as opposition from Benazir Bhutto's Pakistan People's Party (PPP). He remained dependent on the support of the armed forces and of President Ghulam Ishaq Khan, and had to share power with them. Violence and corruption continued to be major themes of the country's political life, but the opposition was not able to exploit them to the full.

The beginning of the year was dominated by the Gulf crisis and war. Nawaz Sharif had to walk a tightrope between his obligations to Saudi Arabia and the allies on the one hand and a passionately pro-Iraqi public opinion on the other. Pakistani troops had been sent to Saudi Arabia at the beginning of the crisis but were kept carefully away from direct involvement in the fighting. Even so, Nawaz Sharif was badly shaken at the end of January when the army chief, General Mirza Aslam Beg, made a speech which by implication was strongly critical of the government stance. With the allied victory, however, Nawaz Sharif was able to weather the crisis. In August General Aslam Beg retired and was replaced as chief of the army staff by General Asif Nawaz Janjua.

A further example of tightrope walking was seen in June with the passage of the Sharia Bill, first introduced during the Zia regime and intended to make Islamic law the basis of all Pakistan's institutions. The final version was in fact severely watered down and included no clear schedule for implementation. Nawaz Sharif thus sought to satisfy the 'Islamic' elements among his supporters while preventing any major disruption to government.

As the year went on, several prominent figures within the IJI emerged as focuses of dissent, among them former prime ministers Muhammad Khan Junejo and Ghulam Mustafa Jatoi. The latter claimed that the October 1990 elections (when he had been in office) had indeed been rigged, as the PPP had always alleged. Charges of corruption and nepotism were made against the government and gained credence from a massive fraud involving cooperative financial institutions which came to light in July and in which the Prime Minister's business interests were allegedly implicated. A notable sex scandal involving in particular the leader of one element of the IJI added to the sleazy atmosphere.

The role played by President Ghulam Ishaq Khan came under attack in some quarters. A speech by him to the National Assembly, shown live on television, was loudly heckled. In November his son-in-law was alleged to have masterminded an assault on a prominent friend of Benazir Bhutto.

Violence remained a dominant feature especially, but not only, in Sind, where kidnappings for ransom, which included foreigners as well as Pakistanis, were reported to be a major deterrent for potential investors. None of the perpetrators was put on trial. At the beginning of October General Fazle Haq, a controversial former governor of North-West Frontier province, was assassinated. A crime wave in the Punjab forced Nawaz Sharif to postpone a visit to Japan in the middle of the year. A constitutional amendment approved by parliament allowed for speedier and more decisive action against the perpetrators of violent crime.

Benazir Bhutto and the PPP did their best to project themselves as viable alternatives, but with only limited success. In part, this was due to their own poor record in office. Benazir Bhutto's husband remained in gaol facing a range of serious charges. The party also had to come to terms with the extent to which its base in the Punjab, the country's largest province, had been eroded by the IJI. In Sind, where it retained a viable position, its local party workers were harassed by the IJI government of Jam Sadiq Ali. Although the PPP tried to hit back—for example, with a general strike in Sind at the beginning of December—it remained on the defensive.

The government's major policy initiative during the year was a radical recasting of the strategy for economic development. In January and February most restrictions on foreign currency transactions and on foreign investment were removed. A new industrial policy was announced under which no questions would be asked about the source of invested funds. This was intended to mobilize at least part of the country's enormous 'black economy' for more productive purposes. At the end of August licences were issued for commercial banks in the private sector. Most striking of all, the government pressed ahead with plans to sell off a large part of public sector industry and banking.

By the end of the year, however, progress had been slow. There was strong resistance from the workers in the units to be privatized, and the speed with which the government sought to push the programme through created further difficulties. Few of the units appeared to be particularly attractive to private investors, although some interest from abroad was shown in the telecommunications sector. The IMF was sufficiently pleased with the way the restructuring programme was going to release the final instalment of the loans agreed in 1988, which had earlier been withheld.

The economy grew, as it had for several years, at around 5 per cent. Trade figures for 1990/91 showed an encouraging increase in exports, although in the second half of 1991 falling cotton prices were a problem. Lower remittances from migrant workers in the Middle East, and other consequences of the Gulf War, had an effect on the current-account deficit, estimated at $2,000 million in 1990/91. Inflation also rose substantially to an estimated 13 per cent in 1990/91. Budgetary difficulties remained, with defence and debt-servicing accounting for the major part of expenditure. The budget deficit decreased to an estimated 5.8 per cent of GDP in 1990/91, still above the target agreed with the IMF.

Pakistan's relations with the United States were cooler than for some years. The aid flow suspended in 1990 (see AR 1990, p. 318) was not resumed, and a visit in November by the US Under-Secretary of State, Reginald Bartholomew, produced little progress on the nuclear issue. Pakistan's leaders felt that Washington was now more interested in a rapprochement with India; indeed, the USA urged Pakistan to settle its differences over Kashmir through bilateral discussions. The Soviet Union, by contrast, took a distinctly more friendly attitude. This was signalled in particular in November when it supported a Pakistan-sponsored resolution at the UN calling for the Indian Ocean to be a nuclear-weapons-free zone.

On Afghanistan, the Pakistan government was generally supportive of the moves towards a comprehensive political settlement, although differences of emphasis persisted between the civilian government and the Inter-Services Intelligence (ISI) agency. Even after the US-USSR agreement in September to halt arms supplies to the Afghan protagonists (see VIII.1.ii), the ISI was involved in fresh mujahideen attacks.

Indo-Pakistan relations were strained throughout the year, with mutual accusations of interference in domestic affairs. There were numerous exchanges of fire across the line of control in Kashmir. However, the two Prime Ministers were restraining forces and they took advantage of the Commonwealth heads of government meeting in October to hold informal talks.

A high profile visit to Iran in September by the President, who talked of a confederation of Islamic states, indicated the direction Pakistan wished to explore in the post-Cold-War world. Along the same lines, an official delegation toured the ex-Soviet Muslim republics of central Asia in September.

iii. BANGLADESH

CAPITAL: Dhaka   AREA: 144,000 sq km   POPULATION: 108,000,000 ('90)
OFFICIAL LANGUAGE: Bengali   POLITICAL SYSTEM: parliamentary democracy
HEAD OF STATE: President Abdur Rahman Biswas (since Oct '91)
RULING PARTIES: Bangladesh Nationalist Party (BNP)
HEAD OF GOVERNMENT: Begum Khaleda Zia, Prime Minister (since March '91)
PRINCIPAL MINISTERS: Mirza Gholam Hafiz (justice), A. S. M. Mustafizur Rahman (foreign affairs), Saifur Rahman (finance), Abdul Matin Choudhry (home), Maj.-Gen. Majedul Haq (agriculture, irrigation & flood control)
INTERNATIONAL ALIGNMENT: NAM, ICO, SAARC, Cwth.
CURRENCY: taka (end-'91 £1=Tk68.00, US$1=Tk36.42)
GNP PER CAPITA: US$180 ('89)
MAIN EXPORT EARNERS: jute, fish

ACTING President Shahabuddin Ahmed, the country's Chief Justice, had been nominated by the three mainstream alliances to take over the presidency on 6 December 1990 on a caretaker basis following the sudden resignation of President Ershad (see AR 1990, p. 320). Charged with arranging 'free and fair elections', President Ahmed came under increasing criticism from some parties for not being 'neutral'. At one point he came near to resigning in disgust at the politicking of the rival parties, but was persuaded by his close aides that his departure might provoke a constitutional crisis. When nominations closed for the 27 February elections, about 80 parties and some 2,800 candidates (including independents) were competing for the 300 elective seats in the 330-member National Assembly (Jatiya Sangsad). The run-up to the election was marked by a lack of clear campaign issues and a preponderance of partisan attacks.

The election was dominated by the competition between the Bangladesh Nationalist Party (BNP) and the Awami League, both of which had boycotted the previous elections in March 1988 (see AR 1988, p. 316). The polling process was observed by groups from the USA,

Japan, the Commonwealth and other South Asian countries. In its report, the 12-member Commonwealth group described the elections as 'palpably free and fair'; other observers saw the election as the most peaceful in the country's history, even though some 15 people were killed in campaign-related clashes. Voting was postponed in two constituencies because nominated candidates died before polling day, while fraud allegations caused re-polling in four others.

In an estimated turnout of 52 per cent, the BNP took 32 per cent of the vote and 138 of the 294 decided seats. The Awami League also polled 32 per cent but achieved only 85 seats (though it later won three of the six re-polled constituencies). The former ruling Jatiya Party of ex-President Ershad won 35 seats, the Jamaat-i-Islami 18, the Communist Party and small formations allied with the Awami League 12, other small parties 3 and independents 3. The BNP also secured most of the 30 additional seats reserved for women (filled by election by the new Assembly), but not until September did it establish a clear overall majority. In by-elections on 11 September for 11 seats vacated by MPs who had won more than one seat in February, the BNP was victorious in five and thus increased its representation to 169 of the 330 seats.

In the aftermath of the February elections, however, there was considerable uncertainty about the next government, as the Awami League challenged the BNP to demonstrate that it could command a parliamentary majority. Eventually, after a promise of support had been given by the Jamaat-i-Islami, the BNP leader, Begum Khaleda Zia, was appointed Prime Minister on 19 March. She was sworn in the following day as the Prime Minister of a BNP government of 11 cabinet ministers and 21 ministers of state. The widow of the late President Ziaur Rahman (assassinated in 1981), Begum Zia became the country's first woman head of government. She faced an Awami League opposition also headed by a woman, namely Sheikh Hasina Wajid, daughter of the first leader of independent Bangladesh, Sheikh Mujibur Rahman (assassinated in 1975). The main task of the new government, said Begum Zia, would be to reverse the economic decline and financial collapse bequeathed by the previous regime.

Begum Zia made known her own preference for a presidential system of government and indicated her willingess to stand as the BNP candidate to succeed acting President Ahmed. However, political opinion coalesced behind the view that a parliamentary form of government should be restored. In a national referendum held on 15 September, the electorate endorsed constitutional measures providing for a return to the parliamentary system, with a prime minister and constitutional head of state. The vote in favour was over 84 per cent, although bad weather resulted in a low turnout of about a third of the eligible electorate. Consequent upon this decision, the National Assembly on 8 October elected its Speaker, Abdur Rahman Biswas, as the country's new President in succession to Chief Justice Ahmed. Mr Biswas received 172 of the 264 votes cast. In a further break with the past, the bulk of the local government structure created in 1982 was abolished on 23 November and a full review of local government institutions initiated.

Bangladesh suffered from both man-made and natural disasters in 1991. In early February the Asian Development Bank placed it (together with India, Sri Lanka, Pakistan and the Philippines) in the category of member countries 'most seriously affected' by the Gulf crisis. On the last day of April cyclone Gorky, blowing at 165 mph and whipping up 20-ft waves, roared across the Bay of Bengal and hit the flat, over-populated coastal regions and islands of Bangladesh. An area the size of south-east England was swamped, between 150,000 and 250,000 people lost their lives and an estimated 5 million were made homeless. The south-eastern city of Chittagong, the country's second-largest, with a population of 3 million, was severely flooded. Some 500 fishing boats and their crews were swept away and a million tonnes of rice were consumed by the sea. It was the worst single cyclone in the 20 years since Bangladesh emerged as an independent state in 1971.

In the external sphere, it was disclosed in August that nine of Bangladesh's embassies abroad had come to virtual standstill financially because of the collapse of the Bank of Credit and Commerce International (BCCI), in which Bangladesh had held substantial foreign accounts (see I.4). On 6 November, after three days of talks in Islamabad, Bangladesh and Pakistan agreed to set up committees to review the implementation of their bilateral economic and trade relations. Begum Zia attended the Commonwealth heads of government meeting in Harare in October (see XI.2) and also played an active part in meetings of the South Asian Association for Regional Cooperation (see XI.6.ii).

Relations between Bangladesh and Burma deteriorated during the last months of 1991, following an exodus of Burmese minority Muslims, known as Rohingyias, fleeing persecution by Rangoon's military regime (see also IX.1.i). By the end of the year more than 20,000 Rohingyias had taken refuge in the border districts of Cox's Bazaar and Bandarban.

iv. NEPAL

CAPITAL: Kathmandu   AREA: 147,000 sq km   POPULATION: 18,400,000 ('89)
OFFICIAL LANGUAGE: Nepali   POLITICAL SYSTEM: parliamentary democracy
HEAD OF STATE: King Birendra Bir Bikram Shah Deva (since '72)
RULING PARTY: Nepali Congress Party
HEAD OF GOVERNMENT: Girja Prasad Koirala, Prime Minister (since May '91)
PRINCIPAL MINISTERS: Sher Bahadur Deupan (home affairs), Mahesh Acharya (finance), Tara Nath Bhatt (justice)
INTERNATIONAL ALIGNMENT: NAM, SAARC
CURRENCY: rupee (end-'91 £1=NRS79.98, US$1=NRS42.84)
GNP PER CAPITA: US$180 ('89)
MAIN EXPORT EARNERS: agricultural products, tourism

AFTER seven months of studied non-participation in the country's day-to-day affairs, King Birendra had promulgated a much-awaited constitution on 9 November 1990 that converted him into a constitutional monarch and formally set the kingdom on a course of multi-party democracy (see AR 1990, p. 325). A somewhat feverish and protracted political campaign ensued, culminating in multi-party elections on 12 May, the first in Nepal for over 30 years. In February the Nepalese government impounded the passports of 46 ministers of the non-party panchayat regime which had ruled the country until the democratic upheaval of April 1990. India's Prime Minister, Chandra Shekhar, paid a three-day official visit to Nepal on 12–15 February, the first by an Indian premier since 1977. He did not fail to commend the process of democratization under way in Nepal.

In the elections the Nepali Congress won 110 seats in the 205-member House of Representatives. The United Communists got 69 seats, the rest being distributed between six other parties and independents. While the Congress polled strongly in rural areas, the Communists swept Kathmandu, where the Congress Prime Minister, K. P. Bhattarai, was unexpectedly defeated by the general secretary of the United Communists, Madan Bhandari. The new Prime Minister was Girja Prasad Koirala (65), the Congress general secretary, who formed a one-party government on 26 May in place of the Congress/Communist coalition which had held office since the restoration of democracy in 1990. Mr Koirala took several other portfolios, including defence, foreign affairs, royal palace affairs, finance and health, though on 5 July he gave the last two to newly-elected colleagues in the upper house.

The Nepali Congress also gained a majority in elections on 26 June to the new National Council, the country's upper house. Of the 60 members, 35 were elected by members of the lower house, 15 were selected from the country's five development zones and ten were directly appointed by the King.

The Nepalese rupee was devalued against the US dollar by 20.96 per cent in two moves on 2 and 3 July, thus shadowing successive devaluations of India's rupee. In mid-July Indian sources reported that Nepal was suffering from a serious cholera epidemic, during which at least 300 had recently died and a further 7,000 were seriously ill.

v. BHUTAN

CAPITAL: Thimphu   AREA: 46,500 sq km   POPULATION: 1,400,000 ('89)
OFFICIAL LANGUAGES: Dzongkha, Lhotsan, English   POLITICAL SYSTEM: monarchy
HEAD OF STATE AND GOVERNMENT: Dragon King Jigme Singye Wangchuk (since '72)
PRINCIPAL MINISTERS: Dawa Tsering (foreign affairs), Namgyel Wangchuk (home affairs), Dorji Tsering (finance)
INTERNATIONAL ALIGNMENT: NAM, SAARC
CURRENCY: ngultrum (end-'91 £1=N48.00, US$1=N25.71)
GNP PER CAPITA: US$180 ('88)
MAIN EXPORT EARNERS: tourism, cement, timber

THIS was a troubled year for King Jigme Singye Wangchuk, who exhibited some uncertainty and unsureness of touch in his conduct of both domestic and foreign affairs.

In early September the King extracted a promise from the Indian government that anti-Bhutan activity would not be permitted by ethnic Nepalese who had fled from Bhutan to West Bengal and Assam. Responding to calls from Bhutan's National Assembly (Tsogdu) to step up moves against dissenting Nepalese activists, the King threatened on 24 October to abdicate if no permanent solution were found.

The King's inability or unwillingness to travel to Colombo in early November to participate in SAARC's annual summit ostensibly caused that meeting to be postponed until late December (see XI.6.ii). In a letter of 17 October, the King had accepted an invitation from President Premadasa of Sri Lanka. On 1 November, however, he wrote again saying that he could not attend because of 'domestic problems', specifically referring to 'current terrorist disturbances in south Bhutan' and to unrest among settlers of Nepali origin.

The 1988 census had recorded Bhutan's population as 1,370,000, of whom 45 per cent were ethnic Nepalese; however, in 1989 King Jigme had asserted that all but 28,000 Nepalese were illegal immigrants. Mass protests and a refugee exodus to India and Nepal had begun in August–September 1990. Thousands of ethnic Nepalese were made stateless in Bhutan by enforcement of the 1985 Citizenship Act, requiring them to show evidence of domicile in Bhutan from before 1958, and by strict enforcement of Buddhist modes and codes.

vi. SRI LANKA

CAPITAL: Colombo   AREA: 64,500 sq km   POPULATION: 16,800,000 ('89)
OFFICIAL LANGUAGES: Sinhala, Tamil, English
POLITICAL SYSTEM: presidential democracy
HEAD OF STATE AND GOVERNMENT: President Ranasinghe Premadasa (since Feb '89)
RULING PARTY: United National Party (UNP)
PRINCIPAL MINISTERS: Dingiri Banda Wijetunge (prime minister, finance, defence), Harold Herath (foreign affairs), A. C. S. Hameed (justice), Festus Perera (home affairs)
INTERNATIONAL ALIGNMENT: NAM, SAARC, Cwth.
CURRENCY: rupee (end-'91 £1=SLRs77.00, US$1=SLRs41.24)
GNP PER CAPITA: US$430 ('89)
MAIN EXPORT EARNERS: tea, rubber, tourism

THERE was no alleviation of civil war conditions in northern and eastern Sri Lanka throughout the year. The activities of the Tamil Tigers had a major impact on south India, where the Tamil Nadu ministry was suspended on 30 January, accused by the central government of being unable to control refugee Sri Lanka Tamils and their armed groups. The assassination of Rajiv Gandhi on 21 May (see VIII.2.i) led to consequent tightening of restrictions on exiled Sri Lanka Tamils in Tamil Nadu and Karnataka. Sri Lanka was regularly criticized for human rights abuses and its relations with critical non-governmental organizations remained tense. Nevertheless, it continued to benefit from considerable overseas aid, especially from Japan.

The year began with a brief ceasefire from 3 to 10 January, during which the Liberation Tigers of Tamil Eelam (LTTE) and the government accused each other of breaches of faith. Fullscale warfare was resumed on 11 January and on 18 February 44 soldiers were killed by LTTE forces in the Mannar district. Defence Minister Ranjan Wijeratne was killed, along with 30 others, in a massive car bomb attack in suburban Colombo on 2 March. Despite denials of involvement by LTTE spokesmen, the assassination of one of their most resolute enemies marked yet another Tiger success. Mr Wijeratne was succeeded as Defence Minister by the Prime Minister, Dingiri Banda Wijetunge.

LTTE forces continued to occupy the Jaffna peninsula throughout the year, despite a major attack launched by the army in early December. The naval base at Karainagar was besieged for four weeks and only relieved on 28 April. The most important military operation, in which at least 2,000 were killed, was the siege of the Elephant Pass army base, which was finally relieved after 25 days on 2 August. This base controlled access to Jaffna, the LTTE headquarters. Another major Tiger attack was on the Defence Ministry operational headquarters in Colombo on 21 June, when a car bomb killed 60 people. As previously, there was massive reaction from the armed forces against civilians, most importantly at Kokkaddicholai in the Batticaloa district, where over 150 were massacred on 12 June, leading to the setting-up of a presidential commission of inquiry on 29 July. Tension between rival Tamil factions caused the deaths of 29 at Vavuniya on 11 March. Representatives of other Tamil groups continued to take an active role in assisting the Sri Lankan armed forces against the Tigers. Among former Tamil exiles who returned were those convicted of attempting to overthrow the Maldives government in 1988 (see AR 1988, p. 327).

Growing concern at these events led to a serious schism in the ruling United National Party (UNP). The party was very successful in winning 192 of 236 local councils on 11 May, with over half the total vote cast. By August critics of President Ranasinghe Premadasa were prepared to attempt his impeachment on a wide variety of charges. On 30 August the President suspended parliament to avoid an impeachment motion supported by two UNP ministers, Lalith Athulathmudali and G. M. Premachandra, and a former minister, Gamini Dissanayake (see AR 1990, p. 323). Allegedly signed by 120 of the 225 members of parliament (enough to secure its tabling under the constitution), the motion accused President Premadasa of bribery, corruption, wiretapping and authoritarianism. The most damaging accusation was that he had armed the Tigers against the Indian Peace-keeping Force during 1987. The rebel UNP leaders campaigned openly on these issues, holding a mass rally in Colombo on 11 September.

After considerable manoeuvring, however, the motion lapsed when Speaker Hanifa Mohamed ruled on 7 October that it did not have sufficient valid signatures. A no-confidence motion was defeated by 123 to 85 on 10 October. The dissident UNP members were expelled from the party and formed a new Democratic United National Front on 3 December. This was the first serious split in the UNP for over 30 years and demonstrated a lack of sympathy for the President's populist style and for the government's record on human rights and resolution of civil conflict. As many as 47 out of 125 UNP parliamentarians were alleged to have indicated their support for the impeachment motion, though most reneged under pressure. Many of the President's opponents urged a return to the parliamentary system of government, which had been replaced by the presidential constitution of 1978 (see AR 1978, p. 273).

Relations with India remained tense, not least because of the involvement of Tamil Tigers in Tamil Nadu, the suspicion that they were responsible for Rajiv Gandhi's assassination, the accusations against President Premadasa and the belief in Sri Lanka that India was encouraging the Tamil rebellion. The South Asian Association for Regional Cooperation meeting, scheduled for 7 November in Colombo, was postponed in the face of Indian reluctance to participate fully (see XI.6.ii). Although the LTTE denied any involvement in the death of Rajiv Gandhi, a group of seven Sri Lanka Tamils committed suicide in Bangalore on 20 August as Indian police closed in on them. The LTTE claimed that they had no interest in assassinating Mr Gandhi and that their representative had met with him on a friendly basis on 5 March. The LTTE leader, Velupillai Prabhakaran, who operated openly in Jaffna throughout the year, denied all knowledge of the Bangalore group on 12 September. However, it was generally believed that the Tigers were actively implicated, and the Tamil Nadu and Karnataka governments insisted that all non-Indian citizens should register with the police.

Relations with Britain deteriorated when the high commissioner, David Gladstone, was declared persona non grata on 30 May for criticizing the conduct of that month's local government elections. In retaliation, Britain suspended £13 million of aid. Delegations from the United Nations and Amnesty International arrived to investigate claims of civil rights abuses, in response to which President Premadasa set up a human rights task force on 23 August. On 11 September Amnesty International reported on mass disappearances, numbering thousands, and called on the government and the Tigers to show more respect for the rights of civilians.

Despite government disarray, prospects for the divided opposition parties did not markedly improve until November, when Chandrika Kumaranatunga, daughter of Sirimavo Bandaranaike, rejoined her mother's Sri Lanka Freedom Party after a rift of seven years (see AR 1984, p. 282).

3. MAURITIUS—SEYCHELLES, COMOROS AND MALDIVES
—MADAGASCAR

i. MAURITIUS

CAPITAL: Port Louis   AREA: 2,040 sq km   POPULATION: 1,100,000 ('89)
OFFICIAL LANGUAGE: English   POLITICAL SYSTEM: parliamentary democracy
HEAD OF STATE: Queen Elizabeth II
GOVERNOR-GENERAL: Sir Veerasamy Ringadoo
RULING PARTIES: coalition of Mauritian Socialist Movement (MSM), Mauritian Militant
    Movement (MMM) and Organization of the Rodrigues People (OPR)
HEAD OF GOVERNMENT: Sir Anerood Jugnauth (MSM), Prime Minister (since '82)
PRINCIPAL MINISTERS: Prem Nababsing (MMM/deputy premier, health), Paul Bérenger
    (MMM/foreign affairs), Jean-Claude de l'Estrac (MMM/planning and development),
    Noel Lee Choeng Lem (MMM/tourism)
INTERNATIONAL ALIGNMENT: NAM, OAU, ACP, Cwth., Francophonie
CURRENCY: rupee (end-'91 £1=MRs27.30, US$1=MRs14.62)
GNP PER CAPITA: US$1,990 ('89)
MAIN EXPORT EARNERS: sugar, textiles, manufactured goods, tourism

SIR Anerood Jugnauth consolidated his dominant political position when he led his Militant Socialist Movement (MSM), in partnership with the Mauritian Militant Movement (MMM), to a resounding victory in an early general election on 15 September. Despite constantly shifting political alignments and the volatility of Mauritian politics, Sir Anerood was only the second Prime Minister in Mauritius's history, his political success owing much to the voters' need to back continuity and economic success. Soon after the election victory the new government announced a constitutional change; Mauritius would become a republic on 12 March 1992, the 24th anniversary of independence. Despite an economic slowdown during 1991, recession did not bite deeply. The island continued to shine brightly compared with the dull aspect of most of its Indian Ocean neighbours; at the end of the year the atmosphere was buoyant.

The MSM/MMM governing coalition, which had been formed in 1990 (see AR 1990, p. 320), had provoked a political crisis when it attempted to bring in a republican constitution. It was far better organized for an election than the opposing alliance of the Labour Party (MLP) and the Mauritian Social Democratic Party (PMSD). Most of the MSM/MMM politicians were old colleagues who had swept aside the Labour Party in the 1982 elections, although Sir Anerood had subsequently formed his own party. The PMSD still retained support among the Creole community, but the MLP was led by the politically inexperienced son of the late Sir Seewoosagur Ramgoolam. The MSM/MMM alliance had, in Sir Anerood and Dr Prem Nababsing (Deputy Premier and leader of the MMM), sufficiently impressive Hindu candidates of the appropriate caste to counterbalance the MLP's Dr Navin Ramgoolam and Sir Satcam Boolell.

The MSM/MMM alliance carried 57 of the 62 elective seats, while the small Organization of the Rodrigues (also in the ruling coalition) retained 2. The opposition MLP/PMSD won only three seats, although they polled 43.7 per cent of the votes in an 84 per cent turnout. Under the electoral rules allowing eight 'best losers' to take seats, to adjust for ethnic balance, the opposition gained four more seats. Some calls for electoral reform focused on the 'best loser' system as an alleged anachronism, but this was not thought to be a priority for the government.

Immediately after the election the government brought in legislation to enlarge the cabinet from 19 to 25 members. Its composition continued broadly to reflect the ethnic balance on the island, with Hindus holding more than half the portfolios. MMM secretary-general Paul Bérenger was appointed Foreign Minister. Governor-General Sir Veerasamy Ringadoo was to become the first President of Mauritius under the new republican constitution. On 27 September the Governor-General announced that the government, in pursuance of its policy of making Mauritius the regional economic centre, would create a free port, extend offshore banking facilities, introduce faster professional training and take steps to ease the current shortage of qualified labour.

ii. SEYCHELLES, COMOROS AND MALDIVES

Seychelles
CAPITAL: Victoria   AREA: 454 sq km   POPULATION: 67,000 ('89)
OFFICIAL LANGUAGE: Creole   POLITICAL SYSTEM: presidential
HEAD OF STATE AND PARTY LEADER: President France-Albert René (since '77)
RULING PARTY: Seychelles People's Progressive Front (SPPF)
CURRENCY: rupee (end-'91 £1=SR9.10, US$1=SR4.87)
GNP PER CAPITA: US$4,230 ('89)
MAIN EXPORT EARNERS: tourism, copra, fish

Comoros
CAPITAL: Moroni   AREA: 1,860 sq km   POPULATION: 458,000 ('89)
OFFICIAL LANGUAGES: Arabic & French   POLITICAL SYSTEM: presidential
HEAD OF STATE AND GOVERNMENT: President Said Mohammed Djohar (since '89)
RULING PARTY: Union for Comorian Progress (UPC)
CURRENCY: CFA franc (end-'91 £1=CFAF484.50, US$1=CFAF259.51)
GNP PER CAPITA: US$460 ('89)
MAIN EXPORT EARNERS: vanilla, agricultural products, tourism

Maldives
CAPITAL: Malé   AREA: 300 sq km   POPULATION: 210,000 ('89)
OFFICIAL LANGUAGE: Divehi   POLITICAL SYSTEM: presidential
HEAD OF STATE AND GOVERNMENT: President Maumoun Abdul Gayoom (since '78)
CURRENCY: rufiya (end-'91 £1=R20.09, US$1=R10.76)
GNP PER CAPITA: US$420 ('89)
MAIN EXPORT EARNERS: fish, coconuts, tourism

AT the April congress of the SEYCHELLES People's Progressive Front (SPPF), the central committee's document for discussion began: 'The SPPF believes in the one-party system and in the socialist option.' It was therefore something of a surprise to find a motion proposed by President France-Albert René himself at an extraordinary congress of the SPPF on 4 December for the introduction of a pluralist political system. However, pressures for a relaxation of one-party control had been building up throughout the year. During the April party congress there had already been one call for a referendum on a multi-party system. The local government elections, which preceded the December congress, had reflected growing disquiet with the government, producing a low turnout and a large number of 'no' votes. President René no doubt had this in mind when he spoke of groups of people no longer prepared to participate in the national political debate within the existing political structure.

It was decided to change the constitution before the end of the year to allow the registration of additional political parties. A constitutional commission was to be elected in July 1992 and there would be a referendum on a new constitution later that year. President René also said that exiled Seychellois would be allowed to return to play a responsible role. Prominent among the returnees was Maxime Ferrari, the former Foreign Minister and leader of the United Democratic Movement (UDM), who had several talks with the President. In fact,

President René was obliged to change the constitution if he wished to continue for a fourth term of office.

The Seychelles economy faltered in 1991. Tourism, its biggest revenue earner, was affected by the Gulf War and the recession in Europe, so that the number of visitors fell to 90,000, well below expectations. This resulted in import restrictions and foreign-exchange controls, which were being gradually eased by the end of the year. Although Seychelles was listed by the UN Security Council as among those countries most affected by the Gulf War, its relatively high per capita income inhibited aid. However, at a Paris conference in February donors pledged substantial sums towards a ten-year environmental plan, designed to preserve the natural beauty of the islands. In his December budget presentation, Finance Minister James Michel noted an 8 per cent increase in the gross domestic product over the previous year and forecast a marked improvement in the economic situation in 1992.

In the COMOROS, there was some suggestion early in the year that the still fragile government of President Said Mohammed Djohar (installed after the assassination of President Abdallah late in 1989) was willing to go ahead with political reform. However, no major evolution took place until after a dramatic coup attempt on 3 August. This took the form of an announcement by the president of the Supreme Court, Ahmed Halidi, purporting to relieve the President of his post on the grounds of his 'grave negligence' (believed to be a reference to the rigging of the 1990 presidential election—see AR 1990, p. 330). Mr Halidi was subsequently placed under house arrest by forces loyal to the government. Peaceful demonstrations in support of President Djohar were marred by the shooting of some young men protesting against his regime. The situation remained tense until November, when an agreement was reached between the government and opposition parties for a national reconciliation process. This envisaged a government of national union, and the convening of a national conference in the course of 1992.

At the beginning of the year the government of the MALDIVES brought in measures to counter the effects of the Gulf War. They included price controls on fuel and basic foodstuffs (sugar, flour and rice) while transport costs rose. There were also power cuts, restrictions on the hours shops and restaurants could remain open and an obligatory 50 per cent reduction in the consumption of oil, in order to preserve stocks. Tourism was affected by the Gulf crisis as well as by the recession in Europe. There was a 6 per cent drop in tourist arrivals in the first six months of 1991, although some tour operators were able to re-route their clients from Europe. The ending of the Gulf conflict enabled the government to restore a 24-hour power service by the end of January. By the beginning of March all the austerity measures had been rescinded.

A severe cyclone caused extensive damage during the last week in

May, especially in the southern and northern atolls. The government appealed for international assistance, reporting damage to more than 3,000 homes and the uprooting of nearly 135,000 plantain trees. The cyclone's wind speed of 90 mph was the highest ever recorded in Maldives; total damage was estimated at $30 million.

During 1991 President Gayoom visited a number of countries in his capacity as chairman of the South Asian Association for Regional Cooperation (SAARC), whose Council of Ministers met in Malé in July (see XI.6.ii). The Maldivian deputy foreign minister, Ibrahim Hussain Zaki, was appointed SAARC secretary-general.

Politically, 1991 was a quiet year for Maldives. Although there was talk of the introduction of a multi-party system, the government took no positive steps in this direction.

iii. MADAGASCAR

CAPITAL: Antananarivo   AREA: 587,000 sq km   POPULATION: 11,300,000 ('89)
OFFICIAL LANGUAGES: Malagasy & French   POLITICAL SYSTEM: presidential
HEAD OF STATE AND GOVERNMENT: President (Adml.) Didier Ratsiraka (since '75)
RULING PARTIES: transitional government including members of Movement for
    Proletarian Power (MFM) and Front for Defence of Malagasy Socialism (MMSM)
PRINCIPAL MINISTERS: Guy Razanamasy (prime minister), Ceasire Rabenoro (foreign
    affairs), Armand Rajaonarivelo (justice), Col. Sylvain Rakotoarison (interior),
    Gerard Rabe Vohitra (finance), Gen. Philippe Ramakavelo (armed forces)
INTERNATIONAL ALIGNMENT: NAM, OAU, ACP, Francophonie
CURRENCY: Malagasy franc (end-'91 £1=FMG2,874.25, US$1=FMG1,539.50)
GNP PER CAPITA: US$230 ('89)
MAIN EXPORT EARNERS: coffee, vanilla, cloves

PRESIDENT Didier Ratsiraka began the year saying this would be one in which reforms on which he had already embarked would be deepened. In fact, in spite of his apparent good intentions, he was faced in June and July with massive demonstrations calling for his dismissal. The crisis blew up suddenly, between 10 and 12 June, while he was out of the country on a visit to North Korea and France. More than 100,000 people gathered in the centre of Antananarivo, calling for the suspension of the 1975 constitution and the convening of a national conference, to decide the country's political future. The President resisted the demands, asserting that there was already a multi-party system and an elected parliament. But he misjudged the strength of the movement against him, becoming the classic model of a 'bunker president', isolated and trapped in his palace while the major towns seemed virtually in the hands of the opposition parties.

Amid widespread strikes and anti-Ratsiraka demonstrations, a state of emergency was declared on 23 July following the formation of a 'transitional government' by the opposition parties, which then tried to occupy six government ministries. The authorities then arrested several leading opposition figures, including the rival prime minister, Albert Zafy. However, President Ratsiraka made a broadcast on 28 July containing several concessions: the dismissal of the government and the organization of a referendum on a new constitution. A new Prime Minister—Guy Razanamasy, said to be politically neutral—was appointed in August, followed by a new government. But this failed to make any immediate impact on the opposition, whose main demands had not been met. Opinion was further inflamed by the killing of several demonstrators by troops during a march on the President's palace on 10 August.

It took another two months of political impasse and economic paralysis before the situation was sufficiently defused for a sort of compromise to be reached. This took the form of a power-sharing agreement, signed on 31 October after two days of intensive discussion between government, opposition, trade union and church leaders. It was agreed that a High State Authority for Transition to the Third Republic would be established, whose 31 members included six from President Ratsiraka's party, 18 from the Hery Velona ('Living Forces') movement of Mr Zafy and seven from a minority tendency in the opposition. The Supreme Council of the Revolution and the National Assembly were dissolved, and two opposition leaders were appointed to head a National Committee for Economic and Social Regeneration, which would advise the Razanamasy government. The transitional period, during which new elections would be held, was to last 18 months.

IX SOUTH-EAST AND EAST ASIA

1. MYANMAR (BURMA)—THAILAND—MALAYSIA—BRUNEI—
SINGAPORE—INDONESIA—PHILIPPINES—VIETNAM—CAMBODIA—LAOS

i. MYANMAR (BURMA)

CAPITAL: Yangon (Rangoon)   AREA: 676,500 sq km   POPULATION: 40,800,000 ('89)
OFFICIAL LANGUAGE: Burmese   POLITICAL SYSTEM: military regime
HEAD OF STATE AND GOVERNMENT: Senior Gen. Saw Maung, Chairman of State Law and Order Restoration Council (SLORC) and Prime Minister (since Sept '88)
PRINCIPAL MINISTERS: U Ohn Gyaw (foreign affairs), Maj.-Gen. Phone Myint (home affairs), Brig.-Gen. David Abel (trade, planning & finance)
CURRENCY: kyat (end-'91 £1=K10.76, US$1=K5.76)
GNP PER CAPITA: US$200 ('86)
MAIN EXPORT EARNERS: teak, rice, minerals

POLITICALLY, Myanmar seemed on hold during 1991. No progress was made towards the drawing up of a new constitution and even the results of the May 1990 national elections (see AR 1990, p. 333) had yet to be finalized. While the military State Law and Order Restoration Council (SLORC) continued to protest that it was as interested as anyone in the emergence of a democratic political system, its critics expressed strong doubts, not least because of the unwillingness of the army to engage in any form of dialogue with the victorious politicians in the majority National League for Democracy (NLD).

The original leadership of the NLD, including former General Tin Oo, U Kyi Maung and Daw Aung San Suu Kyi, remained imprisoned or under house arrest, as did former prime minister U Nu. In December the acting chairman of the NLD, former General Aung Shwe, announced that the party had expelled Suu Kyi because of her alleged contacts with insurgent forces opposed to the government. Several other political parties were barred, including U Nu's League for Democracy and Peace, perhaps because U Nu's son U Aung, an American citizen, was active in Thailand organizing an armed resistance to the regime. The electorally unsuccessful Anti-Fascist People's Freedom League (led by Cho Cho, daughter of former deputy prime minister U Kyaw Nyein) and the National Politics Front for Youth were also banned for contacts with communist and other illegal organizations. The 'parallel government' formed by some NLD representatives under the leadership of Suu Kyi's cousin, Dr Sein Win (of the banned Party for National Democracy), made little progress in its efforts to gain international recognition.

International pressure on the regime remained strong, especially following the announcement in October that Suu Kyi had been awarded the 1991 Nobel Peace Prize. In its citation, the Nobel committee of the Norwegian parliament paid tribute to her 'non-violent struggle for democracy and human rights'. She, of course, was prevented from travelling to Oslo to receive the award in December. Aid from Japan and Western governments remained suspended failing any transfer of power to the NLD, and the United States removed textile trade incentives under a resolution passed by Congress criticizing Myanmar's human rights record. Myanmar's domestic affairs also affected its relations with neighbouring states of the Association of South-East Asian Nations (ASEAN) in that the United States and the European Community tried, without much success, to put pressure on them to apply trade sanctions against Myanmar. However, on behalf of ASEAN, the Philippines Foreign Secretary, Raul Manglapus, did visit Yangon on what was officially billed as a bilateral visit to form a view on the country's future.

Bilateral relations with other neighbours remained largely positive. The continual problem of refugees to and from Bangladesh led to an armed clash between the two countries' armed forces in December (see also VIII.2.iii), but negotiations were quickly opened to attempt to limit the conflict. China continued to be Myanmar's friendliest neighbour, and General Saw Maung, Chairman of the SLORC, and other senior officers paid a successful visit to Beijing in August. As trade between the two countries continued to grow, China also became a major supplier of weapons to Myanmar.

The war against the various insurgents continued unabated. It took on a new dimension in October when significant clashes occurred between government troops and the Karen National Union (KNU) in the delta in and around the town of Bogale. The KNU forces apparently gained access to the area by boat, with the result that communications to and from the region were subsequently interrupted. In other regions the army had greater success, especially in Shan state, where it solidified its control over the former communist-allied minority forces along the international border. Efforts were also undertaken in that area to contain local opium production capacity, a source of concern both for the international community and for the government itself.

ii. THAILAND

CAPITAL: Bangkok   AREA: 513,000 sq km   POPULATION: 55,400,000 ('89)
OFFICIAL LANGUAGE: Thai   POLITICAL SYSTEM: military regime
HEAD OF STATE: King Bhumibol Adulyadej (Rama IX) (since June '46)
HEAD OF GOVERNMENT: Gen. Sunthorn Kongsompong, Chairman of National Peace-Keeping Assembly (since Feb '91)
PRINCIPAL MINISTERS: Anand Panyarachun (prime minister), Adml. Praphat Kritsanachan (defence), Suthee Singsaneh (finance), Arsa Sarasin (foreign affairs), Gen. Issarapong Noonpakdi (interior), Prapass Uaychai (justice)
INTERNATIONAL ALIGNMENT: ASEAN
CURRENCY: baht (end-'91 £1=B44.00, US$1=B23.57)
GNP PER CAPITA: US$1,220 ('89)
MAIN EXPORT EARNERS: textiles, rice, tapioca, rubber, tourism

ON 23 February the military, led by army commander-in-chief General Suchinda Kraprayoon, staged a swift and bloodless coup to remove Prime Minister Chatichai Choonhavan from office. The coup was the first successful such intervention since 1977 and marked the end of a period of increasingly democratic, civilian government. The coup was the culmination of a period of growing tension between the military and Chatichai's government.

Chatichai and Deputy Defence Minister Arthit Kamlang-Ek were apprehended by the military in Bangkok as they were leaving for a meeting with King Bhumibol Adulyadej in Chiang Mai. On the same day, General Sunthorn Kongsompong announced the creation of a National Peace-Keeping Council (NPKC), declared martial law, banned political gatherings, abolished the constitution, and dissolved the cabinet, the Senate and the House of Representatives. The coup was received calmly, both domestically and internationally; many Thais seemed content that a manifestly corrupt government had been removed from power. General Sunthorn headed the NPKC, with General Suchinda, Admiral Praphat Kritsanachan, Air Chief Marshal Kaset Rojananil and Police Chief General Sawasdi Amornvivat as his deputies. General Sunthorn later justified the coup by asserting that the level of corruption and abuse of power was such that the government had become a 'parliamentary dictatorship'. He said a new constitution would be drafted and fresh elections held within six months.

On 1 March the King formally approved an interim constitution, turning the NPKC into a National Peace-Keeping Assembly (NPKA). Elections were scheduled for late 1991 or early 1992. On 2 March the NPKA appointed former diplomat and businessman Anand Panyarachun as interim Prime Minister. Anand's cabinet comprised businessmen and technocrats, bar the important ministries of defence and interior, which were headed by NPKA members. An 'asset verification committee' was created to investigate and bring to trial politicians found to have excessive wealth. On 4 March it was announced that former Prime Minister Chatichai's finances were under investigation, but Mr Chatichai was released from detention on 9 March, as was General Arthit on 16 March. Both left for 'holidays' abroad. Martial law was lifted on 3 May in most areas of the country, and on 9 May the ban on political gatherings was rescinded. On 15 March the King formally appointed a 292-member National Legislative Assembly (NLA), dominated by former and serving military officers. On 8 April a 20-member constitution drafting committee, created by the NLA, held its first meeting.

By the end of the year, political groupings such as the New Aspirations Party (led by Chaovalit Yongchaiyut) and Palang Dharma (led by Chamlong Srimuang) were becoming increasingly outspoken about the delayed appearance of the revised draft constitution. Pro-democracy rallies in Bangkok in November and December, combined with Anand's public expression of disappointment at the work of the constitution drafting committee, led to significant changes in the document. Yet hostility still focused on the role that the appointed Senate could play in dismissing a government. The draft constitution passed its final reading on 7 December. Later, the government announced that a general election would be held on 22 March 1992.

On 19 April all 61 of Thailand's state enterprise unions were dissolved. Union leaders were permitted under new laws to register their organizations as 'associations', subject to Interior Ministry agreement. A new political party, Samakkhi Tham, was registered on 20 June under the leadership of Narong Wongwan but was thought to be a vehicle for the political ambitions of General Suchinda. Ex-Prime Minister Chatichai was replaced as leader of the Social Action Party by Air Chief Marshal Somboon Rahong, who allied the party with Samakkhi Tham.

Economic growth for 1991 was expected to be 7.5–8.5 per cent. The February coup and the Gulf War helped to dampen an over-heated economy. Prime Minister Anand was complimented for the number of new laws and projects introduced during 1991 designed to streamline business and economic activity. The seventh five-year plan (1992–96) was published on 9 September. Average annual GDP growth was expected to be 8.2 per cent over the plan period, during which environmental issues were to be given prominence. New rules announced at the end of the year envisaged tighter control of the approval of large government projects and a reduction of official corruption. The World Bank and International Monetary Fund held their 46th annual meeting in Bangkok on 15–17 October.

iii. MALAYSIA

CAPITAL: Kuala Lumpur   AREA: 132,000 sq km   POPULATION: 17,400,000 ('89)
OFFICIAL LANGUAGE: Bahasa Malaysia   POLITICAL SYSTEM: federal democracy
SUPREME HEAD OF STATE: Sultan Azlan Muhibuddin Shah of Perak (since April '89)
RULING PARTY: National Front coalition
HEAD OF GOVERNMENT: Dr Mahathir Mohamad, Prime Minister (since '81)
PRINCIPAL MINISTERS: Ghafar Baba (deputy premier, development), Abdullah Ahmad Badawi (foreign affairs), Najib Tun Razak (defence), Anwar Ibrahim (finance), Hamid Albar (justice)
INTERNATIONAL ALIGNMENT: NAM, ASEAN, ICO, Cwth.
CURRENCY: ringgit (end-'91 £1=M$5.11, US$1=M$2.74)
GNP PER CAPITA: US$2,160 ('89)
MAIN EXPORT EARNERS: oil, palm oil, timber, rubber, tin

THE politically-dominant United Malays National Organization (UMNO) acted in February to consolidate its financial position through a corporate deal involving M$1,950 million. Renong Berhad, the main holding company for party assets, purchased major stakes in a number of UMNO-controlled concerns, including United Engineers. An important cabinet reshuffle occurred in March following the resignation of Daim Zainuddin as the Minister of Finance. He was replaced by Anwar Ibrahim (hitherto Minister of Education) and his political rival, Abdullah Ahmad Badawi, once an opponent of Prime Minister Mahathir Mohamad, was restored to the cabinet as Minister of Foreign Affairs.

In June Dr Mahathir announced details of his government's New Development Policy to replace the New Economic Policy which had been applied between 1971 and 1990. The new policy was distinguished by an intention to moderate affirmative action (including quotas) in favour of indigenous Malays and to lay greater stress on improved education and training. The target of 30 per cent of corporate assets to be held by Malays was retained, but without a set date, despite their having reached only 20.3 per cent by 1990.

Datuk Joseph Pairin Kitingan, chief minister of Sabah and president of the Parti Bersatu Sabah (PBS), was arrested on 5 January and charged on three counts of corruption. In mid-January Vincent Chung, manager of a company controlled by the state-run Sabah Foundation, was detained under the Internal Security Act for alleged involvement in a plot to take Sabah out of the Federation of Malaysia—a charge which had been levelled against PBS leaders in the wake of its defection from the federal Barisan Nasional (National Front) in 1990 (see AR 1990, p. 337). In May the younger brother of the chief minister, Jeffrey Kitingan, who was director of the Sabah Foundation, was detained under the Internal Security Act on the same grounds. At the end of December Malaysia's Deputy Prime Minister, Ghafar Baba, inaugurated the Sabah Barisan Nasional as an opposition alliance of five political parties. He expressed confidence in its ability to win the next state elections.

Elections for an enlarged state assembly of 56 seats were held in Sarawak at the end of September. The ruling coalition, known as Barisan Tiga, was returned to office with 49 seats. The Parti Pesaka Bumiputra, led by chief minister Abdul Taib Mahmud, won 27 seats, while the Sarawak United People's Party and the Sarawak National Party obtained 16 and 6 seats respectively. The result constituted a major reverse for opposition Parti Bansa Dayak, whose representation dropped from 11 to 7 seats.

Malaysia experienced tension with a number of regional neighbours over territorial issues. In July and December cross-border intrusions by Thai security forces engaged in anti-smuggling operations disturbed bilateral relations. In August joint military exercises with Indonesia generated friction with Singapore (see IX.1.v) and caused the revival of a Malaysian claim to an island at the eastern exit of the Singapore strait. Difficulties also occurred with Indonesia concerning jurisdiction over two islands off the coast of Borneo. A diplomatic row with Australia over a fictional television series, allegedly holding Malaysia in disrepute, was contained when Australia's Foreign Affairs and Trade Minister, Dr Gareth Evans, met Dr Mahathir in Kuala Lumpur in July. Relations with Singapore were repaired somewhat in November when President Wee Kim Wee made the first visit by a Singapore head of state since its independence from Malaysia in 1965.

The circulation of anti-semitic literature was reported in December. Malaysia was among the countries which voted that month against annulling the UN General Assembly resolution equating Zionism with racism.

iv. BRUNEI

CAPITAL: Bandar Seri Bagawan   AREA. 5,765 sq km   POPULATION: 249,000 ('89)
OFFICIAL LANGUAGES: Malay & English   POLITICAL SYSTEM: monarchy
HEAD OF STATE AND GOVERNMENT: Sultan Sir Hassanal Bolkiah (since '67)
PRINCIPAL MINISTERS: Prince Mohammed Bolkiah (foreign affairs), Prince Jefri Bolkiah (finance), Pehin Dato Haji Isa (internal affairs), Pengiran Bahrin (law)
INTERNATIONAL ALIGNMENT: ICO, ASEAN, Cwth.
CURRENCY: Brunei dollar (end-'91 £1=B$3.05, US$1=B$1.63)
GNP PER CAPITA: US$15,390 ('87)
MAIN EXPORT EARNERS: oil and gas

BRUNEI established diplomatic relations with the People's Republic of China on 30 September and with the Soviet Union on 1 October. At the end of November an air transport agreement was concluded with Vietnam. It was reported in that month that the Sultan of Brunei had promised to donate US$5 million to the Margaret Thatcher Foundation.

v. SINGAPORE

CAPITAL: Singapore   AREA: 620 sq km   POPULATION: 2,700,000 ('89)
OFFICIAL LANGUAGES: Malay, Chinese, Tamil & English
POLITICAL SYSTEM: parliamentary
HEAD OF STATE: President Wee Kim Wee (since '85)
RULING PARTY: People's Action Party (PAP)
HEAD OF GOVERNMENT: Goh Chok Tong, Prime Minister (since Nov '90)
PRINCIPAL MINISTERS: Lee Kuan Yew (senior minister), Ong Teng Cheong (deputy premier), Lee Hsien Loong (deputy premier, trade & industry), Wong Kan Seng (foreign affairs), Richard Hu Tsu Tau (finance), Shanmugam Jayakumar (home affairs, law), Yeo Ning Hong (defence)
INTERNATIONAL ALIGNMENT: NAM, ASEAN, Cwth.
CURRENCY: Singapore dollar (end-'91 £1=S$3.05, US$1=S$1.63)
GNP PER CAPITA: US$10,450 ('89)
MAIN EXPORT EARNERS: machinery & equipment, petroleum products, financial services, tourism

PARLIAMENT voted on 3 January, with only one member dissenting, to amend the constitution so as to confer extensive powers of veto over finance and senior governmental and military appointments on the President, who would be elected by popular suffrage. The Presidential Elections Bill, passed at the end of July, provided for voting to take place during the three months preceding the retirement of the current incumbent at the end of September 1993.

General elections were held on 31 August. Prime Minister Goh Chok Tong, who had succeeded Lee Kuan Yew the previous November (see AR 1990, p. 339), represented the occasion as an opportunity to secure a popular mandate in his own right. He openly tied his political standing to reversing the electoral trend against the ruling People's Action Party (PAP), as manifested in the two previous elections. The issue of Mr Goh's credibility was reinforced when Senior Minister Lee Kuan Yew (the former Prime Minister) made a public statement that foreign investors would lose confidence in the island state unless the popular vote for the PAP was increased. At the close of nominations, opposition parties, by agreement among themselves, sought to contest only 40 of the 81 seats. This decision gave the government an absolute majority before any votes were cast and ensured that the occasion had the sense of a by-election on a grand scale.

In the event, the PAP obtained 77 out of 81 seats, losing two to the Social Democratic Party (which retained a seat from the previous parliament) and one to the Workers' Party. Its popular vote showed a continued, if marginal, decline. The votes polled by the PAP, calculated as a percentage of all votes cast in contested constituencies (including spoilt ballots), comprised 59.3 per cent compared with 61.8 per cent in 1988 calculated on the same basis. Prime Minister Goh was clearly shaken by the result, despite the overwhelming majority enjoyed by the PAP in the new parliament. As a consequence, he began to reverse the trend towards a more liberal style of government which he had sought to make his hallmark. At the end of the year, the government banned the import, sale and manufacture of chewing gum. Among the seats lost to the PAP was that of Seet Ai Meet, acting Minister of Community Development, whose portfolio was given in September to Yeo Cheow Tong, the Minister of Health.

A Singapore Airlines airbus was highjacked on 26 March en route from Kuala Lumpur to Singapore. It was seized by four Pakistanis, who demanded the release of prisoners detained in Pakistan, including the husband of former Prime Minister Benazir Bhutto. The plane was stormed at dawn the next day by commandos, who killed all the hijackers and released the passengers and crew unharmed. On 3 May, during a tour of South-East Asia, Prime Minister Toshiki Kaifu of Japan chose Singapore to offer the first explicit apology to the people of Asia by a Japanese head of government for his country's conduct during World War II.

Relations with Malaysia deteriorated in early August following charges by Johore fishermen, backed by the Johore state government, that live artillery shells used in firing exercises by Singaporean soldiers had fallen in Malaysian territorial waters. Shortly after, Malaysia and Indonesia conducted military exercises in southern Johore only 15 miles from Singapore. The location of these exercises and their close coincidence to Singapore's national day (commemorating separation from Malaysia) was construed in the letter columns of the island-state's newspapers as an act of intimidation. The process of charge and counter-charge served to revive publicly Malaysia's claim to Pedra Branca, an island at the eastern exit of the Singapore Strait whose lighthouse had always been operated by the Singapore authorities.

At the end of October, in the wake of the Cambodian peace agreement (see IX.1.ix), Prime Minister Vo Van Kiet of Vietnam visited Singapore. The visit marked the end of nearly 13 years of hostility between the two governments. An agreement was reached on the exchange of diplomatic missions, while Singapore lifted its ban on investment in Vietnam.

vi. INDONESIA

CAPITAL: Jakarta AREA: 1,905,000 sq km POPULATION: 178,200,000 ('89)
OFFICIAL LANGUAGE: Bahasa Indonesia POLITICAL SYSTEM: presidential, army-backed
HEAD OF STATE AND GOVERNMENT: President (Gen. rtd) Suharto (since '68)
RULING PARTY: Joint Secretariat of Functional Groups (Golkar)
PRINCIPAL MINISTERS: Lt-Gen. (rtd) Sudharmono (vice-president), Adml. (rtd) Sudomo (political affairs & security), Radius Prawiro (economy, finance, industry & development), Ali Alatas (foreign affairs), Gen. Rudini (internal affairs), Gen. Beny Murdani (defence & security), J. B. Sumarlin (finance), Lt-Gen. (rtd) Ismail Saleh (justice)
INTERNATIONAL ALIGNMENT: NAM, ASEAN, ICO, OPEC
CURRENCY: rupiah (end-'91 £1=Rp3,717.83, US$1=Rp1,991.34)
GNP PER CAPITA: US$500 ('89)
MAIN EXPORT EARNERS: oil and gas

INDONESIA's human rights record again came under harsh international criticism following the shooting and beating by the army of demonstrators, a foreign aid worker and journalists at an anti-government rally timed to coincide with the visit in November of a UN human rights official to Díli, the capital of East Timor province. An earlier planned visit by an official delegation from Portugal, the former colonial power which, like the United Nations, did not recognize Indonesia's sovereignty over East Timor, had previously been cancelled. Though the army said only 19 were killed in the November clashes, others claimed that more than 100 died and that scores more were wounded and arrested. An official government report, which led to the dismissal of two generals by President Suharto, said that about 50 were killed. The government's response seemed sufficient to allow major aid donors, including the United States and Japan as well as neighbouring Australia, to refrain from imposing sanctions on Indonesia.

Human rights and other domestic issues were highlighted in May when the Dutch chairman of the Inter-Governmental Group on Indonesia (IGGI), the international consortium responsible for coordinating aid to the country, attempted to link future aid to issues such as environmental degradation, labour exploitation and increasing income inequalities. In response a variety of government spokesmen insisted that foreign interference in domestic affairs was not acceptable, while not all the IGGI member governments approved of the linkage. In the end, it was agreed that Indonesia would receive about US$4,750 million in the current fiscal year, up slightly on the previous year. Though new aid was not linked to democratization, pressures in that direction were building up, especially when the government used its extensive powers to place further limits on press freedom during the year. International support for free trade unions also grew as hitherto rare (and still illegal) strikes occurred in several of the new export-oriented industries.

The two-year-old pro-independence and Islamic-oriented rebellion in the north Sumatran province of Aceh seemed to recede during the year as a result of firm military pressures. Reports by July indicated that the government had imposed its grip over the towns and that most of the countryside was peaceful. There remained perhaps 50 to 100 rebels facing an armed force of about 5,000 men in the three most affected northern districts of Aceh. The total number of casualties resulting from the struggle was disputed. Some observers said that more than 1,500 had died, whereas the government put the number at 200 to 400, with only 10 army losses.

The forthcoming June 1992 national elections loomed over the country's politics throughout the year. Though it became likely that 71-year-old President Suharto would stand for another five-year term (and thus potentially extend his rule to more than three decades), other issues remained less certain. To many it seemed that the President had tightened his grip on the country's political life. In September he asserted his authority over his political machine, Golkar, by deleting more liberal and outspoken candidates from the party's list of candidates for the legislature. Though some leading army officers had previously expressed the wish that the President should stand aside, there seemed little likelihood that he would fail to receive the continued support of the politically-powerful armed forces, especially if the army commander, General Try Sustrino, was chosen as his vice-presidential candidate.

The President's efforts to attract support from the more fundamentalist Islamic elements in the electorate were compromised during the year by the government's even-handed approach to the Gulf War (see V.2) as well as by its sponsorship of a national lottery, in contravention of Islamic anti-gambling principles. Any turning-away from the President could lead to increased support for the Islamic-backed Partai Persatuan Pembangunan (PPP), although the party's decline in the 1987 elections meant that it had no chance of gaining governmental influence in present circumstances.

Indonesia continued to enjoy a good rate of economic growth during the year, estimated at about 7 per cent. However, the government's liberalization and deregulation policies evoked criticism from businessmen, who claimed that larger Chinese-owned firms were benefiting disproportionately. This inspired the President to plead for ethnic harmony in his annual Independence Day address in August.

vii. PHILIPPINES

CAPITAL: Manila   AREA: 300,000 sq km   POPULATION: 60,000,000 ('89)
OFFICIAL LANGUAGE: Filipino   POLITICAL SYSTEM: presidential democracy
HEAD OF STATE AND GOVERNMENT: President Corazon Aquino (since Feb '86)
RULING PARTIES: principally People's Struggle (Laban) and United Democratic Organization (UDO)
PRINCIPAL MINISTERS: Salvador Laurel (vice-president), Raul Manglapus (foreign affairs), Gen. Renato de Villa (defence), Franklin Drilon (justice), Jesus Estanislao (finance), Guillermo Carague (budget)
INTERNATIONAL ALIGNMENT: ASEAN
CURRENCY: peso (end-'91 £1=P46.00, US$1=P24.64)
GNP PER CAPITA: US$710 ('89)
MAIN EXPORT EARNERS: electrical goods, textiles, agricultural products, minerals

THE long saga of the Philippines' love–hate relationship with its former colonial master took another turn in 1991 when the Senate on 16 September rejected, by a vote of 12 to 11, a ten-year treaty which would have allowed the United States to maintain its Subic Bay naval base beyond the turn of the century. Having already conceded that the huge Clark airfield was no longer usable following the eruption of nearby Mt Pinatubo in June, the US government had wanted to retain the Subic base. However, the end of the Cold War and the development of alternative, if less complete, basing facilities elsewhere in the region diminished Subic's importance to the Americans, who agreed on 2 October to a phased withdrawal over three years. Though gaining full sovereignty over its territory, the Philippines government would thereby forego $203 million a year in US aid, while nearly 40,000 Filipino workers would lose their jobs as a result of the US departure.

It seemed as if nature continued to conspire against the Philippines in 1991. Following the earthquake in northern Luzon and the super-typhoon in the central and western Visayas in 1990 (see AR 1990, p. 343), the eruption of Mt Pinatubo volcano on 15 June created over 120,000 refugees and displaced temporarily half a million more people. It was feared that post-eruption mudflows would continue to threaten peoples' lives for at least five more years. On 5 November, tropical storm 'Thelma' struck the islands of Leyte and Negros, killing at least 8,000 people as a consequence of high tides and flash floods resulting from deforestation. The series of natural disasters was not only costly in lives and property, but also severely strained the capacity of the government to respond while setting back prospects of economic recovery.

Faced with major foreign issues and natural disasters of these proportions, the government was also forced to confront the sources of political instability in the country. Though support for dissident army officers such as Gregorio 'Gringo' Honasan waned, the 22-year-old communist insurgency led by the 16,000-strong New People's Army (NPA) remained a running sore. Unable to defeat its armed opponents militarily, the government adopted a strategy of negotiations with the rebels, though with little success except in isolated areas. However, the former Reform the Armed Forces Movement (RAM) rebels seemed to be losing both their political support and their *raison d'être* in the run-up to the elections due in May 1992.

The saga of the Marcos family continued during the year with the return on 4 November of Imelda Marcos (minus the remains of her late husband, ex-President Ferdinand Marcos). No sooner had she arrived in the country than she faced the first of several court cases designed to recover for the state some of the US$5,000 million she and her husband were alleged to have stolen during his years in office. Swiss records released in September revealed that $356 million was secreted in two banks in that country.

The domestic political scene was dominated by the race to succeed President Corazon Aquino in the 1992 elections, which would be the first normal electoral contest since the bizarre fall of the Marcos presidency in 1986. The old political warhorses and their parties rapidly came to the fore, especially as the President made it clear that she had no desire to stand again. Amongst the candidates putting themselves forward were Chief Justice Marcelo Fernan for the new Union for Progress; former Senate president Jovito Salonga of the Liberal Party, with Senator Aquilino Pimentel of the PDP-Laban as his running-mate; and former defence secretary Fidel Ramos under the banner of the new People Power Party. The President's party, Lakas ng Democratikong Pilipino, was thought likely to choose former House speaker Ramon Mitra as its candidate, although Mrs Aquino herself indicated her preference for Mr Ramos. The Nationalistas looked set to choose Mrs Aquino's cousin, Eduardo Conjuangco, in preference to Senator Juan Ponce Enrile and Vice-President Salvador Laurel, both near the ends of their political lives. Mrs Marcos also indicated that she would be willing to stand as the candidate of her late husband's New Society Movement.

Whatever happened in the political battles among the old elites, the underlying reality of the Philippines remained one of severe human economic distress. With an economic growth rate of no more than 2.5 per cent during the year, lower than the rate of population growth, and an increasingly large urban society (now 42 per cent of the total), the situation for many, including nearly half of Manila's 8 million people who were squatters, was approaching desperation.

viii. VIETNAM

CAPITAL: Hanoi AREA: 330,000 sq km POPULATION: 64,800,000 ('89)
OFFICIAL LANGUAGE: Vietnamese POLITICAL SYSTEM: socialist republic
HEAD OF STATE: Vo Chi Cong, President of Council of State (since '87)
RULING PARTY: Communist Party of Vietnam (CPV)
PARTY LEADER: Do Muoi, CPV General Secretary (since June '91)
PRINCIPAL MINISTERS: Gen. Vo Van Kiet (premier), Nguyen Manh Cam (foreign affairs), Lt.-Gen. Bui Thien Ngo (interior), Gen. Doan Khue (defence), Hoang Quy (finance), Phan Hien (justice)
INTERNATIONAL ALIGNMENT: NAM
CURRENCY: dong (end-'91 £1=D24,280.56, US$1=D13,005.10)
MAIN EXPORT EARNERS: coal, agricultural products, seafood

THE highlight of the year was the normalization of relations with China, severed since the 1979 border war. A visit to Beijing in August by Deputy Foreign Minister Nguyen Duy Nien paved the way for a meeting in the Chinese capital in November between Vietnamese party leader Do Muoi and Premier Vo Van Kiet on the one hand and Chinese Premier Li Peng and party leader Jiang Zemin on the other, which in turn led to the resumption of full diplomatic relations. The collapse of communism in the Soviet Union was felt to have motivated the rapid rapprochement between the two countries.

The seventh congress of the Communist Party of Vietnam (CPV) on 24–27 June was preceded by intense debate over economic and political policy. A political report and ten-year economic plan were approved. The former stressed that Vietnam would not deviate from the socialist path. The latter noted that, despite some economic successes, the country was still afflicted by high inflation, growing unemployment and poor levels of production. Premier Do Muoi, regarded as a cautious reformer, was appointed as general secretary of the party, replacing Nguyen Van Linh. Foreign Minister Nguyen Co Thach was removed from the politburo due, it was thought, to his opposition to normalization of relations with China. Do Muoi resigned as Premier on 9 August and was replaced by his deputy, Vo Van Kiet, a southerner and enthusiastic reformer. At the same time, the National Assembly appointed Pham Vam Khai as Vice-Premier and Nguyen Manh Cam as Foreign Minister, the latter replacing Nguyen Co Thach.

It was reported on 9 April that the United States had made an offer to normalize relations with Vietnam at a meeting in New York between the US Assistant Secretary of State for East Asia and the Pacific, Richard Soloman, and Vietnam's representative at the UN, Trinh Xuan Lang. The offer involved a four-stage, phased reduction of diplomatic and commercial restrictions, linked to the implementation of the international agreement on Cambodia (see IX.1.ix) and greater information on 2,300 US servicemen missing in action (MIAs). On 19–20 April General John Vessey, special envoy of President Bush, visited Hanoi for talks, during which it was agreed that the US government could set up a temporary office in Vietnam to investigate its MIAs. At a meeting in Paris with Foreign Minister Nguyen Manh Cam on 23 October, US Secretary of State James Baker said the USA was prepared to hold preliminary talks on the normalization of relations.

New economic and trade agreements concluded on 31 January forced Vietnam to pay for Soviet goods in hard currency while abolishing concessionary rates. Soviet aid was to be significantly reduced, to $110 million a year. On 25 October Vietnam's council of ministers banned imports of consumer goods and ordered that imports of strategic goods must be approved at ministerial level. The action was designed to save hard currency. During the year the dong weakened from 6,500 to the US dollar to over 13,000 by end-December. Prices rose by 32 per cent between January and June.

In March it was announced that Bui Tin, an outspoken critic of the government and deputy editor-in-chief of the party newspaper *Nhan Dan*, had been expelled from the CPV. At the end of the year the government announced the release of 16 prominent political prisoners, adding that all such detainees would be released by June 1992. Some 2,000 political prisoners arrested since 1975 were thought to be still held.

On 11–13 June the Japanese Foreign Minister, Taro Nakayama, visited Hanoi for talks with his Vietnamese counterpart, the first visit by a Japanese minister since 1976. A statement of understanding on the repatriation of Vietnamese refugees from Hong Kong was signed between Britain and Vietnam on 29 October (see IX.2.iii). In late October and early November Premier Vo Van Kiet visited Indonesia, Thailand and Singapore, signing a number of diplomatic and economic agreements and restating Vietnam's readiness to join ASEAN. Thai Prime Minister Anand Panyarachun said that he would support Vietnam's application.

ix. CAMBODIA

CAPITAL: Phnom Penh   AREA: 181,000 sq km   POPULATION: 6,800,000 ('89)
STATUS: under administration of UN Transitional Authority in Cambodia (UNTAC); Supreme National Council (SNC), representing four different factions, formed in September 1990 to embody Cambodian 'independence, sovereignty and unity' and represent the country at the UN.
HEAD OF STATE: Prince Norodom Sihanouk, 'Legitimate Head of State' and President of SNC (since Nov '91)
SUPREME NATIONAL COUNCIL FACTIONS: State of Cambodia (SOC), Khmers Rouges (KR), Khmer People's National Liberation Front (KPNLF), Sihanoukists
MEMBERS OF SUPREME NATIONAL COUNCIL: Hun Sen (SOC), Gen. Tea Banh (SOC), Hor Nam Hong (SOC), Maj.-Gen. Sin Sen (SOC), Dit Munty (SOC), Im Chhunlim (SOC), Norodom Ranaridh (Sihanoukist), Khieu Samphan (KR), Son Sen (KR), Son Sann (KPNLF), Ieng Muli (KPNLF)
CURRENCY: riel (end-'91 £1=R1,405.12, US$1=R752.61)

A peace agreement signed on 23 October in Paris by the four warring Cambodian factions, and 15 other members of the International Peace Conference on Cambodia (IPCC), ended 13 years of civil war. Improved relations between China and Vietnam, and the role that Prince Norodom Sihanouk played in the process, were identified as key factors paving the way for the historic agreement. On 17–18 October an extraordinary congress of the ruling Kampuchean People's Revolutionary Party (KPRP) adopted the title Cambodian People's Party (CPP), stressing its democratic and free-market credentials. Towards the year's end, however, diplomats expressed fears that the peace agreement was already under threat, partly due to the failure of the UN to appoint a special representative to oversee the settlement. At a meeting of the Supreme National Council (SNC) in Phnom Penh on 30 December, the parties agreed unanimously to the immediate and full deployment of UN troops.

At the beginning of the year Heng Samrin, the President of the State of Cambodia (SOC), rejected elements of the peace settlement agreed the previous year (see AR 1990, p. 347). He objected in particular to the proposed UN supervision of key ministries and the disarming of all four factions, and called for an explicit condemnation of the 'genocidal' regime of the Khmers Rouges. Fighting then intensified as forces of the KR and the SOC battled to consolidate their positions, prior to the implementation of the peace settlement. Heavy clashes were reported in the north and north-west of the country, particularly around the town of Battambang. In early March a visit to Beijing by members of the rebel National Government of Cambodia (NGC) was thought to have led to a resumption of Chinese arms shipments to the KR. This coincided with a report that Vietnamese troops were being used to stem KR advances, their first such involvement since the withdrawal of Vietnamese troops in September 1989. In April it was announced that the USA had suspended aid to the two non-communist members of the NGC.

From 1 May a voluntary (temporary) ceasefire, proposed by France and Indonesia to help resuscitate the peace talks, gained increasing acceptance. During a meeting of the SNC in Pattaya (east Thailand) on 26 June, a permanent ceasefire was agreed, this being widely viewed as a breakthrough in the interminable wrangling over ending the civil war. It was also agreed that the headquarters of the SNC would move to Phnom Penh under the chairmanship of Prince Sihanouk, who was formally elected to the chairmanship of the SNC in mid-July. To remain neutral, he resigned from his position as president of the NGC.

At a meeting of the SNC in Pattaya on 26–29 August it was agreed that under the peace settlement the armed forces of the four factions would be reduced by 70 per cent and the remainder placed in cantonments under the supervision of a UN Transitional Authority in Cambodia (UNTAC). The SOC agreed to drop its insistence that a reference be made to the KR's 'genocidal regime', and it was accepted that Cambodia would become a multi-party democracy. The five permanent members of the UN Security Council endorsed the plan on 30 August. At another meeting of the SNC in New York on 19 September, delegates further agreed that elections would be held on the basis of proportional representation under UNTAC supervision. This accord removed one of the last major obstacles to a peace agreement and was viewed as a significant conciliatory gesture by the SOC.

UNTAC was charged not only with enforcing the ceasefire and preventing any further arms shipments but also with administering the country until elections in 1993 (by taking over the defence, foreign affairs, finance, public security and information portfolios) and ensuring respect for human rights. The cost of the programme was variously estimated at US$1,000–2,000 million, with Australia, France and Britain pledging military units to enforce the ceasefire. The UN Advance Mission to Cambodia (UNAMIC), consisting mainly of Australian and French troops, arrived in Phnom Penh in November.

Prince Norodom Sihanouk returned to an enthusiastic welcome in Phnom Penh on 14 November. The return on 17 November of Son Sen (KR) was quiet by comparison. Dramatically, on 27 November, a mob attacked the Phnom Penh villa of the KR delegates to the SNC and injured Khieu Samphan. He and his colleague Son Sen were flown to Bangkok the next day. The attack, rumoured to have been orchestrated by Hun Sen (SOC), threatened to sabotage the peace agreement. The KR later played down the incident.

Against this backdrop of political progress, Cambodia's economy remained in disarray. The country's GDP was thought to be 70 per cent of the figure for the late 1960s and there were severe infrastructural bottlenecks: roads and bridges were in poor repair, and there were few skilled people to direct reconstruction. In mid-March it was announced that Soviet economic aid in 1991 would be reduced by 80 per cent to $170 million. By June it was thought that only 100 Soviet advisers remained in the country. Serious flooding in southern provinces, from mid-August to early September, caused extensive damage to the rice crop. On 4 November Cambodia rejoined the UN Interim Mekong Committee, of which Thailand, Vietnam and Laos were also members.

x. LAOS

CAPITAL: Vientiane   AREA: 237,000 sq km   POPULATION: 4,100,000 ('89)
OFFICIAL LANGUAGE: Laotian   POLITICAL SYSTEM: people's republic
HEAD OF STATE AND PARTY LEADER: President Kaysone Phomvihane (since Aug '91), LPRP general secretary (since '75)
RULING PARTY: Lao People's Revolutionary Party (LPRP)
PRINCIPAL MINISTERS: Gen. Khamtay Siphandon (premier), Gen. Phoune Sipaseuth (vice-premier, foreign affairs), Khamphoui Keoboualapha (vice premier, economy, planning & finance), Brig.-Gen. Chouммali Saignakong (defence), Asang Laoli (interior), Kou Souvannamethi (justice)
INTERNATIONAL ALIGNMENT: NAM
CURRENCY: new kip (end-'91 £1=KN1,320.82, US$1=KN707.45)
GNP PER CAPITA: US$180 ('89)
MAIN EXPORT EARNERS: minerals, timber, coffee, electricity

THE Lao People's Revolutionary Party (LPRP) held its fifth congress on 27–29 March, attended by 367 delegates and the general secretaries of the communist parties of Vietnam and Cambodia. Kaysone Phomvihane, the LPRP general secretary, called for the continued implementation of the New Economic Mechanism (NEM) and noted that, despite successes, there were still severe problems associated with poor infrastructure, health care and education, as well as growing budget and trade deficits. He was re-elected as general secretary, consolidating his already strong position, and a new 11-member political bureau was created to replace the abolished secretariat. On 13–15 August the Supreme National Assembly endorsed the first constitution of the Lao People's Democratic Republic (LPDR), providing for a significantly strengthened role for the President. Kaysone Phomvihane was elected as President, while General Khamtay Siphandon filled Kaysone's previous, and now less influential, position of Premier.

On 11–12 March the Thai commander-in-chief, General Suchinda Kraprayoon, visited Vientiane for talks with his Lao counterpart, General Sisavat Keobounphanh, and other government leaders. The meetings led to the withdrawal of Lao and Thai forces from disputed border areas, including Ban Rom Klao, the site of heavy fighting in 1987–88 (see AR 1988, pp. 342–3). On 16 August Laos and Thailand signed a border agreement to foster security cooperation. Earlier, on 29 June, the UNHCR had secured agreement from the Lao and Thai governments to a plan for the repatriation or resettlement of 60,000 Lao refugees living in Thai camps.

It was announced on 8 April that the IMF had approved a loan of $12 million to support the government's IMF-inspired programme of structural readjustment. The year saw the stabilization of the kip at about KN700 : US$1. Soviet economic assistance was suspended at the beginning of the year, with Laos having to pay for Soviet goods in hard currency at non-concessionary rates. Trade with the Soviet Union in 1991 was expected to decline to half the 1990 level. In October a ban on commercial logging was imposed in Laos.

2. CHINA—TAIWAN—HONG KONG—JAPAN—SOUTH KOREA—
NORTH KOREA—MONGOLIA

i. PEOPLE'S REPUBLIC OF CHINA

CAPITAL: Beijing   AREA: 9,600,000 sq km   POPULATION: 1,143,330,000 ('90)
OFFICIAL LANGUAGE: Chinese   POLITICAL SYSTEM: people's republic
HEAD OF STATE: Yang Shangkun, President (since April '88)
RULING PARTY: Chinese Communist Party (CCP)
PARTY LEADER: Jiang Zemin, CCP general secretary (since June '89)
CCP POLITBURO STANDING COMMITTEE: Jiang Zemin, Li Peng, Qiao Shi, Song Ping, Li Ruihuan, Yao Yilin
CENTRAL MILITARY COMMISSION: Jiang Zemin, chairman (since Nov '89)
CENTRAL ADVISORY COMMISSION: Chen Yun, chairman
PRINCIPAL MINISTERS: Li Peng (premier), Yao Yilin, Tian Jiyun & Wu Xueqian (vice-premiers), Qian Qichen (foreign affairs), Qin Jiwei (defence), Zou Jiahua (state planning commission), Wang Bingqian (finance), Jia Chunwang (state security), Cai Cheng (justice)
INTERNATIONAL ALIGNMENT: independent, orientated towards Third World
CURRENCY: renminbi (RMB) denominated in yuan (end-'91 £1=Y10.06, US$1=Y5.39)
GNP PER CAPITA: US$375 ('89)
MAIN EXPORT EARNERS: oil, agricultural products, textiles, light manufactured goods

THROUGHOUT 1991 the Chinese government sought to reaffirm its commitment to reform in economic construction, but gave no hint of any willingness to contemplate political liberalization. Its simultaneous espousal of economic reform and rejection of political change had already created major tensions in its relations with Western nations and Japan—countries on whose technological expertise and assistance it depended for the fulfilment of its economic goals. During 1991 its task was made more difficult by events unfolding elsewhere in the socialist camp. By the end of the year China was the last major country in the world still committed to the tenets of marxism-leninism (in its own case, supplemented by those of Mao Zedong thought and Deng Xiaoping's 'four cardinal principles').

The most explicit statement of China's determination to adhere to the socialist path of development was contained in a speech by Jiang Zemin (general secretary of the CCP), delivered on the 70th anniversary of the foundation of the party on 1 July. He insisted that events during those seven decades had shown that only by following the socialist road could China achieve power and prosperity. Hence the need to 'integrate the fundamental principles of marxism with the concrete realities of the Chinese revolution and national development and keep to our own road'. In the economic sphere, the principle of public ownership of the means of production and the central role of the public sector remained key tenets of China's developmental strategy. Furthermore, planning and market mechanisms, centralization and decentralization must coexist as complementary elements.

The purpose of political reform, said Jiang, was to streamline and enhance the efficiency of the leadership structure and its functional branches and to overcome bureaucratism. He rejected the adoption of political pluralism in China and warned against attempts to infiltrate 'decadent capitalist ideas, values and ways of life', emphasizing instead the need to develop a socialist legal system. Another theme of Jiang's speech was that the party currently confronted many problems in its ideological, political and organizational work. This was reflected in continuing efforts during the year to enhance cadre training and improve the quality of the 50.3 million CCP members. It was revealed that since 1982 discipline inspection commissions at all levels throughout the country had investigated more than 1.5 million cases of inner-party discipline violations—400,000 of these in 1989 and 1990 alone. Each year 0.3 per cent of all CCP members were punished, of whom about 29 per cent were expelled from party membership.

Notwithstanding the renewed emphasis on ideological and political considerations evident since June 1989, the central domestic task clearly remained that of economic construction. The official communique on the seventh five-year plan (1986–90) outlined some of the more recent economic achievements: an expanding revenue base, higher industrial production, greater economic cooperation with overseas countries and higher domestic living standards. But it also conceded that too much emphasis on seeking quick results had contributed to economic overheating and generated severe inflationary pressures. Excessive decentralization, exacerbated by a neglect of ideological and political education, had further weakened the state's ability to regulate and control the economy.

Premier Li Peng gave a characteristically ambiguous assessment of China's current economic situation. Some indicators, he said, afforded room for optimism: growth was accelerating (GNP up 6.1 per cent during the first half of 1991, compared with the same period of the previous year) and industrial production was rising steadily (up 13.5 per cent). Fixed investment showed signs of recovery, with evidence of structural improvements having been made. Serious natural disasters notwithstanding, even the prospects for the 1991 harvest looked good. There was better balance in financial and monetary sectors, while continued progress was recorded in foreign economic relations.

But Li recognized the continued existence of those very problems which had hindered China's economic growth during the 1980s. Notable amongst these were the poor efficiency and low productivity of large and medium-sized state enterprises—units which accounted for almost half of total industrial production and contributed more than 60 per cent of all profits and taxes. Their difficulties were exacerbated by the persistence of 'debt chains' (the phenomenon of interlinked indebtedness amongst several enterprises). Structural economic readjustment had still barely begun and control of fixed investment, as well as of stockpiles of industrial goods, needed to be strengthened.

The Chinese Premier drew attention, too, to the steadily worsening financial situation. Such concern was echoed in Wang Bingqian's reference to the 'unceasing' expansion of the budget deficit and his warning that 'difficult conditions have taken a turn for the worse'. Unless urgent remedial measures were taken, China's fiscal difficulties threatened to impede overall economic progress during 1992.

The existence of the widening gap between purchase prices paid to farmers for their produce and the subsidized price paid by urban residents for basic items had been a severe drain on the national budget in recent years. It was therefore something of a watershed when, on 1 May, the prices of rationed food grains and edible oil were raised by significant margins, though not sufficient to eliminate the previous gap. The impact on urban living standards was cushioned by wage and other cost-of-living adjustments. Despite a rush on state shops to stock up on staple foodstuffs in advance of the price increases (as well as some evidence of speculative purchases), markets remained relatively stable.

Agriculture was the focus of attention from a number of different angles in 1991. Most dramatic was the severe flooding, which affected over 16 million hectares of sown area and caused economic losses valued at 39,800 million yuan. The impact of the disaster was particularly serious in Anhui and Jiangsu provinces, where outbreaks of typhoid, hepatitis, dysentery and malaria posed an additional threat. Hong Kong sources even suggested that public order had broken down in some regions. Yet such was China's vast size that the consequences of even disasters of this magnitude (described as the worst in living memory) were ultimately localized. By the end of the year officials were predicting that the 1991 harvest would be little less than that of 1990.

The agricultural situation was the focus of the deliberations of the eighth plenary session of the CCP central committee, held in November. The communique issued at the end of the meeting emphasized agriculture's place as the foundation of the economy and the basis of political and social stability. From this premise it called for measures to be adopted which would enhance agricultural modernization and further raise farmers' living standards.

The year saw the publication of an outline of the ten-year programme (1991–2000) and eighth five-year plan (1991–95) for national economic and social development. This document saw the 1990s as a pivotal period in the process of China's socialist modernization and economic construction. It was the decade in which, on the basis of the achievements of the 1980s, the 'second stage' of modernization would be realized, so laying the foundation for sustained growth during the 21st century. To this end, the 1990s would witness the further integration of planning and market regulation, improvements in economic management, further structural readjustment and a major expansion in education and the application of science and technology.

The prime macroeconomic target was that the 1980 level of real GNP should be quadrupled by the year 2000. Fulfilment of this target implied an average annual rate of growth of about 6 per cent throughout the 1990s. Grain production was projected to reach 500 million tonnes by the end of the century. The principal welfare goal was to secure living standards commensurate with 'a fairly comfortable life' (a phrase which implied more than merely having enough to eat and sufficient clothes to wear). The document was explicit in its continued commitment to reformist and 'open-door' policies, arguing that these were essential to future success in building 'socialism with Chinese characteristics'. It did, however, concede that the policies of retrenchment, instituted in late 1988, would continue through 1991, becoming increasingly integrated with the policies of reform. It looked forward to steady, sustained and harmonious development: aggregate demand and supply in basic balance and equilibrium achieved throughout the economic system.

Recent years had witnessed strong foreign condemnation of China's human rights record and it was doubtless not coincidental that in November a State Council paper on the subject was published. It argued against a universal interpretation of the concept of human rights, suggesting instead that the issue could only be understood in relation to specific ideologies in individual countries (in China, for example, the most fundamental right was the right to subsistence). Nor were human rights the monopoly of capitalist countries—something to be used as a weapon in order to bring about change in other systems.

In his address to the fourth session of the Seventh National People's Congress, the president of the Supreme People's Court, Ren Jianxin, noted that the adjudication of those implicated in the 'anti-government riots' of 1989 (see AR 1989, pp. 339–40) had been basically completed. Most of those detained, he said, had been dealt with leniently and subsequently released. But 715 people involved in 'serious criminal' offences, as well as 72 others accused of having 'incited and plotted to subvert the government in an attempt to overthrow the socialist system', had been brought to trial in Beijing. In all cases, the strict legality of adjudication procedures had been upheld.

Leniency was not encouraged in the face of what continued to be something of a crime explosion in China. It was revealed, for example, that 450,000 cases of major criminal offences had been filed for investigation during 1990—an 11-fold increase over the 1978 level. Since 1985 the rate of growth of serious crimes had averaged 40.3 per cent a year.

Chinese sources reported the suicide, on 14 May, of Jiang Qing, the widow of Mao Zedong (see XX: OBITUARY). She had been serving a life sentence for her activities during the Cultural Revolution and was regarded within China as the ringleader of the 'Lin Biao-Jiang Qing counter-revolutionary clique', bearing the main responsibility for the excesses of that period (1966–76).

EXTERNAL RELATIONS. China's foreign relations during 1991 were distinguished by a characteristic blend of pragmatism and flexibility. The government faced three major tasks: to accommodate the political upheavals taking place in the Soviet Union; to resume high-level diplomatic contacts with the United States and continue the process of rapprochement with other Western countries and Japan; and to enhance its position in East and South-East Asia.

At the beginning of the year the dominant foreign policy issue was, however, the Gulf crisis. China's consistent position—even after the outbreak of war in the region (see V.2)—was that in the face of the illegal Iraqi invasion of Kuwait every effort should be made to find a peaceful settlement. Hence its repeated calls at the UN for military restraint and the adoption of measures which might lead to negotiations and Iraq's unconditional withdrawal. The Chinese government also viewed the crisis as part of the broader problems of the region and hoped its resolution would be the first step in the settlement of wider issues, embracing Israel and the Arab nations.

On 15 April the CCP general secretary, Jiang Zemin, arrived in Moscow—the most senior Chinese official to visit the Soviet Union since 1957. The importance of the visit, which sought to lend further impetus to the development of bilateral relations, was highlighted by the presence of senior ministers in his party. In the course of the talks, President Mikhail Gorbachev expressed his appreciation of China's support for the Soviet government's policy of *perestroika*. Jiang's response was to underline the importance of reform, but to insist that such changes should conform to a 'correct political orientation and the preservation of stability and unity'. The substantive focus of their discussions was the prospect that existed for further cooperation. Both sides agreed that their countries' geographical proximity, the length of their common border and basic economic complementarities all favoured closer economic ties. Meanwhile, the two Foreign Ministers (Qian Qichen and Aleksandr Bessmertnykh) signed an agreement on the Sino-Soviet border (eastern section) and undertook to continue their talks on remaining border issues, including the question of mutual troop reductions.

China's official response to the attempted coup d'état against President Gorbachev in August (see IV.2.i) was predictably muted. The familiar message was that such matters were the internal affairs of sovereign countries. Even so, following Mr Gorbachev's resumption of power, Qian spoke of his government's determination to respect the choice made by the Soviet people and to seek the further development of friendly ties with the USSR. Foreign Ministry pragmatism was again in evidence on 12 December, when a spokesman spoke of China's desire to develop friendly relations with 'the Soviet Union, as well as the Soviet republics'. On 25 December, following the decision to replace the Soviet Union with a Commonwealth of Independent States, the Chinese government let it be known that it would continue to fulfil its obligations, set out in the various treaties, agreements and other documents signed with the former USSR. It hoped for a reciprocal undertaking by the independent republics. Telegrams were subsequently sent to the foreign ministers of all the newly-independent republics, expressing China's recognition of their new status and reiterating its desire to establish diplomatic relations. By the end of the month, economic and trade agreements had already been signed with Ukraine and Kazakhstan. It was also announced the Wang Jingqing, the former ambassador to the USSR, had been nominated as the new ambassador to the Russian Federation.

For much of the year Sino-American relations remained at a low ebb. In November, however, US Secretary of State James Baker travelled to Beijing—the highest-ranking American official to do so since June 1989. The visit was made without preconditions and clearly signified the ending of the ban on high-level contacts, which had been in force since the Tiananmen Square events of June 1989. Mr Baker's discussions with Li Peng, Qian Qichen and other Chinese officials appeared to result in progress on some, but by no means all, current issues.

The restoration of ties with other Western countries, following the interruption caused by the 1989 political crisis, had already begun in 1990 and continued during 1991. Perhaps the most important single visit to China was that made in September by the British Prime Minister, John Major (see also I.6). The two sides endorsed an agreement on the construction of a new airport for Hong Kong and there were further discussions on ways of preserving the stability of the British colony during the period of transition (see also IX.2.iii). Talks between Mr Major and Li Peng also focused on bilateral relations and international issues of common concern. They demonstrated a commitment on the part of both sides to seek extended trade and economic cooperation. The improved state of bilateral UK-Chinese relations was highlighted in a visit to London by Zou Jiahua (minister in charge of the State Planning Commission) the following month. It was also revealed that Qian Qichen would visit Britain in the spring of 1992.

Reciprocal foreign ministerial visits to Beijing and Tokyo took place in April and June. Even more important was the visit to China which the then Japanese Prime Minister, Toshiki Kaifu, made during August. The Japanese leader noted that 1992 would mark the 20th anniversary of the resumption of diplomatic relations between the two countries and he looked forward to a strengthening of those relations. The most concrete result of Mr Kaifu's visit was an undertaking by the Japanese government to extend loans valued at 130,000 million yen for major infrastructural construction projects in China. But a later request for extra assistance for agriculture, made during Vice-Premier Tian Jiyun's visit to Japan, was less positively received by Japanese officials. A bill submitted to the Japanese Diet, which sought to allow Japanese troops to be dispatched to participate in UN peace-keeping operations overseas, caused considerable anxiety within China (see also IX.2.iv). Chinese protestations seemed to have some effect, in that Japan's Foreign Minister subsequently stated that no troops would be sent without the consent of the Chinese government (in its capacity as one of the permanent members of the UN Security Council).

China had long made it clear that normalization of relations with Vietnam was dependent upon the signing of a political settlement in Cambodia. Less than two weeks after a formal agreement was signed in Paris on 23 October (see IX.1.ix), a senior Vietnamese delegation arrived in Beijing for talks with Chinese leaders. A joint communique announced the normalization of relations between the two countries, which also signed trade and border security agreements (see also IX.1.viii).

Other high-level contacts which signified China's closer relations with South-East Asian countries included visits to Beijing by the President of Singapore and the Thai and Laotian Prime Ministers. Formal relations between China and South Korea also moved a step closer when the Chinese Foreign Minister travelled to Seoul to attend the third ministerial meeting of the Asia-Pacific Economic Cooperation (APEC) group. His presence in the capital provided a perfect cover for him not only to visit the recently-opened Chinese Trade Representative Office but also to meet President Roh Tae Woo. However, Qian himself vigorously denied that their discussions had touched on the possibility of the establishment of diplomatic relations.

Chinese mainland sources welcomed Taiwan's announcement of the end of the 'period of mobilization for the suppression of the communist rebellion' (see IX.2.ii), but argued that the essentially hostile stance of the Taipei authorities had not changed. They rejected the concept of 'one China, two political entities' as a basis for reunification, reaffirming their own commitment to the principle of 'one country, two systems'. There was also predictable Chinese criticism of the suggestion that Taiwan might apply for membership of the United Nations.

ii. TAIWAN

CAPITAL: Taipei   AREA: 35,981 sq km   POPULATION: 20,353,000 ('91)
OFFICIAL LANGUAGE: Chinese   POLITICAL SYSTEM: presidential
HEAD OF STATE AND GOVERNMENT: President Lee Teng-hui (since Jan '88)
RULING PARTY: Kuomintang (KMT)
PRINCIPAL MINISTERS: Gen. Hau Pei-tsun (premier), Fredrick Chien (foreign affairs), Vincent Siew (economic affairs), Wang Chien-shien (finance), Chen Li-an (defence)
CURRENCY: new Taiwan dollar (end-'91 £1=NT$48.15, US$1=NT$25.80)
GNP PER CAPITA: US$7,990 ('90)
MAIN EXPORT EARNERS: manufactured goods, machinery

IN fulfilment of a pledge made during his inaugural address in May 1990 (see AR 1990, p. 357), President Lee Teng-hui on 30 April announced the formal ending of the 'period of mobilization for the suppression of the communist rebellion'. The decision symbolized not only the Taiwanese government's recognition of the authorities in Beijing as a 'political entity which controls the mainland area'—the first time it had officially done so—but also its abandonment of any use of force in effecting China's reunification. Official mainland sources welcomed the decision, but also expressed some doubt that Taipei's essentially anti-communist stand had really changed. Accordingly, President Lee's call for unification talks based on the implementation of liberal democratic policies was little more than rhetorical.

Lee Teng-hui also announced the termination of the 'temporary provisions' which had conferred enormous powers upon the President of Taiwan during the 'rebellion' period and frozen in office some 500 delegates of the National Assembly returned in mainland elections held before 1949. He said that political and constitutional reforms would now be introduced, to provide for the retirement of these 'senior parliamentarians' and the reapportionment of seats in a new 405-member Assembly to be elected in December.

A special session of the National Assembly (8–24 April) duly approved the decision to terminate the 'temporary provisions'. The debate was, however, marred by abuse and violence, following attacks by Democratic Progressive Party (DPP) representatives on alleged 'constitutional blackmail' by elderly members of the Assembly and KMT plans to preserve its control of the political system by undemocratic methods. In the face of a subsequent DPP-inspired boycott and demonstration, the ruling KMT agreed to reconsider part of its constitutional amendment package.

In the run-up to the December elections, the DPP published a manifesto pledging the party to 'build a Taiwan republic with independent sovereignty'—an initiative which some regarded as an attempt to turn the elections into a referendum on Taiwan's independence. Unusually, it elicited the condemnation of both the Beijing and the Taipei authorities and was subsequently admitted by the DPP to have contributed significantly to the party's disappointing performance in the elections. Of the 225 directly-elected Assembly seats contested by 667 candidates on 21 December, 179 were won by the KMT (with 71.2 per cent of total votes cast) and only 41 by the DPP (23.9 per cent). A further 100 seats were reserved on a proportional basis for national and overseas Chinese candidates taking at least 5 per cent of the vote. Of these 75 (including 15 for overseas Chinese) went to KMT candidates and 25 (5 overseas Chinese) to the DPP. The remaining 80 seats were carried over from the previous Assembly.

In April 14 members of the Foundation for Exchanges Across the Taiwan Strait made up the first-ever formal Taiwanese delegation to mainland China. Talks with representatives of the Chinese State Council's Taiwan Affairs Office and other officials focused on issues relating to illegal immigrants, smuggling, piracy, travel and trade. Both sides expressed their satisfaction with the outcome of the discussions, and in November the head of the foundation made a further visit to Beijing.

During the year there was growing public demand for a reapplication for UN membership by Taiwan (which at the end of 1991 was a member of 11 international organizations under the name 'Republic of China'). Official reaction was cautious, arguing that Taiwan's position as a major economic and trading power merited its inclusion in the world body, but suggesting that such a move should be delayed until conditions were more favourable. Meanwhile, Taiwan's priority in its international relations was to seek closer ties with the countries of Eastern Europe and the Soviet Union. To this end, a large delegation travelled in May to Poland, Czechoslovakia, Hungary and the Soviet Union for talks on economic cooperation and aid. During the first four months of 1991, Taiwan's trade with Eastern Europe increased by 82.4 per cent compared with the same period in 1990.

Taiwan's domestic economic performance continued to be relatively disappointing. The rate of GNP increase, having averaged almost 10 per cent a year in 1986–88, slowed to 7.3 per cent in 1989 and fell further to only 5.3 per cent in 1990 (the lowest figure for eight years). During 1991, however, the Executive Yuan approved an ambitious six-year development plan (1991–96) envisaging GNP growth of 7 per cent a year, with per capita income reaching US$13,975 by 1996. These targets were based on an assumed annual inflation rate of 3.5 per cent and an unemployment rate of 2.1 per cent. The plan provided for a major expansion in public sector spending, from 24 per cent of GNP in 1985–90 to more than 50 per cent in 1991–96, and anticipated overall expenditure of $303,000 million on 779 projects, embracing infrastructural construction, energy and heavy industrialization.

iii. HONG KONG

CAPITAL: Victoria   AREA: 1,073 sq km   POPULATION: 5,800,000 ('89)
STATUS: UK dependency due to revert to Chinese sovereignty on 1 July 1997
GOVERNOR: Sir David Wilson
CURRENCY: Hong Kong dollar (end-'91 £1=HK$14.54, US$1=HK$7.78)
GNP PER CAPITA: US$10,350 ('89)
MAIN EXPORT EARNERS: manufactured goods, textiles, financial services

LACK of Chinese government support for plans to construct a new Hong Kong airport on Lantau Island continued to threaten the project's implementation during the first half of the year. High-level talks in Beijing, involving the governor of Hong Kong and subsequently the British Foreign Secretary (Douglas Hurd), failed to achieve a breakthrough. Only after secret deliberations had taken place between a British foreign policy adviser (Sir Percy Cradock) and senior Chinese officials was the issue finally resolved. A memorandum of understanding on the airport project was signed on 4 July and confirmed during Prime Minister Major's visit to Beijing in September (see IX.2.i).

Although the official response to the agreement was enthusiastic, local popular reaction was lukewarm in that its signature was seen by some as presaging greater Chinese involvement in Hong Kong's affairs during the transition period up to 1 July 1997. Under the terms of the memorandum, the Chinese government undertook to support implementation of the HK$16,300 million project and accepted the right of the Hong Kong government to take out associated loans up to a debt limit of HK$500 million, repayable after June 1997. But borrowing above this limit would only be possible with the agreement of the Chinese authorities. In return, it was agreed that the Hong Kong government would maintain its financial reserves at a minimum level of HK$25,000 million as of 30 June 1997. The agreement also provided for the establishment of a joint airport committee (which held its first meeting in November).

For the first time in Hong Kong's history, direct elections were held on 15 September, for 18 of the 60 seats in the Legislative Council (LEGCO). The results showed an overwhelming victory for liberal, pro-democracy candidates, especially those of the United Democrats of Hong Kong (UDHK), which won 12 seats. Allies of the UDHK took a further three seats, while independent candidates won the remaining three. Pro-Beijing nominees failed to record a single success. Many interpreted the results as a vindication of calls for accelerated democratic reform during the transition period. Official Chinese sources were more dismissive and argued that, with a turnout of only 39 per cent, the election results were quite unrepresentative. Moreover, whereas the UK government publicly supported an extension of democracy before 1997, the Beijing authorities argued that an acceleration of political reform would contravene the Basic Law governing Hong Kong's future.

In the wake of the elections, the governor's task of balancing local interests and the demands of the Chinese government was undeniably made more difficult. There were predictable demands for UDHK representation on the executive council, Hong Kong's principal policy-making body. But whether because of UDHK reluctance to accept principles of confidentiality and collective responsibility, or the authorities' desire not to incur Chinese displeasure, the composition of the council remained basically unchanged and continued in its traditional, conservative mould.

The presence in Hong Kong of more than 60,000 Vietnamese 'boat people', held in detention camps, continued to be a source of considerable political and economic embarrassment to the authorities. In October representatives of the Vietnamese and Hong Kong governments and the UN High Commission for Refugees finally reached agreement that those detainees designated as 'economic migrants' should be forcibly repatriated to Vietnam. More than 19,000 had already been so categorized and it was expected that of the 39,000 still to be screened well under 20 per cent were likely to qualify as genuine political refugees. Meanwhile, the influx of refugees into Hong Kong continued, reaching a peak of more than 1,000 in September—the highest monthly figure for 12 years.

The extent of Hong Kong's recent economic difficulties was reflected in the official budget forecast that GDP growth would reach only 3.5 per cent during 1991. Although the projection was subsequently revised upwards to 4 per cent, representing a recovery from the previous two years, it was still well below the previous long-term trend growth rate (over 6 per cent annually since the 1950s). Nevertheless, the visible trade surplus was expected to recover to HK$14 billion in 1991, with sales to China set to increase by some 12 per cent. Increased exports to Japan, Germany and other Asian countries were expected to offset an anticipated decline of 8 per cent in sales to the United States.

Although in decline, inflation continued at a fairly high level, peaking at 13.9 per cent in April. Serious labour shortages in some sectors of Hong Kong's economy were partly to blame. Transferring labour-intensive operations to the Chinese mainland was one way of attacking this problem; another was to import labour. In a policy address to LEGCO on 9 October, the governor revealed that a scheme to introduce overseas workers to those areas of most acute labour shortage was under consideration.

iv. JAPAN

CAPITAL: Tokyo   AREA: 378,000 sq km   POPULATION: 123,100,000 ('89)
OFFICIAL LANGUAGE: Japanese   POLITICAL SYSTEM: parliamentary democracy
HEAD OF STATE: Emperor Tsugu no Miya Akihito (since Jan '89)
RULING PARTY: Liberal-Democratic Party (LDP)
HEAD OF GOVERNMENT: Kiichi Miyazawa, Prime Minister (since Oct '91)
PRINCIPAL MINISTERS: Michio Watanabe (deputy premier, foreign affairs), Takashi Tawara (justice), Tsutomu Hata (finance), Kozo Watanabe (international trade & industry), Masajuro Shiokawa (home affairs)
INTERNATIONAL ALIGNMENT: OECD, security pact with USA
CURRENCY: yen (end-'91 £1=Y234.75, US$1=Y125.74)
GNP PER CAPITA: US$23,810 ('89)
MAIN EXPORT EARNERS: transport and electronic equipment, other manufactured goods, financial services

As in other countries of the world, the new year opened in Japan under the shadow of the Gulf War (see V.2). This posed a particular problem for the Japanese because of their so-called 'peace constitution' and pacifist sentiments, especially among women, which had to be set against their partnership (some would say 'alliance') with the United States and their general wish to take a larger role in world affairs.

When the allied air assault began in mid-January, the cabinet of Toshiki Kaifu promised to make available an extra $9,000 million for the UN effort, bringing Japan's total contribution to $13,000 million. But the pledge had been made without adequate consultation within the ruling Liberal-Democratic Party (LDP) and in advance of obtaining the sanction of the Diet. It therefore generated opposition in these quarters. By the time the brief Gulf ground war began in late February, political circles were in disarray. In order to work out a funding package, for which special taxes would have to be levied, the Kaifu government had to negotiate with Komeito, a centrist party whose support in the upper house was essential in obtaining Diet sanction. It was only after a month of parliamentary debate that the upper house upheld the offer of $9,000 million, on condition that it was used only for providing food for the troops. While, therefore, Japan's financial contribution to the war was generous—indeed, one of the largest—it was relatively slow in coming.

The debates in Japan left the feeling that its contribution was a grudging one, made by the government against much popular opinion. There was international criticism of the lack of a physical presence. On the other hand, Japan's technology, notably its microchips, played a large part in the war effort. Moreover, a flotilla of four Japanese minesweepers was sent to deal with mines in Gulf waters.

Government business was held up because of the Gulf crisis. The budget was delayed in the Diet; the cabinet's plans for reforming politics by changing the electoral system were retarded; and factional infighting embroiled the LDP. Local elections were held during April, when the LDP secured impressive victories in the contests for governorships and prefectural assemblies compared with four years earlier, while the Socialist Party (now renamed in English as the Social Democratic Party of Japan) appeared to be the main loser. But the election for the governorship of Tokyo created a special problem. The LDP incumbent, Shunichi Suzuki, decided to run for a fourth term at the age of 80 but could not get the backing of the national LDP, which supported another, younger, candidate. Mr Suzuki was eventually elected as an independent by a substantial majority, to the great humiliation of the government.

Meanwhile, Mr Kaifu and his ministers had been active on the international scene. The Prime Minister paid a special visit to South Korea in January with a view to improving the relationship by confirming the intention to drop the finger-printing of the 700,000 Korean nationals residing in Japan and promising to consult Seoul over the sensitive negotiations Tokyo was about to conduct with North Korea (see IX.2.vi). In May Mr Kaifu visited China to open a Japanese cultural centre in Beijing, becoming the first leader of an industrialized power to go to China since the Tiananmen Square events of 1989. He then flew on to visit Mongolia.

On 16–19 April came the long-awaited visit to Japan of President Gorbachev of the USSR, accompanied by a large delegation, including Valentin Fyodorov, governor of Sakhalin. There was substantial discussion of territorial issues, although, from his embattled position, Mr Gorbachev could not offer the return of the disputed northern islands for which the Japanese had been hoping. Instead, he gave an undertaking to reduce the number of troops in the islands and to institute a system of visa-free travel. He also proposed, in a speech to the Diet, an Asia-Pacific security plan, embracing the five concerned nations in the region. The Soviet delegation's hopes of substantial financial help were dashed, not least because a satisfactory settlement of the 'northern territories' issue had long been a top priority for the Japanese. As regards post-Gorbachev possibilities, it was noted that Boris Yeltsin of the Russian Federation (in which the disputed islands lie) took the line that the wishes of the islanders, all of them post-war immigrants, should be respected.

In July Mr Kaifu managed to recover some of his own reputation by registering successes on the international stage. He first went to Kennebunkport for further talks with President Bush (with whom he had already had a post-Gulf War conference in California in April) and handed over the final $500 million of the Japanese contribution to the cost of the war. He then attended the London summit of the G7 powers, whose conference communique seemed to be favourable to Japan's contentions, showing reluctance to offer international aid to the Soviet Union. Next Mr Kaifu proceeded to the Hague for the first Japan-EC summit (on 18 July), which issued a declaration advocating closer cooperation and improved political and commercial relations between the two sides. The text stressed the need for 'equitable access [for the parties] to their respective markets' and the removal of 'obstacles, whether structural or otherwise, impeding the expansion of trade'. In a later declaration relating to cars, it was stated that limits on Japanese car imports into the EC would be phased out by 1999.

Mr Kaifu returned to Japan for an extraordinary session of parliament to consider two items of his frustrating domestic agenda. First, he asked for support for three political reform bills, covering the introduction of a system based on single-member constituencies for the lower house as a means of addressing the question of political corruption caused by corporate donations. Those associated with factions in the LDP disliked the reforms for selfish reasons, while the opposition parties opposed them to embarrass the government. Eventually, the bills had to be withdrawn. Second, the government introduced the Peace-Keeping Operations (PKO) Bill, which was designed to permit up to 2,000 Japanese troops to take part in UN peace-keeping operations overseas. The measure was the outcome of lengthy discussions between the LDP and its centrist ally, the Komeito. But the formula it contained only reopened the earlier bitter controversy over the Gulf War. It was accordingly deemed opportune to postpone consideration of the bill until the end of the year.

Early in August the Social Democratic (formerly Socialist) Party announced that its new leader would be Makoto Tanabe, in place of Takako Doi. Miss Doi had received much of the blame for the party's poor performance at the April local elections and for its uncertain attitude towards the Gulf crisis. Nevertheless, during her two years as leader of the main opposition party she had played a charismatic role as one of the few female leaders in post-war Japanese politics.

Another financial scandal unfolded from June onwards. The 'big four' securities companies (Nomura, Nikko, Yamaichi and Daiwa) were shown to have given unfair compensation for stock-market losses to clients, some of dubious reputation. Under threat of Diet investigation, the four companies disclosed the favoured companies. Hence a large number of prominent enterprises (including banks) were seen to be implicated in the irregularities. The Ministry of Finance punished the four companies by suspending them from trading; several senior company officials resigned; and fines were imposed for the violation of ministry directives. While the government could distance itself from the scandal, the widespread nature of the violations was damaging to the money market and to government itself. Eventually, in October, Finance Minister Ryutaro Hashimoto resigned, accepting partial responsibility for the government's weakness in controlling the improprieties.

At the end of September the Emperor and Empress visited Thailand, Malaysia and Indonesia. These were among the countries that Prime Minister Kaifu had visited in April, when he had expressed 'sincere contrition at Japanese past actions that inflicted unbearable suffering and sorrow upon a great many people of the Asian-Pacific region'. This categorical apology, to countries which had been occupied by Japanese troops during World War II, was thought appropriate in view of the imminent 50th anniversary of the start of the war in 1941. It was hoped that the Emperor's visit, the first to Asia by a reigning Japanese emperor, would further enhance relations and signal a new wave of co-prosperity. The three countries visited had all been beneficiaries of considerable Japanese investment.

By the time the extraordinary session of the Diet ended on 4 October, considerable opposition had developed to the Kaifu administration. The Prime Minister's two favoured schemes—political reform and the PKO legislation—had both failed to gain acceptance. Moreover, the new financial scandal had been damaging. Mr Kaifu's term of office as president of the LDP (which automatically carried with it the premiership) was due to expire on 30 October. Whether he could stand for a second term depended on his gaining the backing of the Takeshita faction, on whose support he had relied in the past. Other candidates announced their intention to stand. On 17 October Mr Kaifu cleared the air by announcing his intention to resign. He had come to power as 'Mr Clean' in August 1989 (see AR 1989, p. 352) and remained popular in opinion polls. He had been energetic and relatively successful in foreign relations, but had proved to be weak in party dealings.

Three candidates emerged for the vacancy and conducted a vigorous campaign. The largest faction, that of Mr Takeshita, could not supply a candidate from among its own members but played the decisive part in the vote. The party chose as president 72-year-old Kiichi Miyazawa, an experienced politician who had previously held the portfolios of foreign affairs and finance but who had resigned in 1988 because of the Recruit scandal (see AR, 1988, pp. 355-7). When the Miyazawa government took office on 5 November, members of the Takeshita faction obtained the key ministerial posts.

The beginning of December brought the 50th anniversary of the Japanese attack on Pearl Harbour. With American-Japanese relations at a low ebb, the topic could not fail to attract public debate and press attention in both countries. The issue was kept in proportion because of a conciliatory statement of Foreign Minister Michio Watanabe (made in English to avoid linguistic ambiguity) that 'Japan was deeply remorseful for entering World War II with a surprise attack on Pearl Harbour'. President Bush responded in a speech in Hawaii: 'This is no time for recrimination. The war is over. It is history. We won. And when that was done . . . we made our enemies our friends.'

At the end of the year, when Japanese companies conventionally closed their accounts and planned their future expenditure, the Bank of Japan announced a cut in interest rates by a further half-point.

The object was to kick-start the languishing economy by boosting the housing and stock markets but also to assist the American economy by preventing the yen from rising too fast against the US dollar. In this way Japan sought to create an atmosphere of goodwill for the visit of President Bush to Japan's shores scheduled for January 1992, the first by an American president since 1983 (see also II.1).

v. SOUTH KOREA

CAPITAL: Seoul   AREA: 99,143 sq km   POPULATION: 43,268,000 ('91)
OFFICIAL LANGUAGE: Korean   POLITICAL SYSTEM: presidential
HEAD OF STATE AND GOVERNMENT: President Roh Tae Woo (since Feb '88)
RULING PARTY: Democratic Liberal Party (DLP)
PRINCIPAL MINISTERS: Chung Won Shik (prime minister), Choi Kak Kyu (deputy premier, economic planning), Choi Ho Joong (deputy premier, unification), Lee Sang Ok (foreign affairs), Lee Sahng Yeon (home affairs), Lee Yong-man (finance), Choi Sae Chang (defence), Kim Ki Choon (justice)
CURRENCY: won (end-'91 £1=SKW1,415.12, US$1=SKW757.96)
GNP PER CAPITA: US$5,500 ('90)
MAIN EXPORT EARNERS: automobiles, electronics, ship-building, textiles, footwear

FOR the Republic of Korea (ROK), the year saw a continuation of the international political and economic successes of 1990, while internally the nation was rocked by various domestic problems and crises. On the international level, three major trends were evident. The first was the increasingly close ties which developed between the ex-communist states of Europe (and Mongolia) with the ROK. On 4 January the USSR and ROK governments met to plan long-term policies for economic and political cooperation. As a result of this meeting and subsequent contacts, an agreement was finalized in September for the ROK to make the USSR an export-tied loan of $3,000 million. In addition, an accord on the cooperation on the peaceful uses of nuclear energy was reached on 16 April and an aviation agreement was signed on 29 May.

The most significant diplomatic event in USSR-ROK relations was the summit meeting between Presidents Mikhail Gorbachev and Roh Tae Woo on Cheju Island on 19–20 April, when a comprehensive treaty of cooperation and friendship was discussed. In addition to representatives of the Soviet central government, there were many visits from representatives of the various Soviet republics and cities, most notably the mayor of St Petersburg, Anatoly Sobchak, in early March. Because of the diplomatic and economic importance of ties with a reforming Soviet Union, many Koreans inside and outside the government were deeply worried about the Moscow coup attempt in August (see IV.2.i). President Roh stated that the failure of the coup was a clear victory for the democratic aspirations of the Soviet people.

While relations with East European states such as Poland grew deeper, relations with the People's Republic of China did not develop to the extent that many Koreans had expected. It had been hoped that the establishment of an official Chinese trade office in Seoul on 9 April would lead to formal diplomatic ties by the end of the year (see also IX.2.i). Although this did not materialize, it was widely believed that the Chinese, along with the Soviets, were largely responsible for making the North Koreans reattend the intra-Korean prime ministerial meetings (see below).

Because of its key location in Central Asia, relations with Mongolia were cultivated. A Mongolian economic delegation spent the months of March and April in the ROK learning how to run a market economy. This was followed by a state visit of the Mongolian President in late October, during which the South Koreans agreed to grant various loans to the Mongolians and to give a modern passenger aircraft for the national airline.

The second major diplomatic trend was the move towards the admission of the two Korean states into the United Nations, which had been strongly resisted by the North. In July, however, the North abruptly altered its views and the two states were admitted as full members on 8 August. Unlike Japan, the ROK had become involved in the UN-sponsored Gulf War (see V.2) without public opposition. A team of 154 military medical personnel was sent to the war theatre on 14 January, while the government pledged $280 million to the war effort.

The third major diplomatic trend was the restarting of the 'high-level discussions' between the prime ministers of North and South Korea. North Korea abruptly cancelled the fourth meeting (three had been held in 1990) scheduled to have been held in Pyongyang in February. Under great pressure from China and the Soviet Union, the fourth meeting was eventually held in Pyongyang on 22–25 October, followed by a fifth meeting in Seoul on 10–13 December. The latter resulted in an agreement on a framework for future relations between the two states, as follows: (i) mutual respect and acceptance of the political and social systems of the two halves of Korea; (ii) a mutual non aggression pact; and (iii) economic, cultural and social co-operation. This agreement promised a significant lessening of tensions in the last major flash-point of the Cold War. To underline its importance, President Roh stated on 19 December that there were no longer any US nuclear weapons in Korea (having reportedly received an assurance to this effect during a state visit to the USA on 1–3 July).

While the ROK was successful in the international arena, its domestic political scene remained rocky. President Roh reshuffled his cabinet three times in 1991, following four previous reshuffles in 1988–90. A major land scandal, which implicated a cabinet minister and possibly members of the presidential secretariat, created a crisis which rippled through to the end of the year. The death of a student protester at the hands of the police led to massive nationwide demonstrations in mid-May. In spite of these crises for the government and the ruling party, the two elections for local and provincial officials on 26 March and 20 June resulted in landslide victories for the ruling Democratic Liberal Party (DLP). The results indicated that the general public was even more disillusioned with the opposition parties, the two largest of which merged in early September to form the Democratic Party (DP) headed by Lee Ki Taek.

vi. NORTH KOREA

CAPITAL: Pyongyang   AREA: 122,370 sq km   POPULATION: 22,418,000 ('89)
OFFICIAL LANGUAGE: Korean   POLITICAL SYSTEM: people's republic
RULING PARTY: Korean Workers' Party (KWP)
HEAD OF STATE AND PARTY LEADER: Kim Il Sung, President of Republic and KWP general secretary (since Dec '72 and June '49 respectively)
PRINCIPAL MINISTERS: Yon Hyong Muk (premier), Kim Yong Nam (vice-premier, foreign affairs), Chom Yong Nim (vice-premier, chairman of state planning commission), Vice-Marshall Oh Jin Wu (armed forces), Yung Ki Chong (finance)
CURRENCY: won (end-'90 £1=NKW1.82, US$1=NKW0.97)
GNP PER CAPITA: US$910 ('88)
MAIN EXPORT EARNERS: minerals, metallurgical products, cement, agricultural products, textiles and clothing

NORTH Korea—officially the Democratic People's Republic of Korea (DPRK)—continued to suffer setbacks on the international scene in 1991 due to the diplomatic and economic success of its southern rival (see IX.2.v). The northern government cancelled the fourth 'high-level discussions' between the two states, due to have taken place in February, and mobilized its armed forces on 26 February. However, China and the Soviet Union pressured the North to resume prime ministerial talks with the South in October. The two great powers also persuaded the DPRK to reverse its longstanding policy by agreeing to seek admission to the United Nations, which was accepted on 8 August. The DPRK spent considerable diplomatic energy in 1991 on attempting to establish formal diplomatic relations with Japan, but the attempt foundered on Japan's insistence that recognition was dependent upon the DPRK's fulfilment of treaty obligations to permit inspection of its nuclear facilities.

Li Peng, the Chinese Premier, visited the DPRK on 3–6 May, and Kim Il Sung made an extensive trip through China on 4–15 October. The International Parliamentary Union held its regular meeting in Pyongyang on 29 April–4 May, providing the one diplomatic bright spot of the year. As an indication of the further consolidation of familial power and the inability of the North Korean communist system to change, it was announced on 24 December that Kim Il Sung's son, Kim Jong Il, had been made supreme commander of the Korean People's Army. In the local elections held on 24 November, it was stated that 99.9 per cent of the eligible electors had voted, giving 100 per cent approval to the KWP's candidates.

vii. MONGOLIA

CAPITAL: Ulan Bator   AREA: 1,565,000 sq km   POPULATION: 2,102,000 ('91)
OFFICIAL LANGUAGE: Halh (Khalkha) Mongolian
POLITICAL SYSTEM: transitional
HEAD OF STATE: President Punsalmaagiyn Ochirbat (since Sept '90)
RULING PARTIES: Mongolian People's Revolutionary Party (MPRP), in coalition with Social Democratic (SDP), National Progress (NPP) and Mongolian Democratic (MDP) parties
PRINCIPAL MINISTERS: Dashiyn Byambasüren (prime minister); Davaadorjiyn Ganbold (chief deputy prime minister), Dambiyn Dorligjav (deputy prime minister), Choyjilsürengiyn Pürevdorj (deputy prime minister), Tserenpiliyn Gombosüren (foreign relations), Lt-Gen. Shagalyn Jadambaa (defence), Sed-Ochiryn Bayarbaatar (trade & industry)
INTERNATIONAL ALIGNMENT: NAM
GNP PER CAPITA: US$522 ('90)
MAIN EXPORT EARNERS: livestock, agricultural products, copper ore

MONGOLIA entered a new period of political and economic crisis in 1991 as it moved hesitantly towards consolidation of political pluralism, privatization and a market economy. For much of the year the political scene was dominated by public debate of the draft of the new constitution. Although this focused on such evocative issues as whether the country was to be called the Mongolian People's Republic, the Republic of Mongolia or simply Mongolia, the greatest contention was over the choice of a presidential or a parliamentary form of government, favoured respectively by conservatives and radicals. The annual session of the People's Great Hural (national assembly) opened in early November to approve the constitution but was unable to complete its task by the year's end, although it did opt for parliamentary government with a single chamber.

Racked by factional disputes, the Mongolian People's Revolutionary Party (MPRP) virtually abandoned communism. The party's new programme, adopted at the 20th congress in February, described the MPRP as a 'people's democratic party adhering to socialist ideology'. Gombojavyn Ochirbat (62), elected party chairman in March 1990, was ousted in favour of Ulan Bator first secretary Büdragchaagiyn Dash-Yondon (45).

The attempted Soviet coup in August (see IV.2.i) shook the MPRP's fragile internal unity and upset its delicate relationship with the other government parties. The State Little Hural (standing legislature) condemned the coup and criticized the government paper *Ardyn Erh* and Mongolian radio and television for publishing the coup leaders' statements in full (as the MPRP's paper *Ünen* had done) without telling the public the truth about what was happening in the USSR. MPRP radicals were present when the opposition Democratic Forces, in an Ulan Bator rally, demanded the banning of the MPRP on the grounds that it might stage a similar coup in Mongolia. Following the collapse of the Soviet coup, a special session of the State Little Hural on 28 August adopted a law under which Mongolia's President, Vice-President and senior judicial, defence, diplomatic and government media officials were all banned from membership of any political party. Having ratified the law on 3 September, President Ochirbat gave up his MPRP membership on 10 September.

The public procurator announced shortly afterwards that 12 former members of the MPRP politburo would be tried for corruption and abuse of office. Ex-President Yumjaagiyn Tsedenbal, the former MPRP leader ousted in 1984, who had been declared by a medical commission to be too ill to stand trial, died in Moscow exile in April aged 75. He was buried in Ulan Bator (see XX: OBITUARY). In another echo from the past, a BBC journalist on 22 October reported the discovery near Lake Hövsgöl of a mass grave containing the remains of possibly 5,000 monks thought to have been shot on Stalin's orders under the Choybalsan regime (1936–52). The Hövsgöl provincial authorities later denied the story.

The 21st MPRP congress was originally scheduled for December, 'to discuss reform in response to changes at home and abroad and pressure inside and outside the party' but was postponed as the party finally split. Kinayatyn Dzardyhan, deputy chairman of the State Little Hural, supported by a group of radicals, left the MPRP in November to form the Mongolian Renaissance Party. Mongolia's largest opposition movement, the Democratic Union (DU), elected chief co-ordinator Sanjaasürengiyn Dzorig to the post of president at its June congress. However, Mr Dzorig left the MDU to set up the Republican Party in September; Tsahiagiyn Elbegdorj was made the new DU chief coordinator.

The government privatization commission set up in January decided to issue each Mongolian citizen with share certificates worth T 10,000 and to allow foreign companies to buy shares or complete properties. So-called 'little' privatization began in June with the auctioning of Ulan Bator shops and restaurants but made slow progress, and 'big' privatization of large state industrial enterprises was postponed. Privatization of *negdel* (herding cooperative) property was also approved in June, but the pastures remained state-owned under a land privatization law adopted in October. The new law permitted private and public land ownership under government supervision and leasing of land by foreigners.

The government doubled wages and savings accounts in early 1991 to meet the expected rise in retail prices as controls were lifted. Retail prices went up on average by 34.9 per cent between January and October. Prices of 90 per cent of products and services were freed, and turnover of essential goods still under state control fell to 20 per cent of the total. The budget deficit for the full year was estimated at T 1,400 million. Massive devaluation of the tugrik in June brought the official exchange rate against the pound sterling down from 10.35 to 66.00; by December commercial banks were offering T 155 to the pound. Meanwhile, registered unemployment rose from 31,000 in December 1990 to 54,100 by the end of 1991. Prime Minister Dashiyn Byambasüren expected the economic crisis to continue for two or three years 'till we learn how to live within the limits of our own potential'.

Trade with the Soviet Union, Mongolia's main partner, was cut to one-third of the 1990 level following the transition to hard-currency settlements from 1 January, and the overall foreign-trade deficit at the end of 1991 was estimated at US$40 million. Mongolia experienced acute shortages of petrol, spares, foods and medicines. There were frequent power and heat supply cuts and industrial break-downs, road transport was disrupted and local air services grounded. Newspaper production stoppages because of a shortage of newsprint led to protests that democracy, openness and pluralism were in danger.

Rationing of basic foodstuffs was introduced in Ulan Bator and other main towns in January, followed in May by meat rationing for townspeople. Only 590,000 metric tonnes of grain were procured during the 1991 harvest (a 25 per cent shortfall) and some 70,000 metric tonnes of imported flour were needed to meet domestic needs. Mongolia's herds of cattle, sheep, goats, horses and camels had reached a record 25.4 million by the end of 1990, but severe weather caused heavy stock losses in 1991 and a sharp fall in milk and butter production.

The Mongolia aid conference, convened in Tokyo in September by Japan and the World Bank, granted Mongolia $155 million in short-term aid to meet its immediate needs. Japanese Prime Minister Toshiki Kaifu had visited Mongolia briefly in August, and both Japan and the USA had earlier agreed to provide urgently-needed food and financial aid. Trade and other agreements were signed during President Ochirbat's visit to Washington at the end of January, and Mongolia was accorded most favoured nation status when Prime Minister Byambasüren went to the USA in June.

President Ochirbat flew home from Washington via Moscow, where he and President Gorbachev renewed their commitment to strengthening Mongolian Soviet relations. The Mongolian and Soviet governments agreed in February to update their bilateral economic cooperation agreements, but the big problem of Mongolia's 10,500 million rouble debt to the USSR remained unresolved. The withdrawal of Soviet troops from Mongolia continued amidst Mongolian Green Party demands that the Soviets should make good damage done to the environment. About 3,000 Soviet soldiers were to remain in Mongolia until 1992 to complete the dispatch of equipment.

While Vice-President Gonchigdorj was in Beijing in June, Mongolian and PRC officials signed agreements on the opening of eight new border crossing points. President Yang Shangkun paid a state visit to Mongolia in August—the first by a PRC head of state—during which agreements were concluded on the transit of Mongolian goods through Tianjin port and on postponing Mongolia's debt repayments to China. On the other hand, students from China studying in Mongolia were withdrawn. A visit by the Dalai Lama to Mongolia as the guest of Gandantegchinlen monastery, postponed earlier under pressure from Beijing, took place in September. He told Mongolian Buddhists that Tibet's struggle for independence was encouraged by Mongolia's efforts to throw off communism. The Ministry of Foreign Relations emphasized that the visit was not at government invitation.

X AUSTRALASIA AND SOUTH PACIFIC

1. AUSTRALIA—PAPUA NEW GUINEA

i. AUSTRALIA

CAPITAL: Canberra AREA: 7,687,000 sq km POPULATION: 16,800,000 ('89)
OFFICIAL LANGUAGE: English POLITICAL SYSTEM: federal parliamentary democracy
HEAD OF STATE: Queen Elizabeth II GOVERNOR-GENERAL: William Hayden
RULING PARTY: Australian Labor Party (ALP)
HEAD OF GOVERNMENT: Paul Keating, Prime Minister (since Dec '91)
PRINCIPAL MINISTERS: Gareth Evans (foreign affairs), John Dawkins (treasurer), Ralph Willis (finance), Neal Blewett (trade & overseas development), John Button (industry), Robert Ray (defence), Michael Duffy (attorney-general)
INTERNATIONAL ALIGNMENT: ANZUS, OECD, Cwth.
CURRENCY: Australian dollar (end-'91 £1=A$2.46, US$1=A$1.32)
GNP PER CAPITA: US$14,360 ('89)
MAIN EXPORT EARNERS: minerals, meat and agricultural products, basic manufactures

THE Australian economy remained depressed throughout the year, with unemployment exceeding 10 per cent, drought in many rural areas and a growing realization that the economic policies of the previous decade had not succeeded. The Australian Labor Party (ALP), as the government nationally and in five of the states, saw its popularity waning. In December it removed Bob Hawke from the leadership and as Prime Minister, replacing him by Paul Keating. Corporate Australia remained troubled by instability, media attention being focused for much of the year on the fate of the Fairfax organization (see AR 1990, p. 374). This issue, which involved foreign ownership and cross-media ownership regulations, was finally resolved on 16 December in favour of Conrad Black's Tourang consortium, from which Kerry Packer had been forced to withdraw in defence of his interests in other media. Debate raged throughout the year, leading to a parliamentary inquiry, the intervention of the Australian Broadcasting Tribunal and the publication of a charter of independence by Fairfax journalists. The ALP leadership was generally seen as hostile to the Fairfax press and persuaded the party to modify its previous opposition to overseas involvement.

There were no changes in political control in the states, although in the Australian Capital Territory, where no party had a majority, the Liberals were replaced by the ALP on 6 June without an election. To the surprise of Liberal premier Nick Greiner of New South Wales, his coalition government with the Nationals was almost defeated in the state election of 25 May. The election was called early because of the blocking of legislation in the ALP-dominated upper house, aimed at ending compulsory unionism. The results for the 99-member legislative assembly (lower house) gave the Liberal-National coalition 49 seats (compared with 60 previously), the ALP 46 and others 4. In the upper house the new balance of power rested with the Democrats and the Christian fundamentalist team of Rev Fred Nile. Legal challenges to some lower house results left the premier waiting on a by-election in the new year to determine the viability of his majority. His position was further eroded by the defection of a former Liberal minister, Dr Terry Metherell, on 2 October.

Elsewhere in state politics, the alliance between the ALP and the Greens in Tasmania (see AR 1989, p. 359) disintegrated, although the ALP struggled on as a minority administration. Tasmanian Liberal leader Robin Gray was severely criticized by an inquiry into the bribery scandal surrounding the previous election (see AR 1989, p. 359; and 1990, p. 375). He was replaced by Ray Groom on 17 December. In Victoria and Western Australia, official inquiries into allegations surrounding public and private business scandals continued throughout the year without resolution. In South Australia, the State Bank reported severe losses on 10 February.

National government was dominated by the state of the economy and the associated discontent within the ALP about its leadership and direction. The Liberal opposition, led by professional economist John Hewson, was able to gain considerable advantage but this was not tested at elections. The ALP deputy leader and national Treasurer, Paul Keating, broke his alliance with Mr Hawke and challenged for the leadership, claiming that Mr Hawke had promised this to him before the 1990 election. His initial challenge failed by 66 votes to 44 within the parliamentary party on 3 June. Mr Keating retired to the back benches and was replaced as Treasurer by John Kerin and as deputy leader by Brian Howe. A consistent media campaign kept the leadership issue open, however, and Mr Hawke placed his leadership before the party on 19 December, losing by 51 votes to 56. Mr Hawke retained the support of most of the ALP left, based in Victoria, while Mr Keating was supported by the New South Wales right. There was little ideological difference between the two and the party's elaborate factional system was thrown into disarray by the contest.

Keating reshuffled the government without drastically altering its personnel. The treasurership was taken by John Dawkins, finance by Ralph Willis, employment and education by Kim Beazley and transport and communications by Senator Graham Richardson. Other major ministers remained in place and Mr Howe, from the left, remained deputy leader. Although this was the first occasion on which the ALP had removed a prime minister, there were no immediate repercussions within the party or the trade unions. There was no immediate response to the leadership change in opinion polls, which showed the ALP consistently behind the opposition. Earlier, the ALP had celebrated its centenary in the shadow of the leadership struggle and the worsening economy. Its biennial conference at Hobart on 24 June endorsed the aim of establishing a republic by 1 January 2001 and approved the creation of a public inquiry into print media ownership. It also continued to support a maximum of three uranium mines, despite pressure from the mining industry and from developmentalists within the government.

In other political parties, the Australian Democrats removed their leader, Senator Janet Powell, and replaced her with Senator John Coulter. The major disagreement within the party was over Senator Powell's leadership style and public image, though Senator Coulter was more strongly identified with conservationist and anti-immigration positions. In Queensland, the National and the Liberal parties moved towards an electoral alliance as they searched for a viable opposition to the dominant ALP. On 11 November the Queensland Liberals replaced their parliamentary leader, Denver Beanland, with Joan Sheldon, a new parliamentarian. Sallyanne Atkinson, the Liberal mayor of Brisbane, Australia's largest local authority, was unexpectedly defeated by the ALP in the 23 March elections.

The Democrats worked on a strategy of alliance with the various Green parties throughout the year, but this was not effectively tested in elections. The conservation movement became disillusioned with the ALP over the issue of resource guarantee legislation at the national and state levels. This attempted to guarantee forestry access on a controlled basis and went beyond the strict limitations which the Green movement had fought for in the past. Despite this shift, Prime Minister Hawke persuaded cabinet on 18 June to prevent mining at Coronation Hill in the Northern Territory. This decision was influenced as much by the claim that the site was sacred to the Jawoyn Aborigines as by conservationist concerns about the adjacent Kakadu national park. The Democrats, alone of the four parties in national politics, continued uncritical support of the conservationists.

The main energies of the national government were directed towards the state of the economy. The opposition Liberal and National parties unveiled their economic strategy, 'Fightback', on 21 November. It proposed to halve unemployment, produce 2 million jobs and repay A$13,000 million in public debt. This would be achieved through a 15 per cent goods and services tax, a 30 per cent cut in income tax and the abolition or reduction of other taxes. Commonwealth corporations would be privatized and there would be cuts in wasteful public expenditure. The labour market would be reformed, union influence reduced and private health insurance made more central. By the end of the century tariffs would be reduced to 'negligible levels'. In the meantime, immigration levels would be cut and there would be a greater emphasis on skilled migration.

The changes to tertiary education begun in 1989 were completed, giving

Australia 36 universities in all, twice the number of the previous decade. The government was frustrated in its proposed merger between the Australian National University and the University of Canberra, being unable to secure the passage of legislation in the Senate. The merger which created the Victoria University of Technology in Melbourne also fell apart, with its largest component making alternative arrangements. Universities faced increased enrolments and overcrowding, which many attributed to the effect of youth unemployment.

Of the failed entrepreneurs of the previous decade, Christopher Skase remained in Spain despite repeated invitations to return to face bankruptcy proceedings. Alan Bond was finally served with a bankruptcy notice on 30 December, issued by a consortium of banks (see AR 1989, p. 360). Court proceedings against the former Queensland premier, Sir Joh Bjelke-Petersen, were aborted by the failure of a jury to agree on perjury and corruption charges on 20 October. However, the former Queensland police commissioner, Sir Terence Lewis, was sentenced to 14 years' imprisonment (on 5 August) for corruption. In Canberra, the long inquest into the 1989 murder of police commissioner Colin Winchester concluded on 8 November without being able to establish the identity of the murderer or any motive. John Friedrich, director of the National Safety Council of Victoria, committed suicide on 26 July, frustrating attempts to unravel the complex story of its collapse (see AR 1989, p. 360). News Corporation, owned by Australian-born Rupert Murdoch, was successful on 1 February in rescheduling its debts over a three-year period, thus avoiding problems which might have had severe repercussions on the Australian share market and on media ownership.

The commission of inquiry into Aboriginal deaths in custody reported on 9 May with extensive proposals for changes in arrest and detention procedures. The lengthy report also found evidence of police abuses and urged reconciliation between white and Aboriginal Australia. This aim was endorsed by the Canberra parliament on 5 June with the setting up of a Council for Aboriginal Reconciliation. The Aboriginal and Torres Strait Islander Commission came into operation and elections were held for its regional representatives on 1 March. Aboriginal and immigrant affairs remained relatively quiet, although there were cases of attacks on mosques and synagogues during the Gulf War period and of tension between Serbs and Croats as the war in Yugoslavia intensified. Immigration intake continued to drop, particularly from New Zealand, with net settlement falling below 100,000 for the first time in five years.

Airline deregulation brought a spate of reduced fares and the launch of a third major airline, Compass, which, however, abruptly ceased business through lack of funds and went into provisional liquidation on 20 December. This collapse prompted a popular response in favour of

Compass and against the two established airlines, which were accused of sabotaging its efforts by limiting access at major airports. The national government refused to extend tax concessions to the proposed high-speed train between Sydney and Melbourne, with the result that the project was abandoned by its sponsors. The location of the proposed 'multifunctional polis' was finally agreed in May as Adelaide, though its future remained dependent on Japanese support and interest from other overseas investors.

In foreign policy, Australia continued to press within GATT for the liberalization of world trade, especially as it affected exports of primary produce. The export enhancement schemes of the United States were a particular grievance. Sporting links with South Africa were resumed and the severed air connection restored. The initiative of Foreign Minister Gareth Evans in Cambodia proved fruitful and he participated in signing an agreement between the conflicting parties in Paris in October (see IX.1.ix). Relations with Malaysia and Indonesia remained strained, mainly because of, respectively, critical attitudes in the Australian media and reaction to the military attack on civilians at Díli, East Timor, in November (see IX.1.vi). Good working relations were resumed with China after the downgrading of the previous two years (see AR 1989, p. 357). The active participation of Australia in the Gulf War (see V.2) produced some minor demonstrations and some dissension from the left of the ALP and the Democrats, but seemed otherwise to have broad popular approval and bipartisan support. There was no Australian loss of life.

The massacre of eight people by a gunman at Strathfield in suburban Sydney on 19 August reopened the debate about more restrictive and nationally uniform gun laws, which New South Wales resisted. A series of restrictive measures was agreed at the police ministers' conference on 23 October.

Professor Manning Clark died on 23 May at the age of 76. He was one of the most influential of Australian historians and pioneered the teaching of Australian history. Cardinal Sir James Freeman, the former Catholic archbishop of Sydney, died on 16 March, aged 83. The former Queensland minister, Russell Hinze, died on 29 June and legal proceedings against him accordingly ceased (see AR 1990, p. 375).

ii. PAPUA NEW GUINEA

CAPITAL: Port Moresby AREA: 463,000 sq km POPULATION: 3,800,000 ('89)
OFFICIAL LANGUAGES: Pidgin, Motu, English
POLITICAL SYSTEM: parliamentary democracy
HEAD OF STATE: Queen Elizabeth II GOVERNOR-GENERAL: Wiwa Korowi
RULING PARTIES: coalition headed by Pangu Pati (PP)
HEAD OF GOVERNMENT: Rabbie Namaliu, Prime Minister (since July '88)
PRINCIPAL MINISTERS: Arnold Marsipal (defence), Michael Somare (foreign affairs), Bernard Narakobi (justice), Karl Stack (interior), Matthew Bendumb (home affairs), Paul Pora (finance & planning)
INTERNATIONAL ALIGNMENT: ACP, Cwth.
CURRENCY: kina (end-'91 £1=K1.78, US$1=K0.95)
GNP PER CAPITA: US$890 ('89)
MAIN EXPORT EARNERS: copper, coffee, palm oil, cocoa

THE year brought little respite from the complex of political, economic and social problems which was increasingly characteristic of Papua New Guinea's second decade of independence. The continuing secession crisis on the island of Bougainville, persistently high levels of crime and public disorder, and the relentless self-seeking of political leaders combined to place further pressure on the country's already enfeebled parliamentary democracy.

The stalemate over Bougainville (see AR 1990, p. 377) continued throughout the year, despite apparent agreement being reached in talks held in the Solomon Islands capital of Honiara in January. The absence of a clear leadership structure among the rebels and their lack of articulated demands, beyond vague claims of independence, made effective negotiations difficult. In the meantime, the physical hardships faced by the virtually blockaded islanders continued to mount. The loss of income from the Panguna copper mine remained a major problem for the national economy despite the continued growth of the mining sector in other parts of the country.

The workings of parliament and the behaviour of parliamentarians continued to occupy public attention in 1991. In May, in a move insensitive even by their own remarkable standards over the years, MPs voted themselves large salary increases in the midst of the most serious economic crisis since independence. Protests by students degenerated into rioting. The subsequent student strike led to the closure of the University of Papua New Guinea for the remainder of the year.

In July parliament seized the constitutional nettle which had been a major source of instability since the early 1980s: the virtually unrestricted opportunity available to the opposition to remove a government by a vote of no-confidence. Legislation due to come into effect after the 1992 national elections provided for an extension of the 'grace period', in which a new government was immune from such challenges, from six to 18 months.

A major constitutional crisis was narrowly averted at the beginning of October by the resignation of the governor-general, Sir Vincent

Eri. At the root of the problem was one of Papua New Guinea's most controversial politicians, Deputy Prime Minister Ted Diro (see AR 1989, p. 362; 1990, p. 378). In September Mr Diro was finally found guilty by a special tribunal of 81 counts of corruption dating back several years. The tribunal called for his removal from the government and disqualification from public office for three years. The formal responsibility for Mr Diro's dismissal, however, lay with Sir Vincent Eri, a fellow coastal Papuan and political ally in the People's Action Party. Sir Vincent refused to act, despite demands from both Prime Minister Rabbie Namaliu and opposition leader Paias Wingti that he should do so. Mr Namaliu was therefore forced to dispatch a special envoy to London to petition the Queen (formally head of state) for the governor-general's dismissal. This drastic resort was avoided only at the last moment when Sir Vincent bowed to the inevitable and stood down on 1 October.

The country's frighteningly high crime rate remained a major problem in 1991. A night-time curfew was imposed on the capital, Port Moresby, and other urban centres in an attempt to repeat the temporary success of this expedient in 1985. In August parliament voted to introduce the death penalty for murder, although it was widely felt that executions were unlikely to be carried out in a society so rooted in the humanistic Melanesian traditions of negotiation and concession.

2. NEW ZEALAND—SOUTH PACIFIC

i. NEW ZEALAND

CAPITAL: Wellington   AREA: 270,000 sq km   POPULATION: 3,300,000 ('89)
OFFICIAL LANGUAGE: English   POLITICAL SYSTEM: parliamentary democracy
HEAD OF STATE: Queen Elizabeth II   GOVERNOR-GENERAL: Dame Catherine Tizard
RULING PARTY: National Party (NP)
HEAD OF GOVERNMENT: Jim Bolger, Prime Minister (since Oct '90)
PRINCIPAL MINISTERS: Don McKinnon (deputy premier, foreign affairs), Ruth Richardson (finance), Paul East (attorney-general), Warren Cooper (defence), Doug Graham (justice), Philip Burdon (trade & industry)
INTERNATIONAL ALIGNMENT: ANZUS (suspended), OECD, Cwth.
CURRENCY: New Zealand dollar (end-'91 £1=NZ$3.46, US$1=NZ$1.85)
GNP PER CAPITA: US$12,070 ('89)
MAIN EXPORT EARNERS: meat and meat products, wool, dairy products

THE country was dominated by continuing and deep economic recession in 1991. Although the annual rate of inflation fell to a 28-year low of 2.2 per cent, the contraction was such as to stunt growth and aggravate downturns in key sectors. Construction of all types fell sharply from an already low level, manufacturing output was down and new investment was at its lowest level for a decade. Sharply lower interest rates, which fell to 8 per cent for 90-day money, saw householders, farmers and businesses use these cuts to repay debt or employ slack capacity, ahead of new investment for job creation. The balance of payments improved through a weakening of the local currency, better returns for manufactured exports and declining demand for imports, but serious international trading uncertainties remained. They included a clouded future for New Zealand market access to Europe, doubts whether the GATT Uruguay Round would produce any outcome advantageous for agricultural commodity exporters, and political upheavals in key markets in the Middle East and the Soviet Union.

For government and people alike, the most critical economic indicator remained the country's worsening rate of unemployment. By the final quarter the jobless total exceeded 200,000, or 10.7 per cent of the workforce, with projections showing that the situation would continue to deteriorate. Attempts by the government to provide employment through state-subsidized community work schemes were seen as no more than palliatives. The social and economic costs of the problem were reflected in heightened public consternation over adverse race relations, crimes against property and the person, and growing inequalities of life-style and advantage. Statistics were released which indicated that the top 20 per cent of income earners received nearly half of the country's total income. Moreover, the disparity of earnings between men and women was maintained by government repeal of equal pay legislation.

During Prime Minister Bolger's first full year of office (see AR 1990, pp. 378–80) the most significant and controversial figure within his administration was his Finance Minister, Ruth Richardson. She maintained pressure for a deregulated, market-driven economy, insisting that New Zealand's continued debt levels, poor past growth performance and inability to pay its way allowed no other option than a heavy pruning of state spending. Critics from a variety of sources claimed that this approach aggravated the existing downturn; a New Zealand so drastically 'restructured' according to dry treasury dogma, as favoured by the minister, would leave the country unable to capitalize upon any future upturn in economic fortunes.

In a widely pre-publicized July financial statement (to which she imprudently gave advance billing as being 'the mother of all budgets'), Ruth Richardson took the axe to a wide range of social services. The cuts involved new charges for previously state-funded medical care and hospitalization, removal of housing subsidies and student grants, and lower levels of state assistance for accident compensation. Most devastating for older voters were budget measures that heavily penalized retired persons through an onerous tax regime on any income received beyond state pension payments. This generated a rowdy, but effectively orchestrated, nationwide backlash from so-called 'grey power'. In mass meetings up and down the country, pensioners insisted that in the 1990 election campaign the National Party had given guarantees that their living standards would not be jeopardized. Their hostility fed directly back to the government via its parliamentary caucus: backbenchers repeated in public what they told colleagues, namely, that these measures were a blatant betrayal of the party's 1990 manifesto.

So severe was this response that the government found it politically necessary to dilute tax abatement levels of retired persons' earnings, although this entailed jettisoning prior claims about achieving a balanced budget by 1994. The government also recanted on some of its July budget cuts to health services, so that by the final quarter original estimates of an internal budget deficit for the coming year of NZ$1,700 million had ballooned to NZ$2,750 million. The position was aggravated by lower-than-forecast tax takes caused by the worsening economic downturn.

These developments saw the Bolger government increasingly inflamed and at odds as much with itself as against its formal opponents. Two backbenchers broke away to form a separate political party, while a key Bolger rival in cabinet, Maori Affairs Minister Winston Peters, was dismissed in October for his persistent failure to adhere to collective responsibility over key aspects of economic policy. From the heady days of a massive October 1990 election victory, the nose-dive in the government's standing during the year was remarkable. By the final quarter, Bolger and his administration were languishing at the lowest opinion poll ratings recorded for a prime minister and a government since the inception of polling in New Zealand.

For Michael Moore's Labour opposition, the government's difficulties were a mixed blessing. Third parties, such as the Greens, Jim Anderton's New Labour Party and Matiu Rata's Mana Motuhake, formed themselves into the Alliance, a grouping created for electoral purposes which, by year's end, was rivalling the official opposition in popular support. The key test of these strengths was projected for the February 1992 by-election for Auckland's Tamaki constituency. This was vacated by the November parliamentary resignation of its National member, former prime minister Sir Robert Muldoon, who departed deeply disillusioned with Ruth Richardson's economic policies.

In the field of legislation, workers attacked the Employment Contracts Act as a major assault upon their capacity to organize for collective bargaining and as a bonus for employers determined to hire labour at its cheapest. The act allowed for voluntary unionism where employees could nominate a so-called 'bargaining agent' of their choice to determine contracts of pay and work with employers. While an employer was permitted to choose with whom it could bargain, in the event of an employer's rejection of an agent and subsequent conclusion of an individual contract with an employee, authorities through the

Employment Court were empowered to scrutinize contracts and terms for harshness and unconscionability.

A bill was introduced in October to abolish the Ministry of Maori Affairs and the Iwi Transition Agency and to establish a Ministry of Maori Development. These steps followed controversy within Maoridom concerning allegations by Mr Peters that Maori trust funds, not under his control as minister, had been misused for what he claimed was an unsound business venture involving an American motel chain.

Other adopted or proposed legislation included measures on resources management, immigration, company law reform, reorganization of scientific research, privacy of information, area health administration and management of the energy sector. Parliament was criticized for poor management of its legislative programme and the government for failure to comply with relevant audit procedures.

In the field of foreign relations, the government attempted to repair relations with the United States. It announced a panel that would review the 1986 anti-nuclear legislation whose existence the US government claimed was the major impediment to better relations. For Mr Bolger, a review of that part of the legislation banning nuclear-propelled vessels from visiting New Zealand ports, allied to American announcements that it planned to retire tactical nuclear weapons from its ships anyway, was seen as providing an opening for improved links. The government saw this goal as being furthered by the provision of transport and medical assistance to the multinational force that fought the Gulf War (see V.2). Although Mr Bolger met President Bush briefly at the United Nations on a visit to the United States, the security impasse between the two countries remained, and public opinion continued to favour the retention of a total ban on nuclear entry to New Zealand.

Making a visit to New Zealand, French Prime Minister Michel Rocard apologized for the 1985 *Rainbow Warrior* bombing outrage (see also III.1.i). This was received sceptically, particularly after one of the bombers was later awarded a French decoration. Hopes by both governments concerned that this unsavoury affair might finally be put to rest were delayed in November when the Swiss police, acting on an outstanding warrant, arrested one of the accused saboteurs. Although court proceedings entailing the deposition of briefs by witnesses began in Auckland in December (to comply with the terms of the relevant extradition treaty), the government later decided not to sustain extradition proceedings. This decision, taken in the light of perceived political and trade interests, was hailed by the French government, but derided by Greenpeace as spineless.

New Zealand's relations with Indonesia were tested following the death of a New Zealand national in a November massacre conducted by the Indonesian military in Díli on the island of Timor (see also IX.2.vi).

New Zealand supported Australia in deploring the outrage and calling for a full and impartial investigation of what had occurred.

The government published a white paper on defence that emphasized further links with Australia, rationalization of existing functions to effect savings, a strengthened peace-keeping role and a continued capacity for emergency operations in the South Pacific. Such capacity was mobilized in December when the New Zealand armed forces stepped in to provide immediate relief for Western Samoa in the wake of the devastation caused by Cyclone Val (see X.2.ii).

ii. SOUTH PACIFIC

Marshall Islands
CAPITAL: Dalap-Uliga-Darrit   AREA: 200 sq km   POPULATION: 42,000 ('89)
OFFICIAL LANGUAGE: English   POLITICAL SYSTEM: presidential democracy
HEAD OF STATE AND GOVERNMENT: President Amata Kabua (since '87)
CURRENCY: US dollar
MAIN EXPORT EARNERS: tourism, agricultural products

Federated States of Micronesia
CAPITAL: Palikir   AREA: 702 sq km   POPULATION: 102,000 ('89)
OFFICIAL LANGUAGE: English   POLITICAL SYSTEM: federal presidential democracy
HEAD OF STATE AND GOVERNMENT: President Bailey Olter (since May '91)
CURRENCY: US dollar
MAIN EXPORT EARNERS: phosphates

Western Samoa
CAPITAL: Apia   AREA: 2,830 sq km   POPULATION: 163,000 ('89)
OFFICIAL LANGUAGES: Samoan & English   POLITICAL SYSTEM: monarchy
HEAD OF STATE: Susuga Malietoa Tanumafili II (since '62)
HEAD OF GOVERNMENT: Tofilau Eti Alesana, Prime Minister (since '88)
CURRENCY: tala (end-'91 £1=WS$4.52, US$1=WS$2.42)   GNP PER CAPITA: US$700 ('89)
MAIN EXPORT EARNERS: cocoa, copra, agricultural products, tourism

American Samoa
CAPITAL: Pago Pago   AREA: 197 sq km   POPULATION: 38,000 ('89)
STATUS: unincorporated territory of USA

Cook Islands
CAPITAL: Avarua   AREA: 4,200 sq km   POPULATION: 20,000 ('89)
STATUS: New Zealand associated territory

French Polynesia
CAPITAL: Papeete   AREA: 4,200 sq km   POPULATION: 193,000 ('89)
STATUS: French overseas territory

New Caledonia
CAPITAL: Nouméa   AREA: 19,000 sq km   POPULATION: 162,000 ('89)
STATUS: French overseas territory

Nauru
CAPITAL: Domaneab   AREA: 21.4 sq km   POPULATION: 9,000 ('89)
OFFICIAL LANGUAGES: Nauruan & English   POLITICAL SYSTEM: presidential
HEAD OF STATE AND GOVERNMENT: President Bernard Dowiyogo (since Dec '89)
CURRENCY: Australian dollar   GNP PER CAPITA: US$20,000 ('89)
MAIN EXPORT EARNERS: phosphates

Solomon Islands
CAPITAL: Honiara   AREA: 28,000 sq km   POPULATION: 313,000 ('89)
OFFICIAL LANGUAGE: English   POLITICAL SYSTEM: parliamentary democracy
HEAD OF STATE: Queen Elizabeth II
GOVERNOR-GENERAL: Sir George Lepping
HEAD OF GOVERNMENT: Solomon Mamaloni, Prime Minister (since '89)
CURRENCY: Solomon Islands dollar (end-'91 £1=SI$5.22, US$1=SI$2.80)
GNP PER CAPITA: US$580 ('89)
MAIN EXPORT EARNERS: timber, copra, fish, tourism

Vanuatu
CAPITAL: Port Vila   AREA: 12,000 sq km   POPULATION: 152,000 ('89)
OFFICIAL LANGUAGES: English, French & Bislama
POLITICAL SYSTEM: parliamentary
HEAD OF STATE: President Fred Timakata (since Jan '89)
HEAD OF GOVERNMENT: Maxime Carlot, Prime Minister (since Dec '91)
CURRENCY: vatu (end-'91 £1=VT204.50, US$1=VT109.53)
GNP PER CAPITA: US$860 ('89)
MAIN EXPORT EARNERS: copra, agricultural products, tourism

Kiribati
CAPITAL: Tarawa   AREA: 1,000 sq km   POPULATION: 69,000 ('89)
OFFICIAL LANGUAGE: English   POLITICAL SYSTEM: presidential
HEAD OF STATE AND GOVERNMENT: President Teatao Teannaki (since July '91)
CURRENCY: Australian dollar   GNP PER CAPITA: US$700 ('89)
MAIN EXPORT EARNERS: copra, phosphates, tourism

Fiji
CAPITAL: Suva   AREA: 18,375 sq km   POPULATION: 740,000 ('89)
OFFICIAL LANGUAGES: Fijian & Hindi   POLITICAL SYSTEM: republic
HEAD OF STATE: President Sir Penaia Ganilau (since '87)
HEAD OF GOVERNMENT: Sir Kamisese Mara, Prime Minister (since '87)
CURRENCY: Fiji dollar (end-'91 £1=F$2.75   US$1=F$1.47)
GNP PER CAPITA: US$1,650 ('89)
MAIN EXPORT EARNERS: sugar, agricultural products, tourism

THE South Pacific produced two new independent states in 1991, namely the MARSHALL ISLANDS and the FEDERATED STATES OF MICRONESIA (FSM), both of which were admitted to membership of the United Nations in September. Consisting of 34 atolls and 870 reefs, the Marshall Islands became a UN trust territory under US administration after World War II and in the 1950s gained international fame as the site of US nuclear tests at Bikini Atoll and other locations. Under a free association compact implemented in 1986, the USA remained the controlling power until, in December 1990, the UN Security Council approved the termination of the trusteeship. The islands achieved full independence in 1991 under the leadership of President Amata Kabua, who had held the post since 1987. Made up of over 600 islands, the FSM had had a similar recent history and came to full independence under President Bailey Olter, who was unanimously elected by the federation's National Congress on 11 May.

Only 22 months after the destruction caused by Cyclone Ofa, WESTERN SAMOA was devastated by Cyclone Val, which struck over four days in December. In the immediate aftermath, 12 deaths were confirmed in Western Samoa and one in neighbouring AMERICAN

SAMOA. With damage conservatively estimated at US$450 million, the wreckage of homes, villages, crops, public facilities, communications and roads was comprehensive. Although immediate relief was forthcoming from New Zealand, Australia, France and the United Kingdom, it was predicted that Western Samoa would take years to rebuild itself, so severe was the damage. Earlier, in April, following the first election held under universal suffrage, Tofilau Eti Alesana and his Human Rights Party were returned to power with 30 of the 47 seats at stake. Only two former ministers were retained by the Prime Minister in a major reshaping of his government.

In the COOK ISLANDS, damage to the main island of Rarotonga was inflicted by Cyclone Val, but with no fatalities. Prime Minister Geoffrey Henry's government continued to face financial difficulties over the funding of tourist developments, but his country was approved by securities authorities in Hong Kong as an alternative offshore domicile for locally-listed companies.

In FRENCH POLYNESIA, Cyclone Wasa (the immediate companion of Cyclone Val) claimed two lives, left widespread destruction in the Tubuai Islands south of Tahiti and inflicted major damage on the tourist resort centres of Bora Bora and Huahine. Territorial assembly elections in March saw Gaston Flosse's opposition win a surprising 18 of 41 seats, sufficient for him to form a government in coalition with Emile Vernaudon's faction. This government was soon in trouble, its moves to raise taxes provoking riots among workers in July. M. Flosse then formed a coalition with his old rival Jean Juventin, mayor of Papeete, and M. Vernaudon went into opposition (see also III.1.i).

In NEW CALEDONIA a new high commissioner to the territory, Alain Christnacht, was appointed. Key political figures reappointed included Jacques Lafleur (Rally for Caledonia in the Republic, RPCR) together with Paul Neaoutyine and Rock Wamytan (president and vice-president respectively of the Kanak Socialist Liberation Front, FLNKS). From the FLNKS leaders came several calls for more balanced economic development under the Matignon Plan (see AR 1988, p. 372) to meet indigenous social, educational, and economic needs. M. Neaoutyine, whose Palika party was the second largest in the FLNKS, warned Francis Burck (leader of its largest grouping, the Union Calédonienne) against any adulteration of the 1988 Matignon accords. This occurred when M. Burck, after returning from talks in Paris with President Mitterrand, spoke of an independence for New Caledonia that evolved, meaning a continuing partnership with France rather than a complete break.

At the International Court of Justice, NAURU commenced pleadings against Australia over a longstanding grievance concerning responsibility for restitution of parts of the island exploited for phosphates prior to independence in 1968. Judgment in the case was expected in 1992.

In the SOLOMON ISLANDS, Prime Minister Solomon Mamaloni and

three colleagues were cleared of allegations of misuse of office and powers when arranging a $250 million loan for the country. Regarded as increasingly aloof and arbitrary, Mr Mamaloni survived industrial action by public servants, ministerial sackings, votes of no confidence in parliament and central bank warnings about the serious state of the country's finances, borrowing and spending.

In VANUATU, following mid-year sackings of ministers and senior officials which provoked paralysis in the government and the ruling Vanuaaku Party, Prime Minister Walter Lini was defeated in a September motion of no confidence. He was replaced by Donald Kapolkas pending elections in December. For that contest, Fr Lini formed a new grouping, the National United Party (NUP), which won ten seats in the 46-member Assembly. His longstanding rival, Maxime Carlot, leading the Union of Moderate Parties, won 19 seats, the Vanuaaku Party 10, Barak Sope's grouping 4 and the Tan Union 1. Elected Prime Minister by the Assembly, Mr Carlot then formed a government comprising a coalition of his Moderates and the NUP. Initially, at least, this coalition was supported by, but did not include, Fr Lini.

In July, after a series of ballots, voters in KIRIBATI elected Teatao Teannaki as President to replace Iremia Tabai, whose term had been completed. Earlier elections in May saw 16 new representatives assume responsibilities in the 41-member Assembly.

In FIJI, industrial trouble afflicting the sugar and gold industries remained endemic. This was caused by grievances over remuneration, plans by the government to introduce a value-added tax and decrees discriminating against civil and industrial association. The leader of the 1987 army coup, Sitiveni Rabuka, left the military completely and eventually joined the interim government of Ratu Sir Kamisese Mara as co-deputy premier with responsibilities for home affairs. However, he left the government in November upon assuming the presidency of the Fijian Political Party, one of several parties formed in anticipation of a general election in 1992. Colonel Rabuka's moves revealed a rift between himself and the Prime Minister that grew deeper and more public. Government moves to obtain oil imports directly from Malaysia and Singapore, bypassing traditional company suppliers in Australia and New Zealand, aroused regional controversy among countries fearing that Fiji's initiative would result in their paying higher end-prices.

XI INTERNATIONAL ORGANIZATIONS

1. UNITED NATIONS AND ITS AGENCIES

THE last year of Javier Pérez de Cuellar's ten-year term of office as UN Secretary-General was undoubtedly the busiest 12 months in the history of the organization, even compared with the excitements of 1990 (see AR 1990, pp. 386–97). It covered a period when more and more countries turned to the UN and its specialized agencies for help in defusing military, political and humanitarian crises. At last the UN was seen as an organization that could achieve results where others could not, and the former sense of wordy hopelessness disappeared.

Starting in January with the outbreak of hostilities in the Gulf (see V.2), the UN's political involvement in major issues subsequently extended to El Salvador, Western Sahara, Angola, Cambodia and Yugoslavia, apart from the ongoing problems of Palestine, Cyprus, Afghanistan and Lebanon. As for UN-sponsored humanitarian and economic aid, the areas of famine, refugees and natural disasters were spread across all the continents with the exception of North America.

In his farewell statement to the General Assembly on 17 December, Sr Pérez de Cuellar envisaged the UN as the central agency for upholding the rule of law and for providing necessary international equilibrium and defence against anarchy. For that it would need a cohesive management, equipped with corresponding powers and resources; most of all, it would have to be rescued from the financial bankruptcy it was currently experiencing.

Earlier, at a ceremony at the White House in Washington on 12 December, Sr Pérez de Cuellar was awarded the Medal of Freedom, the highest civil award given by the United States. Presenting the medal, President Bush said that the Secretary-General's life work in service to humanitarian ideals had won him honour the world over. His tenure had marked 'the rebirth of the UN: its emergence as a force for peace'.

46th GENERAL ASSEMBLY. The Assembly began its 46th session on 17 September and elected Samier S. Shihabi, the permanent representative of Saudi Arabia, as its president. In his opening address Mr Shihabi spoke extensively about the growing social and economic disparities in the world.

Seven states were admitted to UN membership: the Democratic People's Republic of (North) Korea, the Republic of (South) Korea, the Federated States of Micronesia, Estonia, Latvia, Lithuania and the Marshall Islands.

In his annual report to the Assembly, the Secretary-General pointed out that during the period under review the Security Council had taken action of 'extraordinary consequence' to reverse the invasion of Kuwait by Iraq and to deter aggression in the future. It had authorized the use of force on a national and coalition basis. However, the experience of operations in the Gulf suggested the need for collective reflection on the question of the future use of powers vested in the Security Council under chapter VII of the UN Charter. He deplored the lack of means at the disposal of the organization to maintain an impartial and effective global watch over situations of potential and incipient conflict. The pool of information available to the Secretary-General was 'wholly inadequate', and it was hardly comprehensible when governments imposed far-reaching and costly responsibilities on the UN but were themselves unwilling to fulfil corresponding financial obligations.

Cape Verde, Hungary, Japan, Morocco and Venezuela were elected as non-permanent members of the Security Council for a two-year term beginning 1 January 1992, to replace the Côte d'Ivoire, Cuba, Romania, Yemen and Zaïre.

On 3 December the General Assembly appointed Boutros Boutros Ghali, the Deputy Prime Minister of Egypt, as the sixth Secretary-General of the UN for a five-year term beginning 1 January 1992. Born in Cairo in 1922 Mr Boutros-Ghali had a long association with international affairs as a politician, diplomat, jurist, scholar and widely-published author. He attended the 1988 Camp David summit conference and had a role in negotiating the resultant peace treaty between Egypt and Israel. In his acceptance speech, Mr Boutros-Ghali expressed appreciation for the opportunity afforded to Africa, through his election, to serve the international community. It was his fervent desire to raise the banner of peace wherever there was under-development, conflict and tension in the world.

As a result of a UK initiative, the Assembly passed a resolution on 19 December establishing the post of a UN emergency relief coordinator, to be appointed by the Secretary-General. The resolution contained guiding principles for improving the UN response to a wide range of international emergencies, and instructed the Secretary-General to establish a central emergency fund in order to strengthen the coordination of UN humanitarian emergency assistance and ensure a rapid response to crises. The fund, proposed at $50 million, would be financed by voluntary contributions.

In a letter dated 24 December, the Russian President, Boris Yeltsin, informed the Secretary-General that the Soviet Union's membership in the UN, including the Security Council and all other organs, would be continued by the Russian Federation, with the support of the countries of the new Commonwealth of Independent States (see IV.2.i). He said the Russian Federation would maintain full responsibility for all the rights and obligations of the former Soviet Union under the Charter, including the financial ones. (Of the ex-Soviet republics, Belorussia and Ukraine had enjoyed UN membership in their own right since 1945.)

FINANCE. Despite repeated appeals to member states by the Secretary-General, as of 31 December the UN was owed over $800 million in payments for both regular and peace-keeping operations. Of that amount, $439.4 million was owed for the regular budget, while an additional $377.2 million was outstanding for peace-keeping. In a report to the General Assembly, Sr Pérez de Cuellar made several proposals to solve the financial crisis. These included charging interest on outstanding contributions and the creation of a $1,000 million UN 'peace endowment fund' of assessed and voluntary contributions to help finance peace-keeping operations. He also, again, requested the Assembly's authorization to borrow commercially.

GULF CRISIS. During the first two weeks of January, Sr Pérez de Cuellar made desperate efforts to avoid the outbreak of war. 'I feel it is my moral duty as Secretary-General of the UN, a peaceful organization, to do everything possible to avoid the worst', he said before flying to Baghdad to meet President Saddam Husain. Between 11 and 13 January the Secretary-General held talks with President Mitterrand and Foreign Minister Roland Dumas of France, Foreign Minister René Felber of Switzerland, the 12 Foreign Ministers of the European Community (EC), Foreign Minister Budimir Loncar of Yugoslavia (also chairman of the Non-Aligned Movement), King Husain of Jordan, former President Daniel Ortega of Nicaragua and Yassir Arafat, chairman of the Palestine Liberation Organization (PLO). He also spoke by telephone to the UK Prime Minister, John Major.

In Sr Pérez de Cuellar's three-hour meeting with President Saddam Husain on 13 January, the latter showed no willingness to withdraw from Kuwait. Finally, on 15 January, the Secretary-General addressed a personal appeal to the Iraqi leader 'to commence, without delay, the total withdrawal of the Iraqi forces from Kuwait'. He concluded by saying that in his final year of office 'no cause would give me greater satisfaction than to set the Middle East as a whole on the road to a just and lasting peace. And no disappointment would be greater and more tragic than to find the nations of the world engaging in a conflict that none of their peoples want.' Following the start of the allied air offensive on 16 January, it emerged that the UN Secretary-General was not informed officially until hostilities had been in progress for several hours.

Already, on 11 January, a UN relief plan for the 1.5 million people expected to leave Iraq and Kuwait in the event of war had been presented at a meeting convened in Geneva by the UN Disaster Relief

Coordinator (UNDRO). As the fighting progressed, the World Food Programme (WFP), the World Health Organization (WHO), the UN Children's Fund (UNICEF), the UN High Commissioner for Refugees (UNHCR) and the UN Development Programme (UNDP) all sent teams of experts and helpers to work on the emergency plan to provide food, medical supplies and shelter for the fleeing refugees. Moreover, the UN Environment Programme (UNEP) and the London-based International Maritime Organization (IMO) became engaged in trying to extinguish the burning Kuwaiti oil wells and to stop the spread of the oil slicks in the Gulf (see also XIV.3). UNDP also set up a Gulf task force for post-war development.

At a Security Council meeting on 28 February, it was announced that a letter had been received from the Iraqi government stating that it agreed 'to comply with resolution 660 and all other Security Council resolutions' (see AR 1990, pp. 561–6). On 2 March the Council, by a vote of 11 to 1 (Cuba) with three abstentions (China, India and Yemen), adopted resolution 686 which demanded that Iraq accept all previous 12 resolutions on the Iraq-Kuwait situation, including the call for an immediate return of all seized Kuwaiti property. It further demanded that Iraq repeal all laws annexing Kuwait, accept liability for war losses and damages, and release all civilian detainees. It also called on Iraq to cease hostile actions, send its military commanders to discuss a cessation of hostilities, arrange for immediate access to and release of all prisoners-of-war, and assist in identifying Iraqi mines, booby traps and other explosives.

Later, the UN received a letter from the Iraqi Foreign Minister, Tariq Aziz, saying that his government would 'fulfil its obligations' under resolution 686, and asked the Security Council to declare a formal ceasefire and lift sanctions against Baghdad. The letter also stated that Iraq would return Kuwaiti gold and paper currency, museum objects and civilian aircraft seized after its occupation of Kuwait on 2 August 1990, as soon as possible.

On 3 April the Security Council, by a vote of 12 to 1 (Cuba) with two abstentions (Ecuador and Yemen), established a formal ceasefire to end the Gulf War by adopting resolution 687, which provided for a formal truce if Iraq agreed to be bound by all its terms (see XIX.1 for full text). The following week the Council unanimously adopted resolution 689 on the modalities for the UN Iraq-Kuwait Observation Mission (UNIKOM) to be sent to a demilitarized zone between the two countries. It was estimated that UNIKOM would eventually consist of up to 1,440 armed and unarmed military personnel provided by member states.

The question of the elimination of Iraq's weapons of mass destruction, as required under resolution 687, led the UN to appoint experts from 19 countries as members of a special commission under the International Atomic Energy Agency (IAEA) to monitor and verify Iraqi compliance.

Its task was to ensure the removal, destruction or decommissioning—at Iraq's expense—not only of any Iraqi nuclear weapons capability but also of biological and chemical weapons and of ballistic missiles. Subsequent on-site inspections in Iraq provoked several incidents, one of which obliged the Security Council to order Iraq to release an IAEA nuclear inspection team from custody together with the documents it had confiscated. As evidence mounted of Iraqi nuclear and other military potential, the Security Council on 11 October unanimously adopted resolution 715 approving a plan submitted by the Secretary-General and the IAEA director-general, Hans Blix, to enforce Iraqi compliance with resolution 687. The plan established probably the most rigorous inspection system ever devised by the UN, involving complete freedom of movement and surveillance rights for UN inspectors in Iraq and verification of all Iraqi imports and exports. The resolution also requested the UN sanctions committee and the IAEA to develop a mechanism for monitoring any future sales or supplies to Iraq that could give it mass destruction weapons potential.

Following the establishment of the ceasefire, a Demarcation Commission and a Compensation Fund were created by the UN, as was a 500-strong UN Guard Force to protect Kurdish refugees. The Demarcation Commission, composed of one representative each from Iraq and Kuwait and three independent experts, had the task of setting up markers to denote the Kuwait-Iraq border according to the 1963 demarcation line registered with the UN. The Geneva-based Compensation Fund, created under Security Council resolution 692 adopted on 20 May by 14 to 0 with Cuba abstaining, was to make restitution to countries and individuals for war damage inflicted by Iraq, to be financed by a 30 per cent levy on Iraq's oil exports. However, prospects of speedy Fund disbursements, on an estimated 2 million claims against Iraq, quickly receded as Iraq continued to argue for a five-year moratorium on the levy and to resist UN conditions for a resumption of its oil exports. On 16 August the Security Council adopted—by 13 votes to 1 (Cuba) with Yemen abstaining—resolution 706 authorizing the sale over six months of Iraqi oil worth $1,600 million, to pay for emergency food and other humanitarian imports. But Iraqi unwillingness to accept UN supervision terms meant that this 'window' had still not been used by the end of the year, when the general UN sanctions regime against Iraq remained in place.

The financial and material resources of the UN relief teams trying to cope with the flood of civilian casualties and refugees resulting from the Gulf conflict and its aftermath were stretched virtually to breaking-point, despite repeated appeals for additional contributions. In a report to the 46th General Assembly, Sr Pérez de Cuellar stated that, in light of the number of other crises demanding urgent attention, it would be 'neither just nor practical' to continue to request funding for humanitarian assistance to Iraq. It was a country, pointed out the Secretary-General, that 'is capable of feeding its people and seeing that their needs are met', especially if it would indicate its willingness to proceed with the oil sales authorized by the Security Council. Nevertheless, it was announced on 26 November that agreement had been reached with the Iraqi government to extend until 30 June 1992 the April 1991 memorandum of understanding providing for UN humanitarian operations in Iraq.

ISRAEL-PALESTINE. Israel's deportation of Palestinians, strict curfews and continued closure of the Palestinian university in retaliation for persistent Palestinian insurgency and strikes did nothing to lessen the ever-present violence in the area and therefore continued to exercise the UN. In March the Security Council issued a statement that its members were 'gravely concerned' by the deteriorating human rights situation for civilians and detainees in the territories occupied by the Israelis since 1967, especially by the effects of the curfews, which prevented Palestinians from going to work. As a result, the UN Relief and Works Agency (UNRWA), whose own employees had been threatened with expulsion, had to bring in emergency supplies of food for Palestinian families. In May the Security Council unanimously adopted a resolution 'deeply deploring' the deportation of four Palestinians and calling for their 'safe and immediate return'.

At Israel's insistence, the UN as such had no role in the Middle East peace conference which opened in Madrid on 30 October, even though it was convened in the framework of Security Council resolution 242 of 1967 (see V.3 and V.4.i). As a positive contribution to the peace process, the General Assembly on 16 December repealed its 1975 resolution (3379) which equated Zionism with racism (see AR 1975, p. 487). The vote was 111 in favour to 25 against, with 13 abstentions.

ANGOLA. In March the government of Angola agreed to the resumption of the UN special relief programme for Angola, and the Secretary-General appealed for immediate international assistance to help almost 2 million people who were under serious threat of starvation due to prolonged drought and civil war. Three months later the Security Council unanimously decided to extend and enlarge the mandate of the UN Angola Verification Mission (UNAVEM), to be called 'UNAVEM-II', to enable it to carry out new verification tasks arising from the peace accords reached between the Angolan government and the opposition Unita forces (see VII.1.vi). In a subsequent report, the Secretary-General stated that the ceasefire in Angola was being respected on both sides and that the Angolan authorities had not requested the UN to provide technical assistance or observers for the forthcoming elections.

EL SALVADOR. The year began with the Secretary-General renewing his efforts to bring about a ceasefire and supervised elections through an agreement between the El Salvador government and the FMLN guerrillas. After prolonged negotiations, sponsored by the Secretary-General, an agreement was finally signed at UN headquarters on 31 December calling for a ceasefire to begin on 1 February 1992 (see II.3.xiii). Earlier, in May, the Security Council had unanimously adopted a resolution establishing a UN Observer Mission in El Salvador (ONUSAL), for an initial 12 months, to monitor all agreements concluded between the government and the FMLN, and include monitoring the human rights situation.

CAMBODIA. The Secretary-General attended the resumed conference on Cambodia in Paris on 23 October and witnessed the signing of the peace agreements which ended the 13-year-old conflict and prepared the country for elections (see IX.1.ix). He said that the Cambodian operation would be the biggest and most complex in the history of the UN. Previously, on 16 October, the Security Council had voted unanimously to establish a UN Advance Mission (UNAMIC) to assist the Cambodian parties in maintaining a ceasefire in preparation for the setting up of the proposed UN Transitional Authority in Cambodia (UNTAC). The UNTAC terms of reference were wide-ranging, including supervising the ceasefire, ensuring a 70 per cent level of disarmament and demobilization, detecting and clearing minefields, controlling the activities of the existing administrative structure and assisting in bringing about the resumption of economic activity.

CYPRUS. Despite convening high-level talks with the leaders of the two communities in Cyprus and representatives of the Greek and Turkish governments, (see III.3.vi), the Secretary-General was baulked in his efforts to formulate an overall framework agreement aimed at solving the Cyprus problem during his term of office. On 23 December the Security Council expressed its appreciation to Sr Pérez de Cuellar 'for his long and tireless efforts to seek a just and lasting solution to the Cyprus question'. The Council restated its support for the convening of a high-level international meeting on Cyprus and extended the mandate of the UN Peacekeeping Force in Cyprus (UNFICYP) until 15 June 1992, while 'noting with concern the chronic financing problem' of the force.

WESTERN SAHARA. In July the Secretary-General informed the Security Council that Morocco and the Polisario Front had finally accepted his proposal for a formal ceasefire to begin on 6 September (see V.6.vi). This followed the setting up by the Council in April of the UN Mission for the Referendum in Western Sahara (MINURSO), which was the first time the UN had been given full responsibility for the organization and conduct of a referendum. According to the UN settlement plan for the area, a transitional period would begin with the ceasefire and end with the proclamation of the results of the referendum.

HORN OF AFRICA. At a meeting of UN humanitarian agencies in Geneva on 3 July on the emergency situation in the Horn of Africa, the Secretary-General said that a report prepared by James Ingram, executive-director of the WFP, should be regarded as a 'call for action—action now'. An inter-agency appeal was made for an additional $250 million to cover the emergency relief, although it was stressed that there could be no end to the famine in Africa while civil conflicts persisted. In September one of the largest food airlifts ever operated by the UN brought relief to Ethiopia, Somalia, Sudan, Djibouti and Kenya, where the lives of many millions of civilians—victims of civil strife, drought, inadequate food supplies and a decimated health and social services structure—were dependent entirely on voluntary donor responses.

SOMALIA. In a related UN operation, the year ended with no sign of peace in the civil war around the capital, Mogadishu, where up to 20,000 people, mostly women and children, had been killed or injured after heavy fighting was resumed on 17 November (see VI.1.ii). A team was sent to the capital by UNICEF to work out contingency plans to expand the relief programme.

ALBANIA. The UNHCR and the International Organization for Migration (IOM) issued an urgent appeal to the international community in August for economic assistance to the Albanian people (see also IV.1.vii). Representatives of both organizations, returning from a mission to Albania, said massive foreign investment was needed to avert an 'economic catastrophe'. In August the UNDP opened a field office in the capital, Tirana, and Albania became the largest recipient of UNDP technical and financial support in ex-communist Europe.

AFGHANISTAN. The Secretary-General welcomed the decision of the Soviet Union and the United States to discontinue their weapons deliveries to all sides in Afghanistan, effective 1 January 1992 (see VIII.1.ii). It came at a time when other developments in the world had resulted in the Afghans becoming 'a forgotten people': 57 projects in the UN Operation Salam programme had been abandoned or scaled down because of a lack of resources.

SUDAN. In March the Secretary-General issued an urgent appeal for $716.6 million in humanitarian relief for some 7.7 million people in

Sudan threatened by drought (see V.6.i). It was agreed that the UN would supervise all relief operations and that the WFP would manage the port-handling and transport of food.

SOUTH AFRICA. At a meeting in Geneva in July, the UN special committee against apartheid called for the maintenance of sanctions against South Africa and 'regretted the premature lifting of sanctions' by the United States and Japan (see VII.3). In a related development, the General Assembly, by a vote of 121 to 2 (UK and USA) with 34 abstentions, urged states to adopt legislation relating to the implementation of the arms embargo on South Africa, and called on them and private financial institutions not to extend new loans and credits. In another resolution, the Assembly urged the Security Council to consider measures against Israel for its violation of the arms embargo against South Africa.

YUGOSLAVIA. Direct UN involvement with the Yugoslav crisis (see IV.1.vi) began on 25 September, when the Security Council called on all states 'to implement immediately a general and complete embargo on all deliveries of weapons and military equipment'. The Council appealed to all parties to settle urgently their disputes peacefully, and the Secretary-General was invited to offer his assistance without delay. In October Sr Pérez de Cuellar asked Cyrus Vance, former US Secretary of State, to be his personal envoy and assist him in his efforts to obtain a ceasefire. When considering a report from the Secretary-General later that month, the Security Council said it was 'concerned about the tragic humanitarian situation' and noted that the arms embargo was not being respected. A high-level mission from UNESCO was sent to Yugoslavia to monitor the protection of the country's cultural and natural heritage, particularly Dubrovnik, which was on the 'world heritage' list. On 21 November the Security Council unanimously adopted a resolution which urged the Yugoslav parties to comply fully with a ceasefire agreement signed in Geneva and endorsed a statement by Mr Vance that a UN peace-keeping operation could not be envisaged without full compliance with the ceasefire agreement. On 31 December Mr Vance made his fifth visit to Yugoslavia to see if the outstanding obstacles could be removed for the deployment of such a force.

DISARMAMENT. Despite the ending of the Cold War, little was achieved at the Disarmament Conference, which began its 1991 session in Geneva in January. The fact that the conference was meeting in the shadow of the Gulf War had an inhibiting effect, especially in the negotiations for a chemical weapons treaty, although it was hoped a comprehensive convention would be agreed before the end of 1992. On

30 October a total of 23 governments pledged almost $1 million at the ninth pledging conference for the UN world disarmament campaign.

HOSTAGES. One area where the UN and Sr Pérez de Cuellar obtained extremely favourable press coverage was the release of nearly all the Western hostages held in the Lebanon (see v.4.v), mainly through the untiring efforts of the Secretary-General's personal envoy, Giandomenico Picco, who received the US President's award for exceptional service for his role in facilitating the releases.

DRUGS. In January the Secretary-General appointed Giorgio Giacomelli of Italy to head the UN International Drug Control Programme. The 45th General Assembly had welcomed the Secretary-General's proposal to unify the UN structures for drug-abuse control so as to enable the organization to strengthen its role as a main focus for concerted international action. One approach to the problem was to provide economic alternatives so that the elimination of the cultivation of poppies and coca would go hand-in-hand with the development of alternative activities, access to markets and the provision of technical assistance and credit. The Minister of Justice of Colombia signed an agreement with Signor Giacomelli in May for a $4 million drug-abuse project which would address the problem of youth unemployment and offer opportunities for personal development, training and counselling. Italy had contributed over $31 million to the UN programme and was the main donor country.

ENVIRONMENT. Two Englishmen were among the winners of the 1991 Global 500 Award—a UNEP prize for environmental achievement. They were Keith Frederick Corbett, who for more than 20 years had championed the cause of reptile and amphibian conservation, and Jonathon Porritt, who had transformed Friends of the Earth into the most authoritative environmental campaigning group in Britain. In June experts from 64 countries and 17 inter-governmental and non-governmental organizations attended a conference of the parties to the Vienna Convention for the Protection of the Ozone Layer, held at UNEP headquarters in Nairobi. They warned that the threat of ozone depletion had increased significantly: a 3 per cent decline during the last decade was greater than that registered earlier and could cause important changes in climate, damage to crops and more skin cancer (see also XIV.3).

WORLD HEALTH ORGANIZATION. The WHO set up a global cholera-control task force at its headquarters in Geneva following estimates that in Latin America between 90 and 120 million people were at risk because of a lack of access to safe water, safe food and sanitation (see also XI.6.v). Also according to WHO projections on the world AIDS epidemic, a total of 30 to 40 million people would be infected with the HIV virus by the year 2000, with 90 per cent of all cases in the developing countries (see also XIV.1). The organization warned that the social, economic and political impacts of the disease could be devastating.

PEACE MESSENGER AWARD. At a ceremony in Coventry (England) on 4 November, the UN Peace Messenger Award was received on behalf of the city by its lord mayor, Councillor Dave Edwards. Coventry became the third British city to win the award (Brighton and Sheffield being the previous recipients).

WOMEN. Concluding its tenth session in Vienna on 1 February, the UN committee on the elimination of discrimination against women called for women workers in family enterprises to be guaranteed payment, social security and social benefits. The committee also recommended that the value of women's domestic work be added to a country's gross national product.

CHERNOBYL. A UN plan to provide long-term economic, social and humanitarian aid for victims of the nuclear power plant accident at Chernobyl (Ukraine) in 1986 (see AR 1986, pp. 100–1, 406–9) was announced on 1 August. The director-general of the UN office in Vienna and coordinator of UN activities relating to Chernobyl, Margaret J. Anstee, said the programme would form the basis for a pledging conference seeking to raise $646 million for 131 projects to mitigate the consequences of the disaster.

2. THE COMMONWEALTH

THE imminence of war in the Gulf in January (see V.2), and then the assassination of Rajiv Gandhi in May (see VIII.2.i), led to the postponement twice of a meeting in London of the Commonwealth's 'high level appraisal group' (HLAG) of ten heads of government. Having originally planned two meetings between the full summits of 1989 and 1991 the group in the end met only on the eve of the Commonwealth heads of government meeting (CHOGM) in Harare (Zimbabwe) on 16–21 October. The HLAG exercise, aimed at reappraising the Commonwealth role in the 1990s and beyond, was therefore almost entirely carried out by a team of senior officials (see AR 1990, p. 397), who met several times during the two years. The HLAG proposals were fully discussed formally in Harare and informally at the CHOGM weekend retreat at Victoria Falls, and pointed the Commonwealth in new directions.

The harmonious Harare CHOGM appeared to mark a turning point in the development of the Commonwealth. For the first time for years, southern Africa was no longer a primary focus of attention. Partly this was because of hopeful developments in South Africa itself (see VII.3), but it also reflected general recognition that the Commonwealth was in danger of being increasingly perceived publicly as only about South Africa.

Commonwealth leaders, including the CHOGM chairman, President Robert Mugabe of Zimbabwe, were determined that, despite the meeting's venue, they should show that the Commonwealth had other roles to play. In this, with the help of the two-year HLAG exercise, they succeeded. South Africa was still a main topic, with Nelson Mandela and other black nationalist leaders being invited to Harare, but now the accent was on planning Commonwealth help for the fully democratic post-apartheid South Africa that at last seemed on the horizon. Sanctions were no longer a divisive issue. The meeting supported economic sanctions for the time being, but what were called people-to-people sanctions were to be lifted and sporting links gradually resumed, as sports organizations in South Africa became integrated. A programme of step-by-step reduction of sanctions agreed by the Commonwealth Committee of Foreign Ministers on Southern Africa meeting in New Delhi on 13–14 September was adopted.

The British dissented on continuing economic sanctions, but Prime Minister John Major minimized the issue so successfully that there remained no serious Commonwealth split. Mr Major took to his first CHOGM a changed, more positive British attitude to the Commonwealth, and his easy style produced a warmer atmosphere than for a long time. Quarrels with Britain, often quite bitter since the Nassau summit of 1985, seemed a thing of the past.

The Commonwealth was now seen as an instrument which could do much to further better government, democracy and human rights—all issues greatly in favour in the West following the Cold War. In the Harare Commonwealth Declaration, laying out a new agenda to supplement the Declaration of Commonwealth Principles drawn up in Singapore in 1971, the leaders pledged to work for democracy, the rule of law, just and honest government, and fundamental human rights.

A start had been made with the dispatch of a Commonwealth group to observe the 1990 elections in Malaysia (see AR 1990, p. 398). A similar group went to Bangladesh for the February elections and declared the process 'palpably free and fair' (see VIII.2.iii), although some imperfections in the voters' roll were noted. The Commonwealth became involved, too, in the Guyana election process (see II.4.ii). In Harare the Lesotho military government asked for Commonwealth help to move to civilian rule in 1992, while President Albert René offered Seychelles as a Commonwealth 'guinea pig' for switching from one-party to multi-party rule (see VIII.3.ii). Commonwealth pressure on President

Daniel Arap Moi helped moves towards multi-party rule in Kenya (see VI.1.iv). In March the Commonwealth Secretariat organized a seminar in Maputo on planning for the first multi-party elections in Mozambique (not a Commonwealth member).

The Harare summit was the best-ever attended. Of the 48 eligible countries, 43 sent heads of state or prime ministers. President Sam Nujoma represented the newest member, Namibia. In agreeing criteria for Commonwealth membership, the leaders shelved an application to join from Cameroon. Uneasy about instability in that country, they decided instead to ask its government whether it could accept the guidelines in the Harare Declaration. It was agreed that the use of English was essential in all Commonwealth business.

Mr Major said Britain would press ahead, unilaterally if necessary, with its plan to relieve the debt of low-income countries, and was supported by Canada. The summit agreed to investigate the setting up of a Commonwealth Bank for Reconstruction and Development. A few days earlier, Commonwealth Finance Ministers, meeting in Kuala Lumpur on 8–10 October, had agreed to promote recommendations made by a group of Commonwealth experts in their report 'Change for the Better: Global Change and Economic Development'.

Non-governmental organizations (NGOs) came into their own in Commonwealth circles during 1991. Governments acknowledged that they should have a wider role in Commonwealth decision-making, and the issue of human rights came to the fore in Harare largely as a result of pressure from the Commonwealth Human Rights Initiative (CHRI) (see AR 1990, p. 399). Its report, entitled 'Put Our World to Rights', called on Commonwealth governments to clean up their human rights records. It won wide public attention. Earlier, the first NGO Forum, with 150 delegates, was convened in Harare on 26–30 August by the Commonwealth Foundation, with the aim of securing for NGOs a greater voice in Commonwealth affairs.

A major step forward was taken to secure the Commonwealth Games on a new footing, following the report of a working party on strengthening Commonwealth sport. Sorely-needed extra funds were pledged in Harare for the Commonwealth Games Federation, and a committee was set up to help raise sporting standards in poor countries and to enable them to host future Commonwealth Games.

In November, at the request of the Harare summit, the Commonwealth Secretary-General, Chief Emeka Anyaoku (Nigeria), visited South Africa to discuss with the government and all the parties how the Commonwealth could help the process of negotiation for a new constitution. He saw President de Klerk, Mr Mandela, Chief Gatsha Buthelezi and other leaders, and Commonwealth observers attended the opening of the Convention for a Democratic South Africa (CODESA) on 20 December.

The Chairman of the Commonwealth Foundation, Robert Stanfield of Canada, retired on 31 December and his place was taken by Sir Richard Luce of Britain, a former (Conservative) Minister for the Arts. Other Commonwealth ministerial meetings in 1991 were: Health Ministers (Geneva, 5 May); Employment and Labour Ministers (Geneva, 4 June); and Agriculture Ministers (Rome, 8 November).

3. EUROPEAN COMMUNITY

THE year began with the member states of the European Community (EC) divided over the Gulf crisis. Some believed the use of force was inevitable to expel the Iraqis from Kuwait, while others were more reluctant. The crisis demonstrated the limits of European solidarity in foreign affairs, provoking wide public criticism. By the end of the year, however, there had been agreement at the Maastricht summit to establish a common foreign and security policy for the prospective European Union, leading to a common defence policy, and the Community was being pushed by the German government into recognition of Croatia and Slovenia.

Whatever the division over the Gulf, subsequent events in Eastern Europe and the Soviet Union gave a new impetus to the development of effective EC policy-making in foreign affairs. The independence movement in the Baltic states, the civil war in Yugoslavia and the disintegration of the Soviet Union all demanded an active response. The Community's capacity to respond effectively to events continued to evolve over the year.

Internal development also continued, with an agreement being reached at Maastricht on the timetable and mechanics of economic and monetary union (EMU), to be achieved at the latest by 1999. In addition, further progress was made on the legislation needed to establish a genuine single European market with effect from 1 January 1993.

GULF CRISIS. Two days before expiry of the UN deadline for Saddam Husain to withdraw from Kuwait, Foreign Minister Jacques Poos, of Luxembourg, as chairman of the EC council of ministers, announced the end of Community efforts to broker a peace agreement. 'The climate does not allow a new peace initiative', he said, after seeing the UN Secretary-General. The Community had twice invited Iraqi Foreign Minister Tariq Aziz for talks, but had been rebuffed on both occasions.

These peace initiatives were viewed sceptically by the British and Dutch, who supported the American view that only force would dislodge the Iraqis from Kuwait. They feared that calls for further peace negotiations would be interpreted as signs of weakness and had themselves committed forces to the Gulf. Italy had sent Tornado warplanes to the crisis zone, while at the same time pushing for talks, whereas Germany, Belgium, Portugal and Spain were not prepared to make any military commitment. President Mitterrand distanced France from the American position until the deadline expired, after which French forces took a full part in the military action. Once war broke out on 16 January, EC foreign ministers issued a statement regretting that the use of force had become necessary. They stressed their wish to ensure peace, stability and development in the region and called for an international peace conference on the Middle East 'at the appropriate moment'. On 28 February they made a joint statement welcoming the suspension of military operations.

The EC maintained a complete economic embargo on Iraq and Kuwait until the war was over. On 4 March the embargo on Kuwait was lifted in accordance with the UN resolution and there was some subsequent relaxation of the ban on trade with Iraq to allow humanitarian aid into the country. As international concern grew over the plight of the Kurds and Shias of Iraq, it was decided to provide 150 million ecu of emergency aid, two-thirds of it from the EC budget.* Mobile assistance teams financed by the Community were later sent to help the resettlement of the Kurds in the UN-protected enclaves in northern Iraq.

The Community had decided in the early stages of the crisis to provide assistance to the so-called front-line states to help them cope with the embargo and with the refugee problem, of which 1,000 million ecus would come from individual member countries and 500 million ecu from the EC budget. In January it was decided 175 million ecu of the EC contribution would go to Egypt and 150 million ecu to Jordan as gifts and 175 million ecu to Turkey as an interest-free loan. A further 250 million ecu was allocated to Israel and to Palestinians in the occupied territories. By the end of the crisis it was estimated that 150,000 Gulf workers had been repatriated to Asia and Africa by means of Community aid.

BALTIC STATES. Rising tension in the Baltic states in January, particularly the killings in Vilnius and Riga in January (see IV.2.ii), provoked a diplomatic reaction from the EC council of ministers, which described the use of force as unacceptable and called on the Soviet authorities to refrain. The European Parliament went further, holding up food aid to the Soviet Union and other assistance for Eastern Europe. As the move to Baltic independence gathered pace, Britain, Spain and some other member states favoured a cautious EC approach, but Germany and Denmark pressed for a more forthright attitude, and their view carried the day. When Baltic independence was conceded in August, the

---

*At end-1991 1 ecu=£0.71 or US$1.34.

Community took the unprecedented step of according full recognition to the three newly-born republics on behalf of all 12 member countries. It called at the same time for open and constructive negotiations between the Baltic states and the Soviet Union to settle outstanding issues.

EC-Baltic talks then began to explore what economic and political help could be given. The three Baltic foreign ministers were invited to join the EC foreign ministers for a meeting on 6 September, when they were told of the Community's willingness to see them join the PHARE programme of assistance for Eastern Europe (see AR 1990, p. 401).

SOVIET UNION. The crisis in the Baltic republics cast a shadow over relations with the Soviet Union and delayed negotiation of the technical assistance programme which had been decided at the Rome EC summit in December 1990 (see AR 1990, p. 402). Ministers eventually agreed the necessary legislation in July, for provision of 400 million ecu for five priority areas: training in public administration and management; energy; financial services; transport; and the distribution of foodstuffs. This programme was put into effect in September after the details had been worked out with the Soviet authorities.

On the day after the Moscow coup of 19 August (see IV.2.i), the foreign ministers of the Community met in Brussels. They condemned the coup and suspended all technical and food aid to the Soviet Union except humanitarian aid. It was also agreed that the association agreements with East European countries would be speeded up and the specific agreements with Poland, Hungary and Czechoslovakia be concluded 'in the near future'. All the EC member states were anxious to coordinate their relations with the USSR at a Community level. News of the collapse of the coup three days later was received 'with profound relief and satisfaction', in the words of a Community communique of 22 August. The EC and its member states rejoiced in the reinstatement of President Gorbachev and the restoration of constitutional order and democratic freedoms. Both Mr Gorbachev and Boris Yeltsin were praised and the aid programmes were reinstated. Subsequently, President Gorbachev sent a request to the president of the EC Commission, Jacques Delors, asking for further food aid and EC support for Soviet participation in international bodies like the IMF.

In recognizing the independence of the Baltic states, the Community underlined their special character as independent nations annexed by the Soviets in 1940. There was a more cautious approach to the other republics such as Georgia, with Spain being particularly nervous of giving too much support to regional separatism. Nervousness at the speed of Soviet disintegration was reflected in the declaration on Ukraine, issued by EC foreign ministers on 2 December. This took note of the independence referendum there and welcomed 'the democratic manner in which the Ukrainian people declared their wish for their republic to attain full sovereignty', while underlining the need for matters to be taken forward in a peaceful, democratic and orderly way. Ukraine was urged to pursue an open and constructive dialogue with Moscow and the other republics to ensure that the Soviet Union's international obligations were carried out, especially its commitments under the Helsinki Final Act including protection of national minorities. Nothing should be done to call into question control of nuclear weapons on the territory of Ukraine, which was expected to join the other republics in accepting joint liability for the USSR's foreign debts.

The Community then took a major new step. On 16 December ministers set out guidelines for recognition of emerging states in Eastern Europe and the Soviet Union. A list of conditions was laid down which was more specific than those previously applied, even by individual countries giving diplomatic recognition. Gaining recognition from the EC and its 12 member states would require respect for UN provisions and Helsinki commitments; guarantees for the rights of ethnic and national groups and minorities; respect for all existing frontiers, 'which can only be changed by peaceful means and by common agreement'; acceptance of commitments on disarmament; and commitment to settle regional disputes by agreement. 'The Community will not recognize entities which are the result of aggression', said the document.

The formation of the Commonwealth of Independent States by most ex-Soviet republics was noted 'with satisfaction' and the resignation of Mr Gorbachev was 'noted'. Eight of the CIS republics were recognized on the last day of the year, having given assurances that they would respect the guidelines. These were Armenia, Azerbaijan, Belorussia/ Belarus, Kazakhstan, Moldavia/Moldova, Turkmenia, Ukraine and Uzbekistan. Recognition was given on the understanding that they would become parties to the non-proliferation treaty (NPT) as non-nuclear states. As the food crisis mounted in Russian cities, it was decided in December to provide 200 million ecu in food and medical aid to Moscow and St Petersburg. Ministers also agreed to guarantee a loan of 1,250 million ecu over three years for purchase of essential supplies, half of which was earmarked to be spent in Eastern and Central European countries.

YUGOSLAVIA. Civil war flared in Yugoslavia (see IV.1.vi) on the eve of the June EC summit in Luxembourg, a conflict on the very borders of the Community which was to test European unity just as negotiations were proceeding for extending Community ambitions in foreign and security policy. The Community's response was the 'troika' of three EC foreign ministers, from Italy, Luxembourg and the Netherlands (respectively the immediately preceding, current and next-in-line holders of the rotating EC presidency). They flew to Belgrade armed with a letter invoking the consultation mechanism of the Conference on Security and

Cooperation in Europe (CSCE) and a threat to cut off aid, securing from the federal Yugoslav government the first of many ceasefire promises. Chancellor Kohl of Germany was especially keen for the Community to act, as was his Foreign Minister, Hans-Dietrich Genscher. Whereas they favoured early recognition for Slovenia and Croatia, the British and French were worried that recognition could provoke new problems, while Greece, bordering Macedonia, feared that nationalist movements in Yugoslavia could provoke an ethnic crisis in northern Greece.

As the situation worsened, the Community continued its efforts to mediate. The 'troika' visited Yugoslavia again, appeals were launched for a cessation of fighting and ceasefire monitors were dispatched (150 of them being deployed in Yugoslavia by August). The European Commission was asked to identify sanctions and rewards which could be applied to different factions. On 27 August the EC foreign ministers stated that the Community and its member states 'could not stand idly by as the bloodshed in Croatia increases day by day' and announced the convening of a peace conference. This met on 7 September at the Hague, under the chairmanship of Lord Carrington (UK), a former secretary-general of NATO. It brought together the Yugoslav federal government and the presidents of the republics in order to 'adopt arrangements to ensure peaceful accommodation of the conflicting aspirations of the Yugoslav peoples'.

The meetings of the Yugoslavia peace conference continued sporadically through the autumn, during which further ceasefires were negotiated only to collapse. The Community attacked the hijacking of the federal presidency by Serbia and Montenegro and said it was not prepared to acknowledge any decisions taken by a body 'which can no longer pretend to speak for the whole of Yugoslavia'. The bombardment of Dubrovnik was condemned. In October a joint statement was issued with the United States and the USSR calling for an end to hostilities. On 8 November the EC suspended its trade and cooperation agreement with Yugoslavia and imposed a number of sanctions, including suspension of benefits under the PHARE programme. The UN Security Council was asked to impose an oil embargo and to improve the effectiveness of an arms embargo.

By mid-December the Germans were determined to grant unilateral recognition to Croatia and Slovenia if the Community failed to act. Accordingly, on 16 December, EC foreign ministers swallowed their misgivings and set 15 January 1992 as the deadline for individual republics to request recognition, which would be granted subject to certain conditions. The UN was asked to send a peace-keeping force.

EASTERN EUROPE. The Soviet Union and Yugoslavia were major preoccupations, but work went on to conclude agreements with the other countries of Eastern Europe. This reflected the Community's belief that economic progress in the newly-established democracies was essential to their stability. There was some resistance on the EC side to making concessions to Poland, Hungary and Czechoslovakia in sensitive agricultural and industrial sectors. Some member countries did not wish to see increased imports of textiles, steel, coal and foodstuffs, since domestic producers were already under pressure. It took the August coup attempt in Moscow to give a new impetus to the talks, which resulted in association agreements being signed on 16 December with Poland, Hungary and Czechoslovakia. These agreements provided for free trade within 10 years and possible EC membership.

POLITICAL UNION. The inter-governmental conferences on political union and economic and monetary union continued in parallel through the year, culminating in agreement on a new treaty at the Maastricht summit on 9–10 December (see also XV.1.ii). The wide-ranging accord was reached under the presidency of the Dutch Prime Minister, Ruud Lubbers. In the words of its opening provisions, the treaty marked 'a new stage in the process of creating an ever-closer Union among the peoples of Europe.' Reference to the Community's 'federal' aim in an early Dutch draft had been attacked by the British, who prevented its inclusion in the final text (see XIX.4). Events on the international scene had pointed up the need for the Community to increase its influence in world affairs. The new draft treaty set as an objective for the Union 'to assert its identity on the international scene, in particular through the implementation of a common foreign and security policy which shall include the eventual framing of a common defence policy'.

There was a fundamental argument from the start of the negotiations over the extent to which foreign and security policy could be brought into the full EC policy-making system. The British and others were opposed, with the result that the final text provided a formula whereby the Commission and European Parliament had a role in the formulation of such policy but without the institutional rights provided by the Treaty of Rome. There would be a gradual implementation of joint action where interests were in common, as long as all member states agreed. The council of ministers itself could decide what policy decisions could be taken by majority vote.

The Community's defence role was a major preoccupation of member states throughout the year (see also XII.2). In June the British and Italians produced a joint paper underlining the importance of a complementary role between the Community and NATO, recognizing the defence identity of the Union while envisaging that the Western European Union (WEU) would be given the liaison role between the EC and NATO. They proposed a strengthening of the WEU and the creation of a rapid reaction force to operate outside the NATO theatre. This was soon followed by a Franco-German plan—presented to the Dutch Prime Minister in a letter from President Mitterrand and Chancellor Kohl—which made no reference to NATO or the Atlantic alliance. Favouring a specifically European defence policy, it included a proposal for setting up an army corps. In the Anglo-Italian proposals, the development of the European identity would reinforce the Atlantic alliance and the WEU would be both the defence identity of the Union and the means to strengthen the European pillar of the alliance. In the Mitterrand-Kohl plan, the WEU would be exclusively responsible to the European Union.

The two extremes of the argument were represented by the British and the French. The former were concerned to do nothing which might provoke the United States into abandoning its commitment to European defence; the latter were keen to establish a European defence policy which was clearly independent of American influence. The Americans expressed their own concern, as when President Bush told his NATO colleagues in Rome on 8 November that 'if your ultimate aim is to provide independently for your own defence, the time to tell us is today'.

It became clear that the WEU provided the key to resolve the problem by being the bridge between the two views. It was decided that the common foreign and security policy would embrace all questions relating to the security of the Union, including framing a defence policy, 'which might in time lead to a common defence'. This policy would respect NATO obligations and there would be a review by 1998. Meanwhile, the WEU would be developed as 'the defence component of the European Union and as the means to strengthen the European pillar of the Atlantic alliance', with the task of formulating a common European defence policy.

The political union treaty also extended the Union's competence to justice and home affairs and to immigration, though mainly outside the framework of the Treaty of Rome. At the same time, there were significant changes to the original treaties. The principle of 'subsidiarity' (see AR 1990, p. 405) featured prominently in the new text, as reassurance to those who feared a Community extending its activities into all policy areas. The concept of European citizenship was introduced and new powers were given to the European Parliament.

Britain's fierce opposition to any new agreement on social policy resulted in a special protocol, negotiated in the closing hours of the summit, which would allow 11 member states to implement legislation in the social field while the United Kingdom stood aside. Warmly welcomed in the British media, this formula promised trouble ahead.

ECONOMIC AND MONETARY UNION. Although Britain also refused to commit itself to the single currency envisaged in the third stage of EMU (as set out in the 1989 Delors plan—see AR 1989, pp. 545-8), the Maastricht summit agreed that this stage would begin 'irrevocably' on 1 January 1999, with the establishment of a European System of Central Banks and the use of the ecu as the single currency. This date could be advanced to 1 July 1997 if more than half the member states met economic performance criteria and a qualified majority agreed to go ahead. The performance criteria required a low public deficit, low inflation, low interest rates and stable exchange rates—conditions which few member states could meet in 1991.

Economic policy would become largely a matter for the European Council and the Council (of economic and finance ministers), which would recommend economic policy guidelines for member states and the Community. Where national economic policies were inconsistent with the guidelines, recommendations would be made to the country concerned. Member states were to avoid excessive budget deficits, any signs of which would be notified to EC ministerial bodies by the Commission. Certain sanctions could then be applied.

The proposed European System of Central Banks would consist of the European Central Bank and the central banks of the member states. Its main task would be to maintain price stability, acting on the same principles as the German Bundesbank, which was the inspiration for the European system. From the beginning of stage three of EMU, it would define and implement Community monetary policy, conduct foreign-exchange operations, hold and manage reserves and promote the smooth operation of payments systems. Stage two preparations would begin on 1 January 1994, when a European monetary institute would be set up consisting of the national central banks. At the same time, member states would begin the process of making their central banks independent.

A special protocol recognized that the UK would not be obliged or committed to move to stage three of EMU without a separate decision to do so by its government and parliament. This formula had been proposed by European Commission vice-president Sir Leon Brittan. At one stage in the negotiations it had been considered as a general provision available to all, but this provoked fierce opposition from France, for whom the establishment of economic and monetary union was an essential goal and which feared that Germany itself—the pivotal state in EMU—might wish to opt out.

The Union Treaty, including EMU, was due to be ratified by national parliaments during 1992, with a view to implementation from 1 January 1993, coinciding with the launch of the single market.

EUROPEAN ECONOMIC AREA. Negotiations were completed in October for the creation of the European Economic Area (EEA) comprising 19 countries and covering the whole of Western Europe, accounting for almost half of total world trade and with a population of nearly 380 million people (see also XI.5.iv). This followed the successful outcome of negotiations in Luxembourg between the 12 EC countries and the seven members of the European Free Trade Association (EFTA). The new treaty was to come into force on 1 January 1993, but this timetable was put at risk when, in December, the European Court of Justice objected on questions of jurisdiction (see XV.1.ii).

SINGLE MARKET. With one full year to go before the single European market deadline of 31 December 1992, a stream of legislation continued to flow from the council of ministers in 1991. Nearly 80 per cent of the required measures had been adopted by the end of 1991, of which 61 per cent were being implemented in national law. During the year ministers adopted far-reaching rules on public procurement, insurance, pharmaceuticals, motor vehicles and indirect taxation. A formula was also agreed, in conjunction with Japan, to regulate the flow of Japanese cars into the Community until 1999. The main problem areas remained frontier controls, veterinary and plant health and some of the banking legislation.

AGRICULTURE. The continuing Uruguay Round negotiations in GATT set the agenda for agricultural policy over the year. The European commissioner responsible for agriculture, Ray MacSharry, proposed a general price reduction and adjustment to production quotas, with compensation related to the areas under cultivation. There was broad acceptance in the council of ministers of the need for fundamental reform, but the draft GATT agreement put forward by GATT director-general Arthur Dunkel in December was rejected because it did not permit direct payment to farmers as compensation for price cuts. Intensive discussions in Brussels throughout December failed to resolve the issue.

ENERGY. A European Energy Charter, the brainchild of Mr Lubbers, was signed at the Hague in December. Its fundamental aim was to encourage cooperation in the energy field across Europe, helping to regenerate the economies of Eastern Europe and to exploit the energy resources of the ex-Soviet Union. All 12 ex-Soviet republics signed, as well as the 12 EC countries and 22 others. The Dutch emphasized the need for a rapid transition to free markets in energy.

The problem of carbon dioxide pollution was examined by EC environment and energy ministers, who asked the European Commission to draw up detailed legislation for an energy tax designed to cut emissions. The Commission had proposed a tax rising to the equivalent of $10 on a barrel of oil by the year 2000 (see also XIV.3).

4. OECD—COMECON—NON-ALIGNED MOVEMENT

i. ORGANIZATION FOR ECONOMIC COOPERATION AND DEVELOPMENT

IT was the year in which the OECD published its first economic survey of a former Eastern bloc country—Hungary, in July. Others were in the pipeline on Czechoslovakia and Poland, to complete the coverage of the three countries in the organization's 'partners in transition' programme. The collapse of the Soviet Union made the work on 'transition' an area of even more compelling interest. The OECD urged that Western responses should include, certainly, the financial and technical aid and investment so much in demand, but also, and in its view most importantly, a commitment to the opening of OECD markets.

This ran at obvious variance with the continuing deadlock in the GATT Uruguay Round of trade talks, where OECD member countries were set one against another. This major embarrassment for the organization remained, in the OECD view, one of the most pressing problems in the international economy. The organization repeatedly urged upon its divided members the importance of a successful conclusion, stressing the support this would give to liberalization of trade in the developing and the former communist world. It also warned of the high costs, for consumers and efficient producers, of 'the protectionist measures which have become all too prevalent' (see also XVIII.2).

Meanwhile, the OECD pursued, still at the level of 'informal dialogue', its relations with the six dynamic Asian economies, or DAEs, which together represented one-third of OECD trade with the non-OECD region. The OECD secretary-general, Jean-Claude Paye, visited three of them—Thailand, South Korea and Hong Kong—in October.

On 2–3 December the annual high-level meeting of the OECD development assistance committee (DAC) focused on 'partnership for sustainable development', gearing up to project the environmental dimension of their development policies at the forthcoming June 1992 UNCED conference in Rio de Janeiro. The DAC's annual statistics published in October showed its members as having provided $54,100 million in official development assistance (ODA) in 1990, an increase of 4 per cent in real terms as compared with 1989. As between the DAC countries, Norway's ODA was again the highest proportion of GNP (1.17 per cent). The USA showed the biggest increase over the 1989 level, of 42 per cent, but a large part of this was due to the forgiving of Egyptian military debt, and the ratio of US ODA to GNP was still only 0.21 per cent, the lowest except for Ireland. Among the other main lenders, Japanese, German, French and Dutch ODA showed an upward trend, but ODA from Italy, Sweden and the UK fell. ODA from the DAC countries was still very much the preponderant element in global lending, although the total from non-DAC (mainly Arab) countries had increased from $6,000 million to nearly $10,000 million in 1990. Total net resource flows from all sources (DAC, non-DAC and multilateral) to developing countries were assessed as up from $123,000 million to $142,000 million.

The OECD's *Employment Outlook* published on 11 July recorded sharply rising unemployment in most member countries, in 1990, after six years of downward movement; further increases in unemployment were expected 'well into the beginning of the upturn'. A relatively recent and very major concern was the impact of international migration into virtually all OECD countries. In Europe the two main trends were immigration from the developing world (changing the net position of southern European countries, traditionally themselves sources of emigration), and from Central and Eastern Europe, where the report expected that political and economic developments would continue to generate 'strong push pressures'. The challenge, it noted, was 'to develop an appropriate balance between migration control policies and active labour market policies'. Estimates for 1991 unemployment rates were that they would remain constant at 7.1 per cent overall; countries furthest above this average were Canada (10.1), Turkey (11.1), Italy (11.3), Ireland (14.7 and rising again) and Spain (15.9 but falling).

The semi-annual OECD *Economic Outlook* was published in June and again on 19 December. In an introductory chapter entitled 'The Path to Recovery', it stated that 'the fundamental conditions for renewed growth at a moderate pace are in place', although the second half of 1991 had fallen short of its June forecast. The OECD aggregate GNP growth rate, given as 2.6 per cent for 1990, would be only 1.1 per cent in 1991 but was expected to rise to 2.2 per cent in 1992 and to 3.3 per cent in 1993.

ii. COUNCIL FOR MUTUAL ECONOMIC ASSISTANCE (CMEA/COMECON)

THE CMEA formally terminated its activities on 26 September 1991, although a dispute over the use and valuation of its assets dragged on until the end of the year. A first attempt to establish a successor agency ended in mysterious circumstances, but a further body was under negotiation.

The penultimate meeting of the CMEA executive committee (its 134th) took place in Moscow in 4–5 January. The German Democratic Republic was no longer a member, having disappeared as a state the previous month, but the other nine were there under the chairmanship of Béla Kádár, the Hungarian Minister of External Economic Relations. Implementing the decision of the 1990 Session (see AR 1990, pp. 408–9), the meeting drafted a statute for a successor Organization of International

Economic Cooperation, selected a list of CMEA documents which would remain in force and declared invalid all others. The 1990 (45th) Session had established a special commission under Hungarian chairmanship for detailed negotiation; its first meeting had been on 11 February 1991. All the documents for the successor organization were approved and premiers were invited, by a letter of the Hungarian Prime Minister dated 14 February, to attend a Session in Budapest at which the documents would be signed. On 22 February, however, they and the CMEA secretariat received a letter from the Hungarian representative saying that 'in the new situation . . . doubts emerged as to the membership of some countries in the new organization, as well as about the tasks of the new organization'. The Soviet government, then dominated by conservatives, was seeking stronger powers for the successor body to the dismay of the East Europeans, especially Poland. The Soviet government changed composition and stance in April, but no inter-member agreement could be reached by the time the final (46th) Session met in Budapest on 28–29 June. Two days before it convened, on 26 June, the USSR Supreme Soviet had resolved to liquidate the CMEA, of whose Moscow headquarters it was the host government.

The agenda of the final CMEA Session was brief. It was resolved that all CMEA institutions and the Council *de jure* would cease to exist within 90 days of the Session. The liquidation took effect on 26 September, but with the issue of CMEA assets unresolved. Basing itself upon an agreement concluded in 1989 with what were then submissive fraternal regimes, the Soviet government insisted that the assets could be disposed of only with the consent of itself, offering successively 31, 45 and 50 million non-convertible roubles for the headquarters building and the adjacent Mir Hotel. However, the other eight members estimated their worth at $400 million in the light of Western firms' keenness to gain office and hotel space in Moscow. They also wanted to keep half the headquarters building for themselves as a trade centre.

After a delay caused by the abortive Moscow coup in August, the liquidation committee held a meeting on 9 September (at which only the chairman, Mr Kádár, represented the non-Soviet membership), but failed to reconcile the conflict of views. A separate coordinating committee, meeting on 18–19 October to draft a statute for an East European Cooperation and Trade Organization, declared that any new body would not seek the Moscow building. The successor agency was explicitly intended to facilitate transition to a market economy with currency convertibility. Discussions on its creation were limited to Bulgaria, Czechoslovakia, Hungary, Poland and Yugoslavia—the last-named having enjoyed special status within the former CMEA. Romania and the three non-European ex-CMEA states (Cuba, Mongolia and Vietnam) were notable exclusions from the consultations.

The liquidation of the CMEA did not imply the termination of the two international banks established under its auspices, as their directors made clear when, on 1 January, transactions ceased in the 'transferable roubles' (TR) used as accounting units (see AR 1990, p. 411). The International Bank for Economic Cooperation (IBEC) reported that when TR disappeared only 80 per cent of members' subscriptions (300 million TR in 1964, half in TR and half in convertible currency) was paid up. The IBEC proceeded to repay members' TR subscriptions and credited their accounts with the ecu equivalent of their convertible tranches. This operation left the bank with a capital of 400 million ecu. The International Investment Bank (IIB) followed the same procedure: its original capital (1,070 million TR in 1972, 70 per cent in TR and 30 per cent in US dollars) had only been paid up as to 50–60 per cent of members' subscriptions. After the 1991 conversions, the IIB's capital stood at 1,300 million ecu.

iii. NON-ALIGNED MOVEMENT

THE first major political gathering of the Non-Aligned Movement (NAM) since the end of the Cold War took place in Accra, as a Conference of Foreign Ministers on 2–7 September, with 97 countries represented. Commentators widely discussed the demise of a Movement that was supposedly redundant in the 'new world order'. At Accra, proposals to merge the NAM with the Group of 77 (the forum for 128 developing countries), or to change the name to the 'Movement of the Third World', were both defeated. In the end, the final declaration asserted that the thaw 'has justified the raison d'être of the Movement', which was as relevant now as at any time. During the emergence of a new order, said the declaration, the Non-Aligned had to reassert themselves 'in order to ensure an equal participation in the creation of such new relations'.

The end of the Cold War was not only an opportunity but also a threatening situation. The 'emerging tendencies towards a unipolar world' and the focus on Europe meant that matters of importance to the Non-Aligned were being marginalized. The new Western influence in the United Nations was seen by some as 'a crisis for the Movement': collectively they called for the Security Council to become 'more democratic and transparent' and for the Non-Aligned to ensure that their own interests were preserved in the process of reforming the UN.

The year produced positive developments in many of the regional problems facing the Movement's membership, notably: improved relations between Guatemala and Belize (see II.3.xiii and II.4.v) and between Venezuela and Guyana; the end of fighting in Ethiopia (see VI.1.i) and El Salvador (see II.3.xiii); and progress towards peaceful solutions to the conflicts in Cambodia (see IX.1.ix) and Western Sahara (see V.6.vi). Even the issues of apartheid and of Palestinian rights were moving in the directions for which the Movement had long campaigned. However, the Non-Aligned had distinct positions on these two issues, which reflected caution over the extent of the substantive change actually taking place. The Accra conference wanted sanctions maintained against South Africa until fundamental constitutional change was under way; they also wanted the Middle East peace conference to be 'under the aegis of the United Nations' (see also V.4.i).

It was not only the continuing desire for a political forum for the Third World that prevented the Movement from deciding to disband. There was also still a general feeling among the members that a high-level political forum for the discussion of development questions was useful. The Accra declaration called for 'greater and more meaningful North-South cooperation' and showed its frustration with demands for 'structural adjustment' of members' economies by arguing that the international community must 'create mechanisms which would require as much attention to the balance of the human condition as we pay to the balance of payments'. Nevertheless, there was little sign that either the formation of joint strategies for negotiating with the North or joint economic activity within the South would begin to return to the level sustained by the Movement in the 1970s.

The most important meeting of developing countries on economic questions in 1991 was only loosely associated with the NAM. This was the second summit of the Group of 15 countries (see AR 1990, pp. 412–3), held in Caracas in November. One striking theme was the linkage made between environmental and development questions. As President Pérez of Venezuela put it in his opening speech, 'if the tropical forests are the heritage of mankind, science and technology should be also'. The practical activities of the G-15 included a meeting of businessmen coinciding with the summit, the establishment of a South Investment, Trade and Technology Data Exchange Centre (SITTDEC), the implementation of several bilateral payments arrangements for mutual trade and the first steps towards a multilateral payments arrangement. Meanwhile, during the year, Julius Nyerere launched the Chinese, Spanish and Portuguese editions of the South Commission report (see AR 1987, p. 404 and 1990, p. 413), with trips to Beijing and to several Latin American countries.

Following the outbreak of the Gulf War (see V.2), the Yugoslavs convened a meeting of 16 foreign ministers of Non-Aligned countries in Belgrade in February. The difficulty this issue presented for the Movement was shown by the fact that it was more than three weeks after the bombing started before the ministers met and that it was an ad hoc group rather than a formal NAM meeting. The resulting efforts of a mission composed of representatives of Cuba, India, Iran and Yugoslavia to visit Baghdad and initiate a peace process were aborted by the start of the ground war. While the NAM had unambiguously asserted Kuwait's right to independence (see AR 1990, pp. 411–2), the Accra conference avoided taking any explicit position on the war against Iraq. Unity was maintained by asserting that, had the Security Council 'applied the same standards of international legitimacy as they did in the Gulf war, the question of Palestine could have been resolved'.

A Programme of Action approved in Accra was aimed at revitalizing the Movement by increasing the level of joint caucusing in the various UN organs, by convening a special conference on environmental questions in preparation for the 1992 UN conference in Brazil (also XIV.3) and by attempting to reactivate the joint NAM programme of economic cooperation.

The disintegration of Yugoslavia had a debilitating effect on the Non-Aligned Movement, as the preoccupation of the Yugoslavs with their internal affairs and the consequent foreign policy ramifications of that crisis meant that they had little time to exercise their central role as chairman of the Movement. Even within the UN diplomatic corps in New York, the NAM Coordinating Bureau was less active and issued few public statements during the year. On the other hand, the election of Boutros Boutros Ghali of Egypt as UN Secretary-General in December (see XI.1) was something of a success for the NAM, which had backed the list of six African candidates from which, among others, the General Assembly made its choice.

The Accra conference, the seventh in the triennial series that started in 1972, saw the NAM increase to 103 members. Chile resumed its membership, which had been suspended since the military coup in 1973. Mongolia, previously an observer, also became a full member. Although Argentina was represented at Accra, its strong identification with the Western world finally led the Argentinians to announce their withdrawal from the Movement in mid-September, bringing the total membership down to 102 countries. One important decision of the conference was to appoint Indonesia to take over as NAM chairman and to host the tenth summit in 1992. The Indonesians had tried at several previous conferences in the 1980s to obtain the leadership. With the decline in the prestige of the radicals and the withdrawal of Nicaragua's candidature, no obstacle remained in their way this time.

5. OTHER EUROPEAN ORGANIZATIONS

i. CONFERENCE ON SECURITY AND COOPERATION IN EUROPE (CSCE)

IN November the Conference on Security and Cooperation in Europe (CSCE) celebrated its first anniversary as a major new multilateral organization in Europe. Founded as a permanent institution in November 1990 (see AR 1990, pp. 575–6), the CSCE traced its origins to the conference of European states plus the USA and Canada which met in Helsinki in 1975. These 35 states signed the Helsinki Final Act, which contained three main sections or 'baskets', the first dealing with security issues, the second with economic and scientific cooperation, and the third with human rights. The Final Act also provided for a series of specialist meetings and follow-up conferences—thus initiating the CSCE 'process'. The Helsinki Final Act did not have the status of international law, and all the documents and statements of the CSCE had to be unanimously agreed by all its participating states. Nonetheless, the CSCE process provided a useful forum for pan-European consultation and dialogue during the years of heightened East-West confrontation in the early 1980s.

With the collapse of communism in Eastern Europe, however, the CSCE acquired a new lease of life. It was now widely seen as a key forum for broad-ranging cooperation in a Europe no longer divided into hostile blocs. Consequently, at the historic Paris summit of CSCE heads of state and government in November 1990, the decision was taken to give the CSCE 'process' a permanent institutional form. The CSCE's new institutions were outlined in the Charter of Paris for a New Europe: a small secretariat was to be established in Prague, along with a Conflict Prevention Centre in Vienna and an Office of Free Elections in Warsaw. A regular series of meetings between participating states was also agreed, thus making the CSCE a more effective forum for institutionalized political consultation and dialogue. A council of CSCE foreign ministers and a committee of senior officials were to meet at least once every six months, whilst heads of state and government were to meet every two years. Finally, it was decided to establish a CSCE Parliamentary Assembly, a proposal further discussed in Madrid in April 1991, when it was agreed to hold the inaugural meeting of the Assembly in Budapest in July 1992.

During 1991 the newly-institutionalized CSCE held a series of specialist meetings and conferences. Three of these were originally provided for in the concluding document of the third CSCE follow-up meeting (held in Vienna between November 1986 and January 1989). From 15 January to 8 February an experts' meeting on the peaceful settlement of disputes was held in Valletta (Malta). This created a 'dispute settlement mechanism' within the CSCE, involving a panel of qualified figures who could provide non-binding 'advice and comment' in cases of dispute between participating states.

From 28 May to 7 June a cultural heritage symposium was held in the historic Polish town of Cracow. This proved much more successful than the previous cultural forum held in Budapest in 1985, when the bitterness of the East-West conflict prevented any meaningful meeting of minds. The concluding document agreed at Cracow reflected the new emerging consensus in Europe on the need for cultural freedom and the preservation of the continent's diverse cultural heritage.

Of even greater significance was the third CSCE conference on 'the human dimension' held in Moscow from 10 September to 4 October (the previous two meetings having been held in Paris in May-June 1989 and Copenhagen in June 1990). This was a memorable occasion, coming as it did so shortly after the failed Soviet putsch of 19–21 August. The Moscow conference reaffirmed that human rights observance was a matter of direct and legitimate international concern. It also further refined the mechanism for the continuous monitoring of human rights which had originally been outlined in the Vienna concluding document. This made possible the involvement of independent experts to help resolve disputes over human rights issues between participating states.

As provided for under the Charter of Paris, two additional inter-sessional meetings also took place in 1991. The first was a meeting of experts on national minorities, held in Geneva on 1–19 July. This facilitated an exchange of national experience on dealing with the rights of national minority groups and agreed a concluding report which stressed that the rights of national minorities could only be adequately guaranteed within a democratic political system. The second was a seminar of experts on democratic institutions, held in Oslo on 4–15 November. Its purpose was to provide a forum for an exchange of information on constitutional law, electoral mechanisms, party systems and the rule of law, and its final report included a number of proposals for practical cooperation.

The themes of the meetings in Geneva and Oslo reflected the new priorities which had emerged in the CSCE since the end of the Cold War. Having previously served as a means of regulating conflict between two ideologically-opposed blocs, the CSCE now provided a framework for developing a new system of international relations in Europe, based on friendly cooperation amongst states committed to the common values of democracy and the rule of law. To this end, a major concern of the CSCE in 1991 was to consolidate democracy as the only system of government of participating states. The meetings in Geneva and Oslo were therefore aimed at providing the young democracies of the former communist states with information, advice and assistance.

Along with its task of setting commonly-agreed standards for democracy and human rights, the CSCE in 1991 also had to deal with a number of pressing regional problems—above all, the civil war in Yugoslavia (see IV.1.vi) and the break-up of the Soviet Union (see IV.2.i). The first meeting of the CSCE council of foreign ministers in Berlin on 19–20 June provided a useful occasion for pan-European consultation on these issues. The Berlin meeting was also significant in two other respects: it admitted Albania as a participating state and it agreed a new CSCE 'emergency mechanism'. This mechanism allowed meetings of the committee of senior officials to be called at short notice without consensus, and endorsed the Valletta report on the peaceful settlement of disputes.

The CSCE's new emergency mechanism was first used in July to discuss the deteriorating situation in Yugoslavia. It was also subsequently invoked in August, September and October, as concern grew about the mounting violence inside Yugoslavia. However, the CSCE's role in the crisis was limited to endorsing initiatives by the European Community (see XI.3). This helped to reinforce the EC's authority in dealing with the warring parties inside Yugoslavia, and also encouraged four other CSCE states, in September, to join the EC in sending teams to monitor the notional ceasefire. But the Yugoslav civil war also illustrated the limitations of the CSCE as an instrument of collective security in the continent, in that it was hamstrung by two factors: first, the consensus principle governing its decision-making; and second, the lack of an effective enforcement mechanism against 'rogue' states.

Nonetheless, the CSCE was seen as one of the success stories of modern European diplomacy. Despite the diverse motives behind its initiation as a 'process' in 1975, the CSCE had emerged as one of the principal institutional pillars of the new Europe—alongside the EC, NATO and the Council of Europe—and seemed destined to remain a key forum for consultation and cooperation between the continent's diverse states.

ii. EUROPEAN BANK FOR RECONSTRUCTION AND DEVELOPMENT (EBRD)

THE European Bank for Reconstruction and Development (EBRD) was established with remarkable dispatch for a major intergovernmental organization: just seven months elapsed between President Mitterrand's proposal (on 25 October 1989) and the agreement to create the bank, reached in Paris on 29 May 1990 (see AR 1990, pp. 134, 411). The pace of change in East European countries, and the urgency of their need for capital inflow and renewed infrastructure and financial services, clearly explained the speed over the EBRD. The bank formally opened its doors in London on 15 April with ceremonies attended by nine heads of state, 17 heads of government, the presidents of the European Community (EC) and of the European Investment Bank (EIB) and the finance ministers of all 39 member states. Membership was classified into 'countries of operations', meaning the European members of the former Council for Mutual Economic Assistance (CMEA/Comecon) plus Yugoslavia, and 'others', who were expected to be the donors. By the end of the year the EBRD board of directors had recommended that Albania be admitted as the 40th member and the eighth country of operations. In September all three Baltic states applied for similar membership, and during 1992 the issue of other republics of the former USSR was certain to be posed.

The EBRD was established with a capital of 10,000 million ecu,* with a majority of shares in the hands of the EC members, the EC itself and the EIB. All members were represented on the board of directors, and the staff, headed by bank's president, Jacques Attali of France, reflected the multinational membership. The EBRD was not quite the first pan-European economic agency, since the UN Economic Commission for Europe had been established in Geneva in 1946 with continent-wide membership and staff from both East and West. Nevertheless, the breadth of participation and personnel of the new bank distinguished it from other international economic bodies, even though these were also keeping pace with change in Europe. Both the IMF and the World Bank were likely to become as comprehensive as the EBRD in Europe with the adhesion of the ex-Soviet republics, while the IMF reported that one out of every six of its economists were working on the European states in economic transition. In December the EC brought itself closer to all-European participation with the signature of association agreements with Czechoslovakia, Hungary and Poland. In November the EBRD itself agreed to serve as the secretariat for the 'Hexagonale' initiative for cross-border and regional cooperation projects between Austria, Czechoslovakia, Hungary, Italy, Poland and Yugoslavia.

By the end of the year the EBRD had accepted 14 investment projects with a commitment of 388 million ecu within an aggregate capital formation of 1,298 million ecu; another 150 projects were under consideration and approval of 25 of these was imminent. Parallel with such banking operations, the bank had initiated technical assistance programmes in seven of its countries of operations (and in the Baltic states) and had adopted, in concert with the governments concerned, strategies on Bulgaria (November), Czechoslovakia (July), Hungary

---

*At end-1991 1 ecu = £0.71 or US$1.34.

(June), Poland (September) and Romania (November). EBRD staff visited Albania in November to prepare an action programme, after earlier visits had ascertained that the new coalition government intended marketization.

iii. COUNCIL OF EUROPE

As the former communist countries of Europe moved slowly towards the establishment of liberal democracies in the place of their former totalitarian regimes, so the Council of Europe's interest became increasingly focused on how the transition could best be aided. The Council's longstanding reputation for the promotion and safeguarding of human rights and democratic ideals, coupled with its pan-European vocation, in turn encouraged the new regimes to use it as a bridge into the wider community of Europe and as a means of conferring legitimacy and acceptance upon themselves. The Spanish chairman-in-office, having made a tour of East European nations with the secretary-general, presented his findings to an extraordinary meeting of the committee of ministers in Madrid on 21 February, where the Council of Europe's relations with these countries was assessed. This was the first meeting in the West attended by Aleksandr Bessmertnykh following his appointment as Soviet Foreign Minister.

Czechoslovakia (officially the Czech and Slovak Federal Republic) became a full member at the Madrid meeting, while Poland achieved full member status at a ministerial meeting on 26 November after a favourable report from the Parliamentary Assembly's observer delegation at the October elections (see IV.1.i). Asked to give an opinion on Bulgaria's application for membership, the Assembly also sent observers to monitor its elections the same month (see IV.1.v) and pronounced them 'free, if not fair'. Romania had attained special guest status in the Assembly, and received a number of visits from Assembly committees. Initial contacts were also made with Albania, which permitted Assembly observation of its elections in March and April (see IV.1.vii) to develop into informal information visits. The speaker of the Albanian National Assembly attended the debate held in Strasbourg on 21 September; following a formal information visit in November, Albania too was granted special guest status.

The situation in the Baltic republics gave much cause for concern in the early part of the year (see IV.2.ii). Following the violence of January and February, the Assembly decided against any immediate pronouncement for fear of making an over-emotional or ill-researched response. The president of the Assembly subsequently led a fact-finding mission to Moscow and the Baltics. Building on the contacts made during this visit, a hearing was arranged, this being the first time that the three republics and the central authorities had met together in an international forum. Following the August coup attempt in Moscow (see IV.2.i), and the Baltic republics' declarations of independence, the restoration of sovereignty was widely welcomed. All three states were granted special guest status and applied for full membership of the Council of Europe.

The conflict in Yugoslavia (see IV.1.vi) dominated the September session of the Assembly. In an attempt to repeat its success with the Baltics, the Assembly invited all sides to participate in a hearing. Sadly, nothing developed beyond ritual insults and sterile posturing. An emergency debate led to a resolution urging that a peace-keeping force should intervene and that declarations of independence by the Yugoslav republics should be recognized. Yugoslavia's special guest status was suspended on 25 November in view of the deterioration in the human rights situation.

Efforts were made to ensure that the Council of Europe's help was as much practical as moral. The 'Demosthenes programme' continued its work of education in the practice of democracy, with increasing emphasis on training those actually responsible for operating democratic institutions. In September the Parliamentary Assembly organized the third Strasbourg conference on parliamentary democracy, which concentrated on the factors necessary to establish and sustain a parliamentary democracy.

The Council of Europe acquired an accepted role in the human dimension of the Conference on Security and Cooperation in Europe (CSCE), and thus contributed to CSCE conferences on cultural heritage, minorities, and democratic institutions, as well as to the main conference on 'the human dimension' held in Moscow and to the ministerial meeting in Berlin (see XI.5.i). The Assembly offered its help and support for the new parliamentary tier of the CSCE, which was established at a conference of parliamentary delegations in Madrid in April.

The Gulf War (see V.2) renewed interest in relations between Europe, the Middle East and Arab states. The Assembly discussed a comprehensive report on the situation of Palestinian refugees, as well as organizing a colloquy on the contribution of Islamic culture to Europe and a Euro-Arab seminar. Towards the end of 1991, the Assembly's committee for the prevention of torture published a highly-critical report on the condition of prisons within the UK as part of its regular programme of checks on member countries' compliance with Council of Europe conventions. Sir John Freeland was elected as the UK member of the European Court of Human Rights in April.

iv. EUROPEAN FREE TRADE ASSOCIATION

THE EFTA ministerial meeting to round off 1991, held in Geneva on 10–11 December, should have been the opportunity for looking forward to the actual implementation of the European Economic Area (EEA). EFTA and the European Community (EC) had managed at last to complete their EEA negotiations, in Luxembourg in the early morning of 23 October. An initialling ceremony was set for 15 December, but there was to be another hurdle. The EC Court of Justice queried whether the regulation of EC-EFTA disputes, by a new EEA legal body, was compatible with its own right to interpret EC law. On 14 December it sent the EEA treaty back for renegotiation accordingly.

The October EEA agreement, to create from January 1993 the world's largest common market of 380 million people, had been described by the current EFTA chairman, Pertti Salolainen, as 'a building-block in the new European architecture'. Mr Salolainen accepted that 'the EC will of course remain the centre of attraction in Europe' but suggested that the EEA was potentially 'an attractive concept for Central and Eastern European countries seeking to become part of the greater European family'. Agreement had come only after the patience of negotiators had been tested by a long deadlock mainly over fish and road freight. Some more EC access to fishing grounds was in the end conceded by Norway, and a very limited amount, on a reciprocal basis, by Iceland, which also got better terms on customs-free access to the EC market for its fish products. Switzerland and Austria made some exceptions to their tightening of restrictions on lorries passing through the Alps; and, sweetening the EEA agreement for the poorer EC countries, EFTA would contribute 2,000 million ecu per year in low-interest loans and 425 million ecu in grants to a 'cohesion fund' for development in disadvantaged regions.

As concluded in October, the EEA treaty was seen as requiring completion of some 40 minor details prior to initialling, signature, and ratification—by the 19 participating countries and the European Parliament. The EEA would follow the principles of free movement of goods, services, people and capital, and the EFTA countries would adopt the *acquis communautaire*, passing into national law some 1,500 EC acts. Non-tariff barriers would be removed, but EFTA countries would not apply the EC's common agricultural, fisheries or coal and steel policy, and would retain sovereign control over their energy resources and production, some stricter environmental controls on chemicals, and state alcohol monopolies in Norway and Sweden. Existing EC rules would apply on consumer protection, education, social policy, company law, anti-trust and competition legislation. There would be free movement of people and mutual recognition of professional qualifications, but Switzerland would have until 1996 to adjust its particularly strict regime on immigration. Capital investment would remain subject to certain restrictions in particularly sensitive areas, such as purchase of real estate by non-nationals in some EFTA countries.

EEA institutions would include an EEA Council (one minister from each of the 19 countries and a representative of the EC Commission, chaired for six months alternately by an EC or an EFTA member), EEA courts (the stumbling block in December) to deal with disputes and to hear appeals on competition rulings, an EEA consultative committee and an EEA joint parliamentary committee. The EEA Council would not be involved in framing EC legislation but would decide by consensus on its wider application throughout the EEA. There would be reviews of the agreement every two years, the first at the end of 1993.

The EEA negotiation had defined the year for EFTA; it preoccupied ministers not only in the negotiating sessions but also at their regular meetings, and dominated the annual EFTA summit meeting, held in Vienna on 24 May. One widespread interpretation of the accord—that EFTA was close to negotiating itself out of existence in all but name—was not shared by the organization's secretariat. It had expanded its staff to 130, and got a budget adopted in May, for the 1991/92 year, which would allow a 40 per cent increase in expenditure.

EFTA did have some progress to record in December, on its external relations: the signature of a free trade agreement with Turkey, to take effect the following April, and joint declarations with Bulgaria, Romania and the three new Baltic states, which were also designed to lead quickly to free trade agreements. However, with the three countries of Central and Eastern Europe which had already signed joint declarations with EFTA, Czechoslovakia, Hungary and Poland, ministers had to content themselves with 'noting substantial progress', since EFTA was not yet in a position to sign the hoped-for free trade agreements.

The conflict in Yugoslavia, meanwhile, had brought a halt to all development on that country's 1990 application for membership of EFTA, which followed the EC lead in freezing all cooperation with Yugoslavia. EFTA did reach a membership total of seven, nevertheless, by the technical step of giving full separate membership on 1 September to Liechtenstein, a participant since 1960 by virtue of its customs union with Switzerland (see also III.2.viii). On the other side of the coin, Sweden had, in July, made its expected application for full EC membership, becoming (after Austria) the second of the EFTA member countries to do so. Moreover, Finland's application was imminent, and both Norway and Switzerland were actively studying the EC's allure.

v. NORDIC COUNCIL

THE 39th session of the Nordic Council was held in Copenhagen on 26 February–1 March. Eight of its recommendations for action by member governments originated from the council of ministers. They included closer cooperation in higher education; the creation of a council for European integration law and a 'secondary-education community'; reorganization of the cultural sector's institutions and financing; and adoption of plans for traffic safety and environmental research. Other recommendations included the development of a joint transport policy, including common policies for rail and the Skaggerak region; closer cooperation on common legislation for bio- and gene-technology; guidelines to achieve 40 per cent representation of women on all Nordic bodies by 1996; and the development of statistical methods and models for measuring 'green' GNP.

The session was attended as guests by the Presidents of Latvia and Estonia and the Vice-President of Lithuania, a gesture of support for Baltic independence which drew an official Soviet protest. Thirteen recommendations concerned the development of closer cooperation with the Baltic littoral states in general and Lithuania, Estonia and Latvia in particular. The Council also wished to see the environmental provisions of the 1974 Baltic Sea convention strengthened. Later in the year, the Nordic Council's presidium supported the now-independent Baltic states' demand for the removal of all Soviet troops from their territories. The presidium also called on the three governments, for their part, to observe international agreements on the rights of ethnic minorities.

Apart from Baltic events, the Nordic Council's general debate was again dominated by relations with the European Community (EC), and in particular the consequences for Nordic cooperation of the prospective EC-EFTA European Economic Area (EEA) and Sweden's forthcoming EC membership application. Some speakers argued that the EEA would promote Nordic integration, not undermine it. There was general support for a 'Nordic clause' in the EEA treaty guaranteeing the continuation of regional cooperation. There was also a general determination to make the institutions of Nordic cooperation more effective, with clearer priorities. To this end the Council adopted recommendations for revisions to the 1962 Helsinki Agreement strengthening the presidium's initiating and coordinating role and explicitly recognizing that international issues came within the Council's scope. Proposals to give it significantly greater budget powers and to create a council of foreign ministers had to be left for further discussion among member governments. They would be dealt with in the council of ministers' report on 'The Nordic area after 1992' being prepared for the 40th session in 1992.

At an extra Nordic Council session at Mariehamn on 13 November, representatives again called for a more effective organization and proposals for action. The presidium responded with a recommendation addressed to the prime ministers attending the meeting. This called on them to define the aims and priorities of Nordic cooperation and to initiate a corresponding revision of the Helsinki Agreement, including the creation of a council of foreign ministers and the establishment of a larger budget, to be concentrated on priority areas.

The prime ministers responded with a 'Mariehamn declaration', in which they announced the appointment of a group of personal representatives to recommend how the existing structures could best be adapted to meet the challenges of the ending of the Cold War, the EEA and the Nordic states' different relations with the EC. Their recommendations would take account of work being done within the Nordic Council and its council of ministers. The general interpretation of this declaration was that at last the challenges facing Nordic cooperation in general and the Nordic Council in particular were to be taken up at the highest political level in preparation for decisions in 1992.

6. AFRICAN, ASIAN, PACIFIC AND AMERICAN REGIONAL ORGANIZATIONS

i. AFRICAN CONFERENCES AND ORGANIZATIONS

THE wind of democratization, in full spate in Africa in the course of 1991, meant that African conferences were more troubled than usual. And in view of the increasingly difficult finances of many states, the continental institutions were often engaged in a struggle for survival.

The Organization of African Unity (OAU) put a brave face on the troubles and signed an ambitious treaty for an African Economic Community at its 27th summit. This was held on 3–5 June in Abuja, the new capital of Nigeria and was the first time an OAU summit had been held away from the Addis Ababa headquarters since the 1981 summit in Nairobi (unless one counts the abortive attempts to meet in Tripoli in 1982). It was in retrospect a prudent move not to go to Addis Ababa, as early June was the week in which President Haile-Maryam Mengistu of Ethiopia fled before a rebel advance (see VI.1.i).

The Ethiopian crisis highlighted the fragility of the thrones of many of those attending the summit. In the previous nine months, at least seven leaders had been overthrown, four by violence (Liberia, Chad, Somalia and Mali) and three, miraculously, by the ballot box (São Tomé and Príncipe, Cape Verde and Benin). There was thus a strange mixture of old warhorses and new democrats, as well as a smattering of the young technocrats, who were increasingly taking over the reins of government in Africa.

Even so, in spite of the turbulence, 34 of the 51 OAU countries were represented in Abuja by their heads of state, though the presences of some were fairly brief. This was in part a tribute to the pulling power of Nigeria, but also to the fact that many wanted to put their signature to the new 79-page African Economic Treaty. This was in many respects a Utopian document for the future—not intended to come into being for another 34 years—but it gave some countries presently in serious difficulties a target to work towards and an ideal to look forward to. Its adoption received official encouragement from UN Secretary-General Pérez de Cuellar, who said it showed the commitment of African countries to establishing a firm foundation for the acceleration of their economic growth and development. It was also supported by World Bank president, Barber Conable, who said that his organization would do everything possible to help in the realization of the treaty's objectives. 'The time has come to move from dreams to deeds', he said.

Many speakers in Abuja bemoaned the present condition of the continent, expressing genuine fears of marginalization from the 'new world order' and from increasing economic integration elsewhere in the world. As the outgoing chairman, President Yoweri Museveni of Uganda, observed: 'The litany of Africa's woes is awesome, painful and agonizing .... While the rest of the world is on its way to modernization, Africa remains a virtual museum piece.'

While the summit pusillanimously skirted round the pressing question of democratization (for fear of offending some of the 'bunker-presidents' present), it did pass resolutions on a number of pressing crises on the continent, such as the situation in Liberia, Rwanda, Ethiopia and Somalia. Not surprisingly, in the case of Somalia (see VII.1.ii), there was strong condemnation of the de facto secession of Northern Somaliland, although the OAU had been signally unable to mediate in what had become an increasingly desperate and murderous conflict. Interim President Amos Sawyer of Liberia received a 21-gun salute from the Nigerians, but this did not assist the peace process in that sad country (see VI.2.v). There was also a declaration on South Africa, after the conference had been addressed by Nelson Mandela of the ANC. However, southern African questions consumed neither the time nor the passion expended at previous African summits. This was perhaps a measure of the change in South Africa (see VII.3), although the conference endorsed the maintenance of most sanctions until real signs of 'irreversible' democratic change were visible.

The democracy issue, interestingly, made a much bigger impact at the summit of the 16-nation Economic Community of West African States (ECOWAS), held likewise in Abuja a month later, when declarations were approved on both democracy and human rights. The grouping, in spite of the conflicts over Liberia, seemed to have a little more dynamism, perhaps inspired, paradoxically, by the common effort involved in the ECOWAS Monitoring Group (ECOMOG) sent in to monitor the ceasefire in Liberia in 1990. This was originally supported by Nigeria, Ghana, Sierra Leone, the Gambia and Guinea, but, as part of the Yamoussoukro peace process, both Burkina Faso and Senegal had committed troops to the ECOMOG by the end of the year. Senegal's 3,000 were actually supported by US funds, indicating US gratitude for the Senegalese contribution to the Gulf War effort (see V.2).

Many Africans read the runes very closely at the Franco-African summit in Paris in November. This was partly because, at the 1990 summit in France (see AR 1990, p. 422), President Mitterrand had linked aid to democracy in such a way as to alarm the hawks of the one-party states. Some of these (in Chad and Mali) subsequently lost power, while others (in Zaïre, Togo, Cameroon and Madagascar) were under fire all through 1991. However, some observers felt that the French pro-democracy line was not as militant in 1991 as in 1990, as expediency gained weight over idealism.

Other groupings in central and east Africa tottered on, while the Arab Maghreb Union, a latecomer that had been moving fast, felt threatened by the rise of Islamic fundamentalism in Algeria (see V.6.iv). The Mano River Union was dead in the water due to the Liberia crisis, while the Senegal River Development Organization suffered from Senegal's row with Mauritania. The Preferential Trade Area (PTA) in east and central Africa seemed in better health than the Southern African Development Coordination Conference (SADCC), which was suffering from an identity crisis because of developments in South Africa. However, a SADCC rethink to take in the 'new South Africa' could make it one of the continent's most ambitious groupings.

For the first time, the Islamic Conference Organization held a summit in black Africa, in Senegal in December. It was notable both for the unusual prominence given to women, and for the absence of some notable Arab leaders (such as the kings of Morocco and Saudi Arabia), which saddened the Senegalese. The Pan-African News Agency (PANA), like many African institutions, suffered from non-payment of subscriptions by member states and ended the year virtually bankrupt.

ii. SOUTH ASIAN ASSOCIATION FOR REGIONAL COOPERATION (SAARC)

IT was another year rather like 1989 (see AR 1989 pp. 406-7), in which it seemed that SAARC would not be able to convene a summit. Ostensibly this was because the King of Bhutan announced that he would be unable to go to Colombo and because of attendant issues of representation, though many commentators deduced that the real cause of the impasse was the prevailing distrust between India's government and that of the would-be host, President Premadasa of Sri Lanka. Thus the SAARC summit, scheduled to begin on 7 November, was put off because of a lack of consensus among member states, though an informal summit of Pakistan, Bangladesh, Sri Lanka and the Maldives took place.

In the event, a one-day SAARC summit was held in Colombo on 21 December and was apparently remarkably rancour-free. A much-accelerated inaugural session, discussions at a retreat and a concluding session were all packed into 24 hours, compared with the customary practice of taking three days. The summit leaders decided to 'strengthen' SAARC by keeping controversial questions such as the idea of a South Asian nuclear-arms-free zone out of their collective deliberations this time. The proclaimed consensus reached by the leaders at the end of their deliberations covered a host of economic and political issues, which was by no means an unusual occurrence at SAARC summits. Yet the high degree of public agreement stood in marked contrast to the disputes and impasse of only a month earlier.

Most of the issues covered by the Colombo declaration were part of SAARC's ongoing agenda of recent years. The need to curb terrorist activities, the Maldivian initiative to seek international consensus on reinforcing the security of small countries, the call to take effective steps to combat narco-terrorism in South Asia, the plea to articulate a collective stand on global and regional environmental issues—all fell into this category. On the environmental issue, in particular, the summit decided to establish a committee to examine the recommendations of a regional study already made on this subject.

The summit leaders also agreed that the SAARC inter-governmental group studying prospects for regional cooperation in trade, manufactures and services should examine further the Sri Lankan proposal for the establishment of a SAARC Preferential Trade Arrangement (SAPTA) by 1997. It was also agreed that a special session of SAARC foreign ministers should be held in Colombo in 1992 to study ways and means of streamlining the working norms of the organization. This would possibly include revisions to SAARC's charter and discussions on how to establish suitable 'external linkages' with other regional organizations such as ASEAN and the European Community. It was agreed to hold the 1992 SAARC summit in Dhaka (Pakistan).

Other meetings held under the auspices of SAARC during the year, included the ninth session of the SAARC council of ministers in Malé in July, when the nomination was approved of the Deputy Foreign Minister of the Maldives, Ibrahim Hussain Zaki, to succeed Kant Kishore Bhargawa of India as SAARC's secretary-general from the end of the year.

iii. SOUTH-EAST ASIAN ORGANIZATIONS

THE Association of South-East Asian Nations (ASEAN) was noticeably less preoccupied with events in Cambodia during 1991. As the warring factions edged towards the signing of a historic peace agreement in October (see IX.1.ix), ASEAN voiced its approval and concentrated its energy on other pressing matters, principally economic affairs. In March President Suharto of Indonesia, Singaporean Prime Minister Goh Chok Tong, Sultan Sir Hassanal Bolkiah of Brunei and Malaysian Prime Minister Mahathir Mohamed convened in Bali for a mini-summit on economic issues. Dr Mahathir used the meeting as an opportunity to promote his ambitious trade bloc initiative, an East Asian Economic Grouping (EAEG), aimed at allying ASEAN with its prosperous northern neighbours, Japan, Taiwan and South Korea. The Malaysian leader contended that the formation of an EAEG would benefit rather than stifle world trade. However, other ASEAN leaders were openly sceptical of the Malaysian proposal. The United States also questioned the initiative, which, it claimed, would divide rather than draw together the trading interests of the wider Pacific area.

Despite the cool reception afforded to the initiative, it was one of a number of plans for enhanced intra-ASEAN economic cooperation which came under discussion at the 24th annual meeting of ASEAN foreign ministers held in Malaysia in July. No proposals were actually adopted, but it was agreed to examine them further in working groups and at the fourth ASEAN summit scheduled to be held in Singapore in January 1992. For the first time, the Soviet Union and China were represented at the meeting. South Korea was accepted as ASEAN's seventh full 'dialogue partner' at the post-ministerial conference (PMC). At the meeting, Japan proposed that the annual PMC should be made a regular forum for dialogue focused on regional security issues.

ASEAN economic ministers held their 23rd annual meeting in Malaysia in October. The ministers agreed on a set of proposals for economic cooperation to be submitted to the fourth ASEAN summit. The agreement on a framework for an Asian Free Trade Area (AFTA) and on the formation of a 'non-institutional' discussion forum, the East Asian Economic Caucus (EAEC), effectively signalled an end to Dr Mahathir's dream of a comprehensive East Asia trade bloc. The AFTA, based on a Thai proposal, would provide for a 15-year transition to free trade in manufactures among ASEAN members. The EAEC, whose participants were not clearly specified, would exist within the broader framework of the Asia-Pacific Economic Cooperation Council (APEC), the Pacific Rim grouping launched by Australia in 1989 (see AR 1989, p. 408).

The third APEC conference was held in South Korea in mid-November. China, Hong Kong and Taiwan (under the name Chinese Taipei) participated in the conference for the first time, raising the number of members to 15. The United States used the conference to reinforce opposition to Dr Mahathir's EAEC proposal. The Malaysian Prime Minister responded by dispatching a low-ranking official to represent Malaysia at the conference. A vaguely-worded final communique committed the APEC members to cooperate to reduce trade barriers both within the region and worldwide, and to identify and promote the region's interests. The communique failed to indicate the level of disagreement among the member countries over their response to the deadlocked GATT Uruguay Round talks. Nevertheless, a separate communique published on the issue backed 'substantial' liberalization of trade, and the members agreed to show 'the necessary flexibility' in the current negotiations.

The 47th session of the UN Economic and Social Commission for Asia and the Pacific (ESCAP) was held in South Korea in April. The conference was attended by over 1,000 delegates, representing the 48 ESCAP members, and had 'industrial restructuring' as its theme. In late 1990 ESCAP had predicted a slowing of economic growth in the Asia and Pacific region. However, in a report published in December the Commission claimed that the region had been well able to withstand the impact of the Gulf War, global recession and stagnant world trade and had emerged with only minor damage. This had been achieved partly through a sharp increase in trade within the region itself, and the report predicted that the region's performance would improve during 1992. The ESCAP findings were reinforced by a report published in December by the Asian Development Bank (ADB), which estimated growth of more than 6 per cent in the region during 1991. The 51-country ADB's annual meeting in Canada in April had failed to agree terms for a controversial replenishment of its soft-loan window, the Asian Development Fund.

iv. SOUTH PACIFIC REGIONAL COOPERATION

AT its annual heads of government meeting held in Palikir, the capital of the newly-independent Federated States of Micronesia (see X.2.ii), the South Pacific Forum elected as its new secretary-general Iremia Tabai, formerly President of Kiribati. The meeting also emphasized the need for better aid delivery, more private investment and stronger trade growth throughout the region (this consonant with the thrust of a 1991 World Bank appraisal of the South Pacific) and stressed the need to articulate South Pacific interests in negotiation of international conventions on climate change and biodiversity. It also condemned continued French nuclear testing in the South Pacific and welcomed binding American assurances for an end to chemical weapons destruction on Johnston Atoll. In other decisions, it supported continued political, social and economic development in New Caledonia pending eventual self-determination, endorsed the applications of the Marshall Islands and the Federated States of Micronesia to the United Nations (both were duly admitted) and approved the establishment of the South Pacific Regional Environmental Programme as a fully autonomous regional body with its headquarters in Western Samoa. The meeting also commended the efforts of the Alliance of Small Island States (AOSIS) in developing a framework convention on climate change.

At its October meeting in Tonga, the South Pacific Commission's annual conference failed to resolve a continuing dispute over the location of the organization's new headquarters, postponing a decision until a meeting scheduled for March 1992. A new director-general was appointed, namely Jacques Iekawe, who prior to this posting was immediate deputy to New Caledonia's high commissioner (appointed by France). The meeting also discussed a management report critical of the organization's operations.

A further regional appointment of note was that of Esekia Solofa from Western Samoa, who was made vice-chancellor of the University of the South Pacific and became the first Pacific Islander to hold the post.

v. LATIN AMERICAN ORGANIZATIONS AND COOPERATION

AT the general assembly of the Organization of American States (OAS), held in Washington, DC on 8 January, Guyana and Belize formally became the 34th and 35th OAS members. Their membership had for many years been delayed by the claims on their territories made by Venezuela and Guatemala respectively.

The 21st OAS general assembly, held in Santiago de Chile on 3–9 June and attended by 34 member states, endorsed the Declaration of Santiago. This document required the OAS permanent council to convene at once following 'any abrupt or irregular interruption of the democratic, political and institutional process, or of the legitimate exercise of power by a democratically-elected government' in any member state. However, the assembly rejected a proposal that all states should immediately sever diplomatic relations with the state in question, supporting instead Mexico's traditional policy (the so-called 'Estrada doctrine') of recognizing any government shown to be in physical control of its national territory.

An admission that the United States had in the past made 'errors' in its Latin American policy by viewing the region through the 'sometimes distorting prism of the Cold War' was made by Lawrence Eagleburger, US Deputy Secretary of State. The admission was the more noteworthy for the fact that he personally had made some of these 'errors'. Following the expulsion from Haiti in October of the OAS secretary-general, João Baena Soares, and six foreign ministers (see II.3.iii), painstaking negotiations brought about a meeting between the contending parties in Bogotá on 22 November, but without success.

The first Ibero-American summit was held at Guadalajara (Mexico) on 18–19 July and was attended by the King of Spain, the Presidents of Portugal and 19 Central and South American republics and the Prime Ministers of Portugal and Spain. The United States was not invited to attend, though the governor of Puerto Rico was. To the irritation of many of those present, the proceedings were dominated by President Fidel Castro Ruz of Cuba. He denounced US domination of Latin America, which he saw in every device for intra-regional cooperation. The final act of the summit, expressing a commitment to joint action, was largely hortatory. However, Argentina and Brazil took advantage of the occasion to sign a bilateral agreement renouncing the manufacture of nuclear weapons. The second of what were intended to be annual conferences would be held in Spain in 1992.

On 26 March the Presidents of Argentina, Brazil, Paraguay and Uruguay, meeting at Asunción, signed an agreement to create a new common market in the Southern Cone with its headquarters in Montevideo. The new grouping, Mercosur, formed a natural development from a series of earlier bilateral accords and had an estimated population of 190,000,000 and a combined GNP of $420,000 million. It aimed to achieve free movement of goods and services by 31 December 1994, commencing with a 47 per cent cut in tariffs in June. On 19 June its members signed a framework free-trade agreement with the United States, and on 20 July Mercosur economy ministers met to discuss anti-dumping policy.

The San José Group of five Central American countries and Panama met for the seventh time with their counterparts from the European Community in Managua on 18–19 March to press for tariff reductions on Community imports of tropical produce from their countries. At the tenth Central American summit in San Salvador on 16–18 June, attended by Panama as a full delegate for the first time, the six republics signed a protocol establishing a Central American Parliament and reaffirming support for the regional peace process. A further agreement was made to reduce certain tariffs. The Parliament (Parlacén) was formally established by Honduras, Guatemala and El Salvador on 28 October.

At a summit meeting of Andean Pact countries on 18 May, heads of government approved the Declaration of Caracas, committing the five states to a free-trade zone by January 1992, and envisaging a fully-integrated common market by 1995.

Regional responses to Latin America's first cholera epidemic since the 1880s included a meeting of the regional health ministers and their Spanish counterpart in Sucre (Bolivia) on 20–23 April. When the initial infection first came ashore at Chimbote (Peru) in January, the outbreak could easily have been contained. Instead, it was allowed to spread, transmitted by fish and shellfish, which had been contaminated by untreated sewage. By the time of the Sucre meeting, over 1,200 had died and some 160,000 had been infected, and the epidemic had already spread to Colombia, Ecuador, Bolivia and Chile. In May it spread to southern Mexico, apparently by way of a light aircraft carrying illegal drugs, and in July to Guatemala. Meanwhile, it had crossed the Andean continental divide to become established in the headwaters of the Amazon. By December it had reached the Brazilian cities of Manaus and Belém and was threatening to devastate the crowded coastal area in the new year.

vi. CARIBBEAN ORGANIZATIONS

THE movement for economic and political integration among English-speaking Caribbean states and territories continued at its customary leisurely pace through 1991, but progress towards the implementation of a common market, planned for 1994, seemed likely to be overtaken by the US drive for a hemispheric free trade zone.

At year's end most of the 13 members of the Caribbean Community (CARICOM) had introduced the common external tariff (CET) which, with the freeing of inter-island trade, was central to the integration process. The CET was designed to simplify procedures, to protect against imports and to boost industrial and agricultural production. The system was introduced on the 1 January target date, set at the 1990 CARICOM summit (see AR 1990, pp. 427–8), only by Trinidad & Tobago. The Organization of Eastern Caribbean States (OECS), grouping the smaller CARICOM members, expressed concern at the inflationary impact of the CET, and several countries delayed implementation. By mid-year seven countries had complied, but by the end of 1991 Grenada, St Lucia, Belize and Montserrat had yet to act.

The first triennial CARICOM regional economic summit conference opened in Trinidad on 27 February. Although intra-CARICOM trade had increased in 1990 (to US$481 million), the total value was less than that of a decade ago. Most island economies remained in recession in 1991, despite increased export production, with unemployment averaging 11 per cent and an aggregate external debt of $11,000 million, equal to the combined CARICOM GNP.

At the annual CARICOM summit in St Kitts on 1–5 July, a trade agreement was reached with Venezuela. Urged on by CARICOM's independent 'think tank', the West Indian Commission, the ritual motions in favour of integration were passed and the 1994 single market target reaffirmed. Moves towards integration had included the opening of the three-centre Caribbean stock exchange in April. The question of expanding CARICOM, as favoured by the United States, was discussed; opposition to the December 1990 coup in Suriname put paid to that country's chances of fuller participation, although it retained observer status. The CARICOM foreign ministers agreed to seek joint representation on 22 international bodies and to establish an economic mission in the Far East.

The US attempt to negotiate on a bilateral basis the terms for each state's participation in the Enterprise for the Americas Initiative (EAI), launched by President Bush in 1990, foundered on the insistence of Prime Minister Manley of Jamaica that the deal should be struck with CARICOM, of which he was the 1990/91 chairman. There was uncertainty as to whether the concepts of a free-trade EAI and protectionist CET could coexist. However, CARICOM acceded en bloc to the EIA package of free trade, free capital movement, official debt relief, economic reform aided by the Inter-American Development Bank, technology transfer and industrial development aid. The agreement, signed in July, set up a US–CARICOM trade and investment council to monitor the opening of markets and to develop common positions on world trade. The EAI, which already had 15 non-CARICOM participants, thus went further than the anti-tariff Caribbean Basin Initiative (renewed in 1990 as CBI–II—see AR 1990, p. 427). The CBI had signally failed to meet the expectations of its 18 Caribbean island participants, whose exports to the United States fell by about 40 per cent in 1983–90 while Central American exports increased by the same amount.

On 2 February the OECS summit in St Lucia addressed the deteriorating balance of trade with the rest of CARICOM in a plan for free inter-OECS trade, the removal of import restrictions and an export-led industrialization strategy developed with the Eastern Caribbean Central Bank. There were agreements on a common fisheries surveillance zone, social security reciprocity and education. In August Grenada rejoined the Eastern Caribbean Supreme Court system.

The inter-governmental Caribbean Tourism Organization (CTO) and the private-sector Caribbean Hotels Association (CHA) continued to explore collective marketing. The CHA called for the creation of a regional airline to supersede the 12 local carriers; CARICOM also favoured rationalization, but the CTO's 15th annual conference in September put off resolution of the issue until mid-1992. The CHA demanded the deregulation of tourism investment and the creation of a Caribbean tourism development bank, and joined the CTO in promoting 'eco-tourism'. The industry had suffered in 1990/91 from recession, increased costs and the effect of the Gulf War.

XII DEFENCE, SECURITY AND ARMS CONTROL

1. NEW PROBLEMS AND WAR IN THE GULF

THE year began with a major war in the Gulf and ended with the complete collapse of the Soviet Union. It was a year in which the United States and its coalition partners won an easy victory against Iraq (see v.2) and the end of the Cold War was more obviously reflected in the policies adopted by the United States and its European allies in NATO. The main security preoccupations were instability in Central Europe, especially the Balkans, and the disintegration of the Soviet Union (see IV.2.i), which raised serious concerns over the command and control of nuclear weapons. Other question marks posed by the demise of the Soviet Union included the future implementation of arms control agreements such as the Strategic Arms Reduction (START) Treaty, signed on 31 July 1991, and the CFE agreement which had been signed at the Paris summit in November 1990 (see AR 1990, pp. 434–8). Perhaps its most important impact, however, was the potential diffusion of nuclear expertise, as Soviet engineers and scientists came onto the open market. Inevitably this exacerbated concerns over nuclear proliferation. In short, 1991 was a year in which the old security preoccupations of the Cold War finally disappeared, only to be replaced by a new set of emerging security concerns.

The appearance of new problems, however, could not obscure the progress made towards a more stable and secure international order. Large steps forward were taken in terms of nuclear arms reductions, while NATO adapted its strategy and force posture to reflect the changed security conditions in Europe. Moreover, the trend towards the emergence of a more independent Western Europe did something to reassure those who were concerned that the demise of the Soviet Union had left what some analysts saw as a 'unipolar' international system, in which the United States was the only military superpower.

Yet the year began on a sombre note. The crisis in the Gulf reached an impasse in January 1991: in spite of a last-minute flurry of diplomatic activity to find a peaceful resolution to the crisis, President Saddam Husain of Iraq proved unwilling to withdraw from Kuwait before the deadline of 15 January imposed by the United Nations. Hostilities began on 16 January, with large-scale air attacks by US and allied forces on Iraqi command and control centres and other key targets in Baghdad and elsewhere. This was the harbinger of things to come, in that air power played the decisive role in the war. The destruction of Iraqi command, control and communication facilities and the degradation of its air defence capabilities, combined with the reluctance of the Iraqi air force to engage in air-to-air combat, allowed the coalition air forces to strike almost at will. The civilian infrastructure, the Iraqi armed forces (including the Republican Guard) and Iraqi nuclear facilities were all severely damaged by what was the most sustained and intense air bombardment in history.

If the war was a victory for the US air force, it was also a triumph for high technology. Although the Patriot anti-missile missile did not perform as well as was claimed during the hostilities, precision-guided munitions, the F-117A 'Stealth' fighters and the Tomahawk cruise missile all proved to be devastatingly effective, while the M-1 tank performed in ways which belied its troubled history. The technological advantage held by the United States meant that the gruelling test of will, in which Saddam Husain had anticipated that he could outlast US forces in a war of attrition, never materialized. The coalition held back from initiating a ground war until there was confidence that Iraqi ground forces had been significantly weakened—and the ground war itself lasted only four days, with Iraqi forces outgunned and outfought. Critics argued that President Bush had stopped too quickly and should have allowed coalition forces to drive to Baghdad and depose Saddam Husain. The President, however, was acutely aware that the 29-nation coalition had been kept together by the very fact that its objective was limited to the liberation of Kuwait.

The conflict in the Gulf also highlighted problems of burden-sharing in US relations with Japan and its West European allies. Britain and France had substantial contingents in the Gulf, but the German constitution prohibited the sending of troops and Japan also proved unwilling to become involved militarily. Under pressure from the United States, however, both Bonn and Tokyo made significant financial contributions to help cover the costs of the war (see III.1.ii and IX.2.iv). Even so, the lack of more direct involvement created deep resentment in Washington.

The impact of the war on the United States was something of a paradox. On the one hand, the dependence on allies for financial support highlighted American economic weakness. On the other, the war was a triumphant exercise in American diplomatic leadership and military strength. As such it provided a form of redemption for the Vietnam War. Mixed with the euphoria and the patriotism which greeted the end of the war, however, was a strong sense of relief. In spite of its victory, the United States did not seem particularly anxious to carry on being the world's policeman. With the war over, it became clear that the downward trend in the US military budget would continue, as Washington attempted to come to terms with the post-Cold War world. This trend became increasingly noticeable when the failure of the August coup in Moscow resulted in the rapid disintegration of the Soviet Union.

2. NATO AND THE EUROPEAN DIMENSION

THE collapse of the Soviet Union continued the process of dismantling the Cold War in Europe which had begun in 1989 with the crumbling of the Berlin Wall. By the end of the year, the only major Cold War institution which remained in Europe was NATO. During 1991, however, that organization initiated a series of reforms which were clearly designed to adjust to a post-Cold War Europe. The changes covered four main areas: force structure, strategy, the relationship with the newly-independent states of Eastern Europe and the balance of effort between Western Europe and the United States. Although the changes in force structure and strategy should ideally have gone together, the former proved easier to achieve than the elaboration of a new strategy for the alliance.

The force structure changes were unveiled at the NATO defence ministers meeting at the end of May and marked a shift from high levels of preparedness to a more relaxed posture with greater emphasis on flexibility and crisis management. The changes included substantial cuts in ready forces and greater reliance on reserves, the creation of multinational corps (in place of the national corps structure) and the development of rapid reaction forces. NATO forces would also be divided into main defence forces, reaction forces and augmentation forces. In addition, de facto changes in nuclear force structure were announced unilaterally by President Bush on 27 September, although this initiative had support from the allies.

The reform of NATO strategy proved more elusive and took rather longer to achieve, not least because of the conceptual difficulties of redefining strategy without an obvious threat on which to focus. Nevertheless, the new strategic concept was made public on 7 November at the NATO heads of government meeting in Rome. The declaration issued by the leaders suggested that security policy was predicated on three mutually-supporting elements: 'dialogue, cooperation and the maintenance of a collective defence capability'. While the military dimension of the alliance would remain, it would serve a much broader concept of security than in the past. As the declaration noted: 'The alliance will maintain its purely defensive purpose, its collective arrangements based on an integrated military structure as well as cooperation and coordination agreements, and for the foreseeable future an appropriate mix of conventional and nuclear forces.' While military forces would be substantially reduced, they would also be given increased mobility to react to a wide range of contingencies, and be organized 'for a flexible build-up . . . [and] for crisis management as well as defence'. The new emphasis on crisis management reflected the inherent uncertainties in post-Cold War Europe, and the need for NATO to consider a much broader range of contingencies than in the past.

The third area of change was the relationship with the states of Central and Eastern Europe, especially Poland, Hungary and Czechoslovakia—all of which were pressing for much closer association with NATO. The final arrangement was a compromise between East European desires for membership of NATO and the reluctance of the alliance to extend its security guarantee. Rather than the East European states being offered associate membership in NATO, a North Atlantic Cooperation Council was established. At the Rome summit in November, the foreign ministers of Bulgaria, Czechoslovakia, Estonia, Hungary, Latvia, Lithuania, Poland, Romania and the Soviet Union were invited to join NATO foreign ministers for a meeting in Brussels in December to thrash out the specific details of this Cooperation Council. The broad outlines were already laid out in the Rome declaration: annual meetings of the Cooperation Council, periodic meetings with the existing North Atlantic Council at the ambassadorial level and additional meetings at ministerial level as circumstances warranted. NATO also identified the key areas where it would try to help the East Europeans: defence planning, democratic concepts of civil–military relations, civil–military coordination of air traffic management and the conversion of defence industries to civilian production. The Brussels meeting itself began the process of institutionalizing the links between the two parts of Europe.

The final, and most vexed, area of change was the shift in the balance of effort and responsibility in NATO from the United States to Western Europe. This shift did not begin in 1991, nor was it completed during the year. Significant progress was made, although at times the process proved to be uncomfortable for governments on both sides of the Atlantic. This was partly because there were different conceptions of what was entailed. In some respects, these could be traced back to the arguments about Atlantic Europe versus European Europe which first became evident in the early 1960s with the clash between the Gaullist vision of an independent or 'third force' Western Europe and the Kennedy administration's 'grand design' for a twin-pillar Atlantic alliance. At that time, though, the debate had more to do with broad philosophy than with practical policy; by 1991 the issue was a much more practical one, as Western Europe moved towards political union and began to consider how defence and security could be included in this process. Moreover, it became clear during the year that several features of the traditional debate had changed.

The Europeans no longer saw defence as a special case which was best put on the backburner until integration had been completed in other areas. Instead, it was seen as an essential component of a comprehensive move towards West European unity. Perhaps even more important was a shift in the balance of influence. In the early 1960s the Federal Republic of Germany depended crucially on the

United States for its security, and was therefore reluctant to do anything which might alienate Washington. It became clear in 1991 that, with the reunification of Germany completed and the Cold War over, Germany no longer felt compelled to side with Washington in its longrunning, if often muted, dispute with Paris over the future shape and role of a West European defence identity. Yet some things remained the same, as Britain continued to give priority to the Atlantic link and to argue that nothing should be done to undermine the continued American commitment to Western Europe (see also I.1). Yet even this was part of an intra-European debate over the nature of the West European defence identity in which Britain was supported by the Netherlands, Portugal and, at critical junctures, Italy.

Perhaps the most crucial difference between the earlier exchanges on a West European defence identity and those of 1991 was that the debate—at both the trans-Atlantic level and the European level—no longer had an abstract quality, but centred around the future role and status of the Western European Union (WEU). This became apparent early in the year. A memorandum from Reginald Bartholomew, the US Under-Secretary of State for International Security Affairs, was sent to European governments prior to the WEU Council meeting of 22 February. In this communication, Mr Bartholomew spelled out concerns that the United States would be marginalized, warned against the creation of a European caucus in NATO and reiterated that nothing should be done to weaken NATO's command structure. Although steps were subsequently taken to mitigate some of the effects of the memorandum, it was clear that it reflected deep-seated American concerns about what was seen as the increasingly exclusive direction of European defence cooperation. Part of the concern was over the proposal that the WEU should become the defence and security arm of the European Community (EC) as it moved towards political union. This notion, which was pushed by France and Germany, generated antipathy rather than enthusiasm in Washington. The US National Security Adviser, Brent Scowcroft, made it clear in April that the United States would be very unhappy if the WEU became 'tied fundamentally to the EC rather than to NATO', arguing that such a development would reduce the American forces in Europe to the status of mercenaries rather than participants 'in the full scope of European security'.

The continuing concerns expressed by American officials were indicative of the perceived drawbacks, for the United States, likely to arise from greater European defence cooperation when this was done on European rather than American terms. A single European voice on security matters, along with an organizational vehicle for expressing it, would challenge the United States' traditional dominance over alliance policy. While this was a price that the Bush administration, in principle, was prepared to pay, in practice it proved more hesitant. The prevailing conception of the WEU in Washington was one that visualized it as an institutionalized caucus within the NATO framework, not as an independent or semi-independent body which could act separately from the United States. In short, the Americans saw the WEU as the European pillar of the Atlantic alliance rather than as a separate entity.

France, however, argued very strongly in favour of establishing the WEU as the EC's defence wing. Moreover, on 16 October Chancellor Kohl of Germany and President Mitterrand of France announced a plan to develop a 'genuine European security and defence identity' in which they explicitly advocated that the WEU should become the 'defence component' of European union (see also III.1.ii). The idea was that the EC nations would form joint military units which would come under the direction of the WEU. In addition, the WEU would develop plans for the deployment of these forces in crisis situations and would start to have joint military exercises. As a first step, a Franco-German corps was to be formed, which Herr Kohl and M. Mitterrand hoped would serve as the 'core of a European corps, to which other armed forces from WEU member states could be added'. In spite of reassuring statements that it posed no threat to NATO and did not contradict 'the assignments NATO has to carry out', the plan did not evoke enthusiasm in Washington and provoked overt hostility in London. This hostility was intensified as France and Germany not only made it clear that they wanted the WEU 'to act in conformity with decisions taken by the EC' but also recommended that the two organizations should establish 'organic links'.

In part, the Kohl–Mitterrand plan was a bargaining ploy for the forthcoming EC summit at Maastricht in December, at which the Community planned to deal with defence as one of the whole panoply of issues related to the aim of European union. In the months prior to Maastricht, there was a great deal of manoeuvring as Britain, the Netherlands, Portugal and Italy indicated their hostility to the idea that the EC would control the WEU, arguing that the WEU should form the European pillar in NATO or at the very least should be the 'bridge' between the Community and NATO.

The prospects for agreement at Maastricht were made somewhat easier though by NATO's Rome declaration, which welcomed 'a reinforcement of the role of the WEU, both as the defence component of the process of European unification and as a means of strengthening the European pillar of the alliance, bearing in mind the different nature of its relations with the alliance and with the European political union'. This formulation provided a suitable compromise partly because it implied that a fundamental choice could be postponed and partly because it simply ignored the tensions between two very different conceptions of the role of the WEU.

Inevitably, differences over the nature and location of a European security identity still played a significant part in the discussions at the Maastricht EC summit—and the defence issue proved to be one of the most difficult items on the agenda. Nevertheless, partly because the Rome declaration had proved a useful framework and partly because there was a desire to prevent divergences over defence detracting from the overall success of the summit, compromise was reached. A formula was found which went a long way to meeting French and German aspirations but which was sufficiently qualified to meet the reservations of Britain and those who supported the British position. The EC leaders agreed to strengthen the WEU and acknowledged that it would be the 'defence component' of European union; at the same time, in response to pressure from Britain, it was accepted that WEU actions had to 'respect the obligations of certain member states under the North Atlantic Treaty and be compatible with the common security and defence policy established within that framework' (see XIX.4 for Maastricht decisions).

In a declaration issued on the occasion of the Maastricht summit, the WEU stated that its members welcomed the development of a European security and defence identity. It also endorsed both concepts of its future by referring to 'the role of the WEU as the defence component of the European union and as the means to strengthen the European pillar of the Atlantic alliance'. More significant than the rhetoric, though, was the WEU's invitation to the three EC states which were not WEU members (Denmark, Greece and the Irish Republic) to accede to the organization.

The American reaction to all this was rather cautious. In welcoming the decision made at Maastricht, President Bush expressed his pleasure that the WEU was to be strengthened, but also reiterated his view that 'NATO will remain the essential forum for consultation among its members'. Yet it was clear by the end of the year that this view was no longer dominant in Western Europe. Although Maastricht allowed the political leaders on both sides of the dispute to return home claiming victory, it was hard to deny that the proponents of 'European Europe' had won at least a partial victory over the supporters of 'Atlantic Europe'. The summit provided no more than a framework and did not resolve many practical questions about the future relationship between the EC and NATO or about the precise role of the WEU. Yet it established a pattern of logic towards a more independent Western Europe, so that although some of NATO's worst fears had not materialized, they had certainly not been dispelled.

If NATO had mixed fortunes in 1991, the newly-institutionalized Conference on Security and Cooperation in Europe (CSCE) (see also XI.5.i) had a bad year. In the aftermath of the Paris summit of November 1990 (see AR 1990, pp. 438, 569–76), it appeared that 1991 would be a year in which the CSCE would develop its crisis prevention and crisis management capabilities quite significantly. This did not occur, and by the end of the year the CSCE seemed a less important component of the emerging European security architecture than at the beginning. The reason was the Yugoslavia crisis (see IV.1.vi). This posed a critical challenge to the CSCE, from which it abdicated, passing the problem to the EC. Although the EC failed to solve the problem, its performance was at least credible. Nevertheless, at the end of the year there was still a strong belief that the CSCE remained a key element in the emerging European security architecture, if only because it provided the sole pan-European security institution.

3. THE START TREATY AND SUBSEQUENT INITIATIVES

IF 1991 was not a good year for peace-keeping, it was a better year from the perspective of arms control, even though this aim seemed increasingly irrelevant as political changes continued to move at a more rapid pace than formal negotiations could match. On 1 June problems over the implementation of the 1990 CFE treaty were sorted out in a meeting between the US Secretary of State, James Baker, and Soviet Foreign Minister, Aleksandr Bessmertnykh. With this and other obstacles out of the way, Presidents Bush and Gorbachev signed the START treaty in Moscow on 31 July, thereby ending a negotiation process which had begun in June 1982. The negotiations had dealt with a whole series of esoteric issues, such as telemetry, down-loading and the definition of new types of missile, and reached final agreement only because of sustained top-level involvement.

The treaty, with its annexes on definitions and protocols on notification, conversion or elimination, throw-weight, a joint compliance and inspection commission, telemetry, and inspection and continuous monitoring, was over 700 pages long (see XIX.2 for details). In substantive terms, it established equal ceilings on the number of strategic weapons which could be deployed by the United States and the Soviet Union and imposed equality in terms of throw-weight—an area where the Soviet Union had traditionally had an advantage, to the great concern of Washington. The main provisions of the treaty were that neither side could deploy more than 1,600 strategic nuclear delivery vehicles (ICBMs, SLBMs and heavy bombers), 6,000 total accountable warheads, 4,900 warheads on ICBMs or SLBMs and 1,100 warheads on mobile ICBMs. In addition, there was a limit of 1,540 warheads on 154 heavy ICBMs (requiring a 50 per cent cut in the Soviet heavy missile force) and a limit on aggregate throw-weight of the ICBMs and SLBMs (requiring close to a 50 per cent cut in Soviet throw-weight). The treaty also established highly intrusive verification procedures, with provision for 12 different types of inspection. Moreover, each side undertook to notify the other of activities associated with its strategic forces.

Although the treaty was criticized in both Washington and Moscow for giving away too much to the other side, the failed August coup in the Soviet Union meant that the emerging technical and strategic judgments were less important than broad political assessments of the treaty. In the last few months of 1991 one argument was that the treaty was moot—that with the collapse of the Soviet Union it was no longer needed. Another view was that the treaty provided at least a partial framework for dealing with the problem of 'internal proliferation' in the former Soviet Union. Not surprisingly, the Bush administration appeared much closer to the latter view than the former. Even so, in the period following the failed coup, as President Gorbachev's efforts to hold the USSR together came to naught, there was a recognition that the START agreement was far from a comprehensive framework to deal with the future of the Soviet nuclear armoury. One American official suggested that the Soviets were in a situation where they had too many nuclear weapons for their own health.

Concerns over the continued dispersal of nuclear weapons in at least four republics (see map on p. 178) provided the background against which, on 27 September, President Bush announced that the United States was taking a series of unilateral steps to reduce the American nuclear arsenal (see also II.1). These measures included the removal of strategic bombers from day-to-day alert status and the return of their weapons to storage areas, and the immediate stand-down of the ICBMs which were to be deactivated under the START treaty, together with a programme for their subsequent elimination at a rate quicker than that designated in the treaty. President Bush also announced that the United States would halt development of the rail-garrison basing mode for the M-X missile and for mobile elements of the Midgetman small ICBM and also cancel its short-range attack missile (SRAM) programme. In addition, the United States would eliminate 1,740 nuclear artillery shells and 1,250 short-range land-based missiles, and would withdraw nuclear weapons, including nuclear-armed cruise missiles, from surface ships and attack submarines.

Although this was a unilateral initiative, President Bush hoped that the Soviet Union would reciprocate. He also reiterated his desire to seek an agreement with the Soviet Union to modify or eliminate all nuclear missiles with multiple warheads (MIRVs). Even so, the great advantage of the unilateral initiative was that it avoided protracted negotiations at a time when the locus of authority in the Soviet Union—indeed its very future—was in doubt. The speech was widely welcomed. Yet there were several things that President Bush very deliberately did not include. The US submarine-launched ballistic missile (SLBM) capability was not affected by the cuts, while the President made it clear that he would still seek full funding for the B-2 'Stealth' bomber. Considerable emphasis was also placed on strategic defence. This was consistent with the way in which the Bush administration, in January 1991, had reoriented the missile defence programme away from President Reagan's Strategic Defence Initiative (SDI) and into a much more modest concept known as 'global protection against limited strikes' (GPALS). The main rationale for GPALS was its potential ability to destroy incoming missiles whether launched accidentally, without authorization or deliberately by a small nuclear power. This rationale was strengthened by the war in the Gulf and by the concerns about command and control of missiles in the disintegrating Soviet Union.

President Gorbachev, on 5 October, responded positively to the Bush initiative. He announced that Moscow was prepared to consider proposals from the United States on non-nuclear anti-missile defence systems, a move that reflected a major shift from earlier Soviet opposition to any attempt to amend the 1972 ABM treaty. He also followed the American lead in removing strategic bombers from alert, standing down over 500 ICBMs (including 134 MIRVed missiles) and halting the further development of mobile missiles. Perhaps even more important, in view of the deteriorating political situation, was his announcement that all nuclear artillery shells and tactical nuclear warheads would be eliminated, while the Soviet Union would remove and store in a central area all nuclear warheads for surface-to-air missiles. President Gorbachev also announced that he would reciprocate the US initiative in relation to surface ships and land-based naval aircraft.

The response of President Bush was that this was 'good news for the world'. Yet with the subsequent disintegration of the Soviet Union, the extent to which these measures would be implemented, and the future of nuclear arms control, remained uncertain. If 1991 had begun on a note of trepidation about the forthcoming war in the Gulf, it ended on a note of even greater anxiety and uncertainty because of the political changes in the Soviet Union.

XIII RELIGION

ORTHODOX REVIVAL. Christmas Day, on 7 January 1991, Orthodox-style, was celebrated openly across the USSR for the first time since the Revolution, with a public holiday in Russia, Belorussia, Ukraine and Moldavia. Patriarch Aleksi II presided at a televised midnight liturgy from the Cathedral of the Epiphany in Moscow, while in Red Square a military band played Christmas carols and there were readings of scripture. On 7 April Easter was also observed publicly, Russian President Boris Yeltsin and Soviet Prime Minister Valentin Pavlov attending midnight service in the cathedral.

In the attempted coup in August (see IV.2.i), dissident priest Fr Gleb Yakunin joined Mr Yeltsin at the Russian parliament telling the crowd: 'God will help you and will help Russia'. On 20 August, Mr Yeltsin appealed to Patriarch Aleksi and 'to all believers in Russia' not to be bystanders, warning of totalitarianism under which the Church would again suffer. The Patriarch replied by questioning the legality of the coup, later excommunicating its leaders and on 26 August celebrating the victory of democracy in the Cathedral of the Assumption in the Kremlin itself, declaring that 'the wrath of God falls on the children of disobedience'. The Moscow Baptist Church's compassion ministries were told to close down but they distributed literature to tank crews. At the funeral of three young men killed in the coup, one of whom was Jewish, they were hailed as Heroes of the Soviet Union, a rabbi read Jewish prayers and Patriarch Aleksi conducted the burial.

The Orthodox Church had gained ground steadily under President Gorbachev and appeared as the ideology of the new state in all but name. Politicians at home and diplomats abroad flocked to churches on Sunday, long-disused Kremlin chapels were opened, and prayer before debate was held at political gatherings. But dangers of triumphalism and intolerance were apparent between office-holders and reformers. As under tsarism, many priests and bishops had been suspected of being police agents under communism. Anti-semitism was rife, embodied in an extreme nationalist group, Pamyat, which claimed St George as its patron. In reaction against nationalism in Orthodoxy, anti-clericalism developed among liberal intelligentsia and in the media. The Church seemed unprepared intellectually and morally, unreformed and lacking independence.

At Easter Cardinal Myroslav Lubachivsky returned to Lvov, centre of Ukrainian Eastern-rite Catholicism, after an absence of 52 years in Rome. There were 864 Catholic churches in the region, 349 Autocephalous Orthodox and 102 Ukrainian Orthodox (see AR 1989, p. 427). Just as Catholic churches functioned as wings of the national movement in Ukraine, so they did in Lithuania, where church ceremonies were attended uncomfortably by former communist politicians. The Lithuanian Roman Catholic Church had been isolated, ignorant of the reforms of the Second Vatican Council and with ill-educated priests. Opposition to both Orthodox and Protestants was expressed in a nationalist Christian Democratic Party.

As statues of Lenin and Marx came tumbling down, the spiritual void left by the collapse of communism opened to many influences. Christian newspapers and magazines appeared with increasing frequency and had wide sales. Prophecies of the last days at the end of the millenium sent some young people to monasteries. In 1916 there were 1,025 monasteries in Russia, in 1985 only 19 survived, but 60 had been opened since. Seventh Day Adventists, persecuted under the tsars and communism, emerged again. American-financed evangelical groups made inroads and Rev Sun Myung Moon of the Unification Church (Moonies) toured Russia and gave large donations to President Gorbachev. The Baha'i religion revived, claiming 22 congregations. Teachers of occult mysteries, prophets, healers and astrologers ran TV shows and claimed sightings of UFOs promising the return of Christ from another planet to destroy the 'failed' world civilization.

NEW ARCHBISHOP. Dr Robert Runcie retired on 31 January after ten years as Archbishop of Canterbury. His successor was Dr George Carey, aged 54, Bishop of Bath and Wells. Regarded as an outsider, not from the public school or Oxbridge background of most Anglican bishops, Dr Carey came from east London, left a school with no O-level examination passes, did national service as a wireless operator, and then worked his way through theological college to a doctorate from London University, later teaching in three colleges as well as ministering in urban parishes. Of the evangelical wing of the Church, Dr Carey was attracted by charismatic movements but claimed to be no fundamentalist. At his enthronement in Canterbury on 19 April Dr Carey urged the importance of witness, recalling the martyrdom there of Thomas à Becket in 1170. His own witness would be to share his faith with young and old, with sick and prisoners, with workers in industry and agriculture. To members of other religions, who were present, Dr Carey said he was compelled to share his faith but after 'listening to sensitive dialogue.'

Dr Runcie had often been criticized as liberal and political, and it was thought Dr Carey would be more conservative. But in a speech on 19 September, after riots at Newcastle, he spoke of them as 'inextricably linked to social deprivation, poor housing and illiteracy', in contrast to governmental dismissal of poverty as a factor in rioting, and he was supported by bishops in Newcastle, Liverpool and Manchester. As controversial was Dr Carey's comment that opponents of women priests were in heresy, later changed to 'serious theological error'. But in his first address to the General Synod the Archbishop called for unity and evangelism.

Dr Richard Harries, Bishop of Oxford, took the Church commissioners to the high court in October to oblige them to put investments on a more 'ethical' basis, but the court refused to interfere. In December the Archbishop, with Cardinal Basil Hume and Chief Rabbi Jonathan Sacks, protested to the Prime Minister against shops being allowed to open illegally on Sundays. A bishops' statement, *Issues in Human Sexuality*, in December, recognized that some clergy were homosexual but urged them to refrain from sexual relationships. In December, also, over 2,000 clergy signed a letter to the Anglican press opposing inter-faith worship and calling for conversion of followers of other religions. The Council of Christians and Jews, among others, opposed this attitude and warned of dangers in a Decade of Evangelism which the churches sponsored, arguing that 'proselytism is the opposite of dialogue'.

Returns of church attendance in England showed a drop of half a million in the last decade. Only 10 per cent of adults, and 15 per cent of children, attended church on an average Sunday. Most main churches suffered decline but Baptists grew by 2 per cent and there was striking growth among 'house churches' as well as in the Pentecostal and Afro-Caribbean churches. On 19 November Terry Waite, the Archbishop's envoy who had been taken hostage in Lebanon in 1987 (see AR 1987, p. 419), was released (see also V.4.v). He said that he had no regrets and his faith had sustained him during years of solitary confinement in chains.

PAPAL ACTIONS. Pope John Paul II visited Poland in June and entered debate on abortion by comparing it to the Holocaust of Jews and the nuclear bombing of Hiroshima, a statement which was strongly criticized. In August he paid the first-ever papal visit to Hungary, where clergy had submitted to the communist regime and knew little of Vatican Council reforms.

In Brazil, in October, the Pope urged resistance to Pentecostalist sects, claiming 20 per cent of Latin America, whose world capital was at São Paulo. Brazil had the largest number of Catholics in the world but the proportion in the whole population had dropped to 76 per cent. There were 382 bishops in Brazil, mostly conservatives appointed by the Vatican. In the USA two thirds of the active bishops were named in this pontificate, with a claimed rule that 'each bishop is more conservative than his predecessor' (see AR 1990, p. 446).

In April Brazilian Franciscan theologian Fr Leonardo Boff was removed from teaching theology and from the editorship of the magazine *Vozes* (see AR 1985, p. 378). It was decreed, he said, 'through third parties, without any reason given. This was the way things were done in the dark days of the totalitarian regimes.' In the Netherlands, the Vatican opposed an experimental New Catechism, made a series of conservative episcopal appointments, and saw the average weekend attendance at Mass sink from 25 to 15 per cent over the last ten years.

Back in Rome, the Pope tried to prevent the Gulf War, calling representatives of all countries involved in it to Rome and urging the nations to 'abandon this bellicose road, negotiate, collaborate'. In London, Cardinal Hume joined Archbishop Runcie in stating that the war was 'regrettable but necessary' (see AR 1990, p. 446). The Pope declared that 'this is not a religious war and cannot be a "holy war"', his stand being welcomed in the Islamic world. Similarly, the Pope deplored the 'crescendo of violence' in Yugoslavia (see V.1.vi). He supported Catholic Croatia's self-determination but preferred negotiation with Orthodox Serbia to unilateral independence.

In May the Pope published his ninth encyclical letter, *Centesimus Annus* (The Hundredth Year), marking the centenary of an encyclical on social concerns by Pope Leo XIII. He warned against purely utilitarian values, insisting that religion was about public as well as private morality.

In December the Pope welcomed President Yeltsin of Russia with full honours as head of state, but was not invited to Moscow in return (see AR 1989, p. 427). In October Russian Patriarch Aleksi II attacked the Vatican for 'proselytism', setting up 'parallel mission structures' in the former USSR and Eastern Europe and reviving Uniate churches. The Pope called a special synod of bishops in December, to which Orthodox were invited; most refused to attend, saying that the Vatican had 'seriously compromised' dialogue with Orthodoxy and had 'distanced itself' from the reforms of the Vatican Council.

CHIEF RABBIS. Immanuel Jakobovits, retiring Chief Rabbi of the United Hebrew Congregations of the British Commonwealth (see AR 1988, p. 437–8), spoke in May of the Israeli incarceration of Palestinians for years as 'a stain on humanity' and suggested enlisting 'the help of friendly Arabs'. For this he was accused of associating with 'Arabists and anti-semites', though many British Jews supported him. Then Lord Jakobovits went to Canada to receive the prestigious Templeton Prize for progress in religion. He was succeeded as Chief Rabbi by Dr Jonathan Sacks, who called for 'a decade of Jewish renewal and revival', parallel to the Christian Decade of Evangelism. Jewish people were divided between hawks and doves in support for Israel, between orthodox and liberals in theology, and there were neglected groups: 'women, the young, intellectuals, the less well-off, the provinces, the small communities.'

In December the UN General Assembly repealed a resolution of 16 years ago which had condemned Zionism as 'a form of racism and racial discrimination' (see also XI.1). A widely-repeated story that Arabs in Israel had cheered when Iraqi Scud missiles flew towards Israeli targets (see V.3) was dismissed as fantasy by the diplomatic editor of the *Jewish Chronicle*, who found no evidence for it in Israeli government statements or media.

Controversy erupted over secrecy surrounding the Dead Sea Scrolls, 800 ancient Hebrew and Aramaic manuscripts discovered in caves at Qumran, east of Jerusalem, from 1947 to 1956. Israeli authorities kept 75 per cent of these unpublished and inaccessible except to a small band of scholars, a policy which Professor Geza Vermes of Oxford called 'the academic scandal *par excellence* of the twentieth century'. The scrolls contained most of the Old Testament books and were said to include ideas comparable to parts of the New Testament. In September the Huntingdon Library in California, which had copies of all the scrolls, decided to make them public, the Oxford Centre for Postgraduate Hebrew Studies becoming the first centre in Europe to obtain a complete set.

ISLAMIC DIVISIONS. The Islamic world was divided during the Gulf War between those who accepted Iraq's claim to defend Islam against the West and those who recognized its aggression against fellow-Muslims in Kuwait, with further differences between Sunni and Shia Muslims and Kurdish patriots. Calling an Islamic conference in Baghdad in January, President Saddam Husain claimed to be taking 'the right path for peace and *jihad* (holy war) not only for Muslims but for all mankind'. Religious groups in Saudi Arabia tried to make life difficult for the allied forces deployed there and urged stricter Islamic laws against some in the middle classes who sought liberalization and against the country's 1.5 million Shias.

Rioting between Muslims and Christians erupted in April and October in northern Nigeria, following several uprisings in the last decade, with some 300 reported killed and 30 churches destroyed. Muslims demanded the imposition of Sharia law and a newspaper declared that 'much of the Bible is false.' New aggressive Christian evangelists, in a book entitled *Who is this Allah?*, argued that he was actually Satan, which angered the people of this largely Muslim area. Traditional Christians quoted statements of the World Council of Churches that Muslims worshipped the true God and the Holy Spirit moved among them.

In Algeria, Muslim fundamentalists rejoiced in the sweeping victory of the Islamic Salvation Front (FIS) in the first round of elections at the end of December (see V.5.iv). At Friday prayers in the mosques this was hailed as 'a day of God', to bring an end to corruption, unemployment and Western practices. In June the Pakistan Senate, overriding objections by churches, other minorities and women's organizations, passed the Sharia Bill establishing Islamic law throughout the country (see VIII.2.ii). In the USSR the number of mosques quadrupled, from 392 in 1985 to 1,500.

On 3 July an Italian translator of Salman Rushdie's *The Satanic Verses* (see AR 1990, p. 448) was stabbed in Milan, and on 12 July the Japanese translator was stabbed to death. In December Mr Rushdie emerged briefly from hiding to fly to the USA to speak at Columbia University. He attacked 'actually existing Islam' as being the 'political and priestly power that at present dominates and stifles Muslim societies', with its literalism and repressive attitudes to women and homosexuals. Admitting that he had 'spoken the Muslim creed before witnesses', he now claimed it was a fantasy to seek the 'modernization of Islam'. He had been wrong to 'suspend—not cancel—a paperback edition' of his book which 'must be freely available'. In reply, Hesham El-Essawy, chairman of an Islamic Society for the Promotion of Religious Tolerance in the UK, said Mr Rushdie had convinced him 'fully, falsely as it turned out, that he was genuinely embracing Islam'. A paperback publication would be 'both a provocation and a confirmation of his opponents' reservations about him', though Rushdie, 'apostate or not, should not be, and should never have been, subject to a death sentence'.

BOOKS OF THE YEAR. A neglected subject was examined by J. Bowker in *The Meanings of Death*, Jennifer Hockey in *Experiences of Death* and K. Grayston in *Dying We Live*, considering biblical teachings. *The Unauthorized Version* by R. L. Fox gave a critical historian's view on truth and fiction in the Bible, Helmut Koester in *Ancient Christian Gospels* described canonical and apocryphal writings, and M. Baigent and R. Leigh sought to expose *The Dead Sea Scrolls Deception*. Two disciplines were compared by I. Barbour in *Religion in an Age of Science* and A. Peacocke in *Theology for a Scientific Age*, while A. Kee considered *Marx and the Failure of Liberation Theology*, arguing that it was not marxist enough. *Women Included* provided a book of feminist prayers with the Lord's Prayer beginning 'Beloved, our Father and Mother', provoking warnings that its use in the Church of England would be illegal. Lord Cheshire treated the problem of suffering in *Where is God in all This?* and R. S. Wistrich wrote on *Antisemitism: the Longest Hatred* while A. Pieris in *Love Meets Wisdom* engaged in Christian-Buddhist dialogue.

XIV THE SCIENCES

1. MEDICAL, SCIENTIFIC AND INDUSTRIAL RESEARCH

ASTRONOMY AND SPACE RESEARCH. On 10 July the longest eclipse of the Sun for more than 130 years provided a rare opportunity for astronomers. The Sun was blocked out by the Moon for seven minutes along a strip curving from Hawaii in the Pacific to the tip of Bajia California off the Mexican west coast, ending in Central America. The eclipse gave astronomers the chance to study what happens in the area immediately surrounding the Sun, something normally impossible because the Sun is far too bright. The 1991 eclipse was especially valuable, not only because the Sun was blocked out for so long, but also because the eclipse passed over one of the world's major observatories, on Mauna Kea in Hawaii. At the end of the year the data obtained, about the solar corona and suspected dust rings around the Sun, were still being analysed.

Also in July astronomers using the 80-metre radio telescope at Jodrell Bank announced the discovery of the what appeared to be good evidence for a planet outside the solar system. The planet, thought to be about ten times the size of the Earth, was said to be in orbit around a neutron star close to the centre of our galaxy the Milky Way. This came as a shock to astronomers, because neutron stars are the 'burnt-out' remains left after stars have exploded in supernovae and thereby would have been expected to have destroyed any planets in orbit around them. Later in the year, in October, the discovery was announced of two more planets in orbit around another neutron star, though doubts were appearing about the first claim.

Several theories to explain the origins of the planets were put forward. They might have been captured from another star by the neutron star's intense gravitational field, they might be the remains of stars stripped down to planetary size by intense radiation from the neutron star or they could have formed from debris from the explosion. Whatever the explanation, the fact that planets had been found in such unpromising places raised hopes that further examples might soon be found in more benevolent surroundings where life could have evolved.

Meanwhile surprising discoveries continued to be made about the planets of our own solar system. By November the space probe *Magellan*, launched in 1989, had surveyed 85 per cent of the surface of Venus with short-wave radar with a resolution of 150 metres, a better survey than that of the large areas of the Earth covered by deep oceans. The surface of Venus appeared crowded with volcanoes, but all clearly extinct, as shown by the sharp outlines of meteorite craters which would otherwise have been obliterated by flows of lava. Some 500 million years ago, earlier craters had all been eliminated by a massive lava flow, caused by some violent event, perhaps the impact of a moon or even planet-sized body.

Another group of radar astronomers, at the US Jet Propulsion Laboratory at Pasadena, found a round spot at the north pole of Mercury which reflected radar very strongly in exactly the way ice does. Although Mercury is the closest planet to the Sun, its poles are at temperatures of around −148°C, because Mercury's orbit has no wobble like that which creates the seasons and periodically warms up the poles on Earth. So the temperature was right for ice, but raised the unanswered question of where the water came from to form that ice.

On 29 October the spacecraft *Galileo*, on its long journey towards Jupiter, took a close look at an asteroid named Gaspra. Another asteroid passed close by the Earth on 18 January and another, known as VG, passed only 450,000 km away on 5 December. Astronomers disagreed about the likelihood of an asteroid impact causing disastrous damage to the human race. Estimates of the likely frequency of events such as the impact which devastated much of Siberia in 1908 varied from once in 100 to once in 2000 years. But experts agreed that disastrous impacts were bound to happen sooner or later and could be averted only by dedicating several telescopes for several years to identify all the asteroids on collision courses with the Earth and then devising plans to divert them into harmless orbits. This could conceivably be combined with a programme to mine the asteroids for their very valuable metal content.

The space telescope *Hubble*, launched in April 1990, continued to be dogged by problems. The most serious had been with the optics, misalignment of mirrors impairing the resolution of the images produced by the telescope. In 1991 two gyroscopes needed to keep the telescope steady in space failed. As with the optical problems, it seemed that the fault could be repaired only by a future shuttle mission.

Meanwhile details were released of so-called adaptive optics systems, developed in secret for the US Strategic Defence Initiative (SDI), which allowed telescopes on Earth to produce images as sharp as, or sharper than, those from *Hubble*, by using computers to compensate for the blurring effects of the atmosphere. If this technology had been declassified earlier the arguments for building and launching *Hubble*, at a far higher cost than ground-based telescopes, would have been much weaker, though the space telescope was still able to return much valuable data unavailable from the ground.

At the end of the year the future of what had been the Soviet space programme was in doubt. Cosmonaut Sergei Krikalyov, who had been in orbit in the *Mir* space station for seven months, faced a landing in a foreign country carrying an illegal document, his communist party card. Could a new Commonwealth authority be set up to salvage the space programme which had given the world the first satellite, the first man in space and the first space station, and would the high cost of continuing space effort be acceptable to citizens near starvation? A mix of commercial sell-off and close scientific collaboration with other nations with space programmes seemed the most hopeful option.

PHYSICS AND CHEMISTRY. On 9 November the international team working with the Joint European Torus (JET) experimental fusion reactor at the research centre at Culham in Oxfordshire announced that it had produced a significant quantity of energy, a million watts of power for two seconds, from the reactor for the first time. This was also the first time that a second isotope of hydrogen, tritium, had been used as well as deuterium. The mix released far more energy than deuterium alone. Like earlier experiments this one involved heating up the fuel to around 200 million degrees Celsius, at which temperature atoms of hydrogen isotopes began to fuse together in the reaction which released energy and which in an uncontrolled form was used in the hydrogen bomb. The JET team warned that commercially-viable power from nuclear fusion was still about fifty years away. The fact that such power stations would not pollute the atmosphere by releasing carbon dioxide to add to the 'greenhouse effect', and that power stations using fusion reactors would cause far fewer problems with the disposal of radioactive materials, were seen as added environmental incentives to press on with fusion research programmes.

A novel form of carbon, synthesized for the first time in 1990, composed of molecules each made up of 60 carbon atoms arranged in a structure like a football, christened Buckminsterfullerine after the American designer of similar-shaped geodesic domes, continued to be the focus of intense attention. Researchers at AT&T Bell laboratories in the USA discovered that 'buckyballs', as the molecules were colloquially known, could act as superconductors. Together with their symmetrical shape and other properties, this discovery opened up new possible applications for buckyballs in microelectronics. Later in the year the crystalline structure of buckyballs was revealed in experiments at Britain's Rutherford Appleton Laboratory. The fact that atoms of other elements could be trapped inside buckyballs suggested more possible uses, among them in new catalysts, lubricants and medicines.

The phenomenon of electrical superconductivity at relatively high temperatures, first discovered in 1987, continued to attract research funding because of the wealth of future practical applications. The world's first electric motor made with high temperature superconducting materials was built and operated in 1991. Its makers, the American Superconducting Corporation, forecast that the first such commercial motors would be available before the end of the century, resulting in massive cost and energy savings.

Dr Muradin Kumakhov of the Moscow Institute of Atomic Energy and Dr Walter Gibson of the State University of New York claimed, convincingly, to have developed the first-ever cheap and simple means of focusing X-rays, with many applications in research, industry and medicine. Kumakhov optics involved passing X-rays through bundles of fine glass tubes bent through very gradual curves, so that the X-rays were constantly reflected off the walls of the tubes without being absorbed. Videos of devices focusing X-rays in this way were demonstrated to the US National Laboratories and to universities and industry and even the more sceptical were showing interest. The company set up by Dr Gibson to exploit Kumakhov optics hoped to see them in use in industry within two or three years, in medicine in four to ten years and in X-ray astronomy within five years.

MEDICINE AND MEDICAL RESEARCH. Figures released by the World Health Organization (WHO) in November showed about 10 million registered cases worldwide of people infected with the human immune virus (HIV) that causes AIDS (acquired immune deficiency syndrome). By 2000 AD there were expected to be 40 million people infected. According to the WHO, 75 per cent of those infected had contracted the disease through heterosexual intercourse, which was the dominant means of transmission in the Third World. Twelve vaccines designed to protect against AIDS were being tested in the USA and Europe and there were plans to test some of them on a larger scale in Brazil, Uganda, Rwanda and Thailand if the first tests showed the vaccines were safe to use. The US Agency for International Development said that, if present trends continued in sub-Saharan Africa, there would be 16 million orphans in the region within five years and the ongoing population increase would be reversed by AIDS alone.

Research continued to provide both discouraging revelations and encouraging developments. Among the former was the discovery, by a team at the Oxford Institute of Molecular Medicine, that infection with HIV is at first held in check by the immune system but that after a while the virus's ability to mutate rapidly, in just the regions identified as foreign by the immune system, overcomes the defences. Among the latter was the announcement, in December, that a trial of two drugs combined—Acyclovir (already used against the virus cytomegalovirus) and Zidovudine, also known as AZT (the main drug used against AIDS)—had shown clear advantages in the first year. While a drug to cure AIDS was not even on the horizon, doctors hoped that by adding more drugs to a 'cocktail' treatment it might be possible to control infection sufficiently to allow those infected to live reasonably normal lives, rather like diabetics.

There was rapid and exciting progress in research into the causes of Alzheimers disease, a form of progressive and incurable senile dementia. Canadian research showed that the progress of the condition could be slowed or arrested by drugs which drained aluminium out of the brain, thereby adding more support to the theory that excessive aluminium in diet could cause the condition. British and American scientists discovered that mice showed symptoms of Alzheimers disease after being stimulated to produce excess amounts of beta amyloid protein.

Meanwhile the research team at St Mary's Hospital Medical School, London, discovered that the brains of ex-boxers with symptoms like those of Alzheimers syndrome also contained similar deposits of beta amyloid protein. This suggested that excessive deposits of the protein, whether caused by physical trauma, genetic abnormality or maybe other factors, was the root cause of the condition. Researchers were working on ways to correct the process producing the excess. But the announcement in December that half the St Mary's research team planned to leave to work in the USA provided a timely reminder that scientists needed modest financial rewards as well as job satisfaction.

Yet another use for the polymerase chain reaction (PCR), the technique which allowed scientists to detect the presence of only a few molecules of any sought-after DNA and to copy it millions of times to make identification easy, was reported in November. Doctors at St James' University Hospital, Leeds, were using PCR to identify single cancer cells in blood taken from patients affected by malignant melanoma. This enabled the spread of cancer to be detected and prevented much earlier. Plans were announced by the WHO for the start of trials of a Chinese herb extract, from the qinghao plant, against malaria. The WHO believed that qinghao offered advantages not only in treating parasites resistant to other drugs, but also because the herb extract was quicker acting than any other therapy. Researchers at the University of Liège developed and tested a new vaccine to protect against rabies. This vaccine was made by inserting genes from rabies virus into the harmless vaccinia (cowpox) virus; this latter virus seemed to be able to protect wild animals against infection and so might offer a means of preventing humans becoming infected with rabies. Animals could be vaccinated by incorporating vaccine in food left out for them to eat.

MOLECULAR BIOLOGY AND GENETICS. Researchers at the Johns Hopkins University School of Medicine reported in October that they had genetically engineered mice so that their immune systems recognized and completely destroyed cancers which had previously been growing in the mice. The team hoped to start tests of the same technique to treat human cancers within a year, using it to try to destroy metastases, cancers which had spread beyond the original tumour.

A private company, DNA Plant Technology of Oakland, California, showed it was possible to protect tomatoes against the effects of freezing by inserting genes taken from flatfish, which are naturally protected against freezing, into the tomato plants. Commercial crops were anticipated in two or three years. Strawberries and cucumbers were next on the list for flatfish antifreeze.

Another biotechnology company, DNX of Princeton, New Jersey, produced pigs with human haemoglobin in their blood by inserting human haemoglobin genes into them. The aim was to separate the human haemoglobin and to use it in solution as an emergency blood substitute for patients whose need was for a blood substitute able to carry oxygen from the lungs, but not for the other, longer-term functions provided by the other constituents of blood. Pigs, DNX believed, could provide haemoglobin in larger quantities, by giving regular blood donations, than could the cell cultures with added human genes which were also being developed for the same purpose. Sheep producing anti-trypsin for the treatment of emphysema into their milk, goats producing the enzyme Tpa used to prevent blood-clotting and cows producing an antibiotic into their milk were also reported during the year.

Professor Alec Jeffreys of Leicester University, inventor of the original DNA 'finger-printing' technique which was revolutionizing forensic science, developed an improved version which was announced by the ICI subsidiary Cellmark, who were exploiting the technology, in November. The new process allowed individual DNA 'finger-prints' to be recorded in digital form, as a string of numbers, and so was eminently suitable for use by police forces to build up libraries of 'finger-prints' for comparison with traces of DNA found in blood or other traces left at the scene of a crime.

In February doctors at the US National Museum of Health and Medicine applied for permission to analyse DNA from bloodstains kept from the assassination of Abraham Lincoln, to see if his gangling build and habitual melancholy had been the consequence of a genetic abnormality causing the inherited condition Marfan syndrome. The doctors argued that others afflicted by the syndrome would be heartened by the knowledge that such a distinguished man had shared their affliction, if so it proved. Others considered it an intrusion. It was the latest of the many ethical conundrums being provided by the onward march of molecular genetics and genetic engineering.

EVOLUTION. The date when fish first invaded the land was pushed back about 10 million years, to around 370 million years ago by an irreverent young zoology demonstrator at the Oxford Museum, who took a fresh look at some long-forgotten Victorian collections of fossils and discovered that fish with legs were crawling around in shallow waters, ready to invade the land, earlier than previously thought. In Dr Per Ahlberg's own words: 'several of my colleagues are now taking a fresh look at grotty old bones in dusty old cabinets and hoping for more important new discoveries.' His own discovery followed that of Dr Michael Coates of the Cambridge Museum, who had shown that one of the first vertebrates to develop legs, Acanthostega, had gills as well as legs and feet with eight toes. It was now clear that, in the course of moving from water to land, fish had evolved complete legs while still being fish in every other way.

NOBEL PRIZES. The 1991 Nobel Prize for medicine was awarded to two German scientists, Erwin Neher of the Max Planck Institute in Göttingen and Bert Sakmann of the Max Planck Institute in Heidelberg, for work which had revealed much about how messages travel between brain cells and from nerves to muscles, especially about the way in which ions flooding into cells set of messages travelling between cells.

The prize for chemistry was awarded to the Swiss Professor Richard Ernst for his work in refining the analytical technique known as NMR, or nuclear magnetic resonance, which had come to be used in virtually every branch of chemistry and in medical imaging.

The prize for physics was awarded to Professor Pierre-Gilles de Gennes of France for his work in developing liquid crystals, laying the foundations for their widespread use in the 1990s in digital watches, pocket calculators and displays of all kinds.

2. INFORMATION TECHNOLOGY

PERSONALITIES. Seldom have the same public impact in information technology (IT) as in, say, politics, but one possible exception was Robert Maxwell, whose death in November 1991 certainly threatened to cause after-shocks in the world of IT (see also I.7 and XX: OBITUARY). Meanwhile, one of the most obvious characteristics observable in the development of computing since its inception, namely progressive miniaturization, had, by 1991, reached such a stage that one of the key themes of the year was the spread of hand-held devices, for which the description 'palm-top' was sometimes used. Technology convergence and integration, other obvious characteristics of the development of computing, were also much in evidence.

THE ELECTRONIC BOOK. Having launched a portable CD-ROM reader, the Data Discman, in July 1990 (see AR 1990, p. 460), the Japanese company Sony waited until the second half of 1991 to launch the product in the United States and Europe (Germany). By that time a number of significant improvements had already been made to the hardware and more than 20 titles were available for use with the device. Thus, for example, the Discman was launched in the United States with a package of three discs, including *Compton's Encyclopaedia*, and in Germany with two discs, a Bertelsmann German dictionary and the Langenscheidt English-German dictionary.

In a shrewd attempt to make the generic term 'electronic book' synonymous with its proprietary hand-held range of products, Sony widely licensed its technology both to other manufacturers, such as Sanyo, Matsushita and Sharp, and to publishers wishing to make their information products available using the Data Discman. In fact, Sony was evidently very conscious of the importance of the availability of appropriate CD-ROM titles for the success of its hardware. With this in mind, at the time of the 1991 Frankfurt Book Fair, Sony was instrumental in launching an International Electronic Book Publishing Committee (IEBPC), ostensibly an independent body but essentially a vehicle for promoting the Sony technology. Nevertheless, many of the leading publishers of Europe participated in the inaugural meeting of the IEBPC.

PALM-TOPS. In parallel with the developments relating to hand-held electronic books, lap-top computers began to give way to palm-top models. As far as miniaturization was concerned, a crucial limit had more or less been reached—not in terms of power (the determining factor in that respect being ultimately the continuing miniaturization of components down to those that functioned at molecular or atomic level) but in terms of convenience to the user, the essential determinant there being the size of the average human finger that operated the keys. Of the models announced in 1991, several, such as those from Hewlett-Packard, Poqet and Distributed Information Processing, could run standard spreadsheet or word processing packages, like Lotus 1–2–3 or WordPerfect, and communicate with other compatible machines.

MULTIMEDIA. During 1991, tangible progress was made towards true 'multimedia' applications—that is, those displaying a seamless integration of text, graphics, still and moving pictures, and high fidelity sound. CD-I (compact disc interactive), long heralded by the Dutch company Philips, working with less vociferous Japanese partners, finally came to market in the United States in October 1991, albeit with only partial screen full motion video (FMV), the elusive full-screen FMV having been promised for later. Despite the long wait, however, initial indications were that by the end of the year CD-I had achieved greater market acceptance than had the rival Commodore product, CDTV (Commodore Dynamic Total Vision—see AR 1990, p. 461), which had been pre-emptively launched in January 1991.

Other moves in the direction of multimedia applications included agreement by a number of companies, including Microsoft, one of the software market leaders, on a hardware and software specification for multimedia personal computers (MPC), which was formally promulgated in the autumn of 1991. At much the same time, International Business Machines (IBM), having declined to endorse Microsoft's MPC, announced its own multimedia personal computer, known as the Ultimedia PC.

CHIP TECHNOLOGY. Following the agreement in 1990 between IBM and the Germany technology company Siemens (see AR 1990, p. 463) to collaborate on the development of a 64-megabit DRAM (dynamic random access memory), the two companies decided in mid-1991 to work together in the manufacture of memory chips. This link effectively killed the likelihood of European companies jointly becoming a force in the world semiconductor market in their own right.

In the search for a wholly electronic replacement for hard and floppy discs (magnetic or optical) which relied upon mechanical drives and were thus something of a constraint upon hand-held computers, the prospects of a chip called the 'flash EPROM' (erasable programmable read only memory) were strongly advocated in 1991. Such chips could be erased by a short 'flash' of electricity and represented a significant advance on basic EPROMs and EEPROMs (electrically erasable PROMs), for which the erasure time was relatively lengthy. Cost and the current inability partially to erase flash EPROMs remained problems, but these were not considered to be insuperable.

A glimpse of the ultimate in miniaturization was given in *Nature* during August 1991. It was reported that research scientists at IBM's research centre in San José, California, had succeeded in moving a single atom of the element xenon from one position to another. In the long term, the discovery of this technique was certain to have important implications for computer switches.

LEGAL AND REGULATORY ISSUES. IT issues were the subject of a number of hard-fought controversies during the year. In particular, the EC Commission, seeking to establish a common framework for the single European market due to be complete by the end of 1992, turned its attention to software, data protection, copyright in databases and satellite broadcasting.

The Software Directive, formally adopted by the EC Council of Ministers in May 1991, had been the centre of a stormy debate over the degree to which 'reverse engineering' should be permissible, that is, the unravelling of proprietary computer programs for the purposes of designing other software or peripherals to work with the original software. Inevitably, a compromise was adopted which permitted the practice in specified circumstances.

Similarly, the Satellite Broadcasting Directive represented a compromise over an issue which had implacably ranged equipment manufacturers, keen to obtain a new source of sales in the form of high definition television (HDTV) sets, against broadcasters, anxious not to incur the costs of an enforced change of transmission standards. In the event, the broadcasters were reasonably satisfied. Use of the D2 version of the MAC (multiplexed analogue components) standard, considered to represent a step towards HD-MAC (the full European HDTV standard), was only to be compulsory for new services from 1995, with no obligation for existing services to switch standard.

EC discussions over data protection and personal privacy and over copyright protection for databases remained unresolved at the end of the year, whilst a storm was already brewing over proposals to liberalize European telecommunications regulations.

THE MAXWELL FACTOR. The death of Robert Maxwell represented something of a loss in the field of IT, unlike in many other areas of activity where investigation and denunciation immediately became the order of the day. Maxwell Communication Corporation (MCC) had been an important contributor to the development of the electronic information industry in the UK, Europe and the USA, with interests in online (InfoLine, Orbit), CD-ROM (Pergamon Compact Solution—which was suddenly axed and the activity transferred to the USA—and a majority stake in Nimbus Records), software (BRS, Molecular Designs) and latterly multimedia (Maxwell Multi Media, in partnership with the Dutch company Philips). Maxwell Satellite Communications had been one of the first six companies granted a specialized satellite service operator's licence in the United Kingdom. MCC was also the lead partner in research under the European Commission's RACE (research and development in advanced communication in Europe) programme. Further development stimulated by these various components of the Maxwell empire was inevitably called into question, at least in the short term, by the rapid collapse of MCC at the end of 1991.

ILLUSION AND REALITY. Hitherto a subject for debate mainly amongst philosophers and literary writers, the relationship between perception and reality took on a new significance in 1991 with the emergence from the research laboratories of an advanced application of computing technology known as 'virtual reality' (VR) or 'cyberspace'. Research into VR had been going on for years, the concept having been mooted by Ivan Sutherand as early as 1965. However, in 1991 VR captured the imagination of a wider public—not just scientists and technologists—partly as a result of media attention and partly through the availability on the market of VR-based games applications.

VR applies sophisticated computer techniques to create three-dimensional simulations of an object which display all the visual, aural and behavioural attributes of that object, a crucial limitation being, of course, the amount of data which can be collected and input concerning the object in question. In addition to objects, which may be observed from the outside, however, it is possible also to simulate complete environments, so that the user may effectively be 'immersed' in the environment and look outwards from the inside.

The visual images and accompanying sounds generated by VR may be viewed and heard using 'ordinary' screens and earphones or speakers. In order to enhance the effect for the user, however, special rooms with all-round screens may be created for particular applications. For other applications, the user may wear on his/her head a rather unwieldy device, which incorporates stereoscopic screens and stereophonic earphones. Such 'data helmets' are sensitive to head movements and the visual displays change as the user's head turns to the left or to the right or up or down. So far as other movements are concerned, garments sensitive to movements or gestures, such as the 'data glove' or even the 'data suit', may be worn. The user may then walk around in the simulated environment and the system will make appropriate adjustments to the video and audio outputs.

Since VR simulations can be computed on the basis of data input to the system as opposed to a photographic record, it is possible to investigate objects or situations from perspectives which would in reality be physically impossible—for example inside an engine. Equally, by using VR techniques in combination with robots with photographic and other sensing equipment, data may safely be gathered on a hazardous environment, for example during a fire, and the situation explored without risk.

VR is still at a fairly early stage of development, but it is clear that there are many avenues to be explored, during which, no doubt, a whole new vocabulary will be coined. Meanwhile, Pirandellians and others may well assert that we are in any case already living in our own artificial reality, blissfully (perhaps wretchedly) oblivious to the data helmets and other paraphernalia in which each member of the human race is imprisoned.

3. ENVIRONMENT

MOST of the year's international governmental activity concerning the environment centred around negotiations over a series of treaties and statements for the June 1992 UN Conference on Environment and Development (UNCED). However, public attention was focused on the effects of the Gulf War, one of the most disastrous human-caused environmental crises in recent history.

Government delegations met in two three-week sessions in March and August in Geneva to prepare for UNCED, while separate groups held several meetings to negotiate framework conventions on greenhouse gases (pollution thought to be warming the atmosphere) and on biological diversity (meaning the conservation of plant and animal species). These treaties, as well as global principles on forest management, were to be ready for the June meeting. All of these negotiations revealed a deep rift between industrial and developing nations, the latter demanding financial help in managing their own environments and in meeting international pollution standards, the former resisting such demands. Negotiations on a global warming treaty, attended by delegates from over 130 nations, saw a general acceptance of the principles of 'appropriate commitments' to reduce emissions of carbon dioxide (CO_2) and other greenhouse gases and on helping developing nations to develop less polluting technologies. However, the US government continued to resist the setting of firm emissions targets and financial help for poorer countries.

In late January, huge quantities of oil were released into the Gulf from Kuwaiti storage tanks during the fighting between Iraqi and allied forces, while Iraqi forces also set alight more than half of Kuwait's active oil wells (see V.2, V.4.vi and V.5.iii). The size of the oil spill, thought to be the worst in history, was estimated at between 5 and 10 million barrels (roughly 11 times the amount of oil release by the *Exxon Valdez* spill in Alaska in 1989—see AR 1989, pp. 45–6, 444). The Gulf was a relatively shallow body of water which cleansed itself very slowly. Sea birds and birds which migrated between Siberia and East Africa, as well as commercial oyster beds, prawns, dugongs (sea cows) dolphins and turtles were all affected, as were coral reefs and other marine ecosystems.

The oil well fires were steadily extinguished by 27 fire-fighting teams from at least nine nations over the course of the year. Initial estimates had suggested this work would take several years, but the last of 732 fires was capped in early November. For eight months, heavy, sooty smoke covered the region. Lung and chest complaints increased dramatically among local people. However, since such smoke contained cancer-causing compounds, health repercussions were expected to be felt for decades to come. There were no substantiated reports of the regional climate change which had been feared as a result of such a cloud, though farming and herding over a large area were expected to suffer from acid rain and poisoned soil and plants.

The year's temperature averages added to the circumstantial evidence supporting pollution-driven global warming, in that 1991 was the second warmest year, after 1990, in nearly 140 years of comparable measurements. Thus, according to the provisional report of the Meteorological Office, the ranking of hottest years was 1990, 1991, 1988, 1983, 1987,

1989, 1944 and 1981. The Met Office noted that 'although it is still too early to link the recent concentration of warm years with the influence of increasing greenhouse gases, international scientific opinion strongly supports the reality of the greenhouse effect, and it is likely that this has played some role in contributing to recent warmth'.

A slight cooling toward the end of the year may have been associated with the major eruption of Mount Pinatubo in the Philippines in June (see IX.1.vii). The series of eruptions increased the amount of dust and aerosols in the stratosphere by 60 to 80 times, according to a report to a meeting of the American Geophysical Union in December. This material could decrease solar radiation and dampen any greenhouse warming over the next three years, an effect which might allow scientists to test their models of the workings of the atmosphere.

UN figures presented to an annual meeting of the International Tropical Timber Organization in June confirmed that the world's rainforests were being cleared at a rate about 50 per cent higher at the end of the decade than at the beginning. In November President Fernando Collor de Mello of Brazil established by decree a 94,000 sq km reserve for the Yanomami people in their traditional forest lands of north-eastern Brazil. This followed years of international protests against broken promises to recognize Yanomami land rights. President Collor had announced in June, following a US visit, that $100 million of his nation's $120,000 million external debt would be converted in 'debt-for-nature' swaps to protect the environment. He said he intended to abolish tax incentives for cattle ranching and farming in the Amazon. His predecessor had also announced the suspension of these incentives shortly before leaving office in March 1990, but they had reportedly been reactivated in early 1991. President Collor also announced the dismissal of the head of the National Indian Foundation, Cantidio Guerreiro Guimaraes. The latter had been internationally criticized for being slow to set the boundaries of a Yanomami reserve and for allowing thousands of gold prospectors to reinvade the area and to bring in diseases such as malaria. Roughly one third of the world's rainforests were in Brazil.

A European protocol on restrictions of emissions of nitrogen oxides (NOx), agreed by the environment ministers of 24 member states of the UN Economic Commission for Europe in 1988, came into force in February. It committed signatories to freeze these emissions at 1987 levels by 1994. NOx, a major pollutant from transport, were associated with 'acid rain' damage, but locally were a threat to human health as they affected the linings of the lungs. A December meeting of the energy and environment ministers of EC countries gave cautious approval for an EC carbon and energy tax, meant to begin in 1993 at a rate equivalent to $3 per barrel of oil, rising by $1 per year to $10 per barrel in 2000 (see XI.3) Major hurdles remained before the plan could be implemented.

In March the United States and Canada signed a clean air agreement calling upon the USA to reduce sulphur dioxide (SO_2) emissions to 1980 levels by the year 2000, and calling upon Canada to reduce such emissions from its seven eastern provinces by the same time (see II.2). This pollution came mainly from coal- and oil-fired power stations and other industrial processes. Canada had been complaining for years about acid rain damage due to US SO_2 emissions. In November the state of California announced new regulations for petrol requiring a 30 per cent reduction in emissions by 1996 and a ban on leaded petrol by January 1992. Due to the size of the state's car market, its requirement for the sale of some emission-free cars was expected to encourage the worldwide development and marketing of efficient electric vehicles.

A June meeting of the signatories of the 1985 Vienna Convention for the Protection of the Ozone Layer in Nairobi heard that ozone depletion had increased significantly since the treaty had entered into force in 1987. There had been a 3 per cent decline in the ozone layer, everywhere except near the Equator, over the past decade, according to the World Meteorological Organization. Some 100,000 people died annually from skin cancer, most of this associated with solar ultra-violet radiation. The US Environmental Protection Agency estimated that for every 1 per cent depletion of the ozone layer, skin cancers rose by 2 per cent. Such radiation also caused cataracts, and a UN report suggested that for every 1 per cent depletion of the ozone layer, another 100,000 people would go blind.

One side-effect of the events in Eastern Europe and the former Soviet Union was an increased flow of information about the design faults and poor maintenance of the type of nuclear reactor involved in the Chernobyl accident of 1986 (see AR 1986, pp. 100–1, 395–6, 406–9). A deputy head of the Soviet State Committee for Atomic Energy Safety, N. A. Steinberg, said that the design of this type of reactor (RBMK 1000) 'blatantly contravenes the requirements of the rules of nuclear safety'. Fifteen reactors of this type remained in operation, while other reactors across Eastern Europe also gave cause for concern. The Austrian and Czechoslovak governments announced in January that they would distribute iodine tablets, intended to combat radiation sickness, in light of growing fears about the safety of some reactors in Czechoslovakia. The UK Atomic Energy Authority reported that in the 'worst case scenario' some 10,000 Soviet citizens and 30,000 people in the rest of the world could be expected to die as a result of Chernobyl.

Sweden had announced in 1988 that it would begin to shut down the country's 12 nuclear plants in 1995. But in early January it reversed that decision, saying it would wait until other sources of energy became viable. It also pledged a large research programme into wind and wood-fired energy systems and into improvements in energy efficiency.

Despite resistance by the United States, an agreement banning mining and mineral extraction in the Antarctic for at least 50 years was signed in Madrid in October. Adopted as a protocol to the 1959 Antarctic Treaty, the agreement also covered issues of waste disposal, marine pollution and wildlife protection. The USA had initially been unwilling to sign without agreement on how to set rules after the 50-year ban. The signing was seen as a victory by environmentalists, and the governments of nations such as Australia and France, which wanted Antarctica to become a 'world park'.

A May meeting of the International Whaling Commission (IWC) agreed to continue the 1985 ban on commercial whaling for another year, while the IWC studied the possibilities of a quota system allowing sustainable catches. Norway and Iceland condemned the decision. The debate was clouded by scientific disagreement over the extent to which whale populations had recovered to levels which would permit allowable harvests. Anti-whaling nations argued that whaling was inherently unethical and that hunting with explosive harpoons, the standard method, was morally unacceptable.

In September, the US administration announced a ban, with immediate effect for South Pacific catches, on the import of fish caught with drift nets. Two months later Japan, whose fleets had been the main users of such nets in the Pacific, agreed to co-sponsor with the United States a UN resolution imposing an indefinite moratorium on the use of these nets from the end of 1992. Environmental groups had long opposed the use of drift nets, which were set to catch salmon, tuna and squid, but also trapped and killed whales, dolphins, turtles, sharks and birds. Japanese drift nets were estimated to have killed 41 million animals other than those they were set to catch in 1990 (before a Japanese ban on the practice came into effect—see AR 1990, p. 425).

The world's population was increasing faster than predicted, according to a May report by the UN Population Fund. Estimated at about 5,400 million in mid-1991, it was expected to reach 6,400 million by 2001. Africa's population continued to grow fastest, with the 650 million Africans of 1991 expected to increase to 900 million by the end of the century (subject to the effect of AIDS).

Whether due to hard financial times, the Gulf War or changing fashions, environmental concern seemed to decline in 1991. The leaders of the Group of Seven dominant democracies devoted most of their 1990 summit to the environment, but at their 1991 meeting the subject got 13 minutes of discussion. Environment sections disappeared from many British bookshops, and once-wealthy US groups such as Greenpeace USA, the National Wildlife Federation and the Sierra Club laid off staff and cut budgets. This decline was accompanied by what many saw as a backlash against the environment on the part of the US government. President George Bush had promised in 1989 that there would be no net loss of wetlands during his term of office. In August 1991 he unveiled a tighter definition of wetlands which would open up some 4 million hectares to developers and farmers.

XV THE LAW

1. INTERNATIONAL LAW—EUROPEAN COMMUNITY LAW

i. INTERNATIONAL LAW

TWO of the most important events of 1991 raised fundamental legal issues. The armed action to drive Iraq out of Kuwait (see v.2) involved questions of the scope of the power of the UN Security Council to authorize action to restore and maintain international peace and security and also questions of the application of the laws of war on occupation, prisoners-of-war, permissible targets and treatment of civilians. The break-up of the USSR (see IV.2.i) raised legal issues concerning the succession of new states to the rights and duties of their predecessor.

The International Court of Justice (ICJ) had more cases before it than ever before, involving a wide diversity of subject matter and of states parties. The Court gave judgment on the merits in one case and accepted one application for provisional measures. Four new cases were brought to the Court.

Portugal sued Australia over the latter's policy on East Timor, a Portuguese colony which had been incorporated into Indonesia in 1976. Portugal claimed that by negotiating and ratifying an agreement with Indonesia relating to the exploration and exploitation of the continental shelf in the area of the Timor Gap, by negotiating the delimitation of that shelf and by the exclusion of any negotiation on those matters with Portugal, Australia had caused serious legal and moral damage to the people of East Timor and to Portugal. This case was based on the alleged duty of Australia to respect the rights of the people of East Timor to self-determination and to permanent sovereignty over its natural resources, and to recognize the powers of Portugal as the state administering the territory of East Timor.

Second, Guinea-Bissau brought a further case against Senegal, asking the Court to declare what should be the line delimiting the whole of their respective maritime territories. Third, Finland instituted proceedings against Denmark in respect of a dispute over the passage of oil rigs through the Great Belt, a strait linking the Baltic to the North Sea. Denmark proposed to construct a bridge over the Great Belt between the islands of Zealand and Fünen (as well as a tunnel). The bridge would exclude drillships and oil rigs over a certain height from passing between the Baltic and the North Sea. Fourth, Qatar brought a case against Bahrain in respect of disputes between them relating to sovereignty over the Hawar islands, sovereign rights over the shoals of Dibal and Qit'at Jaradah and the delimitation of the maritime areas of the two states. This case raised interesting questions, similar to those in the *Guinea-Bissau* v. *Senegal Arbitral Award* case (see AR 1989, p. 448; 1990, p. 468), as to the continuing validity of boundary agreements concluded by colonial powers for their colonies. All four cases would be heard by the full Court.

Proceedings continued in six cases carried over from 1990. Nicaragua withdrew its case against the USA in which it was claiming billions of dollars of reparations; this claim had been based on the Court's 1986 judgment (see AR 1986, p. 412) that the USA had violated international law by its mining of Nicaraguan harbours and support for the Contra rebels. On 12 September Nicaragua informed the Court that it had decided to renounce all further right of action based on the case. This decision was in gratitude for aid given by the USA since President Chamorro's election victory over the Sandinistas in February 1990 (see AR 1990, p. 88).

The one judgment on the merits of a case given by the Court concerned the Arbitral Award of 31 July 1989 (*Guinea-Bissau* v. *Senegal*). The Court's jurisdiction to hear this case under article 36 (2) of the ICJ Statute was not challenged. Guinea-Bissau's main contention was that the Arbitral Award of 31 July 1989 was inexistent because it was not supported by a real majority of the arbitral tribunal. It argued that the declaration by the president of the tribunal contradicted and invalidated his vote in favour of the award. But the Court unanimously rejected this contention on the ground that there was no real contradiction between the declaration and the award. Guinea-Bissau also argued that the award was a nullity because the parties had put two questions to the tribunal and the tribunal had failed to reply to the second question. The two questions included in the agreement to go to arbitration were: (1) Does the agreement concluded by an exchange of letters on 26 April 1960, and which relates to the maritime boundary, have the force of law in the relations between the Republic of Guinea-Bissau and the Republic of Senegal? (2) In the event of a negative answer to the first question, what is the course of the line delimiting the maritime territories appertaining to the Republic of Guinea-Bissau and the Republic of Senegal respectively?

It would have been normal to include in the operative part of the award both the answer to the first question and the decision not to answer the second. Nevertheless, it was clear from the reasoning of the award that the tribunal had decided that, as it had given an affirmative answer to the first question, it did not have to answer the second. So, although the Court recognized that the structure of the award was open to criticism, it held by a majority of 11 to 4 that the award was not flawed by the failure to decide. Although the reasoning had been brief, it was clear and precise, so the award was not void for failure to give reasons.

On 29 July the ICJ made an order in the case concerning *Passage through the Great Belt*, unanimously rejecting Finland's request for the indication of provisional measures that Denmark should refrain from construction works in connection with the planned bridge over the Great Belt. The Court followed its earlier jurisprudence in holding that provisional measures were justified only if there were urgency in the sense that action prejudicial to the rights of either party was likely to be taken before a final decision. The Court found that, according to the planned schedule for construction of the bridge, no physical hindrance to passage through the Great Belt would occur before the end of 1994, and proceedings on the merits would in the normal course be completed before then. Accordingly, provisional measures were not urgently required. But the Court also rejected the Danish argument that, if it ruled in favour of Finland on the merits of the case, any claim by Finland could not be dealt with by an order for restitution but only by damages, because restitution would be excessively onerous. The Court said that, if it were established that the construction of works infringed a legal right, it would not *a priori* exclude the possibility of a judicial finding that such works must be modified or dismantled.

On 7 February the ICJ elected Judge Sir Robert Jennings (UK) and Judge Shigeru Oda (Japan) as its president and vice-president respectively. On 5 December Prince Bola Ajibola (Nigeria) was elected to fill the seat left vacant by the death of Judge Taslim Elias (see XX:OBITUARY), who had been a member of the Court since 1976 and its president in 1981–85.

Three new treaties were concluded on environmental matters. On 29 January the OAU adopted the Convention on the Ban of the Import into Africa and the Control of Trans-boundary Movement of Hazardous Wastes within Africa, intended in particular to ban the import of nuclear waste into African countries. On 25 February the UN adopted the Convention on Environmental Impact Assessment in a Trans-boundary Context. Many states already had domestic laws on environmental impact assessment; this treaty required parties to take account of trans-boundary impact and was intended to enhance international cooperation in assessing environmental impact. On 4 October the signatory states to the 1959 Antarctic Treaty signed the Madrid protocol, providing for a mining ban in Antarctica for 50 years (see XIV.3).

On human rights, the second Optional Protocol to the 1966 International Covenant on Civil and Political Rights providing for the abolition of the death penalty entered into force on 11 July. This supplemented the 1990 OAS protocol to the American Convention on Human Rights to Abolish the Death Penalty (not yet in force) and the Sixth Protocol to the European Convention on Human Rights, (which entered into force on 1 March 1985).

The workload of the European Commission and Court of Human Rights was again very heavy. Discussions took place on the reform of the supervisory system and also on transitional arrangements to prepare for the accession of the states of Eastern Europe. The Court gave its judgment in the *Spycatcher* case on 26 November. It held unanimously that the UK had violated article 10 of the European convention on the right to freedom of expression. After *Spycatcher* had been published in the USA, any confidentiality was lost and the UK court orders maintaining the restriction on the reporting of *Spycatcher* by the British press (see AR 1987, pp. 8–9, 446; 1988, pp. 555–60) were not justified. However, by 14 votes to 10, the Court held that the initial restriction on publication had been permissible under article 10; the lifetime duty of confidentiality imposed by British courts on members of the security services was accepted by the European Court as justified in the interests of national security. The narrow majority reflected the controversial nature of this part of the judgment.

ii. EUROPEAN COMMUNITY LAW

IN a year of mighty events, Europe became ideologically whole again and the centripetal attraction of the European Community, like a great black hole sucking in the surrounding states, became almost irresistible. The old debate among Community jurists between the relative merits of widening or deepening the Community began to lose its sharpness as both processes showed themselves to be inextricably intertwined. And while politics made the headlines, it was law which created the bonds—and some of the difficulties.

This was shown dramatically in relation to expansion. While the association agreements with the Central European states (Poland, Czechoslovakia and Hungary) were duly concluded in December, with a hint of others to follow, it was the EFTA countries which drew most attention. After a further year of hard negotiation, the foreign ministers of the EFTA and EC states finally agreed on all outstanding points in October and decided to sign the definitive text of the European Economic Area (EEA) treaty in late November (see XI.5.iv). It provided for an association between the Community and EFTA (under article 238 EEC) and involved the seven EFTA states accepting as binding internal law the complete *acquis communautaire* relating to the 'four freedoms' (free movement of goods, people, services and capital) as well as the Community's competition rules (both legislation and case law) as at the date of signature of the treaty. Because the Nordic legal systems did not automatically make treaties part of internal law, it was not possible to provide that future Community laws (or case law) should similarly become part of EFTA internal law, and any post-treaty harmonization had to be left unregulated. However, a complex system of judicial review was instituted in an attempt to keep EFTA interpretation of Community law in line with that of the Community's European Court of Justice (ECJ). But this introduced a potentially lethal element. On the one hand, the ECJ feared a dilution of its own exclusive powers (under article 164 EEC); on the other the EFTA states were naturally unwilling to surrender to the ECJ the same sovereign judicial power that it had exercised over the EC states.

Only hours before the projected date of signature of the EEA treaty, the ECJ stated its intention to hold a hearing under article 228(1) EEC, allowing the Court, on application, to issue an opinion on the compatibility with Community law of a draft treaty. In face of this, signature of the treaty had to be postponed. The Court delivered its opinion on 14 December, concluding that the proposed EC-EFTA court and the rules for attaining homogeneity of interpretation of Community law throughout the EEA were not compatible with existing Community law and that therefore the EEA treaty could not be signed by the EC.

By the year's end, urgent negotiations were being devoted to possible amendments of the EEA treaty in order to meet the objections of the ECJ. But the rhythm had been lost and voices immediately began to query the usefulness of the EEA at all, in view of the applications for full EC membership already made by Austria and Sweden (see III.2.iv) and the increasing likelihood that most of the other EFTA states, including Switzerland, would also apply during 1992.

Parallel to these negotiations and events were the Community's higher-profile and more sensitive inter-governmental conferences (IGCs)—on political union and on economic and monetary union (EMU)—which would introduce major changes in, and additions to, the Treaty of Rome and significantly reduce the remaining sovereign powers of the member states. These discussions, too, culminated in a successful political meeting, of the European Council at the Maastricht summit in December, at which the two treaties were agreed (see XI.3 and XIX.4:DOCUMENTS). Subject to final textual polishing by the legal linguists, formal signature was expected to follow in February 1992.

The EMU treaty, by massive amendments to articles 67–73 and 102–109 EEC and numerous additional protocols and statements, set up a European System of Central Banks (ESCB) to be headed by a new European Central Bank, and a European Monetary Institute. All restrictions on movement of capital would be prohibited. The requirement that all economic policy, both national and Community, must be based on the 'principle of open market economy with free competition' was statutorily entrenched. National economic policies would cease to be solely determined by the member states, would have to contribute to Community objectives and would come under the supervisory coordinating control of the Council and Commission. This would include detailed supervision of budgetary discipline and avoidance of excessive government deficits. Monetary policy itself would be determined by the ESCB and include the irrevocable fixing of exchange rates leading to the introduction of a single currency, the ecu, and an exchange-rate policy which would be primarily aimed at maintaining price stability and supporting the general economic policies in the Community. All this would be done in compliance with the following guiding principles: 'stable prices, sound public finance and monetary conditions and a sustainable balance of payments'.

Progress was to be in three stages, the second stage beginning on 1 January 1994 and the third and final stage beginning on a date to be fixed by the Council but no later than 1 January 1999. By a special derogation protocol, the UK was authorized to maintain its separate monetary policy and not to move to the third stage unless it so wished.

The political union treaty was less uncompromising. Although it contained many fundamental changes, it did not introduce a new system of union as wholeheartedly as the EMU treaty did in its field. It did introduce the formal concept of a European Union as the ultimate goal, but did not specify a time-frame for the replacement of the existing Community. It went on to rename the EEC as the 'European Community', removing the conceptual limitation contained in the word 'Economic' (and some of the confusion arising from the Community's assorted titles).

Major constitutional changes included the introduction of a common foreign and security policy, looking forward to the eventual framing of a common defence policy; the introduction of a common citizenship of the Union; the formal inclusion among the Community institutions of the European Council, which would make an annual State of the Union report, and of a Committee of the Regions; and a formal requirement for the Union to 'respect fundamental rights as guaranteed by the European Convention on Human Rights and as they result from the constitutional traditions common to the member states as general principles of Community law'. Of great significance for future integration was the 'federal clause' (not so described) in which a probably vain attempt was made to limit the Community's powers by introducing the new principle of 'subsidiarity' under which EC competence to act was deemed to exist ('only if and insofar as the objectives of the proposed action cannot be sufficiently achieved by the member states and can therefore, by reason of the scale or effects of proposed action, better be achieved by the Community').

Other changes established full freedom of movement and local suffrage for Union citizens and introduced powers to harmonize indirect taxation and to legislate on aliens and visa control over non-Community nationals. In this last context, the 1990 Schengen Treaty between some

EC members (see AR 1990, p. 472), although not openly named, was effectively permitted pending its possible replacement by a Community instrument. Institutional and procedural departures included the introduction of a parliamentary ombudsman; abolition of the five additional commissioners at present appointed by the 'big five' member states; requirement of parliamentary approval for new commissioners; revised legislative procedures (set out in a detailed new article 189b); and revised treaty-making procedures. In addition, new sections were introduced into the treaty on education, research and development, culture, public health, consumer protection and trans-Europe communications (all being specifically within Community competence).

Two important additions were made to judicial procedure. There had hitherto been no effective remedy against a member state which failed to comply with an ECJ judgment. Now the Commission would be able to sue the state for damages under new article 171(2). And hitherto the European Parliament had been excluded from judicial review under article 173, both as plaintiff and as defendant (although the Court had been using some rather creative case law to give it a role). The new treaty remedied the difficulty by expressly including the Parliament in article 173, and indeed the new European Central Bank as well.

Special agreements were also added on implementation of the Community's 1989 Social Charter (see AR 1989, pp. 548–51) among 11 member states (i.e. excluding the UK) and on the involvement of the Western European Union (WEU) as the security and defence arm of the Community (see XII.2).

But Maastricht was not the sum-total of the significant and legal developments in 1991, since the ECJ made a number of important rulings during the year. A private plaintiff was held to have certain rights in damages against a member state which failed to implement a directive (*Francovich*). Member states had certain rights to restrict the export of strategic goods (*Richardt*). The anti-abortion provision in the Irish constitution was not overridden by the freedom to supply services under article 59, EEC, at least when the Irish defendant had no economic link with the English supplier of abortion services (*S.P.U.C. v. Grogan*). To make matters completely safe, the Maastricht summit adopted a special protocol putting article 40.3.3 of the Irish constitution outside the reach of Community law altogether. The UK no longer had unfettered power to alter the baselines for its territorial waters, if that resulted in a worsening of fishery opportunities for Community fishermen (*Commission v. UK*). The Merchant Shipping Act 1988, passed in order to keep Spanish fishermen out of the British fishing quota, infringed the Community's non-discrimination and free establishment rules and so was unenforceable (*Ex parte Factortame*). The use of copyright by the British and Irish broadcasting corporations to prevent other publishers from printing their TV programme schedules was illegal as an abuse of a dominant position (*Magill*). An unemployed migrant worker could be expelled if he had not found work within six months of entry and was not actively seeking work with a genuine chance of finding some (*Antonissen*).

Notwithstanding all the great European events of the year, an English lawyer might be forgiven for concluding by marking the deaths of three distinguished lawyers of German origin who became pillars of the English legal scene, namely Professor Clive Schmitthoff, Professor Georg Schwarzenberger and Dr Francis Mann. They were among a group of lawyers who left Hitler's Germany in the 1930s and found refuge in Britain, where they embraced English law but injected into their work an internationalism which, through sheer example, forced the natives to look beyond the borders of common law. That the British legal profession became so ready, with Britain's accession to the EC, to accept and handle continental legal patterns and concepts was due in great measure to the example of this group. Professors Schmitthoff and Schwarzenberger and Dr Mann, who continued teaching, writing and practising to the end, were almost the last of that extraordinary generation.

2. LAW IN THE UNITED KINGDOM

IN a decision of great constitutional significance, the Court of Appeal held that the immunity from liability for contempt of court afforded to ministers of the Crown did not exclude the possibility of liability being imposed on a minister in his personal capacity; accordingly, a fine was levied on the Home Secretary for breach of an undertaking given to the court[1]. The more traditional boundaries of liability were upheld in *Hague* v. *Deputy Governor of Parkhurst Prison, Weldon* v. *Home Office*[2], where the House of Lords refused to allow a civil action for damages at the suit of prisoners who claimed to have been improperly treated in breach of the prison rules. In *Lonrho plc* v. *Tebbit*[3], however, the Vice-Chancellor did allow the continuance of an action in negligence against a minister of the Crown in respect of an alleged misapplication of his powers; it was stressed, though, that the court had no powers to question any decisions of policy made by the minister. In another action in related litigation, the House of Lords clarified the scope of the tort of conspiracy, holding that an action might lie for damages even where the predominant purpose of the defendant had not been to cause loss to the plaintiff[4].

The interplay of domestic English law with the European Convention of Human Rights was considered by the House of Lords in *Brind* v. *Secretary of State for the Home Department*[5]. In upholding the decision of the Home Secretary to prohibit the direct broadcasting of statements by representatives of proscribed Northern Irish organizations, the House refused to hold that domestic law had to be interpreted in such a way as to give effect to the convention. On the other hand, in *Foster* v. *British Gas plc*[6], the House of Lords followed a ruling of the European Court of Justice[7] and allowed an action based on a European Community directive, effectively outlawing the imposition of different retiring ages on men and women, on the grounds that the defendant company was a quasi-public body.

The law continued to develop its jurisdiction to oversee and control the exercise of power by local authorities and other executive bodies. In *Hazell* v. *Hammersmith and Fulham London Borough Council*[8] the House of Lords held that it had been improper for the defendant council to enter into interest-rate swap agreements as a form of speculative investment, with the result that the council was effectively insulated from losses which it would otherwise have suffered; however, a similar form of speculation by a private investor was held not to be a simple legally-unenforceable gambling arrangement[9]. A simple technical insufficiency in the reasons for an executive decision was held to be not enough to justify the courts' overturning the decision unless genuine loss had been suffered by reason of the insufficiency[10]. In *Johnstone* v. *Bloomsbury Area Health Authority*[11] the Court of Appeal opened the way for the imposition of greater controls over the working hours of junior doctors, holding that they could not be forced to work overtime, even within their nominal contractual duties, if this would have the foreseeable effect of causing injury to their health.

The administration of the legal system began to feel the effects of the coming into force of the *Courts and Legal Services Act 1990*. An application was made by the Law Society for solicitors to be granted limited rights of audience before superior courts; and by an order made under the act foreign lawyers were enabled to enter into partnerships with English lawyers[12]. More controversially, the Queen's Bench Divisional Court refused to recognize the general right of an unrepresented party in proceedings before a magistrates' court to have the assistance of a 'McKenzie'[13] friend: the court upheld the decision of the Leicester justices not to permit two defendants, against whom proceedings were brought for non-payment of the community charge, to be accompanied and advised by a member of the Anti-Poll Tax Federation[14].

The criminal justice system, too, underwent considerable reorganization. The *Criminal Justice Act*, one of the very few significant pieces of legislation of the year, introduced a major reorganization of powers and practices of sentencing. The *Criminal Procedure (Insanity and Unfitness to Plead) Act* heralded a more up-to-date treatment of the mentally-disordered in the criminal process. Further important changes were foreshadowed by the report of Lord Justice Woolf on the operation of the prison service[15], recommending rapid improvements in the condition of prisons and in the systems of keeping discipline in them. A full-scale Royal Commission into the whole working of the criminal justice system was set up after the release of a further six people (the 'Birmingham Six') whose convictions for terrorist-related offences were found to have been unsafe and unsatisfactory[16] (see also I.3).

Judicial activity was particularly marked in the field of criminal law. In a widely-welcomed piece of judicial legislation the House of Lords overturned the long-established rule that a husband could not be guilty of the rape of his wife during the subsistence of the marriage[17]; of no less practical importance was their decision in *R* v. *Savage, R.* v. *Parmenter*[18], clarifying the mental state which has to be established in order to obtain a conviction for a variety of offences under the *Offences Against the Person Act* of 1861. In the Court of Appeal, a move was made towards the clarification of the concept of 'appropriation' in the *Theft Act* of 1968[19]; and in *R* v. *Attewell-Hughes*[20] the precise scope of the offences of deception contained in section two of the *Theft Act* of 1978 was carefully defined. Expanding an earlier decision of the House of Lords which excluded the defence of duress from the crime of murder[21], the Court of Appeal refused to allow the raising of the defence to a charge of attempted murder; the effect of the decision was slightly palliated by the insistence of the court that any duress might be of the utmost importance in determining the proper sentence[22]. After many years of doubt, it was held that the commission of a crime while sleepwalking had to be treated on the same footing as the commission of a crime while insane[23].

In other rulings, an extraterritorial conspiracy to commit a crime in England was held to constitute a crime under English law, even before anything had been done in England pursuant to the agreement[24]; and allegedly careless medical treatment was held not to break the chain of causation between the attack of the accused and the death of the victim[25]. A woman who killed her husband after a prolonged period of domestic violence was held not to be permitted to raise the defence of provocation[26]; but it was made clear this would not preclude the successful raising of a plea of diminished responsibility.

There were two important decisions on the law of criminal evidence: in *Hui Chi-ming* v. *R*[27] the Privy Council ruled that the acquittal of an alleged accomplice in an earlier trial was not admissible as evidence in favour of the accused in a later one; and in *R.* v. *P*[28] the House of Lords explained the scope of the rule allowing the admissibility in evidence of the fact that the accused had been convicted of an offence based on similar facts to those at the base of the present charge.

In the law of torts, the courts began to lay down guidelines covering the situations in which it was proper to make an award of provisional damages rather than a single lump sum[29]; and a rare application for a jury hearing in an action seeking damages for personal injury was refused, reinforcing the principle that jury trials in such cases would almost never be permitted[30]. A looser stance was taken on the exercise of the court's discretion to allow a plaintiff to proceed with an action notwithstanding the lapse of the ordinary period of limitation[31]. In litigation arising out of the Hillsborough football disaster (see AR 1989, pp. 15, 503), the House of Lords reconsidered the circumstances in which damages should be recoverable for nervous shock: recovery was permitted only to plaintiffs with a close emotional bond to the injured parties and who had themselves witnessed the events or their immediate aftermath[32].

By far the most important development in the law of the family was the coming into force in October of the *Children Act* of 1989[33], accompanied by a deluge of rules, orders and guidelines[34]. The act fundamentally altered the balance of power between parents and the state in the upbringing of children, shifting the responsibilities and costs as far as possible on to the parents themselves, whilst at the same time maintaining a flexible and effective overseeing role for the state in order to protect the interests of the children. Further important potential changes in this area flowed from the *Child Support Act*, providing a framework to strengthen the powers of the courts and public authorities to ensure that parental responsibilities are observed. The increasingly bureaucratic nature of the legislation contrasted with the flexible approach of the courts to the exercise of their powers in cases of wardships. In *Re W (A minor)*[35] the Court of Appeal adopted a robust standpoint in refusing to forbid the publication in a newspaper of the circumstances in which a ward of court had been placed for fostering with a homosexual couple, notwithstanding that the child might have been identifiable by inference. By contrast, in *Re R (A Minor)*[36], the same court held that it was open to it to refuse or to give consent to medical treatment for a minor, even though the natural parents of the child would have had no such powers[37].

A number of awkward problems besetting the law of real property were effectively cleared up. In *Spiro* v. *Glencrown Properties Ltd*[38] Hoffman J. adopted an unorthodox interpretation of section two of the *Law of Property (Miscellaneous Provisions) Act* of 1989, thereby avoiding the apparent effect of the statute in preventing the enforcement of many option agreements. In *Billson* v. *Residential Apartments Ltd*[39] the House of Lords adopted a similar purposive construction in holding that the tenant of mortgaged property was entitled to equitable relief against forfeiture of the property under section 146 of the *Law of Property Act 1925* in cases where the landlord had obtained possession of the property by peaceful means; the opposite interpretation, favoured by the Court of Appeal[40], would have permitted many landlords of mortgaged property simply to take the property without compensating the defaulting tenants for its value. More anomalously, the Court of Appeal in *Sen* v. *Headley*[41] held that title to land could effectively be passed by a death-bed gift of the title deeds to the property, providing a potential mechanism for the bypassing of the normal requirement of writing to pass an interest in land. Also potentially problematic was the decision of the House of Lords in *Hammersmith and Fulham London Borough Council* v. *Monk*[42], holding that a local authority tenancy could effectively be determined by one of two joint tenants without the knowledge or consent of the other.

1 *M* v. *Home Office, The Times,* 2 December
2 [1991] 3 All ER 733
3 [1991] 4 All ER 973
4 *Lonrho plc* v. *Fayed* [1991] 3 All ER 303
5 [1991] 1 All ER 720
6 [1991] 2 All ER 705
7 [1990] 3 All ER 897
8 [1991] 1 All ER 545
9 *City Index* v. *Leslie* [1991] 3 All ER 180
10 *Save Britain's Heritage* v. *Secretary of State for the Environment* [1991] 2 All ER 10
11 [1991] 2 All ER 293
12 See (1991) 141 *New Law Journal* 1702
13 See *McKenzie* v. *McKenzie* [1971] p. 33
14 *R* v. *Leicester City Justices, ex parte Barrow* [1991] 2 All ER 437
15 *Prison Disturbances, April 1990. Report on an Enquiry by the Rt Hon Lord Justice Woolf and His Honour Judge Stephen Tumin* (HMSO)
16 See (1991) 140 *New Law Journal* 373
17 *R* v. *R* [1991] 4 All ER 481
18 [1991] 4 All ER 698
19 *R* v. *Gomez* [1991] 3 All ER 394
20 [1991] 4 All ER 810
21 *R* v. *Howe* [1987] 1 All ER 771
22 *R* v. *Gotts* [1991] 2 All ER 1
23 *R* v. *Burgess* [1991] 2 All ER 769
24 *R* v. *Sansom* [1991] 2 All ER 145
25 *R* v. *Cheshire* [1991] 3 All ER 670
26 *R* v. *Thornton* (1991) 141 *New Law Journal* 1223
27 [1991] 3 All ER 897
28 [1991] 3 All ER 337
29 *Willson* v. *Ministry of Defence* [1991] 1 All ER 638
30 *H* v. *Ministry of Defence* [1991] 2 All ER 834
31 *Halford* v. *Brookes* [1991] 3 All ER 559
32 *Alcock* v. *Chief Constable of the South Yorkshire Police* [1991] 4 All ER 907
33 SI 1991/828, 1991/1881, 1991,1990
34 Summarized in (1991) 141 *New Law Journal* 1368
35 (1991) 141 *New Law Journal* 1263
36 [1991] 4 All ER 177
37 See *Gillick* v. *West Norfolk and Wisbech Area Health Authority* [1985] 3 All ER 402
38 [1991] 1 All ER 600

39 (1991) 141 *New Law Journal* 1735
40 [1991] 3 All ER 265
41 [1991] 2 All ER 636
42 (1991) 141 *New Law Journal* 1697

3. LAW IN THE UNITED STATES

IN 1991 attention on law in the media dramatically focused on women's rights on two occasions. Together with the enactment of the *Civil Rights Act* of 1991[1], such attention possibly heightened awareness of the difficulties of protecting such rights. After the hearings before the US Senate judiciary committee concerning the nomination of Judge Clarence Thomas to the Supreme Court, Anita Hill, once employed at the Education Department and later at the Equal Employment Opportunities Commission of the federal government, in both instances under the supervision of Judge Thomas, alleged that Judge Thomas had sexually harassed her on numerous occasions while so employed. In the other case, William Kennedy Smith, nephew of the late President John F. Kennedy, was charged with having raped a woman whom he had met at a bar in Palm Beach and who had accompanied him back to the family residence there. Ms Hill's and other testimony before the Senate judiciary committee and the trial of Mr Smith were reported live on national television. Ultimately, the nomination of Judge Thomas as Supreme Court justice was confirmed by the Senate and a verdict of not guilty returned against Mr Smith by the jury (see also II.1).

The new Civil Rights Act revised the Civil Rights Act of 1964, so that the law would provide substantially as the Supreme Court had construed it in cases prior to 1989 and not as it was construed by that court in several cases in 1989. Under a 1971 ruling, *Griggs v. Duke Power Co.*[2], the Court held that hiring and promotion of women and minorities must be related to their performance of, or their abilities to perform, the job. In 1989, in *Wards Cove Packing Co. v. Antonio*[3], the Court held that employers initially disproved allegations of discrimination by showing that their practices were 'job-related and consistent with business necessity'; after that, the plaintiffs were to prove that the practices were discriminatory by showing that such practices had a 'disparate impact' on them. The new law left the burden of proof with the employers. In *Patterson v. McLean Credit Union*[4] the Court held that the Civil Rights Act of 1964, while it covered hiring and promotion, did not protect an employee against discriminatory assignment of tasks and extra work. The new law clarified that the act extended to everyone all terms and conditions of employment, including privileges and benefits. The enactment of the law perhaps indicated that for the foreseeable future, because the Supreme Court had become dominated by conservative justices, Congress would assume responsibility for developing protection of civil rights. The shift from the Court to Congress was all the more significant because prior versions of the law had been vetoed by President Bush, who favoured the Court's interpretations of the Civil Rights Act of 1964.

State law civil rights protection of homosexuals was expanded with the award by a court in California of a $5.3 million judgment against Shell Oil Company[5], which dismissed an executive who was discovered to be 'gay' after he used an office computer and printer to write a memo on safe-sex rules for a party at his gay sex club; the court found that the executive had been sacked solely because he was a sexually-active homosexual. The judgment, which included $2.3 million in punitive damages, was one of the largest-ever in a gay-related employment case.

The tension between the rights of the unborn and the mother continued to occupy the attention of the courts. In *UAW* v. *Johnson Controls, Inc.*[6] the Supreme Court held that employers could not exclude pregnant women from jobs solely to protect the foetus. The federal courts ruled on the validity of laws which significantly restricted the right to an abortion and which were enacted after the Supreme Court's decision in *Webster* v. *Reproductive Health Services*[7], holding that, after that decision, there was no longer a constitutionally-protected broad right to an abortion under the Court's decision in 1973[8]. One or more of these decisions was expected to reach the Supreme Court and to compel it to decide finally whether the celebrated decision in 1973 was no longer precedent.

In the field of tort law, where developments were often driven by plaintiffs' search for 'deep pockets' and the punitive damages without which few plaintiffs' lawyers could hope to recover their fees and disbursements, judgments were mixed. Two states, California and Wisconsin, held that a homeowner's insurance policy did not cover the sexual molestation by the insured of his child[9] or the transmission of herpes by the insured to another during consensual sexual intercourse[10]. A Colorado court held that McDonald's Corporation, a fast-food restaurant chain, was liable for $210,000 to a mother and her son who were assaulted by a disabled janitor employed at the recommendation of the state's Department of Social Services as part of McDonald's disabled individuals' hiring programme[11]. In another law suit against McDonald's, an Oregon court awarded a $400,000 judgment against the company for injuries caused by a car accident: a 19-year-old employee, who had worked a 12-hour shift after having worked an eight-hour shift the previous night, caused a car accident while driving home, injuring the plaintiff[12].

An appellate court in New York held that a manufacturer might be held liable for unsafe products, even though it did not manufacture such products, if it contributed to the sub-standard nature of such product by lobbying against government regulations affecting the product or by conspiring to minimize public awareness of the unsafeness of the product[13]. The US Supreme Court declined to hold as an unconstitutional denial of due process a $1,077,978 verdict for punitive damages against an insurance company where the agent failed to turn the premiums collected from the insured over to the insurer; as a result the policies lapsed, but the insurer failed to notify the insured of cancellation. The insured incurred medical costs of $2,500, which would have been recovered under the policy. The Court's decision indicated that it was unwilling to prescribe specific standards for limiting punitive damages awards[14]. However, the Court refused to review or reverse decisions of federal appeals courts denying punitive damages to victims of Pan Am flight 103 which was exploded over Lockerbie (Scotland) by a terrorist bomb in 1988 and of KAL flight 103 which was shot down by a Soviet jet fighter in 1983[15].

Three decisions of the US Supreme Court further eroded the rights of accused persons. In *Harmelin* v. *Michigan*[16] the Court held that a life sentence for possession of 672 grams of cocaine, while unusual, was not constitutionally prohibited as cruel and unusual. In another decision, *Payne* v. *Tennessee*[17], the Court held that a court could receive evidence about the effect of a crime on its victim in its decisions about whether to impose the death penalty. In *Coleman* v. *Thompson*[18] the Court held that persons convicted of capital crimes might not be able to apply for writs of *habeas corpus* before a federal court where they had not complied with state court procedural rules; the decision was likely to limit efforts by persons awaiting execution who wished to have their convictions and sentences reconsidered long after their trials.

1 Public Law 102–106
2 401 US 424 (1971)
3 490 US 642 (1989)
4 491 US 164 (1989)
5 *Collins* v. *Shell Oil Co.*, No. 610983–5, Alameda County Superior Court, California
6 No. 89–1215
7 492 US 490 (1989)
8 *Planned Parenthood of Southeastern Pennsylvania Reproductive Health and Counseling Centre* v. *Casey*, No. 90–1662, Third Circuit Court of Appeals; *Guam Society of Obstetricians and Gynaecologists* v. *Ada*, No. 90–16706, Ninth Circuit Court of Appeals; *Sojourner T.* v. *Roemer*, No. 91–3677, Fifth Circuit Court of Appeals; *John L.* v. *Bangerter*, No. 91–C–345G, Federal District Court, Utah
9 *J. C. Penney Casulty Insurance* v. *M.K.*, No. S0110524, California Supreme Court
10 *Loveridge* v. *Chartier*, 468 N.W. 2d 146 (Wis. 1991)
11 M. Charlier and W. Lambert, 'McDonalds Told to Pay $210,000 Damages in Negligent-Hiring Case', *The Wall Street Journal*, 15 March 1991
12 A. Stevens, 'Bosses Fret They May Be Liable For Tired Workers on Road Home', *The Wall Street Journal*, 16 April 1991

13 A. Marcus, 'State Court Allows Industrywide Liability', *The Wall Street Journal*, 25 March 1991
14 *Pacific Mutual Life Insurance Co.* v. *Haslip*, 89–1279
15 *Rein* v. *Pan American World Airways, Inc.*, No. 91–259; *Dooley* v. *Korean Air Lines Ltd*, No. 91–251
16 No. 89–7272
17 No. 90–5721
18 No. 89–7662

XVI THE ARTS

1. OPERA—MUSIC—DANCE/BALLET—THEATRE—CINEMA
TELEVISION & RADIO

i. OPERA

THIS was the year in which the 200th anniversary of the death of Mozart was commemorated in most of the world's opera houses. Productions of the composer's operatic masterpieces were legion, but it was disappointing that the opportunity was not seized to perform more of his unfamiliar early operas. In London, the Royal Opera produced *Mitridate*, by the 14-year-old Mozart, in an imaginative staging by Graham Vick. Apart from this, the most enterprising tribute was that offered by Opera North with *The Jewel Box*, not an authentic Mozart opera but a pastiche concocted by Paul Griffiths who collected seventeen arias and ensembles composed by Mozart for insertion into the operas of other composers, and linked the separate numbers together with spoken dialogue. Other Mozartian highlights of the year included Jonathan Miller's production of *Le Nozze di Figaro* for the Vienna Festival, Nicholas Hytner's *La Clemenza di Tito* at Glyndebourne and, at the Aix-en-Provence Festival, Mozart's earliest work for the stage, *Die Schuldigkeit des ersten Gebots*, which he composed at the age of eleven. Trevor Nunn's *Così fan tutte* at Glyndebourne was unforgivably set on an Edwardian ocean liner; while, also at Glyndebourne, Peter Sellars' *Magic Flute*, transferred to a psychedelic Californian freeway, had to be seen to be disbelieved. The reopening of the newly-restored Tyl theatre in Prague in December was celebrated with a production of *Don Giovanni* which had received its first performance there in 1787.

The Royal Opera began the year with a musically impressive staging of Strauss's *Capriccio*, fashionably updated to the twentieth century, which made nonsense of the text's references to such contemporary composers and playwrights as Gluck and Goldoni. Götz Friedrich's unsatisfactory account of Wagner's *Ring* was brought to a conclusion with a *Götterdämmerung* made notable by Gwyneth Jones's radiant Brünnhilde. José Carreras made a welcome return to Covent Garden after his serious illness, as Samson in Saint-Saens' *Samson et Dalila*, performed in Sidney Nolan's hauntingly beautiful decor, and the appearance of other popular stars such as Hildegarde Behrens (as Tosca) and Placido Domingo (Cavaradossi) did something to mitigate the effect of the new and outrageously high ticket prices. The atonal score of a new opera, *Gawain* by Harrison Birtwistle, much of it in slow or stately tempi, made little effect, but the low point of the Royal Opera's season came with an inept production, imported from Germany, of Meyerbeer's rarely-staged *Les Huguenots*.

The repertoire of English National Opera (ENO) was more enterprising, in productions which ranged from the superb to the arrogantly didactic. David Alden, a director who specialized in attempts to *épater les bourgeois*, mercilessly satirized Stravinsky's masterpiece, *Oedipus rex*, coupling it with a feeble though respectful account of Bartok's *Bluebeard's Castle*. Three operas by Britten were included in the ENO repertoire: a successful revival of *The Turn of the Screw* in Jonathan Miller's sensitive and perceptive staging, a determinedly wrong-headed new production of *Peter Grimes* by Tim Albery, and a revival of the same director's only partly satisfactory *Billy Budd*. A new opera, *Timon of Athens* by Stephen Oliver, turned out to be little more than disposable musical journalism, a revival of Jonathan Miller's delightful reinterpretation of the Gilbert and Sullivan *Mikado* proved as popular as ever, and the company's year ended with a distinctly odd account of the indestructible *Fledermaus*.

Among the best of the productions offered by regional companies were Opera North's *Carmen*, with Sally Burgess in the title-role, Scottish Opera's British premiere of Marc Blitzstein's *Regina*, and Welsh National Opera's *Idomeneo*, magnificently conducted by Charles Mackerras. The new opera which created most excitement was staged in the United States. This was John Corigliano's agreeably eclectic *The Ghosts of Versailles*, the first new work to be commissioned by the Metropolitan Opera since 1967. Corigliano and his librettist, William M. Hoffman, created an opera which moved on two planes of the imagination. The first level was inhabited in the present by ghosts from the time of the French revolution, among them Marie Antoinette, Louis XVI and the playwright Beaumarchais. The second level was that of an opera composed by the ghostly Beaumarchais, featuring the characters from his plays about Figaro and the Almaviva family. Corigliano's score was consistently entertaining, and in its more lyrically reflective moments achieved a highly appealing individual quality. A first-rate cast was headed by Teresa Stratas, Marilyn Horne and Graham Clark, and James Levine presided imperturbably over the superb Metropolitan Opera Orchestra.

In the United Kingdom, public funding for the opera companies remained a lively topic of discussion. The Arts Minister managed to find for the arts in general a larger sum of money than had been expected, but the general view was that the Arts Council subsequently failed to disburse it very wisely. Concern was expressed in the pages of the influential magazine *Opera* and elsewhere about the calibre of people now employed by the Arts Council compared to ten or fifteen years ago, and an admission by the secretary-general of the Council that 'sometimes we get it wrong' was greeted with widespread derision.

Among those who died in 1991 were: the English baritone John Hargreaves who had been a prominent member of the Sadler's Wells Company in the 1950s; the French-Canadian tenor André Turp who sang many of the French and Italian lyric roles at Covent Garden in the Fifties and Sixties; Maria Reining, the Austrian soprano who was a mainstay of the Vienna State Opera in the period before, during and immediately after World War II, a greatly admired Marschallin and Leonore; the producer and lecturer Friedelind Wagner, granddaughter of the composer; Luigi Infantino, the Italian lyric tenor who flourished in the post-World-War-II years; and the Irish tenor, James Johnson, highly popular in the Italian repertory at Sadler's Wells and Covent Garden between 1945 and 1958.

ii. MUSIC

THERE could be no-one who was unaware that 1991 was Mozart year, the 200th anniversary of the composer's death; so it was the music of Mozart that overwhelmed concert-halls, opera houses and television studios worldwide. No doubt the motivation for such a concentration of effort was economic rather than artistic—the musical profession was no more capable of altruism on such a scale than any other human institution. Nevertheless this glut of one composer's music called for no very special effort on the part of musicians or their audiences over the year. Mozart's music had long been securely rooted in the repertories of countless artists and performing organizations, as well as in the popular consciousness, and was universally familiar.

The bicentenary year turned out to have something in it for everyone. Each branch of the musical world contributed to it: the record industry, the academic community, the 'early music' aficionados, the film-makers, the impresarios and agents. All were kept at full stretch as a stream of performances on stage, in the concert-hall, on television and on disc, too numerous to specify, were given throughout the year. Never could there have been more performances of the *Requiem* than there were in December, the actual month of Mozart's death.

Among the numerous festivals given over to the single theme, none was more successful than the Europe-Mozart-Prague festival in September. But inevitably the largest and most comprehensive festival was in America, where the Mozart Bicentennial Programme at the Lincoln Center in New York set out to perform nothing less than Mozart's entire *oeuvre*. As for the record industry, the companies needed no second bidding in issuing, or re-issuing, Mozart recordings. Philips were the most ambitious, issuing the complete works on CD;

and though some fragmentary works required completion before they could be performed, it was stretching the term to claim a 'premiere recording' for a piece which turned out to be nothing more than a modern transcription for orchestra of a piano sketch composed by the eight-year-old Mozart on a visit to London in 1764. The bicentenary showed that there was little if anything still to be uncovered of Mozart's output. Someone managed to discover an autograph sketch in the Library of Congress in Washington, which consisted of the vocal line of *Al desio di chi t'adoro*, for Susanna's revised aria in *The Marriage of Figaro*; but this was hardly new—it was already catalogued in the Koechel list as K.577.

What the bicentenary could do was to challenge fresh insights into the performance of Mozart's music. In particular this was felt by the early music lobby. Many performances were given which used not only 'authentic' instruments, but 'authentic' dress and 'authentic' platform sets. This approach proved controversial, and the trend towards such a limited view of classical music was severely questioned; over 100 years of performance-experience could hardly be forgotten. So it seemed probable that one result of the Mozart bicentenary would be the decline in popularity of the early music movement.

There were other anniversaries in 1991. Among the established composers, it was the centenary of Prokofiev's birth, the 150th anniversary of Dvorcak's. Both were fittingly observed. In London, all seven Prokofiev symphonies were played twice, first in a series of four concerts by the BBC Philharmonic under Edward Downes, next a few months later as part of an ambitious South Bank series under the title *Russian Spring*. The series also provided an opportunity to hear new music by unfamiliar composers such as Boris Tischenko, Elena Firsova, Dmitri Smirnov and Nikolai Roslavets.

The same formula was applied in Prague where Mozart and Dvorak were presented like a double bill at the autumn festival, along with some contemporary Czech composers (Kabeláč, Slavický) and the Hungarian composer Kurtág. At the main festival in May music by Ravel provided an excellent foil for a striking new piece of musical theatre by Kelterborn, *Julia*.

Such a solution to the challenge of contemporary music brought together the two aspects of the musical world which had for long been diametrically opposed: on the one hand day-to-day performances of the standard classics, and on the other, experimental, contemporary works. Great planning and judgment were called for if a new composition was to be inserted in a public concert with some prospect of success with the audience. Wherever new compositions were played, one heard afterwards of unknown works by unknown composers being hailed as masterpieces, or dismissed as worthless, by unknown journalists, for no reason other than the subjective response of the writer. This was compounded by the sheer number of living composers. According to the latest count in the magazine *Composer*, they numbered some 500 in Britain; who knew how many there might be in countries as large as the United States or Russia?

The London magazine, *The Musical Times*, invited its readers to comment on any shortcomings they detected in the musical world. One response, published in December, went to the heart of the problem. It came from Jonathan Harvey, a distinguished composer, one of the very few to work successfully in the electronic field and who was also professor of music at Sussex University. He expressed his deep concern at the prospects facing his composition students, some of whom were greatly gifted. What sort of a profession were they being trained to enter? Would their more ambitious new works ever be heard by them more than perhaps once or twice in their lifetime? The number of composers in the country, which he put as high as 800 (depending on how one defined the term 'composer'), meant that very few, if any, could expect to make a living from composition alone.

Professor Harvey was right in pointing out something which had been known for a long time, but which most preferred to ignore. The statistics for the season 1990/91 in the UK were that, out of the total number of all classical performances, the percentage of works by living British composers was: BBC broadcasts and public concerts 4.25 per cent; all other orchestral concerts 3.1 per cent. Figures for opera, recordings and other smaller events were not available, but assuming they were similar, about 96 per cent of the entire serious musical output of the British Isles in 1991 consisted of music of the past, or music from other countries.

There were one or two statutory premieres of works by British composers: by the London Symphony Orchestra at the start of its Barbican season in September (Tavener's *Dance Lament of the Repentant Thief*); by the City of Birmingham Symphony Orchestra (CBSO) at the opening of the new symphony hall in that city in April (Turnage's *Momentum*). Neither piece was entirely satisfactory; nor were the works commissioned for the promenade concerts by the BBC. Works by Dalby, Nash, Sawer and Wood were given their obligatory first, and probably last, performances. The BBC were much more successful, as in previous years, in giving a platform to new works which had originated elsewhere, such as Lutoslawski's *Chantefleurs et Chantefables*, and Tippet's *Byzantium*. The latter work, a huge setting of the Yeats poem for soprano and orchestra, was brought to London from its premiere in Chicago under Solti, and its second performance in New York, where it was played as part of the celebration to mark the centenary of Carnegie Hall.

Elsewhere the established festivals in England had a fallow year. Maybe, in a period of recession, their concern was survival rather than daring or innovative achievement. This seemed to be the pattern in mainstream concerts as a whole in 1991, with perhaps a tendency towards the large-scale event, aimed at a mass audience, after the manner of pop music concerts. 'Pavarotti in the Park' was one such event in London, spoiled only by torrential rain which kept away many thousands who would otherwise have come to hear their favourite operatic tenor. In the concert hall the season was marked by one or two outstanding Mahler performances. The veteran Klaus Tennstedt gave two performances, of the 6th and 8th Symphonies respectively, while in Birmingham Simon Rattle's performance of the 2nd (*Resurrection*) Symphony confirmed that conductor's predilection for the late romantic repertoire.

A series was devoted to Henze at the Barbican in January, and to the 82-year-old Elliott Carter at the South Bank in April. Notable events elsewhere included the premiere at Bournemouth of Gerard Schurmann's new cello concerto *Gardens of Exile* by the Bournemouth Orchestra, and of Andrzej Panufnik's new String Quartet No.3, *Wycinanki* ('Symmetries'). This had been the test piece in Menuhin's international string quartet competition, and the premiere was given by the winning Wihan Quartet from Czechoslovakia.

The record industry was highly active in 1991. If the larger companies, generally speaking, were occupied with the Mozart bicentenary, it was left to the smaller ones to attend to everything else. Several of them began, tentatively, to record British composers—but always the British composers of yesterday, who were safely dead. The single exception to this trend, and easily the most heart-warming story of the year, if not the greatest music, was provided by the recording by Simon Rattle and the CBSO of Nicholas Maw's 100-minute piece *Odyssey*. Rattle made his contract with EMI conditional on their agreeing to this gigantic project; and there were not many conductors who would be prepared to go to such lengths in support of a composer-colleague.

Among those who died in 1991 were the pianists Claudio Arrau, Rudolf Serkin and Eileen Joyce, the violinist Alfredo Campoli, the composer Andrzej Panufnik, the blind organists Jean Langlais and Helmut Walcha, the American jazz trumpeter and composer Miles Davis and the British pop-singer Freddy Mercury. (For Arrau, Serkin, Joyce, Campoli, Langlais, Panufnik, Walcha and Davis, see XX:OBITUARY.)

BOOKS OF THE YEAR. *A Ravel Reader* by Arbie Orenstein; *Mozart: The Golden Years; Mozart and Vienna; 1791 Mozart's last year* all by H. C. Robbins Landon; *The Mozart Repertory* by Neal Zasland and Fiona Morgan Fein; *The Compleat Mozart* by Neal Zasland and William Cowdery; *The Beethoven Compendium* ed. by Barry Cooper; *Alban Berg, Historical and Analytical Perspectives* ed. by David Gable and Robert P. Morgan.

iii. DANCE/BALLET

ONE trend in the dance world did not change in 1991 and the focus was again on dancers rather than dances. The year would be remembered above all for the deaths of prima ballerina assoluta Margot Fonteyn and of Martha Graham (see XX:OBITUARY), the matriarch of American modern dance. The latter's company gave the first performance of her final creation, *The Eyes of the Goddess*, posthumously in New York.

Anniversaries inevitably attracted attention. Throughout the world Mozart-inspired ballets were created and revived, but none equalled the style and quality of George Balanchine's 1956 *Divertimento No. 15*, still exquisitely performed by New York City Ballet and the Birmingham Royal Ballet. The 150th anniversary of *Giselle* was marked by revivals of well-tried productions and by new versions. Peter Schaufuss's award-winning production for Deutsche Oper Ballett, Berlin (also seen at the Edinburgh Festival) captured the romantic spirit of the work (with pretty designs by Desmond Heeley), although the first act was somewhat busy with the expansion of the peasant pas de deux for eight dancers. At the Paris Opéra (where *Giselle* was created) the traditional text was juxtaposed with an austere, minimalist set by Loïe Le Groumellac which marred the production.

The Paris Opéra was more successful with its programme for the centenary of Bronislava Nijinska's birth. They paired *Les Biches* (with Marie Laurencin's designs superbly reinterpreted) and *Les Noces* with Vaslav Nijinsky's *L'Après-midi d'un faune* and *Le Sacre du printemps* (in the Hodson/Archer reconstruction) to highlight Nijinska's own development on from her brother's work. In contrast, the Royal Ballet performed the same Nijinska ballets with an assured revival of Frederick Ashton's *Scènes de ballet* to show her subsequent influence. The Royal's *Les Noces* continued to set an unrivalled standard, but *Les Biches* no longer showed understanding of Twenties' *moeurs*.

The two major creations for the Royal Ballet were literary ballets, although neither challenged the plays which inspired them. Kenneth MacMillan's *Winter Dreams*, an evocation of Chekhov's *Three Sisters*, had many admirers but only the two pas de deux for Masha (Darcey Bussell) and Vershinin (Irek Mukhamedov) showed the choreographer at his best. *Cyrano* by David Bintley (inspired by the RSC's 1983 production rather than the 1991 film) made a tedious evening in spite of a committed performance by Stephen Jefferies. Otherwise the Royal continued to acquire and perform an extensive Balanchine repertory, although a quartet from Jonathan Burrow's witty *Stoics* enlivened the autumn. A fascinating range of casts illuminated *Manon*, including Viviana Durante, Sylvie Guillem and the incandescent Altynai Asylmuratova as the heroine and Mukhamadov alternating as the cynical Lescaut and the innocent de Grieux.

On two visits to the USA the Royal Ballet won critical praise—indeed it was a year when British companies received more acclamation abroad than at home. Rambert Dance Company had a triumphant season at the Paris Opéra where, at only a few days notice, they replaced Martha Graham's Company which was prevented from travelling by the Gulf War. The remainder of Rambert's year was dominated by the search for an adequate London theatre—Sadler's Wells had long proved too cramped. This resulted in a successful season at the Royalty, including Laurie Booth's *Completely Birdland* and Siobhan Davies's *Plain Song*. Other companies which appeared at this rediscovered venue included Northern Ballet Theatre which showed Christopher Gable's popular new *Romeo and Juliet*, choreographed by the Italian Massimo Moricone; and the Israeli Ballet whose unimaginative repertory was largely by their artistic director, Berta Yampolsky. London Contemporary Dance Theatre continued to show talented dancers in an uninspired repertory (including *Rikud* by Liat Dror and Nir Ben Gal, and *Wind Devil* by Nina Wiener).

English National Ballet also suffered from a lack-lustre repertory. *The Taming of the Shrew* (not John Cranko's best work) was well performed by Lynne Charles (alternating as Kate and Bianca) and the Italian pair, Renata Calderini and Maurizio Bellezza. Vicente Nebrada's dreary *Our Waltzes* and Mauricio Wainrot's *Anne Frank* proved unpopular. At the end of the year the company unveiled a new fast-moving, traditional but unmagical, *Nutcracker* by Ben Stevenson, artistic director of Houston Ballet, in which Thomas Edur and Agnes Oakes (a much-admired Estonian couple) were the Prince and the Snow Queen, and Ludmila Semeniaka (a former Bolshoi star) took over as the Sugar Plum Fairy on 31 December.

The British company that showed the most interesting repertory was Birmingham Royal Ballet (BRB) which went from strength to strength under the inspired leadership of Peter Wright. New creations, William Tuckett's *License My Roving Hands* and Graham Lustig's *Inscape*, were not memorable: but mixed bills were enriched by Paul Taylor's *Airs*, a reworking of MacMillan's *The Burrow*, and above all by a superb reconstruction by Tatiana Leskova of Léonide Massine's *Choreatium*. For audiences, who rarely see any of Massine's works, and then only the lighter, comic works, *Choreatium*, as response to Brahms's Fourth Symphony, was a revelation. BRB included many attractive dancers, and Miyako Yoshida's scintillating technique and notable assurance was a delight.

In the absence of great choreographers, the reconstruction of 'lost works' became increasingly important. Millicent Hodson and Kenneth Archer convincingly reproduced Balanchine's *La Chatte* (with constructivist designs by Naum Gabo and Antoine Pevsner) for Les Grands Ballets Canadiens but, inexplicably, it disappeared after a few performances in Montreal. The Royal Danish Ballet continued its revival of August Bournonville's ballets and Queen Margrethe made lively designs for *A Folk Tale*.

The surprise event in America was Peter Martin's staging of *The Sleeping Beauty* for New York City Ballet. This provided a challenge and a stimulus for the company which led to superb performances in this and other works from Kyra Nichols, Damian Woetzel and the young Ethan Steifel. Most notable was Darci Kistler who was truly fulfilling her early promise; and performances by Kistler and Ben Huys led audiences to the elysium of Balanchine's *Chaconne*.

Economic strictures affected American Ballet Theater so that their *Don Quixote*, staged by Bolshoi star Vladimir Vasiliev, re-used Santo Loquasto's sets and costumes. Enrique Martinez's popular *Coppélia* was revived, now redesigned by Tony Straiges and Patricia Ziprodt. Fewer mixed programmes were given but a revival of Agnes de Mille's *Fall River Legend* provided dramatic opportunities for Cynthia Gregory, Carla Fracci and Sylvie Guillem.

Joint productions became a feature of the dance world. Paul Taylor's *Company B*, a crowd-pleaser to songs by the Andrews Sisters, was premiered by Houston Ballet before Taylor's seasons in New York and London. The other welcome American visitor to Britain was Trisha Brown's Company, the highlight of the flourishing Dance Umbrella. Several smaller companies combined Western styles with Indian classical dance: the most successful in Britain was the Shobana Jeyasingh Dance Company, but Maurice Béjart's involvement in *Trikonam* gave it a high profile.

Béjart's controversial successor in Brussels, Mark Morris, completed his contract with an acclaimed gender-crossing *Nutcracker*, *The Hard Nut*, set in the 1960s. Morris was again active in America, notably with the successful White Oak Project formed around Mikhail Baryshnikov. Wayne Eagling succeeded Rudi van Dantzig as artistic director of Dutch National Ballet after the company had appeared in van Dantzig's *Romeo and Juliet* at the London Coliseum.

Following the collapse of the Entertainment Corporation, the major Russian companies rarely left home although the Kirov (now St Petersburg Ballet) toured the USA, their repertory including Antony Tudor's *Jardin aux lilas*. Nevertheless a host of smaller Russian companies emerged—no less than four toured Britain in the autumn—with eminent dancers redeeming mediocre productions. Yelena Pankova, for example, brought a semblance of style and coherence to Moscow City Ballet's otherwise nonsensical *Sleeping Beauty*, just as she illuminated London City Ballet's *Swan Lake* (after Bourmeister) and its new *Romeo and Juliet* (Stevenson).

Rudolf Nureyev continued to hit the headlines as audiences demanded their money back after his 'farewell tour' in the USA, Britain and

Australia. He in fact appeared in altogether apt works like *Song of a Wayfarer* and *The Moor's Pavane*, but audiences still expected him to dance his youthful roles; the supporting company provided little alternative comfort.

Among those who died during 1991 were Olga Spessivtseva (see XX:OBITUARY) and Tatiana Vecheslova (ballerinas); Ruth Page, John Field, Roman Jasinski (see XX:OBITUARY) and David Poole—all dancers who became artistic directors of significance; Robert Irving, doyen of conductors for dance; Desmond Doyle and Robert Kovich (dancers); and Lyn Stanford (pianist), Edward Stierle (dancer and choreographer with Joffrey), Burton Taylor (ex-ABT dancer), Paul Russell (ex-Harlem and Scottish dancer), Michael Batchelor (ex-Royal dancer) and Adrian Ward Jackson (patron)—all of AIDS.

BOOKS OF THE YEAR. *André Levinson on Dance: Writings from Paris in the Twenties*, Joan Acocella and Lynn Garafola (eds); *I remember Balanchine*, Francis Mason (ed); *Blood Memory: An Autobiography*, by Martha Graham; *Martha: The Life and Work of Martha Graham*, by Agnes de Mille.

iv. THEATRE

THOUGH the recession clearly had an effect upon theatre attendances, no play or musical during the year failed which did not thoroughly deserve to fail, and even several plays of poor quality managed to attract audiences. There continued to be as many productions of Shakespeare as usual, but no one play dominated as, in the previous three years, *The Tempest*, *Hamlet* and *King Lear* had done; the two most impressive stagings were presented not by either the National (NT) or the Royal Shakespeare theatres, but by ex-directors of those institutions now working elsewhere. The great and currently unfashionable virtue of Peter Hall's production of *Twelfth Night* (at the Playhouse) was that it treated the play with respect. Its Illyria was Shakespeare's, neither an exotic Balkan country nor—despite the text's occasional references to a pub at the Elephant 'in the south suburbs'—the playwright's own familiar south London, but a country of the mind.

Such an approach had its dangers, the chief one being that, as in any Shakespeare comedy, those scenes which formally set out to be funny were likely, if left to their own devices, to be tediously unfunny, since Elizabethan notions of humour could hardly fail to appear either ponderous or crude to a modern sensibility. But there is more to comedy than verbal jokes, and *Twelfth Night*'s deepest humour, found in its twists of plot which comment obliquely on human frailty, were brought deftly to the fore by Hall. By contrast, the Royal Shakespeare Company's (RSC) *Twelfth Night* at Stratford was an assault upon the play by a cast whose attempts to minimize the gap between modern dress and anachronistic speech led most of them in the direction of poor articulation and a sloppy disregard of the verse patterns. Apart from giving his actors an occasional piece of superfluous comic business, an inexperienced director (the comedian Griff Rhys Jones) contributed little.

The year's other exceptionally interesting Shakespeare production was Trevor Nunn's *Timon of Athens* at the Young Vic. Once one had recovered from an initial dismay that this was to be a fashionable modern gloss upon the play rather than a serious interpretation of it, there was much to admire. Nunn was adept at moving actors about on a stage—very many well-known directors were not—and his company was first-rate. Timon, that creature of extremes, presents a number of challenges to a performer, all of which were met with ease by David Suchet, who not only signalled confidence and charm in the first half of the play and misanthropic rage in the second, but also contrived miraculously to make these contrasting characteristics seem consistent.

By far the most damage to Shakespeare was done by the English Shakespeare Company, whose offerings included *The Winter's Tale* and *The Merchant of Venice*. The former play, one of Shakespeare's most problematical, was set by its director, Michael Bogdanov, firmly in the twentieth century which, in this instance, made no point at all, and merely caused its audience to wonder why suave contemporary courtiers should be speaking in formal seventeenth-century verse and rushing off to consult the oracle at Delphi. The bear which pursues and eventually eats Antigonus was in this staging not a bear at all, but Leontes.

Tim Luscombe, directing *The Merchant of Venice* for this company, chose to re-set the play in 1938 in a Venice where Mussolini's blackshirted fascists (Antonio's friends Salarino and Solanio among them) were on the rampage, and where the possibility of the play's climactic scene, in which a Jew brings a court action to allow him to cut a pound of flesh from a Christian debtor, was somewhat remote. It was, in any case, an act of the utmost insensitivity to use the ghastly situation of European Jews in the Thirties as a background to Shakespeare's robust yet poetic comedy in which an Elizabethan stage villain is given his come-uppance by a strong-minded Gentile heroine. Luscombe's offence was compounded by his addition of a scene, in dumb show, in which a Jew in yarmulka and prayer-shawl was set upon and viciously beaten up by fascists. This made it difficult to raise even a smile at the antics of Gratiano and his colleagues, or of Portia and Nerissa when dealing with Portia's unwanted suitors. And it made it completely impossible to respond to the comedy in the role of Shylock.

The same company and director also massacred Ben Jonson's masterpiece, *Volpone*, lumbering the play with such props as vacuum cleaners, party poppers, sex-shop lingerie and supermarket trolleys, as well as jokes based on TV commercials, all of which led one critic to wonder whether the director bore some deep personal grudge against the Elizabethan playwrights whose works he had perhaps been forced to learn by heart at school as a punishment.

Classical plays in general tended not to fare well. Gerard Murphy's sexually-hyperactive production of Marlowe's *Edward II* for the RSC was at least not dull, though it was impossible to believe in Simon Russell Beale's petulantly-mincing monarch as the object of either Isabella's or Gaveston's desire. *The Seagull* was given by the Oxford Stage Company in a new version by Mike Alfreds which differed from earlier translations only in almost invariably choosing the most inappropriate word. Chekhov called his play a comedy but it was directed by the perpetrator of this new version as extremely crude farce, and Arkadina, who is meant to be a classical actress, was played in a style considerably closer to Marie Lloyd than to Ellen Terry. However, Dryden's Antony and Cleopatra play, *All for Love*, was given an exemplary production by the enterprising Almeida Theatre. Dryden was certainly no Shakespeare, but his handling of dramatic blank verse in *All for Love* was masterly, and his characterization, not only of the two lovers but also of Antony's friend Dollabella and Cleopatra's eunuch Alexas, provided great opportunities which most of the Almeida cast were quick to seize. Diana Rigg was an admirable Cleopatra, whether skittishly threatening to commit 'some wild extravagance of love in public' or fiercely confronting Antony's wife Octavia.

Other notable revivals included a great rarity, *El Burlador de Sevilla*, by the seventeenth-century Spanish playwright Tirso de Molina, adapted for the RSC by Nick Dear as *The Last Days of Don Juan*, its chief interest for modern audiences lying in the fact that it was the play which introduced the character of the licentious Don Juan; and the more familiar Eugene O'Neill epic, *Long Day's Journey into Night*, produced by the Bristol Old Vic in collaboration with the National Theatre, in which Timothy West gave a superb performance as James Tyrone. There were also two fine revivals of plays by Harold Pinter. *The Homecoming*, first staged in 1965, was vintage Pinter. Indeed, in its teasing ambiguity, its atmosphere of not-too-distant violence, and an enigmatic quality which linked its disparate characters, it could be regarded as this playwright's archetypal play. Twenty-five years after he first staged it, Peter Hall returned to *The Homecoming*, his direction now cleverly emphasizing the play's theatricality. The Almeida Theatre revived Pinter's more recent *Betrayal*, one of his most exquisitely shaped yet most emotionally charged works.

Though no major new play emerged during the year, several were of more than passing interest. Perhaps the most accomplished was

Christopher Hampton's *White Chameleon* (NT), an affectionate quasi-autobiographical account of what life in Alexandria shortly after World War II was like for an amiable engineer, his neurotic wife, his intelligent son (the playwright) and their Muslim servant. Though too slight to serve as an essay on the end of empire, it proved a pleasant enough piece of nostalgia for the joys and pains of childhood, and its portrait of friendly relations between Christians and Muslims was apposite today. David Hare's *Murmuring Judges* (NT) was generally thought to be disappointing, and Arthur Miller's *The Ride Down Mount Morgan* (Wyndham's) seemed to suggest that this fine playwright's remarkable talent might be going into decline.

Three adaptations, though two of them were finally unsatisfactory as plays, all had something to commend them. Steven Berkoff's translation to the stage of Kafka's *The Trial* (NT) was the least successful, for Berkoff had chosen to impose upon the painstakingly-detailed realism of Kafka's novel his own familiar style involving Actors' Studio-type class exercises, slow-motion walks and funny voices. Antony Sher's Joseph K was properly nondescript and colourless (though closer to a Chaplinesque 'little man' than to the character created by the novelist), but in the surroundings of Berkoff's mad expressionist circus his performance counted for little. Keith Dewhurst's *Black Snow* (NT), adapted from a novel by the Russian author and playwright, Mikhail Bulgakov, took a sharply satirical look at the revered figure of Stanislavsky. But Bulgakov's novel was slow-moving and heavy-handed, and by following it too closely Dewhurst produced a play which came alive only in its second half, and thanks mainly to Robin Bailey's hilarious performance as Stanislavsky. *The Cure at Troy* (Tricycle), Seamus Heaney's modern version of Sophocles' *Philoctetes*, was by far the best of these adaptations. It contrived not only to capture the essence of the Sophoclean argument but also, in transferring the action to present-day Belfast, to make a most pungent comment on the current situation in Northern Ireland. In this, Heaney's first work for the stage, the Irish poet's spare, taut verse, as light as air and as transparent, was used to superb effect.

It was a disappointing year in London's fringe theatres, only two new plays revealing any real individuality. Paul Wheeler's *Deceptions* (Kings Head Theatre Club) was a neat little puzzle play, a kind of thriller without thrills in which one was kept wondering who was lying to whom, and why, while its two characters remained locked into a seemingly endless rendition of a duet, 'Any role you can play, I can play better'. *The Pitchfork Disney* by Philip Ridley (Bush) was a weird affair, concocted from early Pinter with a slight touch of Beckett. Images of horror and disgust abounded in this tale of a Cockney brother and sister living in squalor in an atmosphere of unexplained menace.

The new musicals were a sorry lot. *Children of Eden* (Prince Edward), based on episodes from the book of Genesis, was mildly and fitfully entertaining, though Stephen Schwartz's score was singularly lacking in tunefulness. *Matador* suffered from a cliché-ridden plot, lyrics by Edward Seago which rarely managed to rise to the level of doggerel, and songs by Michael Leander which sounded as though they were being hastily improvised by musical illiterates. There was a great deal of haughty flamenco-like posturing and foot-stamping. But by all accounts *The Hunting of the Snark* (Prince Edward) was the worst of the three. All of them were, not surprisingly, commercial failures. On the other hand, revivals of *Carmen Jones*, *The King and I*, and *The Rocky Horror Show* were successful at the box office, and deservedly so.

It was not even a good year for the critics. A prestigious daily newspaper's chief theatre critic was dismissed by his editor, who was shocked by the critic's disrespectful review of *The Wind in the Willows*. In the same newspaper a TV comedy-writer excoriated the entire breed of critics who, he claimed, were joyless parasites feeding on people more talented than themselves, while in a weekly magazine a journalist took the opposite view, accusing theatre reviewers of being too eager to praise the mediocre offerings placed before them.

The death of Dame Peggy Ashcroft (see XX:OBITUARY) robbed the theatre of one of the last of a generation of performers which included Laurence Olivier, Ralph Richardson, Edith Evans and Michael Redgrave. Sir John Gielgud was now the sole survivor of that remarkable collection of great actors.

NEW YORK THEATRE. Three of the most admired contemporary American playwrights produced new plays during the year, all in off-Broadway theatres, Broadway having virtually been taken over by long-run musicals, most of them imported from Britain. A. R. Gurney's *The Old Boy*, set in a prestigious prep school in New England, examined friendship, betrayal and remorse, but in a manner oddly lacking the stylishness and wit of Gurney's earlier plays. Sam Shephard's *States of Shock*, set in a coffee shop whose customers included a colonel, a Vietnam war veteran and a middle-aged couple, suffered from dialogue which could have come from almost any other Sam Shephard play. People and incidents were seldom what they seemed to be, and John Malkovich invested the character of the colonel with his familiar boorish stage personality. *Lips Together, Teeth Apart* by Terence McNally was about the fears and anxieties of modern life, and about death, yet it was also a comedy and a very funny one. McNally was on the way to becoming a minor American Chekhov.

In *Folks Remembers a Missing Page*, J. E. Gaines gave to a solo performer (the playwright himself) a monologue about Harlem, mostly in pre-World War II days, as recollected by an old black derelict. His play was both funny and moving. In *I Hate Hamlet* by Paul Rudnick, the British actor Nicol Williamson gave a virtuoso performance as the ghost of John Barrymore, summoned to come to the aid of a Hollywood actor who was about to play Hamlet in Central Park and, in *Mr Gogol and Mr Preen*, Elaine May wrote an engaging comedy about the world of ideas, explored through a relationship between an aging writer and a vacuum-cleaner salesman.

Important revivals included Harold Pinter's *The Homecoming* with Roy Dotrice as the head of the family, Paul Osborn's charming fantasy *On Borrowed Time* with George C. Scott as the Grandfather, and Arthur Miller's *The Crucible*, directed for the newly founded National Actors Theatre by Tony Randall, with an excellent cast headed by Martin Sheen, Fritz Weaver, Carol Woods and Michael York. The splendid institution of Shakespeare in Central Park, which owed its being to Joe Papp, whose death (see XX:OBITUARY) during the year was a great blow to serious New York Theatre, continued with an *Othello* in which Raul Julia was a dignified Othello, Christopher Walken a superb Iago and Mary Beth Hurt a memorable Emilia. Indoors, at the Public Theatre, a respectful and therefore respectable production of *Pericles* was rightly acclaimed.

Musicals continued to dominate Broadway. The much-heralded *Nick and Nora*, based on *The Thin Man*, the Dashiell Hammett novel which inspired a series of movies in the thirties, opened and closed with ignominious celerity, but the popularity of several Andrew Lloyd Webber musicals and, even worse, the soulless and cynical *Miss Saigon*, showed no signs of abating.

v. CINEMA

IT used to be said that one of the few industries to profit from recession was the film business, since the cinema was the cheapest form of mass entertainment. But 1991 hardly proved that true, largely because television was now the cheapest form of popular entertainment and films had become so costly to make, and so much of a risk enterprise, that even good times seemed precarious.

Hollywood, still the most powerful film industry in the world, if not the biggest (Bollywood in India was now that), did not have a good year, and even Bollywood felt the strain. The rest of the world found 1991 perilous indeed, and none more so than the film-makers of Europe, who found both money and audiences hard to come by.

Hollywood's troubles, chiefly caused by the fact that not enough hits were made, were compounded further by the fact that the average American film, decorated by stars, now cost between $20 and 25 million to produce. With another large sum required for prints and publicity, there was now little profit to be seen until some $70 million had been accrued at the box-office worldwide. Only one in 25 Hollywood films achieved that figure, even if it was often the case that the biggest successes made huge fortunes.

At the end of the year, it was reckoned that almost every Hollywood studio was in the red, despite the success of blockbusters such as James Cameron's special-effects-studded *Terminator II*, Jonathan Demme's horror thriller *The Silence Of The Lambs* and a few other mega-hits including *Robin Hood, Prince of Thieves* and the Oscar-winner for the year, *Dances with Wolves*. And the whole sorry business seemed to be summed up at the year's end by Steven Spielberg's *Hook*, a lavish remake of *Peter Pan* which cost in the region of $70 million to make and which would thus have to be one of the biggest successes of all time to break into profit.

American cinemas sold fewer than a billion tickets for the first time for fifteen years in 1991, only four films reaching the magic $100 million mark, and earnings were down by about six per cent from the previous year. Jeffrey Katzenberg, head of Disney Studios, who had pleaded for major cost-cutting at the beginning of the year, seemed like a prophet at the end of it. Even so, Hollywood continued to expand rather than to contract in the distribution and exhibition fields. If American audiences declined, Europe and Japan, two very large markets, were seen to become more susceptible to American films. This was why Jack Valenti, of the Motion Picture Association of America, refused to countenance any erection of trade barriers against Hollywood films abroad. America, he complained, had only two really successful exports—aeroplanes and films. If these were undermined by protectionist policies, then any US President would be entitled to take retaliatory steps. Consequently, Europe's efforts to prevent American domination foundered and several European countries, including Britain, found that well over 90 per cent of the films shown in their cinemas were now from Hollywood.

This was a serious matter for the European cinema, which now included Russia and the new Commonwealth of Independent States, Turkey and the former Soviet satellite countries. In order to survive, co-production was essential. That often meant making a Russian film with stars from another country or a film like *Meeting Venus*, produced by David Puttnam from Britain and directed by Istvan Szabo from Hungary, with an international cast led by an American (Glenn Close), technicians from several countries and financed from a number of different sources. In the case of this film, there was a genuine attempt not only to make a film which would appeal to a worldwide audience but to do so with a story that had genuine relevance to the whole of Europe—the cultural troubles of the continent being summed up by the trials and tribulations of mounting a production of *Tannhäuser* for the 'Opera Europa' in Paris.

But too often such international co-productions had little relevance to anybody and were unkindly dubbed 'Euro-puddings'. To save the European cinema, the real necessity was still to produce properly national films with international appeal, like France's *Cyrano de Bergerac* and *Delicatessen*, Belgium's *Toto the Hero* and Britain's *Riff-Raff*, which though it was shown only reluctantly in cinemas in its country of origin, won the European Film of the Year Award in November as well as the prestigious International Critics' Prize at the Cannes Festival.

Otherwise, European successes were few and far between, even in their own countries. The once thriving, and state-aided, cinemas of the Soviet Union, Poland, Hungary and Czechoslovakia produced little, because finance was so scarce, and little of note, because of a crisis of confidence as their former audiences streamed into Hollywood films. Only Kryzystof Kieslowski, the Polish director of *The Double Life of Veronica*, had an international success, and that with a film financed largely by France and partly set there. Scandinavia and Germany had very poor years. There was a small revival from a very low point of activity in Italy. Spain seemed to rely largely on the talent of Pedro Almodovar, the eccentric and controversial but highly fashionable director whose new film, *High Heels*, broke records at the Spanish box-office. The French government, though giving much succour to its films, regarded as part and parcel of French culture, was disturbed to find that over 60 per cent of its cinemas were now showing American films. Britain had its worst production year ever as far as the number of films made was concerned, but still managed to produce, often with the aid of television finance, several small-scale artistic successes. Among these were Ken Loach's *Riff-Raff*, Mike Leigh's *Life Is Sweet*, Stephen Poliakoff's *Close My Eyes*, Anthony Minghella's *Truly, Madly, Deeply*, Peter Greenaway's *Prospero's Books* and, leading the way as a box-office success, Alan Parker's *The Commitments*, made in Ireland with American money because no-one would finance it in Britain.

Outside Europe, the huge Indian film industry, mostly centred in Bombay and Madras, continued to fight off the depredations of video and the gradually-expanding government-run television service with a few massive hits and some 900 new films all told, many of which found good export markets in the former Soviet Union, the Middle East and as video releases even further afield. In Australia, where recession bit as hard as anywhere, there were still some notable success stories, like the emergence of Jocelyn Moorhouse, whose first feature *Proof*, made with a very small budget, was much admired all over the world. And Canada, with French-speaking and English-speaking wings, produced some capable efforts, though none able to fight off the US domination of its cinemas.

In China, censorship precluded much meaningful production and it was left to the talented Zhang Yimou to maintain standards with *Raise the Red Lantern*, another of his co-productions, this time with Taiwan, to win golden opinions at festivals but a ban for political impropriety in his own country. The previous year his Sino-Japanese *Ju Dou* had suffered the same fate. Neither Africa nor Latin America had particularly good years—Africa because finance was still so precarious and Latin America because the new generation of film-makers could make a better living on television than in the cinema. There was, however, one outstanding film from Argentina, Maria-Louise Bemberg's *I, the Worst of All*.

What chiefly emerged from 1991 was the general realization that the increasing dominance of Hollywood, even in a poor year for American films, meant that film festivals the world over—and there was a festival somewhere now every week of the year—were responsible for the cultural appreciation and commercial spread of the films of virtually every other nation. The festivals were increasingly regarded as the last line of defence against Hollywood, which though short of finance itself, still had the publicity, distribution and exhibition outlets to outgun anyone else. Consequently, though very few were pessimistic enough to suggest that the cinema was dying—audiences almost everywhere were still too large for that and films could now have a second and third life on video and television—there was beginning to be a realization that a coherent policy was needed to nurture the film cultures of small countries against those of the larger and richer nations. This was not just a matter of financing films in such a way as to protect their national identity, but of aiding cinemas themselves to show a wider choice of fare, with tax breaks and/or quota systems. It was still not widely realized that film, like any other art form that is also an entertainment, needed governmental subsidy to nurture its more imaginative and ground-breaking practitioners.

Among those who died during the year were: David Lean, British film-maker of international successes like *Lawrence of Arabia* and *Dr Zhivago*; Dame Peggy Ashcroft, British star of stage and screen for over fifty years; Joan Bennett, Jean Arthur, Joan Caulfield, Hollywood stars of the Thirties and Forties; Wilfrid Hyde-White, British character actor; Sir Bernard Miles, stage and screen actor and creator of the Mermaid Theatre in London; Don Seigel, American film-maker of the original *Dirty Harry*; American film director Frank Capra; and Yves Montand, French singer and international screen star. (For Lean, Ashcroft, Miles, Capra and Montand, see XX:OBITUARY.)

vi. TELEVISION AND RADIO

BROADCASTING was dominated by the sights and sounds of great events—from the Gulf War to the collapse of the Soviet Union—and by the more gentle charm of nostalgia. The television images that would live longest in the memory were of the almost nightly battles between Scud and Patriot missiles over the skies of Jerusalem and film of 'smart' bombs hitting Baghdad buildings or bridges and the process appearing to turn warfare into a video game. But rather more popular in the UK were the images of rural Kent, conjured up from the novels of H. E. Bates, as *The Darling Buds of May* by Yorkshire Television. The production broke all ratings records for drama, attracting a peak audience of 18.35 million. The series, starring David Jason, finished its first run in May and went on to break a further record when it was released on video in June, selling more than 100,000 copies at £19.99 each.

While popular drama on ITV, everything from *Poirot* to *London's Burning* as well as *The Darling Buds of May*, went from strength to strength, entertainment was overshadowed in a dramatic year by news events and how television and radio covered them. Not only was the Gulf War fought out on television to an unprecedented degree but broadcasters were there when hostages such as John McCarthy and Terry Waite were released and when President Boris Yeltsin of Russia stood out against the Kremlin plotters and saved, for a time, the administration of President Mikhail Gorbachev.

Television, and particularly Ted Turner's Cable News Network (CNN), played a considerable role in the failure of the coup against Mr Gorbachev. According to *Time* magazine, the pictures showing that Mr Yeltsin was alive, well and resisting, rallied the Russians who received CNN and, through word of mouth, a wider population. It also persuaded President George Bush to move from tepid disapproval of the coup to throwing his weight behind the resistance.

The involvement of television in the process of fundamental change in the then USSR could be seen again in an American Broadcasting Company (ABC) programme that went round the world in September. Presidents Gorbachev and Yeltsin sat side-by-side in what was billed as a 'national town meeting', answering questions from American viewers. The broadcast revealed differences on issues such as whose finger should be on the nuclear trigger but surprising agreement on Soviet communism. The Soviet President told the cameras: 'That model has failed which was brought about in our country. And I believe that this is a lesson not only for our people but for all people.'

There was much greater controversy over broadcasters' coverage of the Gulf War. Television and radio reporters were allowed to stay for much of the war in the Iraqi capital and cover, under government restrictions, the allied bombardment of Baghdad. Unlike the others, however, CNN's correspondent, Peter Arnett, was allowed to stay throughout, attracting criticism that the organization was being manipulated by the Iraqi regime. Broadcasters were simultaneously accused of doing the work of the enemy and of sanitizing the violence and the real effects of war. Yet both CNN and the BBC, which ran a rolling news programme on Radio 4 throughout the war and its immediate aftermath, were part of the new phenomenon.

Events were being seen and heard live as they happened rather than being reported hours afterwards or even the next morning. And the audience was worldwide. Viewers of the entire live press conferences of General Norman Schwarzkopf were getting exactly the same information in their living rooms as journalists on the spot thousands of miles away. The power of the single image transfixing a world audience was considered so great that *Time* chose Ted Turner, the man responsible for many of them, as its Man of the Year 'for influencing the dynamic of events and turning viewers into instant witnesses of history'.

During the year the BBC finally set up what it hoped could turn into a British rival to CNN, 24-hours-a-day BBC World Television News. The service began as one of five satellite channels on the Hong Kong STAR TV system available in 38 Asian countries. The BBC was also working on plans to bring the television news service to Africa.

Overall, however, the prophecy made decades ago by Marshall McLuhan, that through television the world was about to become a global village, was still, on most days, a dream. A survey by *Inter Media*, the journal of the International Institute of Communications, on what news the world was watching on its television screens on 19 November—the day Terry Waite returned to the UK—found that most television news was parochial. Asia and Latin America were virtually ignored by the rest of the world and their news in turn was also fiercely local. On 19 November even CNN coverage was almost wholly American.

In the UK the steady growth of cable and satellite television and a very aggressive performance by ITV took BBC Television's share of the audience down towards 40 per cent, and occasionally below, the corporation's worst performance for many years.

In October ITV itself became the story when the winners and losers were announced in the competitive tenders for new 10-year franchises, to run from the beginning of 1993. After years of uncertainty and speculation, the Independent Television Commission (ITC) announced that four of the 16 ITV companies had lost their franchises, including the largest, Thames Television, which had been outbid for the London weekday licence by Carlton Communications, the fast-growing television services company. The other big loser was TV-am, the popular and highly-profitable commercial breakfast station, which bid £14.13 million and was defeated by Sunrise, a consortium including the Walt Disney company and London Weekend Television. The full irony was revealed on 17 October, the day after the announcements, when Bruce Gyngell, the chairman of TV-am, read out a letter from Mrs Margaret Thatcher saying she was 'heartbroken' that the company had lost. The former prime minister added that she was only too painfully aware that she had been responsible for the legislation under which new franchises were granted.

More controversially, the other two losers, TVS Entertainment, holders of the south of England franchise, and neighbouring Television South-West, had submitted the highest bids for their regions and were in effect penalized for bidding too high. The ITC decided it was not satisfied the two could maintain a high-quality programme service throughout the franchise period, with the result that the TVS franchise went to Meridian Broadcasting and the TSW licence to Westcountry Television. Both losers decided to try to fight the decision in the courts, but only TSW was given leave for a judicial review.

There was a wide disparity in the size of bids. Two of the ITV companies, Central in the Midlands and Scottish north of the border, calculated correctly that they would be unopposed and bid just £2,000 each. Two other large ITV companies, Granada and LWT, took enormous risks. Even though both were opposed, LWT bid only £7.58 million and Granada £9 million. They judged, correctly, that their rivals, who each bid around £35 million, would not get over the initial quality threshhold. George Russell, chairman of the ITC, said that, overall, quality had won as a result of the tendering process and claimed that the extra money going to the Treasury out of the ITV system would average only £40 million a year.

The BBC was next in the firing line. The Corporation set up no less than 15 study groups to examine every aspect of its future role in advance of the renegotiation of its Royal Charter in 1996. November saw the first sign of things to come, when the BBC announced a new system of producer choice. The Corporation was creating an internal market for its services so that producers could buy everything needed to make a programme, even studios, on the open market, if that were most cost-effective. Many BBC staff jobs were expected to disappear as a result. John Birt, the deputy director-general, was closely identified with the new policy. After Marmaduke Hussey, chairman of the BBC board of governors, was given an unprecedented second five-year term, the director-general, Michael Checkland, was given only a one-year extension, until March 1993, and Mr Birt was named as his successor.

Despite the general slump in the ratings, several BBC programmes hit their targets. One of those was a September edition of *Panorama* that accused Robert Maxwell of deliberately distorting the share price of Maxwell Communication Corporation and of running dishonest competitions in his papers. Few were as courageous in facing the writs of Robert Maxwell when he was still alive (see XX: OBITUARY).

Channel 4 had a good year with hit comedy programmes such as *Drop the Dead Donkey*, which was set in a television news room and was so fresh that it included jokes on that day's events. But many Channel 4 staff and producers were not amused when it was reported that chief executive Michael Grade had been promised £500,000 to stop him leaving the channel to lead an ITV bid. Although the amount was not confirmed, Mr Grade acknowledged that he had asked to be compensated for taking himself 'off the market'.

The spread of commercial radio continued. By the end of the year more than 120 stations were broadcasting and the first national commercial franchise had been awarded to Classic FM, a popular classical music station. Classic won the 'non-pop' licence by default after the highest bidder, Showtime, which had planned an 'easy-listening' format, failed to raise its finance. The licence for the second of three national commercial stations was advertised before the end of the year and the winner was due to be announced in February 1992.

At BBC Radio praise was heaped on the World Service, not just as a result of its war coverage but also by every returning Western hostage and by President Gorbachev, who listened in during his confinement by the coup plotters in August. Over at Radio 4 the controllers finally plucked up courage to move *Woman's Hour* from the afternoon to the morning, but attempts to change the programme's name were quietly dropped.

Prospects for the merged British Sky Broadcasting improved greatly and by end-1991 the six-channel satellite venture was available in more than 2.7 million homes. BSkyB's top-rated programme by far was the cartoon series *The Simpsons*, which regularly attracted audiences of one million. During the year operating losses were cut from around £11 million a week to less than £2 million and break-even at the operating level was forecast for 1992.

Cable television continued to grow in the UK, largely because of the investment of large American telephone companies, and the number of subscribers, each with access to around 30 channels, passed 225,000. Cable in the US had much larger ambitions. In December Time Warner, the world's largest media company, began building the first 150-channel cable system in New York's Bronx. At the same time, Paramount and Capital Cities/ABC set up a joint venture to bring pay-by-view events to the consumer. Pay-by-view was already available in 20 million American homes and allowed customers to dial a telephone number which unscrambled the transmission of special movies or concerts.

In France the owners of La Cinq, the fifth channel, proved that it really was possible to lose money running conventional television stations. On 31 December La Cinq, whose owners included the Italian media mogul Silvio Berlusconi and Hachette, the French publishing group, announced its intention to file for bankruptcy. Its troubles led to a suggestion from three of France's other television channels that it should be replaced by a French-language news service on international affairs, to be broadcast in France and other French-speaking countries. The news about La Cinq came just as the ITC was putting out its latest thoughts on awarding the licence for Britain's prospective fifth television channel. This was due to go on air before the end of 1994, if the money could be raised.

2. ART—ARCHITECTURE—FASHION

i. ART

THE pattern of the 1990s was already radically different from the 1980s, as the apparently arbitrary categorization of history into neatly-packaged decades for once rang dramatically true. In 1991 the alliance of art, economics and social history became as sharp and stark as any of the academic and critical adherents of the 'new' art history could have wished. The art historian who examined 'material culture' almost exclusively in its socio-economic cultural context, as opposed to art for art's sake, seemed indicated, as aesthetic judgment was submerged by economic catastrophe in the art market.

Because of the commercial euphoria of the 1980s, the new decade was seeing a series of remarkable projects come into being. For example, what used to be West Germany acquired no fewer than three new museums, one of them, at least, quite a different model. In Bremen, the Weserburg, housed in former coffee warehouses on an island in the Weser river, was a 'museum' of modern and contemporary art with no permanent collections; rather, the director, Thomas Deecke, showed collections put together by private connoisseurs and lent to the museum. Frankfurt, now a city of museums, opened a new building also dedicated to the modern and contemporary, designed by the controversial Austrian architect Hans Hollein; this was a city collection, in public ownership. In Aachen, another converted industrial building showed items on a rotating basis from the huge Ludwig collection (some of which was also in the Ludwig Museum in Cologne), rather on the model of the Saatchi collection in London, but on a much bigger scale. Where Charles Saatchi had converted an old industrial paint factory, the Ludwigs had taken over an old umbrella factory for the Ludwig Forum, complete with sculpture garden.

Meanwhile, Berlin was responding to its restoration as Germany's official capital by converting the Hamburger Bahnhof, a disused railway station, into a major showplace for the contemporary. The French were again in the throes of cultural expansion, this time in the provinces: millions (in any currency) were being spent, not least on a nearly-completed new museum for Grenoble, scheduled to open in 1992. On the other side of the world, the first purpose-built major museum for Hong Kong opened in November, concentrating on the history of the colony and Chinese art, but with a gigantic space for travelling shows, inaugurated with (perhaps improbably) a big exhibition of post-war art from France, organized by the Cartier Foundation. T. T. Tsui, a transport millionaire, not only financed the new Chinese gallery, named after him, at the Victoria & Albert Museum in London, but also opened his own very elegant private museum, devoted to Chinese art through the ages, on a floor of a big building in a light industrial area of Kowloon, Hong Kong.

The art market plunged, and there were major 'rationalizations'— meaning redundancies—at the premier auction houses. However, there was also a kind of renaissance of the Renaissance. The Sainsbury Wing, housing the early Renaissance holdings of London's National Gallery, was opened by the Queen in June; and the most expensive painting sold at auction was Titian's *Venus and Adonis* (Christie's, £7.48 million). At the Imelda Marcos sale at Christie's New York in January (held at the order of the US and Philippines governments), a miniature St Catherine by Raphael (?) fetched $1.65 million. Geraldine Norman of *The Independent* reported, however, on the overall commercial scene rather starkly: 'World economic recession, the Gulf War and a series of art scandals in Japan knocked the stuffing out of the art market in 1991.'

The Japanese scandals often involved the fudging of inheritance tax. A major chain of art galleries, owned by Masahiko Sawada, with big stocks of Impressionist and twentieth-century pictures, was submerged in the collapse of his business empire. And at least one major business collection, that of Itoman, an Osaka property company, valued at £200 million, was found to have been improperly used to get round business regulations. Mrs Norman, one of the world's most astute saleroom correspondents, reckoned that in the 1990 season the Japanese had accounted for more than half of the worldwide purchases in Impressionist and twentieth-century fields; in 1991, however, the Japanese virtually disappeared as a market force, not because of economic weakness but because of corporate and business art scandals.

By contrast, the art market was surprisingly solid in more traditional fields, some of which, such as antique silver, made strong comebacks, while furniture, Old Master drawings and paintings, Oriental art and jewellery were steady. Tim Llewellyn, managing director of Sotheby's UK, put it thus (in September): 'If you take out of the equation post-1870 art, the rest of our business is actually up on last year.'

In a year of distressing conflicts, the Gulf War seriously damaged the art and archaeological heritage of Iraq and Kuwait. The conflict in Yugoslavia was devastatingly destructive of architectural and artistic heritage, notably in Dubrovnik, the 'pearl of the Adriatic'. The material culture of Croatia was attacked in a way that suggested to some observers a deliberate attempt by the Serbs at obliteration of the Croatian heritage. Hundreds of churches, not to mention other historic buildings and museums, were reported looted or destroyed. Elsewhere in Eastern Europe, the growing-pains of democracy, and new bureaucracies, left the arts in chaos. The disappearance of art from churches was widely reported.

Even without the chaos of war, and the disturbance of new political alignments, art was at risk. The British publication *Trace*, specializing in the incidence of stolen art worldwide, estimated that in 1991 art worth £3,500 million had disappeared; as regards the financial value of crime, evidently only the drugs trade and computer fraud outranked art theft, with some £50,000–£75,000 million of art unrecovered (1991 estimates). The International Art and Antiques Loss Register (the Art Loss Register) was set up in London in January.

The demise of the blockbuster exhibition—because of the cost of transport and insurance, and the reluctance of lenders to put fragile work at risk—was still confidently predicted. Meanwhile, 1991 saw a quantity of amazing exhibitions worldwide, including a celebration of the year 1492 at the National Gallery, Washington, which did indeed involve the loan of such items as a Leonardo from Poland. Rembrandt travelled to Berlin and Amsterdam, and the biggest-ever exhibition devoted to Toulouse Lautrec was seen at the Hayward, London. But perhaps the sign of the times was the show of Seurat (Grand Palais, Paris; the Metropolitan, New York) in which several major masterpieces were represented by enormous black and white photographs. For example, Seurat's *Bathers* (National Gallery, London) travelled to neither of the venues, nor did Chicago's *Grand Jatte*. Similarly, the Louvre could not move or lend Gericault's mastrpiece, *The Raft of the Medusa*, to the magnificent and unprecedented Gericault retrospective later in the autumn at the Grand Palais.

In Britain, the enormous Japan Festival was marked by numerous art exhibitions up and down the country, of which one of the best was an exhibition of medieval and early Renaissance carved and painted wooden sculptures, at the British Museum. In spite of the turbulence of the Gulf War, other notable shows included the Art of Jordan (Liverpool Museum), the most comprehensive survey ever held, accompanied by the first comprehensive publication in English. Multi-cultural, multi-ethnic art exhibitions gained more attention than usual; Emil Torday and the Art of the Congo at the British Museum's Museum of Mankind won a National Art Collections Fund award, and Mexico's Day of the Dead, at the same museum, received unanimous critical plaudits.

The most comprehensive post-war exhibition of the royal collection, the Queen's Pictures, inaugurated the temporary exhibition galleries at the Sainsbury wing, the National Gallery. It was a good year for women: Gillian Ayres, the British representative, won the leading prize at the Indian Triennale in Delhi; other highlights included Paula

Rego's magnificent mural, *Crivelli's Garden*, at the new restaurant in the Sainsbury Wing, and her marvellous travelling show, Tales from the National Gallery; and Ana Maria Pachecho's unnervingly splendid travelling show of figurative sculpture. One young woman painter, Fiona Rae, and one young woman sculptor, Rachel Whiteread, were shortlisted for the Tate's Turner Prize, won in the event by Anish Kapoor, prizewinner at the 1990 Venice Biennale.

There was controversy in the United States over the conditions attached to the potential Annenberg bequest of Impressionist and post-Impressionist paintings to the Metropolitan Museum, New York. Restrictions included the necessity to show all 53 paintings together at all times, none of which could ever be lent; many thought the Metropolitan had compromised its integrity in apparently acceding to such stipulations. Also in America, the death was announced, in July, of Robert Motherwell, leader of the abstract expressionist school (see XX: OBITUARY).

In Britain, there was a major and successful campaign to save the medieval gold and sapphire Middleham Jewel for the Yorkshire Museum, (£2.5 million), while the amazing piece of furniture, the Badminton Cabinet, commissioned from the Florentine Medici workshops in 1726 by the 3rd Duke of Beaufort, was 'lost' to the Polish-American mega-millionaire collector, Mrs Johnson. Dr Robert Anderson, of the National Museums of Scotland (NMS) was appointed successor to Sir David Wilson as director of the British Museum; the NMS announced controversial plans for the new Museum of Scotland, designed by the architects Benson and Forsyth.

BOOKS OF THE YEAR. *Rembrandt: The Master and his Workshop* (2 volume exhibition catalogue); *The Queen's Pictures* (exhibition catalogue); *Toulouse-Lautrec* (exhibition catalogue); *The Italian Renaissance Interior* by Peter Thornton; *Topics of our Time* by E. H. Gombrich; *A World History of Art* (by Hugh Honour and John Fleming—revised edition); *Impressionist and Post Impressionist Drawing* by Nicholas Wadley; *Van Dyck: Paintings; Van Dyck: Drawings* (edited by Christopher Brown); *Corot in Italy* by Peter Galassi

ii. ARCHITECTURE

DURING 1991 British architects experienced the worst business conditions anyone could remember, resulting in a spate of company collapses, unpaid fees and redundancies. Students signed up for architecture courses in even greater numbers than the year previously; the profession wondered how it would manage to employ its existing personnel, let alone any increase. Against this gloomy background, intellectual battles continued to be fought between modernists, classicists, community architects and the Prince of Wales, most of which involved building rather than the lack of it. The most prominent public event was the completion and opening of the extension to the National Gallery in Trafalgar Square, by the American post-modernists Robert Venturi and Denise Scott Brown. Their design, funded by the Sainsbury family, replaced the competition-winner criticized as a 'monstrous carbuncle on the face of an old friend' by the Prince in 1984 (see AR 1984, p.448). The Venturi building was greeted, on the whole, with approval. The public could admire its use of traditional materials and (occasionally) spectacular interior views, while architects and critics could admire the erudite games-playing of the stone facade.

The second London development unveiled as a result of princely intervention was the proposal for a large commercial scheme next to St Paul's Cathedral at Paternoster Square, produced by a consortium of English, American and Japanese interests. The Prince became involved in the successful attempt to replace an allegedly modernist (in fact neo-classical) design by Arup Associates with one of a classical persuasion. The replacement designs, masterplanned by Terry Farrell, John Simpson and US architect Thomas Beeby, were greeted with great enthusiasm by the general public, alarm by much of the architectural profession and dismay by planning officers in the City of London, who asked for revisions to take account of more than 20 specific criticisms. Whether the Prince shared any of these criticisms was unclear; certainly he made no great speech praising the designs at the opening of an exhibition on the site, but said it was now up to the public to make up its mind on the merits of the classical buildings.

If the Prince recorded victories in London, he failed to put the Scots off their scheme for a National Museum of Scotland, a continuation of an existing building, in Edinburgh. On the morning of the press conference to announce the winners of the biggest competition ever held in Britain, it was announced that the Prince was resigning as a patron of the fund-raising committee—not because he disliked the designs by London-based Scottish architects Benson & Forsyth, but because he felt the competition system was too much dominated by professionals and not enough by lay jurors. Even the Prince's supporters were perplexed by this, and curious about the hamfisted attempt to scupper the proposal, which carried on regardless.

Royal Gold Medallist James Stirling gave an interview in the Scottish press in which he described the Prince as acting like Hitler in appealing to the lowest common denominator; the Royal Incorporation of Architects in Scotland gave Stirling some support, though this was later withdrawn.

Another scheme which progressed during the year was the most direct example of the Prince's interest in architecture: his model village proposal for Poundbury on the outskirts of Dorchester. The scheme, masterplanned by theorist Leon Krier, was redesigned in smaller phases during the year—because of economic reality, said critics; because of ease of planning, said the design team.

Arguments of a different sort pervaded two ongoing debates during 1991: the role of architecture in relation to major public buildings, and the way in which local authorities procured their buildings. The argument about the government as a patron of good architecture came to a head over proposals for the new Inland Revenue headquarters in Nottingham. Originally commissioned on a 'design-and-build' basis, with the contractor playing a lead role and the architects producing designs at speed, the project brought down the wrath of everyone from the local council to the Royal Fine Art Commission and English Heritage. Eventually, to the joy of the Royal Institute of British Architects (which had also been lobbying intensively behind the scenes), the government announced the scrapping of the existing proposals, and the holding of a national competition to produce a building worthy of the site.

In respect of local authority work, the RIBA was less successful. The government announced its intention of introducing 'compulsory competitive tendering' into architectural as well as other local authority services. The objection was raised that the practice offering the lowest price was not necessarily the one that would do it best. The only concession made by the government was its announcement that there would be a 'quality threshold' test for firms competing for work; only then would fee bids be considered. Tendering procedures were carried out in respect of station designs for London's new Jubilee line—involving nearly a dozen new stations by some of the country's brightest architects.

It was a good year for Britain's 'high-tech' architects. Richard Rogers was knighted, gained more work in Japan and worked on ideas for London with the Labour Party. Buildings by Sir Norman Foster which came to fruition included a new wing at the University of East Anglia, Stansted Airport, the new conversion/extension to the Royal Academy and a large office tower in Japan. His Ipswich office building was listed—the first from the 1970s to gain such recognition. But Foster too was hit by the recession and made a third of his staff redundant. The other member of Britain's big three, James Stirling (not himself high-tech), made little progress in the perennial story of attempts by Lord Palumbo to develop his site opposite Mansion House in the City of London. While his client finally won planning permission from the House of Lords, a further setback occurred when it transpired that a road running through part of the site was owned by the City Corporation under a seventeenth-century statute, and that its permission would be needed if the scheme were to proceed. The City had already expressed its opposition to the Stirling scheme, so that its fate looked uncertain at the end of the year.

A conservation drama of a different kind affected Sir Richard Rogers in his attempts to produce a speculative office scheme for Japanese client Daiwa. English Heritage stepped in to list a 1930s telephone exchange on the City site. After a row, the building was de-listed—notably after it emerged that a working example of a similar exchange had survived within a quarter of a mile. Another site which had been a battleground for conservationists, Spitalfields in east London, took a step towards redevelopment with the appointment of US firm Benjamin Thompson Associates as masterplanners, and of a group of British architects to design individual buildings.

The most significant building to open outside London was the International Convention Centre in Birmingham, designed by Renton Howard Wood Levin, complete with arguably the best concert hall in the country. The same practice won the commission to design a major concert hall in Manchester, but saw their BBC current affairs headquarters at White City called off because of funding difficulties.

With work drying up at home, British firms looked abroad for brighter prospects, and found them in Eastern Europe, particularly in newly-vibrant Berlin. Several firms set up offices there, though others with strong Russian links found the future more uncertain following the events of the summer. British practices performed well at the Venice Biennale in the autumn, this year devoted to architecture. A competition for a new bus station 'gateway to Venice' was won by Jeremy Dixon and Edward Jones; James Stirling designed a Biennale bookshop; and Nicholas Grimshaw stole the British show with a model of a proposed airport terminal. The UK did not respond much to European designers: Santiago Calatrava's spectacular proposed bridge design for the East London River Crossing was ignored in favour of a box girder bridge by a British firm.

The Royal Gold Medal for Architecture was won by Colin Stansfield Smith, Hampshire's county architect, who merited the award because of his demonstration that public architecture could be excellent and that it could make use of the best private architects too. The Pritzker Prize went to Robert Venturi in the 25th year since publication of his seminal work *Complexity and Contradiction in Architecture*. The year also saw the announcement of a new architectural award sponsored by Danish brewer Carlsberg. The most valuable in the world, it would give the winner £145,000.

iii. FASHION

IN a year when the fashion industry was hard hit by the Gulf War and the recession, it was a time for those reliable classics like the go-with-everything little twinset, the perfect pair of tailored trousers and the good old-fashioned belted trench coat to make a wonderfully chic comeback. Now, in difficult times, these oldtimers had emerged to become the new status collectables. Aristocratic names like Gucci and Ferragamo hit the 'must have' headlines with a return to a style of glamour to fit the 1990s.

Labels were everything in the fashion business, be it designers or famous houses. When Gucci was in its heyday in the fifties and sixties, stars and royalty flocked to its shops. But when a family financial vendetta brought Gucci to virtual bankruptcy, the glamour had lost its gloss and the customers moved on. Now, under the creative directorship of American Dawn Mello, Gucci was stylish, chic and hot once more. The famous 40-year-old mocassin loafer, with the bridle bit trim, previously available in black or brown only, suddenly appeared in sensational suede colours like yellow and magenta, retailing for £170. It was an overnight success, with copies immediately appearing in the high street, at a quarter of the price. The designer colour explosion was certainly playing the field.

The fashion world, with its incestuous itinerary of spring and autumn ready-to-wear fashion shows in London, Milan, New York and Paris, the couture fashion shows (also twice a year), as well as constant fashion show specials around the world, provoked a supermodel saga. The world's top models like Linda Evangelista (in 1990 a bright blonde, now a pimento redhead), 21-year-old Naomi Campbell (from South London, but now living in New York and working on an accent to match) and Helena Christiansen were accused of being greedy, demanding the kind of big money for catwalk shows that was ruining the industry. However, Vivienne Westwood, who was voted Designer of the Year for the second time in succession at the British Fashion Awards, thought they were worth every penny.

Overall it was not an easy year for the loyal followers of fashion. Lindka Cierach, the couturier who designed the Duchess of York's wedding gown in 1986, went out of business and had a high-profile and bitter trial in which her former employee was convicted of theft charges.

Not everyone let the recession get them down, however, least of all one of the most elegant and richest of the world's fashion designers, Valentino. Celebrating 30 years in the business, a week of lavish partying had Euro-socialites, star-struck aristocracy and movie stars descending on Rome in June. Guest-of-honour was Elizabeth Taylor, who later in the year wore a rather unbecoming Valentino three-shades-of-yellow flounced dress for her wedding to husband number eight. But elsewhere, the recession bit heavily into the retailing sector and, most important of all, buyers were thin on the ground.

Nevertheless, the designers went on creating, with the most wearable of styles quickly sifting down to the high street. From stars to kids, the on-the-street uniform was the ubiquitous black leather jacket worn with jeans, leggings or the still-prevalent short skirt. It was a year of nostalgia, with a revival of some old-time favourites, including Doris Day gingham for summer and good old tweed and tartan for autumn. The little tweed suit came back with a difference though. Instead of being sensibly buttoned up, here it was in sensational colour mixes like orange and pink (the top clash-with-dash of the year), and being shown unbuttoned over a sexy mesh 'body' or an elaborately jewelled and decorated bustier. The 'lingerie look' was definitely one of the sexiest of the year: suddenly those little bias-cut slips, just right for partying, were definitely meant to be seen, and the boned corset was just the thing for evening dressing.

The hemline issue still gave the designers some work to do. For those warmer months the long shaped jacket topped smart shorts and trousers, but by the end of the year the long skirt made a determined push. Draped, slashed or put over a mini underlayer, it was perhaps the beginning of looking at things in a different way.

3. LITERATURE

THE popular choice of Nadine Gordimer as the 1991 winner of the Nobel Prize for literature was not only a rare accolade for a woman—only six female authors had previously received the award since its inception in 1901—but also a symbolic recognition that cultural barriers were breaking down internationally. Gordimer, famous for her short stories and for novels such as *Burger's Daughter, July's People* and *The Conservationist*, could not have won the prize before because South African whites were not accepted within the norms of world citizenship. It was also improbable that a white African writer could have won it until a black African had done so, but that had been achieved in 1986 with the Nigerian Wole Soyinka (see AR 1986, p. 457).

If Nadine Gordimer represented one kind of breakthrough, then so did the marked increase in public interest in writers from Eastern Europe and the collapsing Soviet Union. In the wake of Michael Hamburger's victory for Britain at the tail end of 1990 in the first European Translation Prize, for his version of the poems of Paul Celan, literary translation became more frequent (and *The Independent* introduced a new prize for it). The Schlegel-Tieck Prize was shared for their translations from German between Hugh Young for his version of Edgar Hilsenrath's *The Story of the Last Thought* and John Woods for Christoph Ransmayr's *The Last World*. The Scott Moncrieff Prize was awarded to Brian Pearce for his translation from the French of Paul Veyne's *Bread and Circuses*. And the newly-instituted Bernard Shaw

Prize, established from Shaw's Nobel winnings in 1925, and awarded for translation from Swedish, went to Tom Geddes for Torgny Lindgren's *The Way of a Serpent*. Appropriately, Geddes received the award from Michael Holroyd, himself half Swedish, who in 1991 completed the final volume of his monumental three-part life of Shaw.

An increasing interest in translation existed not only among publishers, for the year saw the effective start of a full programme of work for the British Centre for Literary Translation. This research sanctuary was set up within the University of East Anglia at Norwich, but aspired to be national in its outreach. Similar centres were established a few years ago in Arles (France) and Stralen (Germany), but the insular British were notorious for lacking enthusiasm for such ventures. It was perhaps no surprise, therefore, that it required a German, Max Sebald, to set it up.

The Booker Prize had by now achieved a unique reputation, being the only literary award in Britain to make the headlines overseas. In 1991 the judges seemed to have reached a slightly grudging decision in giving it to the young Nigerian, Ben Okri, whose novel *The Famished Road* thus became the first African novel in English to head international best-seller lists. The Booker judges were much-criticized for not including any women on the shortlist—Angela Carter's *Wise Children* was by general consent one of the most cleverly allusive and life-enhancing books of the year, and it was common knowledge in literary circles that she was dying as she wrote it. Its failure to make the Booker list seemed inexplicable, but so did the resignation from the jury of Nicholas Moseley on the grounds that he did not admire any of the books liked by his fellow judges. This seemed rather peculiar behaviour for one who earlier in the year had himself won the Whitbread Award for his massive novel of twentieth century society and science, *Hopeful Monsters*. On the whole, the Booker assessors over the years had made propitious choices, swinging between novels of the genteel English mainstream and more rumbustious and innovative fictions, usually emanating from the Commonwealth. Okri's book was likely to join Salman Rushdie's *Midnight's Children* and Keri Hulme's *The Bone People* as an imaginative and influential selection.

Okri was likened by many critics, though to his disapproval, to the so-called 'magic realists' of post-modernist fiction—writers declining to countenance the sheerly ordinary and taking surrealist swipes at the constrictions of conventional living. Laurence Norfolk made the most dazzling fictional debut of the year in this mode with his linguistically-scholarly and yet wholly uncerebral novel *Lemprière's Dictionary*. The most debated novelist of the year, however, was Martin Amis, who at last found himself on a Booker shortlist, only to be confounded by accusations of archness and bad taste. *Time's Arrow* was hardly more than a novella in length, but it played with the form of fiction by telling its tale backwards. This was done not in the relatively straightforward way of, say, Harold Pinter in his play *Betrayal*, in which the history of a relationship was seen first at its end and then worked backwards to the moment when its three characters met, but in every nuance and detail. Water ran back into the tap; a baby entered, rather than was delivered from, its mother's womb. What might have been a witty experiment with craft caused some people great offence when it presented the Holocaust of twentieth-century Jewish history as a move away from horror to celebration.

Several leading novelists extended their range. Margaret Drabble, though no longer a fashionable figure (and all the better for it), went to Cambodia for the inspiration of *The Gates of Ivory*, further evidence of a writer tackling big contemporary issues and proving herself unafraid of mixing politics and fiction. Allan Massie's *The Sins of the Father* looked at the impact of Hitler upon some ordinary lives and proved nearly as contentious as Amis's book when Nicholas Moseley made it clear that he thought it should have won the Booker Prize, while the other judges pronounced it dessicated and dull. Timothy Mo's *The Redundancy of Courage* was set in East Timor; Michael Ignatieff, in an under-rated debut, placed *Asya* in the Russian and other revolutions; and Caryl Phillips's *Cambridge*, a novel about slavery in the Caribbean, put paid for ever to the patronizing notion that black writers could only write about black politics. Phillips wrote about a white woman in a language of masterly imitation that never quite collapsed into pastiche.

The best novels were not all so large or historical in their compass. Anita Brookner's *A Closed Eye* looked at two parallel families, one successful, the other not, and maintained her reputation for exquisiteness of feeling, though perhaps a note of impatience with her consistent similarity of method and style began to creep into the customary vast review coverage. Penelope Lively published her most ambitious novel to date; though *City of the Mind* did not please all her admirers, it showed a willingness to explore new territory—in this case London and its past. Julian Barnes was by many considered to be working in a minor key with *Talking It Over*. It was a year in which veteran writers published some of their best work. William Trevor, in particular, was thought to be at the height of his powers with *Reading Turgenev*. There was a facetious celebration of a much-publicized bicentenary with Anthony Burgess's *Mozart and the Wolf Gang*. Even the nonagenarian Naomi Mitchison produced two new books, *The Oath Takers* and *Sea Green Ribbons*, though her prolificity was as nothing to that of the newly-endamed Barbara Cartland, who brought out her 500th title at the time of her 90th birthday. There was a witty satire on metropolitan *literati* from William Cooper, who celebrated his 80th birthday with *Immortality At Any Price*, and distinguished work from Nina Bawden with *Family Money* and from Stanley Middleton with *Beginning to End*.

British fiction, which a decade ago had seemed doomed to miniaturist oblivion, was suddenly bursting forth all over the place, and this in the middle of what publishers considered the worst recession in bookselling they could ever remember. It was good to see some younger novelists consolidating their reputations, among them the thriller-writer Michael Dibdin, with his Oxford-based *Dirty Tricks*, and Maggie Gee, whose *Where Are the Snows* contained a remarkable account of a botched attempt at cross-cultural adoption. But it was also a year of sadness, which saw the deaths of two outstanding talents, Graham Greene and Angus Wilson (see XX:OBITUARY).

Internationally, the best-selling novel of the year was by general consent one of the worst: nothing could prevent the massive advertising campaign for the bogus sequel to Margaret Mitchell's *Gone With the Wind* producing an immediate international hit. No matter that Mitchell herself always declined to gild the lily by telling us in a second book whether Scarlett O'Hara and Rhett Butler came together again. Alexandra Ripley, an unknown writer from a southern American state, was commissioned to tell us. *Scarlett* showed the power of modern marketing techniques and was published in many countries on the same day—a red-letter-day if ever there was one. It continued to be a feature of world publishing that 'airport blockbusters' sold millions of copies, whereas even the most successful serious fiction could expect to sell only in thousands.

Even so, by comparison with poetry, novelists were doing quite well in sales terms. Poetry, according to an article in *The Times* in October, was the national art of the British people, written and read by more individuals than attended football matches. Yet the average poetry book sold in hundreds rather than thousands. There were, of course, exceptions, such as Seamus Heaney and Tony Harrison, both of whom brought an unmodish use of poetry into modern theatre: Heaney with *The Cure at Troy*, a version of the *Philoctetes* of Sophocles, and Harrison, also drawing on classical sources, with his play *The Trackers of Oxyrhynchus*. *Poetry Review* published, in its winter issue, a sparky debate about the predicament of poetry in Britain and America. The touchpaper for this was an article by Dana Gioia entitled 'Can Poetry Matter', which had appeared in the May 1991 issue of *Atlantic Monthly*. He articulated the fear that poetry was becoming the preserve of academics, losing contact with educated audiences. The amazing growth in popular demand for public readings by poets, especially in Britain, suggested that his basic concern was ill-founded, but notions of what poetry was perhaps needed to be enlarged to encompass modes of verse which were manifestly devised for performance. The popularity on the international poetry touring circuits of the likes of La Loca, John Hegley and Benjamin Zephaniah, for example, was bewildering to people who saw poetry as necessarily about words on a printed page. It was easily understood by others who recalled the bardic origins of the form.

Among the best poetry collections of the year were Vernon Scannell's *Time for Fires*, published at the time of his 70th birthday, and P. J. Kavanagh's *An Enchantment*, musings on death which were far from morbid or defeatist. Of younger poets, Sean O'Brien impressed with *HMS Glasshouse*. Two outstanding poets died, namely Roy Fuller (see XX:OBITUARY) and George Barker.

In the field of autobiography, the most serialized and polemical of the year was undoubtedly John Osborne's *Almost a Gentleman*, another class-obsessed memoir in the vein of his earlier volume, *A Better Class of Person*. The bilious tone of Osborne's prose and his apparent hatred for so many of his intimates (including wives, lovers, colleagues and theatre associates) had virtually no parallel in recent times, though it met its scurrilous match in a related genre. This was Kitty Kelley's life of Nancy Reagan, which made headline news with its revelations of infidelities and Lady Macbeth-like ambition. Donald Spoto's *Laurence Olivier: A Biography* was rather in the same vein, with its exposé of a sexual relationship between Olivier and Danny Kaye. Among senior politicians, David Owen led the field with his autobiography, entitled *Time to Declare*. Boris Yeltsin, whose personal star displaced the red star of communism, rushed out an autobiography which managed to take note of the abortive August coup in the Soviet Union only three weeks after the event. Margaret Thatcher was commissioned to write her own life story, but rumours of a world record advance payment proved to be false.

There continued to be a spectacular demand for children's books, though in this field the year was overshadowed by the death in November 1990 of the most successful children's author since Enid Blyton, the droll and conspiratorial Roald Dahl (see AR 1990, pp. 519, 581). A national summer school for teachers and librarians concerned with children's reading was held for the first time in Britain, though such an event had become annual in America. Worldwide, there was concern about apparently-declining standards of children's reading and an alarming growth in illiteracy in Western countries. In Britain, this concern was articulated in a much-publicized speech in Stratford-upon-Avon by Prince Charles, who feared the emergence of a readerless generation unfamiliar with Shakespeare and the classics. Debates about appropriate books to use in the classroom were rife at precisely the moment that a national curriculum was being introduced into British state education.

The recession in publishing was international. In developing nations the dearth of foreign exchange made the purchase of books from abroad virtually impossible, while at the same time limiting prospects for publishing at home. Libraries were forced almost everywhere to cut their spending budgets, thereby putting specialist presses in jeopardy.

A massive relief operation was begun to send books to the republics of the former Soviet Union. There was for the first time a serious move by some mainstream publishers to bring their work out in paperback on the occasion of its first publication rather than in hardback. It looked like a serious crisis everywhere, compounded by growing competition for the book from computer technology (see XIV.2).

The tragic virtual incarceration of Salman Rushdie continued. At the end of 1990 he had announced his conversion to Islam, but before long it became evident that Rushdie's was a cultural commitment rather than an act of faith, and as such it was barely acceptable to liberal Muslims let alone to the *fatweh*-makers of Iran. However, Rushdie showed his resilience by beginning a tentative programme of public appearances. His article 'One man in a doomed balloon' appeared in December, posing the chilling question: 'What is my single life worth?' But there were improvements elsewhere, even if not yet for Rushdie: the Malawian poet Jack Mapanje, for example, was released from prison in his own country after nearly four years without charge.

It was a strong year for fiction and also for poetry books produced by a mixture of mainstream and small presses. Lives of political, royal, literary and show business figures continued to be popular. Books in these categories which were of particular merit or attracted much publicity included the following:

FICTION. Martin Amis, *Time's Arrow* (Cape); J. G. Ballard, *The Kindness of Women* (HarperCollins); Pat Barker, *Regeneration* (Viking); Julian Barnes, *Talking It Over* (Cape); Stan Barstow, *Next of Kin* (Michael Joseph); Nina Bawden, *Family Money* (Gollancz); Anita Brookner, *A Closed Eye* (Cape); Anthony Burgess, *Mozart and the Wolf Gang* (Hutchinson); Philip Callow, *Some Love* (Allison & Busby); Peter Carey, *The Tax Inspector* (Faber); Angela Carter, *Wise Children* (Chatto & Windus); Isobel Colegate, *The Summer of the Royal Visit* (Hamish Hamilton); David Cook, *Second Best* (Faber); William Cooper, *Immortality at Any Price* (Sinclair-Stevenson); Roald Dahl, *Collected Short Stories* (Michael Joseph); Robertson Davies, *Murther and Walking Spirits* (Sinclair-Stevenson); Michael Dibdin, *Dirty Tricks* (Faber); Jenny Diski, *Happily Ever After* (Hamish Hamilton); Roddy Doyle, *The Van* (Secker & Warburg); Margaret Drabble, *The Gates of Ivory* (Viking); Margaret Forster, *The Battle for Christabel* (Chatto & Windus); Michael Frayn, *A Landing on the Sun* (Viking); Stephen Fry, *The Liar* (Heinemann); Jane Gardam, *The Queen of the Tambourine* (Sinclair-Stevenson); Maggie Gee, *Where Are the Snows?* (Heinemann); Julian Gloag, *Love as a Foreign Language* (Sinclair-Stevenson); Michael Ignatieff, *Asya* (Chatto & Windus); Thomas Kenneally, *Flying Hero Class* (Hodder & Stoughton); Balraj Khanna, *Sweet Chillies* (Constable); Jamaica Kincaid, *Lucy* (Cape); Francis King, *The Ant Colony* (Constable); James Kirkup, *Gaijin on the Ginza* (Peter Owen); Penelope Lively, *City of the Mind* (Deutsch); David Lodge, *Paradise News* (Secker & Warburg); Alistair MacLeod, *The Lost Salt Gift of Blood: Collected Stories* (Cape); Moy McCrory, *Those Sailing Ships of His Boyhood Dreams* (Cape); Allan Massie, *The Sins of the Father* (Hutchinson); Stanley Middleton, *Beginning to End* (Hutchinson); Rohinton Mistry, *Such a Long Journey* (Faber); Naomi Mitchison, *The Oath-Takers and Sea-Green Ribbons* (Balnain); Timothy Mo, *The Redundancy of Courage* (Chatto & Windus); Andrew Motion, *Famous for the Creatures* (Viking); Laurence Norfolk, *Lemprière's Dictionary* (Sinclair Stevenson);

Ben Okri, *The Famished Road* (Cape); Caryl Phillips, *Cambridge* (Bloomsbury); Jane Rogers, *Mr Wroe's Virgins* (Faber); Alexandra Ripley, *Scarlett* (Macmillan); William Trevor, *Reading Turgenev* and *Two Lives* (Viking); A. N. Wilson, *Daughters of Albion* (Sinclair-Stevenson)

POETRY. Peter Abbs, *Icons of Time* (Gryphon); Kingsley Amis, *The Measure of Poetry* (Cassell); John Ashbery, *Flow Chart* (Carcanet); Kenneth Baker (ed.), *I Have No Gun But I Can Spit: An Anthology of Satirical and Abusive Verse* (Faber); Judith Chernaik (ed.), *100 Poems on the Underground* (Cassell); Amy Clampit, *Westward* (Faber); Kevin Crossley-Holland, *New and Selected Poems 1965–1990* (Hutchinson); Elaine Feinstein, *City Music* (Hutchinson); John Fuller, *The Mechanical Body* (Chatto & Windus); Duncan Glen, *The Poetry of the Scots: A Bibliographical Guide to Scottish Poetry* (Edinburgh University Press); Philip Gross, *The Sons of the Duke of Nowhere* (Faber); Michael Hamburger, *Roots in the Air* (Anvil); John Hegley, *Can I Come Down Now Dad?* (Methuen); P. J. Kavanagh, *An Enchantment* (Carcanet); Jackie Kay, *The Adoption Papers* (Bloodaxe); Mimi Khalvati, *In White Ink* (Carcanet); Liz Lockhead, *Bagpipe Muzak* (Penguin); Michael Longley, *Poems 1963–1983* (Secker & Warburg); Lachlan Mackinnon, *The Coast of Bohemia* (Chatto & Windus); Edwin Morgan, *Collected Poems* (Carcanet); Peter Mortimer & S. J. Litherland (eds.), Carol Rumens & Richard McKane (translators), *The Poetry of Perestroika* (Ikon Press); Les A. Murray, *Collected Poems* (Carcanet); Tanure Ojaide, *The Blood of Peace* (Heinemann); F. T. Prince, *Collected Poems 1935–1990* (Anvil); Christopher Reid, *In the Echoey Tunnel* (Faber); Vernon Scannell, *A Time for Fires* (Robson); Martin Sorrell (translator), *Modern French Poetry* (Forest); Alice Walker, *Her Blue Body Everything We Know* (Women's Press); Heathcote Williams, *Autogeddon* (Cape); Yevgeny Yevtushenko *The Collected Poems 1952–1990* (Mainstream).

BIOGRAPHIES AND MEMOIRS. (i) Public figures: Princess Alice, *Memories* (Collins & Brown); John Gribbin & Michael White, *A Life in Science: Stephen Hawking* (Viking); Richard Hough, *Winston and Clementine: The Triumph of the Churchills* (Aston); Roy Jenkins, *A Life at the Centre* (Macmillan); Penny Junor, *Queen Elizabeth II 1952–1992* (Conran Octopus); Kitty Kelley, *Nancy Reagan* (Viking); Richard Lamb, *Churchill as War Leader: Right or Wrong?* (Bloomsbury); David Owen, *A Time to Declare* (Michael Joseph); Ronald Reagan, *An American Life* (Arrow). (ii) Show business: Sven Broman, *Garbo on Garbo* (Bloomsbury); Sandra Caron, *Alma Cogan: The Girl with a Laugh in Her Voice* (Bloomsbury); Peter Coleman, *The Real Barrie Humphries* (Coronet); Ava Gardner, *Ava* (Bantam); Katherine Hepburn, *Me: Stories of My Life* (Viking); Vanessa Redgrave, *Vanessa* (Hutchinson); Donald Spoto, *Laurence Olivier: A Biography* (HarperCollins); Nicholas Wapshott, *Rex Harrison* (Chatto & Windus). (iii) Literary lives: Susan Chitty (ed.), *Antonia White: Diaries 1926–1957* (Constable); Artemis Cooper (ed.), *Mr Wu and Mrs Stitch: The Letters of Evelyn Waugh and Diana Cooper 1932–1966* (Hodder & Stoughton); Katherine Duncan-Jones, *Sir Philip Sidney: Courtier Poet* (Hamish Hamilton); Marguerite Duras, *Practicalities* (Flamingo); Pippa Harris (ed.), *The Love Letters of Rupert Brooke and Noel Olivier* (Bloomsbury); Michael Holroyd, *Bernard Shaw, Vol. 3: The Lure of Fantasy* (Chatto & Windus); Hazel Holt, *A Lot to Ask: A Biography of Barbara Pym* (Cardinal); R. W. B. Lewis, *The Jameses* (Deutsch); Diane Wood Middlebrook, *Anne Sexton: A Biography* (Virago); John Osborne, *Almost a Gentleman* (Faber); Laurens van der Post, *About Blady* (Chatto & Windus); Donald Tylden-Wright, *John Aubrey: A Life* (HarperCollins); Michael Shelden, *Orwell: The Authorized Biography* (Heinemann); Martin Stannard '*No Abiding City*': *Evelyn Waugh, 1939–1966* (Dent); Kurt Vonnegut, *Fates Worse than Death: An Autobiographical Collage of the 1980s* (Cape); Auberon Waugh, *Will This Do?* (Century); John Worthen, *D. H. Lawrence: The Early Years, 1885–1912* (CUP).

XVII SPORT

SPORT AND POLITICS. There was an end at last to sport being used as a political football in the debate over South Africa. It had always been questionable behaviour to devise rules against sportsmen which did not apply to businessmen or other visitors. Indeed, the United Nations' sporting blacklist appeared to many to be an example of the discrimination it purported to oppose. Whatever the individual beliefs about this, there was relief that the South African situation had improved to the point where these special sanctions were finally ended (see also VII.3). In July the South Africans were welcomed back by the International Olympic Committee (IOC); and with support from India, the International Cricket Conference (ICC) also lifted its ban. By November the South Africans were playing cricket against India and reaching the final of the Dunhill Nations Golf Cup.

In the case of cricket, there were still anomalies to be overcome. English cricketers who had been penalized for playing there found that there was no remission for past breach of the regulations. The ICC also hesitated to allow the South Africans to take part in the impending World Cup despite the lifting of the ban. While they agonized over this, the Commonwealth summit conference in Harare (Zimbabwe) took the decision for them, giving formal approval to South Africa's participation (see XI.2). That was of particular interest to the prime ministers of Australia and Britain, whose love of cricket had been underlined when they opened the innings together at an impromptu match during the Conference.

An issue often raised by British politicians in the past was revived by a boxing tragedy in London. In a WBO super-middle-weight bout, a bruising encounter ended with Englishman Chris Eubank retaining his world title, but challenger Michael Watson removed to hospital in a critical condition with serious brain damage. This led to renewed demands that boxing be banned.

The good sense of the crackdown on drugs in sport was evident enough after Ben Johnson's reinstatement to run in world athletics. His relatively poor performances underlined the assistance drugs had been to his earlier record-breaking achievements, culminating in his much-publicized Olympic disgrace (see AR 1988, p. 516).

The political upheaval in Eastern Europe started minor tremors in the world of sport as well. The dissolution of the USSR raised queries about which countries were now eligible for various sporting events. The dissolving Yugoslavia had qualified, like the USSR, for the European Nations football finals in 1992, and FIFA debated whether Italy and Denmark should now be promoted into their places. Statesmanlike, the authorities decided to delay a decision while the Olympic movement, too, began to contemplate the break-up of the USSR and Yugoslavia and an influx of new countries.

ASSOCIATION FOOTBALL. The major event off the field was the draw in the USA for the 1994 World Cup to be staged there. On the field, many nations were preoccupied with trying to qualify for the 1992 European Nations Cup finals in Sweden. With only one qualifier from their group, England had a stirring tussle with the Republic of Ireland over two hard-fought games, both of which ended level. Both countries also drew away in Poland, Ireland disappointingly after leading 3–1. A draw there, in their final match, was enough to send England through, but it needed a typical Gary Lineker strike 11 minutes from time to frustrate Ireland. Exasperated, Ireland's English manager, Jack Charlton, commented: 'I will be phoning England's manager in the morning to tell him what a lucky sod he is. England have played crap and are still going to the finals.' There was some justice in the comment, but Graham Taylor could always count on the admirable Lineker to bring poise and class to the team.

For the first time Scotland also qualified for these finals, their decisive match being a 2–2 draw in Switzerland after they had trailed by two goals at half-time. Wales made a brave effort to get there, defeating world champions Germany in their home tie. The resources of the united Germans proved too great, however, for a country about which an American journalist had enquired 'Wales? Is that somewhere in Scotland?' On their own ground Germany won the decisive match 4–1.

Back in Europe after their long ban, English teams showed how hollow had been some of the victories in their absence. Alex Ferguson's Manchester United won the Cup Winners Cup, goals by Steve Bruce and Mark Hughes defeating Barcelona in the final. The UEFA Cup final was, however, an all-Italian affair with Inter-Milan beating Roma. At the start of a new season Liverpool, too, was allowed back into European competition six years after the infamous riot at the Heysel with its Italian casualties. How much their playing skills had been missed was evident as a flood of goals by Welshman Dean Saunders (the most expensive player in the English League) defeated teams from Finland, France and Austria to leave Liverpool, at the year's end, the favourites to take the Cup.

Earlier, Tottenham Hotspur of London had won their eighth FA Cup final, a record in that competition, with its great traditions going back to 1872. Their opponents at Wembley were Nottingham Forest under manager Brian Clough, who had never before taken his team to the final. Fortune had favoured his team in the semi-final when West Ham's central defender was sent off early. The new instruction to referees to send off players committing 'professional' fouls to prevent another scoring was being interpreted sometimes harshly, sometimes leniently, and usually controversially. In this case it certainly ruined the match, Forest winning easily. In the final it was England's most charismatic player, Paul Gascoigne, who deserved to be sent off for a late and violent tackle early in the match. In fact, the only person crippled was Gascoigne, whose serious injury jeopardized his £4 million transfer to Italy. A sympathetic referee felt that penalty enough, and so it seemed when Stuart Pearce scored from the free-kick, provoking an excited commentator to say 'Pearce has the taste of Wembley in his nostrils'. However, a goal by Paul Stewart and an unfortunate own-goal by Des Walker, usually the most reliable of defenders, gave Spurs the Cup. In the Rumbelow's Cup final Ron Atkinson's Sheffield Wednesday beat his old club Manchester United.

In the League, Arsenal were dominant throughout, with even Liverpool faint pursuers. In Anders Limpar, their Swedish import, and England international Alan Smith, Arsenal had lively forwards, but it was a near-impregnable defence which won them their second title in three years.

In Scotland, those old Glasgow rivals, Celtic and Rangers, clashed in the Scottish Cup, Celtic winning 2–0. Clashed was the right word, because four players were sent off in an unruly game. Rangers were truer to their form in winning the League for the fourth time in five years.

RUGBY FOOTBALL. Rugby Union's second world championship was staged at venues in Britain and France with the final at Twickenham. This festival of rugby spread the game's popularity, an estimated 2,000 million people watching the massive TV coverage over the four weeks. The results followed form, the top four rated countries confirming their status. Australia came as co-favourites and proved themselves the best side overall, combining flair in attack with great resolution in defence. England gave them a hard fight in the final, but there was no doubt that victory went to the best team. Holders and co-favourites, the New Zealand All Blacks, lost out to Australia in the semi-finals but had the consolation of beating runners-up, England, in the opening group match. New Zealand and Scotland competed for the third and fourth places, New Zealand finally wearing down the gritty Scots.

A pleasant feature of the group matches was the high standard of unfancied teams like Argentina and Romania. The United States also performed creditably, especially in their determined defence, which limited England's winning margin. The main surprise was the achievement of Western Samoa in running the Australians close, then defeating Wales. The Canadians also played above expectation in qualifying for the quarter-finals and playing entertainingly in a losing battle against New Zealand. The Samoans also found Scotland too strong and it was in the other two quarter-finals that the tense encounters came. Only a late try allowed England to get the better of France in Paris, despite the efforts of Serge Blanco in his final international. In Dublin the Irish fought so fiercely that they led Australia with only four minutes left. Then a tired defence conceded the try which gave the Wallabies a 19–18 win.

For the semi-final the All Blacks were without Martin Jones, who declined to play on a Sunday, and were caught cold by Australia's initial assault. The championship's outstanding player, David Campese, scored a remarkable try and made another, Australian flair proving more effective than New Zealand's 'SAPS' formula of simplicity, accuracy, pressure, support. At Murrayfield England played successfully to the disciplined strength of their formidable pack, though at the end the difference was that Rob Andrew seized his chance to drop a goal while Gavin Hastings for once missed an easy penalty.

Despite being labelled too disciplined and boring, England were in fact the team which played the more entertaining rugby in the Twickenham final. Only outstanding defence prevented them scoring tries as they stormed towards Australia's line throughout much of the second half. In the end, the difference was the one try of the game, scored by Australia's forwards, who made the main contribution to a 12–6 win.

Wigan dominated League rugby, with Ellery Hanley leading them to a fourth successive Challenge Cup win and to the League title as well. To round off their success they beat Australian champions, Penrith, to win the world club cup.

ATHLETICS. The third World Athletics championships staged in Tokyo were so successful that the organizers were considering holding them every two years instead of every four, though many athletes would not welcome a further addition to their already taxing programmes. The great merit of this event was its freedom from the political wrangling and excessive commercialism which had tarnished recent Olympics and that it was not encumbered by a multitude of minor sports. A gold medal in Tokyo did indeed prove that a competitor was the best in the world in a major sport.

The Americans and Russians as usual dominated the championships. By virtue of their ten golds, to add to their eight silvers and eight bronzes, the Americans topped the medals table, but the USSR had more medals in total, with nine golds, nine silvers and ten bronzes. Competing for the first time in these championships as a single nation, Germany was third with five golds; Kenya came fourth with four golds from its domination of long-distance running; and Great Britain came fifth with two golds, two silvers and two bronzes.

Individually, the Games were a triumph for the Americans Carl Lewis and Mike Powell, the only two to break individual world records. Lewis was himself involved in all three new world records. In the 100 m sprint he finished in 9.86 seconds to beat his great rival Leroy Burrell. With two other Americans edging out European champion Linford Christie of Britain (who came fourth), it was no surprise that the American relay team also set a new world record of 37.51 seconds, beating the previous holders, France, into second place, with Britain third.

While the 100 m sprint had a special place in athletics lore, with the winner titled 'fastest man on earth', this time it was the long jump which attracted most attention. Bob Beamon's leap of 8 m 90 cm 23 years earlier had become the longest-standing world record. Achieved at altitude in Mexico, it was regarded as unbeatable until the remarkable Lewis began to threaten it. Lewis's fourth jump in the championship was in fact one centimetre better, but the wind-speed prevented it counting as a record. In the next round, however, Powell jumped 8 m 95 cm without any wind to help him. So he took the record and ensured Lewis's first defeat in the event for a decade.

Britain began, depressingly, with first-round failures for some of its best medal prospects, including Steve Backley in the javelin and Tom McKean in the 400 m, the latter again making an elementary tactical mistake in his heat. Kriss Akabusi then won bronze in the 400 m hurdles, while Sally Gunnell took silver, when the gold beckoned, losing her stride pattern as she approached the fateful last hurdle. Roger Black came off the final bend well in the lead in the 400 m, only to be passed at the finish by American Antonio Pettigrew.

Liz McColgan of Scotland then won the team's first gold with a courageous run in the women's 10,000 m, leading from the front throughout to leave all the others trailing as the humid heat took its toll. That was followed by a surprise win in the final event, the 400 m relay, with Akabusi starting the final leg two yards down on world champion Pettigrew but using his hurdler's strength at the end to power past and win by inches.

Among other outstanding performances were those of Kristin Krabbe of Germany, who beat the previously invincible Merlene Ottey of Jamaica in the ladies 100 m and took the gold in the 200 m as well, with two relay bronzes to follow. American hurdler Greg Foster had his third world championship win and Russia's Sergei Bubka as usual dominated the pole vault, in which he had set so many world records.

The fact that Britain won only two golds after a series of impressive performances in the European championships was a reminder of the higher standards of world competition. But the three leading European nations, the USSR, Germany and Britain, still finished in the top five.

CRICKET. International cricket shook itself free of politics at last when the July meeting of the ICC voted to end the ban on South Africa. The Marylebone Cricket Club (MCC) elected Prime Minister John Major as a member but maintained its ban on women. The best-known England woman cricketer, Rachael Heyhoe-Flint, was rejected and promptly called on the tea-ladies to stage a strike.

An admirable attempt to raise funds for the Memorial Fund for Disaster Relief suffered from English cricket's usual weather problems. The start of this three-year 'crickathon', spearheaded by David Gower, was a September match at Wembley stadium between the Rest of the World, captained by Desmond Haynes of West Indies, and Europe, captained by England's David Gower. The only winner was the rain, which caused the match to be abandoned without a ball being bowled.

English pride also suffered when the Australians achieved overwhelming victory in the Tests in Australia. The worst feature of England's play was an apparent lack of concentration and dedicated effort on which captain Graham Gooch and manager Micky Stewart, had relied to make up for lack of talent. The Jekyll and Hyde nature of England's performance was epitomized in David Gower, who was on occasions brilliant and entertaining, on others wayward and seemingly irresponsible. That view was enhanced when Gower took a flight over the ground on which England were losing a Test match. The escapade amused some but infuriated the officials and put Gower's future Test career in jeopardy. He remained a few runs short of the English record for the overall total of runs in Tests.

With the West Indies having decisively defeated the Australians in the Caribbean, English hopes of doing well against Vivian Richards's visiting team in the summer looked slim indeed. However, England won the one-day international series 3–0 and drew the Test series 2–2. For the final Test at the Oval, Ian Botham was reinstated after a long absence and the left-arm slow bowler, Philip Tufnell, was brought back, despite some disastrous performances in Australia. Tufnell proceeded to play a significant part in England's first home wins against the West Indies for over two decades, taking 6 wickets for 25 runs in the visitors' second innings. To complete a satisfactory season, England then had a decisive win in a single Test against Sri Lanka.

England's noticeable improvement was attributed by some to the revival of spirit and the dedication of younger players like Mark Ramprakesh, especially in the fielding department. But the main reason was the outstanding performance of Graham Gooch and Robin Smith whose batting blunted the West Indies menacing fast bowlers. Smith, in particular, was unrecognizable from the failure he had been in Australia.

In the county championship unfancied Warwickshire led for most of the season, only to be overhauled by Essex in the final few matches. Essex deserved their win, Neil Foster's fast bowling being the most important aspect of a well-balanced team. Foster's 100-plus wickets in the season highlighted England's loss, in that he was banned from Test cricket because of a South African tour.

Hampshire won the NatWest Trophy and Worcestershire the Benson and Hedges final, a commanding innings by Graeme Hick in the latter redeeming a disappointing season for him. The Refuge Assurance Sunday League was won by Nottinghamshire, as Leicestershire faded in the final matches.

Overseas players were again outstanding in English cricket, notably Waqar Younis of Pakistan, a remarkable fast bowling talent, and South African Jimmy Cook, again an outstanding bat. Cook was expected in 1992, to lead the first South African side—from Transvaal—to come to England after the lifting of the ICC ban.

GOLF. The highlight of the golfing year was the Ryder Cup, decided once again by the final singles match. This time a short putt, missed on the last green, finally sank Europe and restored the treasured trophy to America. Europe had started well, Ireland's David Feherty being successful at the opening match and Nick Faldo at last playing up to form to beat Ray Floyd. Colin Montgomerie then staged a remarkable recovery from 4 down with 4 to play to halve his match as Mark Calcavecchia fell victim to nerves. Corey Pavin gave the Americans their first taste of victory, only for Seve Ballesteros to respond with a win which made him Europe's best player with 4½ points out of a possible 5. Then America recovered to lead 6–5 so that everything depended on the last singles match between Bernhard Langer and Hale Irwin. A tied score overall would have meant that Europe retained the Cup. Langer was 2 down to Irwin at the fourteenth, but fought back bravely to be level when they came to the final hole. But putting had always been Langer's Achilles heel: he missed a five-foot putt, enabling America to snatch victory.

The top-rated golfer of the year was the smallest ever to win the prestigious US Masters. Although only 5 ft 4½ ins tall, Welshman Ian Woosnam had such strong arms that he was one of the longest hitters in the game. For all his big hauls of prize money, he had never won a major until he took the famous Green Jacket at Augusta after shaking off the challenge of José-Maria Olazabal and Tom Watson. Woosnam started the season with a record round of 57 on his home course at Oswestry. That was followed by another win on the US tour before his Augusta triumph. Two more wins followed in Europe and as climax he beat the winners of the other three majors in a World Cup head-to-head between the four of them.

For the other three, there were relatively few highlights in the season. Payne Stewart won the US Open and the Dutch Open, but had only one other top ten finish. Ian Baker-Finch's fine last round gave him victory in the British Open, but he had no other such win. John Daly's success in the US PGA was a one-off event, the surprise of the year. At one point he was the ninth reserve for the tournament and he only drove over to the course in the hope that someone would withdraw, a hope which was fulfilled by Nick Price. Daly had no practice, yet his first round was a masterly 69 and he continued to make fun of a course which Jack Nicklaus claimed to be the most difficult he had experienced. However, the Daly lightning did not strike twice in the year, despite the remarkable power of his driving. Woosnam was long, but Daly hit the ball out of sight.

The leading golfer in Europe's Volvo Order of Merit was Seve Ballesteros, back to his best with three tournament wins, including the World Matchplay, and earnings in excess of £500,000. The much-improved Steven Richardson was close behind, followed by Bernhard Langer and Colin Montgomerie, with a dejected Nick Faldo dropping to tenth.

The Dunhill Nations Cup at St Andrew's took on a new significance as the South Africans re-entered international competition after 12 years of political ostracism. Making an immediate impact, they reached the final before losing to Sweden.

MOTOR SPORT. A Grand Prix season which began with every appearance of another runaway win for Ayrton Senna and McLaren-Honda ended with Nigel Mansell and Williams-Renault mounting a spirited challenge which came close to success. In the final analysis, however, it was the first four events which proved decisive, with Senna establishing yet another record by winning all of them. In the first round of the 16-event championship, Senna won with some brilliant driving round the streets of Phoenix. Mansell had come back from retirement in answer to a plea from Williams, backed by much cash, but failed to finish in America.

In Brazil and San Marino, the pattern was repeated: Senna was victorious, while mechanical troubles left Mansell disconsolate and his much publicized come-back looking like a futile gesture. Great fighter as he was, though, Mansell began to repay the Williams' faith by coming second on the difficult Monaco circuit, nursing an engine which cut out intermittently. Senna had won again, but the challenge was clear. By now Williams-Renault had improved the performance and reliability of their cars. In Canada Mansell was leading by more than a minute, with only a few hundred yards to go, when gear failure frustrated him, his only consolation being that Senna, too, was baulked by mechanical failure, for the only time in the season. That bad luck spurred Mansell to a remarkable winning sequence in France, Britain and Germany. His win in France, the 17th of his career, took him ahead of Stirling Moss's previous British record. His win in the British Grand Prix, his fourth, was achieved before a delirious crowd, whose support always seemed to raise his performance.

Senna and McLaren were now under pressure, as Mansell's team-mate Ricardo Patrese was also doing well. Back in Japan, however, Honda's vast research team came up with an entirely new engine. With Shell also improving the petrol, Senna had the extra power he needed to beat Mansell into second place in their next encounter. Senna then won again (and Mansell again broke down) before, in Italy, Mansell lived up to his nickname 'the lion' by storming home first, to the delight of his many Italian fans. In Portugal, Mansell was again leading when an error by the pit-stop crew led to a wheel coming off and disqualification. Mansell battled back, to win the next race in Barcelona, where Senna spun and finished fifth. But more mechanical trouble led to Mansell's retirement in Japan, where Senna was confirmed as champion. The final Grand Prix in Australia was an anticlimax and a disappointing end to an entertaining season. Torrential rain caused more than a dozen cars to crash before the race was called off early, becoming the shortest Grand Prix in history. Senna won the drivers' championship by 24 points and his team-mate Gerhard Berger's win in Japan helped McLaren to win the constructors' championship comfortably enough from Williams. The other one of the big three, Ferrari, had an unhappy season, whereas Benetton and Jordan had moments of success.

TENNIS. The outstanding tennis achievement of the year was France's Davis Cup triumph, its first for 59 years. Yanick Noah proved an inspiring leader and his gamble, in the final against America, of playing Henri Leconte, only just recovered from injury, was a masterstroke. Leconte delighted the rapturous crowd in Lyons by squaring the singles and dominating the doubles. His partner Guy Forget then beat the dispirited Pete Sampras to clinch victory.

Among the men, no player was consistently outstanding. Early in the year Boris Becker became the number one ranked player for the first time when he beat Ivan Lendl to win the final of the Australian Open. The even spread of ability among the men was then evident in Jim Courier's surprise win in France and Michael Stich's even more surprising defeat of Stefan Edberg in the semi-final at Wimbledon followed by a straight sets victory over Becker in the final.

Americans contested the final of the Grand Slam Cup, the most lucrative event in a money-mad sport. Edberg and Becker being unable to participate, Michael Chang and David Wheaton reached the final in search of the $2 million prize. Wheaton, who had reached the semi-final at Wimbledon, proved much too strong for Chang.

Yugoslav-born Monica Seles soon established herself as leading lady by beating Jan Novotna in the Australian Open. The Florida-based 17-year-old was the top-ranked player, but low in the popularity ratings.

Fined for her failure to play at Wimbledon, Seles caused further upset by her comment that she did not talk to lower-ranked players. Steffi Graf recovered her form at Wimbledon, beating Gabriel Sabatini in the final, to give Germany victory in both singles. British tennis remained of depressingly low quality, relieved only by Jeremy Bates and Jo Durie winning the mixed doubles in the Australian Open.

THE TURF. Generous was the horse of the year on the flat, winning the Derby easily, then beating the French Derby winner, Suave Dancer, in the Irish Derby. In the King George VI and Queen Elizabeth Diamond Stakes, Generous won by a wide margin from Sanglamore. Those three fine wins established Generous as exceptional even though failure followed in the Prix de l'Arc de Triomphe, which was won by Suave Dancer.

For the jumpers there was a sad end to the season when the punters' favourite, Desert Orchid, not only failed to win the King George VI Chase for the fifth time but fell close to home while lying last, an unhappy finish to a ten-year career of 34 wins. Mark Pitman rode Garrison Savannah, trained by Jenny Pitman, to victory in the Gold Cup at Cheltenham. Two hours later Pitman broke his pelvis in a heavy fall. He recovered quickly, however, to ride Jenny Pitman's horse Gary in the Grand National and was several lengths clear over the final fence only for Seagram to catch him before the line. Over hurdles, the outstanding horse was Morley Street, who achieved the remarkable double of winning at Cheltenham and in the Breeders' Cup Chase in America.

On the flat, Pat Eddery was again leading jockey, winning his ninth classic and riding his 3000th winner. Lester Piggott, aged 55, completed an exceptional come-back by riding more than 100 winners within a 12-month period. With Generous as his prize horse, Paul Cole was trainer of the year for the first time. As usual, the leading jump jockey was Peter Scudamore with 141 winners despite breaking his leg. Many of those were for trainer Martin Pipe, who was again the leader in his field.

AMERICAN ASPECTS. The Super Bowl XXV American football final gained a unique place in American history. This most popular of all sporting events was in question because of the Gulf War, until President Bush insisted that it went ahead and broadcast a personal message to the huge crowd of spectators. The game was unique, too, in that it proved to be the closest of the 25 games to date and indeed the closest possible, as the New York Giants beat the Buffalo Bills 20–19. In their previous match, the Giants had won through against the favourites, the San Francisco 49ers, with a Matt Bahr field goal in the final seconds. This time it was the Giants who had to watch as Scott Norwood tried for a 47-yard field goal with the last kick of the game. Norwood got the distance, but the ball drifted a few feet wide of the post to deny the Bills. So Bill Purcell's team won through both close encounters, his reserve quarter-back, Jeff Hosteller, being the outstanding player of Super Bowl XXV.

World Series baseball was at present a misnomer since only American or Canadian teams were involved, though the sport was catching on so well that it had been accepted as an Olympic event. The two teams in the seven-match decider this time were the Atlanta Braves and the Minnesota Twins, neither of whom had been highly regarded at the season's start. Unfancied they may have been, but they produced a series of outstanding quality and prolonged tension. The Twins won both opening encounters on their own astroturf. The Braves responded with three wins on the natural grass in their own stadium. Back in Minnesota the series was tied thanks to a brilliant batting performance by the Twins' Kirby Puckett. Even so, extra time was needed to settle it. The decider also went to extra time, with the pitchers so dominant that both sides were scoreless. Only in the tenth inning did the Twins get the home run which sealed their win.

Despite being chosen to host the 1994 World Cup soccer championship, America had no great reputation in the sport. How timely, therefore, that the American ladies should win the first ever women's world football championship. Their experienced front three, Michelle Akers-Stahl, April Heindrichs and Corin Jennings, scored prolifically throughout the qualifying rounds, in which the USA amassed 49 goals without reply. In the finals they won six successive victories and scored 25 times with only five against. A hat-trick by Jennings gave them a 5–2 win over Germany in the semi-final, but they were given a hard fight in the final by Norway. Their 2–1 win in China's Canton stadium, before a 67,000-strong crowd, owed much to talented young mid-fielders Kris Lilly, Mia Hamm and Julie Foudy. But the winning goals came from Akers-Stahl, whose ten goals overall won her the Golden Boot prize as highest scorer in the finals.

XVIII ECONOMIC AND SOCIAL AFFAIRS

1. ECONOMY OF THE USSR/CIS

THE economies of the countries which changed from being the USSR into a new Commonwealth of Independent States (CIS) by the end of 1991 continued to deteriorate in spite of an improvement in the political situation (see IV.2.i). Economic growth had been slowing since the early 1970s, as the command economy started breaking down without anything new being put in its place. In 1990 this turned into a contraction of 6.4 per cent, with a 20 per cent fall in net fixed investment. In 1991 the whole economy of the USSR contracted by an estimated 17 per cent accompanied by a surge in inflation from 10 per cent to 250 per cent, as the price controls of more than 40 years began to be lifted. As Soviet economist Andrei Anikin observed: 'The disintegration of the economy was happening periodically before; now it is happening like an avalanche.'

In a report circulated at the beginning of the year the International Monetary Fund noted that, despite being rich in most natural resources like oil, the Soviet economy was in such a bad state that it could not be reformed without an initial decline in output and employment. Its recommendations included a very sharp reduction in the budget deficit (then 8 per cent of gross domestic product), absorption of excess money holdings (estimated at 250,000 million roubles), a clampdown on credit creation and steps towards positive real interest rates. This was to be accompanied by price liberalization, privatization, trade reforms and changes in the foreign-exchange market. However, political problems (particularly the accelerating disintegration of the Soviet Union and the attempted coup against President Gorbachev) prevented this and the later Yavlinsky Plan from being implemented. The Yavlinsky Plan called for financial assistance from the West in the form of humanitarian aid and foreign currency to support the balance of payments. It pointed out that the West spent more than $250,000 million annually defending itself against Soviet military threats, which were now evaporating. It argued that a small proportion of the 'peace dividend' should be spent on economic assistance to protect the Soviet Union from economic disintegration and civil war.

Some progress was made during the year, including a partial removal of subsidies in April—which trebled the price of meat and more than doubled the price of bread—but political instability prevented radical reforms. During the year earnings from foreign trade fell and imports dropped by 45 per cent compared with 1990, exacerbating already serious shortages of food. The economic crisis also expressed itself in the form of a huge budget deficit, hyper-inflation, empty shops and a near total collapse of the currency. By the end of the year the market rate of 100 roubles to the US dollar valued the weekly salary of a deputy prime minister at about $6. In the powerful military-industrial complex (employing 60 per cent of the workforce in the Moscow area) the problems were compounded by the rapid run-down of military production following the end of the Cold War. Although the military-industrial complex already manufactured consumer goods (including nearly all of the country's television sets and refrigerators), the prospect of turning mainstream military production lines into consumer electronics products presented extreme difficulties.

Fiscal and monetary policy were also in disarray throughout the year. The State Bank had to cover government spending growing much faster than income from taxes, which were being held back by the republics. Government revenues were also curtailed by the collapse of economic growth. Unsurprisingly, the factories which increased production most rapidly in 1990 were those printing money for the government.

It was only at the end of the year that the *perestroika* which former President Mikhail Gorbachev had often talked about, but had failed to deliver, started to be implemented. Following the declaration of the new Commonwealth in December, Boris Yeltsin's government in Russia, by far the largest of the ex-Soviet republics, embarked on one of the most sweeping economic reform programmes ever attempted anywhere in the world. It included the freeing of most prices, an attempt to balance the budget (by removing subsidies and imposing VAT), a big step towards making foreign-exchange earnings fully convertible, and an acceleration of the massive plan for privatization. To mitigate the effects of the programme on poorer people, the government announced that pensions and child support would be raised by 90 per cent.

At the end of 1991 this ambitious plan was still lacking the vital ingredient which gave credibility to Poland's 'shock therapy' two years earlier (see AR 1990, pp. 536–8). Despite public pleas by President Yeltsin for an internationally-backed stabilization programme, the West was not keen to get involved. The plan had three strands involving external economic relations. The first was to bolster Russia's reserves of foreign exchange, which had been drained out completely. The second was to obtain balance-of-payments support to enable the country to buy vital imports. The third was the need for food and humanitarian aid, which the West did provide in limited quantities. It was clear that Russia needed a stabilization fund in order to restore faith in its currency. If all went well, it was argued, the stabilization fund (as had happened in Poland) would not be needed because its mere existence would flush out all the dollars held in secret places as a hedge against inflation.

Experts estimated that the cost of such a stabilization programme for Russia would be some $17,000 million, or less than 7 per cent of the amount the Western nations were spending annually to defend themselves against a military threat which no longer existed. However, President Bush of the USA was reluctant to get into a new international commitment while he was fighting a re-election campaign which put him under great pressure to do more at home. The other big potential contributor, Japan, was also preoccupied with internal domestic politics and was, anyway, reluctant to help Russia until its claims to the southern Kurile Islands had been settled (see IX.2.iv). By the end of 1991 the economic outlook for Russia was looking increasingly bleak.

2. THE INTERNATIONAL ECONOMY

THE economies of the 24-member OECD bloc of industrialized countries expanded by a disappointing 1.1 per cent in 1991 (see also XI.4.i). This compared with a forecast of 2.0 per cent made a year earlier and marked the worst performance since 1982 when negative growth of 0.1 per cent had been recorded. The shortfall was mainly the result of a contraction of 0.7 per cent in the economy of the United States. Both Japan and Germany (the latter boosted by the initial effects of reunification) grew faster than expected. The slowdown was accompanied by a mild improvement in inflation from 4.3 to 4.2 per cent in 1991 and a rise in unemployment (from 6.3 to 7.1 per cent) following seven successive years of reduction. The OECD's aggregate trade deficit fell in 1991, mainly because sharp US and Japanese improvements offset an equally sharp deterioration in Germany. World trade (imports and exports) increased by only 3.3 per cent in 1991 compared with 5.2 per cent in 1990.

Once again the economies of the Far East (most of which, apart from Japan, Australia and New Zealand, were not included in the OECD figures) expanded much faster than the West. China, Indonesia, Malaysia, Singapore, South Korea, Taiwan and Thailand all experienced growth of 6 per cent or more during 1991, apparently unconcerned by the contraction of the biggest market in the world in the United States. Taiwan, a relatively small economy, had foreign-exchange reserves worth $68,000 million at the end of the year, following 11 successive years of trade surplus. This was the second biggest in the world after Japan's $70,000 million. The worst performing area was Eastern Europe, where the problems of adapting from a planned to a market economy produced high unemployment and negative growth of between 2 and 12 per cent in Poland, Czechoslovakia, Hungary and the former USSR.

Among Arab countries, Saudi Arabia fared among the best with economic growth of 8.5 per cent, according to estimates made by the Economist Intelligence Unit (EIU), coupled with inflation of 3.8 per cent. Kuwait was estimated to have expanded by 24 per cent, but from an exceptionally low base level because of effects of the Gulf War. The same conflict saw Iraq's economy contract by an estimated 50 per cent in 1991, following a 25 per cent contraction the previous year, and its inflation rate over the year was estimated at 500 per cent (see also V.4.vi). Elsewhere, according to the EIU, the UAE grew by 6.9 per cent, Egypt by 1.6 per cent, Morocco by 4.5 per cent, Algeria by 2.9 per cent and Tunisia by 2.1 per cent.

In South America Brazil struggled with hyperinflation running at 500 per cent a year, but Argentina's plan of April 1991 succeeded in bringing inflation down to 1.4 per cent in the month of October amid signs of reviving economic activity and an emerging budget surplus. Growth also recovered in Chile, Mexico, Bolivia and Venezuela following the adoption of stabilization programmes.

The biggest rise in stock markets was recorded in Hong Kong, whose bourse rose by 40.7 per cent during the year, followed by Milan (30.8 per cent) and then by Singapore and Australia (at 29 per cent). The bourse with the highest capitalization was Wall Street. It had been overtaken by Tokyo in 1987, but managed to recapture its historic role in 1991 thanks to a 20 per cent rise, while stocks in Tokyo fell by 3.6 per cent.

MONETARY AND FISCAL POLICIES. Monetary policies were eased in the two biggest economies, the United States and Japan, in an attempt to offset a slowdown in economic activity, but interest rates were raised in Germany as the Bundesbank tried to cool down the pressure for increased wages in the wake of reunification. The easing of monetary policy was accompanied by increased permissiveness in fiscal policy. The steady fall in government deficits as a percentage of GNP, which had been such a feature of the 1980s, had ended in 1989; thereafter, the average OECD deficit increased from 1.1 per cent of GNP in 1990 to 2.3 per cent in 1991. The main problems were in Germany, where the difficulty of digesting the eastern sector pushed the government's financial balance from a surplus (excess of income over spending) in 1989 to deficits of 2.5 per cent and 3.7 per cent in 1990 and 1991 respectively. The budget deficit of the United States worsened from 2.4 to 2.7 per cent of GNP in 1991 despite efforts to reduce it.

INTERNATIONAL TRADE. The expansion of the volume of world trade slowed down to 3.3 per cent in 1991, though there were signs of a recovery during the second half of the year. This followed growth of 5.2 per cent and 7.0 per cent in 1990 and 1991 respectively. Exports within the OECD area rose by 2.5 per cent, while imports increased by 3.1 per cent. Exports to non-OECD countries rose by 5.7 per cent. A feature of the year was a 13 per cent rise in imports into Germany, where reunification had caused German companies to shift their efforts from exports to satisfying the newly-expanded home market.

The OECD's trade deficit with the rest of the world improved from $102,000 million in 1990 to $15,000 million in 1991. Markedly improved performances by Japan and the United States were only partially offset by Germany's deficit of $21,000 million (against a surplus of $48,000 million in 1990, before the effects of reunification had had time to take their toll). The biggest current-account surplus among OECD nations (as a percentage of GNP) was recorded by Norway (5.5 per cent) and the worst by Finland (minus 4.7 per cent).

ECONOMIC SUMMIT. The 1991 economic summit of the seven leading industrialized nations (USA, Japan, Germany, France, Italy, UK and Canada) was dominated by two items. The first (not on the official agenda) was the problem of how to help the collapsing Soviet economy as it tried to move from communism to capitalism (see previous chapter). The summit agreed to set up a special committee to monitor events in the Soviet Union, but declined to extend financial aid on a grand scale in the form of a latter-day Marshall Plan. The second priority was the need to reach agreement on the GATT Uruguay Round of trade talks designed to reduce tariff barriers around the world. These talks should have been completed the previous January, but had become stalled on the question of agricultural protectionism. The United States wanted a clear-cut commitment that the European Community would make significant reductions in its huge agricultural subsidies, before it would accept the rest of the package. By the end of 1991 no agreement was in sight.

NOBEL PRIZE FOR ECONOMICS. The 1991 prize was awarded to Professor Ronald Coase (81) of the University of Chicago Law School. Professor Coase, who was born in Britain, proved a popular winner not least because he wrote his work in understandable prose, which some found a welcome relief from the mathematical abstruseness of earlier winners. One of his pioneering works (*The Problem of Social Cost*), published in 1960, explored how conflicts over the use of resources (e.g. if sparks from a locomotive ignited a farmer's field) could be resolved by the buying and selling of property rights rather than by the intervention of the law.

3. THE ECONOMY OF THE UNITED STATES

THE US economy experienced negative growth of 0.7 per cent in 1991, the first shrinkage for nine years, ending the longest expansionary period in peacetime (see also II.1). During the first quarter of the year there was a drop in output of 2.5 per cent (annualized); but by the fourth quarter it had recovered to positive annualized growth of 0.3 per cent, amid signs that the economy was responding to the sharp reduction in interest rates during the year.

The partial recovery late in the year was the result of higher exports and home construction offset by weakness in consumer spending and business investment. Consumer price inflation slowed down to 2.9 per cent in 1991 from 6.2 per cent in 1990 as a result of the Federal Reserve Board's three-year-old 'high wire' policy of seeking to reduce inflation while attempting to avoid a serious recession. The moderation in inflation was helped by the post-Gulf War fall in oil prices and by a sharp deceleration (from 5.2 per cent to 1.6 per cent) in food price increases. Wage pressure moderated from 4 per cent to 3 per cent amid a continuing shake-out of labour.

Fiscal policy, once again, was dominated by the need to get America's ballooning budget deficit down to a manageable level, if not to eliminate it altogether as the Budget Act required. In fact, the deficit rose (from $220,000 million to $269,000 million) even after adding in a $52,000 million surplus on the social security budget. In the private sector the destabilizing growth of debt was reduced as companies started to rebuild the battered balance sheets of the 1980s.

The deficit on the current account of the balance of payments dropped (for the fourth successive year) from $92,000 million in 1990 to only $4,000 million in 1991, thanks to the depressing effect of the recession on imports and to US exports' retaining their improved competitiveness. Unemployment worsened from 5.5 per cent to 6.7 per cent as companies shed labour to offset the effects of the economic slowdown.

OUTPUT AND EMPLOYMENT. With the domestic economy dead in the water, the main propellent of growth, once again, was exports, which managed to expand by 6.9 per cent in value during the year, as against an increase of 2.7 per cent in imports. After allowing for inflation, exports grew by 3.9 per cent and imports by 1.2 per cent. Private sector consumption increased by a very modest 0.3 per cent (in volume terms) and government spending by 0.7 per cent. Every other sector of the economy contracted, notably private sector residential investment, which fell by 11.4 per cent.

Total output rose in the third quarter after three successive declines, helped by the unwinding of the negative economic effects of the Gulf crisis, including a temporary oil price rise and depressed business and consumer confidence. However, a continuing modest recovery in the fourth quarter was not enough to prevent the economy from registering negative growth for the year as a whole. At the end of the year there were fears that the USA had entered the second leg of a 'double dip' recession which could postpone the recovery of world output. For its part, the Fed was confident that output would soon respond to the reduction of interest rates. Employment dropped by 0.5 per cent during 1991, following eight years of continuous growth.

GOVERNMENT POLICY. The easing of monetary policy, which could be traced back to 1989 but which began in earnest in 1990 (see AR 1990, p. 542), continued throughout 1991 as the Fed tried to massage some growth into the economy without reawakening inflationary pressures. By the middle of the year it looked as though the money supply (as measured by M_2) was responding to treatment. But in August monetary growth stalled again amid signs that bank lending was contracting. People appeared to be using the opportunity of lower interest rates to repay their (very high) consumer debts. Since the start of the recession in the summer of 1990, the Fed had eased monetary policy more than a dozen times, including reducing the federal funds rate by 375 basis points. This culminated in a reduction from 4.75 per cent to 4.5 per cent on 6 December 1991. In the same month, the Fed's discount rate was cut to 3.5 per cent. By the end of the year the economy was still locked in the doldrums, but the Fed was reluctant to make further cuts because it believed that previous cuts had stoked up an undercurrent of growth which had not yet emerged from the pipeline.

By the end of the year pressures were also building up for a relaxation of fiscal policy and, in particular, the spending of an increased share of the 'peace dividend' arising from the end of the Cold War with the Soviet Union. This would have the happy effect of boosting the popularity of the Republican Party and of President Bush in the forthcoming congressional and presidential elections. In these circumstances, there was little hope of avoiding a further substantial increase in the budget deficit during 1992, even after allowing for $60,000 billion of expenditure cuts which had not yet been enacted. The ambition of the previous President, Ronald Reagan, to eliminate the deficit entirely by 1993, was now deemed to be impossible.

4. THE ECONOMY OF THE UNITED KINGDOM

THE UK economy contracted by an estimated 2.5 per cent in 1991, after growth of just under 1 per cent the previous year. It was the first year of negative growth since 1981 and marked the end of nine years of continuous expansion, the longest period of uninterrupted growth since the 1960s. The outcome for 1991 was a little worse than the government's (revised) estimates in the March 1991 budget statement, but considerably below the forecasts published in November 1990, when positive economic growth of 0.5 per cent had been envisaged for 1991.

This growth did not materialize because companies cut back sharply on their investment plans in order to rebuild their depleted balance sheets (which at one stage showed record net borrowing of almost £25,000 million). At the same time, the much-mooted revival of consumer spending failed to happen—because potential spenders had become so indebted (mainly on account of mortgage loans tied to their homes) that they were reluctant to borrow any more as long as house prices remained depressed. As a result consumer spending, instead of rising by the forecast 2.5 per cent during 1991, fell by 1.3 per cent in the first half of the year. Investment (in the public and private sectors) fell by 11 per cent in 1991 instead of only 1.5 per cent as had been expected in November 1990.

Most of the fall in output was concentrated in the early months of the year; by the second half, there were signs that the worst was over even though the much-predicted recovery was not yet evident. The main feature of the year was the sharp drop in bank base rates associated with the UK's first year of membership of Europe's fixed exchange rate mechanism (ERM). Interest rates fell from 15 per cent in October 1990, when Britain joined the ERM, to 10.5 per cent in December 1991. However, because of an even steeper fall in retail price inflation (from 10.9 per cent in October 1990 to 4.3 per cent in November 1991), real interest rates still remained stubbornly high.

OUTPUT AND EMPLOYMENT. Unemployment rose every month during 1991 as the recession tightened its grip, to reach 2,604,000 in December (after seasonal adjustments), representing 9.2 per cent of the registered workforce and the highest total for over four years. The recession also brought about a fall of 873,000 in the number of people in employment (to 25.9 million) in the year to September. Just over 500,000 of this reduction was in full-time male jobs, the remainder being in (mainly) part-time female jobs.

Industrial production in the three months to December was 0.5 per cent lower than a year earlier. A decline of 3.5 per cent in manufacturing output was offset by a 7.5 per cent recovery in energy output, partly as a result of North Sea oil platforms coming back on stream after repairs. The fall in overall production concealed some sharp contrasts between sectors. Chemicals and man-made fibres expanded output by 9.1 per cent in the year to December, compared with an 6.6 per cent fall in engineering output and a 6.3 per cent fall in textiles. Investment by manufacturing industry fell by 15 per cent during the year to a level 6.3 per cent below what it was in 1979. Total output in the economy (at constant 1985 factor costs) was 2.4 per cent lower in the calendar year 1991 compared with 1990.

COSTS AND PRICES. The strong inflationary pressures of the previous year abated during 1991 in response to high real interest rates and growing unemployment. The annual rise in retail prices fell from 9 per cent in January to 4.5 per cent in December (having dipped briefly to 3.7 per cent in October). Part of this improvement was due to falling mortgage interest payments. If these were excluded, then the 'underlying' year-on-year rate of inflation was estimated to be 5.8 per cent in November. The outlook for 'input' inflation was rather better, to the extent that the index measuring the cost of industrial raw materials fell by 1 per cent in the year to December.

The annual rate of increase in average earnings fell from 9.75 per cent to 7.25 per cent (in the year to December), still some way above the levels of leading European countries with which the UK would increasingly have to compete. Towards the end of the year there were signs that productivity was improving. The rate of increase in manufacturers' wages and salaries per unit of output fell from 11.6 per cent in April 1991 to 5.0 per cent in November—mainly due to labour-shedding by companies gripped by the recession.

GOVERNMENT POLICY. Monetary policy for much of the year was aimed at keeping sterling as close as possible to the central parity of the ERM (2.95 Deutschmarks to the pound), as a shadowing exercise against the day when the UK moved to the narrower (plus or minus 2.25 per cent) band of the ERM. Britain's entry into the ERM removed most of the 'risk premium' which sterling had carried in the markets. This enabled the authorities to reduce bank base rates in stages (generally following market movements rather than anticipating them) from 15 per cent in January to 10.5 per cent in September. But inflation fell even faster over this period, so real interest rates remained at very high levels, causing distress to over-stretched corporate and personal borrowers. Both the narrow and broad measures of money supply expanded at less than the rate of inflation for most of the year, reflecting the severity of the squeeze. By the end of the year, as the threat of a more prolonged recession loomed, there were increased calls from industry for a relaxation of policy. Credit growth was constrained by the need of banks and individuals to lower their exposure to high-interest debt.

Fiscal policy was broadly neutral in the March 1991 budget (see I.2), which raised VAT from 15 to 17.5 per cent to finance reductions in the community charge (poll tax) and also squeezed company perks. The Autumn Statement accommodated the rise in public spending associated with the recession (such as higher social benefits) while targeting more money to politically-sensitive areas like health. These measures were partly financed by increased projected revenues from privatization proceeds, but mainly by increased government borrowing. In the first nine months of the 1991/92 financial year the public sector borrowing requirement (PSBR) rose to £10,500 million, compared with £2,100 million in 1990/91.

An important feature of the year was the special package negotiated by Prime Minister Major at the Maastricht EC summit in the Netherlands in December. Britain secured agreement from its partners to be able to seek a parliamentary vote before becoming committed to adopting a single European currency later in the decade and also gained exemption from the European Social Charter, whose provisions on working conditions and other matters were deemed potentially harmful by the Conservative government (see I.6, XI.3 and XV.1.ii).

EXTERNAL TRADE. Britain's current-account deficit was £4,800 million in the year to December. This was an improvement on the £15,200 million recorded during 1990, but marked the fifth consecutive year of deficit. The improvement was mainly due to a 4.5 per cent increase in the volume of exports, combined with a modest 1.5 per cent rise in import volume due to the squeeze on consumer spending. One of the features of the year was a sharp rise in exports of motor vehicles, which rose 61 per cent in the year to July. This was due to a combination of permanent factors, notably the increased export output from the new Japanese plants, and temporary ones, such as the decision of multinational groups to divert output from a stagnant UK market to a still-booming European market, particularly in Germany. The boom subsided later in the year, when Europe joined the UK in recession and when the gloomier prospects of growth in the United States diminished the opportunities for strong export growth during 1992.

From a structural point of view, the existence of a deficit at all at this stage in the economic cycle was disappointing. UBS Phillips and Drew, the City analysts, estimated that every other recession year since 1945 had produced a current-account surplus (excluding oil) averaging 1.75 per cent of GDP. In 1991 the current account (on the same basis) was in deficit by 1.75 per cent of GDP. On a more positive note, the UK's trade deficit in manufactured goods, which had been as high as £17,000 million as recently as 1989, was reduced to a little over £3,400 million in 1991.

5. ECONOMIC AND SOCIAL DATA

The statistical data on the following pages record developments from 1986 to the latest year, usually 1991, for which reasonably stable figures were available at the time of going to press. Year headings 1986 to 1991 are printed only at the head of each page and are not repeated over individual tables unless the sequence is broken by extending series of figures over a longer period than elsewhere on the page.

Pages to which the point is relevant include a comparative price index, allowing the current-price figures to be adjusted in accordance with changing values of money.

Unless figures are stated as indicating the position at the *end* of year, they should be taken as annual *totals* or *averages*, according to context.

Tables 2, 3, 4 and 5. Statistics which are normally reported or collected separately in the three UK home jurisdictions (England and Wales, Scotland, and Northern Ireland) have been consolidated into UK series only to show general trends. As the component returns were made at varying times of year and in accordance with differing definitions and regulatory requirements, the series thus consolidated may therefore be subject to error, may not be strictly comparable from year to year, and may be less reliable than the remainder of the data.

Symbols: — = Nil or not applicable .. = not available at time of compilation.

Sources

A. **THE UNITED KINGDOM**
   GOVERNMENT SOURCES
   Annual Abstract of Statistics: Tables 1, 2, 3, 4, 5.
   Monthly Digest of Statistics: Tables 1, 11, 17, 18, 23, 24, 25.
   Financial Statistics: Tables 9, 11, 12, 13, 14, 15, 16, 26.
   Economic Trends: Tables 6, 7, 8, 9, 11, 26.
   Social Trends: Tables 2, 3, 4, 5, 10.
   Department of Employment Gazette: Tables 19, 20, 21, 22.
   Housing and Construction Statistics: Table 5.
   ADDITIONAL SOURCES
   National Institute of Economic and Social Research, *National Institute Economic Review*: Tables 6, 7, 8.
   United Nations: *Monthly Bulletin of Statistics*: Table 1.
   The Financial Times: Tables 13, 15.

B. **THE UNITED STATES**
   GOVERNMENT AND OTHER PUBLIC SOURCES
   Department of Commerce, *Survey of Current Business*: Tables 27, 28, 29, 30, 31, 32, 37, 38, 40.
   Council of Economic Advisers, Joint Economic Committee, *Economic Indicators*: Tables 30, 36.
   Federal Reserve Bulletin: Tables 33, 34, 35.
   ADDITIONAL SOURCES
   A. M. Best Co.: Table 35.
   Insurance Information Institute, New York: Table 35.
   Monthly Labor Review: Tables 38, 39.
   Bureau of Economic Statistics, *Basic Economic Statistics*: Table 39.

C. **INTERNATIONAL COMPARISONS**
   United Nations, *Economic Commission for Europe*: Table 44.
   UN, *Monthly Bulletin of Statistics*: Tables 41, 42.
   World Bank, *World Development Report*: Table 41.
   IMF, *International Financial Statistics*: Tables 41, 43, 44, 45, 46, 47, 48, 49.
   OECD, *Main Economic Indicators*: Table 42.
   Stockholm International Peace Research Institute, *Yearbook*: Table 50.
   OECD, *Labour Force Statistics*: Table 51.

ECONOMIC AND SOCIAL DATA
A. THE UNITED KINGDOM

SOCIAL

1. Population

	1986	1987	1988	1989	1990	1991
Population, mid-year est. ('000)	56,763	56,930	57,065	57,236	57,411	..
Crude birth rate (per 1,000 pop.)	13·3	13·6	13·8	13·6	13·9	..
Crude death rate (per 1,000 pop.)	11·6	11·3	11·4	11·5	11·2	..
Net migration ('000)	+37	+2	−21	+44	+36	..

2. Health

Hospitals:						
staffed beds, end-year ('000)	409·9	388·7	372·9	362·5	337.0	..
waiting list, end-year ('000)(1)	831	806	828	827·0	841·2	830.1
Certifications of death ('000)(2) by:						
ischaemic heart disease	176·8	173·6	171·0	173·4	169.5	..
malignant neoplasm, lungs and bronchus	39·4	39·4	39·4	39·6	39.3	..
road fatality	5·5	5·4	5·1	5·5	5.7	..
accidents at work (number)	537	525	610	475	..	..

(1) End Sept. except 1991, March.
(2) Great Britain.

3. Education

Schools ('000)	35·6	35·4	35·2	34·9	34.8	..
Pupils enrolled ('000) in schools	9,385	9,246	9,101	9,203	9,199	..
maintained primary(1)	4,521	4,550	4,599	4,024	4,807	..
maintained and aided secondary	4,080	3,902	3,701	3,551	3,848	..
assisted and independent	607	619	635	641	613	..
Further education: institutions (number)	3,627	3,252	3,356	3,508	3,318	..
full-time students ('000)	608	624	633	646	690	..
Universities	46	46	46	46	46	..
University students ('000)	310	316	321	334	351	..
First degrees awarded (number)	70,912	71,817	73,756	74,953	..	..
Open University graduates ('000)	8·0	8·0	8·0	8.1	8.1	8.3

(1) Including nursery schools.

4. Law and Order

Police ('000)						
Full-time strength(1)	135·3	136·2	137·3	138·0	139.6	..
Ulster, full-time strength	8·2	8·2	8·2	8·3	8.2	..
Serious offences known to police ('000)(2)	4,324	4,437	4,241·7	4,419·4	5,090.1	..
Persons convicted, all offences ('000)(2)	2,118	1,779	1,777	1,7444	..	..
Burglary or robbery(3)	63	61·4	54·5	49·6	..	..
Handling stolen goods/receiving, theft	187	180	167	138	..	..
Violence against person	44	49	64	57·1	..	..
Traffic offences	1,120	795	774	760	..	..
All summary offences	1,542	1,202	1,204	1,224	..	..
Prisons: average population ('000)	54·3	56·4	57·1	55·41	52.15	..

(1) Police full-time strength: Great Britain only. (2) Because of differences in juridical and penal systems in the three UK jurisdictions, totals of offences are not strictly comparable from year to year: they should be read only as indicating broad trends. (3) Specific offences: England, Wales and N. Ireland.

Overall price index (1985=100)	102·7	107·9	114·9	123·4	133·9	143.0

XVIII.5.A UNITED KINGDOM STATISTICS

	1986	1987	1988	1989	1990	1991
5. Housing						
Dwellings completed ('000)						
by and for public sector(1)	35	34	30	30	33	29
by private sector	167	178	185	177	154	147
Homeless households ('000)(2)	112	118	123	135	156	..
Housing land, private sector,						
weighted ave. price (£/hectare)	231,530	334,070	438,370	430,390	320,960	..
Dwelling prices, average (£)(3)	38,121	44,220	54,280	62,134	66,695	..

(1) Including government departments (police houses, military married quarters, etc.) and approved housing associations and trusts. (2) Accepted by local authorities as in priority need. (3) Of properties newly mortgaged by building societies.

PRICES, INCOME AND EXPENDITURE

6. National Income and Expenditure
(£ million, 1985 prices)

	1986	1987	1988	1989	1990	1991
GDP(1), expenditure basis	317,987	332,179	345,918	353,493	356,332	347,800
income basis(2)	326,963	364,036	404,390	444,106	483,978	..
output basis (1985=100)	103·0	108·1	112·7	115·3	116·6	113·5
average estimate (1985=100)	103·6	108·3	112·8	115·3	116·3	..
Components of gross domestic product:						
Consumers' expenditure	231,172	243,279	261,330	270,575	273,204	267,800
General government consumption	75,106	76,034	76,486	77,182	79,513	81,000
Gross fixed investment	61,813	67,753	76,648	81,845	80,040	70,900
Total final expenditure	475,880	501,318	531,645	550,199	556,042	542,300
Stockbuilding	737	1,158	4,031	2,668	−374	−2,300
Adjustment to factor cost	52,312	55,539	58,312	59,974	60,586	59,600

(1) At factor cost. (2) Current prices, £ 000 million.

7. Fixed Investment
(£ million, 1985 prices, seasonally adjusted)

	1986	1987	1988	1989	1990	1991
Total, all fixed investment	61,813	67,753	76,648	81,845	80,040	70,900
Dwellings	13,622	15,274	18,857	20,076	18,449	..
Private sector	48,937	55,807	65,614	68,907	66,290	..
manufacturing	9,423	10,048	11,198	12,386	12,142	..
other	39,514	45,759	54,416	56,521	54,148	..
Government and public corporations	12,876	11,946	11,034	12,938	13,603	..

8. Personal Income and Expenditure
(£ million, seasonally adjusted, current prices unless otherwise stated)

	1986	1987	1988	1989	1990	1991
Wages, salaries and forces' pay	183,131	200,143	223,250	248,537	275,257	289,791
Current grants	50,920	52,494	54,087	56,793	61,942	71,701
Other personal income(1)	68,453	74,561	87,045	100,662	115,085	118,914
Personal disposable income	263,594	284,608	315,983	351,438	383,020	410,029
Real personal disposable income(2)	252,286	261,301	276,628	291,266	299,685	298,759
Consumers' expenditure	239,535	264,120	296,165	324,348	349,108	368,091
Personal savings ratio(3)	8·5	6·9	5·4	7·1	8·8	10·2

(1) From rent, self-employment (before depreciation and stock appreciation provisions), dividend and interest receipts and charitable receipts from companies. (2) At 1985 prices. (3) Personal savings as % of personal disposable income.

	1986	1987	1988	1989	1990	1991
Overall price index (1985=100)	102·7	107·9	114·9	123·4	133·9	143·0

XVIII ECONOMIC AND SOCIAL AFFAIRS

9. Government Finance(1)
(£ million)

	1986	1987	1988	1989	1990	1991
Revenue(2)	151,305	158,801	174,457	191,371	205,485	220,347
taxes on income	52,442	52,464	58,459	63,015	71,030	77,387
corporation tax	10,708	13,495	15,734	18,537	21,495	21,495
taxes on expenditure	57,687	63,881	69,780	77,190	81,455	77,343
value added tax	19,329	21,377	24,067	27,328	29,483	31,006
taxes on capital(3)	2,356	3,034	3,733	4,118	4,014	3,497
Expenditure(4)	159,776	168,829	177,754	184,592	205,034	222,434
net lending(5)	−2,119	−3,918	−5,231	−5,354	−6,104	−6,404
Deficit(−) or surplus	−8,471	−10,028	−3,297	+6,779	+451	−2,087

(1) Financial years ended 5 April of year indicated. (2) Total current receipts, taxes on capital and other capital receipts. (3) Capital gains, capital transfer tax, estate duty. (4) Total government expenditure, gross domestic capital formation and grants. (5) To private sector, public corporations, and overseas.

10. Public Expenditure
(£ billion, constant 90–91 prices)

	1986	1987	1988	1989	1990	1991
Health and personal social services	29·0	30·3	31·2	32·0	33·0	34·9
Social security	60·9	60·3	57·7	57·5	58·8	64·8
Education	25·9	26·8	27·0	28·4	28·4	29·0
Housing	5·3	5·2	3·8	5·7	4·9	5·5
Defence	23·7	23·3	22·0	22·5	21·8	21·4
Law and order	9·2	9·8	10·1	10·9	11·4	12·0

11. Prices and Costs (index 1985=100)

	1986	1987	1988	1989	1990	1991
Total UK costs per unit of output(1)	102·7	107·9	114·9	123·4	133·9	143·0
Labour costs per unit of output	105·0	109·5	117·2	128·0	141·8	..
Mfg. wages/salaries per unit of output	104·0	105·9	108·6	113·6	123·7	133·4
Import unit values	95·7	98·2	97·5	103·2	107·9	108·4
Wholesale prices, manufactures	104·3	108·3	113·2	119·0	126·0	133·1
Consumer prices	103·4	107·7	113·0	121·8	133·3	141·1
Tax and prices	101·9	104·5	107·5	115·0	124·5	126·2

(1) Used as 'Overall price index' on all pages of UK statistics.

FINANCIAL

12. Monetary Sector(1)
(£ million, amounts outstanding at end of period)

	1986	1987	1988	1989	1990	1991
Notes and coins in circulation	12,824	13,592	14,755	15,362	15,256	15,734
M_0(2) (average)	15,159	15,894	16,377	17,312	18,340	18,859
M_2(3)	168,882	187,104	213,678	234,814	253,403	276,390
M_4(4)	261,073	303,753	357,218	424,017	474,107	501,403
Deposits						
domestic	173,802	210,720	252,108	336,108	372,783	366,201
overseas	493,401	474,211	511,672	610,069	588,277	562,361
Domestic lending						
private sector	206,555	250,782	318,763	432,941	470,461	466,142
public sector	18,102	17,021	15,153	15,140	14,252	14,051
Overseas lending	479,735	460,772	483,726	566,377	545,186	517,283

(1) Institutions recognized as banks or licensed deposit-takers, plus Bank of England banking dept. and other institutions adhering to monetary control arrangements. (2) M_0=Notes and coins in circulation plus banks' till money plus bankers' balance with Bank of England. (3) M_2=Notes and coin plus sterling retail deposits with banks and building societies. (4) M_4= Notes and coin plus all sterling deposits held with UK banks and building societies.

Overall price index (1985=100)	102·7	107·9	114·9	123·4	133·9	143·0

XVIII.5.A UNITED KINGDOM STATISTICS

	1986	1987	1988	1989	1990	1991

13. Interest Rates and Security Yields(1)
(% per annum, end of year)

Treasury bill yield	10·69	8·37	12·91	14·63	13·44	11·00
London clearing banks base rate	11·00	8·50	13·00	15·00	14·00	10·50
2½% consols, gross flat yield(2)	9·47	9·31	9·12	9·22	10·84	9·98
10-year government securities(2)	10·05	9·57	9·67	10·18	11·80	10·11
Ordinary shares, dividend yield(2)	4·01	3·50	4·32	4·24	5·03	4·93
Interbank 3-month deposits	11·25	8·87	12·94	15·13	14·03	10·94
Clearing bank 7-day deposits	6·92	3·58	5·97	6·59	5·11	4·00

(1) Gross redemption yields, unless stated otherwise. For building societies see Table 16. (2) Average during year.

14. Companies
(£ million unless stated)

Total income	67,696	80,794	93,185	103,269	113,982	106,514
Gross trading profit in UK	51,987	61,470	70,136	72,169	74,681	73,359
Total overseas income	7,997	11,386	14,343	18,257	19,244	16,441
Dividends on ord. shares	8,381	11,060	14,669	19,001	22,060	21,803
Net profit	30,617	37,907	42,239	38,046	36,166	35,838
Companies taken over (number)	842	1,527	1,499	1,336	776	..
Total take-over consideration	15,363	16,486	22,742	27,054	8,235	..
Liquidations (number)(1)	14,405	11,439	9,427	10,456	15,051	21,827
Receiverships (number)(1)	7,155	6,994	7,717	8,138	12,058	22,632

(1) England and Wales.

15. The Stock Market
(£ million, unless otherwise stated)

Turnover (£000 mn.)	646·3	1,757·5	1,602·8	1,627·3	1,655·0	1,814·0
ordinary shares (£000 mn.) (4)	181·2	496·1	405·2	564·6	316·0	360·5
New issues, less redemptions(value)						
Government securities	7,169	5,425	−266	−14,113	−8,824	6,384
Local authority issues(1)	−202	−177	−34	−11	−35	−2
UK companies	9,055	15,376	6,693	6,827	2,637	10,445
FT ordinary share index (1935=100)(2)	1,287·11	1,600·01	1,448·73	1,781·41	1,749·4	1,921·9
FT-Actuaries index (750 shares)(3)	782·10	1,025·07	931·67	1,110·29	1,092·4	1,187·3
Industrial, 500 shares	858·57	1,133·51	1,019·76	1,221·71	1,199·1	1,316·5
Financial, 100 shares	590·05	725·37	679·99	763·45	761·6	784·3

(1) Includes public corporation issues. (2) Average during year. (3) 1962=100.
(4) From 1990, UK and Irish only.

16. Building Societies

Interest rates (%): end year:

Paid on shares, ave. actual	8·14	6·51	8·38	9·96	10·06	7·27
Basic rate	5·99	4·02	5·59	6·57	5·77	2·35
Mortgages, ave. charged	12·32	10·34	12·75	14·44	14·34	11·39
Basic rate	12·30	10·30	12·77	14·42	14·48	11·52
Shares and deposits, net (£ min.)	6,592	7,561	13,214	7,735	6,562	6,006
Mortgage advances, net (£ min.)	19,541	15,390	24,737	24,041	24,090	21,039

Overall price index (1985=100)	102·7	107·9	114·9	123·4	133·9	143·0

	1986	1987	1988	1989	1990	1991
17. Industrial Production (Index, average 1985=100, seasonally adjusted)						
All industries	102·2	105·8	109·6	110·0	109·3	106·1
Energy and water	105·0	103·9	99·3	89·8	89·0	92·2
Manufacturing industries	100·9	106·6	114·2	119·0	118·5	112·2
Food, drink and tobacco	100·8	103·2	105·3	105·4	106·3	106·0
Chemicals	101·8	109·0	114·1	119·2	118·3	121·8
Metal manufacture	100·3	108·5	122·0	124·8	121·3	110·4
Engineering and allied	99·1	103·9	112·6	120·3	119·7	110·9
Textiles	100·8	103·9	102·1	98·4	95·9	87·9
Intermediate goods	103·6	106·4	107·9	104·2	103·1	101·6
Consumer goods	101·5	106·8	112·4	114·7	114·0	109·7
Paper, printing, publishing	104·3	114·4	125·0	131·9	133·9	129·1
Construction	103·3	111·4	119·5	124·5	125·7	..
Crude steel (million tonnes)	14·8	17·4	18·9	18·7	17·8	..
Man-made fibres (million tonnes)	0·29	0·27	0·28	0·27	0·27	0·27
Cars ('000)	1,019	1,143	1,227	1,299	1,296	1,237
Motor vehicles, cars imported ('000)(1)	1,054	1,041	1,250	1,310	1,140	..
Commercial vehicles ('000)	229	247	318	327	270	217
Merchant ships(2) completed ('000 gr.t)	106	247	31	106	133	..

(1) Including imported chassis. (2) 100 gross tons and over.

18. Energy

Coal, production (mn. tonnes)	108·1	104·4	104·1	101·1	94·4	96·1
Power station consumption (mn. tonnes)	82·6	86·2	82·5	80·6	82·6	82·0
Electricity generated ('000 mn. kwh.)	282·4	282·7	288·4	292·9	298·5	300·4
by nuclear plant ('000 mn. kwh.)	47·5	44·8	51·7	59·3	55·0	58·5
Natural gas sent out (mn. therms)	19,246	19,814	18,655	18,748	19,373	20,974
Crude oil output ('000 tonnes)(1)	127,200	123,600	114,375	91,800	91,600	91,100
Oil refinery output (mn. tonnes)(2)	69·2	67·7	72·3	73·0	73·9	74·4

(1) Including natural gas liquids. (2) All fuels and other petroleum products.

LABOUR

19. Employment
(millions of persons, in June each year)

Working population(1)	27·86	28·21	28·26	28·50	28·51	28·48
Employed labour force(2)	24·59	24·68	25·92	26·75	26·89	26·17
Employees: production industries	5·66	5·54	5·59	5·55	5·51	5·22
Manufacturing	5·13	5·04	5·12	5·10	5·07	4·78
Transport and communications	1·33	1·33	1·35	1·34	1·35	1·31
Distributive trades	3·49	3·29	3·32	3·41	3·48	3·39
Education and health	3·01	2·91	3·09	3·13	3·16	3·16
Insurance, banking, financial	2·06	2·30	2·44	2·59	2·70	2·60
Public service	1·93	1·98	2·02	1·87	1·89	1·89
Total employees	21·54	21·82	22·10	22·23	22·33	21·66
of whom, females	9·66	9·93	10·16	10·53	10·81	10·61

(1) Including registered unemployed and members of the armed forces. (2) Including employers and self-employed.

Overall price index (1985=100)	102·7	107·9	114·9	123·4	133·9	143·0

XVIII.5.A UNITED KINGDOM STATISTICS

	1986	1987	1988	1989	1990	1991
20. Demand for Labour						
Average index of weekly hours worked, manufacturing industry, 1985=100	96·6	96·1	97·2	96·2	92·4	83·7
Manufacturing employees:						
Total overtime hours worked ('000)(1)	11,720	12,680	13,976	13,380	12,750	10,190
Short time, total hours lost ('000)(1)	485	364	249	302	407	834
Unemployment, excl. school-leavers, adult students (monthly ave. '000)(2)	3,107·2	2,822·3	2,294·5	1,795·5	1,664·6	2,291·9
Percentage of working population	11·2	10·1	8·1	6·4	5·9	8·1
Unfilled vacancies, end-year ('000)	188·8	235·0	238·3	195·4	133·5	123·7
Work-related training programmes ('000)	226	311	343	462	..	..

(1) Great Britain. (2) Seasonally adjusted.

21. Industrial Disputes

	1986	1987	1988	1989	1990	1991
Stoppages (number)(1)(2)	1,053	1,004	770	693	620	342
Workers involved ('000)(3)	538	884	759	727	285	175
Work days lost ('000), all inds., services	1,920	3,546	3,702	4,128	1,903	759

(1) Excluding protest action of a political nature, and stoppages involving fewer than 10 workers and/or lasting less than one day except where the working days lost exceeded 100. (2) Stoppages beginning in year stated. (3) Directly and indirectly, where stoppages occurred; lay-offs elsewhere in consequence are excluded.

22. Wages and Earnings

	1986	1987	1988	1989	1990	1991
Average earnings index (1985=100)						
Whole economy	107·9	116·3	126·5	138·0	151·4	163·5
Manufacturing	107·7	116·3	126·2	137·2	150·2	162·5
Average weekly earnings(1)(2)						
Men						
Manual	174·4	185·5	200·6	217·8	237·2	253·1
Non-manual	244·9	265·9	294·1	323·6	354·9	375·7
All occupations	207·5	224·0	245·8	269·5	295·6	318·9
Women						
Manual	107·5	115·3	123·6	134·9	148·0	159·2
Non-manual	145·7	157·2	175·5	195·0	215·5	236·8
All occupations	137·2	148·1	164·2	182·3	201·5	222·4
Average hours(3)	40·4	40·4	40·6	40·7	40·5	40·0

(1) In all industries and services, full time. From 1991, manual and non-manual based on new standard occupational classification (2) April. (3) All industries and services, all occupations, men and women over 18 years.

23. Productivity
(Index of output per head 1985=100)

	1986	1987	1988	1989	1990	1991
All production industries(1)	105·0	110·1	113·2	113·7	114·4	117·2
Manufacturing	103·0	109·7	116·2	120·8	121·5	121·5
Minerals	107·8	118·3	129·5	128·1	119·4	115·5
Metal manufacture	112·6	131·8	157·2	151·2	135·3	132·0
Engineering	102·5	107·6	115·1	122·9	124·6	123·1
Textiles	100·6	104·4	102·0	102·8	104·8	101·9
Chemicals	104·7	114·8	118·7	122·1	122·0	129·5

(1) Excluding extraction of mineral oil and natural gas.

Overall price index (1985=100)	102·7	107·9	114·9	123·4	133·9	143·0

TRADE

24. Trade by Areas and Main Trading Partners
(£ million; exports fob; imports cif)

	1986	1987	1988	1989	1990	1991
All countries: *exports*	72,810	79,848	81,475	93,771	103,882	104,724
All countries: *imports*	85,662	94,023	106,412	121,888	126,135	118,780
E.E.C.: *exports*	34,943	39,415	40,932	47,540	55,071	59,449
E.E.C.: *imports*	44,506	49,555	55,785	63,807	65,955	61,370
Other Western Europe: *exports*	6,962	7,621	7,412	7,987	9,041	8,679
Other Western Europe: *imports*	11,864	12,884	13,943	15,155	15,745	14,300
North America: *exports*	12,065	12,992	12,623	14,437	14,973	13,151
North America: *imports*	9,994	10,781	12,899	15,929	16,751	15,733
Other developed countries: *exports*	3,614	4,046	4,496	4,519	4,824	4,010
Other developed countries: *imports*	6,861	7,283	8,505	8,514	8,414	8,094
Oil exporting countries: *exports*	5,494	5,223	5,021	5,831	5,575	5,756
Oil exporting countries: *imports*	2,062	1,700	2,087	2,313	2,974	2,787
Other developing countries: *exports*	7,644	8,549	8,630	11,185	12,189	12,130
Other developing countries: *imports*	7,770	9,284	10,471	13,557	13,855	14,155
Soviet Union and E. Eur.: *exports*	1,727	1,571	1,623	1,473	1,480	1,260
Soviet Union and E. Eur.: *imports*	1,865	2,099	2,039	1,781	1,797	1,689
Balance of trade in manufactures	−5,812	−8,254	−9,961	−19,567	−13,722	−6,079

25. Terms of Trade
(Index 1985=100)

Volume of exports(1)	103·8	109·2	112·0	117·3	125·1	126·6
manufactures	103·1	111·3	118·9	132·1	141·4	144·7
Volume of imports(1)	106·9	114·3	130·1	140·9	142·7	138·6
Unit value of exports(1)	90·5	94·3	94·7	101·3	107·0	107·2
manufactures	102·0	106·0	110·0	116·0	121·0	122·0
Unit value of imports(1)	95·7	98·2	97·5	103·2	107·9	108·4
Terms of trade(2)	94·6	96·0	97·1	97·9	99·2	98·9

(1) Seasonally adjusted: Overseas Trade Statistics basis. (2) Export unit value index as percentage of import value index, expressed as an index on the same base.

26. Balance of Payments
(£ million: current transactions seasonally adjusted; remaining data unadjusted)

Exports (f.o.b.)	72,678	79,421	80,772	92,792	102,036	103,704
Imports (f.o.b.)	81,141	89,594	101,587	116,632	120,653	113,823
Visible balance	−8,463	−10,174	−20,815	−23,840	−18,167	−10,119
Invisible balance	+8,509	+7,475	+6,154	+4,217	+3,475	+4,187
Current balance	+46	−2,699	−14,661	−19,623	−15,142	−5,932
Direct investment overseas	−11,728	−19,033	−20,760	−21,521	−8,913	..
Portfolio investment overseas	−23,072	+7,201	−8,600	−31,283	−12,115	..
Bank lending abroad	−53,840	−50,322	−19,267	−27,032	−37,077	..
Direct investment in UK	+4,945	+8,508	+10,236	+17,145	+18,592	..
Portfolio investment in UK	+11,785	+19,210	+14,387	+13,239	+5,070	..
UK overseas bank borrowing	+63,966	+52,814	+34,218	+43,887	+47,153	..
Net change in assets/liabilities	−7,234	−5,810	+9,645	+12,916	+14,636	..
Balancing item	+7,047	−1,651	+5,875	+7,488	+564	..
Official reserves, end of year	14,776	23,490	28,589	23,966	19,935	23,625

Overall price index (1985=100)	102·7	107·9	114·9	123·4	133·9	143·0

XVIII.5.B UNITED STATES STATISTICS   543

B. THE UNITED STATES

27. Population	1986	1987	1988	1989	1990	1991
Population, mid-year est. (mn)	241·60	243·77	246·3	248·8	249·6	..
Crude birth rate (per 1,000 pop.)	15·5	15·7	15·9	16·2	..	..
Crude death rate (per 1,000 pop.)	8·7	8·7	8·8	8·7	..	..

28. Gross National Product
($000 million current)

Gross domestic product	4,269	4,540	4,900	5,244	5,514	5,674
Personal consumption	2,851	3,052	3,296	3,518	3,743	3,889
Gross private domestic investment	718	749	794	838	803	727
Net exports, goods and services	−132	−143	−108	−83	−74	−29
Government purchases	833	881	919	971	1,043	1,088

29. Government Finance
($000 million, seasonally adjusted)

Federal government receipts	828	911	972	1,053	1,105	1,120
from personal taxes(1)	361	406	413	464	482	470
Federal government expenditure	1,034	1,074	1,117	1,187	1,270	1,320
Defence purchases	278	295	298	301	314	323
Grants to state/local govts.	107	103	111	118	131	153
Federal surplus or (−) deficit	−206·8	−161·3	−145·8	−134	−166	−200
State and local govt. receipts	626·3	656·1	701·6	750	724	771
from indirect business tax(1)	298·4	314·0	336·7	356	373	392

(1) Includes related non-tax receipts on national income account.

30. Balance of Payments
($ million)

Merchandise trade balance	−145,058	−159,500	−127,215	−115,917	−108,115	−65,877
Balance on current account(1)	−133,252	−143,700	−126,548	−106,305	−92,123	..
Change in US private assets abroad(2)	97,953	86,364	81,544	104,637	58,524	..
Change in foreign private assets in US(2)	186,011	172,847	180,417	207,925	53,879	..

(1) Includes balance on services and remittances and US government grants other than military.
(2) Includes reinvested earnings of incorporated affiliates.

31. Merchandise Trade by Main Areas
($ million)

All countries: *exports* (f.o.b.)	224,361	252,866	322,245	360,465	393,893	422,788
All countries: *imports* (f.o.b.)	368,700	424,082	440,940	475,329	494,903	488,617
Western Europe: *exports*	60,664	69,718	87,995	98,475	111,375	..
Western Europe: *imports*	89,074	99,934	100,515	102,301	109,450	..
Canada: *exports*	56,984	59,814	70,862	79,746	83,572	..
Canada: *imports*	70,315	71,510	80,921	89,408	93,026	..
Latin America						
exports	30,877	31,574	43,624	48,825	54,272	..
imports	41,426	44,371	51,421	57,438	64,320	..
Japan: *exports*	26,361	28,249	37,732	43,673	47,977	..
imports	80,764	88,074	89,802	93,455	89,667	..

| *Dollar purchasing power (1982–84=100)* | 91·3 | 88·0 | 84·6 | 80·7 | 76·5 | .. |

32. Merchandise Trade by Main Commodity Groups
($ million)

	1986	1987	1988	1989	1990	1991
Exports:						
Machinery and transport equipt.	95,289	108,596	135,135	148,780	172,522	..
Motor vehicles and parts	17,675	19,952	23,972	23,610	26,656	..
Electrical and electronic machinery	20,415	24,359	27,571	32,009	39,807	..
Food and live animals	17,303	19,179	26,415	29,724	29,280	..
Chemicals and pharmaceuticals	22,766	26,381	32,300	36,485	38,983	..
Imports:						
Machinery and transport equipt.	166,240	182,807	201,938	205,761	208,096	..
Motor vehicles and parts	66,201	70,680	71,268	69,340	69,382	..
Food and live animals	22,395	22,224	21,771	20,685	21,932	..
Petroleum and products	39,838	46,724	41,813	52,649	64,561	..
Iron and steel	8,168	8,493	10,274	9,401	..	..

33. Interest Rates
(per cent per annum, annual averages, unless otherwise stated)

Federal Funds rate(1)	6·80	6·66	7·57	9·21	8·10	5·69
Treasury bill rate	5·98	5·82	6·69	8·11	7·50	5·41
Government bond yields: 3–5 years	7·19	7·68	8·26	8·55	8·26	..
Long-term (10 years or more)	8·14	8·39	8·98	8·58	8·74	..
Banks' prime lending rate(2)	8·33	8·22	9·32	10·87	10·00	8·46

(1) Effective rate. (2) Predominant rate charged by commercial banks on short-term loans to large business borrowers with the highest credit rating.

34. Banking, money and credit
($000 million, outstanding at end of year, seasonally adjusted)

Money supply M1(1)	725·4	752·3	790·2	783·4	812·2	..
Money supply M2(2)	2,808	2,910	3,072	3,130·3	3,293·2	..
Money supply M3(3)	3,491	3,677	3,918	3,990·8	4,091·4	..
Currency	180·4	196·4	211·8	217·6	235·5	..
Deposits of commercial banks	2,018	2,009	2,121	2,268	2,363	..
Advances of commercial banks	1,807	1,899	2,021	2,206	2,309	..
Instalment credit	571·8	613·0	667·3	718·9	735·1	728·4
Motor vehicle contracts	246·1	267·2	290·8	290·8	284·6	..
Mortgage debt	2,597	2,943	3,154	3,556	3,856	..

(1) Currency plus demand deposits, travellers cheques, other checkable deposits. (2) M1 plus overnight repurchase agreements, eurodollars, money market mutual fund shares, savings and small time deposits. (3) M2 plus large time deposits and term repurchase agreements.

35. Insurance
($ million, unless otherwise stated)

Property-liability, net premiums written	176,552	193,246	202,015	207,800	217,600	..
Automobile(1)	73,386	81,199	86,379	90,900	..	..
Underwriting gain/loss(2)	−15,913	−7,100	−8,400	−16,500	−23,100	..
Net investment income(3)	21,924	23,960	27,723	31,200	31,400	..
Combined net income(3)	+6,012	+16,860	+19,323	+14,700	+8,300	..
Annual rate of return (%)(4)	13·1	12·8	13·2	8·4	..	..
Life insurance, total assets, end-year	937,551	1,044,459	1,166,870	1,299,800	1,408,208	..

(1) Physical damage and liability, private and commercial. (2) After stockholder and policy-holder dividends and premium rebates. (3) Property, casualty. (4) Per cent of net worth.

Dollar purchasing power (1982–84=100)	91·3	88·0	84·6	80·7	76·5	73·4

XVIII.5.B UNITED STATES STATISTICS

36. Companies(1) ($000 million)	1986	1987	1988	1989	1990	1991
Net profit after taxes	83·1	115·6	154·8	136·5	112·6	..
Cash dividends paid	46·0	49·5	57·1	65·2	63·8	..

(1) Manufacturing corporations, all industries.

37. The Stock Market
($million, unless otherwise stated)

	1986	1987	1988	1989	1990	1991
Turnover (sales), all exchanges	1,705,124	2,284,166	1,584,106	1,844,768	1,611,687	1,776,770
New York Stock Exchange	1,448,235	1,983,311	1,377,711	1,576,899	1,389,084	1,532,979
Stock prices (end-year):						
Combined index (500 stocks)(1)	242·17	247·08	277·7	353·4	330·22	376·18
Industrials (30 stocks)(2)	1,895·95	1,938·83	2,168·6	2,753·2	2,633·7	3,168·8

(1) Standard and Poor Composite 1941–43=10. (2) Dow-Jones Industrial (Oct. 1928=100).

38. Employment
('000 persons)

	1986	1987	1988	1989	1990	1991
Civilian labour force(1)	117,841	119,850	121,666	123,869	124,787	125,303
in non-agricultural industry	106,433	109,229	111,796	114,142	114,728	113,644
in manufacturing industry	18,995	19,112	19,403	19,612	19,063	18,427
in agriculture	3,165	3,210	3,175	3,199	3,186	3,233
unemployed	8,243	7,410	6,695	6,528	6,874	8,426
Industrial stoppages(2) (number)	69	46	40	51	44	40
Workers involved ('000)	533	174	118	452	185	392

(1) Aged 16 years and over. (2) Beginning in the year. Involving 1,000 workers or more.

39. Earnings and Prices

	1986	1987	1988	1989	1990	1991
Average weekly earnings per worker						
(current dollars): mining	525·81	530·85	539·3	569·7	602·0	630·9
contract construction	466·75	479·68	493·1	512·4	526·4	533·8
manufacturing	396·01	406·31	418·4	430·1	442·3	455·0
Average weekly hours per worker						
in manufacturing	40·7	41·0	41·1	41·0	40·8	40·7
Farm prices received (1977=100)	123·0	127·0	138·0	146·0	148·0	..
Wholesale prices (1982=100)	100·2	102·8	106·9	113·6	119·2	121·7
Fuels and power	70·2	70·2	66·7	75·9	85·9	85·2
Consumer prices (1982–4=100)	109·7	113·7	118·4	124·0	130·7	136·2
Food	109·1	113·6	118·3	125·1	132·4	136·3
Dollar purchasing power (1982–84=100)(1)	91·3	88·0	84·6	80·7	76·5	73·4

(1) Based on changes in retail price indexes.

40. Production

	1986	1987	1988	1989	1990	1991
Farm production (1977=100)	111·0	110·0	102·0	114·0	117·0	..
Industrial production (1987=100)	95·3	100·0	105·4	108·1	109·2	107·1
Manufacturing	94·3	100·0	105·8	108·9	109·9	..
Output of main products and manufacturers						
Coal (million tons)	886·0	915·8	950·3	979·6	1,029	993·6
Oil, indigenous (000 barrels/day)	8,727	8,347	8,140	7,613	7,355	7,372
Oil refinery throughput (000 barrels/day)	14,522	14,626	15,020	15,180	..	..
Natural gas ('000 mn. cu. ft.)	16,791	16,540	16,990	17,120	17,830	17,852
Electricity generated ('000 mn. kwh)	2,487	2,572	2,704	2,784	2,807	2,826
Steel, crude (million tonnes)	81·6	89·1	99·9	97·9	96·5	92·0
Aluminium ('000 tonnes)	3,036	3,343	3,944	4,030	4,020	4,000
Cotton yarn ('000 running bales)	9,438	14,359	14,985	11,884	15,064	..
Man-made fibres (millions lbs.)	8,447	8,921	9,119·7	..	..	..
Plastics/resins (millions lbs.)	38,415	32,295	..	..	..	..
Motor cars, factory sales ('000)	7,516	7,085	7,105	6,639	6,604	..

C. INTERNATIONAL COMPARISONS

	Area '000 sq. km.	Population (millions) mid-year estimate 1988	1989	Gross Domestic Product(1) US $ mins(2) 1989	1990
41. Population and GDP, Selected countries					
Argentina	2,767	31·5	31·93	60,314	..
Australia(3)	7,687	16·51	16·83	282,970	295,500
Belgium	31	9·91	9.85	156,853	196,810
Canada	9,976	26·01	26·22	550,351	556,308
China	9,561	1,088·41	1,122·4	422,485	363,773
Denmark	43	5·11	5·13	104,702	130,942
France	552	59·91	56·16	956,443	1,190,403
Germany(4)	357	78·0	62·06	1,189,149	1,487,529
India (incl. India-admin. Kashmir)	3,287	815·6	811·3	272,878	..
Irish Republic	70	3·6	3·51	33,940	42,612
Israel (excl. occupied areas)	22	4·4	4·52	44,362	51,220
Italy	301	57·41	57·52	865,826	..
Japan	378	122·6	123·12	2,833,734	2,938,097
Kuwait(5)	18	2·0	2·05	23,082	..
Netherlands	34	14·8	14·83	223,690	276,896
New Zealand(5)	270	3·3	3·31	41,766	..
Norway	324	4·2	4·23	90,894	105,828
Portugal	92	10·3	10·47	45,525	59,837
Saudi Arabia	2,200	14·0	14·43	82,996	..
South Africa	1,220	34·0	34·51	90,577	101,554
Spain	505	39·0	38·89	380,005	491,386
Sweden	450	8·4	8·49	189,423	257,781
Switzerland	41	6·6	6·65	177,150	224,878
Turkey	781	53·8	56·74	80,423	108,559
USSR	22,403	285·0	..	..	..
UK	244	57·1	57·24	831,672	981,442
USA	9,372	246·3	247·35	5,163,200	5,423,400

(1) Expenditure basis. (2) Converted from national currencies at average exchange rates. (3) Years beginning 1 July. (4) Combines East and West Germany. (5) Years beginning 1 April.

42. World Production
(Index 1980=100)

	1986	1987	1988	1989	1990	1991
Food(1)	115·0	117·0	118·0	122·0	124·0	..
Industrial production(2)	112·0	116·3	122·3	127·1	129·6	..
Crude petroleum, nat. gas	82·6	83·1	87·6	92·6	92·3	..
Manufacturing	115·8	120·6	127·1	131·9	134·6	..
Chemicals	119·3	125·2	133·2	138·3	142·7	..
Paper, printing, publishing	119·9	126·6	133·4	138·2	143·4	..
Textiles	106·1	109·2	110·5	112·2	109·5	..
OECD	110·1	113·4	120·1	124·5	127·1	..
EEC(3)	106·8	109·0	113·6	117·6	120·1	..
Developing market economies(4)	129·6	139·7	150·8	159·1	171·2	..
Caribbean, C. & S. America	109·8	117·3	121·6	131·9	142·9	..
Asia(5)	163·7	181·6	197·7	207·2	226·2	..
France	101·0	104·0	108·1	112·0	113·0	..
Germany, West	107·0	107·0	111·2	117·0	123·0	..
Italy	99·0	103·0	110·8	114·0	114·0	..
UK	110·0	113·0	118·0	119·0	118·0	..
Japan	118·0	122·0	133·5	142·0	149·0	..
Sweden	110·0	114·0	115·1	118·0	114·0	..
USSR	126·1	130·9	134·0	136·0	135·0	..

(1) Excluding China. (2) Excluding China, N. Korea, Vietnam, Albania. (3) Community of Twelve. (4) Manufacturing. (5) Excluding Japan and Israel.

XVIII.5.C INTERNATIONAL COMPARISONS

43. World Trade(1)
($million. Exports f.o.b., imports c.i.f.)

	1986	1987	1988	1989	1990	1991
World(1): exports	2,003,200	2,364,800	2,688,500	2,906,300	3,324,600	..
imports	2,059,100	2,424,800	2,767,600	3,005,300	3,447,800	..
Industrial Countries: exports	1,462,500	1,712,300	1,987,900	2,126,300	2,452,600	..
imports	1,357,200	1,794,300	2,067,500	2,238,800	2,571,200	..
USA: exports	217,307	250,405	322,426	363,812	393,592	..
imports	387,081	424,081	459,542	492,922	516,987	..
Germany, West: exports	243,327	294,168	323,326	341,231	410,104	..
imports	191,084	228,346	250,473	269,702	346,153	..
Japan: exports	210,757	228,631	264,856	273,932	287,581	..
imports	127,553	150,496	187,378	209,715	235,368	..
France: exports	124,948	148,534	167,787	179,397	216,588	..
imports	129,402	158,475	178,857	192,986	234,436	..
UK: exports	106,989	131,239	145,166	152,344	185,170	..
imports	126,330	154,454	189,339	197,730	222,975	..
Other Europe: exports	506,658	599,656	665,620	708,673	855,393	..
imports	529,520	645,564	697,462	767,342	929,431	..
Australia, NZ, S. Afr: exports	46,956	55,238	63,401	68,757	72,953	..
imports	45,156	51,923	62,194	71,550	69,005	..
Less Developed Areas: exports	510,286	624,644	700,550	764,900	848,422	..
imports	521,891	607,561	700,110	744,750	859,103	..
Oil exporters: exports	111,140	128,840	128,320	..	..	..
imports	93,400	91,370	104,790	97,080	112,070	..
Saudi Arabia: exports	20,085	26,975	23,738	28,382	44,417	..
imports	19,112	24,345	21,784	21,154	24,069	..
Other W. Hemisphere: exports	57,324	60,491	73,919	79,281	83,296	..
imports	52,148	59,742	59,937	68,719	75,051	..
Other Middle East(2): exports	14,972	15,700	..	..	..	..
imports	32,004	44,588	39,038	..	..	..
Other Asia: exports	174,856	261,002	323,255	358,187	395,760	..
imports	191,547	260,308	337,460	377,212	418,715	..
Other Africa: exports	23,622	24,218	25,767	..	..	..
imports	27,949	31,316	33,164	..	..	..

(1) Excluding trade of centrally planned countries (see Table 44) (2) Including Egypt. (3) Unweighted average of IMF series for US$ import and export prices in developed countries.

World trade prices (1985=100)(3)	111·0	111·8	112·6	111·8	111·3	..

44. World Trade: E. Europe, USSR, China
($'000 million)

	1986	1987	1988	1989	1990	1991
Eastern Europe: exports	67·07	68·93	69·29	67·06	64·84	..
imports	65·95	66·41	64·65	63·25	65·08	..
USSR: exports	60·04	63·41	62·02	62·29	59·06	..
imports	55·02	53·79	58·04	64·98	64·96	..
China: exports	30·94	39·54	47·54	43·22	51·52	..
imports	42·90	43·39	55·25	48·84	42·35	..

45. Prices of Selected Commodities
(Index 1985=100)

	1986	1987	1988	1989	1990	1991
Aluminium (Canada)	110·5	150·4	244·7	187·4	157·5	125·3
Beef, All origins	97·3	110·8	116·9	119·2	119·0	123·7
Copper, wirebars (London)	96·7	125·7	183·4	200·9	187·8	165·0
Cotton, Egyptian (L'pool)	95·9	99·4	133·2	176·4	183·0	169·9
Gold (London)	115·9	140·8	137·8	120·2	120·9	114·2
Newsprint New York	97·9	106·4	112·7	109·6	106·5	..
Rice, Thai (Bangkok)	96·7	105·7	138·7	147·3	131·9	144·6
Rubber, Malay (Singapore)	106·3	129·8	156·2	127·8	114·0	108·8
Soya Beans, US (R'dam)	92·9	96·1	135·2	122·5	110·0	106·8
Sugar, f.o.b. (Caribbean)	149·3	166·7	251·4	315·9	308·6	221·4
Tin, spot (London)	56·3	60·3	63·3	75·5	53·7	48·5
Wheat (US Gulf Ports)	84·6	83·1	106·9	124·6	99·8	94·1
Wool, greasy (Sydney)	92·0	132·9	219·5	199·3	174·1	..

46. Consumer Prices, Selected Countries
(Index 1985=100)

Argentina	190·0	440·0	1,948	61,933	1,495	..
Australia	109·0	118·0	127·0	136·6	146·4	..
France	102·5	105·9	108·8	112·6	116·4	120·1
Germany(1)	99·8	100·1	101·2	104·0	107·0	111·0
India	108·7	118·3	129·4	137·4	149·7	..
Japan	100·6	100·7	101·4	103·7	106·9	109·7
South Africa	118·6	137·7	155·4	178·2	203·8	..
Sweden	104·2	108·6	114·9	122·2	135·1	..
UK	103·4	107·8	113·0	121·8	133·4	141·1
US	101·9	105·7	109·9	115·2	121·5	126·6

(1) To 1990, West Germany.

World trade prices (1985=100)	111·0	111·8	112·6	111·8	111·3	..

47. Industrial Ordinary Share Prices
(Index 1985=100) average

	1986	1987	1988	1989	1990	1991
Amsterdam	128·7	129·2	119·7	151·4	147·6	
Australia, all exchanges	134·8	193·4	164·6	176·6	166·1	
Canada, all exchanges	111·0	131·5	121·8	140·1	126·1	
Germany, all exchanges(1)	135·2	124·5	104·0	133·0	152·8	
Hong Kong (31 July 1968=100)(2)	2,568	2,292	2,687	2,836	3,053	4,297
Johannesburg	128·0	188·0	148·0	207·0	217·0	
New York	126·2	159·2	147·6	178·2	188.1	214·5
Paris	153·3	177·6	162·1	234·9	207·7	
Tokyo	132·9	196·4	213·9	257·8	218·8	
UK	124·1	163·8	147·6	176·5	172·2	190·2

(1) To 1990, West Germany.
(2) Hang Seng index for Hong Kong Stock Exchange only: last trading day of year.

48. Central Bank Discount Rates
(per cent per annum, end of year)

	1986	1987	1988	1989	1990	1991
Canada	8·47	8·75	8·75	12·46	12.82	7·50
France	9·50	9·50	9·50	10·25	10·25	10·25
Germany(1)	3·50	2·50	3·50	6·00	6·00	8·00
Italy	12·00	12·50	12·50	13·50	12·50	12·00
Japan	3·00	2·50	2·50	3·75	6·00	4·50
Sweden	7·50	7·50	8·50	9·50	11·00	10·00
Switzerland	4·00	2·50	3·50	6·00	6·00	7·00
UK	11·00	8·50	13·00	15·00	14·00	10·50
USA (Federal Reserve Bank of N.Y.)	5·50	6·50	6·50	7·00	7·00	3·50

(1) To 1990, West Germany.

XVIII.5.C INTERNATIONAL COMPARISONS

49. Exchange Rates
(Middle rates at end of year)

Currency units per US dollar / per £

	1987	1988	1989	1990	1991	1990	1991
Australia (Australian dollar)	1·3897	1·1694	1·2655	1·2965	1·3165	2·500	2·458
Belgium-Luxembourg (franc)	38·00	37·26	35·60	30·95	31·36	59·75	58·55
Canada (Canadian dollar)	1·300	1·1907	1·1585	1·1605	1·1593	2·2400	2·1645
China (yuan)(1)	3·722	3·697	4·7001	5·1974	5·3893	9·9011	10·062
France (franc)	5·342	6·057	5·7850	5·0855	5·1901	9·8200	9·6900
Germany W. (Deutschmark)	1·574	1·773	1·6915	1·4950	1·5198	2·8850	2·8375
Italy (lire)	1,165	1,306	1,268·0	1,128·0	1,151·4	2,177·0	2,149·7
Japan (yen)	121·3	124·9	143·80	135·65	125·74	261·75	234·75
Netherlands (guilder)	1·772	2·002	1·9116	1·6865	1,7126	3·2550	3,1975
Portugal (escudo)	129·0	146·2	149·58	134·05	134·76	255·30	251·6
South Africa (rand)	1·988	2·379	2·5480	2·5635	2·7518	4·9373	5·1377
Spain (peseta)	107·75	113·18	109·40	95·55	96·76	183·70	180·65
Sweden (krona)	5·785	6·125	6·1925	5·6250	5·5543	10·8650	10·3700
Switzerland (franc)	1·2755	1·5022	1·5425	1·2750	1·3564	2·4600	2·5325
USSR (rouble)(1)	0·591	0·603	0·6132	0·5655	0·5511	1·0774	1·0290
UK (£)(2)	1·8785	1·8090	1·6125	1·9300	1·8671	..	..

(1) Official fixed or basic parity rate. (2) US dollars per £.

50. Defence Expenditure

Expenditure or budget (US$ mn.)

	1986	1987	1988	1989	1990	% of GDP 1989
France	35,118	36,137	36,105	36,494	36,393	3·7
Germany	34,719	35,320	35,097	35,008	38,016	2·8
Greece	3,152	3,144	3,326	3,116	3,041	6·8
Iran	9,339	7,679	7,353	5,747	5,133	..
Israel	4,318	4,134	3,811	3,830	3,807	9·2
Japan	25,924	27,279	28,521	29,491	30,483	1·0
Saudi Arabia	16,684	16,384	14,887	14,522	15,213	..
South Africa	3,139	3,355	3,468	3,808	3,407	4·2
Sweden	4,357	4,431	4,442	4,508	4,492	2·4
Turkey	2,772	2,647	2,664	2,770	3,418	3·9
USSR(1)	19·1	20·5	20·5	77·3	71·0	..
UK	36,173	35,713	34,629	34,292	32,470	4·1
USA	305,076	300,890	295,841	289,149	268,113	5·8

(1) Official figures, '000 million roubles. Before 1989, military personnel and operations and maintenance only.

51. Employment and Unemployment

Civilian Employment ('000)	1986	1987	1988	1989	1990	1991
USA	109,597	112,440	114,968	117,342	117,914	..
Japan	58,530	59,110	60,110	61,280	62,490	..
W. Germany	25,267	26,626	26,825	27,209	27,946	..
France	20,949	21,018	21,179	21,455	21,733	..
UK	24,434	24,755	25,555	26,376	26,577	..
Unemployment (%)						
OECD	7·9	7·5	6·7	6·2	6·1	..
EEC	11·2	10·8	9·9	9·0	8·4	..
USA	6·9	6·1	5·4	5·2	5·4	..
Japan	2·8	2·8	2·5	2·3	2·1	..
UK	11·6	10·4	8·5	7·1	6·9	..

XIX DOCUMENTS AND REFERENCE

1. GULF CONFLICT: UN CEASEFIRE RESOLUTION

Printed below is the full text of resolution 687 of the UN Security Council containing the terms of the ceasefire which formally ended the Gulf conflict resulting from Iraq's invasion of Kuwait in August 1990. The resolution was adopted on 3 April 1991 by 12 votes to 1 with 2 abstentions. All five permanent Council members (China, France, the UK, the USSR and the USA) voted in favour, together with, from the non-permanent members, Austria, Belgium, Côte d'Ivoire, India, Romania, Zaïre and Zimbabwe. Cuba voted against, while Ecuador and Yemen abstained. (Text supplied by the UN Information Office, London.)

The Security Council,
  Recalling its resolutions 660 (1990), 661 (1990), 662 (1990), 664 (1990), 665 (1990), 666 (1990), 667 (1990), 669 (1990), 670 (1990), 674 (1990), 677 (1990), 678 (1990) and 686 (1991),
  Welcoming the restoration to Kuwait of its sovereignty, independence and territorial integrity and the return of its legitimate government,
  Affirming the commitment of all member states to the sovereignty, territorial integrity and political independence of Kuwait and Iraq, and noting the intention expressed by the member states cooperating with Kuwait under paragraph 2 of resolution 678 (1990) to bring their military presence in Iraq to an end as soon as possible consistent with paragraph 8 of resolution 686 (1991),
  Reaffirming the need to be assured of Iraq's peaceful intentions in light of its unlawful invasion and occupation of Kuwait,
  Taking note of the letter sent by the Foreign Minister of Iraq on 27 February 1991 (S/22275) and those sent pursuant to resolution 686 (1991) (S/22273, S/22276, S/22320, S/22321 and S/22330),
  Noting that Iraq and Kuwait, as independent sovereign states, signed at Baghdad on 4 October 1963 'Agreed Minutes Regarding the Restoration of Friendly Relations, Recognition and Related Matters', thereby recognizing formally the boundary between Iraq and Kuwait and the allocation of islands, which were registered with the United Nations in accordance with Article 102 of the Charter and in which Iraq recognized the independence and complete sovereignty of the state of Kuwait within its borders as specified and accepted in the letter of the Prime Minister of Iraq dated 21 July 1932, and as accepted by the Ruler of Kuwait in his letter dated 10 August 1932,
  Conscious of the need for demarcation of the said boundary,
  Conscious also of the statements by Iraq threatening to use weapons in violation of its obligations under the Geneva Protocol for the Prohibition of the Use in War of Asphyxiating, Poisonous or Other Gases, and of Bacteriological Methods of Warfare, signed at Geneva on 17 June 1925, and of its prior use of chemical weapons and affirming that grave consequences would follow any further use by Iraq of such weapons,
  Recalling that Iraq has subscribed to the declaration adopted by all states participating in the Conference of States Parties to the 1925 Geneva Protocol and Other Interested States, held at Paris from 7 to 11 January 1989, establishing the objective of universal elimination of chemical and biological weapons,
  Recalling further that Iraq has signed the Convention on the Prohibition of the Development, Production and Stockpiling of Bacteriological (Biological) and Toxin Weapons and on Their Destruction, of 10 April 1972,
  Noting the importance of Iraq ratifying this convention,
  Noting moreover the importance of all states adhering to this convention and encouraging its forthcoming review conference to reinforce the authority, efficiency and universal scope of the convention,
  Stressing the importance of an early conclusion by the Conference on Disarmament of its work on a Convention on the Universal Prohibition of Chemical Weapons and of universal adherence thereto,
  Aware of the use by Iraq of ballistic missiles in unprovoked attacks and therefore of the need to take specific measures in regard to such missiles located in Iraq,
  Concerned by the reports in the hands of member states that Iraq has attempted to acquire materials for a nuclear-weapons programme contrary to its obligations under the Treaty on the Non-Proliferation of Nuclear Weapons of 1 July 1968,

XIX.1 GULF CONFLICT: UN CEASEFIRE RESOLUTION 551

Recalling the objective of the establishment of a nuclear-weapons-free zone in the region of the Middle East,

Conscious of the threat which all weapons of mass destruction pose to peace and security in the area and of the need to work towards the establishment in the Middle East of a zone free of such weapons,

Conscious also of the objective of achieving balanced and comprehensive control of armaments in the region,

Conscious further of the importance of achieving the objectives noted above using all available means, including a dialogue among the states of the region,

Noting that resolution 686 (1991) marked the lifting of the measures imposed by resolution 661 (1990) in so far as they applied to Kuwait,

Noting that despite the progress being made in fulfilling the obligations of resolution 686 (1991), many Kuwaiti and third country nationals are still not accounted for and property remains unreturned,

Recalling the International Convention against the Taking of Hostages, opened for signature at New York on 18 December 1979, which categorizes all acts of taking hostages as manifestations of international terrorism,

Deploring threats made by Iraq during the recent conflict to make use of terrorism against targets outside Iraq and the taking of hostages by Iraq,

Taking note with grave concern of the reports of the Secretary-General of 20 March 1991 (S/22366) and 28 March 1991 (S/22409), and conscious of the necessity to meet urgently the humanitarian needs in Kuwait and Iraq,

Bearing in mind its objective of restoring international peace and security in the area as set out in recent Council resolutions,

Conscious of the need to take the following measures acting under Chapter VII of the Charter,

1. Affirms all 13 resolutions noted above, except as expressly changed below to achieve the goals of this resolution, including a formal ceasefire;

A

2. Demands that Iraq and Kuwait respect the inviolability of the international boundary and the allocation of islands set out in the 'Agreed Minutes Between the State of Kuwait and the Republic of Iraq Regarding the Restoration of Friendly Relations, Recognition and Related Matters', signed by them in the exercise of their sovereignty at Baghdad on 4 October 1963 and registered with the United Nations and published by the United Nations in document 7063, United Nations Treaty Series, 1964;

3. Calls on the Secretary-General to lend his assistance to make arrangements with Iraq and Kuwait to demarcate the boundary between Iraq and Kuwait, drawing on appropriate material including the map transmitted by Security Council document S/22412 and to report back to the Security Council within one month;

4. Decides to guarantee the inviolability of the above-mentioned international boundary and to take as appropriate all necessary measures to that end in accordance with the Charter;

B

5. Requests the Secretary-General, after consulting with Iraq and Kuwait, to submit within three days to the Security Council for its approval a plan for the immediate deployment of a United Nations observer unit to monitor the Khor Abdullah and a demilitarized zone, which is hereby established, extending 10 kilometres into Iraq and 5 kilometres into Kuwait from the boundary referred to in the 'Agreed Minutes Between the State of Kuwait and the Republic of Iraq Regarding the Restoration of Friendly Relations, Recognition and Related Matters' of 4 October 1963; to deter violations of the boundary through its presence in and surveillance of the demilitarized zone; to observe any hostile or potentially hostile action mounted from the territory of one state to the other; and for the Secretary-General to report regularly to the Council on the operations of the unit, and immediately if there are serious violations of the zone or potential threats to peace;

6. Notes that as soon as the Secretary-General notifies the Council of the completion of the deployment of the United Nations observer unit, the conditions will be established for the member

states cooperating with Kuwait in accordance with resolution 678 (1990) to bring their military presence in Iraq to an end consistent with resolution 686 (1991);

C

7. Invites Iraq to reaffirm unconditionally its obligations under the Geneva Protocol for the Prohibition of the Use in War of Asphyxiating, Poisonous or Other Gases, and of Bacteriological Methods of Warfare, signed at Geneva on 17 June 1925, and to ratify the Convention on the Prohibition of the Development, Production and Stockpiling of Bacteriological (Biological) and Toxin Weapons and on Their Destruction, of 10 April 1972;

8. Decides that Iraq shall unconditionally accept the destruction, removal, or rendering harmless, under international supervision, of:

(*a*) all chemical and biological weapons and all stocks of agents and all related subsystems and components and all research, development, support and manufacturing facilities;

(*b*) all ballistic missiles with a range greater than 150 kilometres and related major parts, and repair and production facilities;

9. Decides, for the implementation of paragraph 8 above, the following:

(*a*) Iraq shall submit to the Secretary-General, within 15 days of the adoption of this resolution, a declaration of the locations, amounts and types of all items specified in paragraph 8 and agree to urgent, on-site inspection as specified below;

(*b*) the Secretary-General, in consultation with the appropriate governments and, where appropriate, with the director-general of the World Health Organization (WHO), within 45 days of the passage of this resolution, shall develop, and submit to the Council for approval, a plan calling for the completion of the following acts within 45 days of such approval:

(*i*) the forming of a Special Commission, which shall carry out immediate on-site inspection of Iraq's biological, chemical and missile capabilities, based on Iraq's declarations and the designation of any additional locations by the Special Commission itself;

(*ii*) the yielding by Iraq of possession to the Special Commission for destruction, removal or rendering harmless, taking into account the requirements of public safety, of all items specified under paragraph 8(*a*) above including items at the additional locations designated by the Special Commission under paragraph 9(*b*)(*i*) above and the destruction by Iraq, under supervision of the Special Commission, of all its missile capabilities including launchers as specified under paragraph 8(*b*) above;

(*iii*) the provision by the Special Commission of the assistance and cooperation to the director-general of the International Atomic Energy Agency (IAEA) required in paragraphs 12 and 13 below;

10. Decides that Iraq shall unconditionally undertake not to use, develop, construct or acquire any of the items specified in paragraphs 8 and 9 above and requests the Secretary-General, in consultation with the Special Commission, to develop a plan for the future ongoing monitoring and verification of Iraq's compliance with this paragraph, to be submitted to the Council for approval within 120 days of the passage of this resolution;

11. Invites Iraq to reaffirm unconditionally its obligations under the Treaty on the Non-Proliferation of Nuclear Weapons, of 1 July 1968;

12. Decides that Iraq shall unconditionally agree not to acquire or develop nuclear weapons or nuclear-weapons-usable material or any subsystems or components or any research, development, support or manufacturing facilities related to the above; to submit to the Secretary-General and the director-general of the IAEA within 15 days of the adoption of this resolution a declaration of the locations, amounts and types of all items specified above; to place all of its nuclear-weapons-usable materials under the exclusive control, for custody and removal, of the IAEA, with the assistance and cooperation of the Special Commission as provided for in the plan of the Secretary-General discussed in paragraph 9(*b*) above; to accept, in accordance with the arrangements provided for in paragraph 13 below, urgent on-site inspection and the destruction, removal, or rendering harmless as appropriate of all items specified above; and to accept the plan discussed in paragraph 13 below for the future ongoing monitoring and verification of its compliance with these undertakings;

13. Requests the director-general of the IAEA through the Secretary-General, with the assistance and cooperation of the Special Commission as provided for in the plan of the Secretary-General in paragraph 9(*b*) above, to carry out immediate on-site inspection of Iraq's nuclear capabilities based on Iraq's declarations and the designation of any additional locations by the Special Commission; to develop a plan for submission to the Security Council within 45 days calling for the destruction, removal or rendering harmless as appropriate of all items listed in paragraph 12 above; to carry

XIX.1 GULF CONFLICT: UN CEASEFIRE RESOLUTION 553

out the plan within 45 days following approval by the Security Council; and to develop a plan, taking into account the rights and obligations of Iraq under the Treaty on the Non-Proliferation of Nuclear Weapons, of 1 July 1968, for the future ongoing monitoring and verification of Iraq's compliance with paragraph 12 above, including an inventory of all nuclear material in Iraq subject to the Agency's verification and inspections to confirm that IAEA safeguards cover all relevant nuclear activities in Iraq, to be submitted to the Council for approval within 120 days of the passage of this resolution;

14. Takes note that the actions to be taken by Iraq in paragraphs 8, 9, 10, 11, 12 and 13 of this resolution represent steps towards the goal of establishing in the Middle East a zone free from weapons of mass destruction and all missiles for their delivery and the objective of a global ban on chemical weapons;

D

15. Requests the Secretary-General to report to the Security Council on the steps taken to facilitate the return of all Kuwaiti property seized by Iraq, including a list of any property which Kuwait claims has not been returned or which has not been returned intact;

E

16. Reaffirms that Iraq, without prejudice to the debts and obligations of Iraq arising prior to 2 August 1990, which will be addressed through the normal mechanisms, is liable under international law for any direct loss, damage, including environmental damage and the depletion of natural resources, or injury to foreign governments, nationals and corporations, as a result of Iraq's unlawful invasion and occupation of Kuwait;

17. Decides that all Iraqi statements made since 2 August 1990 repudiating its foreign debt are null and void, and demands that Iraq scrupulously adhere to all of its obligations concerning servicing and repayment of its foreign debt;

18. Decides to create a Fund to pay compensation for claims that fall within paragraph 16 above and to establish a Commission that will administer the Fund;

19. Directs the Secretary-General to develop and present to the Council for decision, no later than 30 days following the adoption of this resolution, recommendations for the Fund to meet the requirement for the payment of claims established in accordance with paragraph 18 above and for a programme to implement the decisions in paragraphs 16, 17, and 18 above, including: administration of the Fund; mechanisms for determining the appropriate level of Iraq's contribution to the Fund based on a percentage of the value of the exports of petroleum and petroleum products from Iraq not to exceed a figure to be suggested to the Council by the Secretary-General, taking into account the requirements of the people of Iraq, Iraq's payment capacity as assessed in conjunction with the international financial institutions taking into consideration external debt service, and the needs of the Iraqi economy; arrangements for ensuring that payments are made to the Fund; the process by which funds will be allocated and claims paid; appropriate procedures for evaluating losses, listing claims and verifying their validity and resolving disputed claims in respect of Iraq's liability as specified in paragraph 16 above; and the composition of the Commission designated above;

F

20. Decides, effective immediately, that the prohibitions against the sale or supply to Iraq of commodities or products, other than medicine and health supplies, and prohibitions against financial transactions related thereto, contained in resolution 661 (1990) shall not apply to foodstuffs notified to the committee established by resolution 661 (1990) or, with the approval of that committee, under the simplified and accelerated 'no-objection' procedure, to materials and supplies for essential civilian needs as identified in the report of the Secretary-General dated 20 March 1991 (S/22366), and in any further findings of humanitarian need by the Committee;

21. Decides that the Council shall review the provisions of paragraph 20 above every 60 days in light of the policies and practices of the government of Iraq, including the implementation of all relevant resolutions of the Security Council, for the purpose of determining whether to reduce or lift the prohibitions referred to therein;

22. Decides that upon the approval by the Council of the programme called for in paragraph 19 above and upon Council agreement that Iraq has completed all actions contemplated in paragraphs

8, 9, 10, 11, 12, and 13 above, the prohibitions against the import of commodities and products originating in Iraq and the prohibitions against financial transactions related thereto contained in resolution 661 (1990) shall have no further force or effect;

23. Decides that, pending action by the Council under paragraph 22 above, the committee established by resolution 661 (1990) shall be empowered to approve, when required to assure adequate financial resources on the part of Iraq to carry out the activities under paragraph 20 above, exceptions to the prohibition against the import of commodities and products originating in Iraq;

24. Decides that, in accordance with resolution 661 (1990) and subsequent related resolutions and until a further decision is taken by the Council, all states shall continue to prevent the sale or supply, or promotion or facilitation of such sale or supply, to Iraq by their nationals, or from their territories or using their flag vessels or aircraft, of:

(*a*) arms and related materiel of all types, specifically including the sale or transfer through other means of all forms of conventional military equipment, including for paramilitary forces, and spare parts and components and their means of production, for such equipment;

(*b*) items specified and defined in paragraphs 8 and 12 above not otherwise covered above;

(*c*) technology under licensing or other transfer arrangements used in the production, utilization or stockpiling of items specified in subparagraphs (*a*) and (*b*) above;

(*d*) personnel or materials for training or technical support services relating to the design, development, manufacture, use, maintenance or support of items specified in subparagraphs (*a*) and (*b*) above;

25. Calls upon all states and international organizations to act strictly in accordance with paragraph 24 above, notwithstanding the existence of any contracts, agreements, licences or any other arrangements;

26. Requests the Secretary-General, in consultation with appropriate governments, to develop within 60 days, for approval of the Council, guidelines to facilitate full international implementation of paragraphs 24 and 25 above and paragraph 27 below, and to make them available to all states and to establish a procedure for updating these guidelines periodically;

27. Calls upon all states to maintain such national controls and procedures and to take such other actions consistent with the guidelines to be established by the Security Council under paragraph 26 above as may be necessary to ensure compliance with the terms of paragraph 24 above, and calls upon international organizations to take all appropriate steps to assist in ensuring such full compliance;

28. Agrees to review its decisions in paragraphs 22, 23, 24 and 25 above, except for the items specified and defined in paragraphs 8 and 12 above, on a regular basis and in any case 120 days following passage of this resolution, taking into account Iraq's compliance with this resolution and general progress towards the control of armaments in the region;

29. Decides that all states, including Iraq, shall take the necessary measures to ensure that no claim shall lie at the instance of the government of Iraq, or of any person or body in Iraq, or of any person claiming through or for the benefit of any such person or body, in connection with any contract or other transaction where its performance was affected by reason of the measures taken by the Security Council in resolution 661 (1990) and related resolutions;

G

30. Decides that, in furtherance of its commitment to facilitate the repatriation of all Kuwaiti and third country nationals, Iraq shall extend all necessary cooperation to the International Committee of the Red Cross, providing lists of such persons, facilitating the access of the International Committee of the Red Cross to all such persons wherever located or detained and facilitating the search by the International Committee of the Red Cross for those Kuwaiti and third country nationals still unaccounted for;

31. Invites the International Committee of the Red Cross to keep the Secretary-General apprised as appropriate of all activities undertaken in connection with facilitating the repatriation or return of all Kuwaiti and third country nationals or their remains present in Iraq on or after 2 August 1990;

H

32. Requires Iraq to inform the Council that it will not commit or support any act of international terrorism or allow any organization directed towards commission of such acts to

operate within its territory and to condemn unequivocally and renounce all acts, methods and practices of terrorism;

I

33. Declares that, upon official notification by Iraq to the Secretary-General and to the Security Council of its acceptance of the provisions above, a formal ceasefire is effective between Iraq and Kuwait and the member states cooperating with Kuwait in accordance with resolution 678 (1990);
34. Decides to remain seized of the matter and to take such further steps as may be required for the implementation of this resolution and to secure peace and security in the area.

2. STRATEGIC ARMS REDUCTION (START) TREATY

Printed below is an official summary by the US Information Service of the Strategic Arms Reduction (START) Treaty and associated documents, totalling over 700 pages in all, signed in Moscow on 31 July 1991 by Soviet and US representatives. The treaty document itself and seven associated texts were signed by Presidents Gorbachev of the USSR and Bush of the USA. Three associated documents were signed by James Baker (US Secretary of State) and Aleksandr Bessmertnykh (Soviet Foreign Minister), while the US and Soviet negotiators, Ambassadors Brooks and Nazarkin, exchanged seven letters of understanding related to the START process. (Text supplied by US Information Service.)

Central Limits. The treaty sets equal ceilings on the number of strategic nuclear forces that can be deployed by either side. In addition, the treaty establishes an equal ceiling on ballistic missile throw-weight (a measure of overall capability for ballistic missiles). Each side is limited to no more than:
— 1,600 strategic nuclear delivery vehicles, i.e. deployed intercontinental ballistic missiles (ICBMS), submarine-launched ballistic missiles (SLBMS), and heavy bombers, a limit that is 36 per cent below the Soviet level declared in September 1990 and 29 per cent below the US level.
— 6,000 total accountable warheads, about 41 per cent below the current Soviet level and 43 per cent below the current US level.
— 4,900 accountable warheads deployed on ICBMS or SLBMS, about 48 per cent below the current Soviet level and 40 per cent below the current US level.
— 1,540 accountable warheads deployed on 154 heavy ICBMS, a 50 per cent reduction in current Soviet forces. The United States has no heavy ICBMS.
— 1,100 accountable warheads deployed on mobile ICBMS.
— Aggregate throw-weight of deployed ICBMS and SLBMS equal to about 54 per cent of the current Soviet aggregate throw-weight.

Ballistic Missile Warhead Accountability. The treaty uses detailed counting rules to ensure the accurate accounting of the number of warheads attributed to each type of ballistic missile.
— Each deployed ballistic missile warhead counts as one under the 4,900 ceiling and one under the 6,000 overall warhead ceiling.
— Each side is to allow 10 on-site inspections each year to verify that deployed ballistic missiles contain no more warheads than the number that is attributed to them under the treaty.

Downloading Ballistic Missile Warheads. The treaty also allows for a reduction in the number of warheads on certain ballistic missiles, which will help the sides adapt their existing forces to the new regime. Such 'downloading' is permitted in a carefully structured and limited fashion.
— The United States may download its three-warhead Minuteman III ICBM by either one or two warheads. The Soviet Union has already downloaded its seven warhead SS-N18 SLBM by four warheads.
— In addition, each side may download up to 500 warheads on two other existing types of ballistic missiles, as long as the total number of warheads removed from downloaded missiles does not exceed 1,250 at any one time.

New Types. The treaty places constraints on the characteristics of new types of ballistic missiles to ensure the accuracy of counting rules and preventing undercounting of missile warheads.

— The number of warheads attributed to a new type of ballistic missile must be no less than the number determined by dividing 40 per cent of the missile's total throw-weight by the weight of the lightest RV (re-entry vehicle) tested on that missile.
— The throw-weight attributed to a new type must be no less than the missile's throw-weight capability at specified reference ranges (11,000 km for ICBMs and 9,500 km for SLBMs).

Heavy ICBMs. START places significant restrictions on the Soviet SS-18 heavy ICBM.
— A 50 per cent reduction in the number of Soviet SS-18 ICBMs; a total reduction of 154 of these Soviet missiles.
— New types of heavy ICBMs are banned.
— Downloading of heavy ICBMs is banned.
— Heavy SLBMs and heavy mobile ICBMs are banned.
— Heavy ICBMs will be reduced on a more stringent schedule than other strategic arms.

Mobile ICBMs. Because mobile missiles are more difficult to verify than other types of ballistic missiles, START incorporates a number of special restrictions and notifications with regard to these missiles. These measures will significantly improve confidence that START will be effectively verifiable.
— Non-deployed mobile missiles and non-deployed mobile launchers are numerically and geographically limited so as to limit the possibility for reload and refire.
— The verification regime includes continuous monitoring of mobile ICBM production, restrictions on movements, on-site inspections, and cooperative measures to improve the effectiveness of national technical means of intelligence collection.

Heavy Bombers. Because heavy bombers are stabilizing strategic systems (for example, they are less capable of a short-warning attack than ballistic missiles), START counting rules for weapons on bombers are different than those for ballistic missile warheads.
— Each heavy bomber counts as one strategic nuclear delivery vehicle.
— Each heavy bomber equipped to carry only short-range missiles or gravity bombs is counted as one warhead under the 6,000 limit.
— Each US heavy bomber equipped to carry long-range nuclear ALCMs (air-launched cruise missiles) (up to a maximum of 150 bombers) is counted as 10 warheads even though it may be equipped to carry up to 20 ALCMs.
— A similar discount applies to Soviet heavy bombers equipped to carry long-range nuclear ALCMs. Each such Soviet heavy bomber (up to a maximum of 180) is counted as eight warheads even though it may be equipped to carry up to 16 ALCMs.
— Any heavy bomber equipped for long-range nuclear ALCMs deployed in excess of 150 for the United States or 180 for the Soviet Union will be accountable by the number of ALCMs the heavy bomber is actually equipped to carry.

Verification Regime. Building on recent arms control agreements, START includes extensive and unprecedented verification provisions. This comprehensive verification regime greatly reduces the likelihood that violations would go undetected.
— START bans the encryption and encapsulation of telemetric information and other forms of information denial on flight tests of ballistic missiles. However, strictly limited exemptions to this ban are granted sufficient to protect the flight-testing of sensitive research projects.
— START allows 12 different types of on-site inspections and requires roughly 50 different types of notifications covering production, testing, movement, deployment and destruction of strategic offensive arms.

Treaty Duration. START will have a duration of 15 years, unless it is superseded by a subsequent agreement. If the sides agree, the treaty may be extended for successive five-year periods beyond the 15 years.

Non-circumvention and Third Countries. START prohibits the transfer of strategic offensive arms to third countries, except that the treaty will not interfere with existing patterns of cooperation. In addition, the treaty prohibits the permanent basing of strategic offensive arms outside the national territory of each side.

Air-Launched Cruise Missiles (ALCMs). START does not directly count or limit ALCMs. ALCMs are limited indirectly through their association with heavy bombers.
— Only nuclear-armed ALCMs with a range in excess of 600 km are covered by START.

— Long-range, conventionally-armed ALCMs that are distinguishable from nuclear-armed ALCMs are not affected.
— Long-range nuclear-armed ALCMs may not be located at air bases for heavy bombers not accountable as being equipped for such ALCMs.
— Multiple warhead long-range nuclear ALCMs are banned.

Sea-Launched Cruise Missiles (SLCMs). SLCMs are not constrained by the treaty. However, each side has made a politically binding declaration as to its plans for the deployment of nuclear-armed SLCMs. Conventionally-armed SLCMs are not subject to such a declaration.
— Each side will make an annual declaration of the maximum number of nuclear-armed SLCMs with a range greater than 600 km that it plans to deploy for each of the following five years.
— This number will not be greater than 880 long-range nuclear-armed SLCMs.
— In addition, as a confidence-building measure, nuclear-armed SLCMs with a range of 300–600 km will be the subject of a confidential annual data exchange.

Backfire Bomber. The Soviet Backfire bomber is not constrained by the treaty. However, the Soviet side has made a politically binding declaration that it will not deploy more than 300 air force and 200 naval Backfire bombers, and that these bombers will not be given intercontinental capability.

Magnitude of START-Accountable Reductions. The following are the aggregate data from the Memorandum of Understanding, based upon agreed counting rules in START; also shown are the percentage reductions required under the treaty. Because of the counting rules, the number of heavy bomber weapons actually deployed may be higher than the number shown in the aggregate. These data are effective as of September 1990 and will be updated at entry into force:

	United States		Soviet Union	
	Actual	Reduction	Actual	Reduction
Delivery Vehicles	2,246	29%	2,500	36%
Warheads	10,563	43%	10,271	41%
Ballistic Missile Warheads	8,210	40%	9,416	48%
Heavy ICBMS/Warheads	none	none	308/3080	50%
Throw-weight (metric tons)	2,361.3	none	6,626.3	46%

3. COMMONWEALTH OF INDEPENDENT STATES

The Union of Soviet Socialist Republics (USSR) ceased to exist in December 1991, when a Commonwealth of Independent States (CIS) was established by 11 ex-Soviet republics acting as sovereign entities. Of the 15 original republics, Estonia, Latvia and Lithuania had achieved separate independence earlier in the year, while Georgia declined to join the new CIS. Published below are (i) the Minsk Agreement of 8 December and an accompanying economic policy statement, which were adopted by the Russian Federation, Belorussia and Ukraine and brought the CIS into being; and (ii) the Alma-Ata Declaration of 21 December and an accompanying resolution on UN membership, under which Armenia, Azerbaijan, Kazakhstan, Kirghizia, Moldavia, Tajikistan, Turkmenia and Uzbekistan opted to join the CIS. (Texts supplied by Royal Institute of International Affairs, London.)

THE MINSK DECLARATION

We, the Republic of Belarus, the Russian Federation (RSFSR) and Ukraine, as founder states of the USSR, which signed the 1922 Union Treaty, further described as the high contracting parties, conclude that the USSR has ceased to exist as a subject of international law and a geopolitical reality.
Taking as our basis the historic community of our peoples and the ties which have been established between them, taking into account the bilateral treaties concluded between the high contracting parties;
striving to build democratic law-governed states and intending to develop our relations on the basis of mutual recognition and respect for state sovereignty, the inalienable right to self-determination, the principles of equality and non-interference in internal affairs, repudiation of the use of force

and of economic or any other methods of coercion, settlement of contentious problems by means of mediation and other generally-recognized principles and norms of international law;

considering that further development and strengthening of relations of friendship, good-neighbourliness and mutually beneficial cooperation between our states correspond to the vital national interest of their peoples and serve the cause of peace and security;

confirming our adherence to the goals and principles of the United Nations Charter, the Helsinki Final Act and other documents of the Conference on Security and Cooperation in Europe;

and committing ourselves to observe the generally recognized internal norms on human rights and the rights of peoples,

we have agreed the following:

Art. 1. The high contracting parties form the Commonwealth of Independent States.

Art. 2. The high contracting parties guarantee their citizens equal rights and freedoms regardless of nationality or other distinctions. Each of the high contracting parties guarantees the citizens of the other parties and also persons without citizenship that live on its territory, civil, political, social, economic and cultural rights and freedoms in accordance with generally-recognized international norms of human rights, regardless of national allegiance or other distinctions.

Art. 3. The high contracting parties, desiring to promote the expression, preservation and development of the ethnic, cultural, linguistic and religious individuality of the national minorities resident on their territories and that of the unique ethno-cultural regions that have come into being, take them under their protection.

Art. 4. The high contracting parties will develop the equal and mutually-beneficial cooperation of their peoples and states in the spheres of politics, the economy, culture, education, public health, protection of the environment, science and trade and in the humanitarian and other spheres, will promote the broad exchange of information and will conscientiously and unconditionally observe reciprocal obligations. The parties consider it a necessity to conclude agreements on cooperation in the above spheres.

Art. 5. The high contracting parties recognize and respect one another's territorial integrity and the inviolability of existing borders within the Commonwealth. They guarantee openness of borders, freedom of movement for citizens and of transmission of information within the Commonwealth.

Art. 6. The member-states of the Commonwealth will cooperate in safeguarding international peace and security and in implementing effective measures for reducing weapons and military spending. They seek the elimination of all nuclear weapons and universal total disarmament under strict international control. The parties will respect one another's aspiration to attain the status of a non-nuclear zone and a neutral state.

The member-states of the community will preserve and maintain under united command a common military-strategic space, including unified control over nuclear weapons, the procedure for implementing which is regulated by a special agreement. They also jointly guarantee the necessary conditions for the stationing and functioning of and for material and social provision for the strategic armed forces. The parties contract to pursue a harmonized policy on questions of social protection and pension provision for servicemen and their families.

Art. 7. The high contracting parties recognize that within the sphere of their activities, implemented on an equal basis through the common coordinating institutions of the Commonwealth, will be the following:

—cooperation in the sphere of foreign policy;

—cooperation in forming and developing the united economic area, the common European and Eurasian markets, in the area of customs policy;

—cooperation in developing transport and communication systems;

—cooperation in preservation of environment and participation in creating a comprehensive international system of ecological safety;

—migration policy issues;

—fighting organized crime.

Art. 8. The parties realize the planetary character of the Chernobyl catastrophe and pledge themselves to unite and coordinate their efforts in minimizing and overcoming its consequences. To this end they have decided to conclude a special agreement which will take into consideration the gravity of the consequences of this catastrophe.

Art. 9. Disputes regarding interpretation and application of the norms of this agreement are to be solved by way of negotiations between the appropriate bodies and, when necessary, at the level of heads of the governments and states.

Art. 10. Each of the high contracting parties reserves the right to suspend the validity of the present agreement or individual articles thereof, after informing the parties to the agreement of this a year in advance. The clauses of the present agreement may be addended or amended with the common consent of the high contracting parties.

Art. 11. From the moment that the present agreement is signed, the norms of third states, including the former USSR, are not permitted to be implemented on the territories of the signatory states.

Art. 12. The high contracting parties guarantee the fulfilment of the international obligations binding upon them from the treaties and agreements of the former USSR.

Art. 13. The present agreement does not affect the obligations of the high contracting parties in regard to third states. The present agreement is open for all member-states of the former USSR to join, and also for other states which share the goals and principles of the present agreement.

Art. 14. The city of Minsk is the official location of the coordinating bodies of the Commonwealth. The activities of bodies of the former USSR are discontinued on the territories of the member-states of the Commonwealth.

Executed in the city of Minsk on 8 December 1991 in three copies each in the Belorussian, Russian and Ukrainian languages, the three texts being of equal validity.

For Belorussia	For the Russian Federation	For Ukraine
S. Shushkevich	B. Yeltsin	L. Kravchuk
V. Kebich	G. Burbulis	V. Fokin

MINSK STATEMENT ON ECONOMIC POLICY COORDINATION

It is vitally important to maintain and develop the existing close economic links between our states, in order to stabilize the situation in the economy and pave the way for economic revival. The parties have agreed upon the following:

—to conduct coordinated radical economic reforms aimed at creating fully-fledged market mechanisms, transforming property relations and ensuring freedom of enterprise;
—to refrain from any actions inflicting economic damage upon each other;
—to base economic relations and settlements on the existing unit of currency, the rouble;
—to introduce national currencies on the basis of special agreements that guarantee observance of the parties' economic interests;
—to conclude an inter-bank agreement aimed at restricting monetary emission, ensuring effective control of the money mass, and forming a system of mutual settlements;
—to pursue a coordinated policy of reducing the deficits of the republican budgets;
—to pursue a coordinated policy of price liberalization and of social protection for citizens;
—to undertake joint action aimed at ensuring the unity of the economic space;
—to coordinate foreign economic activities and customs policy, and to ensure freedom of transit;
—to resolve by way of a special agreement the issue of indebtedness of former Union enterprises;
—within 10 days to agree on the amounts of and procedure for financing in 1992 expenditure on defence and on removal of the consequences of the accident at the Chernobyl nuclear power station;
—to request the supreme soviets of the republics that, when formulating taxation policy, they take into account the need for coordination of value-added tax rates;
—to facilitate the establishment of joint ventures (joint-stock companies);
—to draw up during December a mechanism for implementation of inter-republican economic agreements.

For Belorussia	For the Russian Federation	For Ukraine
V. Kebish	G. Burbulis	V. Fokin

THE ALMA-ATA DECLARATION

The independent states: the Azerbaijani Republic, the Republic of Armenia, the Republic of Belorussia, the Republic of Kazakhstan, the Republic of Kirghizia, the Republic of Moldavia, the Russian Federation, the Republic of Tajikistan, Turkmenia, the Republic of Uzbekistan and Ukraine;

seeking to build democratic law-governed states, the relations between which will develop on the basis of mutual recognition and respect for state sovereignty and sovereign equality, the inalienable right to self-determination, principles of equality and non-interference in the internal affairs, the rejection of the use of force, the threat of force and economic and any other methods of pressure, a peaceful settlement of disputes, respect for human rights and freedoms, including the rights of national minorities, a conscientious fulfilment of commitments and other generally recognized principles and standards of international law;

recognizing and respecting each other's territorial integrity and the inviolability of the existing borders;

believing that the strengthening of the relations of friendship, good neighbourliness and mutually advantageous cooperation, which has deep historic roots, meets the basic interests of nations and promotes the cause of peace and security;

being aware of their responsibility for the preservation of civilian peace and inter-ethnic accord;

being loyal to the objectives and principles of the agreement on the creation of the Commonwealth of Independent States;

are making the following statement:

Cooperation between members of the Commonwealth will be carried out in accordance with the principle of equality through coordinating institutions formed on a parity basis and operating in the way established by the agreements between members of the Commonwealth, which is neither a state nor a super-state structure.

In order to ensure international strategic stability and security, allied command of the military-strategic forces and a single control over nuclear weapons will be preserved and the sides will respect each other's desire to attain the status of a non-nuclear and (or) neutral state.

The Commonwealth of Independent States is open, with the agreement of all its participants, to the states–members of the former Soviet Union, as well as to other states sharing the goals and principles of the Commonwealth, which may join it.

The allegiance to cooperation in the formation and development of the common economic space and all-European and Eurasian markets is being confirmed.

With the formation of the Commonwealth of Independent States the USSR ceases to exist. Member states of the Commonwealth guarantee, in accordance with their constitutional procedures, the fulfilment of international obligations, stemming from the treaties and agreements of the former USSR.

Member states of the Commonwealth pledge to observe strictly the principles of this declaration.

For the Azerbaijani Republic: A. Mutalibov; for the Republic of Armenia: L. Ter-Petrosyan; for the Republic of Belorussia: S. Shushkevich; for the Republic of Kazakhstan: N. Nazarbayev; for the Republic of Kirghizia: A. Akayev; for the Republic of Moldavia: M. Snegur; for the Russian Federation: B. Yeltsin; for the Republic of Tajikistan: R. Nabiyev; for Turmenia: S. Niyazov; for Ukraine: L. Kravchuk; for the Republic of Uzbekistan: I. Karimov.

ALMA-ATA RESOLUTION ON UN MEMBERSHIP

The states participating in the Commonwealth, referring to article 12 of the agreement on the creation of the CIS;

and proceeding from the intention of every state to fulfil its obligations according to the UN Charter and participate in the work of this organization as full and equal members;

and taking into account that Belorussia, the USSR and Ukraine were original members of the UN;

and expressing satisfaction with the fact that Belorussia and Ukraine are continuing to participate in the UN as sovereign independent states;

and being filled with the resolution to cooperate in strengthening international peace and security on the basis of the UN charter in the interests of their peoples and the whole international community,

have decided:

1. The Commonwealth states support Russia in continuing the USSR's membership of the

UN, including its permanent membership of the Security Council and of other international organizations.

2. Belorussia, the Russian Federation and Ukraine will give the other Commonwealth states support in resolving the questions of their full and equal membership of the UN and other international organizations. ... [The resolution had the same signatories as the preceding declaration.]

4. MAASTRICHT TREATY ON EUROPEAN UNION

A European Council (heads of government) meeting held in Maastricht (Netherlands) on 9–10 December 1991 reached agreement on draft texts containing important and wide-ranging amendments to the existing European Community (EC) treaties designed to bring about 'an ever-closer Union among the peoples of Europe'. Scheduled for formal signature by the Council of Ministers early in 1992 and then requiring parliamentary ratification in the 12 member states, the Maastricht accord was notable for the exemptions secured by the United Kingdom from its provisions on the goal of economic and monetary union and on a social policy dimension for the EC. The following summary of the accord (the texts of which ran to several hundred pages of complex treaty revision) is based on a briefing issued by the European Commission office in London.

Common Foreign and Security Policy

The opening provisions of the Maastricht accord states that the European Union shall assert its identity on the international scene 'through the implementation of a common foreign and security policy which shall include the eventual framing of a common defence policy'. The policy will be implemented through inter-governmental procedures in the Council of Ministers, fully associating the European Commission with the work and keeping the European Parliament informed, but not using the mechanisms of the treaties. In the area of foreign policy (but not defence), the formal procedure will be for the European Council to give general guidelines for joint action and for the Council of Ministers to implement them, acting unanimously in principle but able to define matters where a qualified majority vote can be used. Joint actions emerging from this procedure will be binding on the positions and actions of members states. Where the Council has not taken any decision on a foreign policy issue, a member state will be free to act and will inform the Council accordingly.

As regards cooperation on defence and security policy, the Western European Union (WEU), currently linking nine of the 12 EC member states, will become 'the defence component of the Union' and the means of strengthening the European pillar of the Atlantic alliance and of formulating a common European defence policy. According to a declaration issued in Maastricht, these objectives will be pursued on the following basis: (i) the policy of the Union should not prejudice national defence polices and should respect NATO obligations; (ii) the new treaty's defence provisions will be revised in 1998 on the basis of a report to be presented to the European Council in 1996; (iii) the WEU is to elaborate and implement decisions and actions of the Union which have defence implications; (iv) the operational role of the WEU will be strengthened by the creation of a planning cell, closer military cooperation, regular meetings of chiefs of defence staff and enhanced cooperation in the armaments field aimed at the creation of a European armaments agency; (v) EC states not currently members of the WEU are invited either to join (in the case of Denmark and Greece) or to take associate membership (Irish Republic); and (vi) the WEU secretariat will move from London to Brussels.

Economic and Monetary Union

Stage 1 of economic and monetary union (EMU), launched on 1 July 1990 under existing EC powers, involves greater coordination of member states' economic and monetary policies, strengthening of the European Monetary System (EMS) and the role of the European currency unit (ecu) and extension of the work of the committee of central bank governors. Implementation of Stages 2 and 3, requiring treaty changes because they involve the creation of new institutions, will take place according to a timetable from which the United Kingdom, under a special protocol, is accorded an 'opt-out' possibility, as follows:

1 January 1994—Stage 2 to begin with the establishment of a European Monetary Institute (EMI).

31 December 1996—Deadline for the Council to decide to launch Stage 3 (including a single currency) and to fix the date, and for the UK to notify the Council whether it intends to move to Stage 3. The Council decision is to be taken by qualified majority, requiring at this stage a 'critical mass' of seven of the 12 member states to meet the convergence criteria (or six if the UK is not participating).

1 January 1998—Further target date for UK notification of non-participation in Stage 3, to apply if the 31 December 1996 deadline for a Council decision has not been met; subject to UK parliamentary requirements, an extension of this further deadline is possible.

1 July 1998—Final deadline for (i) the establishment of a European Central Bank (ECB) and a European System of Central Banks (ESCB), if this has not already happened; (ii) the conferment of independence on national central banks, if the ECB and ESCB are only now being established; and (iii) a Council decision, by qualified majority vote, on which member states meet the convergence criteria for Stage 3 and the single currency.

1 January 1999—Final deadline for 'irrevocable' commencement of Stage 3 of EMU, including a single currency for participating member states.

If the UK opts not to join Stage 3 with other member states, it will retain those monetary and exchange-rate policy powers not subject to EC discipline (while being bound to accept Stage 2 commitments on avoiding excessive public deficit). The UK weighted vote will then be suspended for the purposes of calculating qualified majority Council votes. The UK will have no right to participate in the appointment of ECB officers, and ECB statutes will not apply to the UK. The UK will be free to change its decision and move to Stage 3 at a later date, provided it satisfies the necessary conditions of convergence.

Under the coordination provisions of EMU, member states will regard their respective economic policies as a matter of common concern. EC leaders in the European Council will recommend economic policy guidelines for member states and the Community, while the Council of Ministers will monitor economic developments. Where a national economic policy is inconsistent with the guidelines or jeopardizes EMU, the Council may make recommendations to the member state concerned by a qualified majority vote. Where a member state is in severe difficulties, the Council may agree unanimously on a Commission proposal to grant financial assistance, or by qualified majority if a natural disaster is involved. Member states shall avoid excessive budget deficits, in which context the Commission must monitor government debt and assess whether budgetary discipline is being observed; if there is a risk of excessive deficit, the Commission will inform the Council, which may make recommendations to the member state and require action to be taken. Failure of the member state to comply may trigger further measures, which may include an invitation to the European Investment Bank (EIB) to reconsider its lending policy to the state concerned, a requirement that the state make an interest-free deposit with the Community or the imposition of fines. Council decisions on such measures will be taken by a two-thirds qualified majority vote, with the member state concerned not participating.

By the beginning of Stage 2 on 1 January 1994, member states are required to have adopted programmes to achieve greater economic convergence, especially regarding price stability and sound public finances, and to have initiated the process of making national central banks independent. The EMI to be established on 1 January 1994 will (i) strengthen cooperation between national central banks and coordination of monetary policies, (ii) monitor the EMS, (iii) facilitate use of the ecu, especially through an ecu clearing system, and (iv) prepare for Stage 3 of EMU. The Commission and the EMI will report on member states' progress towards convergence to the European Council, which will decide by 31 December 1996 whether a majority of participating states meet the following four convergence criteria: (i) price stability, defined as a rate of inflation not more than 1.5 per cent above the average of the three best-performing countries; (ii) manageable deficits, defined as a government deficit of not more than 3 per cent of GDP and a public debt of not more than 60 per cent of GDP; (iii) exchange rate stability, defined as observance of the permitted fluctuation margins of the EMS exchange rate mechanism (ERM) for at least two years; and (iv) interest rate convergence, defined as a level not more than 2 per cent above the average of the three lowest rates over the previous year.

If the European Council finds that sufficient member states meet the convergence criteria, it can decide by qualified majority to launch Stage 3 at a particular date. If no date has been fixed by the end of 1997, the ESCB, including the ECB, must be established by 1 July 1998 to replace the EMI. The basic tasks of the ESCB will be (i) to define and implement Community monetary policy, (ii) to conduct foreign-exchange operations, (iii) to hold and manage official foreign reserves of member states (subject to the latter being able to hold working balances of foreign exchange), and (iv) to promote the smooth operation of payment systems. When Stage 3 begins, all the participating states will agree the conversion rates at which their currencies will be irrevocably

XIX.4 MAASTRICHT TREATY ON EUROPEAN UNION

fixed and exchanged for ecus. The ecu will then become a currency in its own right, with its exchange rate relationship with non-EC currencies being determined by unanimous agreement of the Council. The ECB will have the exclusive right to authorize issue of ecu banknotes in the Community, both by the ECB itself or by national central banks. Member states will be able to issue coins, subject to ECB approval and the right of the Council to harmonize denominations and technical specifications. The ECB and the national central banks will be required to be independent, not taking instructions from any EC, government or other source. The Community will speak as one in international negotiations on monetary issues, agreements reached being binding on the ECB and other EC institutions.

Social Chapter Agreement

As a result of UK opposition to the 1989 European Social Charter, the Maastricht summit could not agree on amendment of the existing social articles of the EC treaties with a view to giving legal substance to the Charter. Instead, agreement was reached on a protocol whereby the other 11 member states will be able to implement the 1989 Charter (which became known as the Social Chapter) without reference to the UK. Community institutions can be 'borrowed' for this purpose, with the Commission, Parliament and Court of Justice fulfilling their normal roles and the Council of Ministers taking decisions by unanimity in some cases and by qualified majority vote in others. The preference will be for decisions involving all 12 member states, but where the UK is unable to participate the other 11 can themselves proceed. In the absence of the UK, a qualified majority will consist of 44 votes out of 66, rather than 54 votes out of 76. Work will continue normally on those social policy proposals already under consideration by the Council, such as conditions for pregnant women, working hours and social security rights of migrant workers.

The policy areas where unanimous Council decisions are necessary are: social security and social protection of workers, protection of workers made redundant, representation and collective defence of workers and employers, conditions of employment for third-country nationals and financial contributions for job promotion. Areas where qualified majority voting will apply are: health and safety, working conditions, information and consultation of workers, equality of men and women at work and integration of persons excluded from the labour market. Specific measures must take account of the diverse national practices in the EC, especially in the field of contractual relations, and the need to maintain the competitiveness of the Community's economy. In particular, they must 'avoid imposing administrative, financial and legal constraints in a way which would hold back the creation and development of small and medium-sized undertakings'.

Justice, Home Affairs and Immigration

Under the Maastricht accord, justice and home affairs remain an 'inter-governmental' aspect of Community cooperation rather than one dependent on Commission proposals, although the Commission will be associated with decision-making and has some limited powers of initiative. The provisions identify the following areas of common interest: asylum policy, movement across the EC's external borders, immigration policy, combating drug addiction, combating fraud, judicial cooperation in civil and criminal matters, customs cooperation and police cooperation. These areas are broadly those covered by the Schengen Agreement concluded by the six original EC members (Belgium, France, Germany, Italy, Luxembourg and the Netherlands) in 1990, outside the treaty framework. Their inclusion in the new treaty means that joint positions and joint action can now be taken by the Council, by qualified majority voting if it so decides. Only member states have the power of initiative in criminal matters, although the Commission will be associated with the work and the views of the European Parliament will be 'duly taken into consideration'. The new provisions make special reference to the European Convention on Human Rights and the Convention on the Status of Refugees and also to 'the protection afforded by member states to persons persecuted on political grounds'.

The question of immigration is singled out for a twin-track approach, partly under the Treaty of Rome and partly under inter-governmental cooperation procedures. In the former category, the Council will decide by unanimity, on the basis of a Commission proposal, which third-country nationals require a visa to enter the EC, and a uniform visa format will be established. Qualified majority voting will apply from 1 January 1996; emergency action can be taken for a six-month period to deal with sudden emergencies. Under the latter category, areas of 'common interest' are identified as including: asylum policy, the aim being to harmonize its various aspects by the end of 1993; rues and controls on persons crossing EC external borders; conditions of movement and residence for immigrants; and illegal immigration. An EC-wide system for exchanging information between national police forces (Europol) is to be set up.

New Policy Areas

Some areas of Community policy are expanded in the Union Treaty, and new ones introduced. Some of the main innovations are as follows:

Cohesion. Measures to reduce the gaps between the prosperity of different regions include a Cohesion Fund to be set up by 31 December 1993 to finance projects in fields of environment and transport infrastructure (see Trans-European networks). The Council may decide unanimously where actions are needed outside the structural funds. The fund is designed to help member states whose GDP per capita is less than 90 per cent of the EC average.

Committee of the Regions. This committee will consist of representatives of regional and local authorities. It will be consulted by the Council or the Commission and may submit its own opinion on a matter where it believes that specific regional interests are involved. The Committee will consist of 189 members, ranging from 24 each for the large member states to six for Luxembourg. It will share an organizational structure with the Economic and Social Committee.

Trans-European networks. The Community will contribute to the establishment and development of trans-European networks in transport, telecommunications and energy infrastructures. Support can be given to national programmes, especially through feasibility studies, loan guarantees or interest-rate subsidies, as well as through the Cohesion Fund for transport infrastructure.

Own resources. The Community bodies will examine the 'own resources' system to take better account of the relative prosperity of the poorer member states.

Consumer policy. A high level of protection is envisaged, through internal market measures or specific action.

Culture. The Community is to encourage cooperation in the cultural field, working closely with the Council of Europe. Any incentive measures to be taken must be decided by unanimity in the Council.

Education and vocational training. Community initiatives are envisaged in the areas of education, language teaching, mobility for students and teachers and vocational training policy. They will show respect for member states' responsibility for the content of teaching and organization of education systems and their cultural and linguistic diversity; there will be no EC harmonization of the laws and regulations of member states in these areas.

Environment. There will be a restatement of Community objectives, including promoting measures at an international level. The aim will be a high level of protection 'taking into account the diversity of situations in the various regions of the Community'. A Community inspection procedure will be established for national provisional measures. Qualified majority voting will apply except for fiscal provisions.

Health. The Council will be able to adopt recommendations in the public health field by qualified majority, with the aim of ensuring a high level of human health protection. Member states will coordinate their policies and programmes in conjunction with the Commission.

Industry. The Council may decide by unanimity on measures to help the competitiveness of EC industry, speeding adjustment to structural change, encouraging a favourable environment for cooperation and making better use of innovation, research and technological development. These provisions must not provide a basis for measures which may distort competition.

Insurance. A protocol to the treaty will resolve the confusion over equal pension rights arising from the Barber case in the European Court. There will be no retroactivity of pension rights before 17 May 1990, when the Court made its judgment under the equal pay conditions of the treaty.

Access to information. The Commission is asked to submit a report by the end of 1993 on measures to improve public access to the information available to the EC institutions, on the basis that transparency strengthens the nature of the institutions and the public's confidence in EC administration.

Implementation of EC law. The European Court of Justice will be able to fine a member state for failing to respect a judgment of the Court. It can act on the basis of a reasoned opinion from the Commission, which should tell the Court what lump sum or penalty it thinks appropriate.

National parliaments. More contact is planned between the European Parliament and national parliaments through the exchange of information and granting of appropriate reciprocal facilities. National parliaments should receive Commission proposals in good time.

Ombudsman. The European Parliament is to appoint an ombudsman to look into instances of maladministration by any of the EC institutions except the Court. Individuals, companies and other legal persons will be entitled to lay complaints. The ombudsman will conduct inquiries either on his own initiative or as a result of complaints; where he finds maladministration, he will draw up a report for the institution concerned after receiving their view. The term of office will run concurrently with the European Parliament mandate.

XIX.4 MAASTRICHT TREATY ON EUROPEAN UNION

Other new policies. The Maastricht accord allows for new policies for energy, civil protection and tourism, although no detailed provisions are to be laid down in the near future. These will be examined on the basis of a report from the Commission in 1996. Community action will meantime be based on the existing treaty provisions.

Powers of the European Parliament

In certain major sectors the European Parliament is to have new powers of co-decision with the Council of Ministers allowing it to reject a proposal by an overall majority of its members if agreement cannot be reached between the two institutions in a joint conciliation committee. The new procedure is as follows:

1. The Commission makes a proposal to the European Parliament and the Council of Ministers.
2. Parliament gives its opinion; Council adopts a common position, acting by qualified majority.
3. The Council informs the Parliament of its common position.
4. Parliament has three months in which it can (*a*) approve the common position or take no decision in which case the Council then adopts; (*b*) vote to reject the common position by an absolute majority and inform the Council, which can call a meeting of the conciliation committee comprising equal numbers from Council and Parliament. The Parliament may then (*a*) reject again by absolute majority, so the proposal is not adopted; or (*b*) propose amendments by an absolute majority.
5. If the Parliament proposes amendments at this stage, the Council has a further three months. It may (*a*) approve the amended text by qualified majority (except for amendments opposed by the Commission, which will require unanimity in the Council); or (*b*) refuse to approve, in which case the conciliation committee is convened again.
6. The conciliation committee then has a further six weeks to work on the text. If it approves a joint text, then this is adopted as long as the Parliament votes in favour by a majority of votes cast and the Council approves by qualified majority. Failure by either institution to approve means that the proposal is not adopted.
7. If the conciliation committee fails to agree, the Council has a further six weeks to confirm its original position, perhaps with some Parliament amendments. The Parliament then has a further six weeks following confirmation to reject the text by an absolute majority of members.

The above procedure (which applies mainly to policies where the Council may decide by qualified majority voting) covers the following: (i) internal market legislation, including right of establishment and free circulation of workers; and (ii) common policies for research and development, trans-European networks, training, education, culture, health, consumer affairs and the multi-annual environment programme.

Under other treaty charges, the Commission and its president will be subject to Parliament's approval at the start of their mandate, which is to be for five years rather than four from the beginning of 1995, coinciding with the Parliament's term. The Parliament can request the Commission to submit any proposal where it decides by overall majority vote that new EC legislation is needed. At the request of a quarter of its members, the Parliament can set up a temporary committee of inquiry to investigate contravention or maladministration in implementation of Community law.

The Parliament is to draw up proposals for a uniform election procedure which must be agreed unanimously by the Council. Member states are to agree on the size of the European Parliament in the light of the enlargement of the Community resulting from German unification.

Budgetary Control

Various treaty changes seek to tighten up control of the Community's finances. When proposing new measures, the Commission must give assurances that these can be financed within the limits of EC financial resources. The status of the Court of Auditors is to be increased to that of a full EC institution. The European Parliament will be able to ask the Commission to give evidence regarding spending and financial control, and the Commission will act on the decisions and observations of the Parliament. Governments will deal with fraud affecting the Community's financial interests in the same way that they deal with national fraud.

Citizenship of the Union

A new treaty chapter says: 'Every person holding the nationality of a member state shall be a citizen of the Union. To give such citizenship substance, (i) the Council will take the necessary measures (by unanimous decision) to ensure that every citizen is free to move and reside anywhere within the territory of the member states; (ii) detailed arrangements will be agreed to give all citizens the right to vote, and stand as candidates in, local elections in any member state (by the end of 1994) and in European Parliament elections anywhere in the EC (by the end of 1993); (iii) rules will be agreed by the end of 1993 (and international negotiations initiated) to give Union citizens in a non-EC country the right to diplomatic or consular protection by the representatives of any member state: (iv) citizens will have the right to petition the European Parliament or to apply to the new ombudsman.

Subsidiarity

A new treaty article enshrining the principle of 'subsidiarity' states that in all policy areas which are outside the EC's exclusive jurisdiction the Community will act 'only if and insofar as the objectives of the proposed action cannot be sufficiently achieved by the member states' and can be better achieved by the Community. It adds: 'Any action by the Community shall not go beyond what is necessary to achieve the objectives of the treaty.'

5. UNITED KINGDOM CONSERVATIVE CABINET

(as at 31 December 1991)

Prime Minister, First Lord of the Treasury and Minister for the Civil Service	Rt. Hon. John Major, MP
Lord Chancellor	Rt. Hon. The Lord Mackay of Clashfern
Secretary of State for Foreign and Commonwealth Affairs	Rt. Hon. Douglas Hurd, CBE, MP
Lord Privy Seal and Leader of the House of Lords	Rt. Hon. Lord Waddington of Read, QC
Secretary of State for the Home Department	Rt. Hon. Kenneth Baker, MP
Chancellor of the Exchequer	Rt. Hon. Norman Lamont, MP
Secretary of State for the Environment	Rt. Hon. Michael Heseltine, MP.
Secretary of State for Defence	Rt. Hon. Tom King, MP.
Secretary of State for Education and Science	Rt. Hon. Kenneth Clarke, QC, MP
Lord President of the Council and Leader of the House of Commons	Rt. Hon. John MacGregor, OBE, MP
Secretary of State for Transport	Rt. Hon. Malcolm Rifkind, QC, MP
Secretary of State for Energy	Rt. Hon. John Wakeham, MP
Secretary of State for Social Security	Rt. Hon. Antony Newton, OBE, MP
Chancellor of the Duchy of Lancaster	Rt. Hon. Christopher Patten, MP
Secretary of State for Northern Ireland	Rt. Hon. Peter Brooke, MP
Minister of Agriculture, Fisheries and Food	Rt. Hon. John Selwyn Gummer, MP
Secretary of State for Employment	Rt. Hon. Michael Howard, QC, MP
Secretary of State for Wales	Rt. Hon. David Hunt, MBE, MP
Secretary of State for Trade and Industry	Rt. Hon. Peter Lilley, MP
Secretary of State for Health	Rt. Hon. William Waldegrave, MP
Secretary of State for Scotland	Rt. Hon. Ian Lang, MP
Chief Secretary to the Treasury	Rt. Hon. David Mellor, QC, MP

6. UNITED STATES REPUBLICAN CABINET

(as at 31 December 1991)

President	George Bush
Vice-President	J. Danforth Quayle
Secretary of State	James Baker
Secretary of the Treasury	Nicholas Brady
Secretary of Defence	Richard Cheney
Secretary of the Interior	Manuel Lujan
Attorney-General	William P. Barr
Secretary of Commerce	Robert Mosbacher
Secretary of Labour	Lynn Martin
Secretary of Health & Human Resources	Dr Louis Sullivan
Secretary of Transportation	Andrew Card
Secretary of Education	Lamar Alexander
Secretary of Agriculture	Edward R. Madigan
Secretary of Veteran Affairs	Edward Derwinski
Secretary of Housing and Urban Development	Jack Kemp
Secretary of Energy	James Watkins

CABINET RANK OFFICIALS

Director of the Central Intelligence Agency	Robert Gates
Director of the Office of Management & Budget	Richard Darman
US Permanent Representative at the United Nations	Thomas Pickering
US Trade Representative	Carla Hills
White House Chief of Staff	Samuel Skinner
Chairman of Council of Economic Advisers	Prof. Michael Boskin
National Security Adviser	General Brent Scowcroft

XX OBITUARY

Agar, Eileen (b. 1899), was ranked in the 1930s with André Breton, Paul Eluard, Paul Nash and Pablo Picasso in the European club of surrealist painters. Her immense output continued for 50 years, and spread round the world, in a style which married surrealism with a distillation of nature. Died 17 November

Akhromeyev, Marshal Sergei (b. 1923), was chief of the general staff of the Soviet Union armed forces 1984–88 and thereafter a special military adviser to President Gorbachev. Died by his own hand after the abortive coup d'état, 24 August

Anderson, Carl (b. 1905), American scientist, won the Nobel Prize for physics in 1936 for his demonstration of the existence of positive electrons. With S. H. Neddermeyer he discovered, in 1937, a previously unknown atomic particle which came to be called the meson muon. He was professor and administrator at the California Institute of Technology 1930–77. Died 11 January.

Arrau, Claudio (b. 1905), Chilean-born pianist, was unsurpassed during half a century for combination of technique and interpretative sensitivity. His early teacher, Martin Krause, who had been a pupil of Liszt, said that Arrau had the finest piano talent since that maestro. He gave a public recital in Berlin at the age of 12; his London debut came in 1922. After a spell of psychological depression he resumed his career, mastering the complete piano works of the classical composers from Bach to Schubert. Escaping Nazi Germany for America, he earned worldwide fame in the 1940s. Beethoven remained his favourite subject, but his repertoire was wide, including the 19th-century Romantic school. In 1981, two years after taking US nationality, he made a triumphal return to his native land, which he had refused to visit during the Allende and Pinochet regimes. He recorded many concertos and solo performances, the former under leading conductors who were among his fervent admirers. Died 9 June

Arrupe, Fr Pedro (b. in Spain 1907), was Superior General of the Society of Jesus 1965–83. In 1938 the Order sent him to Japan, where, already a master of Japanese, he witnessed the effect of the atomic bomb on Hiroshima and heroically ministered to its victims. In 1958 he was appointed superior of the new Jesuit province of Japan, and in 1965 was elected the Society's worldwide head. His espousal of 'liberation theology'—the apostolate to the poor and oppressed—and the liberalism of his theological stance offended conservatives in the Curia, but he retained the personal confidence of Pope John Paul II until his retirement. Died 5 February

Ashcroft, Dame Peggy (b. 1907), in her later years was the most revered and best-loved actress on the English stage and in the film world was an international star. Had she retired at 60 she would have been most famed for her acting in Shakespeare and modern classics at the Old Vic, often with John Gielgud, in the 1930s and '40s, and with the Royal Shakespeare Company and George Devine's English Stage Company in the 1950s and '60s; but more recent audiences knew her best for her brilliant performances in films and television series such as *A Passage to India* and *The Jewel in the Crown* (both 1984); she was known, too, for her unceasing espousal of the theatre, of clear speech and intelligent interpretation, and of mainly left-wing political causes, like nuclear disarmament. Among her best-remembered roles had been Desdemona (to Paul Robeson's Othello, 1930), Juliet (1935), Nina in *The Seagull* (1936), The Duchess of Malfi (1944 and 1961), Hedda Gabler (1954), Margaret in *Richard II* (1963) and the Countess of Rousillon in *All's Well* (1981). Died 14 June

Bakhtiar, Shapour (b. 1914), though Prime Minister of Iran for a crucial month in 1978–79, after serving as a high civil servant in the 1940s and in Mossadiq's cabinet 1951–53, spent most of his adult life in exile or in gaol. Educated partly in France, he joined the French army in 1939 and later served in the French Resistance. Returning to Iran in 1946, he soon reached high rank in the public service, but his liberalism earned him dismissal and several spells of imprisonment until the Shah turned to him in desperation, before, on Bakhtiar's advice, fleeing Iran. Overcome by Ayatollah Khomeini's fundamentalist campaign, he escaped to France, where he organized an Iranian resistance movement and became the target of Khomeiniite hit-men. At the third assassination attempt, they succeeded. Died 7 August

Bardeen, Dr John (b. 1908), American scientist, twice shared the Nobel Prize for physics, with Shockley and Brattain in 1956 for their discovery of the transistor, and with Cooper and Schrieffer in 1972 for their work on superconductivity. He was professor of electrical engineering at the University of Illinois 1951–75; in 1977 he was awarded the Presidential Medal of Freedom. Died 30 January

Boyle, Andrew (b. 1919), British author and broadcaster, had two main claims to fame: his book *The Climate of Treason* (1979) identified, at first anonymously, later by name, Sir Anthony Blunt as the 'fourth man' who, with Guy Burgess, Donald Maclean and Kim Philby, had spied for the Soviet Union; and in 1965 he had modernized British radio news presentation with the BBC programme *The World at One*.

He also wrote admired biographies of contemporary figures. Died 22 April

Brickhill, Paul (b. 1916), Australian journalist and author, used his World War II experience as a fighter pilot and prisoner-of-war to write three immensely popular and money-spinning books: *The Great Escape* (1951), *The Dam Busters* (1951) and *Reach for the Sky* (1954), all of which were turned into films. Died 23 April

Bruller, Jean (b. 1902), French author, under the pseudonym Jean Vercors, was a hero of the intellectual resistance in World War II. Wounded as a soldier in an early action, he set up the underground publishing house Editions de Minuit, which produced, among other literary *samizdat*, his own inspiring novel of life under German occupation, *Le silence de la mer* (1941). He told the story of this courageous enterprise in *La bataille du silence* (1967). Died 10 June

Campoli, Alfredo (b. in Italy 1906), British violinist, played all over the world from a wide repertoire of classical and lighter music, making his US debut in 1953. His lyrical style, combined with technical virtuosity, won him great popularity, not least at the 'Proms' and in the USSR. Died 27 March

Capra, Frank (b. in Italy 1897), American film director, had his greatest success in the 1930s, with the comedies *It Happened One Night* (1934), *Mr Deeds Goes to Town* (1936) and *You Can't Take It With You* (1938), all of which won Oscars for direction, the last also for best picture. Other much-applauded films of his in that era were *Platinum Blonde* (1931), *The Bitter Tea of General Yen* (1933) and *Mr Smith Goes to Washington* (1939). He continued making films until 1960, but rarely to the same effect. In 1980 the American Film Institute honoured him with its Life Achievement Award. Died 3 September

Copeland, Miles (b. 1913), American secret agent, an employee of the Central Intelligence Agency or its predecessor 1945–53 and 1955–57, wrote a widely-read book *The Game of Nations*, about the nature and purpose of covert action, on which he disagreed with the CIA establishment. Died 14 January

Cromer, Earl of, KG, GCMG, PC (b. 1918), was governor of the Bank of England 1961–66. Distinguished service with the Grenadier Guards in World War II had been followed by a City career, in the family bank, Baring Bros, and as UK director of the IMF and World Bank (IBRD) 1959–62. Dismissed from the governorship by Prime Minister Wilson, who was galled by his robust criticism of Labour's financial policy, he returned to the City as undisputed leader of its private banking sector, always a stern champion of financial orthodoxy and monetary stability. He was ambassador to Washington 1971–74. Died 16 March

Davis, Miles (b. 1926), American jazz trumpeter and composer, lacked the brilliant skill of a Louis Armstrong, and had an erratic career, but his constant pursuit of the new, as band-leader, instrumentalist and composer, made him one of the great innovative musicians of the jazz and rock eras. Died 28 September

De Lisle, Viscount, VC, KG, PC, GCMG, GCVO (Philip Sidney, b. 1909), was a descendant of the Elizabethan poet and soldier and inheritor of a great Tudor house, Penshurst Place. He won his VC by acts of extraordinary bravery at the Anzio beachhead in 1944. On succeeding to the peerage in 1945, he had been a Conservative MP for less than a year, but became a dynamic Secretary of State for Air 1951–55. He was Governor-General of Australia 1961–65 and thereafter applied his business ability, courage and stern conservative uprightness to the direction of a number of major firms. Died 5 April

Dimitrios I, His Holiness (b. D. Papadopoulos in Turkey 1914), was Ecumenical Patriarch of Constantinople for nearly 20 years from 1972. An apostle of Christian unity, he paid visits to Rome, London and Washington as well as to Orthodox communities in Europe and Near Asia; but he was also at pains to establish the primacy of the Byzantine patriarchate in the whole Orthodox communion. In 1980 he and his guest, Pope John Paul II, initiated a dialogue on doctrinal differences between the Orthodox and Roman Catholic faiths. Died 2 October

Elias, Judge Taslin Olawale (b. 1914), Nigerian lawyer, was president of the World Association of Judges 1975–91 and of the International Court of Justice 1981–85, after two years as its vice-president. Born in Lagos, he studied law in London and became a master of English. Back in Nigeria, he was successively Attorney-General 1960–72, Chief Justice of the Supreme Court and chairman of the advisory judicial committee 1972–75. Meanwhile, he held academic posts in Oxford and Lagos, where he was dean of the university faculty of law. In 1961 he became a member of the International Law Commission, which he chaired in 1970. Died 14 August

Ennals, Martin (b. 1927), British secretary-general of Amnesty International 1968–80, greatly raised both its resources and its worldwide authority in factual exposure of offences against human rights, for which it was awarded the Nobel Peace Prize in 1977. He had been on the staff of UNESCO 1951–59 and secretary-general of the National Council for Civil Liberties 1960–66. Died 5 October

Fawcett, Sir James, DSC (b. 1913), British lawyer, was president 1972–81 of the European Commission of Human Rights, of which he was a member for 22 years from 1962. He had been a legal adviser to the Foreign Office 1945–70, general counsel to the IMF 1955–60, director of studies at Chatham House 1969–76, and professor of international law at King's College, London 1976–80; his published work concerned not only human rights law but also the law of space. Died 24 June

Field, John (b. Greenfield 1921), British ballet dancer and director, brought to ballet not only successful direction but also zeal to spread its enjoyment to a wider public. He was director of the Royal Ballet touring company 1955–70, ballet director at La Scala, Milan 1971–74, artistic director of the Royal Academy of Dancing 1975–79 and of London Festival Ballet 1979–85. Died 3 August

Finniston, Sir Monty, FRS (b. 1912), British engineer, was chief executive (1971–73) and chairman (1973–76) of the nationalized British Steel Corporation. He was a member or chairman of numerous advisory and research institutions, including an official committee of inquiry into the engineering industry (1977–79), whose dynamic and deep-searching report was always linked to his name. Died 2 February

Fonteyn, Dame Margot (b. Margaret Hookham 1919), was not only the topmost ballerina ever produced by Britain but one of the world's greatest of the century. From 1935 she danced leading roles in the Vic-Wells Ballet under the direction of Ninette de Valois, and there developed a creative partnership with the choreographer Frederick Ashton, culminating in Ashton's *Symphonic Variations* (1946). Her dancing in *The Sleeping Beauty* in the Sadler's Wells Ballet's first New York season in 1949 was applauded with unprecedented rapture. Thereafter her status as a prima ballerina assoluta was assured (though not formally ratified until 1979), and besides dancing the great classical roles she won equal acclaim in ballets created for her by Ashton, de Valois, Petit, Cranko and Robert Helpmann, with whom she also had a long dancing partnership. In 1962 a new phase of her art opened when she first danced with Rudolf Nureyev, a continuing partnership of unique rapport despite their difference in age. She retired from dancing in 1979, but continued public life as president of the Royal Academy of Dancing and chancellor of Durham University. Her supremacy was founded less on technique than on the musicality and flexibility of all her movements, her perfect balletic 'line' and her actress's care to steep herself in the character of the role she played.

In 1955 she had married Dr Roberto ('Tito') de Arias, Panama's ambassador to London and an aspirant to high political office, whom she tended devotedly after an attempt on his life in 1964 had left him paralysed; and she spent much of her last years in Panama, impoverished by his disability and later by her own contraction of cancer. Died 21 February

Frisch, Max (b. 1911), Swiss author and dramatist, was best known in the English-speaking world for his plays *The Fire Raisers* (1957) and *Andorra* (1961), and his novel *Stiller*, a grim seriousness limiting the popularity of most of his work. Died 4 April

Fuller, Roy (b. 1912), British poet, succeeded Eliot and Auden as the most esteemed poet of his country. His war poems of 1942–44 established his reputation, but it was not until the late 1950s that his art came to full flower. His *Collected Poems* were published in 1962. Conservative in his literary criticism, though politically marxist until a near-deathbed conversion, he was professor of poetry at Oxford 1968–73. Besides his verse (including poems for children) he published a number of novels, volumes of lectures and several works of autobiography. Meanwhile, he pursued a worldlier career as solicitor and eventually director of a large building society and author of manuals of building society law. He was a governor of the

BBC 1972–79. In 1979 he was awarded the Queen's Gold Medal for Poetry. Died 27 September

Gandhi, Rajiv (b. 1944), was Prime Minister of India 1984–89. The elder son of Prime Minister Mrs Indira Gandhi, by profession an air pilot, he was reluctantly persuaded by her to enter politics after the death of his brother Sanjay in 1980, and when she was murdered in 1984 he took her place. Later that year his Congress (I) party gained an overwhelming majority at a general election, and there were high hopes of a new regime led by a man with modern ideas—he had been educated in engineering in England—free of the taint of corruption. They were sadly disappointed. In face of Sikh violence in Punjab and Tamil violence in Sri Lanka, Rajiv Gandhi appeared uncertain and ill-starred, and his regime was tainted with a corruption scandal. In 1989 it suffered an electoral defeat as devastating as its victory had been massive in 1984. Nevertheless he remained popular, and was on the verge of a return to power when he was assassinated, 22 May

Garcia Robles, Alfonso (b. 1911), Mexican diplomat, shared the Nobel Peace Prize with Alva Myrdal for their persistence in striving for international nuclear disarmament. He had often represented his country as ambassador or at the UN and its subsidiaries before concentrating on that cause, becoming one of the authors of the Non-Proliferation Treaty of 1968. Died 2 September

German, Patriarch (b. Hranislav Djoric 1899), was Patriarch of the Serbian Orthodox Church 1958–89. Under a hostile regime he strengthened and enlivened the Church and fostered its relations with churches in other countries, being elected a president of the World Council of Churches in 1968. Died 27 August

Getz, Stan (b. 1927), American tenor saxophonist, achieved a lyrical tone and style which made him the idol of lovers of 'cool jazz' from the 1950s onwards. A London obituarist called him 'one of the great musical artists of the century'. Died 6 June

Goren, Charles (b. 1901), earned the title 'Mr Bridge' as the top professional expert on the game from the 1930s until his retirement in 1966. Besides publishing a score of books (including *Contract Bridge Complete*, 1942), he was a highly successful international player, for the most part in partnership with Helen Sobel. Died 3 April

Gowing, Sir Lawrence (b. 1918), British painter and art historian, joined in his youth the 'Euston Road' group of artists and continued to paint for the rest of his life, while making a notable career in historical criticism and art administration. His published work included studies of Vermeer (1952), Cézanne (1954), Constable (1960), Turner (1966) and Matisse (1966). He was professor of fine art, University of Durham 1948–58, principal of the Chelsea School of Art 1958–65, deputy director of the Tate Gallery 1965–67, professor of fine art, Leeds University 1967–75, adjunct professor of the history of art, University of Pennsylvania 1977, research fellow at the National Museum of Art, Washington, DC 1985–86. Died 3 February

Graham, Martha (b. 1894), American dancer, choreographer and dance director, began her career as a ballet dancer of modest attainment, and continued to dance, chiefly in her own ballets, until she was 70; but in the 1930s she rose to world fame as choreographer and producer, evolving a creative style of her own, both in ballet composition and in stage design, and building up her own company in New York. She first danced in London in 1954, but her European reputation did not flourish until the 1960s. From then on she inspired the

British school of contemporary dance, while in America she had become a living legend. Of all her countless ballet creations the most lauded and lasting was *Appalachian Spring* (1944). Died 1 April

Greene, Graham, OM, CH (b. 1904), was reckoned by many to be the greatest novelist of his time, and the fact that he was never awarded the Nobel Prize for literature was attributed to prejudice aroused by his leftwing political views and his sceptical religious beliefs. A convert from Anglicanism to the Roman Catholic Church, he disliked its dogmatism and gradually slimmed his faith to little more than belief in God, whom he saw as overlord not only of joy and compassion but also of pain and sorrow. Of suicidal mind after an unhappy boyhood, and plagued by religious doubt, he sublimated his trauma in translating his own fears and loneliness into his fictional characters. A profound melancholy haunts much of his finest work, such as *The Power and the Glory* (1940), *The Heart of the Matter* (1948) and *A Burnt-Out Case* (1961). Nevertheless, his novels as well as his lighter works (e.g. *Travels with My Aunt*, 1939), his plays (*The Living Room*, 1967) and his biography of the 17th-century libertine (*Lord Rochester's Monkey*, 1974) are alive with comedy, even farce.

He was a master of plot, character and situation, but the supreme merit of his genius was the economy of his writing: scenes and situations developed themselves, terse dialogue spoke all that needed speech. Greene was an inveterate traveller, deeply in sympathy with peoples oppressed either by native tyrants or by foreign interference or economic imperialism, and many of his novels had a corresponding background: Mexico (*The Power and the Glory*), Argentina (*The Honorary Consul*, 1973), South-East Asia (*The Quiet American*, 1955), Cuba (*Our Man in Havana*, 1958), Haiti (*The Comedians*, 1966). Among other novels were *The Man Within* (his first, 1929), *Stamboul Train* (1932), *Brighton Rock* (1938), *The Human Factor* (1978), *The Captain and the Enemy* (1988).

Greene was film critic of *The Spectator* 1935–40, its literary editor 1940–41, and a director of two publishing firms. His international honours included that of Chevalier de la Légion d'Honneur. Died 3 April

Han Lih-wu, Dr (b. 1903), was Taiwan's ambassador successively to Greece and Thailand 1968–72, but he was much more than a diplomat. A scholar with degrees from China, the USA and England, his most memorable feat was to rescue the art treasures of the Chinese imperial dynasty, first from the advancing Japanese in 1937 and then from the near-victorious communists in 1949, when he delivered them to Taiwan. He had been a minister in Chiang Kai-shek's Chungking government, with which he threw in his lot when it fled offshore. President of the Sino-British Cultural and Economic Association, founder of the Asian Peoples' Anti-Communist League, the Asia and World Forum and the Chinese Association for Human Rights, he spanned the cultures of East and West. Died 16 February

Hay, Alexandre (b. 1919), Swiss banker, was president of the International Committee of the Red Cross 1976–87, during which period the worldwide activity of the Red Cross more than doubled in scale and the ICRC (a wholly Swiss body) greatly strengthened its links with the national Red Cross organizations, the Red Crescent and UN humanitarian organs. Previously he had been president of the European committee on monetary cooperation 1962–73; subsequently he became president of the Swiss Peace Foundation 1988–91. Died 23 August

Heinesen, William (b. in the Faroe Islands 1900), Danish novelist, poet and barrister, shone brilliantly in the

Scandinavian firmament with work steeped in the lore, history and culture of his island home. Among his best novels were (in their English translations) *The Black Cauldron* (published in Danish 1949), *The Lost Musicians* (1950), *The Kingdom of the Earth* (1952) and *The Good Hope* (1964). Died 12 March

Honda, Soichiro (b. 1906), Japanese engineer and inventor, built the Honda motor company from small beginnings, making motor cycles from 1947 and automobiles from 1957, until, as one of Japan's big three motor manufacturers, it held assets exceeding £4,000 million. Always a fan of motor racing, he made Honda top of the world in Formula One events. Retiring from the company leadership at the age of 65, in 1977 he created the Honda Foundation 'to support the development of technology in harmony with the environment'. Died 5 August

Husák, Gustav (b. 1913), was general secretary of the Czechoslovak Communist Party 1969–87 and President of Czechoslovakia 1975–89. By profession a lawyer, he was a dedicated, ambitious communist from 1933, and a persistent Slovak nationalist. Party rivalries cost him imprisonment from 1954 to 1960, but he rose again to party power and allied himself to Alexander Dubček in 1968. His true colours appeared in the crushing of the Prague Spring, and thenceforward he was the willing tool of his Soviet patrons, subjecting the country to political and religious oppression and economic decline. After Gorbachev succeeded Brezhnev in 1985, he could no longer withstand the tide of popular hatred and thirst for reform. He resigned the presidency and was expelled from the party, but was allowed to live in peace without honour. Died 18 November

Hutchinson, Prof. Evelyn, hon. FRS (b. in England, 1903), American zoologist, was one of the founders of modern ecological science. He taught at Yale University for 45 years, retiring from the Sterling professorship of zoology in 1971. His written work —e.g. his *Introduction to Popular Ecology* (1978)—did not cease, nor did the stream of scientific honours and awards that flowed from the US and other nations. Died 17 May

Idris, Youssef (b. 1927), Egyptian writer, shared with Nobel prize-winner Naguib Mahfouz the credit for a dynamic revival of Arabic literature and drama. In novels, short stories, plays and other writings he portrayed the lives and aspirations of ordinary people, especially women, oppressed by capitalist and Islamic society, and was imprisoned for his pains under President Nasser. Died 1 August

Inoue, Yasushi (b. 1907), Japanese writer, scored immediate success with his first novel *The Hunting Gun* (1949), followed by others, such as *The Bull Fight* (1950), which won Japan's highest literary prize, and *The Roof Tiles of Tempyo* (1959). The latter, and especially his fictional life of Confucius, *Koshi*, reflected his lasting interest in Japan's cultural debt to China. Died 29 January

Irwin, Col. James B. (b. 1930), American lunanaut, spent 67 hours on the Moon, with Col. David Scott, during the Apollo mission of July 1971. His lunar experience had a profound religious effect on him; he became a Baptist preacher, and was obsessed by a search for remnants of Noah's Ark on Mount Ararat. Died 8 August

Jasinski, Roman (b. in Poland 1907), was one of the finest male exponents of classical ballet of his time. Favoured earlier by many of the world's leading ballet producers and choreographers, notably Balanchine, he migrated to the US after World War II and founded the Tulsa Ballet Theatre in Oklahoma. Died 16 April

Jiang Qing (b. Luan Shumeng 1914), widow of Mao Zedong, leader of the Chinese Communist Party, was regarded as the evil genius of the Cultural Revolution of 1966–76. As mistress and later wife of the party leader, she had previously played no prominent public role, though she always worked behind the scene for the subordination of art and literature to marxist ideas; but in 1969 she became officially a member of the Beijing politburo, and her power increased as Mao's health declined. His death in 1976 reversed her fortunes: with three colleagues in the notorious 'Gang of Four' she was arrested and charged with treason. Reprieved from the death sentence in 1983, she was eventually released to her home, where she took her own life, 14 May

Joyce, Eileen (b. in Australia 1912), British pianist, earned worldwide renown in the 1960s for her playing of concertos and other major works, from Beethoven to Shostakovich. Born in poverty of a labouring Irish family, she was discovered by the pianist Backhaus and the composer Percy Grainger, who raised money for her schooling and musical training in Europe. Her debut at the Proms under Sir Henry Wood with a Prokofiev concerto was a sensation. Exhausted and wounded by her efforts, she retired early. Died 25 March

Kaganovich, Lazar (b. 1893), was the last of the powerful Old Bolsheviks. Joining the party in 1908, he was already a regional leader in the revolution of 1917. By 1930 he was a full member of the politburo. The hardest of hardliners and a devotee of Stalin, he retained office after that ogre's death, but was ousted in 1954 for his role in an attempt to unseat Nikita Khrushchev. Died 25 July

Kerr, Sir John, AK, GCMG, GCVO, PC (b. 1914), when Governor-General of Australia (1974–77), in 1975 dismissed the Labor government of Gough Whitlam, which was largely paralysed by an adverse-majority Senate's refusal to vote supply, and invited the opposition leader to form a government, which then called an election and won a big majority. Though vindicated by the best constitutional authority, Sir John incurred the venomous hatred of the Labor Party, and, recognizing that he had become a controversial political figure, resigned his high office. At the peak of his career as barrister and judge he had been Chief Justice of New South Wales 1972–74. Died 24 March

Klasen, Dr Karl (b. 1909), German banker, was president of the Deutsche Bundesbank 1970–77. His determination in 1972 to defend the Deutschmark against the dollar by exchange controls led to the resignation of the economic and finance minister Dr Karl Schiller and demonstrated the central bank's independence of the federal government. Died 22 April

Kosinksi, Jerzy (b. in Poland 1933), American author, was most famed for his novels *The Painted Bird* (1965) and *Being There* (1971), the latter being made into a successful film. An academic sociologist, he was president of American PEN 1973–75 and director of the International League for the Rights of Man. Died 4 May

Land, Edwin (b. 1909), American inventor and business leader, founded the Polaroid Corporation to exploit his inventions, the first of which was the polarizing filter to subdue the glare from over-bright lights. In the 1940s he invented and refined instant photography. Polaroid made him a very rich man, but he disliked publicity and extravagance and gave much money to scientific research. Died 1 March

Langlais, Jean (b. 1909), blind French organist, was from 1945 to 1988 titular master of the famous organ at the Basilique Ste. Clotilde in Paris, where César Franck and his own teacher Charles Tournemire had presided. A brilliant player and teacher, he was also a prolific composer, whose works were performed in many countries. Died 8 May

Lawrence, Dr John (b. 1904), American medical physicist, pioneered the use of nuclear isotopes and emanations in the treatment of cancer and other diseases, and in 1936 founded the Donner laboratory at the University of California for research in nuclear medicine. Died 7 September

Lean, Sir David (b. 1908), British film director, was responsible for some of the most memorable films of the 1940s, '50s and '60s: among them *This Happy Breed* (1943), *Brief Encounter* (1945), *Great Expectations* (1946), *The Sound Barrier* (1952), *The Bridge on the River Kwai* (Oscar-winner, 1957), *Lawrence of Arabia* (Oscar-winner, 1962), *Dr Zhivago* (1965). After an interval of 14 years from *Ryan's Daughter* (1970), he directed one of his finest films, *A Passage to India* (1984). Died 16 April

Lefèbvre, Mgr Marcel (b. 1905), had the distinction, rare among Roman Catholic archbishops, of being excommunicated by the Pope. The causative offence was his consecration of four bishops in 1988, but he had been in conflict with Rome ever since the Second Vatican Council of 1962, which he saw as the Church's capitulation to humanism and modernism, and whose reforms he stubbornly refused to accept, especially its substitution of vernacular rites for the Tridentine Latin Mass. Successive Popes sought reconciliation, but in vain, and in defiance of papal orders Lèfebvre continued to maintain the anti-Vatican II seminary which he had founded in Switzerland. At length, in 1988, he pronounced that the throne of St Peter had been occupied by an anti-Christ, who had committed the mortal sins of liberalism, socialism, modernism and zionism. Ordained priest in 1929, he had been a missionary in West Africa 1932–35 and archbishop of Dakar 1948–62. Died 25 March

Léger, HE Cardinal Paul-Emile (b. 1904), was Archbishop of Montreal from 1950 to 1967, when he resigned to become a missionary priest in Africa. Ecumenical and liberal in his views, both in archiepiscopal office and as a tireless servant and champion of the poor of the world, he exerted great influence, especially in North America. Died 13 November

Lewis, Sir Arthur (b. in St Lucia 1913), West Indian economist, shared the Nobel Prize for economics with Theodore Schultz in 1979. He had taught at the London School of Economics and Manchester University before becoming head of the University College (later University) of the West Indies 1957–63, then returning to academic life at Princeton, where he held successively three professorial chairs. Among his most influential works was *Theory of Economic Growth* (1955). Died 15 June

Lundkvist, Artur (b. 1906), Swedish novelist and poet, was for many years a member of the award committee for the Nobel prize for literature. A marxist and literary modernist, he was reputed to have persistently blackballed the outstanding British novelist Graham Greene (*q.v.*). Died 11 December

Luria, Professor Salvador (b. in Italy 1912), shared the 1969 Nobel Prize for medicine with Delbrück and Hersey for their researches in molecular biology, especially in the control of viral disease. Threatened as a Jew, from the University of Rome he moved to Paris in 1938 and lectured at a number of universities until he joined the Massachusetts Institute of Technology as professor of microbiology 1959–64 and Sedgwick professor of biology 1964–91. Died 6 February

McCone, John A. (b. 1902), American industrialist and government servant, was director of the Central Intelligence Agency 1961–65. He conducted a salutary reform of the agency after a period of discredit, but his most notable feat was to warn of the Soviet intention to site nuclear missiles in Cuba, which eventuated in the Kennedy–Khrushchev confrontation of 1962.

He had been head of big businesses in steel, construction, shipping and shipbuilding, and chairman of the US Atomic Energy Agency Commission 1958–61. Died 14 February

MacLeod of Fuinary, the Very Rev Lord, Bt, MC (b. 1895), Church of Scotland minister, founded in 1938 the Iona Community, where ministers and industrial workers alternated manual work with mission to the urban poor on the Scottish mainland, and inspired the creation, in 1988, of an international centre for reconciliation on the island of Iona, for which money was raised all over the world. Born to wealth and privilege, he was an ardent pacifist and Christian socialist, and a magnificent preacher. A life peerage and the (American) Templeton prize for religion were among the many honours whereby his unique contribution to religious life was recognized. Died 27 June

McMillan, Edwin (b. 1907), American nuclear physicist, shared with Glenn Seaborg the 1951 Nobel Prize for chemistry for their discovery of two previously unknown elements, neptunium and plutonium, the latter, discovered in 1941, being capable of nuclear fission far more powerful than that of uranium-235. He deplored the post-war nuclear arms race, and in 1963 he shared the Atoms for Peace prize with Soviet scientist Vladimir Veksler, his colleague in the invention (1945) of the synchrocyclotron. He worked at the Lawrence laboratory 1934–73, as its head from 1958. Died 7 September

Manzù, Giacomo (b. 1908), Italian sculptor, rejected the abstraction and distortion popular in the art world of his youth in favour of Renaissance realism and emotion. Though an atheist, much of his best work was Christian in subject and site, notably his Door of Death in a Rotterdam church, dedicated to his friend Pope John XXIII. His statue in bronze, *Maternity*, adorns the UN headquarters in New York. Died 17 January

Maxwell, Robert (b. in Central Europe 1923), British newspaper proprietor, rose from extreme poverty and insecurity in face of anti-semitism to become a multi-millionaire, press mogul and confidant of governments. Acquiring different names and half-a-dozen languages on the way, he reached England in 1940, enlisted in the army, rose to officer rank and won the MC for bravery. In 1951 he bought a scientific publishing firm, renamed Pergamon Press, which became the hinge of his financial manoeuvres. These won him control of the British Printing Corporation in 1981 and of the Mirror Group of popular left-inclined newspapers in 1984. Later press ventures included launch of a weekly, *The European*, and purchase of the *New York Daily News*. Zionist and socialist, he was a Labour MP from 1964 to 1970. After his death his affairs were mired in financial scandal and debt. Died 5 November

Miles, Lord (Bernard Miles) (b. 1907), British actor and stage director, founded the Mermaid Theatre at Blackfriars in London in 1959, where he could exercise his own eclectic choice of plays. A versatile as well as successful actor, both on the stage and elsewhere and in many films, he was honoured with a knighthood in 1969 and a life peerage ten years later. Died 14 June

Montand, Yves (b. 1921), French actor and singer, first earned his immense popularity in France as a music-hall singer in the 1940s. From 1952 onwards he won wider fame as an actor, playing in many films in France and, from 1960, in Hollywood, opposite such stars as Simone Signoret (to whom he was married for 34 years), Ingrid Bergman, Marilyn Monroe and Barbara Streisand. Many of his films had a political slant—from the far left he migrated to fierce anti-communism — and as a man of the people risen to popular adoration he had considerable influence. Died 9 November

Motherwell, Robert (b. 1915), American modernist painter, was also an art teacher and editor and director of books and magazines on contemporary art. Retrospectives of his work, mounted by the Museum of Modern Art, New York, toured the Americas and Europe in the 1960s, and another was exhibited by the Royal Academy in 1978. Died 16 July

Nemerov, Howard (b. 1920), American poet, won the Pulitzer Prize for poetry in 1978 and was US poet laureate 1988–90. After serving in the Canadian and US air forces in World War II, he entered an academic career and was a professor at Washington University, St Louis 1969–90. Besides his poetry, which was conservative in style (*Collected Poems*, 1977), he was also much admired for his novels and literary criticism. Died 5 July

O'Faolain, Sean (b. John Whelan, 1900), Irish writer, combined extreme republicanism with liberal revulsion against the deadening grasp of bourgeois Catholic society. This conflict was implicit in much of his work, such as his biographies of Irish nationalist heroes—Hugh O'Neill (*The Great O'Neill*, 1942), Daniel O'Connell (*King of the Beggars*, 1938)—and his editorship 1940–46 of the literary magazine *The Bell* which he had founded; but he was best known to the English-reading public for his masterly short stories, of which a three-volume collection was published 1980–82. Died 21 April

Olav V, HM King (b. 1903), succeeded his father Haakon VII on the throne of Norway in 1957. Born in England, a grandson of Edward VII, and completing his formal education at Balliol College, Oxford, to which he remained devoted, he did much to cement the longstanding friendship between his country and Britain. Evacuated to England after Germany invaded Norway in 1940, he spent the rest of the conflict leading the Norwegian war effort. As king he followed a modest life-style in tune with the character of his people. Died 17 January

Panufnik, Sir Andrzej (b. in Poland 1914), naturalized British composer and conductor, was conductor of the Warsaw Philharmonic 1946–54 and music director of the Birmingham Symphony Orchestra 1957–59. His most creative period of composition followed, its peak being his 8th symphony, *Sinfonia Votiva*, written for the centenary of the Boston Symphony Orchestra in 1981. Died 27 October

Pao, Sir Y. K. (b. in China 1918), moved to Hong Kong in 1949, where he built a great commercial empire based originally on shipping. With a fortune believed to exceed US$3,000 million, he gave munificently to educational and charitable causes, in China as well as Hong Kong. An invaluable link with the Beijing government, he was appointed by the latter to assist in drafting the Basic Law governing the status of Hong Kong after 1997. Died 23 September

Papp, Joseph (b. 1921), American theatre producer, began the Shakespeare Festival in New York, launched free Shakespeare in Central Park and founded the Public Theatre in Astor Place, where his successes included the musicals *Hair* and *A Chorus Line* and high-spirited productions of *Pirates of Penzance* and *Two Gentlemen of Verona*. Died 31 October

Penney, Lord, OM, FRS (b. 1909), as Professor William Penney was one of the scientific team which developed the atomic bomb at Los Alamos in 1944–45. When the USA cut the umbilical cord of British research on atomic weapons, Mr Attlee's government appointed him to design and make Britain's independent atom bomb, which he achieved in 1952. Appointed to the new UK Atomic Energy Authority (UKAEA) in 1954 as member for development of nuclear weapons, he constructed Britain's first hydrogen bomb, successfully tested in the Pacific in 1957. He was member of the UKAEA for research 1959–61, for scientific and technical coordination 1961–64, and its chairman 1964–67. From 1967 to 1973 he was rector of Imperial College of Science and Technology. Died 3 March

Petrov, Vladimir (b. 1907), former Soviet spy, defected in 1954 from the KGB while serving in the Soviet embassy in Canberra, and spent the rest of his life concealed under a new name. Apart from his exposure of associates of the counter-defectors Burgess and Maclean, the extent of his revelations was withheld from the public. Died 14 June

Pirie, Gordon (b. 1931), British track athlete, held five world long-distance records, including those for 3,000 and 5,000 metres (1953 and 1956), but never won an Olympic title. Died 7 December

Ponsford, Bill (b. 1900), Australian cricketer, joined with Don Bradman in a masterly period of Australian batting prowess. His Test average against England in 1934 was 94, and he was specially famous for twice scoring over 400 in an innings in inter-state matches. Died 6 April

Randone, Salvo (b. 1906), was described by a British obituarist as 'the finest classical Italian actor of his time'. From 1941 onwards he was greatly admired for his roles in the plays of Schiller, Goethe, Ibsen and above all Shakespeare, but his most popular performance among Italians was as Henri IV in Pirandello's play. Died 6 March

Revelle, Roger (b. 1909), American scientist, when director (1951–64) of the Scripps Institution of Oceanography in California originated the theory of global warming. In 1964 he launched the international deep-sea drilling project which confirmed the theory of continental drift on the Earth's crust. Later he turned his inquisitive and innovative talents to problems of development in poorer countries, population control, environmental protection and arms limitation, becoming professor of population policy at Harvard (1964–79) and in 1979 professor of science and public policy at the University of California at San Diego. Died 15 July

Richardson, Tony (b. 1928), British stage and film director, came to fame in 1956 as director of John Osborne's *Look Back in Anger* for the new English Stage Company. His alliance with George Devine, the Company's founder, lasted eight years, during which his further successes included *The Entertainer* with Laurence Olivier. Besides cinematic versions of those two plays, among his best films were *Saturday Night and Sunday Morning* and *Tom Jones*, which won him an Oscar for direction. His later output from Hollywood was less distinguished. Died 14 November

Roddenberry, Eugene (Gene) W. (b. 1921), former US army air pilot, invented and scripted the immensely popular space-fiction television series, *Star Trek*, starting in 1966. Died 24 October

Rose, Sir Alec (b. 1908), British greengrocer, sailed single-handed round the world in his yacht *Lively Lady* in 1967–68; although it took him nearly a year, his courage and resource in face of disasters on the way won him great public applause and popularity, which he had never sought. Died 12 January

Sabri, Ali (b. 1920), was Prime Minister of Egypt 1964–65 (after two years in the equivalent post in the presidential council regime) and deputy prime minister 1967–68 under President Nasser and 1970–71 under President Sadat. He had also twice been secretary-general of the Arab Socialist Union. His left-wing stance, however, cost him loss of office and then a charge of plotting to overthrow the government, for which the death sentence was commuted to life imprisonment. Released after 10 years, he died 30 August

Scelba, Mario (b. 1901), was Prime Minister of Italy 1954–55. A founder-member of the Christian Democratic Party and an ardent anti-communist, he had served in previous De Gasperi governments, usually as minister of the interior, and he again held that office under Fanfani 1960–62. Died 29 October

Serkin, Rudolf (b. in Austria 1903), pianist and teacher, was already of world class as soloist when he emigrated to the US in 1939, to become head of piano studies at the Curtis Institute, Philadelphia (1939–68) and its director 1968–76. Among his many memorable recordings, perhaps the finest were of Brahms and Beethoven concertos. Died 8 May

Simms, The Most Rev George (b. 1910), was Archbishop of Armagh and Primate of All Ireland 1969–80; he had been a bishop since 1952 and Archbishop of Dublin since 1957, the youngest living Anglican archbishop. Ecumenical and peace-loving in spirit and action, he was unloved by Protestant extremists, but his Christian care was pastoral, not polemical. He was a world authority on *The Book of Kells*. Died 15 November

Singer, Isaac Bashevis (b. in Poland 1904), was described as the greatest of all writers in Yiddish. In 1935, already the author of the powerful novel *Satan Goray* (published in America 1958), he emigrated to the USA, taking US citizenship in 1943. His short stories became especially famous (*Collected Stories*, 1982), and in 1978 he won the Nobel Prize for literature. Died 24 July

Smallwood, Joseph (b. 1900), as premier of Newfoundland 1949–72, brought the former colony and Dominion into Canada as a province of the confederation. Died 18 December

Spessivtseva, Olga (b. 1895), Russian dancer, was prima ballerina of the Maryinski Ballet and a guest star for Diaghilev, before quitting her native land for the Paris Opéra Ballet 1924–32, where she danced with Aveline and Lifar. Her Giselle, with Dolin, was a sensation in London in 1932, and in 1934 she toured the world with the Pavlova Company; but in 1935 she retired, to end her days, from 1939, in the US, a mental invalid. Died 16 September

Stigler, Professor George (b. 1911), American economist, who won the Nobel Prize for economics in 1982, was a stern analyst of economic phenomena, not identified with any popular school of thought. His most influential books were *The Theory of Price* (1946) and *The Economics of Information* (1961). He was professor of American institutions at the University of Chicago from 1958. Died 1 December

Stone, Sir Richard (b. 1913), British economist, who won the Nobel Prize for economics in 1984, was the first director of the Cambridge University department of applied economics 1944–55, and professor of accounting and finance at Cambridge 1955–80. His early work on national accounting was the basis of the UN system of National Accounts. Died 6 December

Tamayo, Rufino (b. 1899), Mexican artist, was one of a group of Mexican painters, among whom Diego Rivera was the most famous, who created a new, distinctively national school linked to the democratic revolution of 1910. His developing art received growing international recognition, awards and museum purchases from 1950 onwards. In 1981 he gave a vast collection of modern paintings, including many of his own, to the people of Mexico. Died 24 June

Tower, John (b. 1925), Republican US senator from Texas since 1965, was chairman of the Senate armed services committee in the 1980s, and of the 1987 commission appointed to investigate the Iran-Contra arms scandal, which was sharply critical of the White House. In 1989 President Bush nominated him Secretary of Defence, but the Senate rejected him on personal grounds. Died 5 April

Tsedenbal, Yumjaagiyn (b. 1916), was President (chairman of the presidium of the People's Great Hural) of Mongolia 1974–84. A Soviet-trained economist, he had been elected secretary-general of the Mongolian communist party in 1940. From 1952 to 1974 he was Prime Minister of Mongolia, applying a strongly pro-Soviet policy. Suddenly ousted from the presidency in 1984, he prudently retired to Moscow. Died 18 April

Vercors, *see* Bruller.

Voelker, John D. (b. 1903), American jurist and author, was a justice of the supreme court of Michigan (1957–60) when he published his best-selling novel, *Anatomy of Murder*, under the name of Robert Traver, but he was already a successful author of reminiscent books, and continued writing fiction and non-fiction after retiring from the bench. Died 19 March

Wagner, Robert, Jr (b. 1910), as Democratic mayor of New York 1954–65, liberated the city's politics from the grasp of Tammany Hall, colouring them rather with New Deal pink. He was later US ambassador to Spain 1968–69 and presidential envoy to the Vatican 1978–80. Died 12 February

Walcha, Helmut (b. 1907), blind German organist, was among the world's most revered interpreters of the organ music of J. S. Bach, especially the chorale preludes, recording them on the famous organ at the Church of the Three Kings in Frankfurt, where he was organist for over 40 years. Died 11 August

Welensky, Rt Hon Sir Roy, KCMG (b. 1907), was Prime Minister of the Federation of Rhodesia and Nyasaland 1956–63. Starting life as a railway fireman and professional boxer, he entered politics through trade union action, and rose to power by force of personality and plain policy, until blown back by the winds of change in Africa. Died 5 December

Wilson, Sir Angus (b. 1913), British novelist and literary pundit, made his name first with brilliant short stories (*The Wrong Set*, 1949), and then with novels of classical form (*Anglo-Saxon Attitudes*, 1956; *The Middle Age of Mrs Eliot*, 1958). Meanwhile, he had displayed an even greater talent for literary criticism with his *Émile Zola* 1952, followed later by his studies of Dickens (1970) and Kipling (1977). He was lecturer (1963–66) and professor (1966–78) at the University of East Anglia, and also taught at UCLA and other American universities. Died 31 May

Wolfson, Sir Isaac, Bt, FRS (b. 1897), British businessman, was one of the greatest philanthropists of his time. Among his many benefactions from a huge fortune made chiefly from a mail-order and retail store firm, Great Universal Stores, were the foundation of colleges of advanced learning bearing his name at both Oxford and Cambridge, and many gifts to Jewish and Israeli causes. Died 20 June

XXI CHRONICLE OF PRINCIPAL EVENTS IN 1991

A detailed chronology of the Gulf Conflict appears in this volume at V.1.

JANUARY

4   EC foreign ministers met in Luxembourg to consider Gulf crisis; France put forward seven-point peace plan.
    Polish parliament approved appointment of Jan Bielicki as PM.
6   British PM John Major on three-day visit to Gulf.
    In elections in Guatemala, Jorge Serrano Elías elected to succeed Vinicio Cerezo as President.
7   In Haiti, 40 died when army crushed attempted coup by Duvalier loyalists (see 30 Sept.).
    5,000 ethnic Greek Albanians reported to have fled to Greece, amid growing chaos in Albania.
8   In Lithuania, government of Mrs Kazimiera Prunskiene resigned over proposed price rises.
    In UK, two dead, 247 injured, in rush-hour train crash at London's Cannon Street station.
12 Both houses of US Congress voted to authorize military action in Gulf.
    In S. Africa, 35 died when gunmen attacked mourners at ANC wake in township near Johannesburg.
13 UN Secretary-General in Baghdad for talks with Saddam Husain.
    In Lithuania, 13 died when Soviet forces fired on demonstrators protesting at takeover by Soviet troops of public buildings in Vilnius.
    In Portugal, Mário Soares elected President for second term.
14 Soviet parliament confirmed appointment of Valentin Pavlov as PM in succession to Nikolai Ryzhkov; 15 Jan. Aleksandr Bessmertnykh named Foreign Minister.
15 UN resolution 678 (of 29 Nov. 1990), approving use of force in Gulf, became effective, Iraq having failed to meet deadline for withdrawal from Gulf.
    In UK, government had majority of 477 at end of debate on Gulf confrontation.
    Abu Iyad and two other prominent PLO leaders assassinated in Tunis.
16 Allied forces launched massive bombing raids against military targets in Kuwait and Iraq at start of 'Operation Desert Storm' for liberation of Kuwait.
17 King Olav of Norway died aged 87 (see XX: OBITUARY) and was succeeded by his son King Harald V.
18 Iraq launched first Scud missiles against Israel; two died and over 200 were injured in Scud attacks against Israel during Gulf War.
    In Latvia, Soviet commandos attacked Interior Ministry in Riga, killing four pro-independence demonstrators.
    In USSR, 200,000 marched in Moscow in protest against perceived movement towards dictatorship.
21 Iraq paraded allied POWs on TV and announced that they would be used as 'human shields' at strategic targets.
23 Israeli cabinet agreed a policy of non-retaliation against Iraqi Scud missile attacks.
    In USSR, government announced withdrawal of 50 and 100 rouble notes: citizens had three days to change money.
25 Crude oil pumped by Iraq into Gulf formed world's biggest-ever oil slick.
26 President Gorbachev issued decree giving Soviet law-enforcement agencies sweeping new powers to compel economic discipline.

In Somalia, President Barre fled as rebels overran Mogadishu; rebel United Somali Congress (USC) appointed Ali Mahdi Mohammed PM (see 18 Aug., 22 Dec.).
28 Planned Moscow summit between Presidents Bush and Gorbachev, scheduled for Feb. 1991, cancelled because of Gulf War (see 30 July).
29 French Defence Minister Jean-Pierre Chevènement resigned over French involvement in Gulf War; he was succeeded by Pierre Joxe.
In USA, President Bush delivered State of Union address, appealing for nation's support in confronting Iraqi aggression.
In S. Africa, Nelson Mandela (ANC) and Chief Buthelezi (Inkatha) held talks (first for 28 years) in Durban aimed at ending fighting between their supporters: 5,000 had died in past four years.
30 Hundreds of Iraqi soldiers and 12 US marines died in first land battle of Gulf War around town of Khafji on Saudi-Kuwait border.

FEBRUARY

1 In S. Africa, President de Klerk announced immediate repeal of Land Acts, Group Areas Act and Population Registration Act (see 4, 17 June).
More than 1,000 died in earthquake affecting Afghanistan and NW Province of Pakistan.
4 In USA, President Bush sent a proposed $1,450,000 million budget to Congress; it envisaged sharp cuts in defence spending.
6 King Husain of Jordan described Iraqis as victims of this 'savage and large-scale war', a war against all Arabs and Muslims.
7 In UK, IRA mortar bombs caused damage at 10 Downing Street where the cabinet was meeting.
Fr Jean-Bertrand Aristide sworn in as Haiti's first democratically-elected President (see 30 Sept.).
8 US Defence Secretary Cheney and Gen. Colin Powell visited Saudi Arabia to assess allied war effort.
9 In a referendum in Lithuania, voters approved proposal for independence from Moscow (see 6 Sept.).
11 Chancellor Kohl and PM Major held talks in Bonn on Gulf and other issues.
Soviet PM Valentin Pavlov claimed Western banks had been involved in plot to overthrow President Gorbachev.
13 Many Iraqi civilians died when US planes bombed a bunker in Baghdad; allies claimed it was a military communications centre.
15 Iraqi conditional offer to withdraw from Kuwait rejected by President Bush.
17 In Cape Verde, Antonio Mascarenhas Monteiro won presidential election, ending 15 years of PAICV rule.
18 In UK, IRA bomb killed one and injured 38 at London's Victoria Station.
Soviet PM Pavlov, announcing price increases, said retail prices would have to rise an average 60 per cent.
20 In Albania, student protesters tore down statue of former dictator Hoxha; President Alia announced he was taking over all state affairs and would form new government (see 31 March).
Slovenia voted to give local laws precedence over Yugoslav federal legislation (see 25 June).
21 British troops began biggest artillery bombardment since Korean War on Iraqi targets near northern border of Saudi Arabia.
22 President Bush gave Iraq ultimatum to pull out of Kuwait by 23 Feb. or face ground war.
23 In Thailand, government of Chatichai Choonhavan overthrown in bloodless military coup.

24 Allied forces launched ground offensive to liberate Kuwait.
25 Twenty-eight US troops died in Iraqi Scud missile attack in Saudi Arabia.
   Foreign and defence ministers of Warsaw Pact, meeting in Budapest, agreed dissolution of military structure of pact by 31 March (see 1 July).
   In Bulgaria, trial opened in Sofia of former dictator Todor Zhivkov on charges of fraud and embezzlement.
   In USSR, President Gorbachev named a new cabinet.
26 President Saddam announced Iraq's withdrawal from Kuwait, his troops having been routed by allied forces.
27 Allied forces entered Kuwait City and country was declared liberated; allied forces surrounded Republican Guard troops near Basra, having undertaken a massive flanking manoeuvre across southern Iraq.
   Bangladesh held first free national elections for 20 years; Bangladesh National Party, led by Begum Khaleda Zia, obtained largest number of seats (see 20 March).
28 President Bush announced suspension of hostilities in Gulf; Iraq informed UN that it agreed to comply fully with resolution 660 and all other Security Council resolutions; 79 US and 16 British servicemen had died in conflict; Iraqi casualty figures unknown; 175,000 Iraqi POWs were held by allies.

MARCH

2 UN Security Council passed resolution 686 calling for release of all POWs before a final Gulf ceasefire could be signed.
  In Sri Lanka, Deputy Defence Minister Ranjan Wijeratne, a leading opponent of Tamil Tigers, assassinated.
3 Gulf commander Gen. Norman Schwarzkopf and other allied generals met defeated Iraqi commanders in a desert tent to seal end of Gulf War.
  Latvia and Estonia held referendums; both republics voted overwhelmingly for independence (see 6 Sept.).
4 In Gulf, exchange of allied and Iraqi POWs commenced.
  City of Basra reported in hands of anti-government rebels as unrest spread throughout southern Iraq.
5 British PM Major in Moscow for talks with President Gorbachev.
  In UK, Midland Bank became first British bank for 50 years to cut dividend, following slump in profits.
6 PM Major visited Kuwait City and held talks with King of Saudi Arabia.
  President Bush addressed joint session of Congress on ending of Gulf War.
  In India, Chandra Shekhar resigned as PM, his government having lost support of Rajiv Gandhi's Congress (I) party (see 20 May, 20 June).
7 Mrs Margaret Thatcher awarded US Medal of Freedom.
  12,000 Albanian refugees landed at Italian ports in defiance of Italian authorities (see 11 Aug.).
  In UK, at a by-election in Ribble Valley, Liberal Democrats overturned Tory majority of nearly 20,000.
10 In Iraq, 500 rebels reported killed by Republican Guard in Karbala as opposition to regime of Saddam Husain increased in southern Iraq and Kurdish areas.
11 PM Major and Chancellor Kohl held 21st Anglo-German summit in Bonn; Major declared that Britain's place was 'at the very heart of Europe'.
   In Greece, trial opened in Athens of former PM Andreas Papandreou on bribery charges.
15 In Iraq, US troops reoccupied positions in Euphrates valley in attempt to deter Saddam's troops from crushing rebellion.
16 President Bush and PM Major held talks in Bermuda.

17 USSR held a referendum on its own future (six republics refused to take part); Gorbachev gained a slim majority for a renewed federation of socialist sovereign republics; the Russian Republic voted to elect a Russian president by universal suffrage (see 12 June).
Serbian communist leader Slobodan Milosevic resigned from collective Yugoslav presidency, saying his republic would not recognize its decisions.
In election in Finland, Centre Party gained largest number of seats: its leader Esko Aho formed new coalition on 26 April.
18 In Togo, President Eyadema agreed to democratize his 24-year autocratic rule following street protests.
19 In UK, budget day: Chancellor raised VAT to 17.5 per cent to finance £140 reduction in poll tax bills; he increased child benefit and cut corporation tax.
20 Iran and Saudi Arabia resumed diplomatic links, broken in 1987 over deaths of Iranian pilgrims at Mecca.
In Bangladesh, Begum Khaleda Zia sworn in as PM (see 11 June).
21 In UK, Environment Secretary announced demise of community charge (poll tax) (see 23 April).
22 UN sanctions committee agreed to lift restrictions on food and other essentials to Iraq amid mounting fears of famine and epidemics.
24 Nicéphore Soglo defeated President Kerekou in first democratic presidential elections in Benin for 20 years.
25 In Iraq, government forces bombed northern city of Kirkuk, held by Kurdish insurgents; loyalist troops reported to have suppressed Shia rebellion in southern Iraq.
Ulster Unionist leaders agreed to participate in talks with nationalists and Dublin government in first formal N. Ireland initiative for 10 years (see 30 April).
26 President Moussa Traoré of Mali overthrown in military coup; a National Reconciliation Council was set up by Lt-Col. Amadou Toumani.
27 International Olympic Committee announced readmission of S. Africa, after 30-year break.
28 Thousands demonstrated in Moscow in support of Boris Yeltsin, in defiance of Soviet government ban and deployment of troops.
29 In Italy, government of Giulio Andreotti resigned; Italy's 50th post-war government, again led by Andreotti, was sworn in on 13 April.
30 In UK, Oxford won university boat race by 4 lengths.
31 Albania held its first free elections since 1944; ruling Communist Party of Labour obtained parliamentary majority amid allegations of ballot-rigging; President Alia failed to gain election to parliament (see 4 June).
In USSR, Georgia voted overwhelmingly for independence from Moscow.

APRIL

2 British businessman Roger Cooper freed after five years in gaol in Iran for alleged spying.
3 Turkey closed its border with Iraq to prevent entry of some 200,000 Kurds fleeing from advancing Iraqi government troops.
UN Security Council adopted resolution 687 establishing terms of full ceasefire in Gulf.
4 In UK, Labour won by-election at Neath with reduced majority.
Turkey and Iran relaxed border controls as more than one million Kurds fled from advancing Republican Guard.
5 UN Security Council resolution 688 demanded immediate cessation of repression of Kurds; President Bush announced immediate airlift of humanitarian supplies to Kurds.

6 In UK, Grand National won by Seagram at 12–1.
8 European heads of government, in emergency session in Luxembourg, approved £105 million aid package for Kurdish refugees and backed British proposal for 'safe havens' in northern Iraq.
9 Parliament of Georgia voted unanimously to assert its independence from USSR.
  UN Security Council approved resolution 689 on establishment of demilitarized zone between Iraq and Kuwait.
  Iraq vowed to resist creation of Kurdish safe havens by all means.
10 US ordered Saddam to cease all military action north of 36th parallel.
11 Gulf War ceasefire formally came into effect.
  Iraqi forces attacked Kurdish refugees and rebels.
  In Italy, 140 died in fire aboard ferry *Moby Prince* following collision with oil-tanker off Livorno.
14 US Secretary of State announced that US troops had begun withdrawal from southern Iraq to ceasefire buffer zone.
  Iran appealed for international aid: more than one million refugees had fled to its territory from Iraq.
15 EC foreign ministers agreed to lift most remaining sanctions against S. Africa.
  European Bank for Reconstruction and Development (EBRD) officially opened in London.
16 President Gorbachev began four-day visit to Japan, the first by a Soviet leader.
  President Bush announced setting-up of safe havens in northern Iraq for Kurdish refugees under protection of US, French and British troops; operation commenced on 17 April (see 15 July).
19 In UK, Dr George Carey enthroned as 103rd Archbishop of Canterbury.
21 South America reported in grip of worst cholera epidemic this century.
  In UK, London marathon won by Yakov Tolstikov (USSR).
23 President Walesa of Poland on four-day state visit to UK.
  In UK, Environment Secretary announced proposals for new council tax to replace poll tax in 1993.
  President Gorbachev and nine republican leaders signed pact to prevent economic collapse and end strikes; declaration set out timetable for major political changes.
25 Iraq pulled its forces out of northern town of Zakho in response to allied ultimatum; their presence was deterring Kurdish refugees from reaching safe havens.
29 In Bangladesh, some 200,000 people believed dead in country's worst cyclone for 20 years; more died in another cyclone on 2 June.
30 Talks intended to end the political deadlock on N. Ireland opened at Stormont; initiative ended inconclusively on 3 July.
  Kurdish refugees began to move into Western-protected safe havens.
  In Cambodia, UN-backed ceasefire in 12-year civil war came into effect (see 24 June, 23 Oct., 14 Nov.).
  In Lesotho, military leader Maj.-Gen. Justin Lekhanya overthrown and replaced by Col. Elias Ramaema.

MAY

2 In UK local elections, Conservatives lost some 400–500 seats; Labour and Liberal Democrats made advances.
  In Yugoslavia, 12 Croats died in a Serbian-populated village in Croatia, in bloodiest clash between Serbs and Croats since World War II.
6 In Yugoslavia, amid mounting fears of civil war, federal army issued ultimatum threatening to intervene if country's leaders did not end ethnic bloodshed.
7 Spanish PM González on official visit to London.

9   Aleksandr Bessmertnykh arrived in Israel, the first such visit by a Soviet Foreign Minister.
12 In Nepal, first multi-party elections since 1959 won by Congress Party; 26 May G. P. Koirala sworn in as PM.
13 In S. Africa, Mrs Winnie Mandela convicted on eight counts of kidnapping and accessory to assault; she was sentenced to six years in gaol but lodged an appeal.
14 HM Queen Elizabeth II and Prince Philip on state visit to USA; the Queen addressed a joint session of Congress on 16 May.
15 Jiang Zemin, general secretary of Chinese CP, in Moscow for summit talks with Gorbachev; he was first Chinese leader to visit USSR since Mao Zedong in 1957.
    Edith Cresson appointed PM of France following resignation of Michel Rocard.
    Serbian communists blocked election of Stipe Mesić of Croatia as Yugoslavia's first non-communist President but he nevertheless took office on 20 May.
16 In UK by-election, Labour overturned 9,000 Conservative majority at Monmouth.
18 Helen Sharman became first Briton to go into space when she took part in six-day Soviet *Soyuz* mission.
19 Croatian voters approved a proposal that republic should become independent state (see 25 June).
    Chancellor Kohl of Germany on official visit to Washington.
20 Voting began in India's general election (see 20 June).
    In UK, government published white paper *Higher Education: A New Framework* (Cmnd. 1541).
    In UK, government announced legislation to ban importation and ownership of dangerous dogs.
21 Former Indian PM Rajiv Gandhi assassinated in bomb blast at Tamil Nadu election rally (see XX: OBITUARY).
    President Mengistu of Ethiopia fled as rebel forces closed in on Addis Ababa (see 28 May).
22 UK and Albania agreed to resume diplomatic relations broken since end of World War II.
24 Israel launched a massive 30-hour airlift, code-named 'Operation Solomon', to bring 14,000 Ethiopian Jews (Falashas) to Israel.
26 Zviad Gamsakhurdia overwhelmingly elected as President of Georgia (see 25 Dec.).
    In Thailand, 223 died when Lauda Air Boeing 767 crashed.
28 Forces of Ethiopian People's Revolutionary Democratic Front captured Addis Ababa, ending 17 years of marxist rule.
29 In India, P. V. Narasimha Rao elected president of Congress (I) in succession to Rajiv Gandhi (see 20 June).
31 President dos Santos of Angola and Unita leader Jonas Savimbi signed peace agreement in Lisbon, ending 16-year civil war.

JUNE

1   Pope John Paul II began nine-day visit to his native Poland.
3   In N. Ireland, SAS shot dead three IRA gunmen in Co Tyrone.
    Israel launched its most sustained attack for ten years on Palestinian targets in Lebanon.
    OAU summit conference opened in Abuja, Nigeria.
4   In S. Africa, parliament passed composite bill abolishing 1966 Group Areas Act and 1916 and 1936 Land Acts.
    Albanian government resigned following three-week general strike; Ylli Bufi named as caretaker PM (see 11 Dec.).

5 In Algeria, President Chadli declared state of siege amid mounting pre-election violence by Islamic Salvation Front (see 18 June, 26 Dec.).
  In UK, Derby won by Generous at 9–1.
9 Chancellor Kohl of Germany and British PM Major held talks at Chequers on future of Europe.
12 Boris Yeltsin elected President of Russian Federation, its first-ever directly-elected leader; he was inaugurated on 10 July.
  In the Philippines, Mount Pinatubo erupted; at least 350 later reported dead.
  In Bangladesh, former president, Gen. Ershad, gaoled for 10 years for unlicensed possession of arms.
  In Burkina Faso, military leader Blaise Compaoré dissolved revolutionary government and called for adoption of new constitution.
13 Belgian parliament approved constitutional change to allow women to accede to throne for first time since country's independence in 1830.
14 Switzerland celebrated 700 years as a nation state.
15 In India, more than 70 died in attacks by Sikh militants on two trains in Punjab.
17 S. African parliament adopted bill to repeal Population Registration Act, thus ending legal foundation for apartheid.
  In Turkey, Mesut Yilmaz appointed PM in succession to Yildirim Akbulut (see 20 Oct.).
18 In Algeria, Sid Ahmed Ghozali sworn in as new PM (see 26 Dec.).
20 German parliament voted to move country's parliament and government from Bonn to Berlin.
  In India, following delayed elections, P. V. Narasimha Rao appointed PM at head of minority Congress (I) government.
21 In Japan, Mrs Takako Doi resigned as leader of Social Democratic Party.
24 President Mitterrand and PM John Major held talks in Dunkirk on EC and other international issues.
25 Republics of Croatia and Slovenia declared independence from Yugoslavia; on 27 June federal tanks and troops moved into the two republics (see 8 July).
27 Do Muoi appointed secretary-general of Vietnamese Communist Party in succession to veteran leader Nguyen Van Linh.
28 EC heads of government held summit in Luxembourg at which draft treaty on monetary union was discussed.
29 Comecon, Eastern Europe's economic organization, formally dissolved.
  In UK, Mrs Thatcher announced her retirement from House of Commons at next election.

JULY

1 Political arm of Warsaw Pact disbanded by protocol signed in Prague, thus formally ending organization founded in 1955.
2 First national conference of ANC to be held inside S. Africa for 30 years opened in Durban, ending 7 July.
4 In UK, Labour retained seat in by-election at Liverpool Walton; the Militant (Real Labour) candidate was humiliated.
5 In UK, Bank of Credit and Commerce International (BCCI) closed down by Bank of England after discovery of widespread fraud.
  EC foreign ministers meeting at the Hague imposed a total arms embargo on Yugoslavia and agreed to send monitoring mission there.
8 Yugoslav federal government and Slovene leaders accepted peace deal after mediation by EC representatives on island of Brioni.
9 In UK, white paper *Statement on the Defence Estimates* (Cmnd. 1559) proposed

XXI CHRONICLE OF PRINCIPAL EVENTS IN 1991 589

troop levels cuts of 40,000 and to reduce infantry battalions from 55 to 36 (see 23 July).
10 President Bush announced lifting of economic sanctions against S. Africa; International Cricket Council readmitted S. Africa to Test cricket after 20-year ban (see 8 Nov.).
11 In Saudi Arabia, 261 Nigerian pilgrims returning from Mecca died in air crash at Jeddah.
15 Group of Seven (G7) summit conference opened in London, ending 17 July; Soviet President Gorbachev met G7 leaders to appeal for economic aid; summit leaders pledged to complete Uruguay Round of GATT talks by year-end.
In northern Iraq, last allied troops guarding Kurdish safe havens (see 16 April) left for Turkey.
18 In China, more than 50 million acres of farmland submerged in worst flooding since 1930s; at least 1,700 died.
19 S. African authorities admitted making secret donations to Inkatha Freedom Party (see 29 July).
22 In UK, PM Major launched a 'Citizen's Charter' intended to make public services more accountable to customers.
23 In UK, Defence Secretary King announced most radical restructuring of army this century.
President Mubarak of Egypt on four-day state visit to UK.
IMF announced that President Gorbachev had applied for full Soviet membership.
29 In S. Africa, two ministers at centre of illegal Inkatha funding scandal (see 19 July) resigned; 30 July, President de Klerk announced immediate end to covert political funding.
In Yugoslavia, scores reported dead in fighting between Croatian forces and Serbian militiamen (Chetniks).
30 Presidents Bush and Gorbachev began two-day summit in Moscow; on 31 July Strategic Arms Reduction (START) Treaty, reducing nuclear weapons by one third, was signed.
Six Lithuanian border guards murdered by unknown gunmen on frontier with Belorussia.

AUGUST

1 US Secretary of State Baker began new Middle East peace mission; following talks in Jerusalem, Israeli PM Shamir accepted invitation to attend a peace conference (see 30 Oct.).
6 Yugoslav presidency declared unconditional ceasefire in Croatia but clashes continued between Croatian and Serbian forces (see 26 Aug.).
8 Briton John McCarthy, held hostage in Lebanon since 1988, released; on 11 Aug. he handed over letter from Islamic Jihad setting out terms for deal on remaining Western hostages to UN Secretary-General.
Former Iranian PM Shapour Bakhtiar found murdered in Paris (see XX: OBITUARY).
9 Vo Van Kiet appointed PM of Vietnam.
10 Japanese PM Toshiki Kaifu on official visit to China.
11 Italian police and troops fought with Albanian refugees detained at Bari harbour; some 15,000 had arrived in past week and faced deportation.
US hostage, Edward Tracey, released from captivity in Lebanon.
16 Pope John Paul II began four-day visit to Hungary, the first by a Pope since 1052.
18 Remains of Frederick the Great of Prussia reinterred at Sanssouci Palace, Potsdam, 205 years after his death.

18 Ali Mahdi Mohammed sworn in as President of Somalia (see 22 Dec.).
19 In USSR, communist hardliners led by Gennadii Yanaev announced takeover from President Gorbachev; Russian President Yeltsin demanded reinstatement of Gorbachev and assumed control of all government institutions on Russian territory.
20 In Moscow, three died when Soviet tanks moved against anti-coup demonstrators defending Russian parliament in defiance of curfew; European foreign ministers froze economic aid to USSR; Estonia declared independence.
21 In USSR, coup collapsed following widespread resistance led by Boris Yeltsin; conspirators were subsequently arrested (two committed suicide); President Gorbachev announced he was resuming control and returned to Moscow; Latvia declared immediate independence.
23 Addressing Russian parliament, President Gorbachev praised role of Yeltsin in ending coup; Yeltsin suspended activities of Russian Communist Party and extended his authority within Russian Federation; many top Soviet officials sacked in wake of coup.
24 President Gorbachev resigned as general secretary of CPSU, banned party from state organizations and suggested it dissolve itself, condemning its role in abortive coup; he remained Soviet President and appointed Ivan Silayev as PM; Yeltsin ordered seizure of all party and KGB archives in Russia; Ukrainian parliament voted for independence.
25 President Gorbachev announced interim committee of reformers to form new central Soviet government.
26 Yugoslav federal troops and Serbian guerrillas launched assault on Croatian town of Vukovar (see 18 Nov.).
27 British PM Major began three-day visit to President Bush at Kennebunkport; they agreed a six-point programme of aid for USSR.
   Moldavia became eighth republic to announce secession from USSR.
28 President Gorbachev formally dismissed Soviet government and disbanded KGB's collegium, ordering investigation of KGB's role in coup attempt.
29 Soviet parliament suspended CPSU, ending more than 70 years of communist domination of Soviet Union.
30 Azerbaijan declared independence from USSR.
   Lebanese Christian army leader Gen. Michel Aoun arrived in exile in France.
31 In Singapore general election, ruling People's Action Party returned but opposition made gains.

SEPTEMBER

1 British PM Major in Moscow for talks with Presidents Gorbachev and Yeltsin.
2 In USSR, a declaration signed by President Gorbachev and leaders of 10 republics recommended suspension of central government pending new constitution.
3 In China, PM Li Peng and British PM Major signed agreement on new Hong Kong airport; Major subsequently visited Hong Kong.
4 President de Klerk of S. Africa proposed giving blacks the vote for first time under new power-sharing constitution.
   Non-Aligned conference opened in Accra.
5 In USSR, Congress of People's Deputies approved new interim structure of government, thus ending 70-year-old Soviet system.
6 Latvia, Lithuania and Estonia, annexed in 1940, formally granted independence from USSR.
7 EC-sponsored peace conference on Yugoslavia, chaired by Lord Carrington, opened at the Hague; fierce fighting continued in Croatia.

XXI CHRONICLE OF PRINCIPAL EVENTS IN 1991

10 CSCE human rights conference opened in Moscow; delegates from newly-independent Baltic republics joined representatives of 35 other states of Europe and N. America.
11 President Gorbachev announced withdrawal of Soviet troops from Cuba.
Israel released 51 Arab prisoners and bodies of nine others as efforts continued to end hostage problem in Middle East.
13 In Iraq, Mohammed Hamzah al-Zubaydi replaced Saadun Hammadi as PM.
15 At general election in Mauritius, ruling coalition of PM Sir Anerood Jugnauth gained overwhelming majority.
In Sweden, PM Ingvar Carlsson resigned when his Social Democrats lost ground in general election; a centre-right coalition was formed by Moderate Party leader Carl Bildt on 4 Oct.
Hong Kong held first direct elections for colony's legislature (only 18 of 60 seats were contested).
16 Trial of former Panamanian leader Noriega, on drug-trafficking charges, opened in Miami (USA).
17 46th UN General Assembly opened in New York; the three Baltic states, N. & S. Korea, the Federated States of Micronesia and the Marshall Islands were admitted, bringing total UN membership to 166 nations.
19 In Yugoslavia, Croatia and Serbia rejected EC peace efforts.
20 Yugoslav federal army tanks entered Croatia on three fronts in biggest operation since outbreak of fighting on 27 June.
22 Armenia declared independence, the 13th former Soviet republic to do so.
24 Jackie Mann (77) of Britain, held hostage in Lebanon since 1989, was released.
26 In Romania, government led by PM Petre Roman resigned following riots by miners demanding higher wages; Teodor Stolojan named PM on 1 Oct.
27 President Bush outlined proposals for biggest reductions in nuclear armaments since World War II.
30 In Haiti, government of President Aristide overthrown in military coup; 8 Oct. Judge Joseph Nerette sworn in as provisional President.

OCTOBER

1 USSR announced plans to cut its armed forces by nearly half.
City of Leningrad reverted to its pre-revolutionary name, St Petersburg.
Serbian-dominated Yugoslav federal army began siege of historic Croatian port of Dubrovnik.
5 In Zaïre, at least 117 reported dead in rioting against regime of President Mobutu (see 21, 31 Oct.).
President Franjo Tudjman called for mobilization of men of Croatia to defend homeland.
6 In general election in Portugal, ruling Social Democratic Party, led by PM Cavaco Silva, gained outright majority.
7 Yugoslav federal airforce jets attacked Croatian capital Zagreb for first time.
8 HM Queen Elizabeth II in Namibia; nine-day visit to southern Africa was her first since 1947 (before her accession).
Abdur Rahman Biswas elected President of Bangladesh.
13 Bulgarian Socialist Party (formerly Communist Party) overwhelmingly defeated in elections; on 8 Nov. Filip Dimitrov became country's first non-communist PM since 1944.
14 Nobel Peace Prize awarded to Daw Aung San Suu Kyi, Burmese opposition leader under house arrest since 1989.
In UK, the Children Act 1989, most radical reform in law on children for a century, came into force.

15 Serbian and Croatian Presidents held talks in Moscow with President Gorbachev; Bosnia-Hercegovina's parliament voted to declare independence.

In USA, Judge Clarence Thomas confirmed to US Supreme Court despite allegations of sexual harassment made at Senate hearings.

16 Commonwealth heads of government meeting opened in Harare, Zimbabwe; declaration issued on 20 Oct. committed member nations to democracy and upholding of human rights.

In USA, 22 died at restaurant in central Texas in worst mass shooting incident in US history.

18 Eight Soviet republics signed a formal economic union treaty.

20 In Turkey, Süleyman Demirel's True Path Party topped poll in general election; PM Mesut Yilmaz resigned on 21 Oct.

In Swiss elections, governing coalition gained 147 of 200 seats in lower house.

Mozambique's Renamo rebels and government signed peace ageement in Rome, intended to end war which had cost one million lives.

21 US hostage Jesse Turner released after nearly five years in captivity in Beirut.

In Zaïre, President Mobutu sacked Etienne Tshisekedi, opposition leader he had appointed PM on 30 Sept.; many died in subsequent rioting (see 31 Oct.).

22 EC and EFTA countries agreed to form a 19-member free trade zone called the European Economic Area.

23 A Cambodian peace accord, ending 20 years of war, was signed in Paris (see 14 Nov.).

In UK, House of Lords ruled that men could be guilty of marital rape, overturning 250-year principle to the contrary.

27 Poland held first free parliamentary elections since World War II; at year's end no-one had succeeded in forming new government.

In Japan, Kiichi Miyazawa elected president of ruling Liberal-Democratic Party in succession to Toshiki Kaifu; he was appointed PM on 5 Nov.

In Colombian congressional elections, Liberals became largest party in lower house and gained majority in Senate.

29 Presidents Bush and Gorbachev held summit talks, mainly on arms control, in Madrid.

In UK, HM The Queen opened new road bridge at Dartford, first to be built downstream of the City since Tower Bridge.

30 A Middle East Peace conference, intended to end 43 years of Arab-Israeli hostility and to settle Palestinian question, opened in Madrid; three-day opening session, hosted by Presidents Bush and Gorbachev, was attended by Israeli, Arab and PLO leaders; bilateral talks opened subsequently.

31 In Zambia, multi-party elections resulted in the defeat of President Kaunda, who had ruled for 27 years; he was succeeded by Frederick Chiluba.

Zaïre's opposition movement formed rival government and called for international peace-keeping force amid mounting unrest against Mobutu regime.

In Yugoslavia, 50,000 people trapped in Dubrovnik without water and electricity after a month-long siege by federal forces.

In UK, state opening of parliament; Queen's Speech foreshadowed new council tax, legislation on citizen's charter, reform of higher education and tighter procedures on political asylum applications.

NOVEMBER

2 In World Cup rugby final at Twickenham, London, Australia defeated England 12–6.

3 In Madrid, Israeli and Palestinian delegations held first official face-to-face meeting since 1967 Six-Day War.

XXI CHRONICLE OF PRINCIPAL EVENTS IN 1991

4 Imelda Marcos, widow of former President, returned to Philippines after five years in exile, as government filed embezzlement charges against her.
5 Publishing tycoon Robert Maxwell died after falling overboard from his yacht off the Canary Islands (see 5 Dec.).
6 A two-day NATO summit conference opened in Rome; a declaration emphasized need for closer cooperation with emerging democracies in former communist bloc, including USSR.
In the Philippines, some 6,500 believed dead in floods and landslides.
In UK, Chancellor of Exchequer announced extra £1,000 million public spending, particularly for NHS and public transport.
7 In UK by-elections, sitting Tories were defeated by Labour at Langbaurgh and by Liberal Democrats at Kincardine and Deeside.
8 EC foreign ministers, meeting in Rome, decided to impose immediate sanctions on Yugoslavia as siege of Dubrovnik and Vukovar continued.
S. African cricket team arrived in Calcutta to begin first overseas tour since 1965.
10 Serbian-dominated Yugoslav presidency called for UN peace-keeping force to protect Serbs in Croatia.
12 115 reported dead in massacre by Indonesian army in former Portuguese colony of East Timor, annexed by Indonesia in 1976.
13 In Yugoslavia, an EC-brokered ceasefire enabled evacuation of hundreds of civilians from Dubrovnik.
14 Prince Sihanouk returned to Cambodia after 13 years' exile; he was to head Supreme National Council, to include Khmer Rouge representatives, pending elections in 1993 (see 27 Nov.).
17 In Yugoslavia, eastern Croatian town of Vukovar fell to Serbian-dominated federal army; 1,000 had died in 86-day siege.
18 Archbishop of Canterbury's envoy, Terry Waite, kidnapped in Lebanon in 1987, was last British hostage to be freed; all remaining US hostages were released before Christmas; two Germans were still held at year's end.
24 In general election in Belgium, extremists and environmentalists made widespread gains as traditional parties lost ground in protest vote.
Briton Ian Richter freed from gaol in Iraq as Britain freed £70 million of frozen Iraqi assets for humanitarian purposes.
25 In Yugoslavia, 14th ceasefire, brokered by UN envoy Cyrus Vance, came into operation but was ended on 6 Dec. because of continued federal army bombardment of eastern Croatian town Osijek.
26 Poland admitted as 26th member of Council of Europe.
27 Khmer Rouge leader Khieu Samphan forced to flee when attacked by mob on his return to Cambodia; UN Security Council approved resolution to arrange peace-keeping operation in Cambodia.

DECEMBER

1 In Ukraine, electors voted overwhelmingly in favour of independence; Leonid Kravchuk sworn in as President on formal declaration of independence on 5 Dec.
3 At UN General Assembly, Boutros Boutros-Ghali (Egypt) elected Secretary-General with effect from 1 January 1992.
In Kenya, general assembly of ruling KANU party voted to end one-party state after 30 years.
4 US airline, Pan Am, founded in 1927, closed down amid massive debts.
5 In UK, business empire of late Robert Maxwell, including Mirror Group Newspapers and Maxwell Communication Corporation, collapsed with debts of £1,400 million and revelations about misuse of pension funds.

8 Leaders of Russia, Belorussia and Ukraine, meeting in Minsk, agreed formation of Commonwealth of Independent States and proclaimed end of Soviet Union (see 21 Dec.).
In Romania, new post-communist constitution approved overwhelmingly by voters.
9 A two-day summit of EC heads of government opened in Maastricht, Netherlands; a treaty on closer economic and political union was agreed but Britain secured opt-out clauses on plans for single currency and EC social policy measures.
11 Chinese PM Li Peng on six-day visit to India, the first by a Chinese leader since 1960; a deal to reopen cross-border trade (ended in 1962) was agreed.
In Albania, Vilson Ahmeti replaced Ylli Bufi as PM.
14 US Secretary of State Baker in Moscow for talks with Gorbachev, Yeltsin and republican leaders amid mounting concern over control of Soviet nuclear warheads as Soviet Union disintegrated.
15 In Red Sea, 476 Muslim pilgrims died in ferry disaster.
16 In Trinidad & Tobago elections, ruling party defeated by People's National Movement (PNM) led by Patrick Manning.
19 Australian Labor Party ejected Bob Hawke as leader and PM and elected Paul Keating as his successor.
20 In Johannesburg, a multi-party Convention for a Democratic South Africa opened, attended by 19 rival political groups.
In Yugoslavia, Ante Markovic resigned as PM.
21 At a meeting in Alma-Ata, Kazakhstan, eight more former Soviet republics agreed to join new Commonwealth of Independent States set up by Russia, Ukraine and Belorussia; only Georgia had not joined.
22 In Somalia, some 30,000 were reported to have died in civil war following overthrow of President Barre (see 26 Jan.).
Taiwanese Nationalist Party (Kuomintang) gained overwhelming victory in Taiwan's general election.
23 Germany recognized independence of Croatia and Slovenia.
25 Mikhail Gorbachev resigned as President of USSR, which had ceased to exist following formation of Commonwealth of Independent States; control of nuclear weapons was reportedly handed to Russian President Boris Yeltsin.
In Georgia, 56 reported dead in four days of fighting in Tbilisi, where opposition forces sought overthrow of President Gamsakhurdia.
26 In Algeria, first round of multi-party elections resulted in defeat for ruling National Liberation Front (FLN) and victory for the fundamentalist Islamic Salvation Front (FIS).
30 Leaders of the Commonwealth of Independent States, meeting in Minsk, agreed on common strategic nuclear command but affirmed right of each member to form own armed forces.
31 President Bush in Australia at start of 12-day Asia-Pacific tour.

INDEX

Page references in bold indicate location of main coverage.

ABBS, Peter, 513
ABDALA, Ismael, 67
ABDALLAH, Ahmed, 326
ABDUL MEGUID, Esmat, 209
ABDUL NASSER, Khalid, 209
ABDUL WAHHAB, Muhammad, death, 209
ABRAHAM, Gen. Hérard, 79
ABU DHABI, 224, 229
ACOCELLA, Joan, 486
ADAMI, Dr Eddie Fenech, Prime Minister of Malta, 141
ADIMOLA, Andrew, 256
ADYEBO, Isayas, 249
AFGHANISTAN, 60, 222, **309–9,** 315, 316, 382, 389, 583
AFRICAN CONFERENCES & ORGANIZATIONS, 251, 262, 263, 264, 265, 267, 281, 282, 287, 290, **419–21,** 587
AFRICAN ECONOMIC COMMUNITY, 419–20
AGAR, Eileen, obit., 568
AGNELLI, Gianni, 110
AGRAN, Larry, 55
AHERN, Bertie, 117
AHLBERG, Per, 451
AHMAD, Alhaji Abdelkadir, 261
AHMED, Shahabuddin, 316, 318
AHMETI, Vilson, Prime Minister of Albania, 176, 594
AHO, Esko, Prime Minister of Finland, 126, 585
AIDS (Acquired Immune Deficiency Syndrome), 45, 257, 312, 392, 448–9, 486, **488**
AIKHOMU, Augustus, 260
AJIBOLA, Prince Bola, 463
AJMAN, 224
AKABUSI, Kriss, 518
AKBULUT, Yildirim, 149, 588
AKERS-STAHL, Michelle, 524
AKHROMEYEV, Marshal Sergei, obit., 568
AKIHITO, HM Emperor, of Japan, 359–60
AKOL, Lam, 231
ALBANIA, 109, 145, **174–6,** 389, 412, 413, 414, 582, 583, 584, 585, 587, 589, 594
ALBERY, Tim, 478
ALDEN, David, 478
ALESANA, Tofilau Eti, 380
ALEXANDER, Lamar, 49, 567
ALEKSI II, Patriarch, 439, 442
ALFONSÍN FOULKES, Raúl, 67
ALFREDS, Mike, 488
AL IBRAHIM, Ibrahim, 67
ALGERIA, 98, 101, 208, **239–42,** 246, 268, 443, 528, 588, 594
ALI, Abdel-Rahman Ahmed, 251
ALIA, Ramiz, President of Albania, 175–6, 583, 585
ALICE, HRH Princess, 513
ALLIANCE OF SMALL ISLAND STATES (AOSIS), 425
ALMODOVAR, Pedro, 493
ALSOGARAY, Alvaro, 67
ALVAREZ, Enrique, 84
AMERICAN SAMOA, **378, 379–80**
AMINU, Jibril, 262
AMIS, Sir Kingsley, 513
AMIS, Martin, 508–9, 512
AMNESTY INTERNATIONAL, 75, 84, 234, 237, 245, 323
ANAND PANYARACHUN, Prime Minister of Thailand, 331–2, 342
ANDEAN PACT, 426
ANDERSON, Carl, obit., 568
ANDERSON, Robert, 502
ANDERTON, Jim, 376
ANDORRA, **132–2**
ANDREOTTI, Giulio, Prime Minister of Italy, 107–8, 110, 585
ANDREW, Rob, 517
ANGOLA, 137, 283, **287–8,** 382, 387, 587
ANGUKA, Jonah, 253
ANIKIN, Andrei, 525
ANNENBERG, Walter, 502
ANSTEE, Margaret J., 392
ANTALL, József, Prime Minister of Hungary, 159
ANTARCTICA, 459, 463
ANTIGUA & BARBUDA, **91, 93**
ANTONIO, Manuel, 285–6
ANWAR IBRAHIM, Datuk Seri, 333
ANYAOKU, Chief Emeka, 394
ANYONA, George, 252
AOUN, Gen. Michel, 214, 216, 590
AQUINO, Corazon, President of the Philippines, 340
ARAB FUND FOR ECONOMIC & SOCIAL DEVELOPMENT, 238
ARAB-ISRAELI DISPUTE, 58–9, 188, 202, 203–7, 208, 210, 213, 215, 222, 334, 387, 408, 592
ARAB LEAGUE, 206, 209, 236, 240
ARAB MAGHREB UNION (AMU), 207, 233, 243, 421
ARAB STATES OF THE GULF, **224–30,** 236, 252, 306
ARAB WORLD, **204–7**
ARAFAT, Yassir, 205, 213, 384
ARCHER, Kenneth, 483–4
ARCHITECTURE, **502–5**

ARENS, Moshe, 201, 204
ARGANA, Luis Maria, 74
ARGENTINA, **66–8**, 194, 409, 426, 516, 528
ARINGO, Peter Aloo, 254
ARISTIDE, Fr Jean Bertrand, 79, 583, 591
ARMAH, Kwesi, 258
ARMENIA, 173, 174 (*map*), 180, 182, 184, 398, 557, 559–61, 591
ARMS CONTROL & SECURITY (*see also* Conference on Security and Cooperation in Europe, North Atlantic Treaty Organization, Warsaw Pact, Western European Union), arms reductions, 8, 38, 60, 100–1, 390–1, 531; European defence, 400–1, 431–6; Gulf War implications, 429–30; START Treaty, 59, 187–8, 431–3, 555–7
ARNETT, Peter, 495
ARRAU, Claudio, death, 482; obit., 568
ARRUPE, Fr Pedro, obit., 568
ART, **499–502**
ARTHIT KAMLANG-EK, 331–2
ARTHUR, Jean, death, 494
ARZÚ IRIGOYEN, Alvaro, 81
ASAD, Hafiz al-, President of Syria, 212–3
ASHBERY, John, 513
ASHCROFT, Dame Peggy, death, 490, 494; obit., 568
ASHDOWN, Paddy, MP, 16, 26, 31
ASHRAWI, Hannan, 206
ASHTON, Frederick, 483
ASIA PACIFIC ECONOMIC COOPERATION COUNCIL (APEC), 423, 424
ASIAN DEVELOPMENT BANK (ADB), 318, 424
ASIAN FREE TRADE AREA (AFTA), 423
ASSOCIATION OF SOUTH-EAST ASIAN NATIONS (ASEAN), 330, 342, 422, **423**
ASTRONOMY, 445–6
ASYLMURATOVA, Altynai, 483
ATHULATHMUDALI, Lalith, 322
ATKINSON, Ron, 516
ATKINSON, Sallyanne, 370
ATTALI, Jacques, 413
ATUBO, Omara, 256
AUNG SHWE, 329
AUSTRALIA, 194, 334, 337, 344, **368–72**, 378, 380, 381, 423, 459, 461, 486, 514, 516, 517, 519, 522, 523, 527, 528, 594
AUSTRIA, 109, **127–9**, 133, 173, 413, 416, 417, 458, 465, 479, 499, 515, 550
AYDID, Gen. Mohammed Farah, 251
AYLWIN AZÓCAR, Patricio, President of Chile, 71
AYRES, Gillian, 501
AZERBAIJAN, 151, 177, 178 (*map*), 182, 184, 306, 398, 557, 559–61, 590
AZIZ, Tariq, 191–3, 218, 385, 395

BABA, Ghafar, 333
BABANGIDA, Gen. Ibrahim, Head of State of Nigeria, 260, 262

BABANGIDA, Maryam, 262
BABIĆ, Milan, 170
BACKLEY, Steve, 518
BADAWI, Abdullah Ahmad, 333
BADINTER, Robert, 173
BADRAN, Mudar, 211
BAENA SOARES, João, 426
BAHAMAS, **91**
BAHR, Matt, 523
BAHRAIN, **225**, 226, 228, 229, 461
BAIGENT, M., 444
BAILEY, Robin, 489
BAKER, James, US Secretary of State, 58–60, 191, 193, 201–2, 205, 208, 213, 236, 308, 342, 351, 436, 567, 589, 594
BAKER, Kenneth, MP, 513, 566
BAKER-FINCH, Ian, 520
BAKHTIAR, Shapour, death, 99, 306, 589; obit., 569
BAKLANOV, Oleg, 179
BAKOYIANNI, Dora, 144
BALAGUER, Joaquín, 79
BALANCHINE, George, 483–5
BALCEROWICZ, Leszek, 152
BALLARD, J. G., 512
BALLESTEROS, Seve, 520–1
BALLET, *see* Dance/Ballet
BALTIC REPUBLICS, 2, 29, 120, 128, 158, 177, 178 (*map*), 180, 182, 183, **188–90**, 306, 395, 396–7, 413, 414–15, 417, 418, 591
BALZA, Gen. Martín, 68
BANDA, Hastings Kamuzu, President of Malawi, 291
BANGLADESH, 194, **316–18**, 330, 393, 422, 584, 585, 586, 588, 591
BANI-SADR, Abdulhassan, 50
BANK OF CREDIT AND COMMERCE INTERNATIONAL (BCCI), 24–5, 37, 40, 55, 76, 115, 229, 296, 318, 588
BAQUERIZO, Patricio, 74
BARAK, Ehud, 204
BARBADOS, **88–9**
BARBOUR, I., 444
BARDEEN, Dr John, obit., 569
BARKER, George, death, 511
BARKER, Pat, 512
BARNES, Julian, 509, 512
BARR, William P., 567
BARROSO, Durão, 137
BARSTOW, Stan, 512
BARTHOLOMAIOS, Patriarch, 146
BARTHOLOMEW, Reginald, 315, 433
BARRYMORE, John, 491
BARYSHNIKOV, Mikhail, 485
BASHARI, Ibrahim, 235
BASHIR, Lt.-Gen. Omar Hasan Ahmed al-, Head of State of Sudan, 231
BATCHELOR, Michael, death, 486
BATES, H. E., 495
BATES, Jeremy, 523
BAWDEN, Nina, 509, 512

BEALE, Simon Russell, 488
BEAMON, Bob, 518
BEANLAND, Denver, 370
BEAZLEY, Kim, 369
BECKER, Boris, 522
BEEBY, Thomas, 503
BEG, Gen. Mirza Aslam, 313–14
BEHRENS, Hildegarde, 477
BEITH, Alan, MP, 11
BÉJART, Maurice, 485
BEKOW, Nana Oktuwer, 258
BELEZA, Miguel, 138–9
BELGIUM, 33, **111–12**, 194, 280, 281, 396, 493, 550, 588, 593
BELIZE, 81, **89–90**, 407, 425, 427
BELKHAIR, Gen. Larbi, 241
BELLEZZA, Maurizio, 484
BELORUSSIA, 177, 178 (*map*), 182, 183, 384, 398, 439, 557–61
BELSTEAD, Lord, 41
BEMBERG, Maria-Louise, 494
BEN ALI, Gen. Zayn al-Abidine, President of Tunisia, 236–8
BEN DHIA, Abdelaziz, 238
BEN GAL, Nir, 484
BEN YAHYA, Habib, 236
BENHAJ, Ali, 241
BENIN, 272, **273–4**, 419, 585
BENISSAD, Hocine, 240–1
BENN, Tony, MP, 5, 27, 31
BENNETT, Joan, death, 494
BENTSEN, Senator Lloyd, 55
BÉRÉGOVOY, Pierre, 98
BÉRENGER, Paul, 324
BERGER, Gerhard, 522
BERKHOFF, Stephen, 489
BERLUSCONI, Silvio, 498
BERMUDA, 584
BERMÚDEZ VARELA, Enrique, 81
BERRI, Nabih, 216
BESSMERTNYKH, Aleksandr, 58, 180, 350, 436, 582, 587
BHANDARI, Madan, 319
BHARGAWA, Kant Kishore, 422
BHATTARAI, K. P., 319
BHUMIBOL ADULYADEJ, HM King, of Thailand, 331–2
BHUTAN, **320**, 421
BHUTTO, Benazir, 313–14, 336
BIELICKI, Jan Krzysztof, 152, 154
BILDT, Carl, Prime Minister of Sweden, 124–5, 591
BIN-NUN, Avihu, 204
BINGHAM, Lord Justice, 25
BINTLEY, David, 483
BIRD, Vere, Prime Minister of Antigua & Barbuda, 93
BIRENDRA, HM King, of Nepal, 319
BÍLÁDENU, Alexandru, 161
BIRT, John, 497
BIRTWISTLE, Harrison, 477
BISHARA, Abdallah, 226

BISHOP, Maurice, 90
BISWAS, Abdur Rahman, President of Bangladesh, 317–18, 591
BIWOTT, Nicholas, 253
BIYA, Paul, President of Cameroon, 274
BJELKE-PETERSEN, Sir Joh, 371
BLACK, Conrad, 368
BLACK, Roger, 518
BLANCO, Salvador Jorge, 80
BLANCO, Serge, 517
BLITZENSTEIN, Marc, 478
BLIX, Hans, 386
BLOOMFIELD, Sir Kenneth, 40
BLYTON, Enid, 511
BOFF, Fr Leonardo, 441
BOGDANOV, Michael, 487
BOJANG, Dr Lamin, 264
BOLGER, Jim, Prime Minister of New Zealand, 375–7
BOLIVIA, **68–9**, 427, 528
BOLKIAH, Sir Hassanal, Sultan of Brunei, 334, 423
BOLLERS, Sir Harold, 86
BOND, Alan, 371
BONGO, Omar, President of Gabon, 276
BONNET, Gen. Martín, 68
BOOKER PRIZE, 508
BOOLLEL, Sir Satcam, 324
BOOTH, Laurie, 484
BOSCH GAVIÑO, Juan, 79
BOSKIN, Michael, 567
BOSNIA-HERCEGOVINA, 168 (*map*), 170, 172, 173, 592
BOSSANO, Joe, Chief Minister of Gibraltar, 140–1
BOTHA, P. W., 299
BOTHA, R. F. (Pik), 295
BOTHAM, Ian, 519
BOTSWANA, **296**
BOULARES, Habib, 238
BOURASSA, Robert, 63
BOURHAN, Ali Aref, 252
BOURNONVILLE, August, 485
BOUTERSE, Lt.-Col. Desi, 94
BOUTROS GHALI, Boutros, 208, 294, 383, 409, 593
BOWKER, J., 444
BOYLE, Andrew, obit., 569
BRADLEY, Mayor Tom, 48
BRADY, James, 47–8
BRADY, Nicholas, 55, 567
BRAGA DE MACEDO, Jorge, 139
BRAHIMI, Lakhdar, 240
BRAITHWAITE, Nicholas, Prime Minister of Grenada, 90
BRAZIL, **69–70**, 409, 426, 427, 441, 448, 521, 528
BREVEL, Brigit, 103
BRICKHILL, Paul, obit., 569
BRITTAN, Sir Leon, 402
BRITTO RUIZ, Fernando, 72
BROADCASTING, see Television & Radio

BROMAN, Sven, 513
BROOKE, Peter, MP, 40–1, 117, 566
BROOKNER, Anita, 509, 512
BROWN, Christopher, 502
BROWN, Gordon, MP, 12, 14
BROWN, Jerry, 55
BROWN, Trisha, 485
BRUCE, Steve, 515
BRULLER, Jean, obit., 569
BRUNDTLAND, Gro Harlem, Prime Minister of Norway, 122
BRUNEI, **334–5**, 423
BRUNNER, Gerd, 104
BUBKA, Sergei, 518
BUFI, Ylli, 176, 587, 594
BUI TIN, 342
BULGAKOV, Mikhail, 489
BULGARIA, 151, **164–7**, 406, 413, 414, 417, 432, 584, 591
BURCK, Francis, 380
BURGESS, Anthony, 509, 512
BURGESS, Sally, 478
BURKINA FASO, **270–1**, 421, 588
BURMA, see Myanmar
BURRELL, Leroy, 518
BURROW, Jonathan, 483
BURUNDI, **281–2**
BUSEK, Erhard, 128
BUSH, George, President of USA, 567; arms control & defence, 58, 60, 207, 401, 431, 433, 435–8, 589, 591–2; foreign affairs, 29, 59–60, 65, 84, 99, 145–6, 148–9, 171, 187–8, 202, 205–7, 210–11, 213, 234, 244, 288, 302, 341, 358, 360–1, 377, 382, 428, 495, 583–6, 589–90, 594; Gulf War, 44, 47, 56–8, 146, 191–3, 200, 430, 583–4; home affairs, 45–51, 53–56, 460, 474, 523, 527, 583
BUSSELL, Darcey, 483
BUTHELEZI, Chief Mangosuthu, 394, 583
BUYOYA, Pierre, President of Burundi, 282
BYAMBASÜREN, Dashiyn, Prime Minister of Mongolia, 366

CABINDA, 289
CABRAL, Bernardo, 69
CALATRAVA, Santiago, 505
CALCAVECCHIA, Mark, 520
CALDERINI, Renata, 484
CALDERÓN, Ricardo Arias, 83
CALLAGHAN, Lord, 32
CALLOW, Philip, 512
CAMBODIA, 336, 341, **342–4**, 345, 352, 372, 382, 388, 407, 423, 509, 586, 592, 593
CAMERON, James, 492
CAMEROON, **274–5**, 394, 421
CAMILTON, Oscar, 146
CAMPBELL, Naomi, 506

CAMPESE, David, 517
CAMPOLI, Alfred, death, 482; obit., 569
CAMPORA, Anne-Marie, 133
CANADA, **61–5**, 79, 84, 194, 247, 394, 395, 405, 410, 424, 442, 458, 479, 493, 516, 521, 529
CANEPA, Adolfo, 140
CAPE VERDE, 273, **283**, 383, 419, 583
CAPRA, Frank, death, 494; obit., 569
CARCANI, Adil, 175
CARD, Andrew, 567
CARDOSO DE MELLO, Zélia, 69
CAREY, Most Rev Dr George, Archbishop of Canterbury, 440–1, 586
CAREY, Peter, 512
CARIBBEAN BASIN INITIATIVE (CBI), 428
CARIBBEAN COMMUNITY (CARICOM), **427–8**
CARIBBEAN ORGANIZATIONS, **427–8**
CARIBBEAN TOURISM ORGANIZATION, 428
CARLI, Guido, 110
CARLOT, Maxime, 381
CARLSSON, Ingvar, 123–4, 591
ČARNOGURSKÝ, Ján, 156
CARON, Sandra, 513
CARPIO NICOLE, Jorge, 81
CARR, Michael, MP, 13
CARRERAS, José, 477
CARRINGTON, Lord, 173, 399, 590
CARTER, Angela, 508, 512
CARTER, Elliott, 482
CARTER, Jimmy, 265, 290
CARTLAND, Dame Barbara, 509
CARUANA, Peter, 140
CASTRO RUZ, Fidel, President of Cuba, 78, 426
CAULFIELD, Joan, death, 494
CAVACO SILVA, Anibal, Prime Minister of Portugal, 137–9, 591
CAVALLO, Domingo, 66
CAVAZOS, Lauro, 49
CEAUŞESCU, Nicolae, 163
CELAN, Paul, 507
CÉDRAS, Gen. Raoul, 79
CENTRAL AFRICAN REPUBLIC, **276–7**
CENTRAL AMERICA, 51, **80–3**, 426, 428
CENTRAL INTELLIGENCE AGENCY (CIA), 51, 55, 234
CEREZO AREVALO, Vincio, 81, 582
ÇETIN, Hikmet, 150
ÇETINKAYA, Necati, 151
CHAD, 231, 232, 233, **275–6**, 419, 421
CHADLI, Bendjedid, President of Algeria, 239–41, 246, 588
CHAMLONG SRIMUANG, 332
CHAMORRO, Violeta Barrios de, President of Nicaragua, 81, 462
CHANG, Michael, 522
CHAOVALIT YONGCHAIYUT, Gen., 332
CHARLES, Eugenia, Prime Minister of Dominica, 93
CHARLES, Lynne, 484

CHARLTON, Jack, 515
CHATICHAI CHOONHAVAN, Maj.-Gen., 331–2, 583
CHÁVEZ ARAÚJO, Olivero, 84
CHECKLAND, Michael, 497
CHEIFFOU, Amadou, 271
CHENEY, Richard, 192, 199, 567, 583
CHERNAIK, Judith, 513
CHESHIRE, Lord, 444
CHEVALIER BRAVO, Juan, 83
CHEVÈNEMENT, Jean-Pierre, 96, 192, 583
CHIDZERO, Dr Bernard, 294
CHILE, 68, **70–2,** 84, 103, 409, 425, 427, 528
CHILUBA, Frederick, President of Zambia, 290, 592
CHINA, PEOPLE'S REPUBLIC OF, **346–52;** arts, 493–4; Communist Party, 346–7; economy, 345–50; external relations, 29, 224, 232, 307, 312, 313, 330, 341, 343, 346, 351, 352, 353, 354, 355, 356, 358, 361–2, 363, 366, 367, 372, 385, 423; Gulf crisis, 350, 550; Hong Kong, 29, 351, 355
CHIRAC, Jacques, 98
CHITTY, Susan, 513
CHOLERA EPIDEMIC, 426–7
CHRISTIANSEN, Helena, 506
CHRISTIE, Linford, 518
CHRISTNACHT, Alain, 380
CHRONICLE OF 1991, **582–94**
CHRONOLOGY OF GULF WAR, **191–3**
CHRZANOWSKI, Wieslaw, 154
CHUNG, Vincent, 333
CIERACH, Lindka, 506
CINEMA, 45, 118, **491–4**
CLAMPIT, Amy, 513
CLARK, Graham, 478
CLARK, Manning, death, 372
CLARKE, Kenneth, MP, 19, 566
CLAUDE, Sylvio, 79
CLINTON, Governor Bill, 55
CLOSE, Glenn, 492
CLOSE, Seamus, 41
CLOUGH, Brian, 515
COASE, Prof. Ronald, 529
COATES, Michael, 451
COLD WAR, 1, 130, 281, 313, 316, 339, 362, 390, 393, 407, 411, 419, 425, 429, 430, 431, 433, 526, 531
COLE, Paul, 523
COLEGATE, Isobel, 512
COLEMAN, Peter, 513
COLLINS, Gerard, 117
COLLINS, Rudolph, 86
COLLOR DE MELLO, Fernando, President of Brazil, 69, 457
COLOMBIA, **72–3,** 427, 592
COMECON (Council for Mutual Economic Assistance), 157, 158, **405–7,** 413, 588
COMMONWEALTH OF INDEPENDENT STATES (CIS), 177, 178 (*map*), 183–4, 186, 351, 383, 398, 492, 525, 557–61 (*texts*), 594
COMMONWEALTH, THE, 29–30, 140, 142, 259, 290, 292, 294, 303, 316, 317, 318, **392–5,** 442, 514, 592
COMOROS, **325–6**
COMPAORÉ, Capt. Blaise, Head of State of Burkina Faso, 270, 588
CONABLE, Barber, 420
CONDÉ, Alpha, 267
CONFERENCE ON SECURITY & COOPERATION IN EUROPE (CSCE), 133, 158, 171, 172, 190, 398–9, **410–12,** 415, 435–6, 591
CONGO, **277,** 280, 501
CONJUANGCO, Eduardo, 340
CONTÉ, Lansana, President of Guinea, 267
CONTRERAS, Manuel, 71
COOK, David, 512
COOK ISLANDS, **378, 380**
COOK, Jimmy, 520
COOK, Robin, MP, 27
COOPER, Artemis, 513
COOPER, Barry, 482
COOPER, Roger, 306, 585
COOPER, William, 509, 512
COPELAND, Miles, obit., 570
CORBETT, Keith F., 391
CORIGLIANO, John, 478
COSSIGA, Francesco, President of Italy, 108, 110
COSTA RICA, **80,** 83
CÔTE D'IVOIRE, 264, 265, **269–70,** 383, 550
COULTER, Senator John, 370
COUNCIL FOR MUTUAL ECONOMIC ASSISTANCE, *see* COMECON
COUNCIL OF EUROPE, 158, 412, **414–5**
COURIER, Jim, 522
COWDERY, William, 482
CRADOCK, Sir Percy, 355
CRANKO, John, 484
CRANSTON, Senator Alan, 50
CRAXI, Bettino, 107–8
CRESSON, Edith, Prime Minister of France, 97–8, 587
CRISTIANI BURKARD, Alfredo, President of El Salvador, 80
CROATIA, 2, 32, 105, 128, 145, 161, **167–74,** 168 (*map*), 395, 399, 442, 500, 586, 588, 589, 590, 591, 592, 593, 594
CROMER, Earl of, obit., 570
CROSSLEY-HOLLAND, Kevin, 513
CUBA, **77–8,** 79, 188, 224, 287, 383, 385, 386, 406, 408, 426, 550
CUOMO, Governor Mario, 55–6
CYPRUS, 116, 143, **146–8,** 149, 382, 388
CZECHOSLOVAKIA, 2, 100, 109, 110, 152, **155–8,** 159, 160, 194, 354, 397, 400, 404, 406, 413, 414, 417, 432, 458, 464, 480, 482, 493, 527

DAHL, Roald, 512; death, 511
DAHMER, Jeffrey, 45
DAIM ZAINUDDIN, 333
DALAI LAMA, 367
DALBY, Martin, 481
DALY, John, 520–1
DAMANAKI, Maria, 144
DANCE/BALLET, **483–6**
DANIELESCU, George, 162
DANSOKHO, Amath, 266
DARMAN, Richard, 47, 567
DASH-YONDON, Büdragchaagiyn, 364
DAVIES, Robertson, 512
DAVIES, Siobhan, 484
DAVIS, Miles, death, 482; obit., 570
DAWKINS, John, 369
DE BENEDETTI, Carlo, 110
DE KLERK, F. W., President of South Africa, 254, 299–303, 394, 583, 589, 590
DE LA BILLIÈRE, Gen. Sir Peter, 194
DE LISLE, Viscount, obit., 570
DE MICHELIS, Gianni, 109
DE MILLE, Agnes, 485–6
DEAD SEA SCROLLS, 443
DEAR, Nick, 488
DEBY, Idriss, President of Chad, 233, 275–6
DeCONCINI, Thomas, 499
DEECKE, Thomas, 499
DEFENCE ISSUES, **429–38**
DELPIAZZO, Carlos, 76
DELORS, Jacques, President of EC Commission, 22, 170, 397, 401
DEMENTEI, Nikolai, 182
DEMIREL, Süleyman, Prime Minister of Turkey, 147, 150, 592
DEMME, Jonathan, 492
DENG XIAOPING, 346
DENMARK, **118–20**, 194, 301, 396, 435, 461, 463, 514
DENNING, Stephan, 295
DERWINSKI, Edward, 567
DEWAR, Donald, MP, 36
DEWHURST, Keith, 489
DHLAKAMA, Afonso, 284–5
DI TELLA, Guido, 66
DIAKA, Mungul, 280–1
DIBDIN, Michael, 510, 512
DIENSTBIER, Jiri, 156, 158
DIEPGEN, Eberhard, 103
DIMAS, Stavros, 144
DIMITRIOS I, Patriarch, death, 145, 146; obit., 570
DIMITROV, Filip, Prime Minister of Bulgaria, 165
DINKA, Tesfaye, 248
DINKINS, David, 53
DIOUF, Abdou, President of Senegal, 266–7
DIOURI, Abd el Moumen, 244
DIRO, Ted, 374

DISARMAMENT, see Arms Control & Security
DISASTERS & ACCIDENTS (see also Environmental Questions), Chile, 68; Honduras, 83; Iran, 307; Maldives, 326–7; Nepal, 319; New Zealand, 378; Philippines, 339, 457; St Kitts & Nevis, 93; South Pacific, 379–80; USA, 45–6
DISKI, Jenny, 512
DISSANAYAKE, Gamini, 322
DITFURTH, Jutta, 104
DIXON, Jeremy, 505
DJIBOUTI, **251–2**, 389
DJOHAR, Said Mohammed, President of the Comoros, 326
DO MUOI, 341, 588
DOE, Gen. Samuel, 265
DOGAN, Ahmed, 166
DOGAN, Hüsnü, 149
DOI, Takako, 359, 588
DOMINGO, Placido, 477
DOMINICA, **92, 93**
DOMINICAN REPUBLIC, **79–80**
DOS SANTOS, José Eduardo, President of Angola, 287–9, 587
DOTRICE, Roy, 491
DOWNES, Edward, 480
DOYLE, Desmond, death, 486
DOYLE, Roddy, 118, 512
DRABBLE, Margaret, 509, 512
DREGGER, Alfred, 104
DROR, Liat, 484
DRUG-TRAFFICKING, Africa, 209; Americas, 47, 67, 68–9, 72, 75, 77, 84; Asia, 422; sport, 514; UN, 391
DUBAI, 224, 229
DUBČEK, Alexander, 157
DUHALDE, Eduardo, 67
DUKE, David, 56
DUMAS, Roland, 99, 191, 235, 244, 384
DUNCAN-JONES, Katherine, 513
DUNKEL, Arthur, 403
DURÁN, Armando, 77
DURANTE, Viviana, 483
DURAS, Marguerite, 513
DURIE, Jo, 523
DUVALIER, Jean-Claude, 582
DZARDYHAN, Kinayatyn, 365
DZORIG, Sanjaasürengiyn, 365

EAGLEBURGER, Lawrence, 425
EAGLING, Wayne, 485
EAST ASIAN ECONOMIC CAUCUS (EAEC), 423
EAST ASIAN ECONOMIC GROUPING (EAEG), 423
EAST EUROPEAN COOPERATION & TRADE ORGANIZATION (EECTO), 406
EAST TIMOR, 337, 372, 377, 461, 509, 593
EASTERN CARIBBEAN CENTRAL BANK (ECCB), 428

ECEVIT, Bülent, 150
ECONOMIC & SOCIAL AFFAIRS, 525–49; international economy, 527–9; USSR/CIS economy, 525–7; statistical data, 535–49
ECONOMIC & SOCIAL COMMISSION FOR ASIA & THE PACIFIC (ESCAP), 424
ECONOMIC COMMUNITY OF WEST AFRICAN STATES (ECOWAS), 262, 263, 264, 265, 267, 420–1
ECUADOR, 73–4, 385, 427, 550
EDBERG, Stefan, 522
EDDERY, Pat, 523
EDMONDS, John, 26
EDUR, Thomas, 484
EDWARDS, Dave, 392
EDWARDS, Governor Edwin, 56
EDWARDS, Huw, MP, 18, 39
EGYPT, 59, 194, 199, 202, **207–9**, 212, 220, 221, 222, 223, 225, 226, 227, 231, 232, 233, 236, 294, 306, 383, 396, 404, 409, 528, 589, 593
EITAN, Rafael, 203
EL SALVADOR, 80, 81, **82–3**, 382, 388, 407, 426
ELBEGDORJ, Tsahiagiyn, 365
ELIAS, Judge Taslin, death, 463; obit., 570
ELIZABETH II, HM Queen, 9, 254, 292, 374, 500, 587, 591–2
ENDARA GALLIMANY, Guillermo, President of Panama, 83
ENGHOLM, Björn, 104
ENNALS, Martin, obit., 570
ENRILE, Juan Ponce, 340
ENVIRONMENTAL QUESTIONS (*see also* Disasters & Accidents), **455–60**; acid rain, 458; Antarctic, 459; Brazil, 70, 457; Canada-US, 65; drift-net fishing, 459; Germany, 105; global warming, 456–7; Kuwait/Gulf, 192, 193, 198, 221, 228, 385, 456; NAM, 457; nitrogen oxides, 457; ozone layer, 458; nuclear reactors, 458–9; rainforests, 457; UN, 391, 455–6; whaling, 121, 459
EQUATORIAL GUINEA, **278**
ERBAKAN, Necmettin, 150
ERI, Sir Vincent, 373–4
ERITREA, 248–9
ERMAN GONZÁLEZ, Antonio, 66–7
ERNST, Prof. Richard, 451
ERSHAD, Hussain Mohammad, 316–7, 588
ESCOBAR GAVIRIA, Pablo, 72
ESSAWY, Hesham el-, 444
ESTONIA, 178 (*map*), 180, **188–90**, 382, 418, 432, 557, 584, 585, 590
ETHIOPIA, 202, 231, **248–50**, 252, 389, 407, 419, 420, 587
EUBANK, Chris, 514
EUROPEAN BANK FOR RECONSTRUCTION & DEVELOPMENT (EBRD), 9, 174, **412–14**, 586

EUROPEAN COMMUNITY (*see also* European Community Law, Western European Union), **395–403**; agriculture/GATT, 403; Baltic states, 396–7; Central America, 426; defence issues, 9, 106, 109, 135, 400–01, 561; Eastern Europe, 399–400, 464; EBRD, 413; EFTA, 121, 122, 123, 127, 131, 133, 402–3, 416–7, 418, 464–5; EMU/Maastricht summit, 2, 3–4, 28, 30–3, 100, 106, 110, 116, 118, 119, 121, 124, 127, 135, 138–9, 143, 145, 173, 395, **400–2**, **465–6**, **561–6**; energy, 403; environment, 457; external relations, 2–3, 4, 7, 30, 32, 79, 84, 105–6, 115, 124–5, 127, 130, 133, 141–2, 148–9, 153, 160, 161, 166, 170–1, 172–3, 191, 206, 210, 226, 235, 251, 292, 293, 295, 303, 306, 328–9, 330, 358, 359, 395–400, 402–3, 416–7, 418, 422, 426; Gibraltar, 140; Gulf crisis, 7, 384, 395–6; information technology, 453–4; SAARC, 422; Schengen agreement, 466–7; Social Charter, 32, 33, 401, 563; UK, 2, 7, 8–9, 14, 22–3, 26, 28, 29, 30, 31, 32, 33, 38, 400–2, 561–6; USSR, 397–8; Yugoslavia, 105–6, 128, 170–3, 398–9
EUROPEAN COMMUNITY LAW, **464–8**
EUROPEAN COURT OF HUMAN RIGHTS, 413
EUROPEAN COURT OF JUSTICE, 403, 416, **465–8**
EUROPEAN FREE TRADE ASSOCIATION (EFTA), 121, 122, 123, 127, 131, 133, 151, 403, **416–17**, 418, 464, 465, 592
EUROPEAN INVESTMENT BANK (EIB), 238, 413
EVANGELISTA, Linda, 506
EVANS, Gareth, 334, 372
EVERT, Miltiades, 143
EVOLUTION, 450–51
EYADEMA, Gen. Gnassingbe, President of Togo, 272–3, 585

FAHD IBN ABDUL AZIZ, HM King, of Saudi Arabia, 193, 220, 222, 421, 584
FAHIMA, al-Amin Khalifah, 235
FALCONI, Juan, 74
FALDO, Nick, 520–1
FALKLAND ISLANDS/MALVINAS, 5, 194
FARRELL, Terry, 503
FASHION, **505–7**
FAWCETT, Sir James, obit., 570–1
FEDERATED STATES OF MICRONESIA (FSM), 378–9, 382, 424, 425, 591
FEHERTY, David, 520
FEIN, Fiona Morgan, 482
FEINSTEIN, Elaine, 513
FEISSEL, Gustave, 146
FELBER, René, 130
FERGUSON, Alex, 515
FERNAN, Marcelo, 340

INDEX

FERRARI, Maxime, 325
FIELD, Frank, MP, 24
FIELD, John, death, 486; obit., 571
FIELDS, Terry, MP, 26
FIERS, Alan, 51
FIGUEREO PLANCHART, Reinaldo, 77
FIJI, **379, 381**
FILALI, Abdel Latif, 246
FILIZZOLA, Carlos Alberto, 74
FINLAND, 119, 122, **125–7**, 417, 461, 463, 515, 529, 585
FINNISTON, Sir Monty, obit., 571
FIRSOVA, Elena, 480
FITT, Lord, 16
FITZWATER, Marlin, 54
FLEMING, John, 502
FLINT, Julie, 291
FLORAKIS, Kharilaos, 144
FLOSSE, Gaston, 101, 380
FLOYD, Ray, 520
FLYNN, Padraig, 117
FOLEY, Thomas S., 51
FONTEYN, Dame Margot, death, 483; obit., 571
FORD, Gerald, 56
FORDICE, Governor Kirk, 56
FORGET, Guy, 522
FORSTER, Margaret, 512
FOSTER, Greg, 518
FOSTER, Neil, 519–20
FOSTER, Sir Norman, 504
FOUDY, Julie, 524
FOWLER, Sir Norman, MP, 31
FOX, R. L., 444
FRACCI, Carla, 485
FRANCE, **96–101;** arts, 483, 500, 501; broadcasting, 498; Corsica, 97; defence, 100–1; EC, 400–1, 402, 433, 434–5; economy, 97, 98; external relations, 30, 79, 96, 97, 98–101, 110, 126, 135, 153, 163–4, 173, 221, 226, 228, 234–5, 239, 244, 269, 272, 275, 276, 280, 281, 288, 306, 327, 344, 377, 380, 399, 400–1, 404, 424, 430, 550; Gulf crisis, 96, 99–100, 191, 192, 194, 199, 243, 252, 384, 396, 430, 550; immigration, 96, 98; Nobel Prize, 451; overseas possessions, 101, 380, 425; politics, 97; sport, 515, 516, 517, 521, 522, 523
FRANCO BAHAMONDE, Gen. Francisco, 140
FRANCO-AFRICAN CONFERENCE, 421
FRANCOPHONIE, 61, 100, 275, 280, 421
FRANK, Edouard, 276
FRANKLIN, Barbara, 50
FRAYN, Michael, 512
FREELAND, Sir John, 415
FREEMAN, HE Cardinal Sir James, death, 372
FRENCH POLYNESIA, **101, 378, 380**
FRIEDRICH, Götz, 477

FRIEDRICH, John, 371
FRIEL, Brian, 118
FRISCH, Max, obit., 571
FRY, Stephen, 512
FUENMAYOR, Gen. Herminio, 77
FUJAIRAH, 224
FUJIMORI, Alberto Keinya, President of Peru, 75
FULLER, John, 513
FULLER, Roy, death, 511; obit., 571–2
FYODOROV, Valentin, 358

GABLE, Christopher, 484
GABLE, David, 482
GABO, Naum, 484
GABON, **276**
GAINES, J. E., 490
GALASSI, Peter, 502
GALLARDO, Jorge, 74
GAMBIA, THE, **263–4,** 421
GAMSAKHURDIA, Zviad, 183, 587, 594
GANDHI, Indira, 310
GANDHI, Rajiv, 310; death, 309–10, 321–2, 392, 587; obit., 572
GANDHI, Sanjay, 310
GANDHI, Sonia, 310
GARAFOLA, Lynn, 486
GARANG, Col. John, 230
GARCIA, Joe, 141
GARCÍA PÉREZ, Alan, 76
GARCIA ROBLES, Alfonso, obit., 572
GARCÍA VARGAS, Julian, 135
GARDAM, Jane, 512
GARDNER, Ava, 513
GAREL-JONES, Tristan, MP, 140
GASCOIGNE, Paul ('Gazza'), 516
GATES, Daryl, 48
GATES, Robert, 51–2, 567
GAVIRIA TRUJILLO, César, President of Colombia, 72
GAYOOM, Maumoun Abdul, 327
GEBRE-KIDAN, Tesfaye, 248
GEDDES, Tom, 508
GEE, Maggie, 510, 512
GELBARD, Robert, 68
GENERAL AGREEMENT ON TARIFFS & TRADE (GATT), 4, 9, 33, 372, 375, 403, 404, 424, 529, 589
GENNES, Pierre-Gilles de, 451
GENSCHER, Hans-Dietrich, 105, 399
GEORGE, Clair, 51
GEORGIA, 177, 178 (*map*), 180, 183, 184, 397, 585, 586, 587, 594
GEPHARDT, Richard, 55
GERASIMOV, Gennady, 185
GERMAN, Patriarch, obit., 572
GERMAN DEMOCRATIC REPUBLIC (GDR), 405
GERMANY, **102–7;** arts, 499; defence, 8, 106, 105–6, 400–2, 434–5; economy, 33, 100, 102, 106, 527, 528, 529; external relations, 9, 33, 71–2, 102, 103, 104,

105, 110, 119, 126, 135, 152, 153, 158, 161, 166, 173, 187, 215–6, 224, 272, 301, 356, 395, 396, 399, 404, 432–3; Frederick the Great, 107; Gulf crisis, 6, 105, 192, 194, 396; immigration, 103–4; politics, 104; Nobel Prize, 451; terrorism, 103; Yugoslavia, 105–6, 395, 399; sport, 106, 515, 517, 518, 521, 524
GETZ, Stan, obit., 572
GHALIB, Umar Arteh, 250
GHANA, **257–9**, 421
GHANNOUCHI, Rached, 236–8
GHOZALI, Sid-Ahmed, Prime Minister of Algeria, 239–41, 588
GIACOMELLI, Giorgio, 391
GIBRALTAR, 135–6, **139–41**
GIBSON, Walter, 448
GIELGUD, Sir John, 490
GIOIA, Dana, 510
GIRALDO ANGEL, Jaime, 72
GISCARD D'ESTAING, Valéry, 98
GIZENGA, Antoine, 280
GLADSTONE, David, 323
GLEN, Duncan, 513
GLENN, Senator John, 50
GLIGOROV, Kiro, 167
GLOAG, Julian, 512
GODOY, Virgilio, 82
GOGU, Cefin, 145
GOH CHOK TONG, Prime Minister of Singapore, 335, 423
GOLDSTONE, Mr Justice, 301
GOMBRICH, E. H., 502
GONCHIGDORV, Radnaasümbereliyn, 366
GÖNCZ, Árpád, President of Hungary, 160
GONZÁLEZ, Felipe, Prime Minister of Spain, 134–6, 140, 244, 278, 586
GOOCH, Graham, 519
GORBACHEV, Mikhail, President of USSR, 1, 8, 29, 60, 526; arms control & defence, 436, 438, 589, 592, 594; coup, 144, 177, 179–80, 350, 397, 437, 495, 498; foreign affairs, 78, 187–8, 206, 350, 358, 361, 366, 397, 584, 586, 589–92; Gulf War, 186, 192, 583; internal affairs, 181–3, 185, 189–90, 439–40, 582, 584, 586, 590; resignation, 177, 184, 398, 594
GORDIMER, Nadine, 507
GORE, Senator Albert, 50, 55
GOREN, Charles, obit., 572
GOULDING, Marrack, 173
GOULED, Hassan, President of Djibouti, 252
GOWER, David, 519
GOWING, Sir Lawrence, obit., 572
GRADE, Michael, 498
GRAF, Steffi, 106, 523
GRAHAM, Martha, 484, 486; death, 483; obit., 572–3
GRAY, Robin, 369

GRAY, William H., 50
GRAYSTON, K., 444
GREECE, 142, **143–6**, 147, 149, 164, 166, 176, 194, 388, 399, 435, 582, 584
GREENAWAY, Peter, 493
GREENE, Graham, death, 510; obit., 573
GREENLAND, 120
GREENSPAN, Alan, 54
GREGORY, Cynthia, 485
GREINER, Nick, 368
GRENADA, **90**, 186, 427, 428
GRIBBIN, John, 513
GRIFFITHS, Paul, 477
GRIMSHAW, Nicholas, 505
GROOM, Ray, 369
GROSS, Philip, 513
GROUMELLAC, Loië Le, 483
GROUP OF SEVEN (G7), 7, 29, 65, 187, 358, 459, 529, 589
GUATEMALA, **80–1**, 89, 407, 425, 427, 582
GUERRA, Alfonso, 134, 136
GUERREIRO GUIMARÃES, Cantido, 70, 457
GUILLEM, Sylvie, 483, 485
GUINEA, 263, **267**, 421
GUINEA-BISSAU, **283**, 461, 462
GULF COOPERATION COUNCIL (GCC), 206, 207, 212, 221, 225, 226, 228, 229, 230, 243
GULF CRISIS, **194–200, 429–30**; Algeria, 239; Arab world, 204, 207; Australia, 371–2; Austria, 127–8; Bangladesh, 318; Belgium, 111; Canada, 65; Caribbean, 428; ceasefire resolution (687), 550–5 (*text*); chronology, 191–3; Commonwealth, 392; Council of Europe, 415; Cyprus, 146; Djibouti, 252; EC, 395–6; Egypt, 207–9; environment, 192, 193, 198, 221, 228, 385, 456; ESCAP, 424; France, 96, 99–100, 191, 192, 194, 199, 243, 252, 384, 396, 430, 550; GCC, 225–30; Germany, 6, 105, 192, 194, 396; Greece, 146; heritage damage, 500; Indonesia, 338; Iran, 305; Iraq, 217–20; Israel, 200–1; Italy, 109; Japan, 357–9; Jordan, 210–12; S. Korea, 362; Kuwait, 226–9; Lebanon, 214; Libya, 232–3; Luxembourg, 115; Malta, 141, 142; maps, 195; military campaign, 194–200; Morocco, 247; NAM, 408–9; Nigeria, 261; Pakistan, 313, 314; Portugal, 139; Saudi Arabia, 220–22; Senegal, 421; Seychelles, 326; Sierra Leone, 262; Spain, 134; Sudan, 230, 231–2; Syria, 212–4; Tanzania, 256; Thailand, 332; Tunisia, 236, 237, 238; Turkey, 148–9; UK, 5–8, 11, 105, 191, 192, 193, 194, 196, 198, 210, 211, 226, 550; UN, 382, 383, 384–7; USA, 6, 14, 44, 46, 54, 56–8, 99, 191, 192, 193, 194–200, 201, 210, 217–19, 220, 223, 225, 226, 228, 232, 236, 239, 242–3, 305, 395,

429–30, 550; USSR, 186–7; Yemen, 223; Zimbabwe, 293, 294
GULF STATES, see Arab States of the Gulf
GUMMER, John Selwyn, MP, 566
GUNNELL, Sally, 518
GURIRAB, Theo-Ben, 295
GURNEY, A. R., 490
GUTEREZ, Antonio, 138
GUYANA, **86–7**, 393, 407, 425
GUZMÁN ERRÁZURIZ, Jaime, 71
GUZMÁN GUTTIÉREZ, Erwin, 68
GYNGELL, Bruce, 496

HABRÉ, Hissène, 231, 233, 275
HABYARIMANA, Maj.-Gen. Juvénal, President of Rwanda, 282
HACHIMI, Abdelkader, 241
HAIDER, Jörg, 128–9
HAIN, Peter, MP, 39
HAITI, **78–9**, 80, 426, 582, 583, 591
HALIDI, Ahmed, 326
HALL, Sir Peter, 486, 488
HAMAD BIN KHALIFA AL-THANI, Sheikh, Emir of Qatar, 226
HAMBURGER, Michael, 507, 513
HAMM, Mia, 524
HAMMADI, Saadun, 218–9, 243
HAMMETT, Dashiell, 491
HAMPTON, Christopher, 489
HAMROUCHE, Mouloud, 240
HAN LIH-WU, obit., 573
HANLEY, Ellery, 517
HANNIBALSSON, Jón Baldvin, 120
HANS ADAM, Prince, 133
HAQ, Gen. Fazle, 314
HARALD V, HM King, of Norway, 122, 582
HARCOURT, Michael, 64
HARE, David, 489
HARGREAVES, John, death, 479
HARKIN, Senator Tom, 55
HAROUN, Ali, 240
HARRIES, Rt Rev Richard, 441
HARRIS, Pippa, 513
HARRIS OF HIGH CROSS, Lord, 22
HARRISON, Tony, 510
HARVEY, Jonathan, 481
HASHIMOTO, Ryutaro, 359
HASSAN II, HM King, of Morocco, 242–6, 421
HASTINGS, Gavin, 517
HATTERSLEY, Roy, MP, 33
HAUGHEY, Charles, Prime Minister of Irish Republic, 41, 116–7
HAVEL, Václav, President of Czechoslovakia, 100, 155–6
HAWKE, Bob, 368–70, 594
HAY, Alexandre, obit., 573
HAYATOU, Sadou, Prime Minister of Cameroon, 274
HAYNES, Desmond, 519

HAYNES, Richie, 88
HEALEY, Denis, MP, 5
HEANEY, Seamus, 489, 510
HEATH, Edward, MP, 5, 13, 23
HEELEY, Desmond, 483
HEFFER, Eric, MP, death, 24
HEGLEY, John, 510, 513
HEINDRICHS, April, 524
HEINESEN, William, obit., 573–4
HEINZ, Senator John, 56
HENG SAMRIN, 343
HENNARD, George, 48
HENRY, Geoffrey, 380
HENZE, Hans-Werner, 482
HEPBURN, Katherine, 513
HERRIGEL, Otto, 295
HEWSON, John, 369
HESELTINE, Michael, MP, 15, 28, 566
HEXAGONALE, 109, 128, 413
HEYHOE-FLINT, Rachel, 519
HICK, Graeme, 520
HILL, Anita, 53, 473
HILLS, Carla, 567
HILSENRATH, Edgar, 507
HINZE, Russell, death, 372
HOCKEY, Jennifer, 444
HODSON, Millicent, 483–4
HOFFMAN, Mr Justice, 471
HOFFMAN, William M., 478
HOLKERI, Harri, 126
HOLLEIN, Hans, 499
HOLROYD, Michael, 508, 513
HOLT, Hazel, 513
HOLY SEE, see Vatican
HONASAN, Gregorio 'Gringo', 339
HONDA, Soichiro, obit., 574
HONDURAS, **80, 83**, 90, 426
HONECKER, Erich, 72, 103
HONG KONG, 29, 33, 342, 351, **355–6**, 380, 404, 423, 496, 499, 500, 528, 590, 591
HONORAT, Jean-Jacques, 79
HONOUR, Hugh, 502
HORNE, Marilyn, 478
HORTA, Basilio, 137
HOSTELLER, Jeff, 524
HOUGH, Richard, 513
HOUNGBEDJI, Adrien, 274
HOUPHOUËT-BOIGNY, Félix, President of Côte d'Ivoire, 269–70
HOWARD, Michael, MP, 566
HOWE, Brian, 369
HOWE, Sir Geoffrey, MP, 31
HOXHA, Enver, 175
HOYTE, Desmond, President of Guyana, 86–7
HRAWI, Elias, President of Lebanon, 216
HUGHES, Mark, 515
HULME, Keri, 508
HUME, HE Cardinal Basil, 441–2
HUN SEN, 344
HUNGARY, 100, 109, 110, 152, **158–61**, 163, 164, 303, 354, 383, 397, 400, 404,

405, 406, 413, 417, 432, 464, 492, 493, 527, 589
HUNT, David, MP, 38, 566
HURD, Douglas, MP, 9, 16, 22, 28, 30–1, 253, 355, 566
HURRAIBI, Hassan al, 224
HURT, Mary Beth, 491
HURTADO, Fernando, 81
HUSAIN, HM King, of Jordan, 191–2, 210–11, 384, 583
HUSAIN, Saddam, *see under* Saddam Husain,
HUSAINI, Faisal al, 206
HUSÁK, Gustav, obit., 574
HUSSEY, Marmaduke, 497
HUTCHINSON, Prof. Evelyn, obit., 574
HUYS, Ben, 485
HYDE-WHITE, Wilfrid, death, 494
HYTNER, Nicholas, 477

IBERO-AMERICAN SUMMIT, 426
ICELAND, **120–1**, 416, 459
IDRIS, Youssef, obit., 574
IGNATIEFF, Michael, 509, 512
IEKAWE, Jacques, 425
ILEO, Joseph, 279
ILIESCU, Ion, President of Romania, 161–2
IMANYARA, Gitobu, 252
INDIA, 140, **309–13**, 315, 316, 318, 319, 320, 321, 322, 385, 392, 408, 422, 491, 493, 501, 550, 550, 584, 587, 588, 594
INDONESIA, 334, **337–8**, 342, 343, 359, 372, 377, 409, 423, 527, 593
INFANTINO, Luigi, death, 479
INFORMATION TECHNOLOGY, **451–5**
INGRAM, James, 389
INÖNÜ, Erdal, 150
INOUE, Yasushi, obit., 574
INTER-AMERICAN DEVELOPMENT BANK (IDB), 69, 87, 428
INTERNATIONAL ATOMIC ENERGY AGENCY (IAEA), 385, 386
INTERNATIONAL BANK FOR ECONOMIC COOPERATION, 407
INTERNATIONAL BANK FOR RECONSTRUCTION & DEVELOPMENT (IBRD), *see* World Bank
INTERNATIONAL COURT OF JUSTICE (ICJ), 228, 380, **461–3**
INTERNATIONAL DEVELOPMENT ASSOCIATION (IDA), 209, 231
INTERNATIONAL INVESTMENT BANK (IIB), 407
INTERNATIONAL MARITIME ORGANIZATION (IMO), 385
INTERNATIONAL MONETARY FUND (IMF), 89, 153, 163, 209, 214, 238, 241, 242, 266, 291, 292, 297, 312, 315, 332, 345, 397, 413, 589
IONESCU-QUINTUS, Mircea, 162
IRAN, 50, 51, 52, 99, 192, 207, 210, 212, 214, 215, 217, 222, 223, 225, 226, 231, **305–8**, 316, 408, 512, 585, 586, 589
IRAQ, 3, 5, 6, 7, 24, 56, 57, 58, 59, 65, 96, 99, 135, 148, 149, 186, 191, 192, 193, **194–200** (*map* 195), 201, 204–5, 207, 208, 209, 212, 213, **217–20**, 220, 222, 223, 225, 226, 227, 229, 230, 231, 232, 236, 239, 242, 243, 244, 305, 306, 350, 383, 384–7, 395, 396, 409, 429, 430, 443, 456, 461, 495, 500, 528, 550–5, 582, 583, 584, 585, 586, 589, 593
IRELAND, NORTHERN, *see* Northern Ireland,
IRELAND, Republic of, 40–1, **115–18**, 142, 215, 301, 404, 405, 435, 467, 479, 515, 523
IRVING, Robert, death, 486
IRWIN, Col. James B., obit., 574
IRWIN, Hale, 520
ISA BIN SULMAN AL-KHALIFA, Sheikh, Emir of Bahrain, 226
ISLAMIC CONFERENCE ORGANIZATION (ICO), 174, 309, 421
ISLAMIC FUNDAMENTALISM, 88, 205, 208, 210, 211, 214, 224, 230, 232, 234, 236–8, 239–41, 245, 307, 314, 338, 443–8
ISLE OF MAN, 116
ISRAEL, 1, 59, 186, 187, 191, 192, 197, 198, **200–4**, 205, 206, 207, 208, 211, 212, 213, 214, 215, 216, 217, 233, 248, 350, 383, 387, 396, 442, 582, 587, 589, 591
ITALY, 84, **107–11**, 127, 170, 173, 175, 194, 396, 398, 400, 401, 404, 405, 413, 433, 434, 479, 498, 514, 515, 522, 529, 584, 585, 586, 589
ITURRALDE BALLIVIÁN, Carlos, 69
IVORY COAST, *see* Côte d'Ivoire

JABIR, Kamil Abu, 211
JABIR AL-AHMAD AL-JABIR AS-SABAH, Emir of Kuwait, 193, 227
JACKSON, Rev Jesse, 54–5
JAGAN, Cheddi, 86
JAKOBOVITS, Lord, 442
JAMAICA, **85–6**, 428, 518
JANJUA, Gen. Asif Nawaz, 314
JAPAN, **357–61;** arts, 494, 500; economy, 33, 356, 527, 528, 529; external relations, 26, 38, 75, 187, 210, 223, 224, 229, 232, 295, 317, 321, 330, 336, 337, 342, 346, 351, 352, 358, 360, 361, 362, 363, 366, 372, 383, 390, 404, 423, 430; politics, 359, 360; scandals, 359; sport, 522; USA, 360–1
JASINSKI, Roman, death, 486; obit., 574
JASON, David, 495
JATOI, Ghulam Mustapha, 314
JAWARA, Sir Dawda Kairaba, President of the Gambia, 264

JEFFERIES, Stephen, 483
JEFFREYS, Prof. Alec, 450
JEFFRIES, Leonard, 48
JENKINS, Lord (Roy Jenkins), 513
JENNINGS, Corin, 524
JENNINGS, Sir Robert, 463
JERSEY, 116
JEYASINGH, Shobana, 485
JIANG QING, death, 349–50; obit., 574–5
JIANG ZEMIN, General Secretary of Chinese Communist Party, 341, 346, 350, 587
JIGME SINGYE WANGCHUK, HM King, of Bhutan, 320, 421
JOHANSEN, Lars Emil, 120
JOHN PAUL II, HH Pope, 70, 110, 441–2, 587, 589
JOHNSON, Ben, 514
JOHNSON, Earvin 'Magic', 45
JOHNSON, James, death, 479
JOHNSON, Mrs, 502
JOHNSON, Prince Yormie, 265
JOINT EUROPEAN TORUS (JET), 447
JONES, Edward, 505
JONES, Dr Gwyn, 39
JONES, Gwyneth, 477
JONES, Martin, 517
JORDAN, 59, 191, 204, 205, 206, **210–2**, 384, 396, 501, 583
JOXE, Pierre, 96, 192, 583
JOYCE, Eileen, death, 482; obit., 575
JUAN CARLOS, HM King, of Spain, 135–6, 244, 426
JUGNAUTH, Sir Aneerood, Prime Minister of Mauritius, 323–4, 591
JULIA, Raul, 491
JUMBLATT, Walid, 216
JUNEJO, Muhammad Khan, 314
JUNOR, Penny, 513
JUVENTIN, Jean, 380

KABELÁČ, Miloslav, 480
KABUA, Amata, 379
KÁDÁR, Béla, 405–6
KAGANOVICH, Lazar, obit., 575
KAIFU, Toshiki, 336, 351–2, 357–60, 366, 589, 592
KALLEL, Abdullah, 237
KAPOLKAS, Donald, 381
KAPOOR, Anish, 502
KARAMANLIS, Achilleas, 144
KARAMANLIS, Konstantinos, President of Greece, 144
KARAMI, Omar, Prime Minister of Lebanon, 214
KASET ROJANANIL, Air Chief Marshal, 331
KASHMIR, 309, 313, 316
KATZENBERG, Jeffrey, 492
KAUFMAN, Gerald, MP, 27
KAUNDA, Kenneth, 290–1, 592

KAVANAGH, P. J., 511, 513
KAYSONE PHOMVIHANE, President of Laos, 345
KAZAKHSTAN, 151, 177, 178 (*map*), 182, 183, 184, 188, 351, 398, 557, 559–61, 594
KEATING, Charles, 50
KEATING, Paul, Prime Minister of Australia, 368–9, 594
KEE, A., 444
KEFALOYIANNIS, Yannis, 144
KELLEY, Kitty, 511, 513
KELTERBORN, Rudolf, 480
KEMP, Jack, 567
KENEALLY, Thomas, 512
KENNEDY, Senator Edward, 45, 52
KENNEDY, John F., 56, 473
KENNEDY, Laurence, 41
KENYA, 234, **252–4**, 285, 389, 394, 517, 593
KEREKOU, Brig.-Gen. Mathieu, 273, 585
KERIN, John, 369
KERR, Sir John, obit., 575
KERREY, Senator Bob, 55
KHALVATI, Mini, 513
KHAMENEI, Ayatollah Ali, 307
KHAMTAY SIPHANDON, General, 345
KHAN, Ghulam Ishaq, President of Pakistan, 313–4, 316
KHANNA, Balraj, 512
KHIEU SAMPHAN, 344, 593
KIBAKI, Mwai, 254
KIESLOWSKI, Kryzystof, 493
KILFOYLE, Peter, MP, 24
KIM IL SUNG, President of North Korea, 363
KIM JONG IL, 363
KINCAID, Jamaica, 512
KING, Francis, 512
KING, Rodney, 48
KING, Tom, MP, 7–8, 566, 589
KINNOCK, Neil, MP, 5, 10, 14, 16, 17, 24–8, 31–3
KIRGHIZIA, 151, 177, 178 (*map*), 184, 557, 559–61
KIRIBATI, **379, 381**, 424
KIRKUP, James, 512
KIS, János, 160
KISEKKA, Samson, 256
KISTLER, Darcy, 485
KITINGAN, Datuk Joseph Pairan, 333
KITINGAN, Jeffrey, 333
KIYONGA, Crispus, 257
KLASEN, Dr Karl, obit., 575
KLAUS, Václav, 156
KLJUSEV, Nikola, 167
KLOSE, Hans-Ulrich, 104
KOESTER, Helmut, 444
KOFFIGOH, Joseph Kokou, 272–3
KOHL, Helmut, Chancellor of Germany, 9, 71, 102, 104–5, 107, 192, 399, 401, 434, 585–4, 587–8

KOIRALA, Girja Prasad, Prime Minister of Nepal, 319, 587
KOLINGBA, Gen. André, President of Central African Republic, 276–7
KOMBO, Mgr Ernest, 277
KONDOYIANNOPOULOS, Vasilis, 143
KÓNYA, Imre, 159
KOREA, DEMOCRATIC PEOPLE'S REPUBLIC OF (North Korea), 327, 362, **363**, 382, 591
KOREA, REPUBLIC OF (South Korea), 187, 352, 358, **361–3**, 382, 404, 423, 424, 527, 591
KOSINSKI, Jerzy, obit., 575
KOSKOTAS, George, 144
KOSTOV, Ivan, 165
KOTY, Abbas, 276
KOUTSOGIORGAS, Agamemnon, 144
KOVICH, Robert, death, 486
KRABBE, Kristin, 518
KRAVCHUK, Leonid, 593
KRIER, Leon, 503
KRIKALYOV, Sergei, 446–7
KRYUCHKOV, Vladimir, 179
KUMAKHOV, Muradin, 448
KUMARANATUNGA, Chandrika, 323
KUPA, Mihaly, 159
KURDISH QUESTION, 6, 7, 14, 58, 99, 109, 135, 149, 150–1, 217, 218, 219, 305, 386, 396, 443, 585, 586, 589
KURTAG, György, 480
KUWAIT, 1, 5, 6, 56, 57, 148, 186, 191, 192, 193, **194–200**, 204, 210, 212, 217, 219, 220, 221, 223, **225**, 226, 227, 228, 229, 230, 231, 233, 236, 242, 305, 306, 350, 383, 384–6, 395, 396, 409, 429, 430, 443, 456, 461, 500, 527, 550, 582, 583, 584, 586
KYPRIANOU, Spyros, 146

LA LOCA, 510
LACALLE HERRERA, Luis Alberto, President of Uruguay, 76
LAFLEUR, Jacques, 380
LAFONTANT, Roger, 79
LAMB, Richard, 513
LAMONT, Norman, MP, 11–12, 25, 28, 566
LAND, Edwin, obit., 575
LANDSBERGIS, Vytautas, 189
LANG, Ian, MP, 36–7, 566
LANGER, Bernhard, 520–1
LANGLAIS, Jean, death, 482; obit., 575
LAOS, 344, **345**, 352
LATIN AMERICAN ORGANIZATIONS & COOPERATION, **425–7**
LATVIA, 178 (map), 180, **188–90**, 382, 418, 432, 557, 582, 584, 590
LAUREL, Salvador, 340
LAURENCIN, Marie, 483
LAW & LEGAL MATTERS, European Community law, **464–8**; international law, **461–4**; UK law, **468–73**; US law, **473–6**
LAWRENCE, Dr John, obit., 576
LAWSON, Nigel, MP, 14
LAYNIE, Tamirat, Prime Minister of Ethiopia, 249
LE PEN, Jean-Marie, 98
LE PENSEC, Louis, 101
LEAN, Sir David, death, 494; obit., 576
LEANDER, Michael, 490
LEBANON, 2, 7, 149, 205, 212, 213, **214–6**, 382, 441, 589, 590, 591, 593
LECONTE, Henri, 522
LEE KI TAEK, 363
LEE KUAN YEW, 335
LEE TENG-HUI, President of Taiwan, 353
LEFÈBVRE, Mgr Marcel, obit., 576
LÉGER, HE Cardinal, obit., 576
LEIGH, Mike, 493
LEKHANYA, Maj.-Gen. Justin, 297, 586
LENDL, Ivan, 522
LESKOVA, Tatiana, 484
LESOTHO, **297**, 393, 586
LETELIER, Orlando, 71
LETSIE III, HM King, of Lesotho, 297
LEVEY, Gregory, death, 57
LEVINE, James, 478
LEVY, David, 202
LEWIS, Sir Arthur, obit., 576
LEWIS, Carl, 517–8
LEWIS, R. W. B., 513
LEWIS, Sir Terence, 371
LI PENG, Prime Minister of China, 313, 347–8, 351, 363, 590, 594
LIBERIA, 262, 263, **264–5**, 270, 419, 420
LIBYA, 7, 142, 208, 231, **232–5**, 243, 268
LIECHTENSTEIN, **132–3**, 142, 417
LILLEY, Peter, MP, 7, 566
LILLY, Kris, 524
LILOV, Aleksandur, 166
LIMPAR, Anders, 516
LINDGREN, Torgny, 508
LINEKER, Gary, 515
LINI, Walter, Prime Minister of Vanuatu, 381
LISSOUBA, Pascal, 277
LITERATURE, 262, **507–13**
LITHERLAND, S. J., 513
LITHUANIA, 120, 125, 178 (map), 180, **188–90**, 382, 418, 432, 440, 557, 582, 583, 589, 590
LIVELY, Penelope, 509, 512
LLEWELLYN, Tim, 500
LLOYD WEBBER, Andrew, 491
LOACH, Ken, 493
LOCKHEAD, Liz, 513
LODGE, David, 512
LONCAR, Budimir, 384
LONDON CLUB, 261
LONGLEY, Michael, 513
LOQUASTO, Santo, 485
LUBACHIVSKY, HE Cardinal Myroslav, 439

LUBBERS, Ruud, Prime Minister of the Netherlands, 114, 400–1, 403
LUCE, Sir Richard, 395
LUDZHEV, Dimitur, 165
LUJAN, Manuel, 567
LUKANOV, Andrei, 166
LUKYANOV, Anatoly, 180
LUNDKVIST, Artur, obit., 576
LURIA, Prof. Salvador, obit., 576
LUSCOMBE, Tim, 487
LUSTIG, Graham, 484
LUTOSLAWSKI, Witold, 481
LUXEMBOURG, 84, **114–15**, 170, 395, 398, 582, 586, 588

MAATHI, Wangari, 262
McCAIN, Senator John, 50
McCARTHY, John, 7, 495, 589
MACEDONIA, 143, 145, 167, 168 (*map*), 173, 399
McCOLGAN, Liz, 518
McCONE, John A., obit., 576–7
McCRORY, Moy, 512
MacGREGOR, John, MP, 566
McGREGOR OF DURRIS, Lord, 17
MACHAR, Riak, 231
MACHEL, Samora, 286
McKANE, Richard, 513
MACKAY OF CLASHFERN, Lord, 566
McKEAN, Tom, 518
McKENNA, Frank, 64
MACKERRAS, Sir Charles, 478
MacKINNON, Lachlan, 513
MacLEOD, Alistair, 512
MacLEOD OF FUINARY, Very Rev Lord, obit., 577
McLUHAN, Marshall, 496
McMILLAN, Edwin, obit., 577
MacMILLAN, Sir Kenneth, 483–4
McNALLY, Terence, 490
MacSHARRY, Ray, 42, 403
MADAGASCAR, **327–8**, 421
MADANI, Abassi, 240–1
MADIGAN, Edward R., 567
MAGHREB, *see* Arab Maghreb Union
MAHATHIR MOHAMAD, Dr, Prime Minister of Malaysia, 333–4, 423–4
MAHDI, Sayyid Sadiq al-, 230
MAHMOOD, Lesley, 24
MAHMUD, Abdul Taib, 334
MAJID, Ali Hasan al-, 219
MAJOR, John, Prime Minister of UK, 518, 566; EC 8–9, 22–3, 31–3, 110, 534, 584, 588; foreign affairs, 7, 9, 29–30, 41, 351, 355, 393–4, 584, 590; home affairs, 10, 12–16, 18–19, 21–2, 24–8, 37, 589; Gulf War, 5, 191–3, 384, 582–4; Kurds, 7
MALAN, Gen. Magnus, 300, 302
MALAWI, **291–2**
MALAYSIA, **333–4**, 336, 359, 372, 381, 393, 423, 424, 527

MALDIVES, 322, **325–7**, 422
MALDOUM, Abbas Bada, 276
MALI, **268**, 271, 419, 421, 585
MALKOVICH, John, 490
MALTA, **141–2**, 411
MALTA, Rosane, 70
MAMALONI, Solomon, 380–1
MANDELA, Nelson, 300, 303, 393–4, 420, 583
MANDELA, Winnie, 587
MANGLAPUS, Raul, 330
MANLEY, Michael, Prime Minister of Jamaica, 85, 428
MANN, Dr Francis, death, 468
MANN, Jack, 7, 591
MANNING, Patrick, Prime Minister of Trinidad & Tobago, 87, 594
MANO RIVER UNION, 421
MANOS, Stephanos, 144
MANSELL, Nigel, 521–2
MANZ, Johannes, 247
MANZÙ, Giacomo, obit., 577
MAO ZEDONG, 346, 349, 587
MAPANJE, Jack, 292, 512
MARA, Ratu Sir Kamisese, Prime Minister of Fiji, 381
MARCHAND, Philippe, 96
MARCOS, Ferdinand, 340
MARCOS, Imelda, 340, 500, 593
MARGRETHE, HM Queen, of Denmark, 485
MARKOVIĆ, Ante, 167, 171, 594
MARQUES MOREIRA, Marcílio, 69
MARSHALL, Justice Thurgood, 52
MARSHALL ISLANDS, **378–9**, 382, 591
MARTENS, Wilfried, Prime Minister of Belgium, 112
MARTIN, Lynn, 567
MARTIN, Peter, 485
MARTINEZ, Enrique, 485
MARTINEZ CORBALA, Gonzalo, 84
MARTINIQUE, 99
MASCARENHAS MONTEIRO, Antonio, President of Cape Verde, 283, 583
MASIRE, Quett, President of Botswana, 296
MASON, Francis, 486
MASRI, Tahir al, 210–11
MASSIE, Allan, 509, 512
MASSINE, Léonide, 484
MAURITANIA, **269**
MAURITIUS, **323–4**, 591
MAW, Nicholas, 482
MAWHINNEY, Brian, 41
MAWHINNEY, Gordon, 41
MAXWELL, Robert, 17, 497, 593; death, 35, 451, 454, 593; obit., 577
MAY, Elaine, 491
MAZA MARQUEZ, Gen. Miguel, 72
MBA, Casimir Oye, 276
MEADE, Reuben, 93
MEČIAR, Vladimír, 156

MEDICINE & MEDICAL RESEARCH (see also AIDS, Cholera Epidemic), **448–50**
MEDINA PLASCENCIA, Carlos, 84
MEESE, Edward, 51
MEGRAHI, Abdel Basset al-, 234–5
MELLO, Dawn, 506
MELLOR, David, MP, 566
MENCINGER, Jože, 170
MÉNDEZ RUIZ, Col. Ricardo, 81
MENEM, Carlos Saúl, President of Argentina, 66–7
MENEZES, Aristides, 283
MENGISTU HAILE MARYAM, Lt-Col., 248, 250, 419, 587
MENUHIN, Yehudi, 482
MERCOSUR COMMON MARKET, 426
MERCURY, Freddie, death, 482
MESIĆ, Stipe, 169, 172, 587
METHERELL, Dr Terry, 369
MEXICO, 65, 81, 82, **83–4**, 425, 427, 445, 518, 528
MEYER, Roelf, 302
MFANSIBILI, Prince, 298
MICHEL, James, 326
MICHIKO, HM Empress, of Japan, 359
MIDDLEBROOK, Diane Wood, 513
MIDDLETON, Stanley, 509, 512
MILES, Sir Bernard (Lord Miles), death, 494; obit., 577
MILLER, Arthur, 489, 491
MILLER, Jonathan, 477–8
MILONGO, André, 277
MILOSEVIC, Slobodan, 585
MINGHELLA, Anthony, 493
MISTRY, Rohinton, 512
MITCHELL, James, 93
MITCHELL, Margaret, 510
MITCHISON, Naomi, 509, 512
MITRA, Ramon, 340
MITSOTAKIS, Konstantinos, Prime Minister of Greece, 143–4, 146, 149
MITTERRAND, François, President of France, 96–101, 163, 191, 380, 384, 396, 401, 412, 421, 434, 588
MIYAZAWA, Kiichi, Prime Minister of Japan, 360, 592
MO, Timothy, 509, 512
MOBUTU SESE SEKO, President of Zaïre, 279–81, 591–2
MOGAE, Festus, 296
MOHAMED, Hanifa, 322
MOHAMMED, Ali Mahdi, President of Somalia, 250, 251, 583, 590
MOI, Daniel Arap, President of Kenya, 252–4, 394
MOLDAVIA (MOLDOVA), 164, 177, 178 (map), 180, 182, 184, 398, 439, 557, 559–61, 590
MOLECULAR BIOLOGY & GENETICS, **449–50**
MOMOH, Joseph Saidu, President of Sierra Leone, 262–3
MONACO, **132–3**, 521

MONGOLIA, 361, 362, **364–7**, 406, 409
MONTAND, Yves, death, 494; obit., 577–8
MONTEGRIFFO, Peter, 140
MONTENEGRO, 168 (map), 173, 399
MONTGOMERIE, Colin, 520–1
MONTOYA, Marina, 72
MONTSERRAT, **92, 93,** 427
MOON, Rev Sun Myung, 440
MOORE, Michael, 376
MOORHOUSE, Jocelyn, 493
MORAN, Mary C., 53–4
MORÁN FLORES, José Angel, 82
MORGAN, Edwin, 513
MORGAN, Robert P., 482
MORICONE, Massimo, 484
MOROCCO, 194, 208, **242–5,** 246–7, 383, 388, 421, 528
MORRIS, Mark, 485
MORRISON, Danny, 41
MORTIMER, Peter, 513
MOSBACHER, Robert, 50, 567
MOSELEY, Nicholas, 508–9
MOSHOESHOE II, HM King, formerly of Lesotho, 297
MOSS, Stirling, 521
MOTHERWELL, Robert, death, 502; obit., 578
MOTION, Andrew, 512
MOTZFELDT, Jonathan, 120
MOURA, Barros, 138
MOUROU, Abdelfattah, 236, 238
MOZAMBIQUE, 254, 283, **284–7,** 291, 292, 299, 394, 592
MOZART BICENTENARY, 127, 477, 479–80, 482, 483, 509
MSWATI III, HM King, of Swaziland, 298
MUBARAK, Husni, President of Egypt, 207–8, 220, 233, 236, 589
MUGABE, Robert, President of Zimbabwe, 292–4, 393
MUHAMMAD, Ali Nasser, 224
MUITE, Paul, 253
MUKHAMEDOV, Irek, 483
MULDOON, Sir Robert, 376
MULRONEY, Brian, Prime Minister of Canada, 61, 63–5
MURDOCH, Rupert, 371
MURPHY, Gerard, 488
MURRAY, Les A., 513
MUSA, Amr Muhammad, 209
MUSEVENI, Yoweri, President of Uganda, 256, 287, 420
MUSIC, 127, 209, **479–82**
MWINYI, Ali Hassan, President of Tanzania, 255
MYNAMAR (BURMA), 318, **329–30**

NABABSING, Dr Prem, 324
NABLI, Mustapha, 238
NAJIBULLAH, Mohammed, President of Afghanistan, 222, 308
NAKAYAMA, Taro, 342

NAMALIU, Rabbie, Prime Minister of PNG, 374
NAMIBIA, **294–5**, 394, 591
NANO, Fatos, 175–6
NARONG WONGWAN, 332
NASH, Peter Paul, 481
NAURU, **378, 380**
NAYKENE, George, 258
NAZARBAEV, Nursultan, 183, 188
N'DOW N'JIE, Col. Momodou, 264
NEAOUTYINE, Paul, 380
NEBRADA, Vincente, 484
NEEDHAM, Richard, MP, 41
NEHER, Erwin, 451
NEHRU, Jawaharlal, 310
NELLIST, Dave, MP, 26
NEMEROV, Howard, obit., 578
NEPAL, **318–9**, 320, 587
NERETTE, Joseph, 79, 591
NETHERLANDS, THE, 94–5, **113–14**, 170, 194, 395, 398, 400, 401, 403, 404, 433, 434, 442, 452, 520
NEW CALEDONIA, **378, 380**, 425
NEW ZEALAND, 100, 194, 371, **374–8**, 380, 381, 516, 517, 527
NEWTON, Anthony, MP, 566
NEZZAR, Maj.-Gen. Khaled, 240
NGUEMA MBASOGO, Col. Teodoro Obiang, President of Equatorial Guinea, 278
NGUYEN CO THACH, 341
NGUYEN DUY NIEN, 341
NGUYEN MANH CAM, 341–2
NGUYEN VAN LINH, 341, 588
NGUZA KARL I BOND, 279, 281
NICARAGUA, **80, 81–2**, 384, 409, 462
NICHOLS, Kyra, 485
NICKLAUS, Jack, 521
NIGER, 194, 268, **271**, 272, 275, 277
NIGERIA, 222, 230–1, **259–62**, 263, 394, 420, 421, 443, 463, 507, 589
NIJINSKA, Bronislava, 483
NIJINSKY, Vaslav, 483
NILE, Rev Fred, 369
NINN-HANSEN, Erik, 19
NIXON, Richard, 56
NKOBI, Thomas, 303
NKRUMAH, Kwame, 258
NOAH, Yanick, 522
NOBEL PRIZES, economics, 529; literature, 507; peace, 329–30, 591; sciences and medicine, 451
NOLAN, Sidney, 477
NON-ALIGNED MOVEMENT, 259, 313, 384, **407–9**, 590
NORDIC COUNCIL, **418–19**
NORFOLK, Laurence, 508, 512
NORIEGA MORENO, Gen. Manuel, 591
NORMAN, Geraldine, 500
NORTH ATLANTIC COOPERATION COUNCIL, 432
NORTH ATLANTIC TREATY ORGANIZATION (NATO), 1, 7, 8, 9, 30, 32, 106, 109, 119, 152, 158, 160, 399, 400, 401, 412, 429, **431–6**, 593
NORTH, Lt-Col. Oliver, 51–2
NORTHERN IRELAND, 2, 8, 16, **40–3**, 117, 118, 585, 586, 587
NORWAY, **122–3**, 194, 330, 404, 416, 417, 459, 524, 529, 582
NORWOOD, Scott, 523
NOVOTNA, Jan, 522
NUJOMA, Sam, President of Namibia, 394
NUNN, Senator, Sam, 55
NUNN, Trevor, 477, 487
NUREYEV, Rudolf, 485–6
NWOSU, Prof. Humphrey, 260
NYERERE, Dr Julius, 408

OAKES, Agnes, 484
OBEID, Sheikh Abdul Karim, 216
OBITUARIES, **568–81**
O'BRIEN, Sean, 511
OCCHETTO, Achille, 107
ÖCALAN, Abdullah, 149
OCHIRBAT, Gombojavvyn, 364
OCHIRBAT, Punsalmagiyn, President of Mongolia, 362, **365–6**
OCHOA, Jorge Luis, 72
OCHOA ANTICH, Gen. Fernando, 77
ODA, Judge Shigeru, 463
ODINGA, Oginga, 252
ODDSSON, David, Prime Minister of Iceland, 120–1
ODINGA, Oginga, 252–3
O'FAOLAIN, Sean, obit., 578
O'HAGAN, Bernard, 41
OIL (*see also* Organization of Petroleum Exporting Countries), 36, 84, 88, 142, 184, 214, 217, 219, 222, 223, 226, 229, 276, 289, 386–7
OJAIDE, Tanure, 513
OKONGWU, Chu, 261
OKRI, Ben, 262, 508, 513
OLAV V, HM King, of Norway, death, 122, 582; obit., 578
OLAZABAL, José-Maria, 520
OLIVER, Stephen, 478
OLSZEWSKI, Jan, 154
OLTER, Bailey, 379
OMAN, 194, 223, **225**, 226, 228, 229
OMER, Gen. Ishaq Ibrahim, 231
OPERA, **477–9**
ORENSTEIN, Arbie, 482
ORGANIZATION FOR ECONOMIC COOPERATION & DEVELOPMENT (OECD), **404–5**, 527, 528, 529
ORGANIZATION OF AFRICAN UNITY (OAU), 251, 262, 281, 282, 287, 290, **419–20**, 587
ORGANIZATION OF AMERICAN STATES (OAS), 79, **425–6**

ORGANIZATION OF EASTERN CARIBBEAN STATES (OECS), 92, **427–8**
ORGANIZATION OF INTERNATIONAL ECONOMIC COOPERATION (OIEC), 405–6
ORGANIZATION OF PETROLEUM EXPORTING COUNTRIES (OPEC), 92, **427–8**
ORTEGA SAAVEDRA, Daniel, 82, 384
ORTEGA SAAVEDRA, Gen. Humberto, 81
OSBORN, Paul, 491
OSBORNE, John, Chief Minister of Montserrat, 93
OSBORNE, John (playwright), 511, 513
OTTEY, Merlene, 518
OUEDRAOGO, Clément, death, 270–1
OUFKIR, Mohamed, 245
OUKO, Robert, 253–4
OUTTARA, Alassane, 270
OWEN, Dr David, MP, 511, 513
OYUGI, Hezekiah, 253
ÖZAL, Semra, 149
ÖZAL, Türgut, President of Turkey, 146, 148–50

PAASIO, Pertti, 126
PACIFIC REGION, **378–81**, 423–5, 459
PACKER, Kerry, 368
PACHECHO, Ana Maria, 502
PAGE, Ruth, 486
PAKISTAN, 194, 232, 309, **313–6**, 318, 336, 422, 443–4, 520, 583
PALESTINE LIBERATION ORGANIZATION (PLO), 59, 204, 205, 206, 211, 212, 213, 214, 384
PALESTINIAN PEOPLE, 24, 59, 197, 201, 202, 203, 204–6, 210, 211, 213, 214, 215, 216, 227, 382, 387, 396, 408, 409, 415, 442, 587
PALUMBO, Lord (Peter), 504
PAN-AFRICAN NEWS AGENCY (PANA), 421
PANAMA, **81, 83**, 186, 426, 591
PANKIN, Boris, 308–9
PANKOVA, Yelena, 485
PANUFNIK, Sir Andrzej, 482; death, 482; obit., 578
PAO, Sir Y.K., obit., 578
PAPANDREOU, Andreas, 144, 584
PAPARIGA, Aleka, 144
PAPP, Joe, death, 491; obit.; 578
PAPUA NEW GUINEA, **373–4**
PARAGUAY, **74**, 426
PARIS CLUB, 69, 76, 153, 253, 261
PARKER, Alan 118, 493
PASCAL-TROUTILLOT, Ertha, 79
PASHKO, Gramoz, 176
PATRESE, Ricardo, 522
PATTEN, Christopher, MP, 15–16, 23, 28, 566
PAVAROTTI, Luciano, 482
PAVLOV, Valentin, 179, 185, 439, 582–3
PAWAR, Sharad, 311
PAYE, Jean-Claude, 404

PAZ ZAMORA, Jaime, President of Bolivia, 68
PEACOCKE, A., 444
PEARCE, Brian, 507
PEARCE, Stuart, 516
PENNEY, Lord, obit., 578–9
PENTAGONALE, 109
PEREIRA, Aristides, 283
PÉREZ, Carlos Andrés, President of Venezuela, 77, 408
PÉREZ, Dianora, 81
PÉREZ ABELA, Alfonso de los Heros, 76
PÉREZ DE CUELLAR, Javier, UN Secretary-General, 83, 147, 246–7, 382–4, 386–91, 395, 420
PERU, **75–6**, 427
PETERS, Winston, 376–7
PETROV, Vladimir, obit., 579
PETTIGREW, Antonio, 518
PEVSNER, Antoine, 484
PHAM VAM KHAI, 341
PHILIP, HRH Prince, Duke of Edinburgh, 587
PHILIPPINES, 318, 330, **339–40**, 457, 588, 593
PHILLIPS, Caryl, 509, 513
PHYSICS & CHEMISTRY, **447–8, 493**
PICCO, Giandomenico, 391
PICKERING, Thomas R., 567
PIGGOTT, Lester, 523
PILSUDSKI, Marshal, 154
PIMENTEL, Aquilino, 340
PINDLING, Sir Lynden, Prime Minister of the Bahamas, 91
PINOCHET HIRIART, Augusto, 71
PINOCHET UGARTE, Gen. Augusto, 71
PINTO, Harold, 488–9, 491, 509
PINTO DA COSTA, Manuel, 284
PIPE, Martin, 523
PIRIE, Gordon, obit., 579
PITTMAN, Jenny, 523
PITTMAN, Mark, 523
PÖHL, Karl-Otto, 106
POINDEXTER, John, 52
POLAND, 100, 105, 109, 110, 128, **152–4**, 159, 160, 186, 194, 354, 361, 397, 400, 404, 493, 501, 515, 526, 527, 586, 587, 592, 593
POLIAKOFF, Stephen, 493
PONSFORD, Bill, obit., 579
POOLE, David, 486
POOS, Jacques, 115, 395
POPOV, Dimitur, 165
PORRITT, Jonathon, 391
PORTUGAL, **137–9**, 142, 285, 286, 287–8, 396, 426, 433, 434, 461, 522, 582, 591
POSSUELO, Sidney, 70
POWELL, Gen. Colin, 49, 57–8, 192, 199, 583
POWELL, Senator Janet, 370
POWELL, Mike, 517–8
PRABHAKARAN, Vellupillai, 323

PRAPHAT KRITSANACHAN, Admiral, 331
PREFERENTIAL TRADE AREA (PTA), 421
PREMACHANDRA, G. M., 322
PREMADASA, Ranasinghe, President of Sri Lanka, 320, 322–3, 422
PRESCOTT, John, MP, 20
PRÉVAL René, 79
PRICE, George, Prime Minister of Belize, 89
PRICE, Nick, 521
PRIMAKOV, Evgenii, 192, 217
PRINCE, F. T., 513
PRUNSKIENE, Kazimiera, 582
PUCKETT, Kirby, 524
PUERTO RICO, 426
PUGO, Boris, 179; death, 180
PURCELL, Bill, 524
PUTTNAM, David, 492

QABOOS BIN SAID, Sultan, 228
QADAFI, Col. Muammar, Libyan leader, 7, 232–5
QATAR, 194, 198, **225**, 226, 228, 229, 461
QIAN QICHEN, 350–2
QUAYLE, J. Danforth, Vice-President of USA, 49, 295, 567

RABUKA, Sitiveni, 381
RACIAL & ETHNIC CONFLICT, Albania, 176; Australia, 371; Austria, 128–9; Baltic republics, 189–90; Bangladesh, 318; Belgium, 112; Bhutan, 320; Brazil, 70; Bulgaria, 165; Cameroon, 274; Canada, 61; Colombia, 73; Cyprus, 146–8; Czechoslovakia, 155; Denmark, 119; Dominican Republic, 80; Egypt, 209; Ethiopia, 248; France, 96, 98, 244; Germany, 103–4; Greece, 145; Hong Kong, 342, 356; Hungary, 161; Indonesia, 338; Iraq, 218, 305; Israel/occupied territories, 201, 203, 205; Italy, 109; Japan, 358; Lebanon, 215–5; Lesotho, 297; Malaysia, 333; Mali, 268; Mauritania, 269; Mauritius, 324; Morocco, 244; Netherlands, 113; New Caledonia, 380; New Zealand, 377; Nigeria, 261; N. Ireland, 41–2; Peru, 75; Romania, 163: Rwanda, 282; Senegal, 266–7; Somalia, 250–1; South Africa, 299–304; Spain, 136–7, 244; Sri Lanka, 321–2; Switzerland, 130; Togo, 272; Turkey, 149; UK, 6; USA, 44, 46, 48, 42–3, 56; USSR/CIS, 182–4; Yugoslavia, 161, 167–74; Zimbabwe, 294
RAE, Fiona, 502
RAFSANJANI, Hojatoislam Hashemi, President of Iran, 192, 231, 305, 307
RAHMAN, Sheikh Mujibur, 317
RAHMAN, Ziaur, 317
RAMADAN, Taha Yasin, 218
RAMAEMA, Col. Elias, 297, 586

RAMAPHOSA, Cyril, 303
RAMGOOLAM, Dr Navin, 324
RAMGOOLAM, Sir Seewoosagur, 324
RAMOS, Gen. Fidel, 340
RAMPRAKESH, Mark, 519
RANDONE, Salvo, obit., 579
RANSMAYR, Christoph, 507
RAO, P. V. Narasimha, Prime Minister of India, 310–12, 316, 587–8
RAS AL-KHAIMAH, 224
RATA, Matiu, 376
RATSIRAKA, Didier, President of Madagascar, 327–8
RATTLE, Simon, 482
RAWLINGS, Flt.-Lt. Jerry, Head of State of Ghana, 258–9
RAZANAMASY, Guy, 328
RAZIQ, Abd al-, 234
REAGAN, Nancy, 511
REAGAN, Ronald, 50–1, 52, 54, 56, 438, 513, 531
REDGRAVE, Vanessa, 513
REGO, Paula, 501–2
REID, Christopher, 513
REINING, Maria, death, 479
RELIGION (*see also* Islamic Fundamentalism, Vatican), **439–44**
REN JIANXIN, 349
RENÉ, France-Albert, President of Seychelles, 325–6, 393
RETTIG, Raúl, 71
RÉUNION, **101**
REVELLE, Roger, obit., 579
REY, Marie-Michele, 79
REYNOLDS, Albert, 117
RHYS JONES, Griff, 487
RICHARDS, Vivian, 519
RICHARDSON, Senator Graham, 369
RICHARDSON, Ruth, 375–6
RICHARDSON, Steven, 521
RICHARDSON, Tony, obit., 579
RICHTER, Ian, 7, 593
RICO, Aldo, 67
RICO TORO, Col. Faustino, 68
RIDLEY, Nicholas, MP, 22, 31
RIDLEY, Philip, 489
RIEGLE, Senator Donald, 50
RIEGLER, Josef, 128
RIFKIND, Malcolm, MP, 20–21, 566
RIGG, Diana, 488
RINGADOO, Sir Veerasamy, 324
RIPLEY, Alexandra, 510, 513
RIVER GAMBIA DEVELOPMENT ORGANIZATION, 264
ROBBINS LANDON, H. C., 482
ROBINSON, Arthur N., 87
ROBINSON, Mary, President of Republic of Ireland, 118
ROCARD, Michel, 97, 100, 377, 587
RODDENBERRY, Eugene, obit., 579
RODRÍGUEZ, Carlos Rafael, 78
ROEMER, Gov. Buddy, 56

INDEX

ROGERS, Jane, 513
ROGERS, Sir Richard, 504–5
ROH TAE WOO, President of S. Korea, 352, 361–2
ROHWEDDER, Detlev, 103
ROMAN, Petre, 161–3, 591
ROMANIA, **161–4**, 383, 406, 414, 417, 432, 516, 550, 591, 594
ROMANOW, Roy, 64
ROSE, Sir Alec, obit., 579
ROSLAVETS, Nikolai, 480
ROWLAND, Tiny, 291
ROY, Gen. Armand, 247
RUDNICK, Paul, 490
RUHE, Volker, 104
RUMENS, Carol, 513
RUNCIE, Most Rev Dr Robert, 440, 442
RUSHDIE, Salman, 306, 444, 508, 512
RUSSELL, George, 497
RUSSELL, Paul, 486
RUSSIAN FEDERATION, 29, 51, 59, 60, 110, 177, 178 (*map*), 179–86, 188, 190, 309, 312, 351, 358, 383, 439, 440, 442, 492, 526, 527, 557–61, 588, 590, 594
RUTSKOI, Alexander, 181
RWANDA, 257, **281–2**, 420, 448
RYZHKOV, Nikolai, 181, 582

SAADI, Ramón, 67
SAATCHI, Charles, 499
SAAVEDRA BRUNO, Carlos, 68
SABATINI, Gabriela, 523
SABRI, Ali, obit., 579–80
SACKO, Soumana, 268
SACKS, Chief Rabbi Jonathan, 441–2
SADDAM HUSAIN, President of Iraq, 6–7, 14, 58, 99, 148–50, 191–4, 197–201, 204, 208, 210–12, 217–20, 232, 243, 305, 384, 395, 429–30, 443, 582, 584, 586
SAIBOU, Brig. Ali, President of Niger, 271
ST KITTS-NEVIS, **91**, **92–3**, 427
ST LUCIA, **92**, **93**, 427, 428
ST VINCENT & THE GRENADINES, **92**, **93**
SAKMANN, Bert, 451
SALEH, Gen. Ali Abdullah, President of Yemen, 223
SALINAS DE GORTARI, Carlos, President of Mexico, 84
SALMOND, Alex, MP, 37
SALOLAINEN, Perthi, 416
SALONGA, Jovito, 340
SAMARAS, Antonis, 145
SAMPAIO, Dr Jorge, 138
SAMPRAS, Pete, 522
SAN MARINO, **132–3**
SANDIFORD, Erskine, Prime Minister of Barbados, 88–9
SANGUINETTI CAIROLO, Julio Maria, 76
SANKOH, Foday, 263
SANNOUSI, Abdallah, 234

SANTER, Jacques, Prime Minister of Luxembourg, 170
SÃO TOME & PRÍNCIPE, 273, **284**, 419
SASSOU-NGUESSO, Col. Denis, President of Congo, 277
SAUD AL-FAISAL, HRH Prince, 306
SAUDI ARABIA, 158, 191, 192, 193, 194, 195 (*map*), 197, 198, 199, 210, **220–2**, 223, 226, 228, 229, 232, 243, 305, 306, 313, 382, 421, 443, 527, 583, 584, 589
SAUNDERS, Dean, 515
SAVIMBI, Jonas, 287–9, 587
SAW MAUNG, Gen., 330
SAWADA, Masahiko, 500
SAWASDI AMORNVIVAT, Gen., 331
SAWER, David, 481
SAWYER, Dr Amos, 265, 420
SCANNELL, Vernon, 511, 513
SCELBA, Mario, obit., 580
SCHÄUBLE, Wolfgang, 104
SCHAUFUSS, Peter, 483
SCHLESINGER, Helmut, 106
SCHLÜTER, Poul, Prime Minister of Denmark, 119
SCHMITTHOFF, Prof. Clive, death, 468
SCHURMANN, Gerard, 482
SCHWARTZ, Stephen, 490
SCHWARZENBERGER, Prof. Georg, death, 468
SCHWARZKOPF, Gen. Norman, 12, 57–8, 193–4, 198–9, 496, 584
SCIENCES (*see also* Environmental Questions, Information Technology, Medicine & Medical Research, Space Exploration), astronomy & space research, 445–7; evolution, 450–1; molecular biology & genetics, 449–50; Nobel Prizes, 451; physics & chemistry, 447–8
SCOTLAND, 8, 21, 27, **36–8**, 142, 235, 502, 503, 515, 516, 518
SCOTT, George C., 491
SCOTT BROWN, Denise, 503
SCOTTI, Vincenzo, 109
SCOWCROFT, Gen. Brent, 433, 567
SCUDAMORE, Peter, 523
SEAGO, Edward, 490
SEABALD, Max, 508
SEEKIE, Raleigh, 265
SEET AI MEET, 336
SEIGEL, Don, death, 494
SEIN WIN, Dr, 329
SELES, Monica, 522–3
SELLARS, Peter, 477
SEMENIAKA, Ludmila, 484
SENEGAL, 194, 264, **266–7**, 275, 421, 461, 462
SENEGAL RIVER DEVELOPMENT ORGANIZATION, 421
SENEILDÍN, Mohammed Ali, 67
SENNA, Ayrton, 521–2

SERBIA, 2, 145, 161, 167–74, 168 (*map*), 339, 442, 500, 585, 586, 587, 589, 590, 591, 592, 593
SERFATY, Abraham, 245
SERKIN, Rudolf, death, 482; obit., 580
SERRA, Narcis, 134–5
SERRANO ELIAS, Jorge, President of Guatemala, 81, 89, 582
SEYCHELLES, **325–6**, 393
SHAMIR, Yitzhak, Prime Minister of Israel, 202–3, 205, 213
SHARA, Faruq al-, 212
SHARIF, Nawaz, Prime Minister of Pakistan, 313–4, 316
SHARJAH, 224
SHARMAN, Helen, 587
SHARON, Ariel, 203
SHEEN, Martin, 491
SHEKHAR, Chandra, 309–10, 319
SHELDEN, Michael, 513
SHELDON, Joan, 370
SHEPHARD, Sam, 490
SHER, Anthony, 489
SHEVARDNADZE, Eduard, 179, 188
SHIHABI, Samier S., 382
SHIKUKU, Martin, 254
SHOMRON, Gen. Dan, 204
SIERRA LEONE, **262–3**, 421
SIGUA, Tengiz, 183
SIHANOUK, Prince Norodom, 343–4, 593
SILAEV, Ivan, 183
SIMMS, Most Rev George, obit., 580
SIMPSON, John, 503
SINGAPORE, 334, **335–6**, 342, 352, 381, 393, 423, 527, 528, 590
SINGER, Isaac Bashevis, obit., 580
SINGH, Manmohan, 311–2
SINT, Marjanne, 113
SISAVAT KEOBOUNPHANH, Gen. 345
SISULU, Walter, 303
SIYAD BARRE, Maj.-Gen. Mohammed, 250, 283, 594
SKASE, Christopher, 371
SKINNER, Denis, MP, 27
SKINNER, Samuel, 50, 567
SLAVICKÝ, Klement, 480
SLOVAKIA, 155–8
SLOVENIA, 32, 105, 128, 161, **167–74**, 168 (*map*), 395, 399, 583, 588, 594
SMALLWOOD, Joseph, obit., 580
SMIRNOV, Dmitri, 480
SMITH, Alan, 516
SMITH, John, MP (Labour Shadow Chancellor), 11, 14, 27
SMITH, Robin, 519
SMITH, William Kennedy, 45, 473
SOARES, Marío, President of Portugal, 137, 582
SOBCHAK, Anatoly, 361
SOGLO, Nicéphore, President of Benin, 273–4, 585
SOLARI DAMONTE, José, 76

SOLCHAGA, Carlos, 134, 136
SOLOFA, Esekia, 425
SOLOMAN, Richard, 341
SOLOMON ISLANDS, 373, **379**, **380–1**
SOLTI, Sir George, 481
SOMALIA, **250–1**, 252, 389, 419, 420, 583, 590, 594
SOMBOON RAHONG, 332
SON SEN, 344
SOPE, Barak, 381
SORRELL, Martin, 513
SOUFLIAS, Georgios, 143
SOUTH AFRICA, 30, 158, 187, 254, 285, 287, 294, 295, 296, 297, **299–304**, 372, 390, 394, 420, 507, 514, 518, 520, 521, 582, 583, 585, 586, 587, 588, 589, 590, 594
SOUTH ASIAN ASSOCIATION FOR REGIONAL COOPERATION (SAARC), 313, 318, 320, 322, 327, **421–2**
SOUTH COMMISSION, 408
SOUTH PACIFIC COMMISSION, 425
SOUTH PACIFIC FORUM, 425
SOUTH PACIFIC REGIONAL COOPERATION, **424–5**
SOUTH-EAST ASIAN ORGANIZATIONS, **423–4**
SOUTH AFRICAN DEVELOPMENT COORDINATION CONFERENCE (SADCC), 421
SOYINKA, Wole, 507
SPACE EXPLORATION, 47, 127, **445–7**, 587
SPAIN, 67, 77, 133, **134–7**, 140, 142, 194, 206, 244, 246, 247, 278, 295, 371, 396, 397, 405, 414, 426, 427, 467, 493, 586
SPATH, Lothar, 104
SPESSIVTSEVA, Olga, death, 486; obit., 580
SPIELBERG, Steven, 492
SPORT, 21, 39, 106, 259, 302, 372, 394, **514–24**, 585, 586, 588, 592, 593
SPOTO, Donald, 511, 513
SRI LANKA, 310, 313, 318, 320, **321–3**, 422, 519, 584
STANFIELD, Robert, 395
STANFORD, Lyn, 486
STANNARD, Martin, 513
STANSFIELD SMITH, Colin, 505
STARODUBTSEV, Vasily, 179
STEEL, Sir David, MP, 37
STEIFEL, Ethan, 485
STEINBERG, N. A., 458
STEVENSON, Ben, 484–5
STEWART, Micky, 519
STEWART, Paul, 516
STEWART, Payne, 520
STICH, Michael, 106, 522
STIERLE, Edward, 486
STIGLER, Prof. George, obit., 580
STIRLING, James, 504–5
STOICHKOV, Grigor, 166
STOLOJAN, Teodor, Prime Minister of Romania, 162–3, 591

STONE, Sir Richard, obit., 580
STRACHAN, Winifred, 90
STRAIGES, Tony, 485
STRATAS, Teresa, 478
STRAUSS, Robert, 59
SUCHET, David, 487
SUCHINDA KRAPRAYOON, Gen., 331–2, 345
SUDAN, 208, **230–2**, 233, 243, 275, 389–90
SUHARTO, Gen. T. N. J., President of Indonesia, 337–8, 423
SULLIVAN, Louis, 567
SUNQVIST, Ulf, 126
SUNTHORN KONGSOMPONG, 331
SUNUNU, John, 49
SURINAME, **94–5**, 428
SUSTRINO, Gen. Try, 338
SUTHERLAND, Ivan, 454
SUU KYI, Daw Aung San, 329–30, 591
SUZUKI, Shunichi, 358
SWAZILAND, **298**
SWEDEN, 119, 122, **123–5**, 127, 133, 142, 255, 404, 416, 417, 418, 458, 465, 508, 515, 521, 591
SWITZERLAND, **129–32**, 133, 416, 417, 451, 465, 515, 588, 592
SYRIA, 1, 149, 194, 204, 205, 206, 207, 208, **212–14**, 215, 219, 221, 225, 226, 232, 306
SZABO, Istvan, 492

TABAI, Iremia, 381, 424
TAIWAN, 303, 352, **353–4**, 423, 527, 594
TAJIKISTAN, 177, 178 (*map*), 182, 184, 557, 559–61
TAKESHITA, Noburu, 360
TAMARIZ, Diego, 74
TAMAYO, Rufino, obit., 580
TAMBO, Oliver, 303
TANABE, Makoto, 359
TANZANIA, **254–6**, 257, 282, 291
TAVENER, John, 481
TAYA, Col. Moaouia Ould Sidi Mohamed, President of Mauritania, 269
TAYLOR, Burton, 486
TAYLOR, Charles, 263, 265, 270
TAYLOR, Elizabeth, 506
TAYLOR, Graham, 515
TAYLOR, Paul, 485
TAYLOR, Teddy, MP, 234
TEANNIKI, Teato, 381
TEBBIT, Norman, MP, 30, 31, 33
TECHNOLOGY, *see* Information Technology
TEKERE, Edgar, 293
TELEVISION & RADIO, 39, 180, 196, 197, 221, 481, **494–9**
TENNSTEDT, Klaus, 482
THAILAND, **331–2**, 334, 342, 343, 344, 345, 352, 359, 404, 448, 527, 583, 587

THATCHER, Margaret, MP, 2, 6, 9, 10, 11, 13, 14, 18, 21–3, 28, 31–3, 37, 334, 496, 511, 584, 588
THEATRE, 118, **486–91**
THEODORAKIS, Mikis, 145
THOMAS, Judge Clarence, 44, 52–3, 473, 592
THOMAS, Clive, 86
THORNBURGH, Richard, 56
THORNTON, Peter, 502
TIAN JIYUN, 352
TIBET, 367
TIN OO, 329
TIPPETT, Sir Michael, 481
TISCHENKO, Boris, 480
TITO, Josip Broz, 170
TIZYAKOV, Alexander, 179
TLAS, Gen. Mustafa, 213
TOGLIATTI, Palmiro, 110
TOGO, 100, 265, **272–3**, 421, 585
TÖLGYESSY, Péter, 160
TOLSTIKOV, Yakov, 586
TONGA, 425
TÖPFER, Klaus, 105
TORGYAN, József, 159
TORRES Y TORRES LARA, Carlos, 76
TOUIL, Embarek, 245
TOUMANI, Lt.-Col. Amadou, 585
TOURÉ, Amadou Toumani, Head of State of Mali, 268
TOWER, John, obit., 580–1
TRACEY, Edward, 589
TRAORÉ, Gen. Moussa, 268, 585
TREIKI, Ali Abdul al-, 234
TREVOR, William, 509, 513
TRINH XUAN LANG, 341
TRINIDAD & TOBAGO, 30, **87–8**, 427, 594
TROON, John, 253
TROVOADA, Miguel, 284
TSEDENBAL, Yumjaagiyn, death, 365; obit., 581
TSHISEKEDI, Etienne, 279–81, 592
TSONGAS, Paul E., 55
TSUI, T. T., 500
TUCKER, Peter, 262–3
TUCKETT, William, 484
TUDJMAN, Franjo, 171, 591
TUDOR, Antony, 485
TUFNELL, Philip, 519
TUNISIA, 99, 208, **235–8**, 528, 582
TURABI, Hasan al-, 230
TURBAY AYALA, Julio César, 72
TURBAY QUINTERO, Diana, 72
TÜRKEŞ, Alpaslan, 150
TURKEY, 67, 105, 135, 143, 145, 146, 147, **148–51**, 161, 191, 212, 218, 223, 388, 396, 417, 585, 588, 589, 592
TURKMENIA, 151, 177, 178 (*map*), 182, 184, 398, 557, 559–61
TURNAGE, Mark Anthony, 481
TURNER, Jesse, 592
TURNER, Ted, 495–6

TURP, André, 479
TYLDEN-WRIGHT, Donald, 513

U AUNG, 329
U KYAW NYEIN, 329
U KYI MAUNG, 329
U NU, 329
UBALDINI, Saúl, 67
UGANDA, **256–7**, 282, 287, 420, 448
UKRAINE, 59, 158, 164, 177, 178 (*map*), 182–3, 188, 351, 384, 392, 397, 398, 439, 440, 557–61, 590, 593, 594
UMM AL-QAIWAN, 224
UNION OF SOVIET SOCIALIST REPUBLICS (USSR), **177–88** (*see also* COMECON, Warsaw Pact); arts, 507; Baltic republics, 29, 120, 158, 177, 180, 188–90, 396–7, 413, 418; CIS, 177, 183–4, 186, 351, 383, 525, 557–61 (*texts*); coup attempt, 3, 8, 29, 100, 138, 144, 177–80, 411; CPSU, 177, 181; defence, 29, 187–8, 418, 431–2; E. Europe, 152, 155, 157–8, 164, 166, 174; economy, 184–6, **525–7**; external relations, 1, 8, 29, 51, 57, **59–60**, 78, 81, 103, 104, 105, 110, 125, 126, 127, 144, 151, 155, 157–8, 164, 166, 174, 186–8, 202–3, 204, 205, 206, 212, 220, 222, 287, 306, 308, 309, 312, 315, 341, 344, 345, 350, 351, 354, 361, 362, 363, 364, 366, 375, 383–4, 389, 395, 397–8, 399, 400, 414, 423, 432, 436–8; Gulf crisis, 186, 192, 196, 217, 550; religion, 439–40; space, 446–7; sport, 514–5, 517, 518; START Treaty, 436–8, 555–7; UN, 383–4
UNITED ARAB EMIRATES (UAE), 194, **224**, 226, 228, 229
UNITED KINGDOM, **5–43**
EXTERNAL RELATIONS, (*see also* Arms Control & Security, Conference on Security & Cooperation in Europe, European Community, Gulf Crisis, North Atlantic Treaty Organization, Western European Union), Africa, 253, 288, 289, 291, 292, 297, 301, 303, 393; aid, 404; Americas, 74, 86, 87, 90; Asia-Pacific, 9, 323, 342, 344, 351, 380; Commonwealth, 393, 394, 395; Council of Europe, 415; dependencies, 93; diplomatic relations, 174; EC, 2, 7, 8–9, 14, 22–3, 26. 28, 30–3, 38, 109–10, 145, 173, 395, 396, 399, 400–2, 561; E. Europe, 29; G7, 29; Gibraltar, 136, 140; Gulf crisis, 5–8, 11, 105, 191, 192, 193, 194, 196, 198, 210, 211, 226, 550; hostages, 7, 215, 496; Ireland, 40–1, 116, 117; Libya, 234–5; UN, 383, 384, 390, 392; USA, 9, 14, 22, 29, 39
HOME AFFAIRS (*see also* Northern Ireland, Scotland, Wales), architecture, **502–5**, arts, **477–513**; broadcasting, **494–8**; by-elections, 13, 18, 24, 35, 39; Channel tunnel, 21, 38, 142; citizen's charter, 13; defence, 8, 37–8, 42, 106; dogs, 16–17; economy, 9–12, 14, 18–19, 21, 25, 26, 33–6, 37–8, 42–3, **531–4**; education, 19–20; ERM, 10, 23, 532, 533; government, 566 (*list*); law, 468–73; local elections, 15–16, 24; NHS, 17–18, 19, 27, 34, 35, 37, 39; parties, 10, 11, 16, 24, 26–8, 37; poll/council tax, 13, 14, 15, 22, 34, 36; press, 17, 35, 454; religion, 440–1, 442; riots, 25; Rushdie affair, 306, 444, 508, 512; scandals, 24, 25, 35, 37, 40; science & medicine, 447, 449, 450, 452; sport, 21, **514–23**; terrorism, 2, 6, 7, 16, 24, 35, 41–2, 234–5; transport, 20–21, 35; TUC, 26; War Crimes Bill, 17
UNITED NATIONS, **382-92**; (*see also* General Agreement on Tariffs & Trade, International Atomic Energy Agency, International Court of Justice), Afghanistan, 309, 389; Albania, 389; Angola, 287, 288, 387; Arab-Israeli dispute, 202, 205, 206, 208, 213, 215, 222, 334, 387, 408; Cambodia, 343, 388; Chernobyl, 392; China, 350; Cyprus, 146–7, 388; disarmament, 390–1; drugs, 391; East Timor, 337; El Salvador, 83, 388; environment, 391, 455–6, 458, 463; finance, 384; General Assembly, 382–4, 442–3; Gibraltar, 135–6; Gulf crisis, 1, 5, 57, 65, 99, 109, 128, 146, 186, 191, 193, 194, 199, 210, 217, 218, 222, 223, 225, 226, 227, 228, 243, 305, 326, 357, 382, 383, 384–7, 395, 396, 550–5 (*text*); Horn of Africa, 389; hostages, 391; Indian Ocean, 315; Iran-Iraq, 306; Koreas, 362; Kurds, 7, 99, 218, 386; membership, 133, 181, 182, 184, 190, 379, 396, 425; NAM, 407; OAU, 420; refugees, 231, 356; Secretary-General, 208, 382, 383, 409; Somalia, 251, 389; South Africa, 390; Sudan, 389–90; Taiwan, 354; UNDP, 385; UNEP, 385; UNICEF, 385, 389; Vietnam, 341; WHO, 391; women, 392; W. Sahara, 245–7, 388–9; Yugoslavia, 173, 390, 399; Zimbabwe, 294
UNITED STATES OF AMERICA (USA), **44–60**
EXTERNAL RELATIONS (*see also* Arms Control & Security, Conference on Security & Cooperation in Europe, North Atlantic Treaty Organization, Organization of American States), **56–60**; Africa, 248, 253, 255, 265, 272, 281, 285, 287, 288, 289, 290, 295, 298, 390; Arab-Israeli dispute, 1, 58–9, 201–2, 204, 205–6, 207–8, 210, 211, 213, 215, 222; Asia-Pacific, 308, 312, 315, 316, 330, 337, 339, 341–2, 343, 350, 351, 366, 372, 377,

379, 389, 423, 424; Canada, 64, 65, 458; Caribbean/Central America, 78, 79, 81, 83, 84, 86, 87, 92, 427, 428, 462; Europe, 9, 14, 22, 29, 38, 39, 96, 99, 105, 106, 119, 142, 144, 145, 146, 148, 149, 153, 166, 171, 174, 401, 410, 431–3, 529; GATT, 9, 529; Gulf crisis, 6, 14, 44, 46, 54, 56–8, 99, 115, 128, 134, 135, 186, 191, 192, 193, 194–200, 201, 210, 217–19, 220, 223, 225, 226, 228, 232, 236, 239, 242–3, 305, 395, 429–30, 550; hostages, 1–2, 215; Japan, 357, 358, 360, 430; Latin America, 66–7, 68–9, 72, 75, 425–6; Libya, 232, 233, 234–5; Morocco, 243, 244–5; New Zealand, 377; South Africa, 302, 303; START treaty, 429, 436–8, 555–7; UN, 382, 389, 390; USSR/CIS, 51, 57, 59–60, 181, 187–8, 315, 399, 429, 431–3, 555–7
HOME AFFAIRS, **44–56;** appointments, 53, 567 (*list*); arts, 45, 479–80, 483, 485, 490–1, 502, 511; defence, 46–7, 58, 59–60; drugs & crime, 45, 47, 48; disasters, 45–6; economy, 46, 47, 53–5, 404, **529–31;** education, 49; Iran-Contra, 50, 51–2; law, 47, 53, **473–6;** media, 45, 494–5, 498; 'October surprise', 50–1; politics, 44, 55; racial issues, 44, 46, 48, 52–3, 56; scandals/ethics, 45, 49–50, 52–3, 55; science & medicine, 445–6, 448, 449–50; space, 47, 445–6; sport, 45, 516, 518, 520, 522, **523–4;** State of the Union, 46, 49
URUGUAY, **76,** 426
UZBEKISTAN, 155, 177, 178 (*map*), 182, 184, 557, 559–61

VALENTI, Jack, 492
VAN DANTZIG, Rudi, 485
VAN DER POST, Laurens, 513
VANCE, Cyrus, 173–4, 390, 593
VANUATU, **379, 381**
VASILIEV, Vladimir, 485
VASSILIOU, Georgios, President of Cyprus, 146
VATICAN, 110, **132–3,** 174, **441–2**
VECHESLOVA, Tatiana, death, 486
VEIGA, Carlos, 283
VELAYATI, Ali Akbar, 306
VENETIAAN, Ronald, President of Suriname, 94
VENEZUELA, **77,** 79, 383, 407, 408, 425, 427, 528
VENKATARAMAN, Ramaswamy, President of India, 310
VENTURI, Robert, 503, 505
VERMES, Prof. Geza, 443
VERNAUDON, Emile, 101, 380
VESSEY, Gen. John, 341
VEYNE, Paul, 507
VICK, Graham, 477

VEDELA, Gen. Jorge,
VIDENOV, Zhan, 166
VIETNAM, 46, 57, 194, 196, 224, 336, **341–2,** 343, 344, 345, 352, 356, 406, 588, 589
VIEYRA, Desiré, 274
VLOK, Adriaan, 300–2
VOELKER, John D., obit., 581
VO VAN KIET, Prime Minister of Vietnam, 336, 341–2, 589
VOGEL, Hans-Jochen, 104
VONNEGUT, Kurt, 513
VRANITZKY, Dr Fred, Chancellor of Austria, 127–8
VULKOV, Viktor, 165

WADDINGTON OF READ, Lord, 13, 566
WADE, Abdoulaye, 266
WADLEY, Nicholas, 502
WAGNER, Friedelind, death, 479
WAGNER, Robert, obit., 581
WAINROT, Mauricio, 484
WAITE, Terry, 7, 215, 441, 495–6, 593
WAJID, Sheikh Hasina, 317
WAKEHAM, John, MP, 566
WALCHA, Helmut, death, 482; obit., 581
WALDEGRAVE, William, MP, 18, 28, 566
WALDHEIM, Dr Kurt, President of Austria, 129
WALES, 15, 18, 20, 22, 25, 27, 36, **38–9,** 515, 520
WALES, HRH Prince of, 19, 502–3, 511
WALESA, Lech, President of Poland, 152–4, 586
WALKEN, Christopher, 491
WALKER, Alice, 513
WALKER, Des, 516
WALKER, Peter, MP
WALSH, Lawrence E., 51
WALTERS, Sir Alan, 10
WALVIS BAY, 295
WAMYTAN, Rock, 380
WANG BINGQIAN, 348
WANG JINGQING, 351
WAPSHOTT, Nicholas, 513
WARD JACKSON, Adrian, death, 486
WARSAW PACT, 152, 158, 584, 588
WATANABE, Michio, 360
WATKINS, James, 567
WATSON, Michael, 514
WATSON, Tom, 520
WAUGH, Auberon, 513
WEAVER, Fritz, 491
WEBSTER, William, 51, 55
WEE KIM WEE, President of Singapore, 334
WELENSKY, Sir Roy, obit., 581
WEST, Timothy, 488
WEST INDIAN COMMISSION, 428
WEST INDIES, 519
WESTERN EUROPEAN UNION (WEU), 9, 32, 110, 135, 145, 400, 401, **433–5,** 467

WESTERN SAHARA, **245–7**, 382, 388–9, 407
WESTERN SAMOA, **378, 379–80,** 425, 516
WESTERN SUMMIT CONFERENCE (G7), 7, 29, 65, 187, 358, 459, 529, 589
WHALING, 121, 459
WHEATON, David, 522
WHEELER, Paul, 489
WHITE, Michael, 513
WHITEREAD, Rachel, 502
WIJDENBOSCH, Jules, 94
WIJERATNE, Ranjan, death, 321, 584
WIJETUNGE, Dingiri Banda, Prime Minister of Sri Lanka, 321
WILDER, Governor Douglas, 55
WILLIAMS, Heathcote, 513
WILLIAMS, Nicol, 491
WILLIS, Ralph, 369
WILSON, A. N., 513
WILSON, Sir Angus, death, 510; obit., 581
WILSON, Sir David (former director of British Museum), 502
WILSON, Michael, 65
WINA, Arthur, 290
WINCHESTER, Colin, 371
WINDWARD ISLANDS, **92**
WISTRICH, R. S., 444
WIETZEL, Damian, 485
WOFFORD, Harris, 56
WOLF, Markus, 103
WOLFSON, Sir Isaac, obit., 581
WOOD, Hugh, 481
WOODS, Carol, 491
WOODS, John, 507
WOOLF, Lord Justice, 470
WOOSNAM, Ian, 520–1
WORLD BANK (IBRD), 87, 147, 166, 187, 209, 214, 232, 238, 253, 256, 266, 277, 291, 292, 295, 297, 307, 332, 336, 413, 420, 424
WORLD HEALTH ORGANIZATION (WHO), 259, 385, 391–2, 448
WORLD METEOROLOGICAL ORGANIZATION, 458
WORTHEN, John, 513
WRIGHT, Peter, 484

YAKUNIN, Fr Gleb, 439
YAMPOLSKY, Berta, 484
YANEV, Gennadii, 59, 179, 590
YANG SHANGKUN, President of China, 306–7, 366–7
YAVLINSKY, Grigory, 185
YAZOV, Dmitrii, 179

YELTSIN, Boris, President of Russia, 29, 60, 105, 110, 179–81, 183, 186, 188, 190, 358, 383, 397, 439, 442, 495, 511, 526, 585, 588, 590, 594
YEMEN, Republic of, 204, **223–4,** 243, 385, 386, 550
YEO CHEOW TONG, 336
YEVTUSHENKO, Yevgeny, 513
YILMAZ, Mesut, 147, 150, 588, 592
YOMA, Amira, 67
YORK, HRH Duchess of, 506
YORK, Michael, 491
YOSHIDA, Miyako, 484
YOUNG, Hugh, 507
YOUNG, Lord, 12
YOUNIS, Waqar, 520
YUGOSLAVIA, 32, 93, 105, 109, 115, 128, 143, 158, 160, 161, **167–74** (*map* 168), 176, 371, 382, 384, 390, 398–9, 406, 408, 409, 412, 413 415, 417, 436, 442, 500, 514, 515, 522, 583, 585, 586, 587, 588, 589, 590, 591, 592, 593, 594

ZAFY, Albert, 328
ZAHIR SHAH, HM King, formerly of Afghanistan, 308
ZAïRE, 112, **279–81,** 291, 383, 421, 550, 591, 592
ZAKI, Ibrahim Hussain, 327, 422
ZAMBIA, 257, **289–91,** 592
ZANZIBAR, 255, 256
ZAPATA, Fausto, 84
ZASLAND, Neal, 482
ZAYAD BIN SULTAN AL-NAHAYYAN, Shaikh, President of UAE, 228–9
ZENAWI, Meles, President of Ethiopia, 248–9
ZEPHANIAH, Benjamin, 510
ZHANG YIMOU, 493
ZHELEV, Zhelyu, President of Bulgaria, 166–7
ZHIVKOV, Todor, 166, 584
ZIA, Begum Khaleda, Prime Minister of Bangladesh, 317–8, 584–5
ZIA-UL-HAQ, Gen. Mohammad, 314
ZIMBABWE, 29, 248, 286, **292–4,** 392, 393, 514, 550
ZIPRODT, Patricia, 485
ZOU JIAHUA, 351
ZUBAYDI, Hamzah al-, 219, 591
ZUMA, Jacob, 303
ZWANE, Dr Ambrose, 298

REF D 2 .A7 1991